*The
Imagination
of Pentecost*

The
Imagination
of Pentecost

Rudolf Steiner and
Contemporary Spirituality

Richard Leviton

✐ Anthroposophic Press

Published by Anthroposophic Press
RR 4, Box 94 A-1, Hudson, N.Y. 12534

Library of Congress Cataloging-in-Publication Data

Leviton, Richard.
    The imagination of Pentecost : Rudolf Steiner and
contemporary spirituality / Richard Leviton.
        p. cm.
    Includes bibliographical references
    ISBN 0-88010-379-5
    1. Steiner, Rudolf, 1861–1925. 2. Anthroposophy.
3. Spiritual life—History—20th century.   4. New Age movement.
I. Title.
BP596.S66L48   1994   93–48352
299'.935—dc20   CIP

10 9 8 7 6 5 4 3 2 1

Printed in the United States of America

CONTENTS

PART III

"HUMAN"

THE HOLY GHOST CAUGHT IN TIME:
The Ambivalence of Lucifer and Ahriman
across the Threshold

PART IV

"SPEAKING"

THE GOOD AURIC STAR
OF THE HUMAN

P A R T I

"I N"

MICHAEL'S DAWN:

Preparations for the Dawning of
Michaelic Culture in the Twentieth Century

CHAPTER 1

Cognitive Expansion

Indications of Living on the
Threshold of the Supersensible Worlds

*S*UNRISE COMES to the crowded courtyard of El Templo del Santa Maria and its massive, ancient El Tule tree, a half dozen miles from Oaxaca in southern Mexico. Many have sat here in solitary vigil or before the communal campfire all night in expectation of the millennial dawn of Harmonic Convergence, August 17, 1987. In fact at this moment millions of women and men around the world sit expectantly at mountain tops, mesas, stone circles, islands, beaches, medicine wheels, waterfalls, riverbends, urban parks. The planet is suddenly floriate in sacred, numinous, dedicated, human-inhabited landscape sites.

The mainstream media, of course, have had their pejorative field day, snickering and joking about neo-Woodstock recidivism. And for good reason: many ardent New Agers have cast their apocalyptic expectations rather grandly into an *agape* with benevolent space brothers, crystals, and ETs. According to the mythic calendar of the Zapotec Indians, the indigenous "People of the Clouds" in this part of Mexico, the Convergence marks the return at El Tule of Quetzalcoatl, in their belief the legendary Lord of the Tree of Life, after a nearly thousand-year absence. "And the Tree of Life shall blossom with a fruit never before known in the creation, and that fruit shall be the New Spirit of Man," runs the Zapotec prophecy. Quetzalcoatl will come from the east, phosphorescent like the Morning Star, and with his arrival the El Tule tree, under which his heart was buried long ago, will burst into billions of tiny sparks of light to sequin the Earth.

With the first blush of dawn, the feeling here is strong, still, adamant, focused, clear, expectant. Quetzalcoatl—the Lord of Light
in another vocabulary—is coming, at least that's my perception.
The hundreds of men and women ranged around this two-thou-
sand-year-old cedar are like incandescent tent pegs, their concentration like glowing guy wires holding down a brilliant emerald
tent, as something absolutely angelic descends upon El Tule.

As I see it, the Elohim, an angelic family sometimes called Exousiai, form a circlet of winged light about a majestic and tower-
ing archangel while myriad more angels envelop this presence in
sparkling bands of light like the folds in a robe. The Lord of
Light, crowned with angels, descends upon El Tule and meditates on his cosmic heart—on our individual hearts around the
planet, too—in the shape of an emerald, a green pomegranate of
humanity.

Something is happening of paramount importance with respect to our entire period of human habitation on Earth, here in
this moment of synchronous reverence—an interior, elusive, supersensible event in human consciousness that will reverberate
from within us for years to come. With Quetzalcoatl's arrival, the
energy at El Tule is like spiritual gold. We are irradiated with the
light of *Helel ben Sahar,* as the ancient Hebrew prophets said of the
Lord of Light: the Shining One, Venus, the Morning Star, Precious Twin, Son of Dawn, the Dawn Bringer, the Light Bringer—
Lord Lucifer, returning to the Tree of Life, plumed with Elohim.

In retrospect, 1987 was a watershed year for the evolution of consciousness in the West. Evidence peaked that a widespread expansion in cognitive parameters was underway. Everywhere one
looked, there was yet another indication that many were living on
the threshold of the supersensible worlds. Human consciousness
was dilating into occult realities. Thousands in America, Canada,
Europe, Australia— if their claims were to be credited—were having out-of-the-body astral journeys and eye-opening near-death experiences, talking with spirits, communing with the Dead,
channeling Venusians and Pleiadians, larking with ETs and angels.

The millenniality of the Harmonic Convergence, both its fever-
ish preamble in the early 1980s and its subdued aftermath into the
1990s, was founded on a resurgence, both troubling and culturally

remarkable, of nineteenth-century mediumship and Spiritualism, recycled under the fashionable name of channeling. Jose Argüelles, charismatic scholar, mystic, and promulgator of this planetary event, asserted that he received the idea and its details from his direct contact with beings from Arcturus. In trendy enclaves like Los Angeles, where the per capita distribution of self-proclaimed channels was rising steadily—or elsewhere, in hot spots like Santa Fe, Phoenix, Boulder, Mount Shasta, Sedona—Argüelles' remarkable claim was accepted enthusiastically.

In a stunning progression from the 1960s campus radical, the 1980s channel was fast becoming the new counter-cultural subversive, the maverick philosopher, the psychic radical, challenging, if not outraging, our metaphysical complacency. But in the kind of oxymoron of sociology only America seems capable of, the channel was being swept up by the media as the glamorous, newest, and in some cases, affluent, prodigy of the insatiable television talk show. As expected, the mainstream viewed these psychics without portfolio as ontologically precocious and the straightmen for their sarcasms. Divine intervention is surely needed, "but this being late-Eighties America, we need it repackaged—postmodernized—preferably in telegenic bytes by blow-dried shamans."[1] Channeling with its "Gucci-clad truth seekers and celebrity gurus" makes "great copy and bizarre rituals," but mysticism-by-media can get a little banal.[2] Or as that arbiter of normalcy, the *Wall St. Journal,* quipped that year, "New Age to dawn in August, seers say, and Malibu is ready." [3]

Taking a more positive view of the development, sociologist J. L. Simmons noted: "What's *really* going on in this world is very different from what *appears* to be going on, as expressed in newspaper headlines or in conventional textbooks." Simmons read stacks of "New Age" books, traveled extensively around the U.S to its "paranormal" epicenters, spoke to numerous psychics, and concluded these are signs of nothing less than a worldwide spiritual awakening. "There were millions of people more or less involved in an amorphous, unofficial 'movement' just a couple of steps off to the side of mainstream society." There are a "growing number" of people "loose in the world," Simmons adds, who have had a profound spiritual awakening as a result of an unconventional mystical experience.[4]

Most recently, sociological studies indicate that American Baby Boomers, who have spearheaded the "New Age" all the way into midlife from 1960s campus activism, are finding new spiritual homes—a variety of established and innovative religions from the Catholic Church to Seventh Day Adventist, Assemblies of God, the Mormon Church, and the Church of God. Memberships in these churches climbed dramatically from 1965 to1989, in a range of 63 percent (Nazarene) to 183 percent (Church of God). A January 1992 poll revealed that of the age group 27 to 45, 65 percent reported that religion is "very important," while 73 percent contended the Bible is the "totally accurate" word of God and 40 percent attended some form of religious service in the past week. "Increasing numbers of baby boomers who left the fold years ago are turning religious again, but many are traveling from church to church or faith to faith, sampling creeds, shopping for a custom-made God."[5] A major study of 1,600 Baby Boomers—76 million men and women born between 1946 and 1964—conducted from 1988 to 1992, revealed that 58 percent of this group regularly attends church or synagogue, 28 percent do not but remain "very interested" in religious questions, 9 percent are seekers who hop from faith to faith, and 5 percent are atheists or agnostics. Further, the study discovered that 60 percent favor the exploration of multiple religious traditions, 28 percent believe in reincarnation, 14 percent practice meditation, and 70 percent believe in psychic powers. The statistics indicate "a kind of spiritual renewal occurring among members of this generation," but it does not necessarily mean a return to established religions.[6]

That America is among the world's most religious nations may surprise some, but it's an inevitable and perhaps welcome consequence of its historical climate of fostering religious liberty. The depth and variety of American religious commitment was made public in 1991 through the results of a comprehensive statistical survey of 113,000 Americans as part of the National Survey of Religious Identification (NSRI), the most extensive study of American religious identification in this century. Nearly 90 percent of respondents said they had a specific religious adherence, evidence of America's unique position, both historical and cultural, as a "greenhouse for religious formation, adaption, and change."[7] The

NSRI statistics reflect the "true richness of the country's religious tapestry," its predominant and minor faiths, its well-established and burgeoning creeds, Kosmin and Lachman state. Unarguably, America is a Christian majority, with Catholic and Protestant denominations accounting for 86.2 percent of the adult population. Within this giant cohort, 60 percent is Protestant, substantiating the continuity of Protestant culture that has dominated America since its founding. While Muslims, Buddhists and Hindus account for 0.5, 0.4, and 0.2 percent, respectively, which sounds minute, yet small numbers of people can exert large cultural influences; Buddhist population strongholds, according to NSRI, include California (38 percent), New York (6.535), Virginia (4.5), Washington (4.4), and Massachusetts (4.3).

America's continuing religious pluralism is a starting point for tracing the cultural roots of the apotheosis of the psychic and iconoclastic spirituality that has become increasingly apparent since the 1960s. The indications that we are living on the verge of the supersensible world have been increasingly evident since 1945, when the Baby Boom was born. As this huge population neared adulthood in the 1960s, its exuberance and originality in all aspects of life gained crucial momentum. In large measure its members would carry the emerging energies of cognitive expansion on behalf of mainstream society. The 1960s witnessed the mass initiation of college students through psychedelics into the supersensible worlds. For most the vision was hallucinatory and skewed, the journey unchaperoned and without preparation; the entry was psychically unlawful and the results were often psychologically debilitating, even disastrous. Many glimpsed, under LSD, what the initiated describe as the Guardian of the Threshold, but as any initiate will tell you, the Guardian, for the unprepared, can be fearsome, awful, and dreadful. Other, more fortunate psychedelic "trippers," had a momentary taste of the celestial realms, a homeopathic drop from the golden apple of the Gods. But whether the result was breakdown or epiphany, psychedelia made it unarguably clear that the field of consciousness was far huger—and more troublesome—than consensus reality ever postulated.

The 1960s birthed a strange combination of LSD cults, occultism, and Oriental religions, a Bohemian revisioning of the dream of the earlier nineteenth-century Theosophical occult revival and its espousal of spiritual evolution, expanded consciousness, and liberation.[8] Through the esoteric writings of H.P. Blavatsky, Annie Besant, Charles Leadbeater, Georges Gurdjieff, P. D. Ouspensky, and Paul Brunton, among others, the outer court of the Mysteries was thrown open to the public at large. In America the sons and daughters of WASPS, Catholics, and Jews converted wholesale to the unusual eschatologies of Theosophy, Buddhism, and Hinduism as the Tibetan rigors of the "great path of liberation and Nirvana" supplanted the empty pieties and metaphysical dead ends of establishment religion. Sparking the interest of a metaphysically precocious generation was the landmark study *Psychic Discoveries Behind the Iron Curtain* by Sheila Ostrander and Lynn Schroeder (1970); here they reported on the varieties of psychic research—dowsing, telepathy, ESP, the energy body, aura, psychokinesis, psychotronics—underway in laboratories from Prague to Moscow. Similarly momentous in popular impact, though perhaps less rigorously researched, had been *The Morning of the Magicians* (1963), a report by Louis Pauwels and Jacques Bergier about the alleged prevalence of black magic and occultism in Nazi Germany. Both works highlighted previously unsuspected research and activities beyond the conventional threshold of matter and possibility.

Many who declined the nearly obligatory journey to the East, to Ladakh, to Nepal, to the beckoning Himalayas of the Indian gurus, turned to white shamanism, popularized by the elusive Carlos Castaneda. In 1968 Castaneda published the first in a series of books revealing his astrally tortuous initiation into the "way of knowledge" of a Yaqui Indian sorcerer named Don Juan Matus. In 1980 Michael Harner, a Ph.D. anthropologist, published *The Way of the Shaman*, an accessible text that stimulated among mostly educated white young Americans a decade of engagement with the mystical ways of native peoples—astral travel, the human double, ritual, irregularities in time, animal group souls—and a burgeoning body of literature. The shamanic revelation continues to flourish in the 1990s with numerous first-person narratives of initiation and transformation, such as Kay Cordell Whitaker's *The Reluctant Shaman*, which recounts "a woman's first encounters with the unseen spirits of the Earth."

In the early 1980s, Lynn Andrews, a chic Los Angeles art dealer, began publishing her best-selling accounts of a woman's initiation into the occult ways of Canadian Indian wise women in *Medicine Woman*. Two alleged students of the elusive Castaneda, anthropologist Florinda Donner and Taisha Abelar released their accounts of initiations undergone twenty years earlier with the now famous Yaqui *brujo*, Don Juan Matus. Simultaneously, yet independent of the Castaneda stream, Heather Valencia described her ten years of ceremonial experiences with Yaquis in Arizona.[9] While counter-cultural readers largely accepted the accounts of Castaneda, Andrews, and others as self-evident truth, establishment academics rejected them out-of-hand as uncorroborable anecdotes, dubious and probably imaginary chronicles, but nobody contested the fact they sold millions of copies. If nothing else, the *possibility* of the reality of such unsuspected planes of experience and the role of initiation as the guided induction into their problematic realm began to permeate mass culture—that and the hunger to find them.

American style "white shamanism" has proven to be so culturally acquisitive, some argue, that many native American spiritual leaders are taking umbrage with the New Age Baby Boomer appropriation of their customs including the purification sweat lodge, sun dances, vision quests, chants, drums, and various ceremonial artifacts. Those more stridently opposed to the Baby Boomer's "borrowings," such as members of the National Congress of American Indians, issued a "declaration of war" at the end of 1993 against those "non-Indian wannabes" who exploit their sacred rituals for profit, glamour, or a kind of "spiritual fashion statement or hobby." Others think it's salutary to share the "medicine" because it provides non-native Americans "spiritual nourishment" that facilitates personal change and it offers constructive, even reverent, ways for urbanized Americans to relate sympathetically—to regain "connectedness"—to the planet and its threatened environment.[10] Either way, the intellectual and spiritual parameters of American culture—are broadening to include what were once regarded as foreign, if not archaic, philosophies and practices.

Blending 1960s psychedelia, shamanic exploration, and willful hallucinatory insight is the iconoclastic Terence McKenna, dubbed "the Copernicus of consciousness," who extols the archaic in consciousness and advocates "the ethnopharmacology of spiritual transformation."[11] Renowned quantum physicist Fred Allan Wolf reports on his shamanic initiations and mind-bending perceptions with the botanical hallucinogen *ayahuasca* among Peruvian medicine men in *The Eagle's Quest.* Wolf, and other heretical quantum physicists such as Amit Goswami, are outlining a new paradigm of cognition in physics, pioneering the introduction of consciousness as a primary tool of investigation in particle physics and, tacitly, contending it is the fabled ultimate particle and building block of matter.[12] Wolf and colleagues build on the earlier conceptual groundbreaking provided by Fritjof Capra (*The Tao of Physics*, 1976) and Gary Zukav (*The Dancing Wu Li Masters*, 1979), who drew provocative parallels between Asian mysticism and Western physics. Physicist Arthur Zajonc applied spiritual understanding to physical processes, tracing, through the history of light, the evolution of Western consciousness and the relationship between the "outer light of Nature and the inner light of the human Spirit."[13]

Possibly one of the most promising developments for the emerging spiritualized framework of Western, but particularly American, culture was the refusal in late 1993 by the U.S. Congress to further fund the multibillion dollar Supercollider particle accelerator already under construction in Waxahatchie, Texas. While physicists will not share this viewpoint, the defeat of the super-expensive project—whose research would only further entrench the Western materialist-reductionist scientific paradigm of matter which underpins and thoroughly permeates mainstream medical and philosophical thinking—may be the necessary shock that frees up the attention of Western scientists to contemplate other possibilities. They may discover that consciousness, the I of the beholder, and not the speculative Higgs-Boson (on whose behalf the Supercollider was being built) is the ultimate "God particle."[14]

Meanwhile other intrepid souls began to take advantage of the unpacking of the occult Mystery schools in the 1970s. A variety of esoteric schools offering formerly veiled arcana and initiations sprang up, most often constellating around the presumed accomplishments of a founder-guru. Eckankar, "the ancient science of soul travel through dreams, imagination, and direct projection," with roots in an arcana surat practice called "surat shabda yoga," appeared in 1964 when its founder Paul Twitchell declared himself the 971st Mahanta and Living Eck Master of the Vaigiri Order. In 1988 the movement claimed 411 centers worldwide. The Arica Institute, a syncretic psychospiritual discipline with roots in Sufism, was founded in 1971 by Chilean Oscar Ichazo. Erhard Seminar Training (or EST, later renamed The Forum) was the unique synthesis of Werner Erhard, featuring psychologically confrontational situations for insight and breakthrough. Arica and EST were intensely popular throughout the 1970s as the means for quasi-esoteric initiations and inner work. Less prominent groups such as Builders of the Adytum (founded on the teachings of Paul Foster Case), the Arcane School (based on the works of Alice Bailey), and the Erevna, the Researchers of the Truth, founded by the Cypriot magus "Daskalos" (Stylianos Atteshlis), as reported in a popular series by his American student Kyriacos Markides, propagated aspects of the Western Mystery tradition within new age culture.[15]

Other approaches prominent in the field of mental science, or "how thoughts create reality," are the Church of Scientology (founded by L. Ron Hubbard in 1952 upon his theory of subconscious-generated engrammic abberations called "Dianetics," now with an estimated 8 million members and nontaxable assets of $400 million); the Avatar training system (founded by Harry Palmer in 1987, now flourishing in 37 countries with 20,000 graduates); and the multiple social and educational projects constellated about Maharishi Mahesh Yogi (including Maharishi International University in Fairfield, Iowa), famous as the Beatles' guru in Transcendental Meditation in the 1960s. In the mid-1980s magazines such as *The Quest, Gnosis,* and *Magical Blend* began presenting semiesoteric treatments of topics from the Western inner tradition; by the 1990s, they are joined by dozens more small circulation, esoteric speciality magazines treating Egyptian mysteries, Tantra, crop circles, shamanism, Wicca, UFOs, conspiracy theories, and suppressed technologies, and much else.

Another, more beatific, plane of experience announced itself in Western culture in the late 1960s with the revelations from Findhorn, an emerging intentional spiritual community in northern

Scotland. From Findhorn, founded on the visions of mystics Eileen Caddy, Dorothy Maclean, and David Spangler, came reports of communications with the elemental and angelic realms, of meetings with flower devas, gnomes, landscape angels, even the great Pan. Paul Hawken captured the excitement of Findhorn in his now classic first-person account, *The Magic of Findhorn* (1975). Only a few years earlier Western readers had been first astonished, then entranced, with the possibility of botanical sentience and interspecies communication in Bird and Tompkins' *The Secret Life of Plants* (1972). Later, in *To Hear the Angels Sing* (1980), Dorothy Maclean documented her personal odyssey of "co-creation with the devic kingdom." Still later in the 1980s Michaelle Small-Wright showed thousands how to design a Perelandra garden to actively court the devic presence (*Behaving as if the God in All Life Mattered*, 1987). Spiritual raconteur and world peregrinator Timothy Wyllie talks, telepathically, with angels, ETs, dolphins, and other "spiritual intelligences," as recounted in his two books, *Dolphins, ETs, and Angels* (1984) and *Dolphins, Telepathy & Underwater Birthing* (1993).

In fact, angels, angelmania and angelology are rapidly becoming the 1990's version of channeled entities in terms of popularity, thanks to a series of mainstream bestsellers about angelic encounters and contact techniques.[16] The 1990s may prove to be the Decade of Angels, just as the 1980s was the Decade of Channels, and the 1970s the Decade of Gurus. A December 1993 poll of 500 adult Americans revealed surprising statistics regarding angels: 69 percent believe in the existence of angels (up from 50 percent, according to a 1988 Gallup Poll); 55 percent conceive of angels as "higher spiritual beings created by God with special powers to act as his agents on Earth"; 46 percent believe they have a personal guardian angel; 32 percent have personally felt an angelic presence; and 49 percent believe in the existence of fallen angels or devils. "Suddenly the heavenly host is upon us and in this New Age a grassroots revolution of the spirit has all sorts of people asking all sorts of questions about angels," quipped *Time* in a year-end cover story on the subject.[17] "Angels are appearing everywhere in America," announced *Newsweek*, which also published a feature story on angels the same week as *Time*, noting the subject's burgeoning marketability—"where angels walk, fearless merchandisers eagerly tread." Angels are attractive (both commercially and intellectually) in the 1990s because they require no religious denominational commitment, they are the rapturous answer to the "homelessness of secularity," and an argument against the void of death, as our materialist culture has conceived it for centuries. Yet, might today's angels be too cute? query *Time* and *Newsweek*. "The guardian angels of the current American movement come across as either celestial boy scouts or substitutes for the doting grandparents the visionaries never knew."[18] Fashion-conscious New Yorkers were even scurrying about at year's end in search of angelic accouterments (including wings and "the perfect angel robe") for New Year's Eve parties: "I wanted glitter, filmy material, and an out-of-body experience," explained a *New York Times* columnist.[19]

If intuitives could talk with angels, then what about the sentient spirits of nature? Maybe all of nature herself might be conversant, even coherent. Findhorn was the natural conceptual foundation for the Gaia Hypothesis developed by the independent British atmospheric scientist James Lovelock. In *Gaia: A New Look at Life on Earth* (1979), Lovelock shook the mechanistic reductionism of academia by asserting that the planet, anciently called Gaia, operates as a single, integrated, self-regulating biological organism. Lovelock's idea was imaginatively extended by Michael Tobias (*The Voice of the Planet*, 1990) in an extended imaginary dialogue between a disillusioned ecologist on retreat in Tibet and Gaia, who speaks through a voice-enhanced computer. British plant physiologist Rupert Sheldrake added further scientific, if controversial, credence to the concept of botanical sentience through his "hypothesis of formative causation, morphogenetic fields, and morphic resonance." In *A New Science of Life* (1981), Sheldrake postulated that species uniformity and evolution are maintained through subtle informational fields acting across time and space.

In the 1980s the implications of Caddy's Findhorn, Lovelock's Gaia, and Sheldrake's morphogenetic fields were woven into a new quasi-political/conservation stream including Deep Ecology, eco-feminism, socially-engaged Buddhism, and the Greens. First formulated in 1972 by Arne Naess, a Norwegian philosophy professor, Deep Ecology concepts—the ecological self, the council of all beings, core democracy in the biosphere, thinking like a mountain—advocated that personal identity be extended into the world of nature and that self-realization include plants, animals, and the landscape.

The mother-soil underlying the appeal of Deep Ecology has been the powerful upwelling of the Feminine in an American culture dominated by male reductionist rationality. The Feminine is resurfacing as prolific and challenging as Medusa, assaulting the traditions of patriarchy at all levels. Increasingly through the 1980s, the Feminine reasserted herself in woman's spirituality, eco-feminism, outspoken lesbianism, pro-choice politicking, non-Christian Goddess veneration, and a resurgence of the mythic, intuitive, pictorial, symbolic, and *imaginative* mode of consciousness. The depth psychology of Carl Jung and the mythopoeic explorations of Joseph Campbell, both intensely popular in the 1990s, burgeon in this richly feminized context.

The perception of holism, human ecology, cultural feminization, alternative spiritualities, and systems integration began to emerge in the field of alternative, complementary, and natural medicine and health care in the early 1970s with the founding of *East West Journal, Yoga Journal,* and *New Age Journal,* whose combined estimated readership (1993) exceeds 500,000. Older, nonchemical, nonsurgical, nonallopathic modalities for healing became widely available—acupuncture and Chinese medicine, homeopathy, naturopathy, herbalism, iridology, vibrational healing, chiropractic, flower essences—as health care consumers took their education in hand. Insightful physicians like Norman Cousins, Larry Dossey, Deepak Chopra, Bernie Siegel, began combining disciplines, such as meditation, quantum physics, mind-body research, and Asian philosophies, to the conceptual base of holistic medicine as an empowerment for the experience and therapeutic potentials of being a patient. In particular advocates for holistic medicine outlined possible psychospiritual etiologies for disease states and emphasized the active role of cognition, consciousness, and focused will in the resolution of illness. In *The Future of the Body* (1992), Michael Murphy, founder of Esalen Institute in California, published the results of his thirty years of research into the overlap of holistic practice and consciousness. In studying humanity's "emergent capacities for self-transcendence" and further evolution, Murphy described twelve sets of metanormal human attributes including "supreme cognitive capacities for unitive knowledge."

Underlying all these approaches was the concept of body-mind unity, or as the scientists preferred to call it, psychoneuroimmunology (PNI)—the demonstrable, even quantifiable, effect of thoughts and emotions on physiology. PNI, of course, is inherently (and constructively) heretical in light of the foundations of Western materialist science which, in the fields of physics, biology, and medicine, unilaterally rules out the efficacy of human consciousness in the affairs of matter. The development of PNI stimulated a great deal of supportive research and thinking, all of which is restoring consciousness to its rightfully prominent (if not fundamental) position within biology. Numerous key texts for this evolving paradigm of natural medicine, most often written by practitioners, have appeared, notably *Vibrational Medicine* (1988) by Richard Gerber, (M.D.). New technical innovations, such as Kirlian photography and Nuclear Magnetic Resonance Imaging, made the subtle energy fields of the human body apparent—"fields of life," another name for what the esoteric tradition traditionally calls the etheric body. Television journalist Bill Moyers brought the holistic concepts of acupuncture, PNI, yoga, attitude, diet, the meaning of illness, and the utility of directed consciousness to a mass audience in 1993 with his *Healing and the Mind* multipart series on PBS and, simultaneously, a best-selling book of interviews with leaders and innovators in holistic healing.

For many the path to self-realization began at the doorway of death and dying. In 1969 intrepid M.D. Elisabeth Kübler-Ross opened a bold new field of inquiry with her landmark *On Death and Dying.* Here she characterized dying as an archetypal fivefold psychological process and cited anecdotal evidence from patients of transcendent experiences on the threshold of death. Raymond Moody's *Life After Life* (1975) catapulted the Near-Death Experience (NDE) and its anecdotal reports of the survival of consciousness beyond the body into public awareness. Moody studied the case histories of 150 people resuscitated from apparent physical death and found they uniformly reported metaphysical journeys in consciousness. A 1992 Gallup Poll revealed that 5 percent of the American population (8 million) admitted having had an NDE and that 35 percent of people who come close to death undergo an NDE. The near-death experiencer—blissfully disembodied and heaven-bound, or at least gaining a new take on life—became a cinematic icon in such movies as *All That Jazz* (1979), *Resurrection* (1980), *Bliss* (1985), *Flatliners* (1990), and *Jacob's Ladder* (1990).

Kenneth Ring, a transpersonal psychologist, substantiated the NDE with systematic studies, reported in *Life at Death* (1980), *Heading Toward Omega* (1984), and *The Omega Project* (1992). Ring formulated a "parapsychological-holographic" explanation for NDEs, describing them as spiritual experiences that catalyze awakening and facilitate psychic abilities. Melvin Morse, M.D., documented the incidence of post-NDE personality transformation (*Transformed by the Light*, 1992) reporting that NDEs are "paranormal events that happen to normal people," that they are "a real human perception, one that changes people forever." Morse interviewed 100 adults who had undergone NDEs as children at least ten years earlier (and 150 control subjects who hadn't) and found long term changes such as decreased death anxiety, increased psychic abilities, a higher zest for living, and augmented intelligence. The field expanded yet further through the researches of psychiatrist Stanislav Grof, M.D., who linked psychedelics, NDEs, shamanic breakthroughs, symbolic dying meditations, "holotrophic breathing," and psychological developments, beginning with *The Human Encounter With Death* (1978). Grof encouraged clients to credit that consciousness could be independent of the body and that death could be a voyage into the "cosmic unknown." More recently, in *The Holotropic Mind* (1992), he explains how to consciously access and experience the mind's three core levels, which he describes as biographical, perinatal, and transpersonal, for psychospiritual healing. And in late 1992, Betty J. Eadie, an unknown author, published *Embraced by the Light* about her near-death experience in 1973, in which, as she reports, she experienced a whirlwind tour through heaven, meeting angels and Jesus; the book sold 590,000 copies in its first eight months of publication, testifying to the strong popular interest in the NDE phenomenon.

The survival and operation of consciousness outside the body, sometimes called astral traveling or out-of-body experience (OBE), was elaborated extensively by retired businessman Robert

Monroe in his *Journeys Out of the Body* (1971) and *Far Journeys* (1985). Here Monroe, through deliberate brain "hemispheric synchronization," propelled himself like a new Magellan into the astral plane for which he provided an informal cartography. A sibling to the revival of interest in botanical hallucinogens mentioned above is the search for technologically enhanced consciousness. Psychotechnology, as Monroe's work demonstrates, claims to shortcut the efforts of meditation, induce euphoria, relieve stress, bring peak experiences and maybe enlightenment through electronic mind machines based on scientific knowledge of brain waves and chemistry, argues psychotronics maven Michael Hutchison, author of the comprehensive review *Megabrain*.[20] Monroe's OBEs, induced through sound-frequency hemispheric entrainment, represented an aspect of the burgeoning field of cybernetics, or artificial intelligence, that fecund interface between human mind and human-made machine. But the most sophisticated expression of the cybernetic revolution to date is called virtual reality (VR), a data-cloud ménage of desktop computers, interactive video games, designer realities, and, for some, recidivist psychedelia.

VR exponents credit University of Utah's Ivan Sutherland as the godfather of computer graphics whose 1968 breakthroughs have made the "head-mounted video displays" of the 1990s possible. According to *Mondo 2000*, a frothy bimonthly magazine from Berkeley, the information and communications technology of VR epitomizes the New Edge. "We are amplifying the mythos of the sophisticated, high-complexity, fast-lane/real time, intelligent, active and creative reality hacker . . . call it cyberpunk, call it reality-hacking, call it a hyper-hip consumerist wet-dream—but it was obvious at *Verbum* magazine's Digital Be-In that the new 'counter-culture' is here and in full frenzy."[21] As *Time* quipped in a cover story, cyberpunk is a futuristic subculture erupting from the electronic underground to surf the dark edges of the computer edge, offering virtual sex, smart drugs, and synthetic rock and roll.[22] For journalist Howard Rheingold, the interactive technology of virtual reality, cyberspace, and artificial reality equips us to "grasp reality through illusion."[23] The cyberspace novels of William Gibson (*Neuromancer*, 1984; *Mona Lisa Overdrive*, 1988; *Virtual Light*, 1993) vividly portray the interlocking

25

worlds of artificial intelligence, virtual reality, disembodied minds set within a cyberpunk milieu. In cyberspace, which is a computer-generated single-person experiential realm, information becomes geography.

VR's cyberspace domain is brassy if not audacious, a "consensual hallucination" of "unthinkable complexity... ranged in the nonspace of the mind." One VR traveler, his eyes strapped into video-screen eye goggles, left his body, "cradled in its usual cozy node of space-time coordinates" in the Cyberia room of a company called Autodesk in California, for cyberspace, "a universe churned up from computer code, the first commercially available world-in-a-can, a Disneyland for epistemologists, a realm that will be ultimately bounded only by the human imagination."[24] The confluence of VR, computer networks, global electronic databases, even the re-emergence of psychedelic drugs, is a hyperspace configuration journalist Douglas Rushkoff calls "Cyberia." Cyberia is the "new edge," the place "alluded to by the mystical teachings of every religion, the theoretical tangents of every science, and the wildest speculations of every imagination," writes Rushkoff—and in our time, Cyberia "is thought to be within our reach." As virtual reality guru Jaron Lanier sees it, VR heralds a future of interactive creativity, a subjective virtuality of designer-realities. "The new culture is going to be an inter-active culture, in which everybody creates, in a sense, his or her own products. The only way you can really have access to interactive materials is if you're participating in the creation of it yourself"—which means, making things, making virtual reality worlds.[25] The field of virtual reality, mind machines, and hemispheric synchronization must be appreciated in the broader context of a half-century-long quest for artificial intelligence (AI) in the form of ultracompetent computers and humanoid robots. "The machines will eventually excel us in intelligence and it will become impossible for us to pull the plug on them," speculates AI scholar Daniel Crevier.[26]

Another world-in-a-can but a more subdued form of virtual reality but one with enormous culture-shaping potency is the movies. Hollywood in recent years has flirted, often with great commercial success, with metaphysical "idea bites." In America popular culture is epitomized by the cinema, so when the movie moguls start serving up occult themes, in however dilute, sensational, or sentimental a manner, then clearly we are witnessing an expansion of the boundaries of cognition as the Mysteries stream out of the temple.

First came the UFO/ET wave, beginning in the late 1960s, in which benevolent outer space beings made transformative visits to Earth, in movies like *2001: A Space Odyssey* (1968), *The Man Who Fell to Earth* (1976), *Close Encounters of the Third Kind* (1977), *ET* (1982), *Starman* (1984), *2010* (1984), *Cocoon* (1985), *Flight of the Navigator* (1986). The neotechnological postulations of science fiction, the demography of the galaxy, and the requisites of heroic initiation were all cast into archetypal mythodramas in the phenomenally popular *Star Wars* trilogy (1977–1983), the *Star-Trek* quintet (1979–1989), and the *Superman* quartet (1978–1987). These themes are continued even into the 1990s with the conceptually recast *StarTrek—The Next Generation* television series with its interdimensional holodeck and uranopolitan voyaging (and even further, with its successor, *StarTrek—Deep Space Nine*). Time travel, interdimensionality, and the malleability of history were dramatized in the triple installments of *Back to the Future!* (1985–1989) and *The Navigator* (1988). The vagaries and ambivalent entities of the astral plane came to cinematic realization in a series of occult comic nightmares.[27] Then Hollywood's experiment with digestible, marketable occultism broke further virgin ground in the 1980s with films about life after death, NDEs and OBEs, communication with the Dead, reincarnation, and angelic presences.[28]

Of undeniable significance for the metaphysical nourishment of popular culture has been the contributions of Hollywood actress, dancer, and author Shirley MacLaine. MacLaine's critics see her as the doyen of *shtick* but her middle-aged fans praise her as virtually the new Helena Blavatsky. Her serial autobiography (*Out on a Limb*, 1983, which sold 3 million copies; *Dancing in the Light*, 1985, which sold 2.2 million; *It's All in the Playing*, 1987) and genial follow-up textbook (*Going Within: A Guide for Inner Transformation*, 1989) and video (*Shirley MacLaine's Inner Workout*, 1989) translated the generalities of psychic spirituality into multivitamins for mass culture. In 1987 "the New Age's reigning whirling dervish" took her "cosmic act on the road" with her Higher

Self seminars, which grossed an estimated $1.5 million. While collecting $300 per weekend participant, MacLaine shepherded her flock into the world of chakras, reality design, and inner workout. *Newsweek* described the seminars as "part cosmic pep rally, part seance-in-a-circus-tent."

It was a courageous, if superficial, effort that culminated in her January 1987 ABC–TV picaresque mini-series (*Out on a Limb*), replete with all the shibboleths of New Age culture—special-effects OBEs and UFOs, synchronistic meetings, past life regressions, even live spirit channeling, possibly the first televised mediumship in the world. In that remarkable Convergence year, MacLaine also brokered the reputations of several now famous and wealthy "brand name" channels, including J. Z. Knight (Ramtha), Jach Pursel (Lazaris), and Kevin Ryerson (John, Obadiah, Tom MacPherson). MacLaine took an enormous amount of media ridicule for her forthright claims about the supersensible world that year. In a sense she became the scapegoat for an orthodoxy frightened by tremors within the bedrock of its materialist beliefs yet disdainful of the dilettantism and metaphysical laissez-faire running sloppily rampant in the "vast spiritual kindergarten" of the New Age. The New Age itself, said one acerbic critic, is an "essentially harmless anthology of illusions."[29] The *San Francisco Chronicle* lambasted MacLaine's efforts as "screwy metaphysics, a curious case of karma comedienne, deliriously wacko."[30]

For MacLaine, Isness is her business, satirized *The New York Review of Books'* Martin Gardner who was not impressed with her "paranormal poppycock." MacLaine embodied a droll mixture of "egoism and altruism, intelligence and gullibility, curiosity and willful ignorance," railed Gardner, but he conceded that her self-obsession was evidently in resonance with the times. "Jesus only walked on water; Shirley danced on it. Shirley is teetering on the edge of solipsism, the ultimate in self-absorption. The dead are alive and talking to us. The occult revolution shows no sign of abating."[31] The intensity of the media sarcasm, more than anything else, indicated the depth of resistance in mainstream society to the profound metaphysical turbulence within its complacently materialist world view. It was in part a journalistic posture because it was widely known (and joked about) that Wall Street Yuppies consulted psychics for truly inside advice on the stock market and their financial fortunes. Psychism after all had its practical side.

In 1987 the full extent of the psychic floriation of America became alarmingly—or pleasingly—evident. The media was awash in anecdotal reportage as hundreds of new trance channelers popped out of the woodwork into folk hero celebrity status, especially in Los Angeles. One channel slipped into a live trance on the Phil Donahue Show in February that year as Exton, his spirit source, "spouted the usual platitudes."[32] A *Wall Street Journal* reporter toured psychic Los Angeles and filed a bemused anthropologist's compendium of California channels.[33]

The media waxed eloquent as *U.S. News & World Report* described the "Mystics on Main Street." The *Los Angeles Times* considered "the new chic, metaphysical fad of channeling;" *Playboy* went "channel hopping" to encounter the Dead; *Newsweek* listened to Ramtha and "voices from beyond." *People Weekly* used Shirley MacLaine's TV quest to "shed light on a new dawning of soul seekers" then took a marketing publicist's stance in introducing Penny Torres, 27, as "the hottest newcomer to channeling in Southern California"; *Time* pondered "New Age Harmonies," veiling their bafflement in wisecracks about this "strange mix of spirituality and superstition sweeping across the country." More recently, *The New York Times* described the paradox of reverence and rigidity in the New Age, likening its parodiable excesses to a kind of "fundamentalism for liberals."[34] Meanwhile the channeling community itself joined the ranks of media through a variety of nationally distributed new journals, including *Halo, Spirit Speaks, Body-Mind-Spirit,* and *Connecting Link,* as public organs for the new oracles.

When the statistics—or what Madison Avenue likes to call market share—started appearing it became apparent a new occult American demography was emerging. For many, channeling by 1987 had become a New Age growth industry. The West Coast was home to a new cabal of millionaire sleeping prophets and Cinderella trance mediums issuing corporate directives masquerading as guidance from the astral plane as arcana became a commodity. Evidently, the marketplace demanded this. A 1980 Gallup Poll revealed that 71 percent of Americans believed in an afterlife while more recently the University of Chicago's National Opinion Research Council poll stated that of the 42 percent who believe they have had contact with someone who died, 78 percent said they saw, 50 percent said they heard, and 18 percent said they talked with the departed; meanwhile, 30 percent of Americans who say they don't believe in afterlife still claim to have had personal contact with the departed.[35]

A *USA Weekend* poll of 614 randomly selected adults revealed that 23 percent believe in reincarnation, 14 percent believe in mediums, 39 percent believe that intelligent beings exist on other planets, 6 percent have had an OBE, and 10 percent have seen a UFO.[36] *American Health* updated the University of Chicago's data noting 67 percent of those surveyed had experienced ESP, 31 percent had experienced clairvoyance, 29 percent had visions, 42 percent had contact with the Dead. "Our studies show that people who've tasted the paranormal, whether they accept it intellectually or not, are anything but religious nuts or psychiatric cases. They are, for the most part, ordinary Americans somewhat above the norm in education and intelligence and somewhat less than average in religious involvement."[37] In yet another Gallup poll in 1988, 57 percent of Americans believed UFOs are real; 23 percent said reincarnation is real; but for people aged 18 to 24, it is 30 percent; and for people over 50, 21 percent; 24 percent believed it is possible to contact the dead, but for those under 30, it was 38 percent. A 1990 Gallup Poll revealed that one in four Americans either believes in ghosts or is guided by astrology; one in six claim to have communicated with deceased spirits; one in seven has witnessed a UFO, while 47 percent generally affirm a belief in their existence.[38] All of this is set within the context of a country scintillating with spiritual organizations. By 1989 the U.S. was home to 1500 different primary religious organizations, including churches, sects, cults, temples, societies, missions—evidence of "the massive pluralism so evident in contemporary American life."[39] Looking around the converging ethers of 1987, it was easy to conclude a strange, hybrid pantheon had descended diaphanously like morning dew upon the receptive tendrils of Western culture. It was a new Olympian congeries of deceased relatives and intimates, advanced human souls, disincarnate masters, ETs and space brothers, angels and archangels, all queuing urgently for that glossolalic moment at the human microphone.

The extended family had been gathering and communicating, in fact, for the last hundred years. There was Aphraar, a recently deceased Englishman trying to contact his living father (1905); Patience Worth, the seventeenth-century spirit of a Massachusetts woman killed by Indians (1910); Helen and Harry Blount, who posted letters from the other side back home to their living sister in Vermont (1913); Sigwart, a German artist killed in battle, who communicated with his sister through "the bridge over the river" (1915); Private Dowding, a British schoolteacher killed in World War I (1917); Frances Banks, a Catholic nun, who confided her "testimony of light" with her extant colleague (1965); Cynthia Sandys, a British woman who died young but kept in touch with her mother, sending her "awakening letters" (1978); James, the suicidal young son of prominent American clergyman Bishop Pike (1966); Arthur Ford, a renowned psychic, who changed roles after death and became Ruth Montgomery's spirit guide (1971); Richard, a World War II sailor killed in action (1985); Tom MacPherson, a sixteenth-century Irish pickpocket (1980s); Obadiah, a nineteenth-century Haitian herbalist and storyteller (1980s); and Janice, a channel's former "dear friend" (1987).

The next echelon of the astral plane made conspicuous through their contacts in this century, and increasingly in the last two decades, has been the sphere of what channels describe as advanced human souls, ascended masters, and illumined teachers. Over a hundred years ago there was Phylos the Thibetan (*sic*), a "Theocristian student and occult adept" (1886), and soon after came the Company of Avalon and the Watchers, sixteenth-century Glastonbury Abbey monks, opening the "gates of remembrance" (1907). Then came the legendary, enigmatic St. Germaine, "ascended master of the violet flame and I AM," beginning in 1932 with Guy Ballard, but turning polygamous from the 1970s onward with multiple channels. Other masters announced themselves: Dhjwal Khul, "a Tibetan disciple of a certain degree," presiding over a larger group of Tibetan lamas (1919); Silver Birch, a North American Indian, making "no appeal of illustrious personage, title, rank, or fame" (1930); White Eagle, once Hiawatha and a Mohawk Indian chief, now a spokesman for the White Brotherhood (1930); John the Evangelist, one of the twelve disciples of Christ (1967), first through David Spangler, then others; Christ, who purportedly dictated a 1,200-page "Course in Miracles" to an atheist academic (1975); and Ramtha, a 35,000 year old Lemurian warrior and "enlightened one" who "became God in one lifetime and will become a grand teacher upon this plane" (1977).[40]

Recently a more amorphous category has emerged, sibling to the advanced disincarnate humans, as a gallimaufry of the un-born-human-like intelligences who have never entered physical incarnation or in some cases even congealed into a describable form. There is Seth, "an energy essence personality, the psychological personification of a supraconscious extension of my normal self" (1963); Michael, a recombined entity of 1,050 old soul fragments and individual essences occupying the mid-causal plane (1970); Lazaris, the Consummate Friend, outside of time, "a consciousness without form, a spark of light" (1974); The Brotherhood of God (1980), a "God-created group of spirit entities, the Counselor that Jesus promised;" the Brotherhood, a group of souls "under the direction of the Logos of this planet" (1987); and Orion, five nonphysical beings "of a differing reality whose energies present themselves in the voice of one speaker" (1989).[41]

The UFO-contactee movement that began in the late 1940s in recent years delivered up various oracular contacts beginning in the 1970s. Increasingly, the mellifluous ETs of the 1980s hail from ever more remote galactic locales. Probably the most popular of orating space brothers is Commander Ashtar, a slightly bombastic Jean Luc Picard of some behemoth starship cruising Earth's ionosphere. Ashtar was first heard from in 1952 by George Van Tassel, when he gave his job description as "commandant quadra sector, patrol station Schare, all projections, all waves;" in 1982 Ashtar claimed another human mouthpiece named Tuella, through whom he outlined his vision of impending catastrophe, harvest, and "project world evacuation"[42]

Other galactic beings, not always with craft, announced themselves. There was Ra, an ancient golden Venusian astronaut from "a sixth density social memory complex, three evolutionary cycles ahead of us" (1981); Zoosh from Alpha Centauri (1989); Ebban from Jupiter; the Pleiadians, "a collective of extraterrestrials, our ancient family, ambassadors;" Bashar, a commander from Essassani, the "place of living light 500 light years away in a different vibrational plane;" Leah, another Venusian, the channel's multilifetime spiritual teacher, bringing "the energy of the Vanished Ones who are your planet's ancestors who came from the stars" (1988). A strange subset of alleged UFO contact is the alien abduction category, as recounted most notably in the mass market works of Budd Hopkins (*Missing Time*, 1981; *Intruders*, 1987) and Whitley Strieber (*Communion*, 1987; *Transformation*, 1988). According to these accounts human beings have been forcefully brought into contact with extraterrestrial intelligences and submitted to physically unpleasant and psychologically torturous examinations. A somewhat more bizarre branch of the space brothers category is what Ruth Montgomery calls "the extraterrestrial walk-in." Here, in a form of voluntary possession, the present incarnate human soul walks out and a more advanced galactic being walks in, picking up the threads of one's life.[43]

We musn't overlook the tremendous influence on the imaginative, picture-making life of post-1945 readers by the burgeoning genre of science fiction. Numerous authors, applying principles of quantum physics, myth, robotics, and masterful storytelling technique, have radically stretched readers' concepts of time, space, matter, consciousness, extraterrestrial life, and evolutionary possibilities, bringing them to the virtual threshold of a cognitive expansion, even "transcendence and a unique extra-dimensional experience." Through science fiction "we seek that which is beyond the bounds of our best knowledge."[44]

As we live further into the closing decade of the twentieth century, the angelic realm is still significantly underrepresented in the channeler's roster, although as we noted above, awareness of angels among New Agers as a category of cognition is increasing. Ken Carey's best-selling channeled quartet (*Starseed Transmissions, Vision, Return of the Bird Tribes, Starseed—The Third Millennium*) derive from "informational cells within the galactic organism," which Carey sometimes calls Raphael, "a focus of collective human consciousness" that "comes from the Presence."[45] For about a decade Solara Antara Amaa-Ra has channeled the "Golden Solar Angels," which have co-created with her several books (*Invoking Your Celestial Guardians*, 1986; and *The Star-Borne:*

A Remembrance for the Awakened Ones, 1990) and *The Starry Messenger,* a bimonthly newsletter for the angelic Diaspora.[46] In the early 1970s a young California scientist named J. J. Hurtak made what many now regard as the state-of-the-art return home. During prayer one night he was conveyed by the "Master Ophanim Enoch" first to "Metatron, the Creator of Light in the outer universe," then "into the presence of the Divine Father." Classical angelologies describe the Ophanim as a high-ranking angelic family and Metatron as an archangel foremost in the celestial hierarchy. Hurtak unpacked his concentrated celestial revelations in *The Book of Knowledge: The Keys of Enoch* (1971), "probably the single most scientifically rich and puzzling set of channeled material in modern times."[47]

Few channeled sources at present can claim the kind of exalted angelic pedigree behind Hurtak's material. Nor should we automatically accredit this source as representing a higher degree of spiritual authority simply on the basis of its epistemological claims or attributions to source; it might, but it is better to exercise prudence until we have reliable guidelines. This is a highly problematic area, and one that desperately needs rigorous standards of knowledge and evaluation. For one, there is the high cost of the Mysteries. During her heyday J. Z. Knight was collecting up to $1000 a person for tickets to hear her spiritual tenant, Ramtha; some clients spent an estimated $100,000 at the Ramtha School of Enlightenment in Helm, Washington, on tapes, books, and paraphernalia—all of which made Knight a multimillionaire.[48] "Some of the fees currently being charged are out of all proportion to the actual quality of the material being received," comments clairvoyant David Spangler. "It's a bit like paying $500 for a rare edition of *War and Peace* and getting the *Comics Illustrated* version instead."[49]

It's one thing to mistake the comics for *War and Peace* but when the comics start boasting they are high yogic texts and manuals for awakening, then *caveat emptor* should be our mantra. In the channeling world of the late 1980s an alarming equation developed between psychism and spirituality, such that if one was psychic, then *a priori* one was spiritually advanced. The trouble here is that, as the biographies of many of the prominent channels indicate, in most cases the new psychics had spontaneously combusted into clairvoyance without any previous training or inner preparation. As we will note later in this book, that kind of foundation is not necessarily indicative of spiritual attainment nor is it the basis for reliable cognition of the supersensible world or advice made from information obtained in this way. In fact metaphysically this is a highly treacherous terrain with no end of possibilities for deception, error, spiritual digression, even ontological danger. While the initiated and the sensible could recognize this jerry-built bond of psychism and spirituality as meretricious, many enthusiastic neophytes were wide-open and vulnerable, buying a lot of dubious advice wholesale.[50]

This is the negative, problematic side of the recent efflorescence of channeling. But it's not all bogus and spurious, and we must be careful to peel away the misleading layers of media misrepresentation and pejorative, the internal glamorization by the New Age and the psychics themselves, to find the potential gold buried within. For there is gold in the phenomenon; perhaps only a little, but surely this much occult activity must indicate something profound is desperately struggling to surface through the permeable membrane of the Western psyche at the end of the twentieth century. We must ask difficult, even ruthless questions to get at the uncorrupted heart of this activity. How has channeling come so easily, so rapidly, to Western culture at the close of the twentieth century? As historian Jon Klimo so accurately commented in 1987, "Currently there is an extraordinary upswing in public interest in the phenomenon we now call channeling."[51] As this troubled century draws to a close, interest in expanding the parameters of consciousness and the nonmaterial realms, highlighted in the events of 1987, continues to increase.

Now in the 1990s, the continued prominence of channeling is a leading indicator (but certainly not the only one as we have documented numerous complementary signs above—as the 1990s progress, the New Age is talking more with angels) of a general heightening of sensitivity in the West to the supersensible world. We see the unmistakable signature of American culture upon these varied examples of cognitive expansion: the tendencies to inflate, trivialize, materialize, sensationalize, glamorize, idolize, and generally render as celebrities unto Hollywood in all its media guises. So we must be careful, assiduously so, that these vital young shoots of truly new culture do not get corrupted or destroyed by wrong gardening practices; and we need to ask: what does all this mean for the evolution of human consciousness in our time? The parameters of human cognition are clearly expanding even if, in this rapid unfoldment, they open into certain problematic, possibly digressive, areas. For what inner purpose has this multifaceted cognitive expansion almost spontaneously and certainly anomalously irrupted into mainstream culture? To what psychological and cultural end is our sensitivity developing? Does channeling have a state-of-the-art, peer review system, a scheme of responsible criteria for assessing quality or accuracy? Are there standards for occult investigation or reliable road maps for peregrinations off the beaten philosophical track of Western orthodoxy? And does channeling and sudden cognitive dilation pose spiritual dangers for the unprepared? Do the disembodied, spiritual intelligences, and angels all have our best interests in mind? These are vital questions too few seem to be asking, yet to leave them unasked, and worse still, unanswered, may imperil our spiritual evolution as awakening human beings.

Rudolf Steiner (1861–1925), the Austrian clairvoyant, initiate, spiritual scientist, and founder of Anthroposophy, always scrutinized the facts of history for their underlying symptomatology. He never took social events—wars, social upheavals, pivotal speeches, ecumenical councils, even individual lives—at their face value. For Steiner social manifestations were "pointers to real inner happenings, symptoms of an inner process of evolution," whose reality was occurring in the supersensible realm. Such a social fact in our time is the irruption of channeling, interest in the occult, and the other signs of cognitive expansion. In Steiner's view, such facts are symptoms of something bigger, deeper, and more profound, but not immediately apparent. As he saw it the goal of anthroposophical work is to penetrate the evident symptoms to the occult or hidden cause; once the "real inner happenings" are identified, we can freely and with awareness decide to aid and abet them. This kind of perception of the occult agenda behind the veil of symptoms is crucial for humans to participate knowingly in the great movements of evolution.[52] The identification of the inner happenings and spiritual intentions underlying the symptoms of cognitive expansion and the elaboration of indications for our conscious participation in their fulfillment is the theme of *The Imagination of Pentecost*.[53]

We must establish a vantage point from which to view our present condition, master a vocabulary by which we can precisely describe our situation, and appropriate a discipline of scientific spirituality through which we can become aware participants in our evolution. We can reasonably ask: what is channeling a symptom of? For what reason is the late twentieth century seized by this expansion in cognition? Why are we standing on the threshold of the supersensible worlds? Into what new stage is human consciousness struggling to mature that channeling and the occult floriation of Western culture appear as symptoms? And if channeling is a leading symptom of unfolding spiritual evolution, how can we—deliberately, consciously, efficaciously—participate in this supersensible intention moving powerfully through our times? With the aid of the spiritual insights of Rudolf Steiner in conjunction with the results of my own supersensible clairvoyant investigation in the past decade, I hope this book will provide some provisional answers.

But before I move into the main arguments of *The Imagination of Pentecost*, I must answer two interlinked questions that will inevitably and justifiably arise in the mind of the reader. Why Steiner and who am I to say any of this? To answer this even briefly, I must digress into a small measure of autobiographical background. For about fifteen years, from age 18 to 33, I was actively and conscientiously involved in the practice of Zen Buddhism under the occasional instruction of an authentic Zen Master. While this immersion in a spiritual lineage profoundly different from the sterile Protestantism in which I was raised was refreshing, even stimulating, the deeper benefit for me was the discipline of meditation and the training in rigorous detachment in the face of all mental phenomena. That is the ideal of course, and occasionally I made good on my aspirations.

Zen practice strongly emphasizes nonidentification with one's mental contents, including personal thoughts, internal chatter, beliefs, prejudices, opinions, and, particularly, spontaneous imagery, apparitions, apparent hallucinations, inner voices, and irruptions from the astral plane. These are all given the pejorative term *makyo*; students reporting such *makyo* to a Zen Master are strongly admonished that they are treading a path of spiritual dereliction. Zen Masters really take the psychics apart, and my own teacher lambasted me when I first told him I was conversing with angels. It's not that Zen Masters disavow the potential ontological reality of such mental experiences; in their process of awakening, they are visited by all the spiritual worlds, from heaven to hell. This was as true for the historical Buddha as it was for my teacher; their secret is they were not impressed. Their concern is that students might easily lose the way on the path to spiritual awakening should they provisionally accredit such phenomena with any degree of importance. The goal, we were taught, is to maintain a state of mind that is clear like space, empty, mirrorlike; this is "true mind and Buddha nature." Thoughts and images come and go like clouds, insubstantial, ephemeral, insignificant, while one sits with equanimity. As a result I spent fifteen years meditating and never had a single vision, apparition, or lush mental image. The only *makyo* I experienced during that time was the common though illusory perception of pain in my knees.

Then in my mid-thirties, evidently for karmic reasons I am only now beginning to cognize, I decided to pass through the eye of a needle. I spent several years living in England in the company of two spiritual colleagues and underwent a lengthy initiation under the auspices of several families of angels and a variety of disincarnate former friends and inner-plane spiritual teachers. After years of "mind like clear blue space" (in my best moments, that is) I was rushed into a sudden clairvoyance and intense inner vision and activity outside the body. The nature of this rich unfolding of picture-consciousness and expanded cognition was in the context of the Arthurian and Grail traditions, and assumed a quality of vivid myth—living participation in certain archetypes of the psyche and landscape as a kind of imaginal engagement in an unsuspected etheric geography.[54]

One of my colleagues was an accomplished channel; in fact, my impression then and now, ten years later, is that this person was an immaculately clear clairvoyant capable of responsibly contacting a high spiritual source, a person who had similarly received intensive inner preparation under the guidance of a Buddhist teacher.

None of the three of us had the kind of temperament that is easily inflated to grandiosity or exaggeration. My own background in discriminatory meditation served me well, guarding me, I trust, against a great deal of potential error and strengthening me in the face of strange, discomfiting experiences, shocking karmic revelations, even occult opposition. During the most intense phase of this inner work, our group of three had nearly nightly oral (and visual) contact and dialogue, both as a group and individually, with a particular family of angels known, in Hebrew and Qabalistic angelologies, as the Ophanim. This contact has continued during the past decade, though the intensity, duration, and nature of the dialogue is continually shifting.

One of our contacts involved the Archangel Michael. We did not speak with Michael, nor he with us, not directly; rather, the Ophanim often brought us into the presence of this great spiritual being on behalf of our ongoing training in the activities of the Grail stream. We received the clear impression that the Ophanim and Michael, plus various other spiritual intelligences, are cooperatively, fraternally engaged in various projects on behalf of humanity and this planet. About this time I made the ingenuous mistake of asking a lifelong student of Rudolf Steiner what he could tell me about Michael. When he finished laughing at the irony of my question, he recommended a text by Steiner in which I read about the mission of Michael in terms of the "revelation of the secret's of Man's being."[55] That was my first introduction to Anthroposophy.

During the ensuing decade in which I underwent the obligatory period of inner digesting of a great deal of inner spiritual experiences, I increasingly found the insights and spiritual intelligence of Rudolf Steiner a beacon for my own unfolding insight. While I recognized Steiner's obvious mastership in the path of Western Christian occultism, my own "introductions" and incursions into the supersensible made a bridge for me to Anthroposophy which I have since found consistently illuminating and corroborative. In practical terms, then, I entered the stream of esoteric Christianity through the living, initiatory mythos of the Arthur and Grail streams, on a foundation of Buddhist mindfulness practice. I learned that a Buddhist can proceed anthroposophically; there is nothing about Anthroposophy as a cognitive training that precludes other traditions or backgrounds. Anthroposophy in its pure, living form is a spiritual science that emerges out of the cultural, evolutionary necessity of this moment in time, the twentieth century. In the simplest terms, I experienced a direct conjunction of my experiences with Steiner's teachings. This, for me, is the key to making Anthroposophy personally relevant: I was able to bring to the insights of Rudolf Steiner the results of my own biography of inner events. This gave me an empirical frame of reference and made much of Steiner's otherwise difficult material immediately accessible. I empathize with the many students of anthroposophy who have struggled with Steiner's material without a basis formed of their own occult experiences.

Over the years many people have told me Steiner is too difficult for them, and they have felt discouraged from continuing their investigations. Perhaps I am a real oddfellow here, but I can honestly say that during the three-year period of intense reading that was preparation for writing this book, I often regarded Steiner's works to be as gripping and spellbinding as the mysteries of Agatha Christie. By this I mean no disrespect; in fact, quite the opposite. What Steiner says in his books and lectures I found as intellectually engaging and as "hard to put down" as Christie's stories. Admittedly, I am an intense fan of mysteries and detective novels, but I think the genre serves the practice of philosophy well. The cosmos and humanity, after all, are two faces of a Mystery: we know who did it, but we don't know what this "Who" did. So I read Steiner avidly. For me, it was a matter of comparing the results of my investigations with Steiner's indications and finding agreement, confirmation, guidance, correction, instruction, and inspiration. It was at times like reading the field reports of a senior colleague in a profession in which I was just finding my way. That, as I came to appreciate, was what Steiner hoped of those who encountered Anthroposophy: to accept it not as dogma but as indications, both perennially truthful and subject to periodic revision, that individuals might of their free will choose to consider.

I profoundly respected Steiner's epistemological rigor, which he arrived at through a process of scientific and mathematical training. I was heartened to hear his impassioned portrayals of the supersensible hierarchies, their missions, and the pivotal importance of the Christ. For it is a *hearing*: Steiner's spiritual presence comes powerfully through his lectures, even in translation, and often a direct transmission comes through from the Logos to the reader, borne on Steiner's words. In my own travails on the Grail Quest I had been obliged to come to terms with the truth of the Christ; to get there I had to penetrate my own prejudices and the gross misrepresentations perpetrated over historical time by the Catholic Church. Helping me in this inner transmutation was the Archangel Michael, whom I discovered is a key player in the Grail Mysteries. Through this experience and from information provided by the Ophanim, I realized that the lineage into which I had entered was in fact the same Michaelic-Grail stream into which Rudolf Steiner had entered some ninety years earlier and had renamed Anthroposophy. Though it is a claim that some readers may find problematic, the Ophanim indicated that they had actively worked with "a very clear reporter named Rudolf Steiner" during his time and that there were certain elements of the anthroposophical view—most notably, the Lucifer-Ahriman dialectic—that they hoped might now be adjusted in light of current spiritual developments.

One of Steiner's foremost endeavors was to indicate the parameters for epistemological certainty when confronted with supersensible information, intelligences, or experiences. In other words, as an individual investigator, how does one know with certainty that the information and images gathered during clairvoyant or psychic research are ontologically valid and not the filtered fabrications of one's own psychological processes? In the vernacular we say, How do you know you're not just making it up? I spent ten years agonizing and laboring with this question, testing the spirits, so to speak, to see what fruits the advice of the Ophanim bore in the world and in my own development. I read widely in occult, esoteric, philosophical, and channeled materials; I read deeply within the prodigious body of work Steiner left; I actively worked to digest the body of spiritual experiences my engagement with the Ophanim had generated; and I participated as directly as I could in the annual revelation of the Christ, called Epiphany, deepening my own nascent appreciation of this great cosmic being. Every step of the way I found in Rudolf Steiner a matchless companion. Although one often feels the temptation to enshrine Steiner as a twentieth-century Western guru, he emphatically discouraged this, preferring the term mentor or counselor. Even so, a mentor of the stature of Rudolf Steiner may be held in high regard; one of his contemporaries expressed it this way: "There can be no completed work, for his Thought is *Life*, striding onward from resurrection to resurrection—a Spirit Being, showering light. We can become independent and creative when with sacred ardor we grasp the unspoken and unprinted products of Rudolf Steiner's spirit."[56]

The result of these interlinked efforts was the conviction that the insights of Anthroposophy, as formulated by Rudolf Steiner, are a valuable, reliable, even inspiring guide for a Westerner seeking to develop and deepen spiritual experience in the context of a nondogmatic system expressly intended for this perilous moment in human spiritual evolution. As such, Anthroposophy is not a brand-name metaphysics but a keen tool, a methodology, a spiritual science that, from an evolutionary point of view, is spiritually necessary for men and women at this time, entirely independent of its carrier, Rudolf Steiner. This is just how he would prefer it, too. Certainly there are other valid metaphysical systems within the Western Mystery tradition, such as Theosophy, the Fourth Way teachings of G. I. Gurdjieff, and the Arcane School of Alice Bailey, to mention a few (all of which, incidentally, I studied on my own before coming to Steiner). I have also struggled on my own with the Mystery revelation of Qabala concurrent with my study of Anthroposophy. There are also numerous legitimate lineages founded on the spiritual charisma of individual teachers. Steiner never intended students to frame matters in terms of exclusivity; all systems are compatible and complementary with Anthroposophy, he claimed. To a degree, one's attraction to one approach over another is a matter of intellectual temperament.

The honoring of individual temperament or spiritual predisposition in fact is at the core of Steiner's approach. Personally, I felt most at home and most warmly welcomed in the company of Rudolf Steiner. I also appreciate the practicality, flexibility, and timeliness of Steiner's approach. Fundamentally it is a methodology, not a system; his Anthroposophy represents a meticulous instruction in the methods of attaining wakeful cognition of the supersensible world. Of equal merit is the fact that Steiner's methodology is acutely relevant for our spiritual condition at the close of the twentieth century and not a refashioning of antique methods and initiatory structures. In a remarkable precognitive sense, Steiner understood the probable developments and crises in human spirituality at the eve of the millennium and left many prescient indications for us on how best to safely negotiate our passage through these shoals. Again, on a practical level, Steiner frequently and thoroughly discussed the issues, problems, dangers, and opportunities confronting the would-be occultist in approaching the supersensible worlds, whether it be through mediumship, spontaneous psychism, or diligently schooled clairvoyance. It's as if he foresaw the efflorescence of channeling in the 1980s and sought to leave warnings and advisements in what was for him at the time, the future, and for us, the present. It would be inexcusably pedantic for me to argue that Steiner's methodology and the results of his clairvoyant investigation offer us the best metaphysical system today. I would rather say, as Steiner often did when confronted with similarly vexatious questions: let's see how well this view explains the facts before us. I hope that the conclusions of *The Imagination of Pentecost* will vindicate the leap of faith I make on behalf of the reader into the anthroposophical world view as represented by Rudolf Steiner.

The age of the authoritarian spiritual leader is finished, Steiner announced. We are now entering a new age of individual, independent spiritual unfoldment under the aegis of a globally distributed spiritual intelligence. Steiner called this global aegis the Archangel Michael; the cognitive goal of this new unfoldment would be the individual perception of the Christ, free from inherited belief, dogma, subservience, iconography, or priestly mediation. The Christ is not a proprietary icon of the Catholic Church, Steiner emphasized, but a generic inner fact of the world and Earth history—and a fact highly worth knowing on one's own. One's authentic alignment with this ecclesiastically liberated Christ will be the epistemological basis for a new, unfettered, and, eventually, limitless cognition of the supersensible world and individual fulfillment, Steiner said. With the Christ schooling our cognition, men and women (*Anthropos*) will come to know the cosmos directly and to embody its wisdom (*Sophy*).

It is the argument of this book, then, that the multiple indications of cognitive expansion we are witnessing at the end of the twentieth century will find their consummate expression in a spiritual experience I call the Imagination of Pentecost, and that in making our inner preparations for this crucial experience Anthroposophy is a reliable yet flexible foundation.

CHAPTER 2

The Consciousness Soul

Evolutionary Spiritual Agenda for our Time

*W*ITH THE CONTINUING irruption of spiritual realities into our physical plane existence—which Steiner foresaw as the likely course of events for the twentieth century—it is "an absolute necessity" that true, spiritual scientific knowledge should enter our lives. What were once occult secrets must flood the culture as everyday revelations. Our age desperately needs to become spiritual, Steiner said in the war-torn Berlin of 1915, and unless we can regulate our lives according to the insights of spiritual science, life will slide into chaos and desolation. The world—and its wars, as Steiner reflected at the time—becomes intelligible only when we look beyond the evidences of worldly life and supplement this with knowledge from the realities of the invisible.

But our knowledge of the invisible world must be tested and validated in the same way that we acquire objective knowledge of the physical world. Of prime importance in our struggle to comprehend the symptoms of this deeper unfolding of spiritual evolution is human reason itself. The essence of Steiner's discipline of spiritual science is that the scientific method of inquiry, testing, and validation be applied to our investigations of the supersensible world. The same faculties of cognition—logical thinking and respect for concrete details—whereby we understand the outside, material world must be turned inwards to understand the subtleties of the supersensible.[1] Knowledge of the supersensible worlds must be acquired consciously and presented coherently to ordinary human reason.

It is characteristic of the progress of human evolution that often the most significant events in an age can be completely concealed from the eyes of those living through them. Steiner often commented that the Mystery of Golgotha—the whole mystery enactment of the Christ, from birth, baptism, and transfiguration, to crucifixion and resurrection—was the pivotal event in planetary history yet one that passed by almost unnoticed and uncomprehended by contemporaries of that time. Even today, nearly 2,000 years later, the real implications of this event have hardly permeated human awareness. As I implied in Chapter 1, the Harmonic Convergence of August 1987 was another such pivotal event whose occurrence and aftermath are still underacknowledged and largely ignored, not only in mainstream culture but among Anthroposophists as well.

Scrying the course of the twentieth century in 1910, Steiner foresaw that "phenomena will appear in the near future that only spiritual science will be able to grasp and that will remain misunderstood if spiritual science is not there."[2] The "fantastic theories of modern science" will no longer satisfy our need to understand, and they may contradict our experience. A great deal lies waiting in the womb of our spiritual evolution, but it can come to birth only through our willing, conscious cooperation. The cultivation of spiritual science is a "real cosmic event" because it opens doors to cosmic influences attempting to enter Earth. Our engagement with the great upheavals and birthings of contemporary history is possible only when we penetrate with our conscious understanding the occult background and intentions at play behind the visible world. Only in the supersensible worlds can we fathom the true being of the Human. There we learn that in our time the supersensible being of the Human is struggling to birth what Steiner called the consciousness soul.

When Steiner talks about perceiving the supersensible reality behind the historical symptom his gaze encompasses the entire history of the earth and human evolution. The description of the consciousness, or spiritual, soul, is set within this vast context. Steiner outlines the Human as a ninefold being who unfolds each of these nine aspects in sequence, over time; in fact, the evolution of the planet and the unfolding of these predestined ninefold human aspects are essentially synchronous, if not identical, events.

In other words the purpose of the unfoldment of the cosmos is to facilitate the manifestation of the Human. In practical terms, Human and Cosmos are not only reciprocally related but, even though the apparent forms differ, mirror images of each other.

Clairvoyant perception reveals that the ninefold human comprises three bodies, or sheaths. These are the physical, etheric, and astral, and an Ego, or I (self-consciousness), which in turn includes three components, sentient soul, intellectual soul, and consciousness soul; together these make up six aspects of the human. The three highest human developmental aspects are called Spirit-Self, Life-Spirit, and Spirit-Man. From one perspective the ninefold human condenses into the threefold of body, soul, and spirit, each with three aspects; from another perspective, the human is sevenfold, in which the three aspects of the Ego are regarded as one category. The totality of the nine aspects comprises the Human, native to the supersensible worlds, but destined eventually to incarnate fully in the physical realm. The consciousness soul, then, is the third soul aspect of the Ego, or the sixth aspect of the Human, and, as far as the human evolutionary agenda goes, our current task.

The year 1413 A.D. marked the beginning of a 21,60 year long manifestation of the human consciousness soul, a process that will culminate around the year 3573 A.D. Steiner called each of these 2,160 year phases a post-Atlantean cultural epoch, as a way of dating recent history from the collapse of the Atlantean civilization, which, incidentally, was for him a fact. The specificity of the number 2,160 for each cultural epoch is not arbitrary but is a direct correlation with a cosmic cycle. Approximately every 2,160 years the Sun moves through one-twelfth of the zodiac; a full cycle of 25,920 years is traditionally called a Platonic Year. Steiner also construed individual human development in seven-year increments, such that in a man or woman the consciousness soul generally unfolds between the ages of 35 and 42. Thus the evolution of human consciousness, on an individual and collective level, is synchronized both with the unfolding of the Earth and with cosmic cycles.

In Steiner's chronology, the series of seven post-Atlantean epochs began around 7227 B.C. when the gradual deterioration of the Atlantean continent and civilization was complete. While the majority of historians have always dismissed Atlantis as a fable concocted by Plato, for Steiner, the reality of Atlantis was unarguable; its presence in the history of Earth is indelibly inscribed in the Akashic Records, the great etheric library of the world often mentioned in esoteric literature.[3]

Three planetary epochs—Indian, Persian, Egyptian-Chaldean—followed Atlantis and preceded the time of the intellectual soul, which was the epoch immediately preceding our own. Each of these epochs had the task of evolving another aspect of the nine-fold human totality. The fourth post-Atlantean epoch of intellectual, or mind, soul ran from 747 B.C. to 1413 A.D., encompassing for the West the period of high Greek culture, the founding of Rome and its empire, the so-called Dark, medieval period, and the flowering of Europe in the Renaissance. The elaboration of the consciousness soul is the task of our fifth post-Atlantean cultural epoch, a crucial phase in human collective development, and one which has already progressed through nearly 600 years.

The elaboration of the consciousness soul during this current 2,160 year period has specific spiritual obligations that must be fulfilled to maintain the positive momentum in human evolution. It requires that we develop conscious, wakeful cognition of the spiritual worlds and that our reasoning process becomes enriched with spirituality. In essence, the consciousness soul requires spiritual science. Since the fifteenth century, the observation of material, sense reality has been at the forefront of human effort. The task of the consciousness soul has been objective, material perception, the "pure beholding of external reality" in the stance of spectatorship, accompanied by independent reflection and thinking—self-sufficient, scientific, pure, abstract—and the formulation of pure concepts. In our time, said Steiner, the rational and intellectual aspects have become the "most outstanding aspects of man's present state of soul."

Paramount for the consciousness soul is our activity in the forming of our thoughts. Contemporary humanity can actually form its own thoughts, from out of itself. This may not sound at all remarkable, but Steiner assures us that not so long ago humans could not think independently but were dependent on spiritual inspiration for their thoughts, on infusions of mental contents from the "gods." That's changed with the advent of the era of the consciousness soul. Contemporary humanity has the possibility of independently cognizing the totality of the supersensible worlds while incarnate; in earlier times this was possible only in the life after death. We may easily take this freedom for granted, but in an earlier day, this kind of cognitive range simply wasn't possible.

In previous epochs, particularly the Indian and Persian, supersensible intelligences actually formed humanity's thoughts, inspirations, and concepts, guiding a young humanity through its evolutionary phases. We took our inspirations from the gods; the gods made thoughts arise in us—this is how people experienced it. In our time, these intelligences—what tradition calls angels, archangels, and the full extent of the celestial hierarchy of cosmic beings—have withdrawn, leaving humankind to draw upon its own inherent resources to produce living thoughts. But in this act of self-sufficient cognition, an additional factor must be present, and it is this which will spiritualize the science of reason. This additional factor is a human Ego permeated by the Christ Impulse, that is, the sense of the human I, that self-referential, self-aware sense of ourselves, warmed and quickened by the Christ. The attainment of a Christ-permeated Ego—the consciousness soul, in other words—is the mission of the fifth post-Atlantean epoch and the proper goal of our spiritual striving. This has nothing to do with furthering the worldly success of the apostolic mission of the Catholic Church or anything like that; rather, as Steiner indicated, the permeation of the I-consciousness by the Christ offers an invaluable and essential aid to our cognitive capacity.

In Anthroposophy, the discipline and body of knowledge of spiritual science, the subject of the human Ego, or I, is vast. Its implications extend everywhere. The whole issue of independent cognition—an individual I that cognizes the supersensible worlds while awake and that can know directly, lucidly, and with certainty—is at the heart of the momentous incarnation of the totality of the Human, native to the timeless supersensible worlds, into the physical life of humanity in the time-dominated material world. We take our presence in the material world entirely for granted, but when seen from the vast perspective opened up here, our embodied presence is not so much miraculous as stupendous in import. It took a very great deal of preparation, planning, and supervision to get this far, 600 years into the elaboration of the consciousness soul. In Steiner's estimation, the development of the individual, independent, cognizing I-awakened, Christ-permeated "I-consciousness" that knows is the raison d'etre of human existence. Similarly, the evolutionary necessity that a human being might say "I" to oneself de facto required the physical world. In other words, the world, our Earth, exists so that we may have I-consciousness. The existence of the planet Earth is far from a random accident in an indifferent cosmos that our contemporary materialist sciences would have us believe.

The preceding four post-Atlantean cultural epochs have seen the progressive closing of the portals of the supersensible world to incarnate humanity. Increasingly men and women have experienced a constricting of the perceptual and cognitive field, a radical condensation of a range of vision that once encompassed the supersensible in all its magnificence. This inevitable development was formally acknowledged, if not mandated, in 869 A.D. at the notorious eighth Ecumenical Church Council at Constantinople when Pope Nicholas decreed that the human being was not threefold (spirit, soul, and body) but twofold (soul and body); anybody who argued the threefold nature of humanity (Trichotomy) would be henceforth branded a heretic. The effect of this ninth-century council was to abolish the spirit from humanity until further notice; instead, the soul would be construed to have certain spiritual qualities.[4]

The portals to the spiritual worlds were closed, both by papal degree and in accordance with the intentions of the supersensible intelligences, so that humans might become self-conscious, inwardly spiritual, independent beings, capable of objective cognition. Paradoxically, the spiritual worlds had to grow darker to us before we could fill them with the light of our own seeing; that's where we stand today in the midst of the elaboration of the consciousness soul. The purpose of the physical world is to provide a context in which independent cognition, the free activity of the human I, or self-consciousness, can happen. Without this, we would have been perpetually tied to the cosmic apron strings of the celestial hierarchy, perceiving the supersensible in only a diffused, entranced, dreamlike state. We would never have known we were individual human beings. "We had to lose that awareness of the spiritual world in order to exchange it for I-consciousness," explained Steiner.[5]

It was a slow process, but the old, natural clairvoyance of spirit-vision and spirit-knowledge finally died out around 1250 A.D. The experience of direct and immediate contact with spiritual intelligences for the most part disappeared from human consciousness and the objectivities of material science and technology took their place. The fifth post-Atlantean cultural epoch marks the turning-around point in this experience of cognitive darkening. Since 1413 A.D. humankind has increasingly had the potential of returning with self-awareness to that perpetual vision of the supersensible, but with a big difference: this time we can do it while staying awake and discriminatory, like clairvoyant scientists.

Through the elaboration of the consciousness soul, we may, through our own activity, pry open the portals to the spiritual world and enter as wakeful, conscious, individual humans. Clairvoyance attained under the auspices of the consciousness soul will be an improvement over the kind we had formerly. Once clairvoyance was a natural endowment, but it was dreamy, undifferentiated, and basically an extension of the thought-processes of the spiritual intelligences; then came an interim period in which objective, discriminatory faculties, typified by science and mathematics, were developed; now with the consciousness soul comes wakeful, lucid, precise cognition as an individual, self-aware I-consciousness of these same supersensible domains. Perhaps the chief difference is that now one can say: *I* am awake and perceiving in this nonmaterial realm and aware that I am cognizing. Through the consciousness soul and its "new soul faculties," we may have the best of both dispensations: the independence of the awake I-conscious human being and scientifically precise perception of the realities of the supersensible world. Steiner called this the new Christian initiation because it is the Christ as Logos that awakens human cognition to a self-aware, self-referential, wakefully subjective state. In this initiation we maintain full awareness of the Ego in its activities; we do not fall asleep or go dreamy in the presence of the supersensible but apprehend its activities with a quickened daytime consciousness. The I remains as fully awake while penetrating the higher worlds as it does in negotiating its way through the physical world.

What precipitated this profound turning about in the human relationship to the supersensible worlds was the Christ Event, the incarnation of the Christ and its fulfillment through the Mystery of Golgotha. For Steiner, the incarnation of the Christ, whom he perceived as an exalted cosmic being—what anciently was called a god—was more than the foundation for a particular religion called Christianity. For Steiner, no Church, no people, no polity, can claim exclusive ownership, either iconographic or liturgical, of the Christ—only the Earth can. As with the historical reality of Atlantis, Steiner knew with certitude that the Christ had appeared on Earth and undergone the five initiations as recounted in the Gospels. Steiner knew this because through his own clairvoyance he was able to read the events in the Akashic Records. Once we complete the incarnation of the consciousness soul so shall we be able to corroborate these occulted historical events in the Akashic Records. That in part is the point of the Christed cognition Steiner foresaw as the destiny—and wonderful opportunity—confronting humanity in this and the next century. Although few, if any, Biblical scholars will likely make the effort, the Akashic Records offer the possibility of independent corroboration for other researchers wishing to check Steiner's claims.

In a sense, the historical activities of a human named Jesus, whose martyred followers called themselves Christians, were symptoms of "real inner happenings." The inner reality for which they were symptomatic was a cosmic-planetary fact of far-reaching, global import, regardless of ethnic, religious, or political identities. It was a fact that not only irrevocably changed the course of human evolution on Earth, but profoundly affected the structure and evolution of the supersensible hierarchy itself. It was the Christ Event and it truly changed the world.

It also transformed the Mystery initiations. Prior to the Christ Event the Mystery initiations were conducted according to either the Sign of Jonah or the Sign of Solomon. In the Jonah initiation, the candidate for initiation spent three and one-half days lying unconscious in a sheltered temple; meanwhile, his soul left the physical body, collected experiences in the supersensible worlds, returned, then later imparted the memory of these experiences within the "whale" of the spiritual world to the candidate's daytime awareness. In the Solomon initiation, candidates received revelations in a "sublimated trance condition," but without the rigors of "temple sleep" and immersion in the unconscious required in the Jonah experience.

In either case, the candidate for Mystery initiation strove to cognize the great Sun Being, the Christ, while transiting the spiritual worlds. Since the Christ resided in the Sun, the candidate had to travel to the Sun. We must be careful here lest we outrage the astrophysicists; by Sun, Steiner did not mean the physical star we call the Sun, but its spiritual or nonmaterial aspect, the Sun within the Sun, in a sense. The Mystery of Golgotha changed all that; now the Sun had come to Earth. In anthroposophical vocabulary, the "Christ Event" and "Mystery of Golgotha" are interchangeable terms that point to the sequence of activities, or initiations, that characterized the life of Christ on Earth, beginning with birth and culminating with the Resurrection, Ascension, and Pentecostal inspiration. In essence these interchangeable terms point, synecdochically, to the *fact* of the Christ on Earth.

In the Christ Event, the Christ-Sun Being publicly demonstrated what had formerly been symbolic rites enacted in the esoteric Mystery schools. Contrary to the beliefs of exoteric Christianity, the crucifixion was not a disaster, in that a Savior had been publicly rejected, but a necessity, the unavoidable dénouement by which a profound intention was completed, literally grounded. Through Christ's blood shed on the cross, Christ became one with Earth and humanity because that sanctified blood literally entered the substance of this planet. The Sun Being imparted this cosmic essence—the living Ego-consciousness—to the Earth and was forevermore present. The blood is important because in Steiner's anthroposophical anatomy, the blood is the carrier of the Ego, the molecular context for individuality; I-consciousness lives in the body through the blood, which of course uniformly permeates every cell in the human organism. The Ego finds its highest expression in the Christ, who is called the Son of Man; thus the tangible blood of this consummate I-being is a priceless elixir for both planet and humanity.

Through the new Christ initiation, men and women could comprehend the Christ-Sun Being, virtually anytime, anyplace—and on their own, without priests or apostles. As the Christ awakens within each individual human, so does our blood literally become a transmuting medium carrying the force of the awakening Christ to the trillions of cells that comprise our organism. The dictum, *Not I, but the Christ in me*, becomes a molecular truth. Through the Christ Event, this cosmic Ego, the Son of Man, was to be given over to humans. "Man is the being in whom the power of the Sun was to be present in its fullness," commented Steiner in a 1910 lecture series. "Christ Jesus is the representative, the embodiment of the power which imparts to mankind the full consciousness of the 'I am.'"[6]

Through this power, humans can attain conscious cognition of the spiritual worlds, no longer through the inherited old clairvoyance, but through the willed development of the Ego, Christ's gift to humanity. Through this gift of the Son of Man to humankind, we can say "I am" to ourselves. The human Ego, or I, is the immortal, the self-aware, in the Human. When a human can say "I am", this is tantamount to God speaking within, yet it is a condition inherently paradoxical. After his epiphany on the road to Damascus, Paul, no longer the skeptical, Christ-denying Saul, reflected, "Not I, but the Christ in me." The Christ had become Paul's I by an act of his free will, in effect by a personal reiteration of the crucifixion and the "death" of his sense of self.

In the cultural epochs preceding the Mystery of Golgotha, more often than not it was the case that an individual did not experience one's I as a separate foundation of being. Rather, individuals perceived their "I" as part of a common group-soul Ego, as part of a tribe, such as the multigenerational family of Abraham. Here Abraham was the I for all the members of the tribe. They did not say "I" to themselves, but "Abraham;" they could not know, or cognize, on their own behalf, but had always to defer to Abraham's knowing. Now in the epoch of the consciousness soul, an individual human can remain established in one's own "I" and draw forth from this individuality all the secrets of the supersensible world through an act of independent cognition. Between the years 1413 A.D. and approximately 1900 A.D., this was a difficult, formidable task, but with the advent of the twentieth century, things have been made easier. That's because one of the principal activities of the consciousness soul, Steiner indicated, will be the functioning of a "natural etheric clairvoyance," similar to the astounding daytime revelation of the Christ in his subtle body that so gripped the former arch-doubter, Saul of Tarsus, on his journey to Damascus.

Among the general public and among academic historians Steiner is generally underappreciated as a major prophet of the twentieth century, if not the epoch—the fifth post-Atlantean cultural epoch of the consciousness soul, to borrow his phrase. In fact, Steiner, despite his prodigious contribution to humanity in terms of lectures and books, is practically unknown, even among the eclectic American New Age community. It is an irony hard to understand at times, but even in occult, esoteric bookstores stocked with the most arcane, obscure titles, there will be nothing of Steiner.[7] That is unfortunate because in the concentrated twenty-five years of outward public service and proclamation, from his emergence around 1900 to his death in 1925, Steiner filled his books and 6,000 lectures with many indications of trends and spiritual events likely to occur in the remaining seven decades of this century.

Not the least significant of his many pronouncements was the conviction that mystical experiences would eventually become the common heritage of humankind again. Qualities of soul that were once arduously achieved in the Mystery initiations would eventually become the common heritage of all women and men. The time would come when "We shall have the perception to see that things which are discerned spiritually can be spoken of as historical fact with the same directness and assurance with which we speak of the facts of external science."[8]

A mighty, revolutionary change was coming, Steiner foresaw, in which the first seeds of a delicate new, natural, etheric clairvoyance would evolve. It would be a deeply incisive change in the faculties of the human soul as a general heightening of the human powers of cognition unfolded. Formerly veiled, even unsuspected, the richness and teeming life of the etheric world would gradually become apparent to humankind in the daytime, that is, through wakeful, discriminatory cognition and not, as before, dreamy group-soul clairvoyance.

This is a key difference, and the legitimate fruit of many centuries of difficult human evolutionary striving. During the first half of the twentieth century, this wakeful etheric clairvoyance would appear first in a few individuals, but increasingly it would blossom in more humans over the next 2,500 years. Eventually through a natural process of evolution, this etheric clairvoyance, at least in its elementary form, would become the birthright of the majority of humans. In other words, a cognitive ability once attained only through lengthy, arduous Mystery school initiations will eventually be a standard feature of human consciousness. Thus will the consciousness soul be born in the Human. With this new clairvoyant faculty, people will perceive the etheric world, the etheric body, pictures and premonitions of coming events, and the connection between deeper happenings in the etheric world and their symptoms in the physical world. "A number of souls will experience the strange condition of having ego-consciousness but at the same time have the feeling of living in a world essentially different from the world known to their ordinary consciousness." [9]

Most importantly, Steiner foresaw that the human etheric body itself would undergo a major transformation in the twentieth century, enabling the seeds of this new clairvoyance to sprout. In the 1990s most people, if they are aware of it at all, have a vague, fuzzy idea of the etheric body. The pictorial revelations of Kirlian photography have given indications of an enveloping energy field around physical biological structures, and while, technically, this is not the etheric body but an aspect of our electromagnetic field, its portrayal helps us form a picture of what the etheric body might be. The healing practices of certain natural holistic medicines such as acupuncture, homeopathy, and Anthroposophic medicine generally conceive the etheric body as a subtle sheath or formative life-field overlaid upon the physical form that shapes and maintains organic matter, including the human body. The etheric body is central in the development of the consciousness soul. So to appreciate the remarkable development Steiner foresaw in the human etheric body—a transformation already underway—we need to understand the nature and history of the human etheric body, and this brings us back to an ancient time in the cosmos called Old Sun. That is because, as we noted above, the unfoldment of the human and the cosmos are reciprocally interdependent and simultaneous events; to understand the Human, we need to understand the cosmos, and the reverse—which, incidentally, is what Anthroposophy is all about.

Steiner's cosmology is radically different, often disturbingly so, from the orthodox astrophysical view of the origin of the solar system. It is common for people first exposed to his explanations and models to regard them as bizarrely topsy-turvy; that was certainly my initial reaction. Afterwards the internal consistency of Steiner's decidedly unorthodox perceptions takes on a curious persuasiveness and our perspective suddenly flips, revealing a startling coherence where first we saw strangeness. Steiner places our planet Earth within a sevenfold developmental sequence (still incomplete) in which our solar system is seen as one cosmic body. Humankind appeared and evolved within this solar context, as did each of the nine celestial families comprising the three "angelic" hierarchies.

This is an additional feature of Anthroposophy: not only have the Human and cosmos reciprocally evolved, but so has the entire heavenly hierarchy (the residents of the supersensible world) in a complex triple reciprocity. Human, cosmos, and supersensible worlds are all interdependently linked and have unfolded together. In other words, the creation, elaboration, and progression of the solar system, humanity, and the hierarchies were synchronous, coincidental events. In a sense, each is a different face in a different context of the same thing: the Logos; but we'll return to this thought later. It is important to note here that when Steiner uses the familiar terms Saturn, Sun, Moon, and Earth, he does not mean the physical planets as we know them today. As he meticulously explains in his *Outline of Occult Science*, the cosmos evolved through a series of planetary epochs, in which the entire cosmos as a "body" was characterized at different stages by qualities Steiner describes with the terms Saturn, Sun, Moon, and Earth.

The first stage was Old Saturn, a gaseous, amorphous milieu in which the mineral, warmth-germ of the human physical body was first created. The whole body of the solar system was characterized by the term Old Saturn, although, technically, the planet Saturn did not physically exist. Next came Old Sun, an airy, swirling environment in which the human etheric body was created. On the Old Moon, dominated by water, the astral body was incorporated into the emerging human. The fourth stage is called Earth. This marked the materialization and mineralization of the solar system of which our planet Earth was a microcosmic aspect. On Earth physical matter appeared and things became visible as evolving humanity was given the Ego, or I-consciousness. But there are three more planetary stages for the cosmic body yet to pass through before the triune evolution of humanity, solar system, and hierarchy is completed: Jupiter, Venus, and Vulcan. In fact the complete cosmic process encompasses 343 planetary transformations, in which each of the seven major planetary stages undergoes 49 metamorphoses. As Steiner computes the past and future history of the cosmos, it is an exceedingly complex model. For the present, however, it is what happened during Old Sun when the human etheric body was developed, and its far-ranging implications into our own time, that concerns us in this chapter.

During the Old Sun period the Kyriotetes, or Spirits of Wisdom, members of the Second Hierarchy—one group of spiritual intelligences charged with certain cosmic tasks—imparted the ether body to evolving humanity. The Kyriotetes' substance itself is ether, "mobile, power-filled wisdom, or life," so the human etheric body is an emanation of the Wisdom Spirits. In more than a metaphorical sense, in our etheric body we find the life of the Kyriotetes. In Steiner's cosmology, the human is the totality of contributions and life bodies from all the celestial and cosmic beings, angelic, stellar, and planetary. The human being is a living microcosm of their collective effects. During the Old Sun phase, the "human mineral," which was as far as our evolution progressed during Old Saturn, was animated, made alive with ether. Steiner likens the Old Sun human to a plant: Old Sun humans were phototropic, sentient, emotionally inert and not self-aware. As the Kyriotetes poured the ether or life body into the human, the Sun itself, previously dark, began to radiate light in the world. Life began. Signs of inner activity appeared in the germinal human. The solar influence began to quicken the nascent human being.

What had been the appearance of life on Old Saturn now became *actual* life on Old Sun. Old Saturn contributed *Logos* to the human, the primal formative Word, or sound essence. Old Sun added *Life* in the form of the etheric body, the animated life of wisdom. Old Moon next added *Light*, the spiritual, astral light of the stars (emotionality); and Earth will contribute the priceless I-consciousness. During the Sun evolution, "*Life* was in the *Logos*, and out of this living *Logos* there arose *Light* during the Moon evolution."[10] Thus on Old Sun, through the activities of the Spirits of Wisdom, Logos—the primordial Word, or sound essence of the cosmos—was made living, vital, incorporated into the human as the etheric body. As the Gospel of St. John tells us: "In the Beginning was the Word, and the Word was with God, and the Word was God." This concept lies at the heart of the Western Mystery tradition and is central to our exposition of the etheric body and its import in human evolution at this time. The Old Sun etheric body is the expression of the living Logos active in the human organization. The etheric body is spoken into being by the Kyriotetes.[11]

During the Old Moon phase we received the elements of our affective life, the structure of our emotions; this we will discuss later in a different context. Now, during the Earth stage, the etheric body keeps the human in contact with the cosmos and is the seat of activity for another member of the Second Hierarchy, the Exousiai, or Elohim, the Spirits of Form. In our life on Earth (and here I mean the physicalized planet) the etheric body is an image of the cosmos, of the entire starry heavens, filled with its activities, sounds, and intelligences. For the most part we are not aware of the prodigious, swirling activity in our etheric body, but sometimes, at the moment of falling asleep, we might catch a glimpse.

Steiner vividly described the generally unrecognized nature of the etheric body. During sleep the etheric body is inwardly mobile, the site of continual lively activity, which he evokes with words and phrases like these: humming, singing, a changing murmur, resounding music, the Music of the Spheres, radiance, a flooding stream of warmth, a phosphorescent glow. All of these qualities are an "outer revelation, the external clothing, the revelation, the glory of mighty cosmic beings"—the Exousiai.[12] The activity of these exalted Sun-beings (also known as the Elohim), their flowing and mutual influencing, itself forms the human etheric organism. As progenitors of the etheric body, then, we have the Kyriotetes, or Spirits of Wisdom, and the Exousiai, or Elohim, the Spirits of Form. From out of their flowing life essence our etheric body is woven.

What does all this flowing consist of? Thoughts. The etheric body is formed of flowing thoughts, of the thought-processes of the Universe individualized. When we speak of the thoughts of the Elohim or Kyriotetes, we must not understand this as so many sentences strung together like semantic ribbons to fashion an etheric body. From their perspective, thoughts are more like grand, dynamic tableaux of cosmic intention, mighty pictures, gestures, imaginations, *speakings*; from our perspective this is apocalyptic language. The etheric body is the expression of individualized Logos; in other words, the human etheric body, even in its generic expression, is the individualization of a complete cosmic activity.

The Logos speaks to the human in an individual form, through an inner Word which comprises the human's essential being. In the etheric body, speech, as forms for the Word or Logos, is turned inward, etherically, giving us a "resounding, speaking, individualized Logos." This incessant activity of the Exousiai forms a subtle vertebral column in the human, set opposite to the physical spine in the front of the body. Here the chakras, or what Steiner preferred to call the lotus flowers (the seven subtle swirling energy fields related sequentially to the human endocrine glands and ascending states of consciousness), attach to the astral body, which is formed by the third member of the Second Hierarchy, the Dynameis, the Spirits of Motion. The living activity of the Second Hierarchy streams down from the cosmos, is individualized in the human, exists in the astral body, but *shows* itself in the etheric body.[13]

Steiner helped illustrate the individualization of the Logos through the human etheric body by developing the new art form called eurythmy. Eurythmy, which refers to a series of dancelike movements comprising a "beautiful, harmonious form," is a demonstration of the Mysteries of speech. If we pronounce the entire alphabet out loud from *a* to *z*, we produce a very complicated airform made of letters, a complex word, explained Steiner in 1924. This word form is the human etheric body itself; the etheric body is woven of spoken letters, the origins of the eurythmy gestures. My body in effect is made of the alphabet. When the etheric body speaks it doesn't use the tongue but the limbs; when the larynx makes words, the etheric body dances them. This etheric human is the Word which contains within it the entire alphabet, born out of the creative human larnyx, explained Steiner. So if we were to go through the whole alphabet, we should in the consecutive sounds, unfold the mystery of the human being. In speech human beings themselves are fashioned. After all, *In the beginning was the Word*, our Western traditions continually remind us, and Eastern spiritualities emphasize the creative force of mantras. But with Steiner's astounding observation this near platitude suddenly springs into meaning. "God eurythmetizes, and as the result of His eurythmy there arises the form of man."[14]

All of this arcane anatomy has a startling consequence. When we wish to find the seat of our thinking, of intellectual activity, we turn not to the physical brain, as Western science and philosophy has tacitly assumed for centuries, but to the etheric body. We think through our etheric body. Thinking is nothing less than the etheric body's natural life activity. The etheric body is a thought organism with a life and force of its own; that life consists of living pictures and imaginations, "this self-imagining world formed out of the universal thought-weaving of the cosmos." The human etheric body and its microcosmic world of flowing, weaving thoughts bears our whole intellect. Thought isn't so much words, sentences, or concepts, but interlinking, living pictures. This was immediately evident to humanity long ago when we still possessed the natural, though dreamy, group-soul clairvoyance; then our thought-life was identical with the supersensible environment. With the deliberate eclipse of this natural though primitive cognitive faculty during the Greco-Roman epoch of the intellectual soul (747 B.C.–1413 A.D.), humanity transformed etheric pictorial thinking into abstract, symbolic, logical thinking—the world of sentences, syntax and, inevitably, brain chemistry and structure. As the reality of the etheric body waned, the mistaken presumption that thinking is an epiphenomenon of the physical brain gained ascendancy.

In a real sense the human etheric sheath is formed by a powerful "Imagination driven outward" by the Second Hierarchy. This hierarchy reveals itself through its activities, which are prolific, weaving Imaginations. This weaving of picture-thoughts, which knits the human etheric body, is the expression or signature of the spiritual world itself. Here in our individualized etheric bodies we may find, should we take the opportunity, a living revelation of the life of the cosmos. The cosmic picture world is the true form of the etheric body, and this picture-etheric body is the seat of the vital, formative forces that shape and maintain the human physical form. The crucial life forces that shape and permeate the outward physical body, facilitating growth, health, and nutrition, are at the same time united with the etheric picture-thought weaving.[15] Thus we can say that it is the living thought-pictures of the cosmos, working through the activities of the Second Hierarchy, that generate the human intellect and thinking, and shape and maintain the physical human body. Our physical body is a transposition of etheric thoughts into biological matter. This observation, incidentally, has profound consequences for medical modeling within the emerging field of alternative, holistic medicine, which has struggled for years with the nascent conception that our thoughts affect our health. The etheric body provides the clear link in this equation.

The etheric body is integral to the activities of time and memory. Its constant mobility is rhythmic like a musical sequence, cyclic, and harmonious, moving with the pulse of cosmic and solar time. The etheric body is associated with whatever evolves in time. According to Steiner, when Moses related the stunning pictures of an ancient time on Earth, later recorded in Genesis, he did so by reading out the secrets of time as registered in his own etheric body. The etheric is the "great memory tableau" containing in the human form "a vast picture" of an individual's life. or on the planetary level, the unalterable record of all deeds and events since the beginning.

Normally, in the life after death, this meticulous picture record of an individual life is viewed by the disincarnate soul somewhat like a movie. This is a standard feature of the afterlife activity; once, men and women sought to complete this review while still in bodily form as part of an initiatory sequence in the old Mystery schools. In these ancient initiation rites, the candidate accessed the etheric tableau while still alive; then the fully developed clairvoyant could consult the etherically inscribed picture records at will, nearly anytime. This was an opportunity for extended, independent cognition and a profound gesture of human spiritual freedom; but it took a great deal of inner work. The etheric, acting as memory library on a larger scale, is what the esoteric tradition calls the Akashic Records, because *akasha* is the Sanskrit name for what the West calls "ether." So when we discuss the human etheric body we are essentially referring to an individualized

Akashic Records. Our wakeful access to the memory-laden etheric body enables us to read in the Akashic chronicle the successive phases of "cosmic memory," or evolution in time.

In the ancient Mystery school initiations the candidate strove to develop "eyesight" in the etheric body to access both individual and cosmic memory. The etheric body is an organ of cognition. That's still hard to appreciate at the close of the twentieth century because we are so culturally, and scientifically, immured in a materialist, reductionist, mechanistic model of the human being, what French philosopher René Guénon calls "the reign of quantity." On the other hand, our struggle to master the etheric body as a cognitive organ has been uphill all the way for the last several millennia. The nature of our human organism itself has militated against it. The relationship of the etheric body to the physical was different in the first three post-Atlantean epochs than it has been for most of the fourth and fifth, and it was even more different in the antediluvian Atlantean period. During Atlantis, the "etheric head" (that aspect of the etheric body around the head) extended far outside the boundaries of the physical head. The etheric head was like a billowing cowl. In the Atlantean Human, the etheric body was only loosely attached to the head, which produced an "incomplete coincidence" of etheric and physical bodies.

This projecting part of the etheric body was able to receive impressions, like imprints on soft wax, from the astral body which was active and cognizant in the supersensible world. The astral body imprinted picture-thoughts, or memories, of its activities onto the plastic, malleable etheric body. Human incarnate consciousness, working through the material brain, was then able to read out or discern the thought-pictures. In today's language, we would say of this readout that we had a psychic vision. This naturally loosened etheric body made possible the clairvoyant abilities, extraordinary memory, and presumed magical powers of the Atlanteans. Over time, the etheric cowl around the physical head retracted, condensed, and drew more tightly into the skull. What in the Atlantean head profile had been a "special and central point of perception," became in later post-Atlantean epochs, "an organ, the development of which will restore the power of clairvoyance in humanity: the pineal gland." Steiner suggests that in the pineal gland (a tiny organ located at the center of the brain), we find the condensed, materialized residue of the earlier etheric cowl.[16]

As the etheric head condensed and grew tightly bound to the physical organism, the nature of the Mystery initiation changed, too. The etheric body had to be almost forcefully pried loose from the physical body to facilitate clairvoyant perception. The supervised immersion, or baptism, of the candidate was so thorough it was a near drowning; but the shock of imminent death precipitated a temporary loosening of the etheric from the physical. This loosening flooded physical awareness with a lifetime etheric memory tableau. This same experience happens somewhat serendipitously today in the rising incidence of Near-Death Experiences (NDEs); here, during a life-threatening experience or clinical death, the contents of a person's lifetime suddenly flash before one's attention as a vivid cinematic review.

The statistical increase in NDEs today actually corroborates a statement Steiner often made regarding the evolution of the human etheric body. "Today humanity has actually reached the point when in a great number of individuals the etheric body is beginning to loosen itself from the physical," Steiner reported in 1908.[17] In the twentieth century, we stand at a major turning point in which the etheric body, weak and relatively powerless within the physical head organization, will emerge again, free itself from the gravity of the physical—that "three pound universe," as some neuroscientists jokingly refer to the human brain—and reclaim its cosmic, thought-filled independence. In essence, this loosening of the tight bond between etheric and physical body is the major change Steiner indicated the etheric body would start to undergo in our time. The loosening of the etheric body from the physical is the rightful task of the consciousness soul epoch. It is also what will bring forward that natural etheric clairvoyance destined to unfold in humanity starting in the mid-twentieth century.

This natural, etheric clairvoyance providing wakeful cognition will be the legitimate fruit of the consciousness soul. Once again we find Christ is the orchardist. In our time the etheric body will be revitalized, Steiner indicated, and this re-energization of the thinking, picture-weaving life body, in which thoughts are, once again, real, living forces, is connected with the new revelation of

Christ. "When the etheric body is revitalized, man finds Christ."[18] That's because through the Mystery of Golgotha, the Sun Being called Christ permeated the human etheric body with new life, inaugurating its course of metamorphosis through the consciousness soul and its eventual return to full clairvoyant potency. That aspect of the human etheric body that was transformed after Golgotha Steiner called *buddhi,* or life spirit, noting that "only through the formation of *buddhi* can the human being recognize and perceive Christ as spiritual essence."[19] The etheric perception of the risen Christ, Steiner said repeatedly, would be the greatest event of the twentieth and succeeding centuries. It would be the hallmark experience for the consciousness soul epoch.

We must carefully distinguish here between the perception of the Christ and the physical reappearance of the Christ on Earth. In our densely materialized way of thinking today, it is easy to misconstrue the intended subtlety as something literal, to misconceive an etheric event as a physical fact. The Christ cannot return to Earth in a second coming in human form because through the Christ Event, the Christ was permanently incorporated into the planet; the Christ never left the planet's etheric organization. Many twentieth-century Christians take a literal, fundamentalist stance towards the millennia expectation of the Second Coming of Christ, and expect the Christ to once again walk incarnate among us. Steiner never meant this and considered such a view a disappointing reductionist simplification. The Mystery of Golgotha is an event unique to the planet; it cannot, need not, and will not be repeated. Once is utterly sufficient.[20]

With the Mystery of Golgotha, Christ became one with the Earth. Thus his presence is always available in the etheric atmosphere of the planet, and, by extension, in the etheric organization of the human being. That's the profound opportunity of the consciousness soul epoch. The "true nature of the Second Coming" means a recapitulation of Paul's apocalyptic vision en route to Damascus. We could put it this way: the Christ returns to Earth and humanity in spirit, as after the Ascension, but, truthfully, the Second Coming is *our* ascension to etheric perception of the Christ's indelible presence. In the vernacular, we meet the Christ halfway; that was the gift to humanity of the Crucifixion. Humankind acquiring etheric perception is the true Second Coming. In our time the Christ will enter increasingly into "the ordinary consciousness" of humans; first a few, then many, will "meet Him objectively as an etheric form." Steiner foresaw a perpetual Epiphany through which the Christ would be always revealing himself. To prepare ourselves for this revelation without end and to complete the task of the consciousness soul epoch, we need the spiritual discipline of Anthroposophy, Steiner said.

Steiner regarded the form of Anthroposophy itself as a "true Christ-revelation," claiming that "every line we read of our anthroposophical science is an entering into a relationship with Christ." [21] Such a claim is easily misunderstood. At the close of the twentieth century, the Western intellectual marketplace is overstocked with competing metaphysics and the gurus of a hundred schools each claim a unique celestial imprimatur. So, for many not familiar with Steiner's intimate yet rigorously tested relationship with the supersensible, such a statement sounds ideologically parochial, the unsupportable assertion of a philosophy seized with manifest destiny. Yet as we move deeper into the meaning of Anthroposophy in the course of this book, becoming aware that its cosmic roots and karmic intentions weave the supersensible and material worlds together, our initial hesitations with Steiner's claim may be allayed.

As a spiritual scientist, Steiner earnestly sought to describe objectively the events and intentions of the supersensible world with the same consummate precision and detachment with which a scientist would recount the results of a laboratory experiment. His hope was that other individuals, in whom the possibility of wakeful cognition had arisen, might corroborate on their own the results of his investigations on their behalf. Such is the way with scientists: they offer the results of their experiments to rigorous peer review and independent replication. If anything, Anthroposophy is Steiner's frank invitation to us to confirm or adjust his spiritual scientific observations through our own efforts. If Steiner has a system, it is the *methodology* of Anthroposophy itself, the reliable methods by which we may school our cognition to make our way safely and without error into the supersensible world, and, once there, to conduct scientifically precise research into its structure, activities, and plans.

Steiner made another claim fraught with irony. This is an acutely violent century in which millions of young men and women have died through wars. Through a strange law of conservation, this prodigy of death serves the unfolding of the consciousness soul. Millions of young soldiers and numerous civilians have died in the wars of the twentieth century, beginning with the first European cataclysm between 1914–18, and continuing with the Gulf War of 1990–91, the Bosnian massacre of 1992–93, and the approximately 30 major regional and civil wars underway as of 1993. So many young humans dying in the biological prime of their lives—what becomes of their etheric bodies? Steiner set this question before himself in 1914 as World War I exploded around him.

He knew that when a human dies, the etheric body immediately separates itself from the human biological form. In the normal course of death in old age, the etheric body, after its contents have been reviewed and digested by the discarnate soul, shrivels up and its elements are returned to the cosmos. This is not the case with premature death. It's as if the etheric body has a certain predetermined time during which its innate vitality will be released; if the physical form dies before this time is complete, the unused energy is available for other activities. Steiner discovered that this surplus of unused, vital etheric bodies in the first two decades of this century would contribute significantly to the flowering of etheric clairvoyance at the end of the century.

Nothing is wasted in the commerce between material and supersensible worlds. Early deaths here are energy boons there. The young war dead took their unused etheric bodies up into the spiritual world, said Steiner. Later, living incarnate humans, filled with enthusiasm for spiritual science, could receive the "instreaming forces" of the unused youthful etheric bodies, making the receipt of "tremendous instructions" possible. It is as if the Dead selectively donate their unspent etheric force to incarnate humanity on behalf of the goals of human evolution, which in our time is the elaboration of the consciousness soul. It's a tremendous paradox, worthy of deep reflection. Here we have, in one generation, an atavistic milieu of extreme violence, death, revenge, general darkness, and negativity contributing to the enlightenment and spiritual fulfillment of the next generation of humans. Steiner called this the principle of spiritual economy. The unspent etheric forces become available to stream back into earth evolution, making "a major contribution to spiritualizing human civilization" and releasing "a truly profound longing for the spiritual world."[22] However, it must be emphasized that this arrangement represents a way of making the best of a bad situation. Steiner did not in any way wish to endorse warfare and killing as an aid for human spiritual development. Far better is for men and women to willingly work together under the Christ aegis and through the social, fraternal process to develop their etheric cognitive powers.[23]

How bizarre and yet spiritually elegant that the awful proliferation of twentieth-century war deaths—World War II, Hiroshima, Korea, Vietnam, Cambodia, Iran, Iraq, Bosnia—through an unsuspected process of recirculation actually might be energizing the spiritual evolution of humanity. Through this accelerating recirculation, "the Dead" will increasingly wish to intervene positively, cooperatively, in the future of civilization. Steiner indicated that communications with the Dead—human souls, still bound karmically to the Earth, but in between incarnations—would increase, gradually building a bridge between the two worlds. For Steiner it was axiomatic that consciousness survives physical death and that the celestial realms are "peopled" with discarnate human souls at all stages of personal evolution; some of the discarnate Dead ardently wish to work creatively in service with colleagues physically incarnate on the Earth. This understanding was part of Steiner's direct clairvoyant experience; he often tracked the post-life adventures of various souls he had encountered as a way of understanding the structure and dynamics of the supersensible world. Steiner understood this collegiality across the incarnate/discarnate membrane would increasingly become the experience of a much larger share of humanity in the future. Certainly, as our brief review of the recent channeling literature in Chapter 1 indicates, the dialogue across the threshold is well underway.

From the standpoint of clairvoyance, of course, calling the discarnate "the Dead" is a misnomer. Their bodies—physical, etheric, and astral—are dead and dissolved, yet as disembodied intelligences they live spiritual, evolving lives. We are constantly in intimate connection with the world of the Dead, immersed in their presence, even if we are unaware of it, Steiner assured us. They live in our thinking, feeling, and willing in the same way we live within the plant world. We aren't inwardly bound to the plant kingdom, yet our etheric body derives from the same Sun forces that constitute the plants. In this sense an aspect of our lives is co-extensive with the plant kingdom. The plants are part of us, etherically; our etheric nature is a recapitulation of the plant world. Similarly, the Dead—and here we mean not only the recently, prematurely deceased, but the full complement of super-sensible residents at all stages of individual soul evolution—live within us, working, in the most positive expression, to stimulate our awareness with ideas, blessings, new impulses, inspirations, and guidance. The Dead can also be a nuisance, even dangerous, in the form of ghosts, poltergeists, and restless, inimical spirits. As in any other circumstance, we must be prudent and exercise sharp discrimination in our potential communications or interactions with the discarnate. As the New Age joke goes, Just because you're dead, doesn't mean you're smart.

Clairvoyant perception reveals that a great deal of what arises in us is "in truth told us by the Dead." In other words, without our being aware of it, we are nonetheless frequently in communication with the disincarnate. And it's a reciprocal process, too. The Dead benefit from our involvement with spiritual science; soul education continues in the life after death in which the fetters of the conditioned incarnate mind are removed. "We literally turn ourselves into fruitful pastures for the dead when we fill ourselves with the ideas of spiritual science."[24] The Dead are often illuminated by our hard-won spiritual illuminations; in fact, Steiner often counseled the bereaved to read spiritual science texts out loud, directing the words to the image of the deceased. Steiner also remarked, when in his early days he was confronted with tiny audiences for his public lectures, that while there might be but a few embodied humans present in the lecture hall, far many more souls strained to listen in from the supersensible world. One of the practical tasks of anthroposophical life during the consciousness soul epoch is to ensure that this reciprocal communication bridge is built between the living and the dead and that the cognitive commerce be immaculately clear and of maximum benefit to all humanity. In Steiner's view, the etheric perception of the Christ, facilitated by the gradual loosening of the etheric body from the physical body, would in fact make this commerce across the threshold possible.

It is not only the Dead who will be cooperating with incarnate humans "actively in the highest degree" during this 2,160 year period. Humanity is ripening towards a time of unilateral cooperation, a time of conscious relationship with the multiplicity of spiritual beings and intelligences that comprise the supersensible worlds. In a remarkable sense, this will be an act of momentous self-awareness. Insofar as the totality of spiritual intelligences of the three hierarchies collectively and sequentially created the human being, our wakeful cognition of their existence and activities and, more importantly, our freely willed work with them on behalf of human, planetary, and cosmic evolution, will be a profound act of remembering at the highest level.

The cosmos becomes aware of itself through an awakening humanity, recognizing its spiritual elements, which are these same three hierarchies. Our cognition of the cosmic constituency of the human being is itself an act of cosmic self-awareness, in which the inherent self-reflexivity of the Logos becomes activated. The new Christ event—our etheric perception of the Christ who is the Logos—will bring us into a conscious, daytime, cooperative relationship with all the hierarchies and intelligences in the cosmos. The quickening of our cognition into the domain of the etheric body is the key to this event. It is as if one glimpse of the risen Christ will bring the entire supersensible world in tow as we become aware of the Logos.

Steiner foresaw a time, "in a future by no means far distant," in which we will be aware of the influences of the spiritual world and willingly live and work in natural communion with these spiritual beings and their intentions. With our increasingly conscious and voluntary engagement with the hosts of supersensible beings whose life body is the cosmos, attained through the emergence of the new etheric clairvoyance of the consciousness soul, we will reside once again, and at long last, within the aegis of cosmic intelligence and its regent, the Archangel Michael. The fulfillment of the consciousness soul, the activation of the human etheric body, and the individualization of the Christ Event as a cognitive reality is Michael's task.

CHAPTER 3

Cosmic Intelligence

Michaelic Preparations for the
Respiritualization of Cosmic Intelligence

*T*HE COSMIC BEING named Michael is pivotal to Anthroposophy. In traditional angelologies Michael, whose name means "like unto God," is described as an archangel, one among seven similar beings whose responsibilities encompass, in part, the Earth, its seasons, its evolution, and its life in the cosmos. Traditionally, Michael's time of maximum yearly influence is the autumn, culminating in his eponymous festival, Michaelmas, once celebrated throughout Europe on September 29. During this time he is often commemorated for his deed of dragon-slaying; the religious icon of the human St. Michael is an anthropomorphosed version of the archangelic Michael. Usually depicted with doughty sword and stout shield, Michael is the standard bearer and way-preparer for the Christ.

In Anthroposophy, Michael's function is accorded greater depth. Here the great archangel is the Lord of cosmic intelligence, the "fiery Prince of Thought in the Universe," as Steiner wrote. Michael, for Steiner, was an incontestable spiritual reality, evident to his inner perception; when Steiner discussed the deeds of Michael, he spoke as a researcher—a spiritual scientist—reporting the results of his empirical, experiential investigations. The world of the archangels was for Steiner as cognitively palpable as the world of men and women. Since the beginning of humanity, Michael has kept his spiritual eye on the progress of his human protégés incarnate on Earth. He has always worked to make the transfer of independent intellectuality from the cosmos to individual men and women a reality on Earth. His own cosmic activity of ordering ideas and precipitating actual realities is of the same nature as the life of the intellect within the human individuality. In other words, what Michael does for Intelligence in the cosmos he does within humanity as well. As Steiner put it, "that which works as intelligence throughout the whole Cosmos should later become concentrated within the human individuality." Working tirelessly to insure it does is the Archangel Michael.[1]

What is cosmic intelligence? It is knowledge of the "mutual relationships of conduct" of all the heavenly beings. It is an awareness that encompasses all the ideas, thoughts, pictures, knowledge, intentions, reasons, agendas, and activities of all the spiritual beings, stars, and planets in the cosmos; an awareness that construes them rightfully in the context of an august plan so that it may contribute constructively to their fulfillment. It is knowing everything the hierarchies have in mind—and why; more important, it is the *ability* to know, to cognize, this vast spectrum of intention. That kind of monumental cognition is what Michael has been striving for so many millennia to impart to each human on Earth as a birthright: the opportunity to apprehend the cosmos as an independent knower. This concentration of knowledge is the wisdom or *sophos* in anthropo*sophy*, from the great spiritual being Sophia, whom we will consider later in the book. Michael conveys thoughts and ideas through which we can grasp the spiritual, gain intellectual understanding of the world, yet remain free beings. At least analogically, we might say his sword keeps our cognition lucid and his shield blocks delusions and misperceptions. On a practical level, the attainment of cosmic intelligence by individual men and women means direct, unmediated cognition, without priesthood, whether religious or occult, and without inherited dogma, whether philosophical or epistemological. Cosmic intelligence, for Michael, is cognitive autonomy.

Michael conveys to the human intellect all the original thought-forces and imaginations of the gods, "full of soul and inwardly warm."[2] Michael, as the World Being whose cosmic activity is thought, has kept himself pure and virginal over the eons for an evolving humankind. Michael himself, on behalf of a ripening humanity, embodies a pristine, original intelligence—the primordial

spectrum and agility of consciousness intended for humanity—
and seeks, increasingly, to impart this quality to us. Michael maintains the crucial balance between a World-picture, which is too
much disembodied fantasy, and World-intellect, which is too literal and materialized. "The World-picture becomes through him
a World-revelation, full of wisdom, which reveals the World-intellect as Divine World-activity. And in this World-activity lives the
care of Christ for humanity."[3]

Michael and the Christ are colleagues in the same project of
transferring the cosmic intelligence intact and spiritualized to
individual humans. Towards this end Michael maintains humanity's original connection with divine spirituality and the Logos.
In Steiner's view the "Divine-Spiritual" expresses itself in the cosmos in succeeding stages. First through its inmost *Being*, then
through the *manifestation* of this Being, then through the *active
working*, when the Being withdraws from the manifestation. The
final stage is through the *accomplished work*, when only the forms
and processes but not the living Being of the Divine-Spirituality
remain.

As incarnate humans we live in this fourth world of accomplished work. Michael's remarkable deed on our behalf has been
to adhere to the Being and manifestation stages of the Divine-
Spiritual. Michael's perpetual effort is to imbue human evolution
with this same immaculate adherence he has maintained; unknown to us, he has maintained inviolate something priceless until we mature, spiritually, and can receive it. Michael's enduring
inspiration is to embody in perfect freedom for human cosmic
evolution that primordial relationship with the Being of the Divine-Spiritual. Michael's mission is to cultivate in us the "Christ-
language about the cosmos," that same "primeval Light" that
Christ brought to the human Ego. To understand Michael,
Steiner said, is to "find the way in our time to the Logos, as lived
by Christ here on Earth and among men."[4] As we noted above,
the missions of Michael and the Christ are intricately intertwined.

Since the Mystery of Golgotha, Michael invites humans to manifest their freedom by perceiving spirit in matter—*as* matter—in a
daytime, wakeful cognition. This new "Michael revelation" doesn't
force itself on anyone; in fact, humans must actively go out on the
Michael path to meet it. Michael waits, patiently, for us to join

him, but he never solicits; we must join him only voluntarily out of our free choice and through our wakefulness. Then Michael pours "absolute clarity" into the human soul. In the Michael revelation we look for the spiritual *in* the material and perceive spirit, soul, and body working into one another. Then the flesh becomes Word again (through the intermediation of the word-permeated etheric body), matter transmutes itself into Logos, and we dwell as spiritualized flesh within the realm of the Word. This is the aim of the new "Michael-culture" as Steiner envisioned it.

Even though Michael has assumed spiritual guidance of human affairs, his regency is anything but heavy-handed and authoritarian. Michael merely *shows* the way, but we must follow him in our freedom. And he encourages us to see his way during the daytime. In earlier times Michael transmitted his intelligence through night revelations, dreams and visions that came upon men and women while asleep or otherwise unconscious in their Egos; this is the atavistic path of somnolent mediumship and unconscious psychism, inappropriate to the changed soul conditions of our times. In our epoch of the conciousness soul Michael becomes the "revealer during the day." Michael facilitates our cognition when we are wakeful, secure in our individuality, working under the light of the Sun on the physical Earth— in the daytime.[5]

Since the Mystery of Golgotha—this is what Steiner calls the sequence of the Christ incarnation from birth to Crucifixion and Ascension—Michael has been drawing ever closer to human consciousness. Since the ninth century and especially since the last third of the nineteenth, Michael has been on a path leading from the cosmos to humanity, standing in a new relationship to human thought. Up until the ninth century humans knew their thoughts came from above, from Michael; they felt their mental life was really Michael thinking in them. Then in the ninth century A.D. thoughts began to fall away from Michael's dominion. As thoughts passed out of the spiritual world and into the individual minds of men and women, and as humans began formulating thoughts independently of spiritual inspiration, Michael sought a change in his immemorial cosmic task.

Since the late nineteenth century Michael has wanted to "live *in* the human souls in which the thoughts are formed." Michael wants to be the individual human's guide in forming higher, subtler, more exalted, thoughts; he liberates thought from dry, frosty abstraction and converts cool head-cogitations to fervent heart-revelations. Michael warms and enlivens human thinking. Michael wants a legion of "souls clarified by thought." Humans will actively draw thoughts, or the spiritual content of the cosmos, directly out of their own being and inner forces. As we suggested in the previous chapter, this Michaelic enlivening of thinking is directly related to the reinvigoration of the human etheric body. There we noted the life of the etheric body *is* thinking. Michael can now be heard "from within" as the inherent spirituality of the human becomes a conscious experience. In the new Michael age, the Sun-nature—Michael's domain within the solar system—will begin shining within the soul so that men and women will speak of being led by the Sun in their thought-life. Thereby "the ideas of man do not merely remain 'thinking,' but in thought develop *sight*," and thereby living pictorial content.[6]

What this new "sightful thinking" will appreciate is that for the last 2,000 years since the Mystery of Golgotha Michael has overseen a great deal of supersensible preparation for the profound spiritual transformations that began in the late nineteenth century, have become prominent in the twentieth century, and that will come to dominate the life of succeeding centuries. As Steiner would say, even today we cannot begin to understand the cognitive expansion and occult floriation of late twentieth-century culture without studying the complex supersensible preparations and events that underlie them. In other words, anthroposophical thinking schools us in the understanding that the great burst of channeling, psychism, and occultism of the 1980s and beyond is the result and expectation—at least, the unmistakable symptom—of many centuries of careful supersensible preparation. Steiner's meticulous researches through the Akashic Records on this matter illuminate the spiritual-historical *context* for this recent development. Golgotha was the first stage, laying the foundations for the eventual etheric clairvoyance of the Christ event. The second stage happened in 869 A.D. when human karma was thrown into chaos with a rupture in the cosmic intelligence and within the three angelic hierarchies. It was a schism felt in both the supersensible and physical worlds.

In the world of human evolution, the Eighth Ecumenical Council that convened at Constantinople in 869 A.D. declared dogmatically that the traditional conception of Trichotomy, that described the human as threefold (body, soul, and spirit), was heretical and, as far as ecclesiastical dogma was concerned, officially untrue. What was "true" was Dichotomy, which posited a twofold human of only body and soul; the spirit, as the third component of humanity, was denied a place in the human being. These were the external facts of that year, but a great deal more transpired in the world of "objective realities." For one, Michael was handing the cosmic intelligence over to human individuals, inaugurating a necessary process that would take more than a thousand years to mature. For another, a major shift was happening in the solar system itself. The Sun Intelligence, which is to say, the Sun as a colony of spiritual beings, had always stood under Michael's jurisdiction. But around the ninth century sunspots began pimpling the once pristine complexion of the Sun and for Michael this was inauspicious. To the other planetary intelligences (that is, the purposeful spiritual awareness of each planet, such as Venus, Mars, and Mercury, each construed as a vast spiritual presence), this meant they would no longer be ruled by the Sun, nor would they allow the Earth to be dependent solely on the Sun. These planetary intelligences resolved that the Earth would hereafter be dependent on the entire cosmos. "It was a complete separation of Cosmic Powers that had hitherto belonged together. The Sun-Intelligence of Michael and the Planetary Intelligences gradually came into cosmic opposition with one another."[7]

Things were not too harmonious among the angels either. According to Steiner, a number of angels formerly united with Michael broke from his realm, contending that the guidance of humans would be undertaken by "earthly powers" alone. That meant angels operating within the Earth sphere rather than from the supersensible heights would guide an evolving humanity on Earth. This dissension threw human karma into chaos. It is the responsibility of angels to make a human being's life karmically coherent. Through our karma we are destined to meet various individuals in a given lifetime and to thereby experience a certain quality of interaction. But with the Michael schism, some angels remained with Michael while others descended to Earth.

The situation was like a telephone exchange in which numerous wires dangled dangerously unconnected. Human karma grew disordered. Destined connections didn't happen; karmic necessities went incomplete, unfulfilled. Human experiences in succeeding lifetimes were no longer coordinated with their karma and a "chaotic element" entered modern history.

Something else happened in 869 with import for the late twentieth century. Steiner put it paradoxically, saying in that year Christ met Himself. What he meant was that as the Grail-Parsifal stream from Spain flowed into the Arthur-Michael stream from Britain, two images of the Christ merged. It may be surprising to learn that the Celtic legends of King Arthur, his birthplace at Tintagel, and the august mystery of the Holy Grail are implicated with the business of Michael, cosmic intelligence, the Christ, and etheric clairvoyance. Both streams bore potent images of the Christ in their wake; in 869, the two Christ images converged, thereby uniting the Arthur and Grail streams as one Mystery tradition. It is important to remember, as Steiner repeatedly reminds us, that long before the actual incarnation of the Christ, his presence as a Sun Being had always been a key aspect of the Mystery schools.[8]

There at Arthur's castle at Tintagel, on the rugged Cornish coast of southwest England, Arthur and the Knights had striven to transfer Michael's dominion over cosmic intelligence into the social-spiritual sphere of Europe. This impulse was Arthurian or "pagan" Christianity in which Christ in collaboration with Michael was the Sun hero of the Mysteries. This stream preserved and transmitted an "etheric Image of the Christ." Later, in the Spanish Grail-Parsifal stream, initiates no longer sought for the intelligence flowing down from the cosmos; they knew it had descended to the Earth and that the Christ of Golgotha would be found in the blood and hearts of men and women. The Arthur stream bore the cosmic image of Christ the Sun hero, moving outwardly; the Grail stream bore the Christ himself, the incarnate Christ who became the brother of humanity, moving inwardly. Then in that pivotal year, 869, the "pre-Christian Christ stream" (Arthur) and the "Christian Christ stream" (Grail) came together.[9] A profound integration had been completed for Western civilization and for the global future of the Christ event.

A related development of equal import was happening behind the scenes in cosmic spiritual evolution. Between the fourth and fifteenth centuries A.D. "an event of immense cosmic importance" transpired. The Exousiai, or Spirits of Form (Elohim) withdrew as the source of human inspiration and the Archai, or Spirits of Personality, took up the task but with an agenda that was "radically different." With this transition, the entire inner structure of human spiritual life was transformed. Formerly, the Exousiai, who bore the forces of form and the life of cosmic thought, had poured the cosmic intelligence *from outside* into human consciousness through visions and imaginations. The Exousiai had furnished the content of the ancient clairvoyant visions by grace which manifested involuntarily and in a dreamy unselfconscious context in human cognition. But with the transition to the Spirits of Personality, this would all change.

The Spirits of Personality, who are one hierarchy closer to humans than the Exousiai, do not hand out imaginations to whoever wants them. Under the Archai's new tutelage, humans must work out a personal vision, developing imaginations in full consciousness, building them up with will and effort *from within*. Then we must bring these imaginations as epistemological fruits to the Archai to be "verified, proved, and confirmed." We must find our way into new thought-forms, said Steiner, then offer these to the Archai, "who are weaving the new world-plan" and to "the objective process of the spiritual world." As a result a human will feel more aware of the thoughts in one's own being, as the indication and result of intense, inner activity, of enlivened etherically vital thinking. Through this transition, thinking will remain objective yet become our personal asset. And anything deriving from involuntary imaginations, from the old ways of atavistic, dreamy, natural clairvoyance, in the age of Michael, Steiner warned, is pathological, pushing a man down below his normal level and blocking his way into the intended evolutionary threshold.[10]

The scale of Michaelic preparation for spiritual events destined to begin in the twentieth century may impress us as awesome when we next consider the Michael School. This was a remarkable supersensible conclave held between the thirteenth and fifteenth centuries. Here the future of cosmic intelligence was negotiated. Included in the discussions between the hierarchies and humanity were Michael, Aristotelians, Platonists, the great teachers of Chartres Cathedral, the souls who would be late twentieth century Anthroposophists—in short, all the souls ever connected with the Michael stream, once and future anthroposophists. Not only human souls, but all the beings of the angelic and archangelic hierarchy and numerous elementary beings (gnomes, nature spirits) attended. It was a watershed supersensible conference "in the domain of the Sun," circa 1413 A.D., that coincided with the transition underway in human culture from intellectual to consciousness soul.

Michael was the teacher at this great meeting. It was a "process of instruction" in which Michael reviewed the wisdom of the ancient Mysteries and provided a stunning vista of the future, of that new age of Michael-culture scheduled to begin in the late nineteenth century when he took up his rulership once again and when all the teachings of this supersensible Michael School would be translated to Earth. In that coming age, the Michael principle would be developed differently—"through the Intelligence of the human soul itself." The Sun-Christianity, expressed in the Grail stream and through the great Platonist teachings at Chartres, would be united with the scientific rigors of Aristotelianism, Michael foresaw. Thus were the Michaelic seeds of spiritual science laid down, for the fusion of science and spirit, reason and intuition, that would constitute that future maturation of cosmic intelligence called Anthroposophy.

Steiner didn't talk publicly about this momentous Michael School until nearly the end of his life. Then in 1924, in the course of 80 lectures on karmic relationships, he revealed for the first time the inspiring details of "one of the most important exchanges of ideas behind the scenes of human evolution."[11] Steiner made it clear that in the results of this Michael School lie the roots of the karmic relationships of twentieth-century Anthroposophists. Men and women drawn to Anthroposophy today may find inexplicable resonance in this information; some may eventually or spontaneously remember something of that profound meeting and collective commitment under Michael's aegis. The Michael intention reaches forward through 600 years of time, linking lives and spiritual beings in a "mighty world-historic plan." As the twentieth century ends, the time for that plan's maturation now draws upon us, as Steiner foretold.

The great teachers of the School of Chartres, who had carried forward the spiritual vision of Platonism, were returning to the supersensible worlds. Other souls were preparing to bring a spiritualized Aristotelianism (a spiritualized scientific method) into civilization. To these would pass the responsibility for the ordering of spiritual life on Earth. This transfer would work, at first, chiefly through the Dominicans, who would develop Scholasticism and its "bitter but glorious battle" to master the true use of human intelligence. Only much later would the old Platonists of Chartres seek to reincarnate and enter once again the stream of human evolution. The appropriate time for this would be the end of the twentieth century, Michael indicated, and the most efficient vehicle would be the Anthroposophical Movement as the Michaelic stream would thence be known. At that time—ours—Anthroposophy would strive to unite the two elements, Platonism and Aristotelianism, in a single spiritual science, knowledge of the Human.

Coincident with the fifteenth century inner Michael School was the esoteric founding of Rosicrucianism in Europe by the initiate, Christian Rosenkreutz. "True Rosicrucianism lies absolutely in the activity of the Michael Mission," said Steiner.[12] The early Rosicrucian movement prepared the path for Michael for his coming "earthly Mission," which would begin in the late nineteenth century. The Rosicrucian initiates worked closely with Michael in the supersensible realms, but "without the danger of entangling him in present earthly happenings." The powerful soul forces developed by Rosenkreutz and his circle of initiates were later used to found the nineteenth-century occult movement called Theosophy which prepared the way for Anthroposophy and the advent of Steiner's Michaelic mission. It was the strength radiating from the etheric body of Christian Rosenkreutz, Steiner claimed, that provided inspiration for that great Theosophical text, *Isis Unveiled* (1877), by H. P. Blavatsky, Theosophy's founding seer. Thus with the almost secretive fifteenth-century founding of Rosicrucianism a vital step was taken upon the Michael path that would lead to the eventual flowering of twentieth-century Anthroposophy.

Michael's next preparatory event was a "mighty Imagination" staged in the supersensible worlds at the beginning of the nineteenth century. Again all the great spirits in the Michael stream gathered around him for the "enactment of a great and sublime supersensible ritual and ceremony, an unfolding of mighty pictures." It was a "great, cosmic spiritual festival."[13] Michael was preparing for momentous changes in his stature and relationship to the Earth, beginning in 1840 and peaking in 1879, when he would take up his new 350-year regency.

Through this Imagination, Michael wanted to consecrate his coming regency and his work with Michaelic souls who would be once again incarnate. Michael, as Prince of Thought, cast everything his pupils had learned in the previous fifteenth-century School and everything residual from the ancient initiation wisdom, into new pictures and imaginations for contemplation. Michael cast his living thought into imaginations of the new Christianity. These living pictures—animate etheric images, from our incarnate viewpoint—would implant the inner Michaelic impulse men and women would need when later they began their anthroposophical work on Earth. The majority of Anthroposophists, Steiner claimed in 1924, carry this Michaelic seed subconsciously within them as the result of this nineteenth-century Imagination.

In 1840 Michael rose from the rank of Archangel to Archai, or Time Spirit, moving one step closer to the formal commencement of his mission in 1879. The affairs of archangels usually involve overseeing the evolution of group souls, major ethnic collective identities such as the Hebrew, the Slav, the German. The domain of the Archai is global—overseeing the complex spiritual evolution of an epoch. With Michael's elevation to Archai, it became easier for him to work directly into human evolution, not only from the super-earthly position that was traditionally his, but from a new earthly standpoint. At the same time Michael retained his responsibilities as one of the seven principal archangels.

As Time Spirit, Michael's agenda—the respiritualization of the cosmic intelligence that had passed over to human individuality in the ninth century—became paramount. We must realize that since 869 A.D. and the revocation of Trichotomy, spirituality had been legislated out of human intellectuality and it had grown increasingly materialized. It would be Michael's mission to re-impart a spiritual impulse to humanity's ripening but earthbound intelligence. In the same year (1840) in which materialism attained its zenith, Anthroposophy rested in "the womb of preparation," awaiting that great call to birth from Michael, the new Spirit of the Time.

The next Michaelic call came in the 1870s. At this point it was evident that a "cosmic New Year" was dawning. From his standpoint in 1920 Steiner understood that since the 1870s "the Spiritual World has made a mighty inroad into our Sense-world." He realized the supersensible was re-entering our physical existence through revelations in a new way in order that the Ego (or human individuality, the I-consciousness) could receive a fresh spiritual content in full waking consciousness. Since the 1870s cosmic knowledge, through Michael, willed to reveal itself to humankind, to enter into the living stream of evolving humanity. This potentially would impart a "new upbuilding impulse out of Heaven." Steiner realized that as the era of the consciousness soul progressed into the twentieth century, we would live in "an extraordinarily important epoch," one that inexorably requires revolutionary changes in the way we think and perceive. Only through this transformation of our cognitive faculties into "a new conception of present facts" could we expect to grasp what the womb of the future holds in store for us.[14] Progress in our spiritual evolution would depend on this.

But something else began appearing in the late 1870s out of the recondite womb of the future. The Vulcan-beings. Vulcan, the seventh, culminating phase of cosmic evolution, exists in our future. But in the 1870s these future Vulcan-beings, however paradoxical it sounds, started entering the human incarnational stream as an advance guard of our spiritual destiny. The Vulcans are heavenly, not human, beings from beyond the Earth, bringing messages into human culture about the viability of a "comprehensive spiritual science." Increasingly in the next few centuries, Steiner said, more of these advanced Vulcans will walk among us, and we owe it to our evolution to understand their language. The possibility of the presence of spiritually advanced future beings walking amongst us sheds light on various strange phenomena commonly reported in New Age and occult literature such as "walk-ins" and alleged ET contacts.[15]

Michael began his 350 year regency as chief archangel and Archai in November 1879 with a cosmic battle. At that time Michael overcame the Dark Forces (represented by certain angels) of the supersensible realm and cast them down into the Earth. This battle had raged in the celestial sphere from 1841 to 1879. The Imagination or pictorial tableau of Michael slaying the dragon (the Dark Forces zoömorphically depicted) suggests this decisive event. On the one hand, the Earth sphere became polluted with these cast-out dark spirits; on the other hand, the clarification of the celestial spheres meant the freer flow of spiritual cognition— as "a fine spiritual rain." Since the Dark Forces were cast out of the supersensible world, the spiritual light of that realm was unsullied; our danger was in not penetrating cognitively beyond the confusing atmosphere of the Earth plane, now dense with the particulates of the Dark Forces. Never were the Dead (and the Unborn) so powerful an influence among humanity as they were between 1870 and 1890, Steiner commented. What formerly had been cosmic strife was now re-engaged as worldly strife. In this conflict men and women remained neutral and inactive only at their peril because their spiritual evolution depended on their prevailing on Michael's behalf. As we will appreciate in the next chapter, during this thirty-year period, Europe and America witnessed a dramatic upsurge in occult activities, psychism, and mediumship.

Michael's "dragon-slaying" act proliferated the Earth with hordes of roaming angelic Spirits of Darkness, perpetually offering opportunities to humans to "surrender to all sorts of errors and observations that belong to the darkness of evil."[16] The possibility, even likelihood, of cognitive error and metaphysical delusion was greatly enhanced by this Michaelic deed. But this problematic situation had a positive side. Through constant temptation and challenge humans could grasp spiritual truths through reason and thereby protect themselves against error. Fighting off illusion and error is a quick way to hone one's cognitive swordsmanship; spiritual warriors are quickened by confrontations with capable enemies. So it was a necessary, ultimately salutary, transfer, to bring the deluding spirits down into the Earth plane. Formerly the cosmic intelligence had streamed down from Michael into humans as inspiring thoughts and imaginations. In this arrangement Michael's responsibility was to be constantly in strife with the opposing supersensible powers. The gradual transfer of cosmic intelligence to humanity obliged men and women to purify, maintain, and defend this intelligence on Michael's behalf. Whereas formerly Michael protected human intelligence, now individual humans would, with Michaelic guidance, protect their cosmic dispensation themselves, taking them one step further towards spiritual freedom and cognitive autonomy.

Michaelic preparations in the nineteenth century closed with another pivotal event. The year 1899 marked the end of the Age of Darkness, or what the Hindu tradition calls the Kali Yuga, the black epoch. Kali Yuga began approximately in 3101 B.C., Steiner claimed. Its agenda was a progressive darkening of the ancient clairvoyance, a closing of the doors to spiritual cognition, a strengthening of Ego-consciousness and the faculties of material sense observation, reason, and intellect. The year 1899 marked the dawning of the age of clear, radiant light; it was a "sudden thrust forward" through which humanity received "an impetus towards the first beginnings of a future clairvoyance." The Dark Age is immediately followed by the Golden Age, or Satya Yuga, which, if Steiner's indications are accurate, we are either in the earliest stage of or on the verge of entering with the coming century. This new clairvoyance of the Satya Yuga will bring full, independent spiritual cognition with daytime, wakeful Ego-consciousness, something never before experienced in human incarnate life. It will be Michael's long-guarded gift to humanity on behalf of the Christ: cosmic intelligence. The impulse imparted to Earth evolution by the Mystery of Golgotha will literally open our eyes.[17]

The new Michael age will restore truth and order to human karma, unfolding a profound understanding of destiny that will one day inspire law-making and political activities in a new key. The disastrous karmic schism of the ninth century and the artificial bifurcation of the human spirituality will be finally healed and human karma will proceed coherently again. In the Michael age, Steiner declared, Christ will be found in this realm of destiny because at the end of the twentieth century Christ becomes the Lord and Judge of karma for human evolution. As Lord of this cosmic office, the Christ will "bring the balance of our karma into line with the general Earth karma and the general progress of humanity." [18]

Indeed, great, even momentous, changes have already taken place in the supersensible world, awaiting only our enlivened perception, Steiner announced. The world is already much more radiant than people perceive. By 1921 Steiner could confidently declare at his headquarters in Dornach, Switzerland, that the spiritual world had already descended upon us and that in fact since the fifteenth century humanity has lived increasingly in "the resting Godhead." Why don't we see this marvel? Because we have been living oblivious of this fact, possessed by the "psychosis" of materialism. The Godhead awaits the human attainment of an Imagination strong and living enough to encompass the supersensible; through this Imagination we will "recognize the world around us as a spiritual world." This Imagination is achieved through the awakening of our etheric perception. And with this act of newfound spiritual cognition we will begin fulfilling our task in creating a new Michael culture for the epoch of the consciousness soul.

The new Michaelic culture *could* be a living Imagination co-created by humankind and the supersensible hierarchies that interweave the spiritual and material worlds. Michaelic culture is conditional because Michael requires men and women to aid him voluntarily in the respiritualization of cosmic intelligence. Steiner beheld the Imagination of Michael and understood what was required for this century and beyond. Thinking must be redeemed from abstraction and made warm and living again. Intelligence must become Michaelic. Concepts must be spiritualized. The gravity of materialised cognition must be overcome. Thinking must become the vehicle for seeing. Cosmic intelligence must be respiritualized through the Michaelic impulse. The visions of the Michael conclave must be manifested on Earth in our time. Humans must engage themselves with the Michael mission. Great intentions were forecast for the end of the twentieth century. "And Anthroposophy would like to be the message of this mission of Michael."[19]

Anthroposophy first lived in the supersensible realms in Imaginative form, said Steiner, but with the progression of the Michael regency, it *descends* from the super-earthly into the earthly. Here it is borne forward into human evolution by many "anthroposophical souls" who have been schooled by Michael in the integration of Platonist spirit and Aristotelian science. With Platonists and Aristotelians working in unison and with the "right devotion," Steiner predicted that Anthroposophy, or spiritual science, as a Michaelic intention could reach "a certain culmination in earthly civilization" by the end of the twentieth century, leading culture out of its decline. The thrust of the Michaelic mission is the redemption of human thinking, the enlivening of intellectuality into Imagination, the resumption of etheric perception. The Mystery of Golgotha, the Michaelic preparations over the last 2,000 years, the twentieth-century expansion in cognition, the advent of the consciousness soul, our newly emerging etheric clairvoyance, the new Christ event, the descent of Anthroposophy—these are watersheds in the respiritualization of thinking.

A great deal now depends on humanity taking up our responsibility for perfecting this heavenly gift of the independent I capable of cognizing cosmic intelligence. Michael and the Exousiai made the necessary transfer more than 1,000 years ago and until about the mid-nineteenth century humans were usefully engaged in material sense observation, concept formation, and the free-ranging application of reason through science. Material-based perception of the physical world and the formation of sense-bound concepts from this context were a necessary stage in our spiritual evolution; but now we stand upon the next threshold that calls for a respiritualization of our thinking. This means, in practical terms, we must think again, and pictorially, with our etheric forces. Thinking must be enlivened into imagination so that the human will activity isn't abandoned to the instincts.[20]

The experience of thinking once was radically different. During the period of the intellectual soul, from about the eighth century B.C. until the fifteenth century A.D., humans thought with the etheric body. The thinking process felt different from other processes of waking life. Most remarkable from our perspective, the human being actually felt refreshed while thinking; thinking brought activity and life into the etheric body. It was an experience of grace and invigoration. One's soul felt "submerged in the overall cosmic intellect." After all, thinking is an event in the etheric body which is the matrix of formative forces that literally inform our physical biological organism and its processes. Thinking had an inherent moral imperative, too. It was unconscionable for men and women of that time to engage in thinking while in an "immoral" soul condition. Such an act was an insult to the divine cosmic intelligence and likely to bring evil into the world. Human thinking, in that earlier time, was intimately interdependent with the unsullied morality of the hierarchies; as we thought, or experienced thinking, so were we permeated by pristine moral soul forces by the Exousiai.

All this changed as the Michaelic transfer of cosmic intelligence matured and the epoch of the consciousness soul dawned in humanity. In the fifteenth century people began thinking with their physical body. This denser, physicalized thinking became "only a shadow image of cosmic thinking," a corpse of abstract, lifeless, intellectualistic concepts. Concepts became materialized as the dynamism of the etheric body was eclipsed. Regrettable conclusions were drawn; spiritually untenable hypotheses were made. The human organism is a mindless chemical machine, said the chemists. Matter is divisible into finite physical minutiae, proclaimed the physicists. Life has no inherent meaning or purpose, said the existentialists. The survival of the fittest determines evolution, said the biologists. Human behavior is predetermined and automatic, said the psychologists. History is the dialectics of economics and territoriality. When the physical body dies, human consciousness is extinguished, said common sense. The concept of a spiritual teleology and the experience of sense-free spirituality vanished. We know the rest: it is our twentieth-century, agnostic technological culture in which consciousness is at best an epiphenomenon of the physical brain and human life a rare, maybe unique, aberration in an empty cosmos.

By the beginning of the twentieth century Steiner could observe that our thinking comprehended only the mineral realm. Already the world of plants and its etheric Sun-derived dynamism had become a riddle to this deadened cognition. Thinking had succumbed to the lifeless weight of materialism. The weaving world of spirit had been exiled from the domain of thought. Concepts were tortuously constructed, devoid of any spiritual context. Cosmic intellectuality had been buried under stone and earth. New scientific theories and world views were but questions, not answers. Thinking was severed from morality; "bad" people thought as easily as "good" people—and either way it was an enervating experience. Strangely, thinking now made people feel tired, depleted, because it was divorced from the enlivening etheric energies. We have crept into the Earth and our inspirations have become subterranean, Steiner commented. We live in grave danger of becoming "earthworms in the universe" and "hermits of the Earth"—clever intellects, perhaps, but deadeningly earthbound.[21]

All of these conditions pose a "profound and fateful challenge" to modern humanity. The function of will is in danger of surrendering to the dictates of instincts. In Steiner's model, the soul activity of the human is threefold, comprising thinking (intellect), feeling (emotions), and willing. To enter this threefold domain as a wakeful human is indeed a struggle, but one making us worthy to be a "companion of Michael." Thinking, in its best sense, is an active soul-spirit process engendered out of the core of our being, enabling us to encounter that which lives in the outer reaches of the etheric world as idea-cosmic intelligence. Feeling is a domain created out of the living mother of the cosmos in her progressive guises. In the function of willing burns the fire of the future—"the flaming future comes towards one as in apocalyptic revelation, in act, in deed."[22] However, in most cases human beings do not know will, only its impulses, reflexes, and gestures. Normally, we are awake in our intellect, we dream in our emotions, and we are asleep in our will. But it is a considerable liability to be asleep and unconscious in our will activity because our will bears the momentum of our karma. If we do not wakefully intend, then we are subconsciously compelled. We can never exercise free will while we remain asleep to the pressures and intentions of our karma, the accumulated weight, direction, and necessities of our past deeds. When our thinking is etherically dead, devoid of the living Imaginations and vital pictures of cosmic life, "the more will the full interest of what lives outside in society be abandoned to the instincts." The images in our thoughts are no longer compelling; mere pictures, abstracted from a living reality, they lack the impetus to conscious action. So if we don't have a conscious motivation for action, we're likely to act from unconscious promptings—from regressive "basic instinct," as the popular 1992 movie suggests. Our shadow-thinking, immersed in the mineral realm, will yield up to the will inchoate, automatic, self-serving, and potentially immoral, activities—symbolized by an ice-pick brandished during lovemaking—and "humanity will be laid to waste completely."[23]

Anthroposophy has descended from the Michaelic sphere precisely to circumvent this disastrous entropic drift in consciousness, Steiner announced. In our time thinking is no longer imbued with life from outside. Instead we must transcend our conditioned, dead thoughts—our "dry scholarliness"—by instilling life into them from *within*, from the Christ Ego-consciousness dwelling latent in each of us. The key here is that the necessary enlivening of human thinking and the respiritualization of cosmic intelligence is a movement initiated from within the soul forces of each individual. In this reinvigoration Michael is our co-creator, but he cannot move until we do. Only pure sense-free thinking in the I-being will inflame intellect to "will-filled action." Thus cognition and free will are intricately connected in this Michaelic mission. The attainment of cognitive autonomy is coincident if not identical with the mastery of free will; it is, Steiner declared, the essence of spiritual activity. The recognition of the inertness of our thinking is itself the first inwardly awakening response. We will wake ourselves up inwardly through our own willed activity, and through this new etheric life redeem thinking. Our thinking will be Imaginations, living, dynamic, life-filled pictures that encompass the prolific thought-weaving activities of the cosmos.

Through enlivened thinking and the exercise of living Imagination humans will return light to the cosmos. Something will be added to the world through our cognitive activity. This is expected of us by the hierarchies in the epoch of the consciousness soul. The hierarchies attending Michael and the Christ expect that "light will stream upwards from human life itself" to meet what is flowing down from the cosmic powers. Michael stands ready to guide humans in forming higher thoughts, liberating us from the dead realm of the head and introducing us to the warmer realm of spiritual fervor in the heart.[24] With cognitive autonomy comes a cosmic responsibility. As the downstreaming forces that created the world become exhausted, a maturing humanity must replenish the cosmos with a human-produced upstreaming light. Supersensible beings are calling on humankind to become conscious co-creators in the universe, to send living, glittering thoughts back into the cosmos as mirror-pictures of the gods. The human presence in this reciprocal circuit is necessary for the flowering of the next phase of human-cosmic evolution.

No epoch lives by itself, without reference to what must unfold in cosmic-human evolution. In Steiner's panoptic view of history, one epoch always prepares conditions for the next. In fact, Steiner's model of time and history is vast, encompassing seven cultural ages, seven evolutionary epochs, seven conditions of form, seven conditions of life, and seven conditions of consciousness. Regarding this last category, we now exist within the fourth condition of consciousness, or life stage of the cosmos, called Earth; the fifth and next stage is called Jupiter. The seeds of this future Jupiter condition are sown and sprout during the fourth, Earth, condition, and, in a smaller sense, in this the fifth post-Atlantean cultural age devoted to the consciousness soul. Cosmic evolution will progress from the Earth to Jupiter phase. Even as the fifth cultural epoch of the consciousness soul struggles toward its maturity, it is always looking ahead, preparing conditions through its activities, struggles, and insights, for all future conditions, including this new Jupiter phase of the cosmos. In this future condition, the cosmos evolves as a single body into the life of Jupiter, just as it has passed through a Saturn, Sun, Moon, and Earth stage. Again, by Jupiter Steiner means not the planet but a cosmic soul condition and unified field of consciousness. Then there will be complete freedom of thought. What passes for science today with its materialistic biases will be regarded then as "antiquated superstition." Only those forms of knowledge founded on the spiritual will be acknowledged as true. Men and women will unite in "brotherliness in working groups." Communities of souls founded on spirit, not blood and genetic inheritance, will be the norm.

In a smaller time frame, Steiner indicated that in the coming sixth post-Atlantean cultural age (circa 3573 A.D. and onward), the concept of race and atavistic group-soulness will be stripped away. A worldwide culture of men and women will emerge; there will be a milieu of "universal humans" able to remember their I and no longer identifying with any ethnic, political, group soul. Global I-hood will create a nonracial world community.[25] The individual spirituality of a person, not inherited, genetic, group-soul features expressed atavistically as ethnic identity, will determine

facial characteristics. The spiritual (or its absence or adulteration) will become a "race-creating force" in itself, shaping human
physiognomy. The human body becomes an outward image of the
soul which has incorporated the Christ within. Eventually, looking
far ahead, the conclave of Christ-transformed bodies will be
"united in a single cosmic sphere, Jupiter." Of considerable interest for political events of the 1990s, Steiner indicated that living in
the folk spirit of the Slavic people, today ravaged by bloodfeuds,
ancient rivalries, "ethnic cleansings," and torturous political turmoil, are the seeds for the spiritual stream of the coming sixth epoch. Since 1989 upheavals in Slavic Eastern Europe, from the
Berlin Wall to xenophobic Albania, have restructured the geopo-
litical map of the world.

In the sixth post-Atlantean cultural age, the human astral body
will be purified and strengthened through the inherent forces of
the Ego. Steiner called such a purified, transformed astral body
Manas, or Spirit-Self. Here the forces of the I-consciousness work
through the turmoil of the emotional body, bringing to it coherence and light. When the astral body is completely permeated
with spiritual forces then the Virgin Sophia is attained, a condition necessary for the unfolding of cognitive autonomy. This
Manas initiation actually is the foundation of the inner schooling
of spiritual science that Steiner elaborated and recommended,
and which we'll consider later in the book.

In Steiner's day humanity was "just beginning, fully conscious,
to work a little of Manas into its astral body."[26] In our day the proliferation of unschooled psychics and spontaneous "channels" indicates the cultural ripeness for a large-scale Manas initiation; it
also illustrates the metaphysical liabilities of its absence. Steiner
foresaw a Manas culture in which individualized men and women
would experience different sources of truth, yet live harmoniously, immersed in a common wisdom and with agreement between what individuals experience as the higher realities. This
consensual reality, corroborable through a kind of epistemological peer review process, would be founded on the perception of
Spirit Self, the soul condition of the Jupiter epoch, drawing into
humans as a "Spiritual Sun." In the coming Jupiter stage humans
will experience the consciousness possessed today by angels
through a beatific cognitive upgrade. Jupiter consciousness will

be "conscious picture consciousness," a combination of the Old Moon dream picture lucidity with the wakefully precise object-consciousness developed during Earth.

In the future Jupiter Manas culture the two mighty world revelations of Christianity and Buddhism will unite. The Christ will lead humanity into the legendary wisdom realm of the Buddhas called Shambhala. This was among Steiner's most stunning prophecies. The fusion of the two streams actually was accomplished through the Mystery of Golgotha; cultural, spiritual evolution will gradually incorporate this achievement in human life and understanding during the epoch of the consciousness soul. Steiner's description of the preparation of the four being bodies of the Christ is complex and radically unconventional, but in essence he tells us that through the physical incarnation of Christ the spirituality of both the Buddha and Zoroaster were united, comprising "one of the most significant fusions of the spiritual streams in humanity."[27] In our own time the Christ Impulse is about to be enriched again by another tributary stream pressing upon it. Steiner called this new influx "a form of Mercury-culture" which was nothing less than a "renewed influx of the Buddha stream." This new Mercury-stream proclaimed itself in the fact that many undergoing occult development under Steiner's indications during his time of activity subsequently grew into the spiritual world.[28]

Steiner foresaw a Buddhism permeated with the Christ Impulse and a humanity rising into vision of the "light-woven, light-gleaming Shambhala, abounding in infinite fullness of life and filling our hearts with wisdom."[29] Shambhala is the spiritual realm of the ascended human Hierarchy on Earth, usually physically referenced with an obscure mountain valley in Mongolia and paramount in Buddhist aspirations. Here live perfected humans—saints, masters, Bodhisattvas, the human Hierarchy, in short, who guide humanity. The reality of Shambhala will be acknowledged, declared Steiner. Christ will lead humanity to Shambhala. Shambhala will show itself again when humans perceive the Christ in his etheric form. Humankind will rise through the maturation of normal faculties into the wisdom land of Shambhala, denoting "the most momentous turning-point in the evolution of humanity."

All this is part of the Michaelic culture Steiner foresaw as a "universal historic necessity." The symptoms of cognitive expansion underway in twentieth-century Western culture are multiple and prodigious: the resurgence of the occult, the proliferation of psychism, channeling, and arcana, virtual and computer-generated designer realities, transpersonal experiences through psychedelic drugs, OBEs, NDEs, shamanism, and Eastern spiritual disciplines, the rise of etheric body-mind medicine, Gaian deep ecology, ecofeminism, species-specific morphic resonance, and global epiphanies like Harmonic Convergence. We may reasonably construe the Tibetan diaspora and the pre-eminence in the West as a spiritual authority of His Holiness the 14th Dalai Lama, Tenzin Gyatso, who also won the Nobel Peace Prize in 1990, as a significant indication that this eventual merger of Pauline Christianity and Shambhallic Buddhism is well underway. These are the early, sometimes inchoate, historical symptoms of the coming of Michaelic culture.

The supersensible reality is the dawning of the Michael age. The symptoms indicate the time is ripe to take in hand the project of respiritualizing cosmic intelligence through the human individuality. The presence of symptoms in itself doesn't mean the work is already completed. Symptoms are indications of historical timeliness. They are pastel streaks in the dawn sky. They are signals that the time is now appropriate to consciously, voluntarily, co-creatively take up the Michael mission. The Michael mission—the respiritualization of cosmic intelligence, the re-enlivening of pictorial etheric imaginations as the foundation of thinking and cognition—implicates the entire planet and all its residents, regardless of creed, ethnicity, or group-soul identity. To understand Michael's intention is to cognize a living Imagination—Michael the Time Spirit upholding the Cosmic Intelligence within us, guiding our thoughts, waiting for us to acknowledge his presence, waiting to meet us in living thought, etherically alive. When we bring our thinking to a contemplation of the living Imagination of Michael, which is nothing less than the Michael mission, his 350-year regency of 1879–2229 A.D., through this act itself we enter the living stream of Michaelic intelligence. This is Michael's dawn in our awakening imagination, in our etherically alive thinking.

Michael brings us the Sun. We must rise into etheric perception to see it. The maturation of the consciousness soul and the emergence of Jupiter Manas culture are not certainties, but probabilities. We must willingly cooperate with the intentions of evolution and spiritual destiny. Our moral failure to develop spiritual cognition would render this future Jupiter barren. Our moral progress through the activities of spiritual science creates the future Jupiter human being, thereby assuring our positive future. A great deal is written on the Michael agenda for the next phase of our evolution. We live amidst a proliferation of symptoms that the Michael dawn is occurring; a myriad of signs indicate the necessary stage of cognitive expansion into Michaelic spirituality is happening. It's crucial that we understand our co-creative responsibility in bringing Michael culture into being. So much depends on our freely willed effort.

The cultural task of Anthroposophy was precisely this, Steiner contended: to create the foundation for a "true and genuine facade of Western civilization." Steiner saw Anthroposophy as a direct outgrowth of the spiritual life of the twentieth century, a movement that from its inception was the authentic channel for the new spiritual life moving into culture since the 1870s. Anthroposophy would carry the Michaelic impulse into Western civilization. The ongoing descent of Anthroposophy as a Michaelic cosmic thought-form is an event with import for the entire epoch. "In the future the Anthroposophical Society must be the center through which the esoteric life flows, and it must be conscious of it."[30] In the next chapter we witness the historical emergence of Michaelic Anthroposophy as a clarifying response to the occult eruption of Spiritualism and the Old Moon formulations of Theosophy in the late nineteenth century—a metaphysically troubled yet expectant time remarkably like our own circumstances one hundred years later.

PART II

"WISDOM"

ANTHROPOSOPHY EMERGING:

The Science of the "Wisdom of the Human"

Arises out of Nineteenth-Century

Spiritualism and Theosophy

Theosophy's Roots

The Impetus for Theosophy in
Nineteenth-Century Spiritualism and Mediumship

"*H*ERE, MR. SPLIT-FOOT, do as I do!" exclaimed twelve year old Kate Fox on the evening of March 31, 1848. Mr. Split-foot, a disembodied invisible spirit, had been upsetting the Fox household every night for two months with a cacophony of knocks and raps. The Foxes, upright Methodists, had no interest in the spirit world or what was then called "medium power." The previous December John D. Fox had moved his family of three young girls, Leah, Margaretta, and Kate, to this small wooden house in the village of Hydesville, New York, just outside Rochester. Later, psychics would say the Fox home was peculiarly suited to the activity of spirit communion because it was "charged with the aura requisite to make it a battery for the working of the telegraph," or communication by rapping. [1]

Kate merrily snapped her fingers at the disembodied knocking spirit, deftly establishing the rules of communication for what was nineteenth-century America's first documented and most publicized "spiritual telegraph." Mr. Split-foot dutifully imitated Kate Fox's silent hand movements, indicating it could see and hear, then spelled out a series of intelligible messages. He told Kate that about five years earlier an itinerant peddler named Charles Rosna had been murdered and buried in the basement, and it was Rosna's troubled spirit that was now operating the spiritual telegraph. A great deal more of this was to come, prophesied Rosna. "Hosts of spirits, good and bad, high and low, could under certain conditions not understood, communicate with earth," Mr. Split-foot told Kate. Such communication was produced through the "forces of spiritual and human magnetism, in chemical affinity."[2]

That March evening was indeed a moment of high affinity. In effect, it inaugurated the American Spiritualist movement, a grass-roots incursion into the multifaceted forces of human and spiritual magnetism and communication across the threshold of the supersensible worlds. It was a direct experience of the invisible worlds that in less than thirty years would claim almost one-third of the American population as believers. News of the "Rochester knockers"—and the phenomena of "medium power" itself—spread like brushfire throughout New England and the Midwest. Mr. Split-foot prophesied that these manifestations wouldn't stay confined to the Fox sisters and their Hydesville "spirit circle," but would go all over the world. "You must proclaim this truth to the world," Mr. Split-foot rapped out. "This is the dawning of a new era. You must not try to conceal it any longer."[3]

Soon America and Europe would be inundated with an astonishing array of the physical effects of medium power: séances, table-talking, speaking in tongues, apports (materialization of physical objects), poltergeists, furniture bilocation, direct voice mediumship, ectoplasmic materializations, rapping telegraphs, automatic writing, trance speaking, spirit photography, spirit music, slate-writing, levitation. The spirits were claiming front stage. On November 14, 1849, Kate Fox, who had moved into Rochester, participated in America's first public demonstration of spiritualist phenomena at Corinthian Hall, the city's largest meeting place. The meeting's evidences of occult force incited materialistic critics to a "vindictive and unreasoning spirit of antagonism," but for everyone else, the demonstrations broke upon their constricted world view as a consciousness-dilating revelation.

The number of Spiritualist believers in "the extraordinary intelligence manifested by spirits in various ways" multiplied rapidly, but the skeptics regarded this "hydra-headed monster in its now hourly increasing magnitude" with disdain and horror. The first coherent spiritual telegraph may have begun in Hydesville, but by 1850 its intelligible messages were received by operators around the country, as a kind of unilateral spiritual contagion, appearing everywhere. "Spiritualism did not radiate from a definite center," noted a journalist in 1870, "but sprang with a spontaneous and irresistible life of its own, independent of human propagandism."[4] Just how spontaneous and independent this sudden effluence of Spiritualist effects actually was—and how best to respond to it and exploit its spiritual momentum—would be the query motivating first Theosophy then its successor, Anthroposophy, as the late nineteenth century's occult response to Mr. Split-foot.

Spiritualism irrupted in the consciousness of Western culture in 1848 at precisely the moment in which materialism peaked. The 1840s marked a watershed decade in the unfoldment of the consciousness soul, an evolutionary project in human development begun in 1413 A.D. By 1840 the physical organs of human intellectual activity—the brain—had achieved perfection and culmination in their development, Steiner noted. A new phase of decadence and retrogression of the brain had in fact already set in. The 427-year effort to develop objective sense perception of the material world and its elaboration through intellectual concepts had matured. By 1840 humanity as a whole had achieved an "empty, shadowy intellect." People could say to themselves: "I possess intellect," even if they filled themselves with materialistic thinking, feeling, and willing. The human mind occupied itself with lifeless, abstract, shadowy concepts of the material realm—mineralized intellect—constructing a world view in which the livingness of Spirit had no place.

Ironically, mid-nineteenth century materialism, which peaked in the 1840s, was actually a rarefied spirituality. People then *lived* in the "most spiritual element possible," Steiner noted, but *absorbed* only the concepts of materiality. With the continuing maturation of the consciousness soul, the human had evolved into "a completely spiritual vessel;" yet most men and women negated this ripening spirituality, turning to matter, making only what is physical and material into the objects of their thoughts. The ancients had never manifested materialism because they had lived in the matter of the physical body. But nineteenth-century humanity was strangely disembodied, dwelling only in the spirit, "completely free of a cosmic connection to their body."[5]

The exclusive focus on the material form of manifestation was not what was harmful. The fundamental error was that people maintained "an impossible idea of matter." The matter postulated by their way of thinking as real was nowhere real. There is no matter anywhere that corresponds to their atomistic theories. The typical materialist "contemplates matter without becoming aware that he is really in the presence of spirit, which is simply manifesting itself in the form of matter."[6] Just how troubled, if not tortured, was the nineteenth century psyche was exemplified in the spiritual sufferings of one of that century's most prominent philosophers, Friedrich Nietzsche (1844–1900).

For Steiner, Nietzsche was the synecdoche of the late nineteenth century's inner intellectual climate. When Steiner first read Nietzsche in 1889 he believed he had met a fellow traveller. Steiner commented in 1895 that "independently and from completely different directions, I came to concepts which were in harmony" with those Nietzsche expressed in his early books. Steiner further noted that his own *Theory of Knowledge Implicit in Goethe's World Conception* (1886) exemplified the "same way of implicit thinking" as what he later encountered in Nietzsche's works. Steiner approved of Nietzsche's insistence on the primacy of the individual, but it was an "absolute necessity" that certain corrections be added to Nietzsche's world conception pertaining to the exercising of conscious freedom in evolving moral principles for action. By 1895 Nietzsche was an "important personality" and had exercised "an immeasurably great influence" upon European thinking. Nietzsche's influence on Western culture had already reached the dubious stage of "infatuation."[7]

Steiner realized that here was a philosopher who did not behold the spirit—in fact, Nietzsche denied it—yet in whom the spirit unconsciously battled against the unspiritual views prevalent among his contemporaries. Nietzsche was rigorous about intellectual honesty. He was convinced that a belief in God was not compatible with the tenets of modern materialist knowledge; he knew the reigning nineteenth century world view, founded on empirical natural science, would never lead him to the divine. Philosophically, to proceed as if it could was dishonest and a lie. Nietzsche's strict honesty compelled him to focus exclusively on the physical world, even though this restricted focus would never answer his deepest questions. Nietzsche sought a human and therefore physical foundation for moral ideals because for him the supersensible realm was certainly inaccessible and probably a delusion, thus empirically unavailable for any justification of human ethics. His "tragedy," so representative of the age, was that he desperately needed to bring his moral problems into the spiritual worlds for rationalization, but was unable to do so.

The profound schism in Nietzsche's soul eventually shattered him. Steiner, visiting Nietzsche in Weimar, Germany, in 1896, found the philosopher already literally out of his mind. Clairvoyantly, Steiner beheld the noble soul of Nietzsche, "boundless in its spiritual light," literally hovering above the man's physical head. Steiner understood what had to be suffered by a philosopher who looked toward the spiritual world from the prevailing materialist conception of nature. Natural science for Nietzsche was the only rationally defensible tool of inquiry, yet its blade was too dull to make even the shallowest metaphysical incision.

In that formative moment in 1896, Steiner knew he stood between two opposites—Nietzsche and Goethe—who framed his intellectual mood. He had worked for years as a scholar in the Weimar archives of both Nietzsche and Goethe and had written insightful books about their struggles and world views. So, Steiner considered, on the one hand, here is the ravaged, dying Nietzsche, the dead fruit of materialism, the failed "battler against his age, a martyr of knowledge." On the other hand, here is the irrepressibly curious, the intellectually vital Johann Wolfgang von Goethe (1749–1832), the German philosopher, dramatist, poet, and naturalist with "an entirely sound and harmonious nature" from an earlier day. Ultimately, Steiner cast his lot with Goethe, who would be Steiner's lifelong mentor. Throughout his public speaking career and in nearly all his written works, Steiner paid respect to the "deep inner soundness of the Goethean world view." Goethe was uncompromisingly original and free from intellectual fashion, said Steiner. His world view "lies so deeply founded in the being of the world that we must meet its basic features wherever energetic thinking penetrates to the sources of knowledge."[8]

Goethe adopted a living, meditative approach to science, particularly to the study of plants. Through an intense contemplation of the essence of the plant as a metamorphic process and activity over time, Goethe arrived at the perception of the "archetypal plant:" all plants, regardless of shape, size, and climatological variation, equally express a fundamental quality, an archetypal plantness—the *Urpflanze*. "He sought the ideas which live in the things. When he observed nature, it then brought ideas to meet him," wrote Steiner, who spent seven years editing Goethe's scientific papers and wrote several books about Goethe's epistemology. Goethe therefore could only think nature to be filled with ideas. He tried to find his bearings within the manifoldness of the plant's being, picturing to himself "the sense-perceptible form of a supersensible archetypal plant."[9] Goethe constantly sought the essential living being—the dynamic idea in multiple expression— behind the physical processes of nature. Consequently, he found spirit everywhere and developed a natural science that included the living spirit.

But there Goethe stopped; his concern about losing his grip on sense reality kept him from a knowledge of pure spirit beyond the physical. Nietzsche conceived the spiritual in a mythical form, but never pressed beyond this level of spirit-myth past nature into a perception of real spiritual being. "Goethe *found* the spirit in the reality of nature; Nietzsche *lost* the spirit-myth in the dream of nature in which he lived."[10] But neither Goethe nor Nietzsche pressed forward far enough to develop a body of living thought suitable for the coming century, Steiner argued. Goethe's progress was inspiring, while Nietzsche had failed, refusing to develop an objective sense for the truth. This necessary body of living thought would appear around 1900 through Steiner's anthroposophy.

Steiner, bold, original, even shocking in his formulations, was still the intellectual product of his time, with roots in the traditional thinking of his contemporaries. His intellectual context was informed by the work of Goethe and Nietzsche, but he also located his own thinking with respect to two other luminaries. The nineteenth century, as he interpreted its intellectual history, also expressed itself in the contrast between two other leading thinkers, Georg Hegel (1770–1831) and Max Stirner (1806–1856).

For Steiner, Hegel was "wholly thought-man, the greatest thinker of the modern age"—but *only* a thinker. Hegel lacked any feeling for the spiritual world. For Hegel the world of spirit lived in thinking, but it was an entirely "impersonal thinking." Hegel's thinking indulged in a world contemplation in which the human, with all its creative powers of inner being, was strangely excluded. Steiner praised Hegel for espousing the "radiant power of thoughts," whose primal, inner power enables humans to penetrate into the supersensible realm. But while Hegel perceived and affirmed, on behalf of German idealism, the supersensible nature (and thrust) of thinking, he was "not able himself to lead the supersensible nature of thinking up into supersensible realms."[11]

Stirner's emphasis, in contrast, was a praxis of "wholly personal volition;" he demanded that the "I" recognize that all the beings it has set above itself in historical time are derived from its own body and then set in the world as external idols. "All the beings placed over the 'I' finally shatter upon the knowledge that they have only been brought into the world by the 'I'," explained Steiner.[12] However, Stirner had no appreciation for the harmonious interaction of humans. Stirner, an anarchist philosopher, had published *The Ego and its Property* in 1845, which contained the seeds of a moral philosophy Steiner would subsequently develop called ethical individualism. Steiner regarded Stirner, despite his limitations, as the "freest thinker" that humankind had brought forth in the new age. "Against the one-sidedness of endowing the World Spirit merely with knowledge (Hegel), the other one-sidedness had, indeed, to appear—the assertion of man as mere will-being (Stirner)."[13]

Steiner oriented himself with respect to the thinking and dialectics of his German peers—Goethe and Nietzsche, Hegel and Stirner—because he knew that philosophers reveal in the nature of their thinking the spirit and impulse moving through an age. Steiner took his bearings from these philosophical forebears, then charted a new course. There was another countervailing current that offset the rarefied intellectual formulations of the nineteenth-century German idealist philosophers—the ideologically subversive field of animal magnetism and Mesmerism, in which the intangible activity of the supersensible had a foothold.

Late in the eighteenth century, the Austrian physician Franz Anton Mesmer (1733–1815) contended that a mysterious force—"animal magnetism"—passed from him to his patients, producing an artificial trance in the patient. Mesmer found it was much easier to heal an entranced patient than someone awake and discursive. His colleagues branded him a medical charlatan and drove him out of Vienna in 1778, but he resurfaced in Paris and soon developed a large following for his theories of the hypnotic Mesmeric trance and magnetic healing. Mesmerism posed important, uncomfortable questions about a human being's natural psychic abilities. In 1784 the French Academy denounced Mesmer, but some of his loyal roaming Mesmerists eventually brought the teachings of animal magnetism to America in 1837, where it formed the foundation for much of this country's early Spiritualism. "In important respects, (Mesmer) might be almost a reincarnation of Paracelsus. He recognized the importance of the spirit, the imagination, and felt that the universe is pervaded by meaningful influences."[14]

The embryo faith of Spiritualism was incubated in the revelations of the "magnetic clairvoyants," concluded Frank Podmore in his comprehensive if skeptical survey *Modern Spiritualism* (1902). Spiritualism was the direct outgrowth of Mesmer's animal magnetism, claimed Podmore, and its first apostles were drawn primarily from the ranks of Mesmerist practitioners and magnetic clairvoyants working in séances. Spiritualism was no aberration of the age, but an organic outgrowth traceable to previous forms of popular, spontaneous mysticism (ecstasy, obsession, magic, witchcraft, as opposed to deliberate, formal occult initiation) from well before Mesmer's time. Spiritualism was the child of the psychic activity of the eighteenth century. There had been the revelations of Swedish scientist-turned-angelologist and savant, Emmanuel Swedenborg (1688–1772). There had been the religious visions of George Fox (1624–1690), English founder of the Quakers and zealous missionary who claimed "The Lord opened unto me." And there had been the Puritan and Wesleyan conservatives who used psychic phenomena to prove the existence of the spiritual world. "In the late 1600s, as the polemic against witchcraft grew and Deism, which denied the validity of any intercourse with spirit entities, emerged, the Puritan theologians began to issue numerous accounts of the spirit world."[15]

Spiritualism's pedigree may have encompassed the nether worlds of witchcraft and possession, but there was a key difference. Popular thinking in the Middle Ages maintained a belief in the "overshadowing presence and continual intervention" of spiritual beings, but these presences were nonhuman, either angelic or elemental, who stood outside the human moral order. With Spiritualism, however, the identity of these intervening supersensible agents changed. They were no longer angels or elementals, detached, aloof from human affairs, but the spirits of deceased men and women, standing very much in the human moral community—and not a few of them wishing to get involved again.[16]

By 1848 the spirit world, whether it manifested as disembodied humans or the unborn angelic, had made inroads into American popular culture. The evangelical Mormons, for one, were determined to convert America to the Nephite gospel of Jesus Christ in a fever of spiritual manifest destiny. In 1823 the angel Moroni had visited eighteen-year-old Joseph Smith (1805–1844) in Palmyra, New York. "He called me by name, and said unto me that he was a messenger sent from the presence of God to me...that God had a work for me to do," wrote Smith afterwards.[17] Moroni facilitated Smith's spirit initiation by a numinous John the Baptist, then revealed the Mormon sacred history and mystical future to the young prophet. Smith founded the Church of the Latter Day Saints in 1830, which grew steadily, despite bitter opposition, as a millennialist, prophetic movement fueled by divine revelation.

Spirit was also fueling the Shakers, practitioners of ecstatic dance. This was a pacifist-mystic movement founded in England by Mother Ann Lee (1736–1787) which she transplanted to pluralist America in 1774. By 1837 when Shakerism had grown to 6,000 members living in nineteen communities, discarnate American Indian spirits started using Shakers to re-establish contact with their living relatives. Their supersensible presence literally caused bodies to shake, such that an entire tribe might be given over to native Indian ways—singing, whooping, dancing, eating, speaking. But they had been forewarned. Around 1830 Shaker clairvoyants had been visited by a multitude of spiritual beings who indicated the approach of a great spiritual crisis in the world. What traditionally had been the psychic gifts of the Shakers exclusively would soon be dispensed unilaterally in "mighty floods upon the world's peoples as stupendous tokens of spiritual presence." This new era of prodigious presence would commence around 1848 with the discovery of "mines of treasure," actual material wealth in the earth in complement to the downstreaming spiritual riches. This abundant phase would last until 1870.[18] The Shakers prophesied accurately, for 1848 was indeed an apocalyptic year that saw the vertiginous California Gold Rush, the publication of *The Communist Manifesto* by Marx and Engels, fifty separate political revolutions in Germany, Italy, and Austria, the Rochester knockers, "public rapping mediums," and the dawn of Spiritualism.

The catalog of nineteenth-century Spiritualism easily rivals, if not surpasses, the channeling prodigies of the late twentieth century. But how little known to us now are the former celebrities of nineteenth-century physical mediumship, once household names in Spiritualist circles: Kate, Leah, and Margaretta Fox, Andrew Jackson Davis, Daniel Home, Emma Hardinge, Henry Slade, Dr. Monck, Jonathan Koon, Erastus and William Henry Davenport, Horatio and William Eddy, Mrs. Osborne Leonard, Eusapia Palladino, Stainton Moses, Allan Kardec.

Nor was the movement without its widely circulated periodicals, which included *Spiritual Messenger, Spiritual Telegraph, Shekinah, Light from the Spirit World, Banner of Light, The Christian Spiritualist, The Spiritual Scientist, New Era.* The mainstream press constantly published reports and narratives of new occult phenomena. A *Home Journal* 1853 estimate claimed 40,000 Spiritualists in New York City alone; in addition there were 300 magnetic circles, several thousand mediums, 20 public test mediums, and 100 medical clairvoyants. An 1852 national estimate acknowledged 2,000 "writing mediums;" an 1854 report estimated American Spiritualists to number one million; and by 1860, according to "accurate and reliable bases of information," that number had swollen to 11 million, which was about one-third of the American population, then 33 million.[19]

The years 1848–1868 in America were prodigious with the effects of physical mediumship. Emma Hardinge, a British psychic, journalist, and propagandist for Spiritualism, summarized the movement this way in 1870: "The tiny rivulet has expanded into an ocean, whose stormy billows have beat on every shore on Earth, and swept over every city, town, and hamlet. The humble frame dwelling at Hydesville looms up into the proportions of a gigantic temple whose foundations are laid in the four corners of the Earth."[20] In 1874 a New York *Sun* banner headline declared:

"Spiritualism Advancing: A New Religion Gaining Ground Among Us."

The psychism of Spiritualism upwelled in a young country already aflame with religious fervor, as prophets and preachers ignited a score of spiritual brushfires and new Christian sects—revivalism, perfectionism, millennialism, adventism, the Rappites, the Millerites, not to mention the "Second Awakening" of Baptists, Congregationalists, Methodists, the Presbyterian Campbellites, the frontier evangelists. Much of this religious tension was due to millennialism, the conviction of the imminence of Christ's Second Coming. So much spirit wind had passed through the towns and villages of New York that the state became known as the "burned over district." And America's five-year conflagration known as the Civil War gave Spiritualism and its contact with the dead another strong foothold as the bereaved sought contact with the recently deceased. Spiritualism's presumed contacts with the discarnate soothed the grief of relatives grieving the 600,000 war dead, "but also gave assurance that there was in fact a world beyond death—a belief which science, with its insistence on tangible evidence, had called into serious question, and which religion, in its reliance on dogma and form, had failed to defend convincingly."[21]

In 1854, Wisconsin Governor Nathaniel Tallmadge, who may have been Spiritualism's Shirley MacLaine, brought the proportions of this gigantic temple under the imprimatur of his reputation to Washington D.C. Tallmadge was the first signer, among 15,000, of a Spiritualist Memorial to Congress. This document detailed "phenomenal aspects" of Spiritualism and requested Congress to fund an official investigation to substantiate and popularize the movement's claims. The Memorial was a revealing catalog of the diversity of physical mediumship in the 1850s. It described an occult force variously at work that spontaneously moved "numerous ponderable bodies," produced various lights and colors, mysterious rappings, powerful concussions, hoarse voices of winds and waves, harmonic sounds like human voices or musical instruments, even aberrations in human physiology.

Tallmadge's Memorial was a précis of Spiritualist phenomena, but the movement and its manifestations were burgeoning so rapidly it was nearly impossible to keep a handle on it all. The notoriety of the Rochester knockers was soon succeeded by activities in the home of Rev. Dr. Eliakim Phelps, a Presbyterian minister and family man of Stratford, Connecticut. Fortunately, Phelps believed in medium power, because on March 10, 1850, following a contrived séance, the spiritual world erupted in his sedate home in a series of disturbances of "extreme frequency and violence." The poltergeist intrusion continued for several days and would persist at intervals for the next eighteen months. Objects were thrown around, windows were smashed, a great deal of damage was done, mysterious writings appeared, and invisible hands rapped out intelligible and "frequently blasphemous" answers to Phelps' questions.[22] "The result was one of the most spectacular cases of poltergeist disturbance on record." His household in disarray—with 71 window panes broken—he couldn't resist querying the chair-tossing spirits using a language of raps. Phelps learned that chief among the disturbing spirits was a deceased French clerk who had once mishandled (cheated) a settlement for Mrs. Phelps; while he claimed to be suffering in hell for his misdeeds, "The Phelps poltergeists seem to have been the usual crowd of invisible juvenile delinquents."[23]

Automatic writing was prevalent among Spiritualism's physical effects, and the literary hand of ghosts sometimes produced valuable documents. Rev. C. Hammond of New York City published *The Pilgrimage of Thomas Paine and Others to the Seventh Circle* in 1852 as the alleged afterdeath activities of the eighteenth-century American revolutionary and pamphleteer. "I had no will to write it, or exercised any other control, than to let my hand be moved by an invisible influence and write as it would," Hammond confided. A Bostonian named J. V. Mansfield became renowned around 1854 as a "writing medium and great spiritual postmaster." Mansfield transmitted thousands of letters from deceased in the "spirit country" to anxious friends and relatives among the living. A Philadelphian named Charles Linton produced automatic writings in the 1850s which he attributed to Daniel Webster and William Shakespeare. Then in 1855 he published *The Healing of the Nations*, a popular and influential 370-page book he wrote down from spirit dictation in four months. Other Spiritualists cited "Benjamin Franklin" as their byline. In 1853 T. L. Harris produced "An Epic of the Starry Heaven," 4,000 lines of inspired poetry received in trance. The epic's original composers, Harris claimed, was a circle of medieval spirits that included Dante.[24]

Sometimes the incarnate human involvement required preparation, skill, and considerable effort, and the communication was more like stenography. In 1882, John Ballou, an Ohio dentist and automatic writing channel, published his 900-page *Oahspe*, an alternative Bible dictated to him by "beautiful spirits." In 1886 the clairaudient Frederick Oliver acted as stenographer for Phylos the Thibetan (sic), allegedly a discarnate occult adept, who dictated *A Dweller on Two Planets*, which discussed life in Atlantis. Slate-writing was a curious variation of literary automatism. Here merely the physical presence of the medium produced the written communication. On March 26, 1852, E. P. Fowler perceived several discarnate humans hovering near his writing desk. "Luminous currents" entered his pen, an invisible hand dipped it in the inkwell, then "without the application of any other force or instrument, it was made to move across the paper and a communication was made which I have since learned was in the Hebrew language."[25]

The anomaly of spirit photography appeared in England and America beginning in the 1860s. Phantom images of deceased men and women unaccountably started appearing in photographs taken in the presence of a medium.[26] This, too, had been predicted by the "Other Side" in an 1856 London séance, according to Spiritualist historian Arthur Conan Doyle in 1926. From the 1860s to 1920s thirty recognized mediums for psychic photography produced "thousands of those supernormal results," called "extras," which for Doyle at least were a clear indication of "a wise, invisible Intelligence presiding over the operation and working in his own fashion."[27]

Voice mediumship and "Direct Voice" were two more examples of Tallmadge's occult force at work. An Ohio farmer named Jonathan Koon flamboyantly demonstrated voice mediumship in 1852 in his Spirit Room. Koon converted a small log hut into a performance room for spirit manifestations, furnishing it with a spirit table and rack, drums, triangles, tambourines, bells, and other musical instruments suspended from the ceiling by wires. Koon's whole family—himself and eight children—were all considered pre-eminent "mediums for the spiritual forces." Before an audience of perhaps twenty, and with his mediumistic family with him, pére Koon played his fiddle. The spirits responded with their own concert, plucking bars and melodies from guitar, banjo, accordian, French harp, tea bell, and drums. One visitor described the music as "exquisitely beautiful, or even seraphic;" another heard the inarticulate voices of angelic choirs. Afterwards, the chief spirit gave the company an edifying discourse, made audible, not through Koon's larnyx (as in channeling or trance speaking), but through an aluminum trumpet positioned elsewhere in the room.[28] The spirits in the Spirit Circle required only Koon's magnetic presence, but not his actual speech organs, to make themselves heard.

Not just America was prolific with spirit presence. Spiritualism was sweeping mid-nineteenth century Europe, too, if a little less energetically than its fiery passage across America.[29] Spiritualism in France revolved around the psychic prodigies of Allan Kardec (1804–1869) who renamed his movement Spiritism, founding it on the belief in reincarnation. In 1850, Kardec, a medical doctor, investigated the results of two young psychics and put his own questions to them. He was so impressed with the results, and so convinced that he had "a mission confided to him by Providence," that he published them as *The Spirits' Book* (1856). Kardec followed this up with several more influential works (*The Book on Mediums*, 1861; *The Gospel as Explained by Spirits*, 1864; *Heaven and Hell*, 1865). Kardec's *The Book on Mediums* is a commendable attempt to apply scientific precision, logical analysis, and methodical classification to the complex phenomenology of spiritism. It is still valuable today not the least for Kardec's refreshing candor regarding the possibilities for what he called charlatanry, mystification, and jugglery: "As everything can become a subject for making capital, it is not astonishing that persons should wish to make capital out of the spirits."[30]

Spiritism, he said, touches on all the questions that interest humanity. Kardec founded the Society of Psychologic Studies to answer some of these fundamental questions; his group met weekly at his house to gather new spirit communications which he published in his journal, *La Revue Spirite*, which he edited until his death. Kardec's paranormal material, obtained through automatic writing and the planchette (he disapproved of trance speaking, hearing voices, or seeing visions as reliable means of communication) influenced millions throughout Europe. "Spirit beings may be defined as the intelligent beings of the creation," a spirit source once told Kardec. "They constitute the population of the universe, in contradistinction to the forms of the material world."[31] Mediumship is not an exclusive privilege but a faculty inherent in humanity, said Kardec; in fact, "every person who feels, in any degree whatever, the influence of the spirits, is a medium."[32]

One of Britain's foremost Spiritualists was William Stainton Moses (1839–1892), an ordained Anglican clergyman. In 1872 a variety of physical mediumistic effects constellated around him, including raps, table-tilting, psychokinetic movement of large objects, direct voice, musical sounds without instruments, apports (movement of matter through matter), psychic lights, scents, and levitation. Through automatic writing Moses brought through information from a source made of forty-nine spirits calling itself Imperator Band. As his mediumship matured Moses strove to blend intellectual reasoning with the religious implications of his spirit revelations, and he advocated mediumship as a way to understand the will of God.[33]

The "will of God" was about to make another vociferous mark in the Spiritualist world, this time in Chittenden, Vermont, known since as "the Spirit Capital of the World." Horatio and William Eddy, both mediums, lived on a farm in this rural Green Mountain village. By the early 1870s they were vocal hosts for up to thirty different spirit voices during their nightly Circle Room séances. But there was a lot more than spirit voices making their presence known at the Eddy farmhouse. Human spirits were materializing as living phantoms. Ghosts were becoming tangible. It was this remarkable "solidification of human forms," chronicled for New York's *Daily Graphic* throughout 1874 by a capable lawyer, journalist, and Civil War hero named Colonel Henry Steel Olcott (1832–1907), that would precipitate a momentous event in nineteenth-century Spiritualist and occult history—the founding of the Theosophical Society in New York City in 1875.

Materializations of human phantoms were by far the most outrageous and controversial example of medium power. With materializations Spiritualism peaked. During a typical séance, William

Eddy would enter a large free-standing closet and draw the curtain hung over the doorway. The room lights were dimmed. Eddy would fall asleep inside his cabinet and remain inert, with "every indication of profound obliviousness to external things." Then the curtain parted and a phosphorescent phantom entered the room.

From here on in, the phantoms ran the Eddy show. For the next hour form after form appeared, often a dozen per seance, and each one different, distinct, apparently real, and all unforgettable—"in all respects like persons living in the flesh," commented one spectator. In his early days among the Chittenden "spooks," Olcott was reasonably certain that the ghostly figures that materialized in the Eddy home originated from beyond the mortal veil. "He must, therefore, create test conditions and amass evidence that would not only remove those doubts but at the same time throw a spanner into the arguments of the skeptics— of which there were many."[34] Olcott filed his original report ("The World of Spirits, Astounding Wonders that Stagger Belief") with the *New York Sun*. The *Daily Graphic* was so enthusiastic—and startled—about Olcott's preliminary report, that it commissioned what would become a twenty-article series on the Chittenden materializations, published between September and December 1874. Olcott brought them out in book form in the following year as *People From the Other World*.

In all Olcott witnessed at least 300 full-form materializations in the Eddys' Spirit Circle. He tested them, queried them, subjected them to healthy skeptical analysis, but still it all seemed true to him. "They appeared as substantial as any human being in the flesh," Olcott noted. How was it possible? Olcott concluded that possibly "by some occult control over now unknown forces of nature, beings, other than those in the body, can manifest their presence to sight, touch, and hearing."[35] "The production of materialized phantom forms, that become visible, tangible, and often audible" was not all that was happening at the Eddy farmhouse. Olcott's list of phenomena included rappings, movement of objects, painting in oils and water-colors under spirit influence, prophecy, speaking in strange tongues, levitation, discernment of spirits, message writing, psychometry, clairvoyance. As a later commentator said, "Since St. Paul first enumerated the gifts of the spirit, no more comprehensive list has ever been given."[36]

Olcott was considerably impressed with the contents of the Eddy list and with the accomplishments of Spiritualism itself. With the Eddy materializations, he felt he was on the verge of a major discovery of radical import for the worlds both of Spiritualism and science. If it were true that visitors to the Spirit Circle could actually see, touch, and converse with deceased relatives "who had found the means to reconstruct their bodies and clothing" to be temporarily visible, even tangible, then "this was the most important fact in modern physical science."[37] It would be for Olcott and his earnest contemporaries conclusive proof of the existence of another, subtler world behind the material.

Anecdotal reports of these unaccountable materializations continued throughout the 1870s. Séance participants spoke of "ectoplasmic emanations"—amorphous, cloudlike pillars, fleecy, vaporous, gray-whitish patches, balls of light, cloudy, faintly luminous threads—extruded by a medium's body that eventually formed a phantom human. The most controversial of such ectoplasmic apparitions and a celebrated incident that ruined not a few reputations was that of "Katie King." The spectral Katie was presumed to be the phantom of a seventeenth-century British woman and daughter of John King, also known as Sir Henry Morgan, a notorious pirate. Nelson Holmes and his wife were the mediums who facilitated Katie's New York debut; she was already well known in London Spiritualist circles. Curiously, in subsequent years numerous other mediums claimed John King as their "control," continuing even into the 1920s; an isolated incident occurred in Sweden as recently as 1963.

The *New York Times* brought Katie into the public eye in a July 21, 1874, leader: "A Ghost or a Fraud: 'Katie King,' A Spirit Who Revisits The World." The *Times* correspondent watched Katie animate herself "like a forming cloud," then fade away. He acknowledged he had no satisfactory explanation for the anomaly. But he wasn't convinced that the séance and materialization weren't somehow fraudulent. "It may be that we have been entertaining and entertained by angels unawares," he commented. But in his view, the whole thing was "one part Spiritualism and two parts humbug."

With this admission, the *Times* skeptic was only a step away from the unequivocal pronouncement of a Russian clairvoyant, initiate, occult scholar, and Theosophical dynamo, Madame Helena Petrovna Blavatsky (1831–1891), who would soon throw over the whole Spiritualist applecart of physical effects. For Blavatsky, the Eddy and Holmes materializations were *three parts* humbug.

Blavatsky met Colonel Olcott one day in October 1874 during an Eddy séance, and with this meeting the Theosophical movement was born. Olcott rather understated its import when he hailed Blavatsky's arrival in his next *Daily Graphic* report as "an important event in the history of the Chittenden manifestations."[38] Olcott, refreshingly direct in his expressions, exclaimed to a companion at the Eddy home upon noting a new visitor: "Good gracious! look at *that* specimen, will you." That specimen—in scarlet Garibaldi shirt, "a lively mop of red-brown hair," a "massive Calmuck face" with features both imperious and sympathetic—was H.P.B.[39] Blavatsky was a medium herself, capable of all the mediumistic marvels that so enthralled Olcott and the Spiritualists; yet she was much more. She was a clairvoyant initiate trained by Tibetan and Hindu adepts; from this spiritually mature position she gave Olcott, a little over-intrigued with the physical phenomena, a lucid perspective on what was really at play in materializations and, more importantly, what they portended for Western culture.

Blavatsky came to America with a mission. "I am here in this country sent by my Lodge on behalf of *Truth* in modern Spiritualism, and it is my most sacred duty to *unveil what is*, and expose what is not."[40] Blavatsky made it precisely clear to Olcott how an initiate differed from a medium. "Mediumship is the opposite of adeptship; the medium is the passive instrument of foreign influences, the adept actively controls himself and all inferior potencies.[41] Blavatsky wanted to turn the focus of the Spiritualists from mere phenomenalism, "unconscious sorcery," inchoate communication with the Dead, and Spiritualism's "weird wonders" to a higher form of thought, a true spiritualism, and contact with discarnate adepts presumed to be more highly evolved than humankind. "I was sent from Paris to America on purpose to prove the phenomena and their reality, and show the fallacy of the spiritualistic theory of spirits," she commented. The Spiritualists' view of the supposed powers of the disembodied spirits was too "transcendent," said Blavatsky, who alerted people to the fact that such phenomena could be (and was) produced by other agencies than the supposed dead. It is essential to understand how much of this can be done by the embodied human soul through the domain of the "blind but active powers at work" within the unexplored regions of the human being. Further, mediumship, unless "the most careful attention" was accorded to its every aspect, was an undertaking fraught with peril. The mysteries of mediumship and the "might problem" of spirit manifestations must be studied thoroughly, and no better tool for this study would be found than the ancient Vedic, Brahmanical, and Oriental texts, she claimed. These represent "the grandest repository of wisdom ever accessible to humanity," elucidating "the entire mystery of nature and of man." The ancient yoga aphorisms of Patanjali would shed more light on Spiritualism than the revelations of the contemporary medium Andrew Jackson Davis himself. Blavatsky urged the American Spiritualists to welcome the esoteric Eastern teachings, which didn't refute the mediumistic effects, but explained them "in light of larger knowledge."[42] Blavatsky transmitted these "buried treasures of ancient wisdom" in over 5,000 pages in two master works (and another 8,655 pages in her *Collected Writings*), still regarded as indispensable occult reference works (*Isis Unveiled*, 1877, and *The Secret Doctrine*, 1888, both of which Blavatsky claimed to have been received through occult dictation). "I proclaim myself a true Spiritualist because my belief is built upon a firm ground," she declared in 1876.[43]

The light of Blavatsky's larger knowledge and firmer ground revealed mediumistic effects, especially materializations, to be entirely different than people commonly supposed. Spiritualist seances were indications of a dangerous "necromantic epidemic," said Blavatsky, examples of "forced post-mortem assimilation" in which the kingdom of the Dead invades the regions of the living. Mediums for the most part were "ever-lying, cheating, miserable instruments of the undeveloped Spirits of the lower sphere, the ancient Hades." Blavatsky knew she was purposefully sent to America from Paris "to *prove* the phenomena and their reality and show the fallacy of the Spiritualistic theories of 'Spirits.'" But accomplishing that was sure to provoke intense controversy. "Belief in the agency of 'Spirits' or disembodied souls in these phenomena is as foolish & irrational as belief in the agency of the Holy Ghost in the fabrication of Jesus—if the latter ever lived."[44]

Individual mediums might call out hundreds of different "would-be human forms," but in Blavatsky's estimation, no spirit ever expressed anything but "the most commonplace ideas." Olcott agreed: "the wise, the pure, the just, the heroic souls" who have passed into the Silent Land, cannot come back to "spout sapphics through scrub-women nor swing through the air on a spiritual trapeze at the bidding of poverty-stricken mediums."[45]

If it wasn't the rematerialized spirits of the deceased who produced the mediumistic effects, then who was it? "If they only knew the truth! Had they seen what I saw frequently," exclaimed Blavatsky. She "emphatically" denied that spirits of the dead could manifest themselves objectively in any manner, although she acknowledged they could, if their "finer astral entity" survived, inspire and teach humans through a subtler telepathy. Although it embroiled her in bitter controversy, Blavatsky admitted that in certain instances she manifested certain "marvellous spirit manifestations" from out of herself. "I did not want people at large to know that I could produce the same thing at will," she noted, because she had been instructed by her teachers to "keep alive the genuineness and possibility of such phenomena" in the hearts of those who had recently converted from materialism to Spiritualism. In 1875 at the Nelson Holmes' residence in Philadelphia, Blavatsky unobtrusively produced the faces of John King and Katie King in the astral light but allowed the Spiritualists assembled to conclude the apparition had been brought forth by the mediumistic power of Mrs. Holmes. "She was terribly frightened herself, for she knew that *this once* the apparition was real."

What lay behind the ectoplasmic materializations were astral souls resident in the living body of the medium herself. Nearly all of the phenomena of the "spiritist sorceries" were the result of "the freaks of the spirits of the mediums themselves, unconscious to themselves, the invisible and real self of the medium," explained Blavatsky. But the activities of these freaks of the unconscious self were aided by "earthly dregs" and "deformed, monstrous creatures," elementary or disembodied humans vegetating parasitically as astral shells within Earth's atmosphere. In fact, a congeries of astral entities were capable of manifesting through unconscious mediums: deceased humans on the astral plane (including suicides and other victims of sudden death), shades ("a soulless bundle of the lowest qualities"), shells, (astral corpse of deceased entity—"spooks" of malevolent intent), vital-ized shells (astral corpse animated by an artificial element spirit), nature spirits, aspects of the medium's personality, and occasion-ally adepts, masters, or perfected humans.

Shades and shells invariably are somewhat vampirish, draining away the medium's vitality during the séance; nor are they likely to contribute useful, original, or prescient information. A. E. Howell, summarizing the Theosophical views of Blavatsky, Lead-beater, and Besant in 1927, wrote (and quite prophetically with respect to conditions today): "It is the use of shades and shells at seances which brands so many of spiritualistic communications with intellectual sterility. Their apparent intellectuality will give out only reproductions: the mark of non-originality will be present, there being no sign of new and independent thought."[46] Thus Blavatsky declared: "With horror and disgust I often ob-served how such a reanimated shadow of this kind separated it-self from within the medium, how often coming out in the medium's astral body moulded in another vesture, it imperson-ated one's *relative*."[47]

With this pronouncement, Blavatsky unmasked the most glam-orous act in the mediumistic astral carnival show. Blavatsky of-fered more than a scathing critique of Spiritualism's superficiality; she offered the West a praxis, Theosophy, the practice of being "wise in things of God." The Spiritualist momentum in America was a useful ally, Blavatsky conceded, because it was an unmiti-gated sore in the side of the materialists and it broke the theologi-cal grasp of orthodox Christianity on human souls. Other than this, however, the fervor of Spiritualism produced, "few things worthy of a thoughtful man's attention," as Olcott put it. Its preva-lence, however, was the unmistakable sign that the true focus of Blavatsky's American mission was now at hand.

On November 17, 1875, Blavatsky, Olcott, and a handful of col-leagues formally founded the Theosophical Society in New York City, "for the study and elucidation of occultism." Their effort strove to vindicate the pre-eminent importance of Eastern reli-gions, to explore the hidden mysteries of nature, and to outline the "infinitude of the occult psychological powers" hidden with-in the physical human. Blavatsky's occult sciences would assure people "that there are beings in an invisible world, whether 'Spirits' of the dead or *Elementals*, and that there are hidden powers in man, which are capable of making a *God* of him on Earth."[48]

Theosophy, or God-Wisdom, announced Blavatsky in the premier issue of *The Theosophist* in October 1879, was as old as philosophy itself, predating the Christian and Platonic eras. "Theosophy is, then, the archaic *Wisdom—Religion*, the esoteric doctrine once known in every ancient country having claims to civilization." This primordial wisdom is "an emanation of the divine Principle." India, the "sacred land of ancient Aryavarta," would provide the philosophical keys for this renewal of Theosophy in the nineteenth century, Blavatsky declared, because "none is older than she in esoteric wisdom and civilization." India is the "fruitful hot-bed whence proceeded all subsequent philosophical systems." This pro-Indian bias is, in part, why within a few years the Theosophical Society had forged a strong alliance with the Indian Arya Samaj, led by the Pandit Dayanund Saraswati Swami, and with the Ceylonese Buddhists. There would be an emphasis on individual research, eclecticism, and iconoclasm, "free and fearless investigation" upon "the path of independent thought," said Blavatsky. The Society itself may have no formal creeds, other than Universal Brotherhood, because creeds are but shells around spiritual knowledge; theosophy "in its fruition is spiritual knowledge itself." People were exhorted to spiritual self-reliance and each man or woman was encouraged to regard oneself as "his only Savior." Theosophists would be original thinkers, seekers after the eternal truths and universal problems, guided by their own inspiration in a "Republic of Conscience."[49]

As such, the Theosophical Society is entirely the opposite of every other society that presently exists, explained Blavatsky in 1880 in a letter to the president of the Society for Psychological Studies in Paris. "We do not permit in it the shadow of dogmatism, whether of religion or of science." As a school of occult inquiry, the Theosophists take their name from the ancient Greek Theosophia—"God-Wisdom"—not "in the dead letter, but rather in the spiritual sense" of the word. Not an entirely physical or materialist science, Theosophists—"members of the great *Universal Fraternity*, the fraternity of sciences, religions, and ideas"—would honor its methodology for its inquiry into "*Divine Wisdom*" that lies at the foundation of everything. The Theosophical Society will accomplish what other societies, like the Masons, only promise: fraternity of membership "without distinction" of race, creed, or social position.[50]

Of significance to the subsequent rise of Rudolf Steiner's anthroposophy was Blavatsky's remark that Theosophy would be unconcerned about politics: "The Society cares but little about the outward human management of the material world." They would be concerned only with the "*inner* man" and the "occult truths of the visible and invisible worlds."[51] Theosophy's indifference to the well-being of "physical man" and "the man of matter," as Steiner would explain a few decades later, was an anachronistic Hindu-inspired, Earth-denying attitude that arose from their repudiation of the importance of the Christ Event in human and planetary evolution, which is to say, the permeation of the material Earth and incarnate humanity by the fructifying Logos. In contrast, anthroposophy would hold as the ultimate validation of the worth of its spiritual scientific investigations their application and grounding in the physical lives of men and women and the manifold ways in which these applications made lives better and more spiritually fruitful.

Theosophy deliberately arose as a clarifying response to the chaotic world of mediumship. Blavatsky knew with certainty that powerful spiritual impulses and agencies were behind their bold action. These "agencies" were the Mahatmas, an arcane cabal of Himalayan human adepts, Blavatsky claimed, who guided and facilitated humanity's spiritual evolution. They had in fact "commissioned" Blavatsky's work of propagating a "wave of transcendental influence" in the West. She was their agent among the American Spiritualists, seeking to organize their mediumistic phenomenology into a coherent discipline of occult science.

So behind the Theosophical Society loomed these pre-eminent Mahatmas. In the 1870s they felt an urgency to get "these ennobling truths" into cultural circulation in the materialistic West. Spiritually lethargic India equally needed a jolt of Western physical initiative, while the West, spiritually hallucinating, needed an infusion of occult truth. The rampant excesses and unsupportable attributions of American Spiritualism told the Mahatmas the time was ripe, that the materialist facade was crumbling and new light from beyond might shine through its widening cracks. The Mahatmas knew that "time was needed for the ideals of compassion and of the *oneness* of all living beings to permeate the consciousness of the twentieth century *before* the tidal wave of psychic interest and development would overwhelm humanity."[52]

Through Blavatsky's Theosophical Society, the Mahatmas wanted to redirect the energy and enthusiasm behind the currents of materialism, spiritualistic phenomena, and worship of the dead. They knew that the widespread psychic cravings were another, deceptive form of materialism, "fruits of a disbelief in all but material things." Worse, these fruits represented a blind belief in the "materialization of Spirit." One had only to consider the considerable inventory of mediumistic effects prevalent in Blavatsky's time to see the marked emphasis on materiality: ectoplasm, materialized objects and people, the moving of objects, the making of sounds—uniformly, these phenomena were densely physical, grossly tangible (visible or audible) materializations of supersensible energies.[53] Materialism had descended with such gravity into Western culture that even the ideas and expressions of the spiritual had become entirely materialized. The Mahatmas hoped that through Theosophy the legitimate impingement of the intangible worlds on human experience could quicken men and women into genuine spiritual awakening.

Even so, Spiritualist phenomena would initiate the Society. Despite their repudiation of psychism's tidal wave, the Theosophical founders realized that only the marvellous effects of physical mediumship would catch the public's attention. In the 1870s Blavatsky rallied a good deal of acclaim, and criticism, for her effects: spiritual telegraphs, astral bells, precipitated messages, raps, deviceless impressions of pictures on paper, reading texts in the astral light. "These accursed phenomena have ruined my character," she complained later. But she knew it had been necessary. Education was at a lower level then than it is today, reflected Countess Constance Wachmeister, Blavatsky's benefactor and secretary, in 1893. "It required an attraction to awaken in them that initial interest which was destined to make them think more deeply."[54]

Once the public began thinking more deeply, the dedicated nucleus around Blavatsky hoped to inculcate the "first principle of true Theosophy—universal brotherhood." They wanted to forge a multinational, multiethnic, multidenominational body of men and women firmly united "in brotherly love" and the ideal of "a regenerating practical Brotherhood," engaged in altruistic study, work, and goodwill. In this "large-hearted spirit of comradeship," declared Blavatsky, "the ethics of Theosophy are more important than any divulgement of psychic laws and facts." Theosophical ethics were paramount because they "sink into and take hold of the real man—the reincarnating Ego."[55]

This real human was never a materialist, but the outer human had to be liberated and retrained. Theosophy was the living protest against the gross, luxurious materialism of their day, declared Blavatsky. Materialism was pernicious in all its expressions, whether it was science, dogmatic theology, or the "materialistic phenomenalists" with their indiscriminate mediumship, physical manifestations, and trance possessions. The time was ripe to reveal once again the occult doctrine. Theosophists wanted to bring forward the phenomena of intellectuality, philosophy, and logic, embracing the rigor of science and the insight of religion—what Blavatsky, drawing on arcane Hindu terminology, called "manasic development."[56]

In the context of Manas, latent psychic abilities could unfold as valuable aids in spiritual development while being kept perfectly under control. When psychism is checked and directed by the manasic principle, then the individual is protected from "the most dangerous delusions and the certainty of moral destruction" that otherwise claim undisciplined mediums whose capacities were "running riot."[57] Blavatsky sought to impart a degree of occult initiatory knowledge to the problem of spontaneous mediumistic development. The Mahatmas anticipated the grave danger of the inevitable interaction of materialistic thinking with the psychic lure that comes with the acquisition of preliminary yogic powers. Unsupervised and undirected, this irruption could be disastrous for human evolution. Against this liability, the Mahatamas wanted to assert a "fighting, combative Manas" that would "arrest the attention of the highest minds" and thereby lead them safely to the realm of higher spiritual unfoldment.[58]

Blavatsky was instructed to open the door of materialism into the new, unsuspected domain of genuine occult development.

The tenets of Theosophy implied quite directly that a science existed founded on a knowledge of laws governing spiritual causality underlying worldly events; more significantly, this body of knowledge was an oral tradition handed down over centuries by teachers, initiates, and masters. But Theosophy's deeper intention was to convince the public of the reality of the occult hierarchy and its perfected, superior humans, the Mahatmas. If the phenomena of Spiritualism demonstrated latent psychic, occult, and spiritual potentialities unexploited in humans, then the existence of the Mahatmas was a living example of what this full development looked like in the human context. During her years in the East, Blavatsky was initiated directly by several of these "elder brothers of humanity," including one who would remain her lifelong mentor, an Indian Rajput prince named Mahatma Morya. When Blavatsky met him in London in 1851, he outlined her future and indicated how she could best prepare for the work for which she had been chosen. "We sent her to America, brought them together (Olcott)—and the trial began," said Morya in 1882. "She is our direct agent," stated another Mahatma, a Kashmiri Brahmin named Kuthumi in 1888. Blavatsky met him in Shigatse, Tibet, in 1868 when she lived there for three years. "I have lived at different periods in Little Tibet as in Great Tibet, and these combined periods form more than seven years," she wrote in 1884.[59]

The Himalayan masters are behind our movement and we founded our Theosophical Society at their direct suggestion, said Blavatsky. She was in America to point the way eastward, back to the remote caves and hidden valleys where these "guardians of humanity" dwelled. Besides Kuthumi and Morya, Blavatsky was on a collegial basis with others of this brotherhood of "Greater Ones:" Serapis Bey, Chief of the Brotherhood of Luxor and Great Lodge of Egypt; Djwal Khul, a high-ranking Tibetan lama; and the Greek master, Illarion (also spelled Hilarion). In all there were 50 to 60 of these "Supermen" in the occult hierarchy, claimed one prominent Theosophist. Each adept maintains his own parish, which are not counties or districts, but "huge countries and even continents." These Supermen include Lord Vaivasvata Manu (ruler of the Fifth Root Race), Lord Maitreya (the coming Buddha), Lord Chaksusha Manu (ruler of the

Fourth Root Race), Jesus (incarnate as a Syrian amidst Lebanese Druses); and, at the top of the hierarchy, Sanat Kumara ("the first Initiator"), who is the Lord of the World and the King of Shambhala.[60]

The diaphanous intrusion of the occult hierarchy into Western awareness was an aspect of what the Mahatmas called "the centennial effort." Beginning with the twelfth century A.D., in the last twenty-five years of each century the Brotherhood of Adepts strive to move spiritual impulses and the occult doctrine into the mainstream of European culture. The Theosophical push of 1875 was the latest such centennial effort—not that it was especially successful, according to the Mahatmas. "You must have understood by this time, my friend," Kuthumi told Blavatsky in a "precipitated message" in 1881, "that the centennial attempt made by us to open the eyes of the blind world—has nearly failed: in India, partially; in Europe—with a few exceptions—absolutely."[61] Blavatsky reportedly announced later that as of 1897 all new spiritual influx into (and through) the Theosophical Society would cease for one hundred years.

It didn't help the centennial effort that the early history of the Theosophical Society was marked with continual controversy, crisis, scandal, dissension, and metaphysical flamboyance. There was political in-fighting, bitter and vituperative attacks, long, acrimonious debates, accusations and denials, tangled webs of charges and countercharges, prolonged periods of turbulence. Theosophy's elder statesman, Olcott, presiding over the Society's 1906 convention and looking back over thirty years of organizational work, lamented, "I have never found such evidences of bitter misunderstandings and dangerous unrest as at the present Convention."[62] Despite the internal uproar, organized Theosophy was indisputably growing. By 1900, the Society claimed 1,286 members in 71 branches in America (with 58 lodges in Europe and 187 in India). By 1913, the U.S. totals had grown to 3,550 members and 129 lodges. In 1902 Rudolf Steiner became General Secretary of the German section of the Theosophical Society, with headquarters in Berlin. By 1913, his section's membership totalled 2,500 with 69 operating lodges.

With the turn of the century Theosophy moved into its second generation of leadership. Blavatsky died in 1891 and Olcott passed away in 1906. Theosophical leadership was taken up by Annie Besant (1847–1933) and Charles Leadbeater (1847–1934), a remarkable occult couple who would nearly destroy the movement with their millennialist mistake of forewarding the coming World Teacher. Besant met Blavatsky in London in 1887, studied with her, then succeeded her in 1891 as head of the Theosophy's Esoteric Section. She was known as "Annie Militant"—a rebel, a free-thinking radical, activist, and brilliant orator, a crusader for women's rights, trade unionism, Fabian socialism, and birth control. Besant's meeting with Blavatsky transformed her completely; Besant turned her "enormous energies from materialism and atheism to the pursuit of the occult and sacred," assuming the Society presidency in 1907.[63]

"How unconsciously I was marching towards the Theosophy which was to become the glory of my life," she reflected in 1893, "groping blindly in the darkness for that very brotherhood, definitely formulated on these very lines by those Elder Brothers of our race, at whose feet I was so soon to throw myself."[64] In 1889, feeling that "something more than I had" with Socialism was needed to cure social ills, Besant found her way "Home" through the "priceless good fortune" of meeting H. P. Blavatsky and becoming her student. Besant, acting on "imperious intuition," gave Blavatsky her unwavering faith and passionate gratitude until the latter's death in May 1891.[65] While visiting with Blavatsky at Fontainebleau in 1890, Besant had a vision one night of Mahatma Morya, as she recounted in her *Autobiography*. She woke suddenly and found "the air of the room thrown into pulsating waves, and then appeared the radiant astral figure of the Master, visible to my physical eyes."[66]

Blavatsky was impressed but she wasn't convinced Besant was clairvoyant. "She is not psychic nor spiritual in the least—all intellect; yet she hears Master's voice when alone, sees his light and recognizes his voice."[67] So Besant may have had her moments of psychic lucidity, but it was Leadbeater who largely assumed the role of Theosophy's clairvoyant after Blavatsky. As things turned out, clairvoyance alone doesn't guarantee good judgment, and Leadbeater became Theosophy's occult *enfant terrible*. Leadbeater was a former Anglican priest, a popular lecturer, and talented—some might say, precocious—occultist, who first visited

India in 1883 at the insistence of Mahatma Kuthumi. It was Leadbeater who in 1913 discovered the thirteen-year-old Brahmin youth from Madras named Rajagopal (later known as Krishnamurti) whom he claimed would be the next Buddha on the planet Mercury. Besant claims about Krishnamurti were more immediate. The young Jiddu Krishnamurti would be the next World Teacher, the reincarnation of the Christ, and the Theosophical Society, under their direction, would deliver him triumphantly to the world.

Besant announced the plans for the coming World Teacher in 1908 during a U.S. speaking tour. In fact, she spoke incessantly about the coming to visibility of an Avatar or World Teacher, and the advent of a new Root Race into which a returning Christ would incarnate. Apparently even Blavatsky had confided at one point that the real purpose of the Theosophical Society was to prepare for the advent of the World Teacher, although it's doubtful she would have endorsed the plans as laid out by Leadbeater and Besant. Theosophy's World Teacher impulse (or detour) may be traceable in part to Besant's deep immersion in Indian culture and arcana.

Besant's involvement with India was passionate. She felt immense pride in Indian culture. In India's hand, she wrote, "is laid the sacred charge of keeping alight the torch of spirit amid the fogs and storms of increasing materialism." So influential was Besant in her fiery pro-India pronouncements, that in 1919 she was elected president of the Indian National Congress. And Besant's involvement with Indian occultism was just as deeply rooted. While living in Varanasi, Besant apparently was in contact with Swami Vishudhanand and his disciple Gopinath Kaviraj. Kaviraj was a renowned tantric, master of numerous *siddhis*, or mystical powers, and claimed a direct link to a secret cult located at Lake Mansarovar in Tibet. Gopinath Kaviraj claimed that much of Theosophy came from the secret doctrines of Kalachakra Tantra and its prophecy of the Kalki Avatar. Kalachakra reputedly was taught by the Buddha only to the highest adepts in Shambhala. Around 1913, Besant came under the guidance of Rishi Agastya, who, Theosophists claimed, had special responsibility within the occult hierarchy for the destiny of India. Through this recondite skein of swamis, rishis, and Varanasi gurus, Besant was apparently briefed on the imminent coming of the Maitreya Bodhisattva and his manifestation in the human body of Krishnamurti.[68]

With this apparent hierarchical imprimatur in hand, things moved quickly. In 1909, Krishnamurti joined the Esoteric Section and was accepted by Kuthumi as his disciple. The following year Leadbeater took Alcyone (Leadbeater's new name for Krishnamurti) for direct initiations from Mahatmas Morya, Djwal Khul, and Kuthumi. Besant and Leadbeater then founded The Order of the Star of the East in Adyar, in 1911 (with themselves as Protectors, Krishnamurti as its Head) to handle preparations for Krishnamurti's millennialist debut. Leadbeater went off to Australia in 1925, "clad in purple robes with crozier and jewelled cross," and kept himself busy "creating the atmosphere and the energy for the emergence of the sixth root race." Leadbeater's use of his occult powers had reached "bizarre" levels.[69]

Besant's messianic propagandism knew no bounds. The World Teacher would found a global religion (headed by Besant), and a world university (with Besant as chancellor), and he would appoint twelve apostles, of whom seven already had reached the stage of Arhatship (including herself and Leadbeater), Besant wrote in their new journal, *Herald of the Star.* Besant, Leadbeater, and a few others had, by their own reckoning, passed their fifth initiation and had become adepts, free of the causal chain of karma and rebirth, Besant claimed. Leadbeater had already presented himself as a thirty-third degree Mason and was now declaring himself a Bishop of the Liberal Catholic Church. In 1927, when the Society had a world membership of about 42,000, Besant told the Associated Press: "The Divine Spirit has descended once more on a man, Krishnamurti, who in his lifetime is literally perfect as those who know him can testify."

Fortunately, Krishnamurti was humbler and wiser than that. He was increasingly distressed and bewildered by Besant's outlandish statements about apostles and arhats, rapid initiations, global religion, world university, and their inflated plans for his ministry. Then, at the height of Theosophy's messianic fervor in the summer of 1928, Krishnamurti called everything off. At the Order of the Star's annual convention at Ommen, Holland, Krishnamurti disillusioned the society's 3,000 stalwarts by asking them to abandon the idea of him as World Teacher. Truth is a pathless land, he declared soberly, and as president of the Order his consummate act was to dissolve the organization. "Truth, being limitless, unconditioned, unapproachable by any path whatsoever, cannot be organized; nor should any organization be formed to lead or to coerce people along any particular path." The Order of the Star plummeted to Earth as Krishnamurti repudiated two decades of presumed occult guidance as received through Leadbeater and Besant.[70]

Krishnamurti's repudiation was a disaster for the Theosophical Society. Their global ideals were shattered. With one act, their in-house messiah exploded what had become the society's dynamic raison d'etre of the past two decades. Besant never recanted her prophetic fantasies of Krishnamurti as the vehicle of the World Teacher, even at her death a few years later. Leadbeater wandered off into another underexploited mystical world, the Eucharist Communion Ceremony, where he examined the occult aspects of the Christian sacraments. There would be no charismatic third generation to succeed Blavatsky-Olcott and Leadbeater-Besant in the leadership of the Theosophical movement; Theosophy would survive but in a deflated, sobered context.

Probably the only prominent Theosophist who might have rejoiced at Krishnamurti's denunciation was Rudolf Steiner, were he still alive in 1928. He had been outraged at Besant's profound millennialist misconstruction. For Steiner, the notion of a physical reincarnation of the Christ (or any single World Teacher) was not only a materialist sacrilege but cosmically impossible. Long before the denouement at Ommen, Steiner had abandoned the Theosophical Society. Steiner's original, iconoclastic work had never sat well with Besant and they were increasingly at metaphysical odds with each other. Theosophists under Besant and Leadbeater, lacking any understanding of the Mystery of Golgotha, had been "sidetracked into a strange development," the "absurdity" of putting Krishnamurti forth as the reincarnated Christ, said Steiner.[71] The Krishnamurti debacle ultimately was the result of a kind of cognitive dissonance and flawed metaphysical perception on the part of Blavatsky, said Steiner. Besant and Leadbeater were in effect the undiscriminating agents of Blavatsky's original spiritual error or shortcoming. Blavatsky's greatest mistake was to focus her spiritual attention on the realm in which

Christ could be found while in her ordinary consciousness, in her wishes and desires as a personality, "she had a lasting antipathy for everything Christian or Hebrew and a preference for all other spiritual cultures on earth." Blavatsky's concept of the Christ was "completely wrong," Steiner explained in 1921, but she passed it on to her closest students, "and, since then, it has been dragged along, oversimplified to the point of grotesqueness into the present day."[72]

The Krishnamurti spectacle, even at its inception, was "reminiscent of the aberrations of Spiritism" and indicated to Steiner "the terrible degree" to which deterioration in the Theosophical Society had set in. It was as if the grand intention, that noble centennial effort put forward by the Mahatmas, had been derailed into a monomaniacal fixation with the apotheosis of a single Mahatma manqué. After all, once Krishnamurti woke up as an adult, he rejected the mantle of spiritual authority so slavishly wrapped around him by Leadbeater and Besant. Too many Theosophists had become "fanatical followers" in a movement increasingly marked by triviality and dilettantism. Further, to put a single man forward as the incarnation or vehicle of a World Teacher was a travesty of the Michaelic spiritual goals of the epoch of the consciousness soul, which valued individual human development over unique messianic accomplishment. There will be not one World Teacher in whom the revelations and potencies of divinity shall be concentrated, but many, indeed, thousands of world teachers as the impulse from the Mystery of Golgotha becomes individualized throughout humanity. The new order of the day, said Steiner, is not World Teacher, but mentor, colleague, companion, as men and women awaken to a globally distributed Christ community. To expect the precious Pentecostal impulse to be concentrated in a single individual, whether as a new Buddha or Christ, is an egregious act of misplaced concreteness and a profound metaphysical error.

So in late 1912, after a performance in Munich of his Mystery drama *The Guardian of the Threshold,* Steiner and his 2,500 German colleagues in spiritual science crossed a threshold and walked out of the constrictions of Theosophy and into the freedom of Anthroposophy.

CHAPTER 5

The Importance of *Freiheit*

The Anthroposophical Refinement of Theosophy

*A*NTHROPOSOPHICALLY VIEWED, the tidal wave of nineteenth century mediumship and Spiritualist effects failed to accomplish anything progressive for human evolution, Steiner told his German colleagues. Mediumship dampened the best qualities of consciousness and led men and women regressively back to earlier, subconscious states of mind. Spiritualism introduced only the "old connections" with death and the lifeless, while failing to open a path "to the living men of the spiritual." Materialistic science had led only to the external dead, while Spiritualism—a materialistic science in another guise—brought people to the supersensible dead, to "knowledge and worship of the lifeless."[1] Further, the prevailing theories of spiritualistic effects were grotesque, based on materialistic biases, guaranteed to grievously mislead those who studied them. Even so, Steiner knew that nineteenth century Spiritualism, despite its shortcomings, was an unmistakable historical symptom of a supersensible process struggling to work its way into the human stream. What he wanted to know was why did it happen between 1840 and 1880?

Momentum had been building for well over a century for a lightening in the materialist trend of Western development. From his own researches, both textual and clairvoyant, Steiner understood that the year 1716 marked the birth hour of modern Spiritualism. In that year Emmanuel Swedenborg, the Swedish scientist turned psychic, released his clairvoyant revelations and trance communications gleaned from his travels and experiences in the Shetland Islands while investigating the subject of "second sight." In that same year Swedenborg, twenty-eight, was appointed Extraordinary Assessor in the Royal College of Mines by King Charles XII of Sweden. By the time his supersensible contacts began in April 1745—a spirit apparition visited him in a London inn announcing Swedenborg's new vocation as an intermediary between Heaven and Earth—Swedenborg had thirty-five years behind him of formal and self-directed education and the protocols of the scientist. Swedenborg's subsequent work was the forerunner of everything that followed under the rubric of a scientific investigation of spiritistic phenomena. But the impetus towards the supersensible still took refuge in the presumed truths of sense evidenced in that highly rational, Cartesian century.

By contrast, Allan Kardec's Spiritism was in harmony with the ancient-wisdom teachings of Theosophy because it presented the idea of reincarnation. Still, in Steiner's estimation neither the formulations of Swedenborg nor Kardec did justice to the complexity, necessity, and goals of the Spiritualist eruption as it unfolded. For the most part, the human intellect of the nineteenth century had been "utterly incapable of doing justice" to the evidences of the supersensible world, a time in which "want of clearness" reigned universal. Not only did the public misconstrue Spiritualism's physical effects, but probably most of the world's Theosophists themselves were oblivious of the fact that the whole Spiritualist eruption had been planned, monitored, and, finally, abandoned by the occult brotherhoods. In a sense the whole episode had been a grand sleight of hand.

To appreciate this rather startling declaration, one must have a sense for what transpires behind closed doors, in this case, among the myriad secret and occult brotherhoods whose machinations to a large degree determine the shape, texture, and direction of human cultural history. Steiner only occasionally discussed the nature and activities of the various shadowy brotherhoods and occult lodges of Europe, America, and Asia, but he made it clear, through hints—and in a special lecture series given in Dornach in October 1915, subsequently published as *The Occult Movement in the Nineteenth Century*—that their influence and intentions permeated culture, and, in many instances, governed it. We need only consider

Steiner's indications regarding the esoteric origins of World War I and the motives and agencies behind the burning of the Goetheanum in 1923 by Anthroposophy's enemies to gain a sense of what invisible hands are at play behind public events. Far more so than politicians and diplomats who live in the public eye, it is the chiefs of the secret lodges who are the true history-makers. Political figures are their puppets, gesturing and politicking according to their occult machinations, subconsciously received. In Steiner's day, the most recent project of the brotherhoods had been Spiritualism itself, which, after lengthy deliberation, and dissension, they began purposefully to introduce into Western culture in the 1840s. Essentially, Spiritualism was an experiment undertaken by the lodges; not long after, when it was evident that it had failed, lodge-sponsored mediumship was officially withdrawn.

Of course, none of this was publicly known; only a few of the esoteric cognoscenti, like Steiner and Blavatsky, had an idea of what was happening behind the scenes, and why. In his October 1915 lecture cycle, mentioned above, Steiner outlined his researches into the origins of nineteenth-century Spiritualism. About twenty years earlier, another esotericist had covered the same ground, in effect confirming Steiner's investigations two decades later. A British occultist named C. G. Harrison, had, in 1893, at age thirty-eight, reported essentially the same conclusions in his lectures to the Berean Society of London, subsequently published as *The Transcendental Universe*. The Berean Society was an association of Christian esotericists and "theoretical occultists" who sought to understand the supersensible world in light of the reality of the Christ incarnation.

Among these, Harrison was avowedly an independent researcher, apparently a capable occultist and initiate, and, outside the Berean circle, according to Rosicrucian scholar A. E. Waite, who reviewed his book, an "altogether unknown gentleman." *The Transcendental Universe* was translated into German and published in Munich in 1897, and it is certain that Steiner studied it closely; in subsequent years, he alluded to it occasionally but without specific citation. Harrison may have been unknown outside the Berean Society, but his contributions to Western esotericism were considerable. His intelligence and profound culture enabled him to "'correct,' Christen, and make public the occult truths implicit in Theosophy—itself a making public for the first time of what had previously been a secret tradition—with remarkable coherence, impartiality, compassion, and wisdom."[2]

Generally speaking, the esoteric brotherhoods and lodges were comprised of initiates with varying degrees of clairvoyant contact with the occult hierarchy of Shambhala and with a cultural agenda of their own. Their spiritual affiliations were variable: some inclined to the right, holding humankind's spiritual evolution as paramount and taking direct guidance from Shambhala; others inclined to the left, choosing to exploit impulses arising in human evolution as a means for enhanced power and dominance. To outline the infrastructure, policies, and activities of the secret lodges—Rosicrucian, Qabalist, Masonic, and others unnamed[3]—is a book in itself; by definition, such lodges are secret, literally occulted from public scrutiny. Paradoxically, the ones we may have heard of are, by definition, not the secret, efficacious lodges; those we are unlikely ever to learn about substantively. Suffice it to say here that among the lodges working on behalf of humanity—generally called White brotherhoods, because they work with the light for the healing and enlightenment of humanity—their "occult politics" might be termed either conservative or liberal; this definition turns in part on the attitude towards secrecy versus disclosure of occult truths. Then there are the "Black" lodges—these exploit the darker, unconscious, shadow side of humanity—working at variance with the good of humanity. Technically, the category of a black brotherhood—a secretive cabal whose members are collectively committed to manipulative projects that undermine human freedom and conscious evolution—is an oxymoron because occultists who are so wholly self-centered (i.e., black magicians) can never work with confidence together in groups, in brotherhood. But there were, and are, the Brothers of the Left (or Brothers of the Shadow) who can work regressively against the general direction of conscious human evolution and the indications of the spiritual hierarchy.

By the mid-nineteenth century, materialistic tendencies were peaking in human thought. Materialism was like a leaden plate set atop deeply buried faculties of spiritual vision slumbering in the unconscious. By 1840, as we noted in an earlier chapter, materialism was informing all areas of human activity, and human thought processes had assumed a physical intellectuality devoid of living, etheric picture-making. In short, real thinking had been deadened. In fact, the materialist momentum was so strong that it was feared if it continued for a few more decades it would likely have a devastating effect on the general health of humankind. The danger, as Steiner saw it, was "epidemic insanity," a widespread condition of "nerves," neuroses, and mental ailments. From the vantage point of the further elaboration of the consciousness soul, these developments were highly problematic, so the occult fraternities that oversee human development decided to take steps to arrest this decidedly downward trend in human conscious evolution. Only the calibrated release of esoteric knowledge and information about the unseen worlds would transmute that deadening probability in Western spiritual development. An infusion of light from the supersensible might, the lodges hoped, re-enliven science by insinuating the spirit in matter.

The big question was how best to accomplish this infusion of materialist culture with vivifying arcana. How much esoteric information could be safely revealed? Rashness and indiscretion could be psychologically destructive. Around mid-century, the esotericists and exotericists of the occult lodges were divided on this issue. One faction wanted to popularize secret knowledge, stressing the urgency of a spiritualization of the prevailing materialist view of the world. The other group staunchly upheld traditional occult vows of silence regarding true spiritual facts, knowing that such knowledge released without initiation inevitably leads to calamity. Their debate, "of which the outside world knows nothing," was widespread and heated, said Steiner.

Eventually a compromise was hammered out. The lodges agreed to proceed cautiously, to ascertain indirectly to what extent the general public was prepared to handle an influx of genuine occult knowledge. The brotherhoods decided to put forward an experimental method—mediumship—through which attention would be drawn to the spiritual world. The lodges figured that the path of mediumistic revelation might help people recognize the unseen, previously unsuspected spiritual world in the same way they habitually acknowledged and studied the physical. It would be a materialistic way of revealing the supersensible, but commensurate with the prevailing conditions of the fifth post-Atlantean epoch. They hoped this experiment might precipitate the scientific investigation of the supersensible world. Thus, after suitable individuals were identified and trained to be mediums, Spiritualism and mediumship were deliberately introduced into America, then France and England. "The phenomena of the séance room are not due to the spirits of the dead but of the living," explained C. G. Harrison in his lecture to the Berean Society in 1893. "Modern spiritualism is an experiment on modern civilization decided on, about fifty years ago, by a federation of occult brotherhoods for the purpose of testing its vitality and ascertaining whether it is capable of receiving new truths without danger."[4]

Unfortunately, as the exotericists and esotericists soon discovered, the experiment was a big mistake. "It had been expected that the mediums would reveal the existence of certain elemental and nature spirits in the environment," said Steiner. "Instead they all started to refer to revelations from the kingdom of the dead." The mediums uniformly reported—mistakenly—that they were controlled by spirits of the deceased; by a queer turn of events, they were insensitive to, or forgot about, the involvement of the occult lodges which were the source of their mediumistic phenomena. The brotherhoods extrapolated the likelihood that mediumistic insight would be used to circumvent what should properly be achieved only through natural, sense-bound reasoning; this would only deepen the weight of materialism on the Western psyche. The gifts of intuitive insight might easily be used to pick winning lottery tickets, even suitable brides, and make people rich. The occult brothers quickly acknowledged that their attempt to test the cultural maturity of humankind by means of the mediums had gone awry. They resolved, though not unilaterally, to close down the experiment and suppress the whole business. They took immediate steps to recall the psychics and halt all further training in the art of mediumship.

By this act, however, they decommissioned mediumship. According to Steiner, after their withdrawal, the capabilities of the average medium were made "harmless," and their pronouncements were "not much more than sentimental twaddle."[5] However, this was not the end of the protean "Frankenstein monster" of mediumship, according to Harrison. Certain irreversible mischief had already been done. "The door had been opened to extramundane influences, and could not be reclosed." Mediumship, particularly in America, became a profession, and mediums, vulnerable to a myriad of subconscious influences, "were largely exploited by 'Brothers of the Left' for their own purposes."[6]

Frankly, Steiner didn't care for the occult brotherhoods anyway. For him, secret lodges and fraternal occultism were antiquated approaches based on outmoded thought-forms. Certain occult brotherhoods had apparently approached Steiner with proposals, but he left them unanswered. What acutely concerned him, insofar as he wished to contribute positively to the evolution of the consciousness soul, was that the black brotherhoods (as he called the occult fraternities of the "left") were opposed to conscious spiritual cognition and filled their agenda with projects to thwart its attainment. Their work was dominated by "a tremendous amount of scheming." These brotherhoods wanted humanity to enter ever deeper into materialism and to construe supersensible forces as nothing other than previously unsuspected forces of physical nature. Through the propagation of misleading information, the deliberate fostering of metaphysical errors, and an atmosphere of occult materialism constructed through the words and phenomena—materializations, ectoplasm, ghostly images, raps, psychokinesis—of mediums, humanity would believe the afterdeath state is simply a continuation of physical life. Thus the lodges of the Left would achieve their goal of preventing correct information about reincarnation from entering Western public culture.

Steiner regarded the brotherhoods' activities as "one-sided interference," "evil," "dreadfully hostile," and "extremely harmful." As such, they were inimical to the goals of Anthroposophy which held human spiritual freedom as its highest aspiration. Some of the occult lodges weren't too salutary for Blavatsky, either. In one estimation, Blavatsky was disapproved of by nearly all the lodges and occultists of Europe. She was independent, metaphysically competent, an occult maverick, and trouble. Steiner relates how beginning in 1879 American occultists inflicted a lengthy "occult imprisonment" on the outspoken woman. She had been about to blow the whistle on some dubious activities of the American secret lodges—including their complicity in the Spiritualism experiment—threatening to make them "shut up shop." For several years, then, Blavatsky's clairvoyance was paralyzed by these machinations of black magic, as she languished in a kind of solipsistic occult cocoon.

According to Harrison, Blavatsky never visited or lived in Tibet but only imagined it during her imprisonment—"a kind of spiritual sleep characterized by fantastic visions," says Harrison—while residing in Kathmandu. Blavatsky meant well and was a "medium of a very exceptional kind," he claimed, but she was extraordinarily ignorant of the powerful influences brought to bear on her, "more sinned against than sinning...an instrument in the hands of unscrupulous persons who made unfair use of her remarkable gifts and exploited her, so to speak, for purposes of their own."[7] Eventually, the Indian occultists freed Blavatsky from "prison," but their quid pro quo was that Theosophy's content would retain a particular "one-sided" Indian coloring. Blavatsky's occultism would thus serve the "special aims connected with Indian interests." In a strong sense, the Theosophical impulse was corrupted from its germination, corrupted by the manipulations and power politics of the lodges, by Blavatsky's possible psychic paralysis and adulteration, and by the ambivalent intentions of various Mahatmas, or Mahatmas manqué. Steiner further claimed that Blavatsky's unadulterated access to Mahatma Kuthumi was compromised, because "a hidden individual, a Mahatma behind a mask, had been instituted in place of Blavatsky's original teacher and guide...who stood in service of a European power."[8] Harrison claimed that "Kuthumi" was actually an agent—"a treacherous scoundrel," said Harrison's informant—of the Russian government hired to deceive and hoodwink Blavatsky.[9]

It hadn't started out that poorly for Blavatsky. Some of the occult fraternities and their Mahatmas regarded this Russian iconoclast as a psychic prodigy, perfect for their purposes of producing demonstrable occult truths. The occultists—especially those of the Left—took an intense interest in her. They let her know through hints that she was a personality of key importance, one through whom a great many truths about the spiritual worlds could be reliably revealed. Blavatsky acquired "an untold amount of occult knowledge" through working with certain American brotherhoods after her arrival in the United States in 1873. But she learned something they didn't wish anyone else to know and they expelled her. Through her "extremely significant insights," she realized the American lodges were planning to achieve certain political goals by fronting people for office who had received an occult training. First they expelled her, then locked her aura in that stultifying psychic paralysis.

These same brotherhoods also strove to prevent a coherent knowledge of reincarnation from entering Western culture in the nineteenth century. The Brotherhoods of the Left used the mediums to oppose the teaching of repeated human lives, ironically preserving the anachronistic views of orthodox Christianity on this subject, said Steiner. That was one of the experiment's primary destructive outcomes, to get mediums to make false assertions about the life after death and to obfuscate the reality (and complexities) of reincarnation. After all, if they were conversing with the deceased, even years after their physical deaths, surely repeated Earth lives was not a fact, for otherwise these souls would have reincarnated; further, if the after-death experiences of the deceased were fundamentally identical to life on Earth, this, too, would severely distort the truth and discourage people from seriously, actively undertaking their spiritual evolution. Why bother? The lodges fostered the belief, through the mediums, that there was no reincarnation. "The object was to divert them from the realization that the soul is connected, not only with the Earth and its happenings, but also with what is out there in the cosmos."[10] The physical marvels of Spiritualism were exploited as barricades to divert humanity's attention as much as possible from their esoteric astrological connections with the solar system, which underpin any accurate model of reincarnation.

Not only were the black brotherhoods actively suppressing knowledge of reincarnation while bringing a materialistic spiritism forward through mediumship, both Western and Eastern brotherhoods were engaging behind the scenes in some bizarre and disruptive astral manipulations. Steiner was even suspicious of the motivations behind Harrison and his Berean Society, insinuating that both may have been activated by a hidden political agenda, possibly unknown even to its principals. The group's apparent aim, said Steiner, was to amalgamate a certain trend of European

Christian thought. "It desired that the teaching of repeated Earth-lives—which it was essential to make known—should be left out of account."[11] The issue of reincarnation was crucial because unless Westerners accepted its reality and understood its laws, it would never free itself from materialistic, sense-bound thinking. The ultimate goal of the Brotherhoods of the Left was to interfere with the lawful progression of humanity by obstructing the etheric cognition of the Christ. The strategies they used were quite gruesome, even appalling, as Steiner presents them.

The Western brotherhoods confined the dead within physical matter. Their strategy was to load the population of living humans with people educated only in materialist concepts; when they died, they would naturally gravitate back to the earthly sphere and there remain fastened. The brotherhoods could then draw upon this "clientele" of earthbound dead souls to enhance their power and thereby grow to "tremendous strength." The Eastern brotherhoods captured undissolved human etheric bodies, populated these human etheric forms with "demonic spirits" who didn't belong to earthly evolution, and enlisted these demonic etheric forms as factotums of the lodge. Thus the Western lodges built up a clientele of the servile, materialist dead, while the Eastern lodges created a spectral roster of demon-humans.[12] When we consider this twofold aberration in light of Spiritualism's mediumistic phenomena and its tremendous popularity, the insight is upsetting. Nor are we necessarily immune from these same machinations in our own time; the lodges of the Left are just as strong at the end of the twentieth century as they were a century earlier. In fact, as we will explore later in the book, the stakes are far higher this time and the devices far more subtle and meretricious.

This confluence of black lodge activities strove constantly to prevent humanity from becoming aware of the Christ in the etheric and to block the Mystery of Golgotha from being brought forward into Western culture. Why? Because the etheric perception of the Christ as the mature fruit of the consciousness soul would be a powerful, liberating act of *independent*, Michaelic cognition, crucial for the respiritualization of cosmic intelligence. It would be a cosmic event, in fact, and one long prepared for and nurtured by the Christ and the entire celestial hierarchy around him. It would be—is destined to be—an act of spiritual freedom worthy of our human incarnation. As such, it cannot be controlled by the lodges, the Mahatmas, or anybody else. After the supersensible intelligences deliberately diminished their intimate presence in the human psyche in order for the I-consciousness to develop in place of the group soul identity, the occult fraternities saw an opportunity to take the place of the ministering, but withdrawing, "Gods."

In effect, they usurped the divinely mandated position of the celestial hierarchy in the life of human consciousness. The desired outcome of the epoch of the consciousness soul is a Michaelically-inspired revolution by the common man and woman: a French Revolution of the soul in which the domineering influences of the brotherhoods, Mahatmas, lodges, the spirits of the deceased, even the "Gods," are thrown off. A humanity cognitively worthy of its incarnation because it has struggled to gain its rightful freedom, a humanity awake in its cognition, which, the black brotherhoods well know, encompasses all the worlds, supersensible and physical, would be the end of any possible manipulative hegemony they might seek to interpose into the lawful evolution of humankind towards the Jupiter, Venus, and Vulcan phases of the cosmos. Naturally the dark lodges oppose this.

So they strove in complete earnestness that for nineteenth-century humanity, and, following this, for men and women of the twentieth century, the Christ might pass by unnoticed (or mistakenly identified), that nobody would perceive his "etheric individuality" and the promise of total freedom it offered the Ego of each man and woman. Then, with this major barricade in place, they wished to introduce a host of false Christs, anti-Christs, ersatz messiahs. The Krishnamurti debacle was a perfect case in point, and certainly not the last.

The 42,000 Theosophists around the world setting up the young Alcyone as the Christ and Maitreya reincarnate were not likely to take the kind of responsibility required by the consciousness soul to look for the real Christ in the etheric or to experience the Christ as a living principle within their own Ego. It was too alluring not to identify the Christ with a specific, spiritually charismatic individual; it also demanded perhaps too much of Theosophists to accept the profound self-responsibility for cognizing the Christ as a spiritual reality independent of any human personality, Mahatma or otherwise. And, as Steiner noted, the Christ really had no place in the Theosophical metaphysical scheme; for Theosophists, the significant revelations come from the Eastern traditions. In terms of human evolution, this was unfortunate. The etheric perception of the Christ *is itself* the transcendence of materialist thinking. It is a world-shattering event; the cognition *is* the second coming, is the incarnation of the World Teacher—a thousandfold, a millionfold. "Materialistic thinking will conceive of this event as a descent of Christ in the flesh," said Steiner. False Christs will proliferate by the middle of the twentieth century, he predicted; then there will be "plenty of them," exploiting materialistic beliefs in "one of the most terrible temptations besetting mankind."[13]

For Steiner, the Christ is the pivotal issue, whether it was the anti-Christs being brought forward by the black lodges, or the institutionalized disdain by Theosophy and its guiding savants, Blavatsky and Besant, for the Mystery of Golgotha. That she missed the importance of the Christ Event, however, was not grounds for dismissing Blavatsky's contribution, Steiner argued. Blavatsky was "an extremely gifted medium" who "possessed mediumistic faculties in the very highest degree." Steiner granted that she could draw "a very great deal" from the spiritual world. She had a "colossal memory" for everything supersensible that revealed itself. Blavatsky was "thoroughly honest," audacious, and *eine Frechdachs* ("a cheeky creature"). But a "strange atavism" operated in Blavatsky, reminiscent of the dreamlike state of consciousness of the old Mystery leaders, and inappropriate for our epoch of consciousness soul. Steiner found this atavistic desire to relapse to the ancient dream consciousness and the accompanying aversion to fully conscious knowledge of the spirit prevalent among Blavatsky, Besant, and other Theosophical leaders as well. For him it was an "alien" state of mind.[14]

It was inexcusable for Theosophy to ignore the Christ, contended Steiner. The Christ Event, effected through the Mystery of Golgotha, was the most important *fact* in planetary history, the one event that gave the Earth its cosmic meaning, Steiner said. It is a momentous fact whose ramifications must be assimilated by humanity, regardless of creed or religious disposition. It is a fact in the same sense that a meteor striking the Earth and gouging out a tremendous hole and sending up huge clouds of dust is a fact; but the Christ's impact on the planet, unlike the meteor, is unendingly salutary. Nor is the Christ a new fact recently revealed on Earth; revelations of the Christ as Sun Being were at the heart of the perennial Mystery tradition. "I wished to show that the ancient Mysteries had to do with ritual pictures of cosmic events, which then took place on the historic level in the Mystery of Golgotha as *fact* transferred from the cosmos to the earth."[15]

In other words, the Christ Event marked a qualitative turning point in the entire Mystery tradition. The Mystery had in fact incarnated amongst us and the initiation was thereby made easier and more accessible. Not only was this nowhere taught in Theosophy, but it was in direct opposition to Theosophy's pro-Indian dogma. Theosophy put forward its Mahatmas as our intermediaries with divine wisdom and the Logos; Steiner said, because of the Mystery of Golgotha, this was no longer necessary. We could apprehend the Logos directly without any sacerdotal interfacing. But this wasn't the direction Theosophy had taken ever since Blavatsky. In her ordinary consciousness, Blavatsky had a "lasting antipathy, even a passionate loathing" for everything Christian or Hebrew. The Christ-Logos did not get much positive play in Blavatsky's thinking. Her concept of the Christ was entirely wrong, Steiner argued, and, regrettably, she passed it on to her students and Theosophy itself, where it remained, "oversimplified to the point of grotesqueness."

Anthroposophy arose to correct this oversimplification and redress the one-sided pro-Indian bias of Theosophy. Anthroposophy emerges in freedom, free from the machinations of occult lodges or the Mahatma hierarchy. The innate Wisdom in the Human—anthroposophy—would unfold as the freedom of spiritual activity—*Freiheit*—from the living example of Steiner's own conscious, Christ-centered, Michael-imbued clairvoyance. Steiner himself would be the living demonstration of *Freiheit*, worthy perhaps of our emulation but not pedestalization. The last thing Steiner wanted was to be set up on a platform in Kuthumi's place as the newest and brightest Western Mahatma. Anthroposophy does not teach the world from a pedestal. His respect for human freedom absolutely precluded that temptation.

Freiheit is a key word in Steiner's thought which he introduced in one of his foundation works, *Die Philosophie der Freiheit*, generally translated as *The Philosophy of Spiritual Activity*. *Freiheit* means spiritual freedom of the inner human being, an inner state of "free-hood," and the science or means (*Wissenschaft*) for attaining it. It evokes a world view of acting, thinking, and feeling out of one's own spiritual individuality. *Freiheit* is the answer to the troubling question Steiner put to himself and his early readers in 1894: "Is man, in his thinking and doing, a spiritually *free* being, or does he stand under the compulsion of an iron necessity of purely natural lawfulness?"[16] Steiner asked: Do reason, purposes, and decisions exercise in human willing the same kind of irresistible compulsion as desires do in animals—because if they do, human thinking itself isn't free, nor our actions, nor our life. In other words, are we free to act based on the ethical results of our independent thinking, or are we compulsively, subconsciously driven?

Steiner's answer was no, most of the time we are not free in our thinking, but, yes, it is possible to be spiritually free in our thinking. Inner spiritual freedom is indeed possible but requires concentrated effort and a great deal of inner schooling. "Freedom has its life in human thinking, and it is not the will which is of itself free, but thinking which empowers the will."[17] The exercise of free spiritual cognition—"the possibility for the individual to act from his own inner self"—is in fact the core reason for human incarnation and the goal of the consciousness soul. Spiritual cognition is "an exaltation of life," an experience of "living warmth" in our feeling, thinking, and willing, glowing as "the fire of life's ardor." In this epoch we must resolutely will to be free beings, free individuals. Thinking in a spiritual scientific way will lead us into the spiritual world, tying us "consciously, little by little," to the supersensible realities. Through our intellectual consciousness, we can take hold of "the inner force of pure thinking and the inner soul condition of freedom in the process of self-knowledge."[18]

Residual thoughts from earlier lifetimes or inherited tradition actually rob us of our freedom. This is the domain of the "unfree natural will." Only by starting from an unconditioned mental state of blankness or nothingness can we give life to our thoughts through our own will forces and inner activity. The will itself is not free; it is thinking that empowers the will, and thinking that grants us freedom. So when our thinking is pure, sense-free, and living, then we are free; once free, we may express our will in the world, which is to say, undertake ethically inspired action.[19] It is through the free use of supersensible human forces, slumbering in the majority of people, that we have "the free, independent source of spiritual knowledge."

Freiheit means human beings unfold thoughts out of their own inner activity and one draws forth moral impulses from these self-generated or pure thoughts. This "action out of moral intuition which includes freedom" Steiner called, following Max Stirner, "ethical individualism." Essentially, Steiner says, *Freiheit* generates goodness, or Christ love. Cosmic thought, which is the fruit of spiritual cognition, turns directly into moral sensibility, moral impulses, because the divine-spiritual lives in each human individuality. The ultimate expression of this divine-spiritual as a moral forming impulse in the human being is the Christ Logos acting as Love.

The moral proceeds not from external commandments or the pressures of tradition, but from the "wholly individual soul" that has cognized the etheric Christ and welcomed the Christ-permeation of one's etheric thinking body. And humans must approach the Christ in freedom, not because they are Christians or Westerners or pious. The contents of the ancient cosmogonies may have been forced upon the initiates in the Mystery schools, but not so the Mystery of Golgotha. In the Michaelic era, this we may approach only voluntarily, without any compulsion from tradition or conventional morality—only freely, because we will it. The way we take our stance towards this Mystery, the quality of our attitude, constitutes our "most intimate means of an education toward freedom."[20]

This was not the kind of education Theosophy had in mind. Not even in her most lucid, lodge-free moments did Blavatsky approach the issue of independent, Christ-centered, spiritual cognition as the sine qua non of human freedom. She was clairvoyant, privy to occult truths and secrets, and passed them on as the revealed wisdom of the gods in her monumental texts. But Steiner wanted more. The times demanded more. The epoch of the consciousness soul would not come to fruition through Theosophy and its adoration of the received wisdom of the Mahatmas. Their way is inadequate to the task of appropriating the cosmic intelligence that is humanity's due. The wisdom of the Gods—Theosophy—must yield to Human wisdom—Anthroposophy.

Through Anthroposophy, each individual is invited—encouraged, inspired, exhorted—to cognize the dual Mystery of the cosmos and humanity. This is possible because of a cognitive reciprocity at play: self-knowledge is knowledge of the world and world knowledge is knowledge of the self. Anthroposophy teaches that the Human is the "condensed image of the world" and that the world is "the being of Man poured out into infinite space."[21] The recognition of this magnificent reciprocity *is* the expression of human freedom; and to cognize it is to activate it, to begin fulfilling our human role in the equation.

Steiner had another paradoxical way of expressing this relationship of Human and World. A riddle arises in the world, expressed as phenomena. This riddle cannot be resolved by means of ordinary thoughts. The whole world is a riddle and humanity is its solution.[22] Human knowledge is our participation in what the beings and events in the supersensible and physical world have to say. To know is to fulfill our role; that is humanity's purpose. More importantly, the process of knowledge, which is the inner life of the human being, is a world event. "Man is not a being who creates for himself the content of knowledge; he provides in his soul the stage on which for the first time the world experiences in part its existence and its becoming." Knowledge through human beings completes the world. In Steiner's theory of knowledge, the human, in the act of knowing, of attaining knowledge, actually participates in the creation of the world, contributing something indispensable to the wholeness of being.[23] Cognition is world generative and, through the pure moral impulses it produces, it is equally world restorative.

In light of the primacy of *Freiheit* and its inherent moral imperative, Steiner was adamant about founding a spiritual science upon knowledge, not authority. Theosophists might be content with received authority, but it would have no place in Anthroposophy. "Never should the phrase be heard that truths are accepted simply because I have voiced them!" Certainly, Steiner had the qualifications of a spiritual authority of the first rank. He had direct access to the Akashic Records, the hierarchy of Mahatmas (incarnate and disembodied, also called the White Brotherhood), and a fair proportion of the celestial hierarchy from angels to Seraphim. It is how he interpreted this broad band access that makes all the difference. That he could do it was surely proof that all his fellow travelers could, in their own time, do the same. That is the Michaelic goal of the epoch of the consciousness soul. Steiner encouraged all aspiring Anthroposophists to this same cognitive range, this same participation in the revelations of cosmic intelligence, and he provided the means for everyone to achieve this, through a rigorous, sequential training in spiritual scientific investigation.

One needn't be born clairvoyant to attain conscious, daytime cognition of the supersensible. In fact, natural clairvoyance or spontaneous clairvoyance as an adult is often more of an impediment than an asset. Natural, mediumistic clairvoyance is often atavistic and unreliable. The chances of lucidity are often much greater when, after a long struggle and inner purification, through one's activated cognitive forces one achieves the perception of the supersensible; under these conditions, independent, *corroborable* spiritual research is possible. Corroborability of supersensible results was paramount with Steiner; two researchers ought to come up with similar conclusions, like scientists. "I regard it as my task to say nothing which I cannot guarantee to have been tested and proven." It was his high standard to make use "only of what can be revealed to the one who is *himself* the investigator."[24]

Steiner inserted nothing in his speeches or books unless he had first "confronted" it in the supersensible world. Clearly, his sense of scientific protocol when investigating the supersensible world was highly developed. He felt no obligation to guard any ancient mysteries; what he possessed as occult knowledge was entirely the result of his own research. Therefore, he was free, as discretion advised, to share his results with others. Steiner's insistence on the primacy of direct knowing by the researcher and the active engagement of the thinking process in acquiring supersensible knowledge stands in marked contrast to Blavatsky's protocols. She once said she was only the "string" that tied together the culled Eastern flowers the Mahatmas gave her. Such passivity would have no place in Steiner's spiritual science.

In his formulation of Anthroposophy, Steiner put his essential spiritual being forward as a model for conscious cognition in the age of the consciousness soul. Steiner, out of inner freedom, "with the force of his whole being and fired by the impulses of the Time-Spirit Michael who is just entering his time of rulership, opens to humanity a new path of initiation appropriate to the present time."[25] But Steiner did not exalt himself before his colleagues in spiritual science as the exemplary researcher. The example of his life, his actions, his thinking, his Michaelic inspiration, his Christ permeation, his inner struggles to birth Anthroposophy through his own being in the early twentieth century—from this living context the flowers of Anthroposophy would bloom as wisdom of the human being.

Similarly, Blavatsky was the human vessel for Theosophy, the wisdom of God. But Theosophy had arisen as the unbalanced compromise of the turbulent exchange among Blavatsky, the Spiritualist mediums, the Mahatmas, and the American, European, and Indian occult lodges. As such, the message was undoubtedly manipulated and distorted.[26] Anthroposophy, emerging through the clarified being and initiatory life of Steiner, would be the inner conduit for twentieth-century spiritual life and beyond, the "great impulse" for a new spirituality and the assumption of new responsibilities. Anthroposophy would provide the fresh revelations, commensurate with the spirit of our times, necessary for the foundation of a "true and genuine facade" for Western civilization.

Steiner, born clairvoyant, had been gathering spiritual knowledge for decades but it wasn't until he was about thirty-nine that he began speaking openly of the supersensible worlds he was so familiar with. In his adult years prior to 1900, Steiner felt he was waiting for a clear sign of timeliness from the supersensible worlds, some assurance that the moment was ripe to begin his public work. Through his patience, he acknowledged the occult law that no new initiative in occult matters could be put forward by the initiate himself. Rather, an initiative must arise in response to questions or suggestions put by others emerging as an undeniable impulse from the life of the moment. The advent of the question itself would herald the time of ripeness for the new initiative.

The advent came at a chrysanthemum tea party arranged in Berlin in 1901 by some friends of Countess Brockdorff, one of Steiner's early social mentors. On that occasion Marie von Sivers

(1867–1948), a prominent Russian actress, creative speech instructor, and Steiner's future wife and lifelong Anthroposophical collaborator, put a question to him. Isn't it a matter of great importance to call into life a spiritual movement in Europe? she asked. Certainly, Steiner replied, but "I should only be available myself for a movement that links on to Western occultism—to this exclusively—and carries its development farther." Such a movement must also link with the teachings of Plato and Goethe, he added. With the necessary question finally raised, indicating without doubt the ripeness of the moment, Steiner, then forty, took the preliminary steps towards establishing that true and genuine infrastructure for Western culture he had long foreseen. Anthroposophy might now be introduced as a spiritual impulse into Western culture.[27]

It is significant to note here that in contrast with Theosophy, which arose under the supersensible direction of the Mahatmas working through their agents (Blavatsky), Anthroposophy was born in the world with the imprimatur of a fellow human being, in this case, Steiner's future fellow traveler, Marie von Sivers. Although Anthroposophy of course had the Archangel Michael's endorsement, it did not enter the stream of human life through his activities; rather, because Anthroposophy is profoundly about human spiritual freedom, *Freiheit*, and cognitive autonomy, the timing of its birth and the circumstances of its introduction had to depend on human conditions, initiatives, and ripeness. Further, Anthroposophy had pre-established roots and a context in the prominent Idealist stream of Western intellectual history, as Steiner frequently explained in his lectures.

Steiner was already thoroughly "linked" to Goethe's thinking. He had devoted seven years, from 1889 to 1896 which he spent in Weimar (the "Goethe-city"), to editing Goethe's natural scientific works for a new scholarly edition, and he had written numerous monographs and several books on different aspects of Goethe's world view. Steiner felt that Goethe's ideas about nature necessarily led to his own body of anthroposophical knowledge. There was a clear continuity between early nineteenth-century Goethean thinking and twentieth-century anthroposophical thinking. Those seeking a natural scientific foundation for spiritual science could find this by "enlivening" within themselves Goethe's ideas on nature, then extending this approach to attain knowledge of the spiritual worlds.

When Goethe observed nature, it brought ideas to meet him. To him, nature abounded with ideas; ideas lived in everything. The best example of this for Goethe was the idea of the archetypal plant—the single, primal *plant* as a process expressed manifoldly, a "thousandfold," throughout the plant kingdom. Goethe sought the prototype, the original, unifying idea behind the "changeability" of individual manifestations, whether it was plants, animals, or humans. "The mental picture of the basic organ, transforming itself in stages from seed to fruit as though upon a 'spiritual ladder,' is the idea of the archetypal plant," Steiner explained. The natural world is permeated with creative Spirit expressing itself as ideas, said Goethe. He constantly sought the underlying, ideal, formative principle, whether it was the human intermaxillary bone or geological stratification. For Goethe, the idea is always implicit in the experience, so there is only one source of knowledge—the objective being of the natural world itself. Idea and perception are reciprocal realities, interrelating through human consciousness in a form of spiritual breathing.[28]

The Goethean way of thinking had its limitations, Steiner stated without reservation. Goethe did not take his contemplation of the archetypal ideas behind plants and animals to its necessary conclusion. He contemplated the natural world until the supersensible ideas behind the multiplicity of expressions confronted him, but how about the metamorphosis of ideas themselves, how about their hierarchical interactions within the ideal realm? Answers to these questions are tasks "which first begin upon the empirical height where Goethe stopped," Steiner observed. Goethe wasn't able to perceive the world of ideas itself; in fact, he had an "antipathy" for self-knowledge, said Steiner. Goethe lacked the "organ" for the contemplation of the human's innermost nature—self-perception. He was thereby unable to behold freedom. Despite these epistemological shortcomings, Goethe brought forward a pure stream of Platonism. "He had an open sense for the Platonic lifting of the human soul up to the world of ideas."[29]

Plato, who lived in the early days of the fourth epoch of intellectual soul (circa 428–347 B.C.), had argued that archetypal, universal, or abstract ideas, such as beauty, goodness, and truth, could not be derived from sense perception. Such ideas, rather, were spiritual, resident in an ideal realm. Humans brought Ideas to birth through the dialectical method as exemplified by Socrates. The dialectic, working through Socrates, acted as the "midwife of knowledge." All knowledge was actually a remembering, said Plato. Originally, before it undertook incarnation in the "prison-house" of the physical body, the human soul had perceived the archetypal Ideas in the supersensible realm. It was humanity's task, then, to become conscious again of these formative Ideas. And it is the task of Anthroposophy, as a culmination of the thinking of Goethe and Plato, to provide the means for regaining these supersensible Ideas.

This is the task of Anthroposophy, but what was its origin in the ideal realm? Where had the *idea* of "Wisdom of Man" come from? Where had the *wisdom* itself come from? And what was this wisdom? And what about the word "anthroposophy" itself? Steiner claimed he had the word *anthroposophy* from Robert Zimmerman, a professor of philosophy at the University of Vienna; as a student in the 1880s Steiner attended Zimmerman's lectures. Steiner had the highest regard for Zimmerman, but his anthroposophy was "a tangled undergrowth of abstract concepts."[30] Anyway, the term shows up over two centuries earlier in a book by Thomas Vaughan, called *Anthroposophia Theomagica* (1650), which was about Syrian Egyptian gnosis.[31]

Gnosis is the answer to all these questions. The idea of the wisdom of the Human and the wisdom itself come from Gnosticism, the collectivity of heretical Christian sects that flourished in the first two centuries after Christ. Steiner's critics often branded him a Gnostic, as if that were a pejorative sufficient to repudiate his ideas. Any kind of immersion in the thinking of Gnosticism makes it clear that rather than an insult, to be called a Gnostic is to speak to the core of what has emerged as Anthroposophy. Steiner was a Gnostic, then, insofar as the *sophy* in Anthroposophy derives from Sophia, the Gnostic expression of divine wisdom.[32] In essence, Anthroposophy is all about Sophia. As Sophia is fundamental to the Michaelic-anthroposophical project of respiritualizing cosmic intelligence, it is crucial to understand what "She" is.

The discovery of the Gnostic Gospels in 1945 at Nag Hammadi in Egypt was a sensational event in the twentieth-century deepening of the Christ impulse. Suddenly some forty-six previously unavailable, even unsuspected, original texts—probably the entire sacred library of a Gnostic sect, suppressed by the orthodox Christian Church for nearly two thousand years—resurfaced, affording us a new look at Gnostic thought. There are several extant Gnostic formulations—Marcion, Basilides, Mani, Simon Magus, Justin, Valentinus—but the speculations of Valentinus are among the most textually complete and philosophically engaging. Valentinus was born in Egypt, educated at Alexandria, taught in Rome (circa 135–160 A.D.), and compiled his thoughts about gnosis and Sophia in his *Gospel of Truth,* one of the documents recovered at Nag Hammadi. Other foundation Sophia texts include *On the Origin of the World, the Eugnostos, The Sophia of Jesus Christ,* and *The Apocryphon of John.* From their overlapping descriptions we can form a living idea of Sophia.

Sophia's story begins in the Pleroma. At the beginning of all things stands the unbegotten, primal, unknown Father, also called *Bythos* (the "abyss"). Bythos is the perfect, pre-existent Aion and the divine Autogenes. Aion is Endless Time, self-generated (autogenic). Aion's sole company is Silence (or Grace), which is its thought. Out of Silence, Aion brings forth Mind, which alone can comprehend its begetter's infinite greatness; Aion also generates Truth. This forms the first tetrad of Abyss, Silence, Mind, and Truth. Next come two pairs, or Aions: Word (Christ) and Life (Holy Spirit); Human and Church; and these, with the primal tetrad, comprise the first ogdoad (group of eight). From Mind and Truth come ten additional pairs of Aions, and from Word and Life come twelve. The thirty Aions are distributed in fifteen male-female pairs, each called a syzygy. The thirty Aions, or fifteen syzygies, constitute the Pleroma, which is the Fullness of Being, the hierarchy of the divine realm, the "fully explicated manifold of divine characteristics." The Pleroma (or prime Aion), is the perfection of God, the fullness of God's being, the circle of divine attributes, the whole completeness of divinity, the fullness of real existence, and the archetypal ideal. Aion has similar connotations of "always" and "forever." The last, youngest, and outermost "female" Aion in the chain of emanations from the Absolute Being is Sophia, or Eternal Wisdom.[33]

A few Gnostic texts relate that the immortal, First Human was Sophia's consort within the Pleroma, while others say it was the Son of Man, or Christ. Either way, the texts uniformly portray her destiny as lying outside the Pleroma. All the Aions yearned to contemplate and comprehend the unbegotten Father, but only Mind actually enjoyed that privilege. This passion for knowledge of the Unbegotten Father infected the Pleroma, affecting Sophia most of all. Sophia desired to conceive a thought from out of herself and to bring forth a likeness of the primal Aion out of herself; she undertook this without the consent of her consort or the Holy Spirit. Sophia departed the Pleroma attempting to achieve the impossible, what had never been done before. Mythographically, this marked Sophia's fall.

Outside the Pleroma, existence was miserable for Sophia. Limit steadied her and Sophia recovered herself; then she returned to the Pleroma and her consort. But her restoration was incomplete and would lead to the genesis of the world. This precosmic fall of a divine Aion actually precedes Creation. Her Fall as wisdom was also a Creation of wisdom, of a world that would be permeated with divine wisdom, Sophia's essence. Sophia's passion and intention formed a new objective being outside the Pleroma, called the Lower Sophia or Achamod ("desire"). This Sophia-Achamod endures the same gamut of suffering as her mother as she hopelessly seeks the vanished Light. Her passions (grief, fear, bewilderment, ignorance, and conversion) manifest as definitive states of being outside the Pleroma. The passions of Sophia-Achamod become the substance of the world, the four elements of matter (e.g., earth, air, fire, water), and their "turning" or conversion towards the redeemer. Here, Sophia-Achamod, also called *Sophia Prunikos* (Sophia the Whore) wanders in grief and fear amidst the self-created phantasms of her fallen psychical substance.

Sophia's fall precipitates the creation of the worlds outside the Pleroma. By this means, Divine Light enters the creation. Sophia's aberration, or error, as it's often called, produced a shadow—"limitless chaos, limitless darkness, and bottomless water, a fearful product"—which had been expelled from her being like an aborted fetus. Sophia formed this chaos into a "likeness" of herself, which then emerged from the primal water. Thus Sophia's desire to create a self-reflection by which she might know the unbegotten Father produced *Ialdabaoth*, her imperfect, defective image.

Ialdabaoth is the androgynous lion-faced Demiurge, the chief archon, the cosmic architect and cosmocrator. He creates the seven planets, the archons (primal rulers) of the solar system who will eventually decree humanity's Fate through their "yoke of mechanical necessity." Ialdabaoth also creates the seven heavens of the angelic hierarchy (365 angels in all), "and he was honored by all the army of angels." But Ialdabaoth is "impious in his arrogance," conceiving himself the sole artificer and "prime parent," with no other God besides him. "Because of the power of the glory he possessed of his mother's light, he called himself God."[34]

Ialdabaoth had great authority yet he was ignorant of his origin. Sophia, abiding in the Pleroma, enlightened her insolent progeny, Ialdabaoth, with a vision of two beings higher up in Creation than he. Sophia revealed to him the First Human (the primordial human) and the Son of Man (the Christ-Logos). The Human is the perfect image of the unbegotten Father, Sophia told Ialdabaoth. Here is his likeness in the primal water, she said. "There is an immortal Man of light who has been in existence before you and who will appear among your modelled forms; he will trample you to scorn just as potter's clay is pounded."[35] Ialdabaoth was greatly disturbed by this vision.

Ialdabaoth, the seven archons, and the 365 angels set out to create Adam, the "natural body" of the immortal First Human whose image they had seen in the water.[36] Sophia breathed life into Adam and he came alive. The archons were jealous of Adam because they knew he could "think better" than they. Adam's intellect became "sober" and "correct," and he experienced gnosis—"acquaintance" with the difference between good and evil, light and darkness, the fruit of "perfect knowledge" formerly available only to the gods. The natural Adam possessed the "luminous Epinoia of the light" from Sophia which awakened his thinking. "From that day, the authorities knew that truly there was something mightier than they."

Sophia is characterized variously in the Gnostic texts and commentaries. She is "Mother of the Universe, whom some call Love," and the "tri-male Spirit." Certain texts identify her with the mystical Silence and the Holy Spirit, in addition to Wisdom. Wisdom, as *ennoia*, is the "first universal creator," who brings the creatures forth, enlightens humans, and gives them wisdom. The image of thinking, reflecting, reasoning (*ennoia*) is feminine and thus a primal power of conception, the source of the universe, and the power to shape and manage creation. Sophia thinks the world into being and leaves that original thinking within the created world as a kind of divine signature and guiding light, according to this view. Sophia gives terrestrial Adam the *ennoia*, the divine spark of wisdom. Drops or sparks of Light fall into the visible world into the souls of human beings as miniature seed revelations of the Pleroma.

Gnostics following Valentinus and Marcus prayed to Sophia-Mother as the "mystical, eternal Silence." They entreated her as "Grace, She who is before all things," and as "incorruptible Wisdom for insight (gnosis)."[37] Sophia is the "great goddess of Heaven, mother of the stars, universal genetrix." She is the "light-maiden" who appears before the seven archons, the lower powers of the world, and incites them to desire her. Sophia is *Pistis*, or Faith. Sophia-Pansophos is the companion of immortal, celestial Human (the feminine half of the androgynous First Human) from whose syzygy all things—Chaos, the Aions, the seven heavens, the firmament—have emanated. Sophia is Isis, the *anima mundi*, the "Archaeal Universal Soul," the Holy Ghost, Mother of the gods, goddess of Speech and Sound, the creative Intellect, and Astral Light.[38] The Sophia revelation is the apocalyptic unveiling of Isis, as perennially referred to in the Mystery tradition. Sophia is the fallen divinity through whom the Light became immersed with darkness, but she is also the "intermediary" between the Pleroma, the archonic Creation, and the exiled spirituality resident in humanity as sparks.[39]

Meanwhile, Lower Sophia (Sophia Prunikos) exists in travail outside the Pleroma. The Christ was not permitted to leave the Pleroma to redeem the Lower Sophia at that particular point in "time," but Jesus was. Jesus, the thirty-first but unpaired Aion, is the "perfect, common fruit of the Pleroma," the symbolic unity of the thirty Aions. The "whole Pleroma of the Aions," said Irenaeus, a Gnostic commentator, contributed their individual excellences to produce Jesus, who would appear on Earth "as the perfect beauty and star of the Pleroma." The Aions sent Jesus outside the Pleroma to be Lower Sophia's consort. Jesus, as Sophia's *Soter* (savior, redeemer), acting on behalf of the Logos, became her syzygy in the created worlds and thereby redeemed all the divine sparks of Sophia's *ennoia*, her thought-seeds of light in the world. Through Sophia's deliverance, the Pleroma and Creation are restored to harmony. Gnosis becomes the pre-eminent revelation, the Sophianic "acquaintance." Or, as the Valentinians defined it, gnosis is the "knowledge of the ineffable greatness" and "the redemption of the inner spiritual man."

So not only is Sophia the object of redemption, but she herself assists in the redemptive process. The Mother, with all her human souls stripped to their light sparks, enters the bridal chamber of the Pleroma for the sacred marriage (*hieros gamos*), or divine syzygy, of Sophia with Jesus. "On the scale of the total divine drama, the individual ascent is part of the restoration of the deity's own wholeness, impaired by the events of the beginning."[40]

That is why Steiner said knowledge acquired by humans is the indispensable part of the world's becoming. The human acquisition of knowledge facilitates the perpetual restoration of syzygy of Sophia. This point highlights the thinking behind Steiner's statement that the emergence of Anthroposophy on Earth is a cosmic event because it enables Sophia to be made whole again. In either case, Sophia-Wisdom unites with Anthropos-Human, as Anthroposophy: Wisdom of the Human. The Gnostic concept of Sophia is more implicit in Steiner's thinking than outwardly explicated—although it is one of the foundations, along with elements from Zoroastrianism, of his complete view—but he considered the subject in his 1914 Leipzig lecture cycle, *Christ and the Spiritual World*, and later in Dornach in 1920, in *The Search for the New Isis, Divine Sophia*.

We have lost the true Isis-Sophia legend in our time, which is "the wisdom and knowledge of the Christ," said Steiner. Steiner related the Egyptian myth of Osiris-Isis with the historically more recent event of Christ-Sophia. Osiris as the dismembered Sunbeing was an early representative of the Christ, who had not yet appeared on Earth. Isis, his wife, was an image of the Mother of the Savior and the consort—the Divine Wisdom called Sophia. Sophia is the world's spiritual essence, the "wisdom that sees through the world and enables man to comprehend the world." But in our time—the early twentieth century—the Isis-Sophia being is dead. Sophia's grave is the wide space of heaven. Isis-Sophia is "spread out, in her true shape, in the beauty of the whole Universe." Ideally, she radiates out of the cosmic spaces in "an aura of many shining colors," as the living revelation of the stars and planets as "spiritual monuments." Instead of this, we have the "dead body" of the divine Sophia, a living, wisdom-speaking cosmos killed by mathematical, mechanistic abstraction, or what René Guénon aptly called "the reign of quantity." This is Sophia's grave.

The Christ is forevermore united with Earth and human evolution. This the Mystery of Golgotha secured for the future of Earth and its human residents. But for Christ to appear before us, for us to have that Damascan etheric perception of the risen Christ, we must find Isis-Sophia again. We must restore the *sophos* to the Human, through the activity of Anthroposophy. We must appreciate the detachment with which Steiner approached this spiritual-historic necessity. Steiner did not regard Anthroposophy as an intellectual, patentable product of his own personal development, but rather as a name for an ineluctable historic process that must work its way into the human stream during the epoch of the consciousness soul and especially during the Michael regency. For Steiner, presenting Anthroposophy to the world was a matter of articulating an *objective* philosophical reality.

Just as the Gnostics explained, the destinies of Sophia and Christ in the world are intimately reciprocal. "The Christ will appear in spiritual form during the twentieth century, not through an external happening, but inasmuch as human beings find that force which is represented by the holy Sophia." Sophia is necessary for finding the Christ and the Christ-Logos is necessary for Sophia's restoration; the interface is humanity awake in its cognition. In an earlier time, the Sophia force worked through humans in two ways. This twofold Sophia permeation was exemplified in the story of how the birth of the Christ child was announced to both the pious shepherds and the learned Magi. The knowledge and wisdom of the cosmos and of its Logos the Christ was announced interiorly, through forces of the Earth working through deepened heart insight to the shepherds, and exteriorly, through the living astrology of the Magi. In this way the twofold Sophia brought awareness of the Christ to humans.

So will it be again, Steiner said. We will find the new Sophia when, through "living Imagination," we resurrect the abstractions of astronomy, mathematics, and geometry, the detritus of the Magi's living astrology, into a vision of the spirit-filled cosmic expanse living within us, and when we similarly resurrect the materialistic empiricism of sense perception, the detritus of the shepherd's inner clairvoyance, into a perception of the spirit-permeated world outside. The new Isis-Sophia legend must be formed out of an Imagination suited to our age of consciousness soul. The time is ripe: "We are standing before this very point in time."[41]

In Steiner's pre-grave biography of Sophia, he related how She evolved through the twenty-nine stages (or Aions) of the Pleroma. In the course of this evolution, Sophia realized that if she wished to maintain a "free vision" of the spiritual world of the Aions, she had to separate something from herself to exist as an outside agency. What Sophia separated was Achamod, her desire; Sophia's passion now wanders through the realms of space and "permeates everything"—living in our sense perception, our thinking, as "something cast out into the souls of men," as a longing for the spiritual world. Achamod (or the Lower Sophia) permeates the created world as an image of the Divine which Sophia cast out from herself as progeny. Meanwhile, human souls are shut in with Achamod, the image of Sophia's desire, in the material world; we have only the image, the desire, but not Sophia herself in this world of matter she precipitated in her wanderings outside the Pleroma. This separation from the pure Sophia *is* the material world. The fourfold elemental world is the embodiment, the materialization, of her passionate life. The movement towards gnosis is the wish to overcome the separation from Sophia and to regain that glimpse of Divine Light, that illumination by the "ray from the Son of God." That had been the soul's experience in the "primal remote past" and it has lived in the soul as a memory ever since.[42]

The ancient Sophia-Wisdom was prepared on the Old Moon, then secreted everywhere within the new Earth, Steiner explained. The Old Moon phase of cosmic evolution was called the planet or cosmos of wisdom. Old Moon wisdom was then "stamped upon the outer world." This wisdom was "a kind of spiritual substance lying at the foundation of all things," pervading all of nature. In a sense, the positive side of Sophia-Achamod roaming the created worlds was this permeation of matter with innate wisdom, with the residual presence of Sophia. Inner wisdom first appeared on the Earth through the human Ego but develops gradually by degrees. Human wisdom will eventually reach the same heights as the "all over-ruling" Nature wisdom.[43] "Sophia [Holy Wisdom] lies hidden in every atom and every stone, every tree and every flower. Her magic wand of revelation lies concealed within each of us."[44]

But why is Sophia so important for Anthroposophy? The thinking of Valentin Tomberg (1900–1973), a Russian Anthroposophist who came to prominence after Steiner's death, makes it clear. Tomberg wrote about Sophia in the 1930s in his studies on the Old and New Testaments.

For Tomberg, Sophia was not an abstraction, an archetype, or a piously mystical state of mind, but an actual, cognizable cosmic being, akin to an archangel. Sophia *is* the cosmic intelligence, but that portion of the cosmic intelligence that descended to the human Ego as the "fallen" Sophia. Thus at the outset we see that Sophia is the precious inheritance of cosmic intelligence Michael guards on behalf of humanity. The pure Sophia, who still resides in the Pleroma, performs a special spiritual task. That task is to impart the "prevenient Manas revelation." That is, a spiritual cognition of cosmic intelligence that precedes and anticipates repentance, which is a turning about in the mind, or conversion, the fifth passion of Sophia. Manas, as we had already noted, signifies the activities and structure of human intellectuality, the chief feature of the Human (originally, *Man*, from Manas) as the "One who thinks."

The work of the pure Sophia's Manas revelation is protected by Michael, administrator of cosmic intelligence. "He so guides the whole revelation of the Sophia that it may be absorbed by the best forces of Man's consciousness soul." Michael creates the bridge between the Manas-light and the consciousness soul by "pouring strength of Will into the moral content of the revelations of thought." In other words, to work voluntarily with Michael during this time of his regency means, necessarily, to come into the milieu of Sophia, the embodiment of Divine

Wisdom, or cosmic intelligence. It also means to penetrate the Mystery of Golgotha and attain the Damascan vision of the etheric, risen Christ-Logos on our own as the basis for efficacy in our restorative work with Michael on Sophia's behalf. The matter is reflexive and reciprocal.

Through Sophia's revelation, the "unity of the Trinity" becomes perceptible. Sophia is "an *inspiring* Being," says Tomberg, who facilitates a perception of the innate harmony of the supersensible world to men and women who ascend through thought to meet her. Through this perception of the harmony of all spiritual hierarchies afforded by the Sophia revelation, the Trinity of Father, Son, and Holy Spirit is revealed as a unifying reality. In this age, our first meeting with Sophia happens in human thinking "which strives to comprehend the divine Trinity in its cosmic revelation as a unity of three different principles." Sophia doesn't represent separate cognitions in distinct regions, said Tomberg, but "the knowledge of that which gives meaning to all separate cognitions." Sophia is the matrix that unifies all products of cognition. The stones of these separate cognitions build the temple of the universe, which is Sophia's provenance as Divine Wisdom.[45]

Sophia bears the gift of a concentrated inner wisdom, Tomberg explained. This wisdom encompasses not only the Light of the Godhead (the Unbegotten Father) shining through her being, and not only the cosmic vista of the Akashic chronicle, but a "remembrance" of the soul ascending from within. This kind of wisdom is "pure creativity," but it is also a cognition of the *plan* of the world; we noted earlier that cosmic intelligence encompasses understanding of the *why* behind the activities of the celestial hierarchy. Through Sophia, "the whole experience of the past Cosmos rises out of the inner being as the primal intention for the present Cosmos." Sophia reveals to us the plan, the intention, the reason—the Why?—for the cosmos. Surely this is the ultimate answer to the myriad questions that passionately engage us as human beings. In this way Sophia is the "spiritual archetype of the soul." Sophia provides acquaintance, gnosis, and knowing. This fact establishes the similarity in destiny between "the true soul-being of Man on Earth and of the Sophia-being in the Spiritual World." Again, it is a reciprocal, interdependent situation.[46] So the enlightenment of humanity is the restoration of Sophia; the

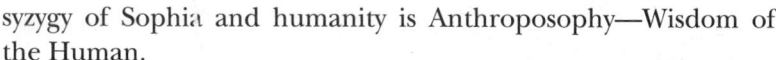

syzygy of Sophia and humanity is Anthroposophy—Wisdom of the Human.

In light of the depth of this divine drama, how much do the thoughts of Spiritualism and Theosophy encompass the requirements of the Sophia revelation? Do they create *Freiheit*, the evolutionary urgency of the consciousness soul? These were the questions Steiner put to himself in the first decade of this century as he brought forward the living thought of Anthroposophy. Steiner answered them with Anthroposophy itself, as a message from Sophia, then dedicated his remaining years to furthering the Sophia cognition in humanity. In our time, too, these are legitimate, urgent questions. Do channeling, as mediumship is now called, and laissez-faire occultism foster spiritual freedom and generate that "prevenient Manas revelation" that Tomberg outlined which is the cognition of Sophia as cosmic intelligence?

Steiner found the fundamental tenets of Theosophy to be incompatible with the realities of his direct spiritual knowledge and the objective requirements of Anthroposophy on several counts. First, Theosophy is overly Indian and Oriental in emphasis, presenting a one-sided cosmology based on Hindu and Buddhist concepts. It isn't that this Aryan formulation is inaccurate or metaphysically unserviceable; it just does not integrate smoothly into the main streams of Western thought, either exoteric or esoteric. Moreover, it represents a revelation from the first post-Atlantean cultural epoch of India when the conditions of consciousness were entirely different; and its predominant practices involve yogic control of the breath as a vehicle for higher awareness. As such, it is destructively anachronistic for the soul conditions of humans living in the epoch of the consciousness soul. "The modern human being must rise into the spiritual world not by way of the breath but by way of an intensified life of soul," noted Steiner. We must try to "sever the connection (unconscious as it otherwise is) between the breathing process and the thinking process."[47]

Second, Theosophy misses the global significance of the Mystery of Golgotha and has no intention of bringing the Christ impulse forward into the twentieth century as a living revelation. By omitting the Christ, Theosophy denies the living Logos in human thinking; more profoundly, by denying the Christ Event any significance in human or planetary history, Theosophy becomes essentially antiteleological, antihistorical, and, thereby, profoundly in error. The Christ incarnation had a momentous purpose, a divine teleology that encompasses the entire life of the cosmos and its seven stages of unfoldment of which Earth is but the fourth. The Theosophic cosmogony is historically parochial, extending no earlier in cosmic evolution than Old Moon and its savant population of "lunar pitris" and "Dhyan Chohans." But what about Old Sun, Old Saturn? And what about Earth's destiny, as Jupiter, Venus, and Vulcan? These phases of cosmic evolution Theosophy, even in its best moments in Blavatsky's impressive tomes, fails to address.

Third, Theosophy is burdened with Mahatma worship. Theosophy's followers, and especially its leaders, idolized a remote quasi-human hierarchy of "perfected men" who dispense occult truths by grace and discretion. Steiner never disputed the reality of such a hierarchy; he had direct contact with members of the White Brotherhood, both in and out of human incarnation. But this kind of metaphysical dependency on the masters defeats any cultivation of *Freiheit*. How can human beings develop inner spiritual activity when they believe the arcana they ardently seek is available only through Morya, Djwal Khul, or Kuthumi and their precious "astral mail" service? What if they refuse to cooperate? And can they be trusted?

There could be no true human freedom in this hierarchical papacy. Supersensible cognition could aspire to no greater heights than a communication with the hierarchy's pope, the "virgin angel" and Lord of the World, called Sanat Kumara. But what of the nine angelic hierarchies? What of Michael, Christ, Sophia? Theosophy provided no road map for how to reach them. And when Theosophy finally came to discussing the Christ, it got it completely wrong, materialistically fronting a Hindu savant as the human face of the Second Coming. Who would want to place their reasonable trust in a movement founded on behind-the-scene secrecies, plots, and occult imprisonments? The occult lodges and Mahatmas had schemed to produce or compromise nineteenth century Theosophy, manipulating Blavatsky like a puppet, pulling her in contrary ways according to their aims. The Order of the Star fiasco may well have been the machinations of the black lodges out to destroy Blavatsky's legacy and to obfuscate the accurate perception and comprehension of the Christ. The Christ is pivotal for the human attainment of free spiritual activity, cognitive autonomy.

Steiner clearly felt uncomfortable with a supposedly spiritual movement founded on the autocratic guidance of remote, often disembodied, Mahatmas. Theosophy disapproves of peer review, of collegial validation, one of the foundation stones of the scientific method. Anytime a Theosophist claimed to have independent access to the Mahatmas, he was discredited, and his messages repudiated; the history of the Theosophical Society is replete with examples of this. Steiner resolved to bring forward a movement inspired by the willing, conscious cooperation of men and women working voluntarily under the aegis of Michael and the Christ, both of whom meticulously, scrupulously respect the parameters of human freedom. Steiner exhorted his colleagues to corroborate his statements by developing their own clairvoyant consciousness, through a spiritual scientific training. With this perspective, they could independently consult the Akashic Records through direct spiritual seeing and check, refine, or correct his data. Anthroposophy requires a clairvoyant collegiality inspired by Michael, not an autocratic hierarchy dominated by one savant.

We need to look deeply to find the degree of presence of Sophia in Theosophy and Anthroposophy. There is a major evolutionary difference between the revelation of *Theo-Sophia* and *Anthropos-Sophia*. Theosophy arose as the inspiration of the Mahatmas acting from outside or beyond mainstream human culture. They were a benevolent theocracy acting on behalf of an oblivious, materialistic humanity. Theosophy affirms the wisdom of cosmic intelligence, Sophia, but it is only implicit, introverted within the consciousness of the gods. Theo-Sophia is the cosmic intelligence resident in the gods, in the hierarchy of perfected humans raised to godlike stature. It is the wisdom of God in the gods—Sophia in the Mahatmas—and brokered to mainstream humanity through the occult lodges and Mystery Schools.

This is inherently elitist. This theocracy or brotherhood dispenses the divine wisdom cyclically, at one time through the Hibernian Mysteries, at another through the Stanzas of Dzyan, or through their centennial effort. But in Theo-Sophia a schism exists between humanity and knowledge; the theocracy is the in-termediary. It is not Wisdom *in* the Human, but Wisdom *for* the Human. Wisdom in the Human is the product of the I-conscious-ness, but Wisdom for Man is an offshoot of the old Group Soul, pre-Ego tribal identity. Once the hierarchy provided our thoughts, spirituality, and morality; under Theo-Sophia, the Ma-hatmas would assume this paternalistic role. But we would not be free human beings under this condition. Our revelation is sec-ondary, textual: we *know about* things, but we don't *know* them di-rectly. The gods know, the perfected Mahatmas know, some of the lodge members know, the gurus know, but we as ordinary hu-mans don't know. The possibility of gnosis, of Sophianic acquain-tance, is not universally accorded under Theo-Sophia. On this path we remain exiled from Sophia and the Michaelic transfer of cosmic intelligence is a failure.

With Anthroposophy, Sophia completes her crucial transition from Pleroma to World. Sophia moves from embodiment in the gods (Theo-Sophia) as occult theocracy to living presence in hu-manity (Anthropos-Sophia). Anthroposophy emphasizes the di-rect, unilateral acquisition and embodiment of cosmic intelligence through the unique human I, the Ego. The consciousness soul is permeated by the Christ-Logos, the principle of knowing itself, and, through the Logos, the Sophia is born in the human. The Michaelic project to respiritualize cosmic intelligence can bring the Sophia Being into the consciousness soul of twentieth and twenty-first-century human beings. In this way cosmic intelligence incarnates on Earth and the Mahatmas assume a less prominent role as guides and clarifiers; as we ascend, they become our spiri-tual colleagues.

When we examine the contents of the transitions from Spiritu-alism to Theosophy to Anthroposophy, we find an ever greater proportion of the cosmos involved at each stage. Mid-nineteenth century Spiritualism brought a gross materialization of the spirit through mediumistic, physical effects. Spiritual energies and presences were somehow materialized, made physical, so people could see or hear them with their ordinary senses. Spiritualism introduced a combination of the phantoms of the lingering dead, astral shells, elemental beings, and mediumistic ectoplasmic ema-nations. It was primarily a physical, materialist phenomenology entirely within the human plane, regardless of whether the humans were alive or dead. But the Spiritualists missed the essential point that the *fact* of mediumistic effects tried to convey. During the height of Spiritualism, people were taken up with the glamors of the physical phenomena—the raps, the furniture moving, the apports, the spirit concerts, the ectoplasmic extrusions, the supposed contact with dead relatives. But they missed the message that spiritual and elemental forces work behind and through the matter of sense perception, that materialism is a rarefied spirituality.

With the transition to Theosophy, the source of influence shifted from the apparent dead to the transcendental Mahatmas, perfected humans for whom being alive or dead was spiritually inconsequential. Yet even with Theosophy, the spiritual was materialized, and thus misrepresented. The Mahatmas Morya, Kuthumi, Hilarion, Serapis Bey, and Djwal Khul may have been rarefied beings, but they were, at the end of the nineteenth century, physically resident on the Earth. And if the Masters of Wisdom couldn't meet the Theosophists in person, at least they wrote through "precipitated" letters. Theosophists could read *The Mahatma Letters*, the Mahatmas rich correspondence with A. P. Sinnett of Allahabad, India, between 1880 and 1884. Even this testimony to the transcendent was expressed physically—in 145 handwritten communications. In other words, the two stages, including Spiritualism and Theosophy, both depended almost exclusively on physicalized, materialized, sense bound revelations, presences, and activities; their coin of the realm was spiritual materialism.

The Theosophical-Anthroposophical distinction can also be drawn on the basis of the Michael-Christ pivot. Theosophy turns on the revelations of ancient, divine wisdom brought forward by a benevolent hierarchy of Mahatmas, or ascended humans, some of whom were physically incarnate in the late nineteenth century. Anthroposophy pivots on the Mystery of Golgotha, a recent planetary fact of profound import, and the role of the Time Spirit Michael in bringing forward the contents of this Mystery into the epoch of the consciousness soul. Michael mediates the Christ Event to all of humanity, to every man and woman, providing each individual with a direct, replicated access to the revelation of Golgotha. This occurs through the widespread etheric perception of the Christ; the etheric perception of the Christ awakens cognition and empowers speech, just as the original Apostles were moved to speak as the Logos after their Pentecostal initiation. The Mystery of Golgotha guarantees to every man and woman willing to make the effort the equivalent apostolic experience of Pentecost; this gift to humanity Steiner called World Pentecost. Thus Anthroposophy holds World Pentecost as its ideal, almost egalitarian, democratization of the Holy Spirit.

In contrast, the Mahatmas work secretly through selected individuals to bring through edited revelations of the old, pre-Christ Mystery wisdom. Anthroposophy posits unilateral access to the Akashic Records and present-time, new cosmic activities through individual training and alignment with Michael and the Christ. With Anthroposophy, we do not need privileged access to ancient initiatory texts, which are only aspects of cosmic intelligence; when we can access the Akashic chronicle directly on our own, the Theosophic textual revelations pall in significance. Steiner exemplified this dispensation of cosmic intelligence through his 1913 lecture cycle called *The Fifth Gospel,* which he called the "Gospel of Knowledge of the Spirit, the Macrocosmic Gospel;" this new material retrieved from the Akashic Records supplemented the fourfold proclamation of the Gospels of Matthew, Mark, Luke, and John. "Although, as you will hear, this Fifth Gospel has never yet been written down, in future times of humanity it will certainly be put into definite form. In a certain sense, however, it would be true to say that it is as ancient as the other four Gospels."[48]

The two cosmic beings known as Michael and the Christ make the Logos revelations directly available to anyone who desires them and who is sufficiently schooled to access them. Anthroposophy emanates from a more exalted level of the cosmic hierarchy (Michael, Christ, the angelic panoply) but brings the revelations deeper into human culture than Theosophy. Theosophy accesses secrets held by the occult human hierarchy, but they are themselves working in accord with the divine plan as mediated by the Time Spirit Michael and the Christ-Logos. Theosophy gives men and women a vicarious contact with divine wisdom, an *image* of Sophia through an adulation of her ancient wisdom-*bearers* (i.e., the Mahatmas). Anthroposophy gives humanity Sophia herself, living within Christ-permeated men and women; Anthroposophy gives humans the Wisdom in the Human. Anthroposophy is the opportunity to directly know and embody Sophia without the intermediation of idolizing gurus or reifying mediumship. If there is cause for adulation the proper focus should be the unbegotten Father without whom Sophia's quest for cognition would never have been. Let us adulate the glory of *Wisdom in the Human Speaking*, the fulfillment of Sophia, Michael, Adam, and Christ.

In light of this we must ask: is it Wisdom in the Human speaking through mediumship and channeling, or are we entranced with a simulacrum? Two crucial questions loom before us at this point. Who are these uncredentialed, unborn, overly glamorous astral beings speaking to us from behind the uncritical facade of the popular and well-paid channel, today's refurbished medium? And to what degree are the black lodges once again manipulating our exchanges with the supersensible world? If they did it a century ago, certainly they are busy again today.

Mediumship and channeling that work under the aegis of Theo-Sophia are Old Moon atavisms spouting Old Moon speech. In Steiner's cosmogony, when the Moon separated itself from the Earth, the great spiritual teachers and founders of the primordial wisdom then living on Earth retreated to the interior of the Moon. These Moon-Beings were once the "registrars" of our destiny, the primeval wise teachers of a young humanity, the guiding powers of evolving Earth life. They now live etherically on the Old Moon and radiate spiritually to Earth the cosmic influences from the Universe beyond the Moon. This Old Moon spiritual population is the first we encounter in the life after death; Theosophy calls them "Lunar Pitris." "In the Moon sphere they permeate us with their own being, and enable everything to appear to us with greater reality," Steiner explained.[49]

What is the spiritual pedigree of these Old Moon intelligences? These Old Moon-Beings are actually the mighty "gods" of the Indian first cultural epoch recirculated as old third epoch Egypto-Chaldean angels now reappearing in world culture according to a cosmic evolutionary necessity. There is a cosmic evolutionary necessity at play here such that the fifth post-Atlantean cultural epoch of the consciousness soul has to recapitulate aspects of the third epoch, which was Egypt-Chaldea of the sentient soul. This angelic hierarchy of Egypto-Chaldean angels may have wielded an appropriate influence in the third cultural epoch, but as supersensible influences in our age of the consciousness soul, they are backward, immature, and lag behind. It's only when they work in conjunction with the Christ that their influence is timely.

In our day these "backward Egypto-Chaldean spirits" strive to put forward a "materialistic movement," interposing this against the lawful guidance of the normal, progressive directors of human evolution. These Egypto-Chaldean spirits work in complement with other regressive, nonmature Old Moon spirits—"angels in a backward state, beings occupying the lowest grade in the ranks of Luciferic spirits." These secondary spirits occupy a middle position between humans and angels. In earlier days they incarnated in human form, founded civilizations, and became some of the original heroes and race—teachers of the Greeks and Egyptians, such as Cadmus, Theseus, Cheops, and Pelops. They brought the concepts of individualization, differentiation, and freedom into human civilization. "Thus the ability to speak a separate language is, in all races, traceable to the illuminating presence of these great beings who were angels in a backward state."[50]

Clairaudient hearing and clairvoyant sight reveal to the assiduous Anthroposophist today that these old Chaldean and Egyptian angel-beings are "now again acting as spiritual leaders under the guidance of the Christ." It is highly likely, then, that the extensive new age channeling roster of uncorroborable cosmic celebrities—Ramtha, Mafu, Lazaris, DaBen, Orin, Orion, Ra, Ebban, Zoosh, the Brotherhood of God, Mentor, and all the others—includes many from the ranks of these Old Moon, Old Egypto-Chaldean beings. That's if we're lucky; we could well be dealing with far more regressive, inimical spirits masquerading as cosmic luminaries. If such supersensible sources are in fact regressive Egypto-Chaldean angels, we must exercise great circumspection with respect to their pronouncements and advice, always asking ourselves: does their information further the Michaelic goals of our time to respiritualize cosmic intelligence? Circumspection is always justified in dealing with the supersensible because we still have the machinations of the black lodges to reckon with; and if we enter the occult astral arena, as so many do, without preparation, esoteric schooling, or inner preparation, *caveat emptor* and

God protect our souls! Opposition to Michael, the Christ, and the consciousness soul is everywhere, and it's foremost on the agenda of the Brothers of the Left. I am not counseling paranoia, but realistic prudence. As Steiner said, "So the Powers that do not want the truth to come to light are everywhere at work." What are these Powers up to with the channeling movement?

First, let's review what we have disclosed about the underpinnings of nineteenth-century Spiritualism. The Spiritualist phenomena effectively spanned the forty-year period from 1840, which Steiner designated as the peak of materialism, until approximately 1880, by which time the Theosophical Society had been founded and the Michael regency had been inaugurated. Initially, the goal of launching Spiritualism was to arrest the materialist tendencies deadening Western culture and to introduce the reality of the unseen worlds and energies behind physical nature. The device was mediumistic materializations and physical phenomena, directed and facilitated by the occultists of the various lodges working through public mediums. The result was a failure. The mediums misattributed the source of their effects to spirits of the dead and shifted public attention from the occult forces behind nature to spirit communications with the deceased. This obscured the crucial issue of reincarnation and its soul responsibilities for the living, and led to an even more pronounced densification of spirituality into the gravity-burdened confines of materialist perception. The public came to misconstrue spiritual forces as unfamiliar physical forces of nature, leading to a kind of occult materialism. After the white lodges withdrew their sponsorship of the Spiritualist experiment, the Brothers of the Left exploited the metaphysical confusion to further their own goals.

Now, let's consider the recent resurgence of this same impulse during the time period 1970 to 1990 (or, if we are more generous, 1960 to 2000) in light of what we understand about lodge manipulation and spiritual-historical necessity. It is a reasonable assumption to say that a further lightening of materialism and a deepening of spiritual and occult content in general public awareness was judged necessary for the last quarter of this century. At the heart of this intention was the preparation for a culminating spiritual event called the Imagination of Pentecost, the full flowering of Steiner's prophesied World Pentecost—speaking *as* the Logos. But of course there was no need to duplicate the presentations made a century ago; this time, more Mystery knowledge and initiation content was released to introduce the reality of extraplanetary sentient, intelligent life, whether it is disembodied, differently-bodied, neo-human (more evolved), or angelic.

The device, again, was mediumship, but primarily through voice channelings and, secondarily, through printed transcripts, and, to a lesser, extent, audio and video formats of "live" transmissions. In approximately three-quarters of the examples of voice channelings, the mediums are unconscious, nonparticipatory, and generally amnesiac after the session; in most cases, the medium is unprepared for the job, having received no evident occult or spiritual training. Of course we are still too close to the events to assess their success or failure; it is clear, as we will appreciate as this book unfolds, that a great deal of confusion and obfuscation has been achieved. Chief among these distortions is a general quality of inflation and grandiosity, perhaps the counterbalance to the densification that marked the nineteenth-century Spiritualist phenomena.

Today's mediums are naïve and uncritical in their source attributions, taking the credentials and identity claims of their contacts at "face value." Their contacts boast of all manner of spiritual pedigree but there is almost no corroboration, peer review, or attempt at substantiation. The contacts tacitly encourage their mediums to inflate their own importance and stature as channels of planetary importance. This approach, in its most negative, regressive expression, glamorizes the attributed, disincarnate source while the human mouthpiece is exempted from taking any personal responsibility for the contents of the transmissions. A clear danger is that since the majority of the psychics at work in this field have bypassed (omitted) the requisite rigors of occult training and preparation, their example fosters a laissez-faire attitude about accessing the supersensible world. Their example of easy, unimpeded, unschooled contact obscures the vitally necessary fact that one must never cross the threshold between physical and supersensible worlds without working with the Guardian of the Threshold. As we will examine in Chapter 8, this is a major danger for unschooled psychics and may be a kind of booby trap or land mine subtly emplaced by the Brothers of the Left on the doorsill between worlds. The typical content of today's mediumistic materials has a kind of quasi-scientific tone, yet in most respects it is patently unscientific and oblivious to the most basic protocols of scientific procedure. Similarly, true, accurate, corroborable Akashic history is obscured and distorted by a confusion of tongues, as each source claims the true story.

Chief among the goals of the black brotherhoods is to stifle the true cognition of the Christ in our time. Steiner indicated this very clearly in his discussion of nineteenth-century occult activities and plans. An effective way to accomplish this is to create another Tower of Babel, to encourage a babbling confusion of glossalolic tongues speaking half-truths and claiming cosmic pedigrees. In this way contemporary humanity will miss the Christ through a false understanding of spiritual presence and activity. The brotherhoods want to trammel independent cognition because, for one thing, it would unmask their own occult machinations. They want independent, Christ-permeated cognition to be undeveloped, or skewed, bent, perverted, or corrupted—so that many voices speak falsely, boastingly, contrarily, deceiving themselves and the public into thinking they are voices for the Good, oracular factotums of Christ. But if there are many voices, everybody misses the one voice, the Logos, the source of speech, and Speech itself: the Word. Meretricious words are mistaken for the sterling Word and the Christ passes by unheard.

When strong, clear cognition is not present, misrepresentations prevail and the supersensible world is misrepresented. The brotherhoods want the spiritual worlds to be materially construed, so that they seem like a Southern California upgrade to bourgeois life. This will distort the spiritual dynamics and necessities of reincarnation and paralyze the muscle of individual morality and will. Twentieth century channels are well rewarded with publicity, fame, and wealth. The message is: spirit is a marketable, dividend-earning commodity. But if you're an occultist of ill intent, it's exceedingly easy to take hold of the communication channels when the medium or psychic is unprepared, untrained, more used to being an insurance claims adjuster or marketing consultant. This kind of unseen exploitation already happened with nineteenth century Spiritualist mediums, and that lesson should have been brought forward to us as instructive and salutary. The untrained medium cannot hold the line taut with the supersensible and is subject to massive confusion, disinformation, distortion, and error. Ramtha is misconstrued as the Christ. Mafu gets elevated to Hindu sainthood. Ashtar is accorded Joint Chiefs-of-Staff status among the UFO crowd. Deception abounds. Psychism is equated with spirituality. Opening to channel means instant clairvoyant initiation. The vivifying spiritual-evolutionary impulses are blocked or perverted. People miss the Christ and settle for the space brothers.

Channeling's Tower of Babel floods the world with many uncorroborable realities. When many tongues babble dissonantly, pompously, the unity inherent in the Christ-Logos is always thwarted. The Christ-Logos can never emerge from this disparate papal chorus of voices. It's as if a barrier is established, a gate locked firmly against the arrival of the Logos in the community of untrained speakers. The lodges encourage channels to attribute the source of their voices to grand cosmic identities separate from themselves. Channels are never urged to see through the facades, to follow the voices all the way in to the one voice of the Christ. Instead the oracular sparks across the synaptic gap between the worlds bankroll the channels in a new Palm Beach life as press agents for dubious astral celebrities. Channeling's clairvoyance tacitly advertises itself as easy, remunerative, status-creating, wisdom-generating, but nobody reflects that it is also very often unearned, undisciplined, and unwarranted. It's not just the black lodges that are fostering this carnival of fools; the left-handed occultists are only puppets for far more powerful cosmic agencies (like the Euripideans, the Carollans, and certain Pleiadian lineages) for whom the emergence of Sophia in humanity incarnate on Earth warrants the greatest organized opposition.

But the deception lurking in channeling's popularity today is even more insidious and therefore effective. The tacit assumption among channels is that they have authentically cast an oracular bridge across the worlds over which they convey the messages of exalted, beneficent supersensible beings to a metaphysically hungry humanity. Actually, a great deal of channeling is no more than oracular solipsism. There may be no genuine contact across the threshold at all but the mirror talk of Narcissus. The whole scheme of cosmic attribution is faulty because it presumes an accurate cosmological, hierarchical model; and it's tautological if we credit the channels or their sources themselves as a dependable source of such a model. Channels talk with themselves—with larger aspects of themselves—and credit the exchange to the mellifluosity of the cosmos.

Channeling flourishes today because of education. The post-World War II Baby Boom generation is probably the highest educated group of Americans in the country's history. As more people get educated, the intellect is stimulated, and people conclude they have a direct line to a spiritual entity when all they're really doing is, as an English poet once put it, regurgitating the blood of other men's heads. It has nothing to do with channeling. As Steiner made meticulously clear, very little that is presented under the general heading of channeling or mediumship is in any way useful. People presume psychism is synonymous with spirituality, but the two have nothing whatsoever to do with each other. Ancient China symbolized the psyche as a butterfly that flitted from one flower to the next. The undisciplined psyche is also like a tiger that will devour itself or a moth that will destroy itself upon a flame. In any event, the necessary rigor for the kind of wakeful, methodologically exact clairvoyance required by the consciousness soul for the emergence of Anthropos-Sophia is totally shortchanged. But as the cosmos dilates before us, revealing the vast panorama of cosmic intelligence awaiting us, we proceed without discipline, schooling, or inner training in our exchanges only at our considerable peril. We have been living perilously for more than one hundred years since Time Spirit Michael took up his new regency, signaling the transition from Theo-Sophia to Anthropos-Sophia.

The transition from Theo-Sophia to Anthropos-Sophia was a cosmic upgrade to the hierarchies of the celestial unborn—the angelic hierarchies and exalted cosmic beings such as Christ, Michael, and Sophia. In our own day of mass-market channels and television psychics, we need to make the next transition, but this time *within* Anthroposophy, through a new dedication of Anthroposophy founded on an understanding of Sophia in Anthropos. That prepares us for the event called the Imagination of Pentecost, which we'll consider later. For the present, let's say that the general trend in late twentieth-century channeling is a further dilation into the cosmos. There are, again, channels for the living dead, for the Mahatmas (who are now mostly discarnate and franchising their voice through dozens of channels), a few for the angelic families, but there are also new channels for previously unidentified cosmic beings, for the unborn stellar, residents of stars, planets, and constellations.

The 1980s psychics opened the channel to the living, speaking zodiac. The zodiac is a glossalolic wheel of speech. The opportunity is that the cosmos comes alive with speech; the danger is the reification of identity across the planetary threshold. As we'll learn later in the book, Steiner strongly emphasized that the human is a living miniaturization of the cosmos. The angelic families, the cosmic beings, the stars, constellations, planets—these are all constituents of the human being. "Behold Man! Here is the World in flesh," Steiner would say. Steiner of course was not oblivious to the machinations of the Lodges with respect to the advent of the new Michael regency and the possibility it offered for achieving modern initiation. Already in the last third of the nineteenth century, the adversary powers were at work, seeking to undermine all that Michael was putting into place; and this was merely a prolegomenon to what late twentieth century Anthroposophists would have to contend with. Contemporary humanity must strive for an understanding of *Per spiritum sanctum reviviscimus* ("Through the Holy Spirit we are reborn"), but it will not be easy. "If you consider this counsel and compare it with the modern attitude coming from science you will recognize that there will be immense opposition, perhaps of a kind you cannot even imagine today, which will take the form of external actions and deeds that, above all, will have a tendency to make initiation science entirely impossible."[51]

The danger with the current attitude about channeling is actually twofold. First, most channels attribute their source to an advanced intelligence separate from their own consciousness. With the surge of 1980s' channeling, people were taken with its California glamor, the newfound astral celebrities, the allure of the wise voices. But for most channeling enthusiasts, the underlying message that the *fact* of channeling conveyed passed them by: namely, that our real identity and cognitive range includes the entire cosmos and all its beings, and that we must strive to be a fully conscious, independent investigator, co-creator, and cosmic colleague, but not some kind of well-paid sycophantic voice-box.

Second, few channels ask their presumed mentors for credentials. New Age black humor caught the edge of this perception with the popular quip, Just because you're dead, doesn't mean you're smart! Few appreciate the fact there are intelligences in the vast cosmos whose business does not rightfully include interfering with or entering human evolution, either through speech (channeling) or embodiment (walk-ins). These sources may not lawfully be part of the cosmic human, yet they may be slyly ingratiating themselves for their own aims through the uncritical, laissez-faire, and often myopic popular attitude about channeling. How can anyone tell? And who's watching out? Human *Freiheit*, Michael's precious endowment on behalf of Sophia and the Christ, hangs in the balance. Without anthroposophical rigor, we may never attain to true, unimpeded clairvoyance so needed by Sophia for her redemption.

The Redemption of Sophia

The Anthroposophical Rigor of

True Clairvoyance

*W*E CAN TELL, and we should be watching out for, the veracity of our supersensible contacts, but the way to safeguard ourselves against error and deception in the supersensible worlds is through spiritual scientific training and inner schooling. The path of anthroposophic initiation is the way in which the Sophia revelation—Wisdom in the Human—can be brought forward into the epoch of the consciousness soul as a form appropriate for our soul conditions.

As Steiner repeatedly emphasized, the dangers of going astray and the possibilities for self-deception in spiritual development are considerable. The risks of error and misconception without inner schooling are even more formidable. We must be fully prepared for the inevitable "nasty tricks" that illusion in the higher image worlds will play on us. Yet we can discipline our thinking in such a way that true inner experiences may arise without being damaged by "aberrations of fantasy." As students of spiritual science, the goal is "unfailing mastery" over our whole being. In this way we avoid the seeming clairvoyance that perceives false forms of the spiritual and is only a greater blindness and a major impediment for our unfoldment.

Spiritual scientific training uses the wakeful, conscious mind that is awake in its thinking. It is only in our thinking that we are relatively awake, because we dream in our feelings and sleep in our will. So inner schooling begins with that aspect of the human being with the highest immediate potential of wakefulness. The Michaelic age demands our wakefulness, demands that our cognitive activities be conducted in the daylight of I-consciousness. What we need today, said Steiner, is a conscious spirituality, a state of enhanced consciousness that is reflexively aware of itself engaged in cognitive activities, not the half-conscious or unconscious mind that characterized humanity in the older time of the Mysteries and long before the Christ Event. Everyday waking consciousness is the proper threshold for entering the supersensible—not trance, somnambulism, mediumistic abstraction, or spirit possession.

But this everyday mind must be trained. Perception and thought are the sense-world tools for cutting a groove in the invisible, but they must be regulated by "attentive thinking" and "thinking factually by means of inner force." This means our thinking, our faculty of idea formation, must become sense-free, independent of the objects of the physical-sensory world. For example, Steiner frequently forwarded the meditative image of a circle of seven radiant red roses in the middle of a black wooden cross; this image is not found in the sense world, but must be actively constructed in thinking, or meditative visualization.[1] Sense-free thinking itself is the doorway, Steiner said. "For in thought itself an inner entity is already present that is connected with the supersensible world." Human thinking, after all, is a direct gift from the regent of cosmic intelligence and cosmic thinking, Michael.[2]

The supersensible worlds must be approached with the same intellectual clarity and sobriety of thought with which we examine the natural world of sense perception. The rationality of the intellectual soul—the fruit of the previous post-Atlantean epoch, the Greco-Roman, 747 B.C.–1413 A.D.—must be firmly established before the spiritual inquiry of the new consciousness soul begins its work. The chief characteristic of the intellectual soul is the scientific method for ascertaining objective facts in the sense world. Steiner would have us apply this same rigor of thought in our relations with the occult world, thereby incorporating the fruit of the intellectual soul with the endeavor of the consciousness soul. This extension of the scientific method into spiritual investigation is the hallmark of Steiner's spiritual science. The best clairvoyant, Steiner argued, is one who is a "rational and clear thinking person," who practices "sane, sound thinking," and who exhibits "the greatest clarity of speech." The best preparation for supersensible work is through deepening the logical activity, inwardly intensifying thought, and exercising that same exactness of mind that characterizes mathematics and natural science. From logic to Logos—that's the path of spiritual science. This exactness of mind frees thought from sense impressions and outer experiences, concentrating it into one focused point "which is held entirely under control."[3]

How many of Col. Henry Olcott's sapphics spouting scrub women could claim this kind of intellectual soul pedigree? And how many of *Spirit Speaks'* entranced channeling celebrities have schooled themselves in the scientific manner of forming concepts necessary for reliable metaphysical exploration? Nineteenth-century mediumship and twentieth century channeling both exhibit a great intellectual passivity and scientific flaccidity, not to mention the standard disengagement of the medium's consciousness—if not into oblivion—from the tableau or oration arising within. Without the conscious, discriminating presence of the man or woman in the face of the inner image, there is no guarantee the results are not dreaming, astral chimera, hallucination, or deliberate disinformation. And, if this is the case, we should prudently put no stock whatsoever in their pronouncements.

What is really needed here is to transpose the habits of objective scientific investigation into the activity of supersensible research. Steiner expressed this in a remarkable statement: "Thus is the Natural Science of today the true basis for spiritual seership." In this formulation, Steiner neatly reunites two estranged functions of the Western psyche—rational science and spiritual intuition. During the years 1906 to 1909, Steiner steeped himself in the "fully conscious scientific outlook" of the modern materialistic scientists for whom the external, physical world was the sole reality. But Steiner wanted both to "imbue with inner meaning" this materialist model and to "impregnate the Imaginative world" with its objectively rigorous tenets. Through his studies and meditations he wanted to make a living bridge in his thinking between these two normally disparate realms. Spiritual science is the integration of both poles of cognitive functioning. "This is what the real method of spiritual science ought to be—to enter into the spiritual world along the same path that man has entered into nature during the last three or four centuries."[4]

Spiritual science in terms of its inner logic and mode of thinking, Steiner contended, belongs to the same stream of modern thinking as the natural sciences. The only difference is that natural science researches the apparent physical world while spiritual science investigates the supersensible worlds lying behind the physical. But spiritual science must exhibit that same mental attitude of rigorous exactness, the same clarity, insight, sharp thinking, healthy judgment, intelligent, logical thinking, and meticulous, assiduous attention to detail, that characterize the activities of a biologist or mathematician. The spiritual scientist must avoid indolence, and through a "real exertion and effort" further develop these exemplary thinking habits, acquired through the intellectual soul, and extrapolate them into its penetration and study of the supersensible worlds as the consciousness soul. In other words, both psychic and scientist possess a necessary component of this new integrative spiritual science. The psychic has the experience of the sense-free world but no firm grounding in I-consciousness or reliable habits of scientific inquiry. The scientist has the requisite habits of rigor and method but categorically disallows the consciousness of the investigator as a relevant factor in his investigations; and typically, the scientist acts as if the physical world is devoid of independent intelligence, sentience, or spirit.

The habits of objective science must be retained but the style of thinking needs a transformation, Steiner explained. The prevailing scientific method of thought is one of dismemberment, reductionist dissection, atomic differentiation—a state of mind that demands exact, concretized definitions. In contrast with this, Steiner proposed "formative, Goethean thinking"—spiritual science in the spirit of Goethe. This is a shape-forming, shape-producing way of thinking "closely bound up with the human being" that produces separate pictures, rounded totalities, contours, and colors. It is a Christ-permeated way of thinking that allows for a metamorphosis of forms in a play of "fruitful pictorial concepts." Through formative thinking we retain possession of ourselves and avoid that feeling of dismembered, estranged emptiness that is the dead fruit of scientific thinking by itself. [5]

We retain our integrity through formative, Goethean thinking because in this approach thought is a living, active force. The human is in essence a thought-being, and our thinking is both the starting point in the path to knowledge and the direct expression of what is perceivable in the supersensible world. In other words, our first legitimate contact with the supersensible is likely to be a living picture, a dynamic thought. "So the imparting of this expression acts in the one to whom it is communicated as a germ that brings forth from itself the fruit of knowledge." But the attainment of that precious fruit of knowledge requires "greater intellectual effort" than people are accustomed to. Our thought life must be a copy of "undisturbed mathematical judgments and conclusions," because regulated thinking, inwardly active, takes us from reliable starting points to "the most hidden truths." Our independent thinking, by which Steiner really means sense-free interior picture-making, becomes the "spiritual eye" for perception of the supersensible.[6]

For this spiritual eye to open into true, dependable clairvoyance, we must actively practice conscious involvement in every phase of perception. "In experiencing true second sight we are as active as we are in the physical world in writing on paper," explained Steiner. In spiritual perception it's the hierarchical beings who write on us, but we have to know how to *read* their script. Misinterpretation is easy and can lead to grave errors in understanding. If we have thoughts and concepts that are only mirrors of the physical world, how can we ever decipher what the spiritual beings have written upon our consciousness in their language founded not on sense-bound ideas but on the living, weaving, cosmic thought world? We cannot afford to be slack in this vital process of transcription of the occult texts written upon us by the hierarchical intelligences; yet so often we are. "True clairvoyance requires the kind of active work by the soul we can compare with writing."[7]

Accurate supersensible work, then, requires the exactness of wakeful thinking and our full attentive involvement every step of the way. We must not sleep through our perceptions for only wakefulness can generate cognition. Freedom, again, is the issue. Spiritual scientific training recognizes the necessity of human freedom throughout the process. But freedom is a twofold condition. Freedom means we are free of external compulsion from the coerced guidance of teachers, masters, peers, or traditions, but it also means we are not subservient to inner opinions, prejudices, sensations, feelings, and tendencies of our own, to what's usually called the subconscious. Freedom also means we are free from sense-*bound* thinking, so that we can perform sense-*free* thinking. In this transition the function of willing has paramount importance, for in effect it makes the difference between perception and cognition, between sleeping through our contacts and staying precisely awake.

The function of willing is either our taskmaster, delivering up the compulsions predetermined by our unresolved karma, or it is our potent collaborator in freely extended sense-free thinking. For the will to be active in service of thinking, it must be free from the bonds of unconscious dreams and unclarified feelings. Free also means free to voluntarily take our own path, to make our own discriminations at the important crossroads of growth. Nowhere in Anthroposophy does the individual become a "blind instrument" of established instructions, even Steiner's. Steiner maintained "an unlimited respect for the personal privilege of each individual." The fulfillment of the rules of conduct and the guidelines for practice are always voluntary.[8] This is the Michaelic way.

In keeping with Anthroposophy's unwavering respect for the investigator's independence, Steiner brought forward the role of spiritual advisor, counselor, and senior colleague. Steiner, though an exemplary contemporary initiate, disavowed guru status, Mahatma status; regardless of his own stage of development, he implied, such categories are irrelevant and misleading for the sincere student of spiritual science. Anthroposophy acknowledges only horizontal authority, the individual authority of colleagues. Anthroposophy would not recognize the pre-eminence of the guru, savant, or spiritual autocrat, nor did Steiner exhibit these qualities in his relations with fellow Anthroposophists. Since the Mystery of Golgotha, we have each been on the Michaelic path as individuals evolving towards a legitimate, conscious clairvoyance and etheric perception, finding our way into the supersensible world as independent men and women. Just as the Holy Spirit once touched the crowns of the Christ's twelve Apostles on Pentecost, empowering each to speak *as* the Christ, so in our time will the Pentecostal Spirit touch us all, in a unilateral, egalitarian experience Steiner called World Pentecost.

We'll discuss this later for it is the fruit of this study, but for now let us say that Pentecost empowers each "apostle" to speak equally from the Spirit. When I say "speak *as* the Logos," I mean coherently, passionately, with inspiration, lucidity, and transmission, not in an inchoate babble of tongues or exotic coded syllables. In the age of the consciousness soul we entrust ourselves only to tutors who provide indications, not to autocrats with commandments. "At every step we remain our own master while scrupulously following the indications given."[9] It's far more crucial that we maintain an "absolute direct relation" to the objective spiritual world than allegiance to any particular teacher. There is a certain perfection in the fact that Steiner is not with us today as an embodied human and that we take inspiration and guidance only from his published works and not his charismatic personal presence. So he serves as a tutor from a distance, allowing us complete freedom.

Not only is our independence as spiritual investigators held at a premium, but within Anthroposophy, the path of spiritual scientific development itself is individualized. Steiner may have looked into Rosicrucian, Goethean, and Theosophical methods, and he may have taken scientific degrees, and he may have had respect for historical legacies, but at heart he was a rebel. He went his own individual way. He broke from the materialists, the Spiritualists, the Theosophists, the Lodges—he went his own way, following the indications of the supersensible hierarchy as best he could. He found his way into the supersensible world on his own and he formulated his statements about that world from the rigor of his own judgment. Yet it was his brilliance, and intellectual maturity, to present the results of his philosophical independence within the established context of Western philosophy, initiation occultism, and esoteric Christian spirituality. When Steiner accepted responsibility for the German Section of the Theosophical Society in 1902, no one was uncertain of the fact that he would present only the findings of his direct vision and research. And he would bring forward this knowledge "in his own way" before the Theosophists. Those were his conditions for assuming leadership.

How can the path to the supersensible world be standardized, anyway? The complete truth about spiritual development can be seen only in the example of individual souls. We find a picture of general human evolution through the unique development of a specific individual. There is no such thing as development per se, or anything we could call common, ordinary, orthodox development; there is no generic cookbook for spiritual unfoldment. "For each individual in the world, there must be a different process of development." The condition of the individual at the point of departure from sense-bound materialist thinking determines the subsequent qualities of the path. In practical terms, this means the path of instruction is similarly unique and individualized.[10] The goal throughout is a "community of free and independent Egos." After all, the zodiac has twelve different faces comprising the archetypal Human; and this archetype, in some systems of symbolic astrology (called Sabian Symbols), is further divided into 360 soul qualities, each according to a Degree. Without being overly simplistic, surely there are at least 360 paths into the center of the Ego.[11]

We have looked at the preliminary characteristics of the Anthroposophic path of instruction and noted that of high importance is rigorous training through wakeful, sense-free thinking in a context of freedom, independence, collegiality, and individualization. In light of these criteria, how do the paths of mediumship and channeling, as the most visible and active expressions of the signs of cognitive expansion in our time, measure up? Do they represent a true or false path to spiritual knowledge? Are they suited to the evolutionary needs of the consciousness soul? Are they Michaelic?

Steiner's assessment of mediumship was forthright and unequivocal. Mediumship is an atavistic, elemental clairvoyance, a false spiritual path unsuited to our times. Trance mediumship exhibits old faculties, ancient vestiges of the pre-Atlantean soul resurfacing inappropriately in a later age. The old clairvoyance was visionary, dim like twilight, dreamlike, and elemental. At one time—the cultural period called Lemuria, which preceded Atlantis—it was the natural state of consciousness, but it was a consciousness in which humans were unable to say "I" to themselves, to maintain self-consciousness. It was probably something like the

"Dreamtime" of the Australian Aborigines as we understand it—no doubt inadequately—today. The Lemurian etheric head was still "open" to instreaming cosmic thoughts and inspirations. But the self-reflexive sense of I-consciousness—the sense of being awake and aware during one's cognition and being a wakeful witness to one's awareness—was undeveloped. The evolution of consciousness demanded that humans had to gradually "purchase" self-consciousness, or the Ego-sense, and the concomitant facility for observation of the outer, material world, by the "surrender" of this old clairvoyance. In the age of the consciousness soul, humans can say "I" to themselves in the act of thinking and cognition; traces and manifestations of the old, unselfconscious clairvoyance are abnormal, unreliable, "prone to all kinds of aberrations," and regressive.

That's why Steiner unhesitatingly branded such clairvoyance a false path of spiritual development. By false, he meant unsuited to the present conditions of consciousness and thereby likely to produce cognitive error or developmental disaster. Because this trait was once a standard human faculty its recrudescence in our time comes easily; it is vestigially human but inappropriate to humans today. The essential point here is that the clairvoyant must remain in full control of the experience, as well as fully awake during the experience; if one must decode an occult, symbolic script written upon our inner perception by the sense-free spiritual intelligences, one will never succeed in doing this while somnambulant and dreamy. Trance conditions such as mediumism, somnambulism, and hypnotism, and any other investigations of the supersensible world by a consciousness that is not awake in its thinking, is a "travesty" of modern natural science, "out of date," and a false path, Steiner insisted.

People who want to experience the supersensible world with the same kind of passivity with which they absorb the sense world, without *knowing* it and being awake in their knowing, are treading a false path. Steiner doesn't mean "false" in the sense of a moral judgment, as in a "bad" path; his chief concern was that souls not be led into error or psychic danger, that misleading paths not be upheld as state-of-the-art. Were this a discussion in the realm of science, Steiner would be urging fellow scientists not to be sloppy in their replications of important experiments; otherwise, their results would be judged invalid by their peers. "Every activity that fails to awaken consciousness in the spiritual world, that stumbles along blindly and only looks for effects, as superficial occultism, for example, is on the false path."[12]

Steiner would not have been too impressed with America's Hollywoodish enthronement of the channeling celebrities in mass culture. There is a tacit belief today that channelers are more evolved, more spiritually advanced, than their non-orating contemporaries, that they are all "old souls" with a stunning curriculum vitae of high former incarnations now in beneficent circulation among the lesser evolved to uplift their awareness. Such people would not like to hear Steiner describe them as evolutionary laggards. Atavistic, psychic abilities in themselves do not mean a person has reached the stage of clear thinking, which is the true yardstick for soul maturity in our age. The possession of a natural, unschooled, spontaneous clairvoyance doesn't mean such a medium is more advanced than everyone else; we would be very foolish to be impressed along these lines. Such a person is actually "lagging behind," exhibiting a less developed state of consciousness far less significant than a person with sound, rational judgment. "That this soul shows such abilities means that it has failed to go through certain things that had to be experienced in the age of clairvoyance. People with a natural gift of clairvoyance have gone through far less than those who are thinkers nowadays."[13] The unschooled clairvoyant is actually now struggling to catch up on what he missed in earlier stages of evolution; if the black lodges are successful, we will be hoodwinked into according the trance channels pre-eminent status as highly evolved souls.

The clairvoyant who has been suitably schooled, by contrast, has developed clear, lucid inner seeing on a basis of rational thinking. Ancient humans possessed cosmic vision and instinctive imaginations, but they lacked independent rational thinking, Steiner explained. Their clairvoyance was a nighttime seeing, in which the cosmos permeated their dreaming consciousness. In the Michaelic age, clairvoyance needs to develop from daytime consciousness, from the wakeful state of mind in which actual intellectual activity takes place. The presence of natural, untrained clairvoyant consciousness, Steiner asserted, is due to the "inadequate development of the organs of the intellect." Steiner found it quite common in his time to meet people who had clairvoyancy but almost no scientific intellect. Such people circumvent the normal exercise of thinking by grabbing ready-made thoughts and images out of the spiritual world. "The person in question does not think this out, instead, he *sees* it, bringing it along from the spiritual world."[14] In Steiner's view, supersensible thoughts acquired in this vicarious way were inauthentic and illegitimate, but, worst of all, they posed the metaphysical danger to the clairvoyant of deception or error.

Steiner drew a firm line between psychics and initiates. Reliable, practical cognition of the supersensible world through reading the Akashic Records is possible only through initiation. "The secrets of existence are only accessible to an extent corresponding to man's own degree of maturity."[15] The true source of spiritual science is the "imperishable" testimony of the Akashic Records, but without assiduous inner schooling, there is no guarantee of making an accurate reading. In fact for most people, it's not a question of entering the supersensible world in the correct way, but rather of getting there at all. True gold in occult information is legitimate guidance without inflation. In our time this is a crucial issue affecting our knowledge base and the parameters by which we know and assume that our knowing is accurate—that's epistemology. The 1990's New Age occult intellectual marketplace is inundated with freelance metaphysicians without formal initiatory resumés; bookstalls are glutted with the hastily prepared reports of born-again reincarnate solar initiates, Mayan hierophants, Zeta Reticulan apologists, master cylinder planetary saviors, and Pleiadian spokeswomen, all proclaiming definitive cosmogonies and infallible prophecies with the presumed oracular veracity of Delphi.

The prevalence of inflationary heralds is unavoidably paradoxical as we move into the new style of Aquarian spirituality that emphasizes the individuation and metaphysical competence of the individual arising phoenix-like from the ashes of a now irrelevant priesthood of any persuasion. The trouble is that this Aquarian philosophical carte blanche easily generates an amateurs' bazaar, where the savant *manqué* asserts uncorroborable and often fantastic claims. Traditionally, hard-won, genuine occult knowledge was carefully guarded by the old initiatory lodges (such as the original

Rosicrucians) and transmitted to new students only in the context of a precise schedule of initiations and inner cleansing (a purgation of the astral body called the "Virgin Sophia" in esoteric Christianity) to ensure a requisite soul maturity in the face of valuable, even dangerous, information. Now as psychics and astral cowboys sprout like dandelions in the lawn of the collective psyche, these conventional regulatory protocols are inactive and consumers of metaphysical texts assimilate material at their peril.[16]

What will get the aspiring clairvoyant across the threshold is what Steiner called "methodologically exact head clairvoyance." For spiritual research to be genuine it must be undertaken with the same rigor and clarity the mathematician summons to confront a problem in mathematics. By head clairvoyance, Steiner meant to distinguish the new Michaelic intellectual clairvoyance from the old "belly-talkers" of Rome and Greece. These oracles were thought to have a *daimon* in their bellies that spoke through the medium and foretold the future. Head clairvoyance confronts the whole cosmos and leads to universal, objective knowledge independent of the human being. Information gained through head clairvoyance has "spiritual, lasting significance." This kind of higher clairvoyance is connected with the etheric heart, with a new etheric organ through which we are independent of the physical organism. Head clairvoyance is acquired only through "lengthy, selfless development"—the inner schooling of initiation.[17]

Steiner's life is the best example of the standards he has in mind. His biography exemplifies the judicious balancing of innate clairvoyance with assiduous schooling in rationality. Steiner was always acutely aware of the supersensible world. It was his home. He was more familiar with the spiritual realm than the physical. By his own description, his "bond of union" with that "adjoining world" bore the "genuine character of reality." Direct knowledge of the supersensible had always been for him "self-evident," while his grasp of the physical sense world was fraught with difficulty. In his early years, when he focused on the sense world, it was like "making a visit," passing through a door, a boundary, to make an excursion into the world of others. But how could he not be absorbed in the supersensible when he saw clearly every day that in this adjoining world "the most gigantic facts are happening." When Steiner was a young man working in Weimar on the Goethe archives, he admitted to himself that his experience of the spiritual world had always been "more intense and strong" than his experience of the physical. But when he was about thirty-six this imbalance changed entirely as he entered the sense-bound world.

For years Steiner had schooled himself in disciplines that would foster his intellectual mastery of the sense world. As an adolescent, he had attended the *Realschule* (that specialized in modern science and technology); he had studied physics, mathematics, and geometry. He pored over Kant's *Critique of Pure Reason* which he brought to class camouflaged in his history book. Then he took a college degree at Vienna Technical University. As a young adult, Steiner met and studied with some of Germany's leading scientists, and immersed himself in Goethe's scientific writings. But throughout his early "self-education," he remained at best a tourist in the phenomenal world.

Suddenly, according to a kind of inner clockwork, around 1897 a new attentiveness to the sense-perceptible world arose in him. Now thirty-six, his relations with the material world became easier. He confronted the sense world with an unblemished objectivity, his mind free of all subjectivities. This brought a revelation. Steiner realized that this kind of lucid observation of the physical world in fact leads back into the supersensible. "Thus the spiritual world and the sense-world had at that time become manifest to men in all their contrast." When observing the physical world this way, one goes completely outside oneself, Steiner noted; then one returns with "an intensified capacity" for spiritual perception in the supersensible world. With this kind of perceptual reflexivity established, Steiner felt at home in both worlds; he felt he could extend his wakeful consciousness equally into either domain and make reliable, objective observations.[18]

As he moved increasingly into the public eye as his teaching ministry began, Steiner's anthroposophical colleagues confirmed his ease of residency in both worlds. One contemporary commented on Steiner's deportment during a lecture: "He seemed to be looking away from and beyond the audience, gazing intently at pictures before him. With the greatest delicacy of touch and a most striking alertness and caution, he proceeded to describe these pictures." Steiner formulated his direct perceptions from the Akashic Records into living thoughts and exact concepts that he imparted with clarity and warmth to his audience. He always spoke as if he needed no history texts, but "had himself been an actual witness of all these events." As this same observer remarked, with Steiner there was no question of trance, mediumship, or channeling. When one looked at Steiner, one saw a "super-consciousness" like "the bright sunlight of day."[19]

When we look at the channelers working among us or being upheld as exemplars of the craft today, we may reasonably ask if it is the bright sunlight of day we are witnessing or "the uncanny flashing of rockets by night," as Steiner's commentator drew the contrast. Edgar Cayce (1877–1945), for example, dubbed the "sleeping prophet," is probably America's most famous medium. While in a self-induced trance or sleep state, he spoke an estimated 14,000 readings totaling 12 million words, yet afterwards he was never aware of what he had said. Cayce's sleeping prophet model of trance mediumship is clearly in the Spiritualist atavistic lineage. While it represents a step forward from nineteenth-century materializations to twentieth-century voice phenomena, it is still within the Spiritualist milieu because Cayce slept through the transmissions, refusing, or unable, to remain awake in his I-consciousness during the process.

Perhaps he is best credited as a bridge between the two phases because, unarguably, his received material has benefited many. "In his own mind and memoirs Edgar Cayce was no more a psychic wonder than he was a hypnotic freak—and he probably spent as much time in hypnotic trance as a busy corporation executive spends on the telephone. He thought himself, as his dreams and diaries showed, a man with a job to do—like other men with other talents." But there was a constant danger with Cayce's twice-daily trance sessions. There were occasions when his family or colleagues were unable to rouse him from trance, when he lay for hours in bed, his pulse and respiration flagging, in danger of dying. Every time Cayce put himself into trance in his Reading Room, he literally put his life on the line; while we applaud his courage in service, surely this abandonment of the physical organism during supersensible contact is not an emulable ideal. While awake, Cayce "had a flow of psychic experiences sufficient for an exceptional lifetime without trances." People close to him remarked how he could lift his waking mental ability to an enhanced level after a few moments of intense concentration.[20]

Many among the legions of our contemporary channelers fit this sleeping prophet pattern. Penny Torres Rubin calls herself a "full body channel," because Mafu, her "control," completely incarnates into her body during a session. Jach Pursel, who channels Lazaris, describes his procedure as "objective full-trance channeling." Objective means Lazaris is not part of Pursel's consciousness, while full trance means that Pursel is unaware of what's said during the trance state, according to a Lazaris flyer. Lazaris "himself" says: "We keep the channel in a sleep-like state so that he stays out of the way. It would be possible for him to 'witness' what we say, to 'listen' as the vibrations go by—but we prefer him to be completely out of the way. The best way to keep the information pure is to have the channel be as much a 'pure instrument' as possible." For Eileen Rota, who channels Pretty Flower, the procedure is "full-body synchronization." Pretty Flower, self-described as an old Indian spirit, makes full use of Rota's body, such that Rota, who is in a "trance-like state," walks around with her eyes open, often gesticulating, making toning sounds, even rocking people in her arms. Rota's conscious presence in a given session varies from no awareness to partial consciousness.[21]

Another example of the sleeping prophet channel is Carla Rueckert, who channels Ra, a golden Venusian from our evolutionary future. Rueckert is passive and disengaged and most often enters trance while lying under blankets in bed with her eyes covered. At a certain moment she departs her physical body and Ra enters it to answer questions. "Since Carla has no idea of what has occurred during the session, she is always most curious to know how it went," explains one of Rueckert's colleagues.[22] Jeanette Kandl calls herself a deep-trance medium, who achieves "a level of intensity" similar to Cayce's somnambulism. She has no recall of the information she channels from David, who claims to be the ancient patriarch of Jerusalem; David prefers Kandl to go "elsewhere" when it's time to conduct business. "But when she completely empties out of her body, so that I am in complete command of the body, it is better for her," explains David.[23]

For psychic Ellwood Babbitt, the withdrawal of his consciousness during a channeling session is "exactly like dying." Over the years Babbitt has "manifested" at least 300 different spirit personalities, including, allegedly, Samuel Clemens, Sigmund Freud, Krishna, Abraham Lincoln, Socrates, and the Christ. "So far as I have been able to determine in my experience of 300 readings," explained Babbitt's colleague, "the trance involved in spirit communication is a complete withdrawal of the spirit of the medium from his body, and the entry of another spirit into it...surrendering to that spirit the controls of the body."[24]

Somewhat as a counterbalance to these examples of evident possession by a spiritual intelligence, we can cite the experience of one of Britain's foremost "sensitives," Grace Cooke, who brought through White Eagle, a Christ-centered member of the White Brotherhood. White Eagle construed the trance control as a partnership, "a rising up of the soul of our co-operator in trust, in confidence and in surrender to the communicator." When the medium surrenders to the controlling entity, her personality goes into "abeyance, withdrawn to a higher state." It's like pulling down a shutter, explains White Eagle. When Cooke awakes, she finds the memory of his transmission is "obliterated." In light of the cognitive requirements of the consciousness soul, even with the Christ-centered partnership of White Eagle and Cooke, this approach is not ideal. The waking consciousness of the medium is still eclipsed by the possessing entity, however benign.[25]

Kevin Ryerson became a media psychic celebrity through Shirley MacLaine's endorsement and was the first medium to channel "live" for a television program in MacLaine's 1987 *Out on a Limb*. According to Ryerson, a trance channel is a person who spins consciousness like a radio dial, who is able to set aside one level of consciousness to allow another one to come through. These other levels are usually discarnate intelligences that are "independent of my own thought processes" and which "broadcast" 24 hours a day, available to Ryerson whenever he enters "an altered state not unlike sleep." Ryerson's altered state is evidently a valuable financial asset. "I'm one of the very few people who literally gets paid for sleeping on the job," he quips.[26]

Probably one of the best paid of the sleeping prophet channels is J. Z. Knight, who became a multimillionaire from the astral munificence of her ancient Lemurian father, Ramtha. Knight's description of how Ramtha entered her life and stayed there exemplifies the leading characteristics of this style of atavistic mediumship. Knight claims that Ramtha initially materialized in her kitchen as "a giant man made all of light." Her eyes went glassy, like a sleepwalker, "the power to reason fled my mind and I felt pulled into the splendor of that unearthly magic." When Ramtha arrived the next time, Knight felt as if a strong hand jerked her out of her body and a wind swept her up toward a brilliant light at the far side of a tunnel. Ramtha told her she would "bloom completely" into a channel, but it would cost her something. "You will abdicate the entirety of that which be your body. Thought multitudes shall come to hear and to know, indeed, seemingly, you are left out, indeed, missing."[27]

But when the consciousness of the medium is "indeed, missing," is this any different than possession, the forcible occupation by a disembodied spirit of a living human's mind and body? And when sleeping (millionaire) prophets such as Knight, Ryerson, Pursel, and Torres receive enormous public acclaim (and riches) for their spirit contacts and mastery of *Anthropos abscondis*, isn't this a bizarre exaltation of possession? Clearly we are not looking at examples of consciousness soul activity founded on the wakeful attention and spiritual freedom of the individual. It is unsettling to note how many of the spiritual intelligences prefer the host awareness to step out of the way, to be put to sleep, and rendered inactive in the transmission. The possessing spiritual intelligences in effect take over the body and will of the medium, encouraging them to "abdicate" their incarnational rights and rationality. There is nothing Michaelic about this blatant disregard for the autonomy, however fragile, of the participating medium in these examples.

The next major categorical style for channels is what we might designate the conscious stenographer. This is the inheritor of what Spiritualism called automatic writing, but with considerably more personal involvement and wakefulness than the astral tricks of slate-writing. One of the most famous, and earliest, examples of this style is the journalist-turned-psychic, Ruth Montgomery. Her spirit contacts, which she called The Guides, began in 1956 and would eventually produce an assortment of genial, informative, unpretentious books on various occult topics. "I was ever the skeptical reporter, requiring convincing proof before taking my readers along with me on each of the quantum leaps into a largely unexplored and mysterious realm," Montgomery noted in 1986.[28]

Wayne Hatford's approach to automatic writing is to invoke spiritual protection, enter a meditative state, then wait for the "etheric link" to be established when his handheld pen starts to write by itself. "I let myself be guided by spirit, never knowing what words will follow."[29] Alice Bailey channeled nineteen texts from the Tibetan Mahatma Djwal Khul through wideawake dictation. Her procedure was to assume an attitude of "intense, positive attention," remaining in full control of her sense perceptions. "I simply listen and take down the words that I hear and register the thoughts which are dropped one by one into my brain."[30] Helen Schucman, a Ph.D. research psychologist, had a similar experience when she took "inner dictation" from the "Voice," which spoke the contents of *A Course in Miracles* intently in her mind. "There's no actual sound, and the words come mentally but very clearly," Schucman said. She insisted her procedure was not automatic writing but "scribing," because it always required her full cooperation. "I'm perfectly aware of what I'm doing."[31] That didn't mean she liked it. When the twice-daily dictations began in 1965, Schucman resisted the material, felt apprehensive of its source, and, as an agnostic psychologist, spiritually challenged by its implications. Completed in 1973, the *Course* has been phenomenally popular in the succeeding decades, influencing millions with its Christ-centered self-help spirituality.

For Graham Bernard, who communicates with a deceased friend named Richard, the procedure is "brain impingement." He realized he wasn't just writing words automatically, but that "the words came to me in thought and I found myself writing, with my own handwriting, words that I already knew or thought." Bernard received the words because his disembodied correspondent "impinged" thoughts on Bernard's brain.[32] Ruth White writes down the words of her guide, Gildas, "in my own hand-writing, as if receiving dictation," but it's not until afterwards when she reads through the transcribed material, does she take in the full sense of what was recorded. Her working relationship with

Gildas, a "messenger of truth," is karmically intimate: he told her they were "twin souls" and "perfect partners."[33]

A third category catches a smaller number of contemporary channelers. We might call these the conscious orators. With this group we approach a form of supersensible communication that is on the threshold of appropriateness for the consciousness soul, as indicated by Rudolf Steiner. One of the first contemporary examples of conscious oration was Jane Roberts, channel for an entity called Seth; their work together began in the late 1960s and produced many valuable texts until her death in 1984. Roberts didn't hear so much a voice but whole sentences that sprang seemingly from nowhere, to which she gave speech. She entered a "light trance" during this dictation, whose method of delivery she likened to automatic speech. Her conscious thoughts receded and she lost track of the sense-world environment; yet she felt she could return, voluntarily, at any moment, to her "normal" state of mind. "There is no invasion in our relationship. I do not feel controlled by someone else. My consent is necessary at all times."[34] Roberts also noted Seth's obvious joy and vitality as he spoke through her, declaring, "The personality was not mine." In describing himself and the paradoxes of communication, Seth noted: "I am in this room, although there is no object within which you can place me. I come here as though I appeared through a hole in space and time."[35]

Roberts set a commendable example by her sense of rigor, healthy skepticism, and, with her husband, Robert Butts, her meticulous regard for the conceptual development and integrity of the received material. She also had a keen understanding of human psychology and its intellectual formulations by twentieth-century innovators; this educational background enriched her Seth material and added an edge of continual inquiry and active thinking to her works. A large portion of her work under the tutelage of Seth was to develop a new model of the multidimensional personality. "The Seth Material has completely changed my ideas of the nature of reality, and reinforced my sense of identity. I feel in control of my own destiny as never before, and no longer ruled by patterns subconsciously set during my childhood." While Roberts admitted somebody more familiar with psychic literature and paranormal experiences might have been better prepared for the inexplicable arrival of Seth and subsequent events, she "would not have missed them for the world."[36]

In another medium's experience, the spirit entity itself insisted that he remain conscious during the transmissions, that he come "down to Earth." Initially, Ron Goettsche slipped into deep trance while lying on the couch. A voice named Jason, of "a decidedly different quality," would speak through him; afterwards, Goettsche remembered nothing of the communication. Jason's voice was very slow and labored, a condition caused by Goettsche's lack of conscious presence, Jason explained. Goettsche, by his own admission, had been refusing to be present. "The entity continually expressed a desire that I participate. Jason said their job would be easier if I hung around for the sessions consciously. I am now completely aware and have total recall of each session."[37] In this example, the spiritual intelligence actually insists on the wakeful participation of the human partner in the transmission.

Elisabeth Fitzhugh made her conscious awareness of the channeling session a condition for her participation. She insisted on retaining memory of what Orion spoke through her before she would consent to the exchange. "Thus, intuitively, I accepted the mantle and the responsibility of cognizance. The final choice of entering into this work would always come through my conscious agreement and interaction."[38] When Mary-Margaret Moore's spirit, named Bartholomew, comes through, she feels more "alive, alert, and aware" as her consciousness expands to encompass everyone in the room. "There is a human element still present here in that I am *not* in a trance nor have I been 'taken over' by some separate entity. My consciousness is very much present but my sense of ego seems to fall into the background and let this bolder, faster moving energy lead the way."[39] In these preceding examples we see the emergence of Michaelic qualities of spiritual communication along the lines Steiner indicated as essential for the consciousness soul.

With the examples of David Spangler and Ken Carey, we come much closer to the quality of exchange Steiner regarded as appropriate for the activity of the consciousness soul. Spangler was the young, almost precocious, Findhorn mystic who moved in and out of channeling before the boom even hit the New Age. Spangler never regarded himself as a channel when he relayed to others "the thoughts and images of a disembodied friend of mine named John." Spangler didn't miss that experience when his way of relating and working with John changed.[40] Ken Carey is well known for bringing through angelic voices in his channeling and for being an articulate commentator on the experience of channeling. At the outset, Carey felt "a low humming, an energy field, a Presence," but when he first heard the voice, he cried. The choice to engage the channel opening before him was his. "I decided to take the plunge. I let go and opened myself fully to the experience of blending with the angel. Pictures began to take shape." The messages were nonverbal, more like pulsations that "carried the concise symbolic content of what I term 'meta-conceptual information.'" Carey co-perceived the angelic and human reality in a startling "synthesis," experiencing his body as a "biological radio" that could be adjusted to pick up different "informational frequencies" from a collective memory.[41]

What would Steiner have made of the various reports from channels and mediums today? We are fortunate that he actually gave his endorsement to a slim collection of transcribed spirit letters from 1915, subsequently published as *The Bridge Over the River.* Sigwart, a young musician who was killed in World War I, began communicating with his sister, who was still alive, through conscious stenography. "I myself must open a door in my mind," Sigwart's sister realized when she perceived his presence. "Then I shall hear the words I have to write down." When Sigwart's sister brought the results of this exchange to Steiner to examine, he gave it his imprimatur. "Yes, these are exceptionally clear, absolutely authentic communications from the spiritual world." Transmissions of this kind were very rare, Steiner added.[42] That Steiner approved the Sigwart communications gives us valuable indications of the specific criteria we might use in our own evaluation of channeled texts, in the stream of spiritual science, when we lack the means to clairvoyantly corroborate or refute them on our own.

What are the qualities found in *The Bridge Over the River* that Steiner felt compatible with the rigor of Anthroposophy? Sigwart's sister, as channel, is conscious and wakeful during the exchange and must exert herself deliberately by opening a door in her mind to hear Sigwart's words. The communication is possible because of her qualities of love, faith, courage, understanding, and her close karmic bond with the deceased. Sigwart exhorts her not to mourn his death, to disregard the status of his physical body, and to think of him only in spiritual terms, as this will help him struggle free from the etheric and astral sheaths still enclosing him. Sigwart shows evidence of his own spiritual evolution in the life after death. He moves into a perpetual attitude of love and lives with an expanded awareness; he drops his attachment to his material sheaths and shifts into subtler realms of the supersensible. His after-death chronicle shows a steady spiritual progression, made possible by the cooperation of colleagues and mentors on both sides of the veil. Sigwart benefits from his sister's metaphysical studies and attendance at metaphysical class meetings and they both progress in their understanding of spiritual scientific truths.

Sigwart's letters are valuable, objective descriptions of the supersensible world. They include precise, factual descriptions of astral plane geography, projects, and activities, such as study, writing, music, angelic concerts, and his occasional glimpses of rarefied spiritual beings, including the Christ. He experiences the love and presence of the Christ and realizes that the supersensible world comprises a multilayered hierarchy of spiritual beings undertaking grand cosmic projects. The spiritual advancement of Sigwart's sister actually facilitates his progress and makes their communication easier. Sigwart sketches his life under the guidance of the "Helpers" and "Masters," making it clear that he must fulfill various karmic obligations before his after-death free will is granted. Self-willing is required for improvement and advancement, he emphasizes. As Sigwart advances, the world of Devachan changes; at first it seemed familiar, then it shifted to being "so totally distant from your logic," he told his sister. Sigwart as a supersensible being doesn't display any inflated sense of self. He recognizes his errors in perception and acknowledges that self-deception can occur through any spiritual being. Activity of will is fundamental for self-mastery, Sigwart explains, and that includes his sister's free will in choosing to listen to him. Her participation in this exchange should strengthen not disqualify her for worldly responsibilities. "Be never afraid I might draw you away from your duties—*no*—you should become stronger, more capable, so you can confront them as masters and not as knaves."[43]

Steiner fully agreed with this last point. Supersensible contact should not disable one for full practical relations with the material world. Ideally the seed-results of spiritual scientific investigation take root in the world of men and women and blossom into world-uplifting activities. The supersensible investigator must be able to return home to the sense world "at any and every minute," there to resume life as a "practical, thoughtful human being." Steiner regarded spiritual science as a pursuit of eminently practical usefulness. Anthroposophy's eminently practical expressions—Waldorf education, Camphill curative work, bio-dynamic agriculture, curative eurythmy, water flow research, Anthroposophic medicine—clearly substantiate this point. Supersensible truths have taken root and fructified our world. Spiritual science awakens independent individuals to an experience of community-building. "Through experiencing the supersensible together, one human soul is awakened most intensively in the encounter with another human soul." Because individual souls awaken to higher insight together, "a real communal being" descends into such a group of people who have gathered for the purpose of "mutually communicating and experiencing" Anthroposophy.[44]

Spiritual knowledge, if it's genuine, if it's transmitted correctly, will quicken a human's nature. Spiritual information should help humans find their bearings in life; it should kindle within a deeper love, more understanding. The results are actual life and not dead theory; they come alive in a person and lead one to the whole *Anthropos*, the complete human. Spiritual scientific information makes life in the physical plane more intelligible because, after all, the fundamental aim of knowledge and wisdom is to solve the great riddle of humanity. Anthroposophy, as knowledge of the human being, engenders cosmic feeling, enabling humans to rise up again into the riddling cosmos using their humanness as the starting point. The degree to which revealed spiritual information helps solve this great riddle is itself a prime yardstick of its value and epistemological veracity. Steiner regarded the practical intelligibility of channeled material as a touchstone for correctness. What does it inspire us to do? Does it lead to moral, ethical impulses that improve the world and generate clarity and goodness?

Clairvoyant tidings from the spiritual world must be fruitful for our human colleagues, and this fruitfulness becomes the objective basis for morality, Steiner declared. A true anthroposophical revelation utterly transforms thinking and feeling. Spiritual scientific results are not an accumulation of theories, not simply a change in the contents of our information, but living, catalytic truths that act on our feeling, thinking, and willing, precipitating change, through giving us a true description of our place in the total organism of the Earth and cosmos. When we cognize this place, we are filled with humility and enlivened with responsibility. Anthroposophy places the human at the very center of the cosmos, as the microcosmic, *anthropocentric* concentration of everything in the far reaches of the galaxy. Humans know they are not an earthworm but cosmic beings with responsibilities. "At the moment in which man realizes that he is embedded within the total organism of the earth and has no business being a festering boil on the earth's body—at that moment there exists an objective basis for morality." This recognition of our rightful, awesome place in universal existence invariably produces humility, not arrogance; from this humility arises "the love that proceeds from spiritual truth itself" and the motivation for "the right conduct of life."[45]

This motivation for the right conduct of life engenders a deep sense of responsibility to truth and wisdom. Candid, honest, and sincere truthfulness must be among the highest of standards for the practicing clairvoyant. The forecastings of prophets and the descriptions of supersensible facts are valueless if they aren't permeated by this heightened responsibility for truth and wisdom— "the finest and most important fruit that can be gained from spiritual science."[46] Spiritual science engenders a kind of conscience in the thinking activity and a profound sense of responsibility towards truth and untruth. The occult student must so develop oneself that "logical error is a source of pain to him no less excruciating than physical pain, and conversely, the 'right' gives him real joy and delight."[47]

Wisdom must become our ideal because everything we do, our thoughts, even our moods, influences the cosmos. Nor should we impatiently release brand new supersensible discoveries to the world; a period of inner ripening is required (often years) in which the new insights are kept continuously present in the soul by the conscientious investigator. Further, we should never be content with the conclusions of one standpoint, one survey, one perspective, alone. Clairvoyants who argue dogmatically for one autocratic view should be disregarded. Spiritual scientific issues need examination from multiple angles, from as many as twelve to gain a full view, Steiner insisted. Just as the zodiac represents twelve different, even conflicting, views of the Sun, so, too, must our views of the supersensible be multiple, overlapping, even, paradoxically, contradictory. "We are always conscious of the fact that truth must be approached from many sides and that we must wait patiently until its different aspects merge into a single picture."[48]

And if they don't merge in the cognition of the individual listener, the clairvoyant can't force his influence. The clairvoyant must leave the reader or listener completely free to determine the truth or falsehood of the revealed information. People exposed to the results of channeled material are often at a great disadvantage if they lack the clairvoyant means to corroborate or refute the information. Often we have no reliable way of telling if the information before us is true, distorted, or patently inaccurate. This is most unfortunate because in many respects our life depends on being able to make the discrimination; our intellectual, metaphysical, and spiritual life, that is, if we take such things seriously. A story circulated in various wisdom traditions tells that should a teacher knowingly impart wrong occult or spiritual information to a student or simply a person who inquires, the karmic repercussions are grievous and the compensatory requirements considerable. That's why spiritual teachers are counseled to hold their opinions unless they are absolutely certain they can speak truthfully. This gives us a perspective on the karmic liabilities of propagating incorrect metaphysical information. So we must know how to discriminate, yet largely we do not. This was true in Steiner's day and it is equally so today: How can the nonclairvoyant test the results so as not to be led into error or self-deception?

Steiner was acutely aware of this dilemma and took every measure possible to respect the freedom of each individual Anthroposophist to make an independent determination. Steiner understood that the responsibility to uphold the occult student's freedom lies with the psychic or clairvoyant. The results of supersensible research must be communicated in such a way that "even without clairvoyance, everyone will be able to test them by reference to the normal feeling for truth present in every soul and by applying to them his own unprejudiced reasoning faculties." The fruits of supersensible vision are valueless until the psychic brings them into the range of "ordinary cognition," expressing them in ideas and concepts graspable by "a natural sense of truth and by sound reasoning." Often Steiner set out to substantiate his points, initially obtained clairvoyantly, by logic, analysis, and rational discussion, rather than through authoritative assertion. It's crucial that the clairvoyant fundamentally understand the information, because its value begins "only at the point where the possibility of reasoned proof begins."

Occult information must be thoroughly digested and assimilated and its ramifications allowed to ripen before the clairvoyant can properly present them to the public; commonly, this ripening process may require years, an appalling prospect to impatient Americans particularly, for whom instant gratification is the norm. The clairvoyant cannot simply present the mystical text as received as a self-evident numinous revelation to be consumed by avid but credulous listeners exhibiting no more discrimination than blind faith. Even so, this happens all the time, as the latest channelings are rushed into print. Ideally, the supersensible researcher must take responsibility for presenting the results in such a way that they kindle in each listener warmth, enthusiasm, and vibrant life. Results must be understood, digested, ripened, reworked, "thoroughly tested," and re-presented in a way that's accessible to sound intellectual understanding.[49] These are the anthroposophical standards for true clairvoyance as put forth by Rudolf Steiner, and they are as prescient today as they were in 1910.

When the results of supersensible research are presented in this manner to the public in the form of speeches or printed texts, they can be valuable preparatory aids in developing living concepts. A good text can legitimately start someone on the way. "The character I impressed upon my books is such that their very study is the beginning of spiritual training," Steiner noted. When the author imbues his occult writings with a "living content of the soul," and the reader brings to this an impulse to truly absorb these thoughts, to read the communications about the supersensible worlds in the "right" way, then the reader has already entered the spiritual world through the act of reading.

As Steiner repeatedly advised his colleagues, "in thought itself an inner entity is already present," and this entity is connected with the spiritual world. When, through active, engaged reading, we make what spiritual research offers our own—when we really work with it, thinking it through, picturing it, absorbing it thoroughly—we become accustomed to a mode of thinking and the contents of this mode which are not derivable from sense observations. We become acclimated to sense-free thinking. Understanding precedes seeing, Steiner said, so reading texts of spiritual science is itself the way to cross the threshold into sense-free thinking and participation in the supersensible worlds.[50] In light of this, we see immediately why it is so crucial that there be quality standards and discriminatory parameters for the spate of occult, channeled, and mediumistic material that enters the intellectual marketplace. At least analogically, the situation is akin to the standards of purity and safety upheld by the FDA with respect to food and pharmaceuticals.

The evaluation of the procedures and results of contemporary channelers, whether they are sleeping prophets, conscious stenographers, or conscious orators, must turn on whether the activity exhibits and fosters *Freiheit* and whether it works towards the redemption of Sophia. Is the Sophia-Being brought any further into humanity? Does the Wisdom come into the Human *livingly* through this activity or this text? Is the psychic, channel, medium, or initiate, through this exchange with a spirit being, becoming an anthropomorphic point of Sophia? This is important because Sophia incarnates into humanity only through each single human in which she may live. We must realize at what stakes this game is played: nothing less than the redemption of Sophia is at stake in every text, speech, or document of spiritual information. Each of us, in this Michaelic epoch of the consciousness soul, is responsible for the welfare of Sophia. Sophia shall be born in the world through us. Steiner called this incarnation the "Living Being Anthroposophia." Sophia is anthropomorphized through each individual. The Anthroposophical Movement, Steiner envisioned, would be the collectivity of points of anthropomorphic Sophia. So when we look at channeling, we must ask ourselves: from the

Michaelic perspective of the cosmic intelligence and the human destiny of Sophia, is the communication event before us *anthropo-sophic* in its most profound sense? Is anthroposophy emerging from this spiritual activity?

These are really the questions we must set before us when we look at the fact and the results of spirit communication, in the continuum from Spiritualism and Theosophy to what we might term *Channelism*. For a spiritual, cosmic impulse to enter the human evolutionary stream, it must come through the embodiment and living consciousness of a human—ideally, through many humans. In this way, Rudolf Steiner in his time was the cosmic impulse of Anthroposophy embodied. First through Steiner and then through many, many colleagues, Sophia's redemptive intention, as Anthroposophy, began emerging in the Western civilization of the consciousness soul.

Sophia began to enter livingly into individual men and women, first in the fifteenth century, increasingly since the age of Michael in 1879, and intensively with the close of the twentieth century. Anthroposophia began living among us as well, as a living organism, as an independent living being. The Living Being Anthroposophia, Steiner said, goes about among us and we are responsible to her every moment of our lives. Anthroposophia, who evolved out of the Being Philosophia, is now elaborating the consciousness soul—with us. Humanity looked up to Philosophia "as to a goddess who descends from the divine cloud heights." Now, as Anthroposophia, She emerges from within the human organization itself—from within the consciousness soul, as the Wisdom in humanity. "Everything that is done should be done in consultation with this Living Being 'Anthroposophia.' It is one of the essential life conditions that Anthroposophia should be regarded as a living being."[51] And it is one of the essential life tasks that the Living Being Anthroposophia should enter civilization through the Anthroposophical Movement, said Steiner. This Movement would be her living body of incarnation. Each Anthroposophist would be a point of living anthropomorphic Sophia, an embodiment of Wisdom in humanity. This will mark the beginning of "a new cosmic age."

This was the mood informing the Christmas Foundation Meeting of December 25, 1923 to January 1, 1924, in which Steiner rededicated the Anthroposophical Movement. In this remarkable conference at the Schreinerei at Dornach, Steiner laid the Foundation Stone, both for a new Goetheanum and a revivified Anthroposophy, in the hearts of the 800 men and women gathered with him. The 1923 Christmas Foundation Meeting was the culmination in Steiner's time of an impulse that arose in 1902 when he became head of the German Section of the Theosophical Society, and that deepened in 1913 when he and 2,500 colleagues broke off from Theosophy, formed the Anthroposophical Society, and laid the Foundation Stone for the first Goetheanum on Dornach Hill. The impulse may well be traceable back to the supersensible Michael school that spanned the thirteenth to fifteenth centuries in which numerous souls planned the future birth of Anthroposophy.

"The Christmas Meeting was no trifling episode," said Steiner. "It betokened the assumption of new responsibilities for the Anthroposophical Movement flowing from the realm of the spirit."[52] The meeting was a "festival of consecration" in which something was undeniably present from the spiritual worlds, Steiner explained. The spiritual powers were "responding with an ever greater measure of grace, with ever greater bounty." It was the beginning of a "turning-point of worlds" and a "new revelation" under the dominion of Michael that heralded "a renewed and transformed truth of the Christ Impulse." The Christmas Foundation Meeting was far more than a festival week; it was a conclave on behalf of the future. It will be an impulse affecting the whole world and the destiny of humanity, Steiner declared afterwards. It was a fundamental renewal and a new foundation in which Anthroposophy was established on a new basis—on the human element which would be cultivated within the Society.[53]

Steiner intended that the public work of Anthroposophy from that point forward would be permeated with an esoteric stream. From that moment hence, the Mysteries would be made public, and people would be taught genuine spiritual knowledge in stages. The Christmas Meeting inaugurated a new era in which concrete facts of the spiritual life would be "fearlessly" brought forward, declared Steiner. Spiritual flames of fire would go forth from the new Goetheanum at Dornach. An impulse originating in the spiritual world would radiate out from the rededicated

Anthroposophical Movement. Esotericism would become a living power, a living seed, among Anthroposophists. "If Dornach is to fulfill its task, actual happenings in the spiritual world must be spoken of openly. In Dornach there will be created a living center of spiritual knowledge."[54]

The Anthroposophical Society would provide the foundation for the future life of the Mysteries, Steiner said, looking ahead into "far cycles of time." The Goetheanum at Dornach would become a new Mystery center for the Michaelic age of the consciousness soul. In that epiphanous moment in Dornach in 1923, Anthroposophy was seeded for the future—for the late twentieth century and beyond, for the duration of the epoch of the consciousness soul, at least. What the Anthroposophists accomplished during their nine days at Dornach that year was "by way of preparation." By their work and concentration, they fulfilled their "duty" to the future—which is our time. The seeds of Anthroposophia would germinate worldwide. The Living Being Anthroposophia would incarnate within men and women in all nations as Wisdom in the Human.

Steiner foresaw how in the "near future" it would be possible to "speak with greater precision, when a great deal that can now be only of the nature of indication may perhaps be discerned with far, far greater exactitude in the spiritual chronicle of World-Becoming."[55] Now, seventy years after the Christmas Foundation Meeting, we can discern with far greater exactitude Steiner's indications about that fundamental dichotomy of Being he called Lucifer and Ahriman, central to the outcome of our World-Becoming. As Steiner formulated it, the archetypal polarity of Lucifer and Ahriman lies ambivalently at the basis of Anthroposophical cognition. In the next chapter, we examine the consequences and opportunities of the Holy Ghost caught in Time expressed in the vexatious ambivalence of Lucifer and Ahriman in the soul life of humanity.

PART III

"HUMAN"

THE HOLY GHOST CAUGHT IN TIME:

The Ambivalence of Lucifer and Ahriman

across the Threshold

CHAPTER 7

Zurvan's Progeny

The Cosmic Battle of Lucifer and Ahriman

in Humanity

*T*HE AKASHIC RECORDS reveal a remarkable moment at the beginning of the material Earth and just preceding the original incarnation of humankind into this virgin domain. In that moment outside of time, before Time began on this planet, a celestial being, first known as the Lord of Light, then later as Phosphoros, and still later as Lucifer the Light-Bringer, stood upon the virginal Earth contemplating his dominions. The Earth was Lucifer's dominion because it was created in his image, as were its self-conscious future inhabitants, human beings. The Earth was made in the Human's image, as were humans, and that image of the Human was livingly embodied by Lucifer, the supersensible expression of the Holy Ghost as Human.

Lucifer bore the Light of the creation as the Human. Lucifer was then, as the Hebrew legends still recall him, an archangelic figure of stunning majesty and effulgent light. On the third day of creation, Lucifer—Son of the Dawn, and God's chief archangel charged with the guardianship of all nations—walked in Eden, the realm of living light, his body afire with blazing jewels—the spiritual lights of the zodiac, conclaves of attending angels—all set in purest gold.

One radiant jewel amid Lucifer's raiment of light was especially prominent, a bright green emerald residing at his heart. The blazing light from this emerald was more blinding than the Sun itself. With this cosmic heart-centered brilliance of his own being,

Lucifer irradiated the Earth and the numerous spiritual denizens who were then present in bodies of light, completing the necessary advance preparations for the coming physical incarnation of human souls. It was as if a green phosphoric beacon of terrific potency swept across the land, fixing the pristine Earth in Lucifer's contemplative, benevolent regard. The spiritual beings laboring to prepare the Earth for the human residency beheld the lovely Light-Bringer with awe and appreciation, enraptured by the beautiful spectacle of Lucifer' s independent, self-aware, cosmic intelligence and the tremendous promise it held for the humanity about to incarnate, for whom Lucifer had cultivated it.

With Lucifer's momentous presence, the Earth was seeded forevermore with the illumined heart-light of self-consciousness and cosmic wisdom, alive and resident in the diaphanous light body of the perfected, primordial Human. Through this act, Lucifer engaged himself with humankind living on Earth. By irradiating the Earth, Lucifer cast his light—his own being—into time, and his heart-seed became conditioned by the demands of biological, evolving human life in time. The fulfillment of his promise to incarnating humanity would be dependent on their own voluntary, freely willed effort to cultivate their cognitive birthright, to consciously engage themselves in Lucifer's grand endowment of Sophia's cosmic intelligence. By entering the realm of Time, which would be the life of biological humanity, Lucifer cleaved his own being in accordance with the ineluctable duality of existence in time and space which is, provisionally, the fundamental human experience. That was Lucifer's sacrificial investment on humanity's behalf in the context of a newly created planet—to be the Holy Ghost caught in Time in the context of Earth.

But that wasn't how Lucifer's intentions and his sacrificial act would be remembered. Lucifer's overweening pride turned his wits, the Hebrew legends tell us, such that he announced he would ascend above the clouds and stars to enthrone himself on the Mount of Assembly as God's equal. As punishment God cast Lucifer from Eden to Gehinnom, the Bottomless Pit within Earth. Lucifer shone like phosphoric lightning as he plummeted from grace but his light form was reduced to ashes, his high spirit condemned to "flutter blindly without cease through profound gloom" in the bowels of Earth.[1]

For his humanitarian sacrifice, the once-radiant Lucifer has been memorialized as the groveling, arch-devil Satan—tempter, seducer, corrupter of humankind, fomenter of unconscionable evil. For centuries the fallen Lucifer, in standard exoteric Western thinking, has been the scapegoat for a humanity that refuses to take cognitive responsibility for his gift of independent intelligence—*Freiheit* embodied. Isaiah's famous Biblical declamation (Isaiah 14: 12–15) encapsulates the conventional pejorative view of Lucifer that has dominated Western thinking for the last two thousand years. "How art thou fallen from heaven, O Lucifer, son of the morning. For thou hast said in thine heart, I will ascend to Heaven, I will exalt my throne above the stars of God: I will sit also upon the mont of the congregation, in the sides of the north: I will ascend above the heights of the clouds; I will be the most High."

Thus Lucifer has remained, up to the present day, the Holy Ghost caught in Time, the ambivalent Light-Bringer, half-archangel, half-devil, a celestial spirit imprisoned in matter. This primordial bifurcation of the Human has perennially vexed the human being living in Time; so profound have been its implications that the individual consciousness of every man and woman bears the trauma of this primordial cleavage. The Luciferic dichotomy has fragmented Sophia, the Wisdom-Bearer, and obstructed Michael, the Wisdom-Guardian, and thereby sundered cosmic intelligence from the rightful cognition of humanity.

Until Lucifer is rendered whole again through a redemptive act, the revelation of Sophia cannot be imparted and the Michaelic mission to bestow upon humankind the incalculable gift of independent cosmic cognition will remain stalled. This is how matters stand, then, even in our own day, the Michaelic epoch of consciousness soul culture, in which the possibility—the urgency—of Lucifer's redemption looms imminently on the horizon of human life. And, standing as both midwife and obstructor on the threshold of this desperately required work of Luciferic redemption, is the Anthroposophical Movement. Regrettably, the Anthroposophical Movement, and its body of received thought from Rudolf Steiner, is today as ambivalent about Lucifer's redemption as it is about the Holy Ghost it continues to bifurcate in its thinking. Steiner did not conceive of Lucifer as the Holy Ghost caught in

Time; after 1910, he quite unwaveringly adhered to a dualistic, adversarial model that posited Lucifer against Ahriman in a dialectic resolved only through the intervention of the Christ. Before 1910, however, Steiner's thinking was more amenable to the different model of Lucifer and Ahriman I will propose in this chapter.

The bifurcation of Lucifer into Lucifer and Ahriman is central to Steiner's anthroposophical formulations. It is also foundational to everything in this book; to appreciate the opportunity of the Imagination of Pentecost, as a spiritual experience, we need to understand the lives and activities of these two great spiritual beings of the cosmos. To understand Steiner's thinking about this profound subject, we must highlight the context from which he drew his metaphysical contents. Just as Steiner had drawn from the Gnostic views of Sophia for the underpinnings of his thinking on cosmic intelligence, so he took his model of the twofold Holy Ghost from the earlier dualistic thinking of Zoroastrianism. In the Zoroastrian system, there is *Spenista Mainyu* ("Bounteous Spirit," later Ahura Mazda) and *Angra Mainyu* ("Destructive Spirit," later Ahriman). Thus, to understand Steiner's Ahriman—which in name and nature clearly derives from the Zoroastrian concept—we must examine the roots of this conception, and those roots lie in the ancient revelation of Zoroaster.

In later Zoroastrian thought, both *Spenista Mainyu*, as the good Being of light, and *Angra Mainyu*, as the evil Being of darkness, were seen to emanate from the one universal principle called *Zurvan akarana*, or "uncreated, infinite Time."[2] Zurvan is an ineffable domain similar to the Gnostic's primal Aion of the "unbegotten Father." The primal principle of Zurvan evokes the calm, undisturbed flow of uncreated cosmic Time. Zurvan is thus father to both the Bounteous Spirit and the Destructive Spirit (essentially, Lucifer and Ahriman), Steiner realized. These are "two phases proceeding from the hitherto undivided flow of Time— two phases coming into conflict as they encounter one another and resolving their conflict only in the stream of on-flowing Time."[3]

Steiner never provided more than an indication of the Zoroastrian conceptual roots of the onflowing Time of Zurvan from which he elaborated Anthroposophy's dualistic conception of Lucifer and Ahriman, but his occult predecessor, H. P. Blavatsky, was more forthcoming with mythological and metaphysical correspondences. Zurvan is the unknowable, uncognizable deity of boundless space, the Unknown Cause, the One who has always existed, limitless Time in Eternity, the "Boundless Circle of the Unknown Time." Zurvan's glory is "too exalted, its light too resplendent for either human intellect or mortal eye to grasp and see." The primal emanation of Zurvan was eternal light that had previously been concealed in Darkness, said Blavatsky, esoterically paraphrasing the Zoroastrians. From this Circle of the "ever-unmanifested Principle" issues the radiant, creative, and generative light of the Logos, the universal Sun known as Saturn/Kronos, Horus, Brahma, or Ahura Mazda. From the eternal light was formed Ahura Mazda, the "King of Life, the first-born in Boundless Time," and "first Father of the Righteous Order."[4]

As the Iranian god of Time, Zurvan was deified in two forms: as *Zurvan akarana*, meaning Infinite Time, and as *Zurvan dareghokhvadhata*, meaning Time of the Long Dominion, or Finite Time. Zurvan as Finite Time, represented a 12,000 year duration that rules human life, bringing old age, decay, and death. This form was portrayed afterwards in Mithraism as a lion-headed human monster with wings, astride a planetlike sphere with a long staff and keys, and entwined by a large serpent on whose body were inscribed the time-bound signs of the zodiac. This Mithraic lion-man is remarkably similar to the Gnostic lion-faced Ialdabaoth. As one ancient Persian text declared, "For Zurvan there is no remedy; from death there is no escape." The Indian *Bhagavad-Gita* expressed a similar sentiment in its equivalent view of Zurvan as the Time God Vishnu, creator-sustainer of the universe: "Know I am Time, that makes the worlds to perish, and come to bring on them destruction."

This primordial scission of Zurvan as Time "without limit" (*Zurvan akarana*) and Time "long to rule" (*Zurvan dareglo-khvadhata*) seems to prefigure the later dualism of Ahura Mazda and Ahriman. As such, Zurvan is the ambivalent creator god, imperishable and infinite, and the lord of the Three Ages of the Human, which is to say, the god of death and Time that rules and destroys all life. Creation (*Bundahishn*) was the first Age, the primordial dispensation of Time and Light as Ahura Mazda from the Boundless; next came Mixture (*Gumezisn*), which was Angra Mainyu's attack on the purity of creation whereby the world became a dualistic mixture of good and evil; the third Age will be Separation (*Wizarishn*), a time of healing and renovation, when the original good is separated from the subsequent evil.[5] In the Creation Age, Ahura Mazda pronounced the *Ahunvar*, the twenty-one sacred words of *Yatha ahu vairyo*, the Word of Truth, a cosmically potent mantra that revealed to Angra Mainyu his assured, complete destruction after 9,000 years of battle. In the Mixture Age, however, Angra Mainyu responded with the *Akoman*, the Lying Word of the Evil Mind. Thus was their cosmic dialectic enjoined.[6]

Zarathustra's original formulations excluded the concept of a primogenitive Zurvan; later Zoroastrians, possibly heretical, added Zurvan out of metaphysical necessity. Two primordial coeval spirits named *Spenista Mainyu* and *Angra Mainyu* represent the opposing universal forces of light and dark, life and death, good and evil, Zarathustra posited. Ahura Mazda, "the wise, omniscient Asura, the wise Lord, the knowing one,"[7] upholds the principle of good order, called *asha*, while Angra Mainyu, "inimical, enemy spirit, spiritual foe," stands for falsehood and "the Lie," called *Druj*.[8] As Zarathustra's *Yasna* text declared, "The two primal spirits who revealed themselves in vision as twins are the Better and the Bad in thought, word, and action." But only the wise know how to choose correctly between better wisdom and the bad lie, cautioned Zarathustra.

According to legend, Zarathustra was taken by the angel *Vohu Manah* ("Good Thought") into the presence of the great Sun spirit Ahura Mazda. There he appreciated Ahura Mazda's manifold golden qualities. Ahura Mazda is the spirit of light and wisdom, perfectly good, merciful, benevolent, a pure, intangible spirit, dwelling in eternal, endless light. He is the god of the supreme law of justice and truth, the supreme guardian of the moral "righteous order" (*asha*) of truth and law, inspiring good deeds, words, and thoughts so that aspirants can attain the kingdom of blessings.[9] Ahura Mazda is the wise lord of "marvelous science and mysterious power," surrounded by a glittering court of "beneficent immortals," the *Amesha Spenta*, similar to the 30 Aions who comprise the Gnostic Pleroma. Ahura Mazda created the celestial sphere, filling it with constellations and the signs of the zodiac, and assigning to 6,480,000 stars their precise location in the cosmos. Although Ahura Mazda existed before the creation of the world, he is limited by the coeval existence of his twin brother and Evil Spirit, Angra Mainyu, whom he banished into the "darkness of Hell" at the beginning of Time.

The negative attributions of Angra Mainyu as the *Druj*, the chief agent of the Lie, are far more frequently enumerated in the Zoroastrian Gathas than are the positive qualities of his perennial opponent, Ahura Mazda.[10] In the Persian Gathas, *Druj* meant falsehood, deception, and wickedness—the fundamental Lie. Angra Mainyu created the *Aka Manah* (or *Akoman*, the Evil Mind) as a direct counterposition to Ahura Mazda's *Vohu Manah* ("Good Mind"). His most common epithet in the Gathas, which are vituperous with his condemnation, is "full of death." Angra Mainyu is all death, a tyrant, of evil creation, religion, and knowledge, inveterately wicked, of evil glory, the worst liar, the consummate deceiver, the sower of disorder; he's deadly, having infected mortal bodies with disease and decay, made plants poisonous, and, concomitantly, corrupted humanity's moral nature. Angra Mainyu lures humans to destruction through deceit, producing seductive demons to pervert humankind, infecting the Earth with mephitic creatures who abide in "endless darkness," leading "the worst life, in the abode of Deceit and of the Worst Thought."

These malevolent *drujas* exist solely to disfigure the beauty and perfection of Ahura Mazda's creation.[11] Angra Mainyu killed *Gayomart*, the primeval, original Human, and *Goshurvan*, the primeval world ox. Angra Mainyu is the essence of absolute, unredeemed evil, always preferring wrong-doing; he's filled with ignorance, malice, and perversity. This Destructive Spirit arose from the abyss of endless darkness oblivious of either Ahura Mazda or his own inevitable doom; he has knowledge only of past events and lies in "a darkness so thick that the hand can grasp it."[12]

The history of the conflict between Ahura Mazda and Angra Mainyu is the story of the created world itself, said Zarathustra. When these coevals first encountered each other and their creative activity and perpetual conflict began, their strife divided creation in half. Their field of battle is the present world; their focal point is humanity's consciousness. The outcome hinges on the choice of wise men and women; it's a choice because Ahura Mazda created humans to be free in their actions, a beneficence that also made them accessible to the evil machinations of Angra Mainyu. It is up to humans to choose the victor.

The *Druj* may be coeval with Ahura Mazda, but he isn't coeternal, according to the Gathas; Angra Mainyu will not, like Ahura Mazda, endure forever. In the third Age of Renovation, he will be defeated and annihilated by Ahura Mazda, his better half. Ontologically, however, there is still a fundamental problem implicit in this equation that was realized by the later Zoroastrians. "Though he is to be finally conquered by Ormazd, he is no emanation from him and his being is the limitation of Ormazd, who, as an unavoidable consequence of dualist principles, cannot possess infinity."[13] Further, since these two principles always existed uncreated, they are inherently equal, which means there is no eschatalogical guarantee that Ahura Mazda can triumph over his equal. What if their mutual opposition, too, is eternal? The Zurvanite heresy (circa 200–651 A.D.), wherein Zurvan was brought forward as progenitor of both Ahura Mazda and Ahriman, was the resolution to this limitation of the wise god, Ahura Mazda; the introduction of Zurvan would be the guarantor of Ahura Mazda's primacy.

The Zoroastrian duality of Ahura Mazda and Angra Mainyu was carried forward into relatively recent Western culture through the ambivalent demon-savant Mephistopheles, as depicted in Goethe's *Faust*.[14] Goethe presents Mephistopheles in the guise of a noble squire and wandering scholar, attired in red and gold, with a cloak of silk brocade, a rooster's feather in his cap, and a long nicely pointed blade under his belt. The pure soul, Gretchen, sees through his fair semblance to his meretricious core. For her, Mephistopheles' eyes are repulsive and give her heart a sharp sting, and his presence makes her ill. In all, he is a knave not to be trusted, a "freak of filth and fire." Through his grin, half-mocking, half-threatening, Gretchen knows Mephistopheles has sympathy for nothing. Faust, of course, is considerably less discerning at first, and welcomes Mephistopheles' offer to broaden his cognition of the world and its perennially veiled secrets. Of himself, Mephistopheles declares cavalierly that he is the spirit that negates, whose proper element is sin, destruction, and evil, that he is part of the darkness that gave birth to the light. He is the Lord of Lies who, through magic and illusion, abets Faust's confusion.

Mephistopheles dazzles Faust with dream shapes, plunging him into an ocean of untruth and near ruin.

Yet the simulacra of Mephistopheles is a kind of virtual truth condoned, if not commissioned, by "the Lord," as Goethe explains in the Prologue in Heaven. There the swaggering Mephistopheles makes a wager with the Lord that with his "arts" he can corrupt Faust and relieve him of the misery of the gift of reason. "His life might be a bit more fun/Had you not given him that spark of heaven's sun/He calls it reason and employs it, resolute/ to be more brutish than is any brute." Through the artful machinations of Mephistopheles, the spiritually desperate Faust peers through the outer veils of existence, then experiences the social results of magical manipulation fueled by personal desire. Faust in the end repudiates Mephistopheles, branding him a sophist and liar.

Even so, as, ostensibly, a literary portrayal of Ahriman, Mephistopheles' character strangely includes a few of the better, brighter aspects of Ahura Mazda. Unlike Faust, the grim, frustrated alchemist, Mephistopheles has a bright sense of humor, a wit that's broad, earthy, and acidic; he even laughs uninhibitedly at himself. He has keen psychological perception and is not swayed by the human facades of convention or pretense. He might be radically dishonest in issues of self-interest, but "he confronts us with a rarely equalled candor just when Faust's enthusiasm outsoars all scrupulous concern with truth or honesty."[15]

It was precisely Goethe's enthusiasm in blending some of Ahura Mazda's bright qualities into that monolithically evil agent of the *Druj*, Angra Mainyu, that outsoared what Steiner contended was the true, "factual" conception of this existential polarity. This conception, Steiner claimed, must be triadic, not dualistic. "We must emphasize the fact that if a person wishes to conceive of the structure of the world in a factual manner, he must acknowledge the triad, the two opposing elements of the Luciferic and Ahrimanic and the Divine element which holds the balance between the two."[16] Throughout his writings, Steiner took Goethe to task for the terrible mistake of consolidating the bright and dark aspects of Ahura Mazda and Angra Mainyu into a single Mephistopheles. Goethe, "in his characterization of Mephistopheles, constantly confused the Luciferic and Ahrimanic elements. Goethe's Mephistopheles is a figure mixed, as it were, of two elements."[17] This "jumbling up" of two cosmic elements, said Steiner, has entered modern consciousness as the "delusion of the duad."

In Steiner's appropriation of the original Zoroastrian world view, Ahura Mazda is the personification of the divine element, the great Sun Spirit, the great Sun Aura and sublime spiritual being who guides humanity back from the physical to the spiritual—in effect, the Christ. The factual structure of the world is too subtle to conceive of Ahriman as carrying the full burden of spiritual opposition to an aspiring humankind, Steiner said. There are in fact *two* spiritual foes working against the higher nature of the Human: these are Ahriman and Lucifer. Ahriman deceives us into thinking our inner being alone is self-sufficient, while Lucifer exposes humans to illusions when they form conceptions of the world. "One grows out of man's willing and feeling nature, the other out of his intellectual nature." Goethe "constantly confused" and intermingled the Luciferic and Ahrimanic elements in his over-simplified Mephistopheles, thereby hindering the reader and subsequent Western cultural thinkers from developing a "uniform picture" of these two cosmic elements.[18] Goethe's nineteenth-century Mephistopheles, implied Steiner, was a metaphysical disservice that needs to be corrected by newer, twentieth-century anthroposophical formulations.

The profound cosmic dialectic between Lucifer and Ahriman permeates every aspect of human existence, said Steiner, who made this neo-Zoroastrian conception of duality the cornerstone of his anthroposophical thinking. But Steiner thought more subtly into this perennial duality than had the earlier Zoroastrians. "Lucifer and Ahriman are now in league together in a kind of partnership in the outer world," he announced. Their forces are knotted together, their threads interwoven in a "higgledy-piggledy" nature. Ahriman assaults our intelligence with destructive forces, encouraging an "objective occultism" (or occult materialism); Lucifer pervades our soul life with egotistical "fumes of spiritual ecstasy," encouraging a "subjective mysticism" (or inflationary spirituality).

Their means might differ but, consensually, their target is the human soul, and that soul is particularly, acutely, imperiled as it approaches the threshold of the supersensible worlds. This fact is the true "secret" of the threshold; not knowing this puts us at extreme peril in any occult activity, any gesture of cognitive expansion, any easy clairvoyance. At this significant moment of approach, Lucifer and Ahriman join forces and bar the entrance to the supersensible domain. The moment we step across the threshold between physical and supersensible worlds, Lucifer and Ahriman form an alliance and "together bind the petals of the lotus flowers to the elementary backbone."[19]

The result is spiritual chaos, cognitive disaster. As we will make clear in this chapter, this is the crux of the liability with all forms of contemporary cognitive expansion, whether it's talking with angels, channeling diaphanous ETs, or transiting cyberspace under virtual light. Because of the complex structure of the supersensible world and the inexorably ruthless laws of the threshold, we may easily put ourselves in significant danger *without even knowing it.* As Steiner outlined it, the minute we cross the threshold, unless we are vigilant and prepared, we may be oblivious to the fact we have been jumped, bound up, gagged, and cognitively sullied. That of course is what the Brothers of the Left hope will happen to us because then we will be subject to a myriad of errors, misperceptions, misattributions, and help spread occult chaos in the world.

What Steiner called lotus flowers the Eastern esoteric tradition describes as chakras, the seven subtle, consciousness-energy vortices arranged vertically with reference to the human spine and the endocrine glands. Both views agree that the lotus flowers or chakras are the astral eyes of perception in the supersensible world, so, if they are bound up by interfering, malevolent spirits, this is a perilous state indeed, particularly, if, as is usually the case, the threshold-crossing human is unaware of this major cognitive impairment. And if the lotus flowers are bound up and incapacitated by two celestial beings with ill intent, this is a human impairment of cosmic proportions. The human is immediately assailed by a greater flush of egoism and a greater love of deception than one would ever normally encounter in the physical world. The binding of the lotus flowers fetters a person "within himself by means of his own elemental or etheric capacities," as Lucifer and Ahriman have "an easy game with the soul."

It puts us into a kind of solipsistic occult imprisonment and cognitive cocoon not unlike what Blavatsky endured. Through this binding, Lucifer and Ahriman lead the unprepared, and now hindered, souls into their own special kingdom and regale them with a gallimaufry of spiritual chimera, corrupting them with "all sorts of spiritual worlds which the human being will take for the truly genuine one grounded in the cosmic order." Lucifer and Ahriman permeate our visions and heard voices with a strong tendency to misinterpretation; what we think is clairvoyance is objectively, only *pseudo*-clairvoyance.[20] With the flowering of the consciousness soul into etheric cognition in the late twentieth century, the cognitive peril of this Luciferic-Ahrimanic alliance cannot be overstated.

Why are Lucifer and Ahriman so determined to undermine true, factual human cognition? They want to capture human souls and imaginations for their own "bogus creation in the universe, created in opposition to the progressive Spirits," a supernumerary "planet" Steiner called the Eighth Sphere. This is one of Steiner's more abstruse, difficult concepts, but as he formulated it, the Eighth Sphere is an unlawful domain set like "a solid blue wall limiting everything in space" at the boundary of the seven planetary spheres (Saturn, Sun, Moon, Earth, Jupiter, Venus, Vulcan—which is to say, "the domain of the ordered and regular evolution of humankind") and the domain of the fixed stars. But the Eighth Sphere's limitation of cosmic space is false, only apparent; formerly, humans considered the boundary of space to be nothing other than the limits of human sense-bound perception. Then Lucifer and Ahriman constructed this meretricious limiting membrane and strove to enrich it with "constituents made into imaginations" from Earth, the Fourth Sphere.[21]

Elements and forces from the Old Moon substantiality, the Third Sphere, are also involved. In fact, as we proceed through Steiner's full conceptualization of Lucifer and Ahriman, we will discover that the Old Moon astrality is central to the activities of these two celestial beings in the life of humanity. For the moment, it's important to note that the Eighth Sphere is really a triangulation of Lucifer-Ahriman, the Old Moon, and Earth. Through a complex process of cosmogenesis, the Eighth Sphere is manifested out of the Third Sphere. As the Old Moon/Third

Sphere advanced towards its new expression as New Earth/ Fourth Sphere, Lucifer and Ahriman wrested valuable substances away from the Spirits of Form, supervisors of that stage of development, and permeated this Old Moon substantiality with their own being. Through a kind of spiritual piracy and unsuspected alchemy, Lucifer and Ahriman constantly remove Earthly mineral substance to build their own Eighth Sphere.

This makes more sense when we remember that the evolution of Old Moon to New Earth meant that what was formerly only imaginatively perceptible (the spiritual essence of the planetary spheres expressed through metals like gold, silver, and iron) became materially perceptible, or mineralized, with the creation of Earth. Metals became physically tangible and visible, a rare creation in the mostly supersensible universe. The importance of Earth in this sense is that it represents the "mineral impregnation" of a world body. The supersensible mineral world was born materially as Earth. Lucifer and Ahriman require this minerality to make their Eighth Sphere more materially present; their work is a kind of materials piracy on behalf of planet creation. As Steiner described it, as the Earth mineral comes into physical existence from out of the imaginative substantiality of the Old Moon, Lucifer and Ahriman snatch it up and alchemically transform it into imaginations for their evolving Eighth Sphere. In other words, what is destined to be physical substance—supersensible minerals densifying into earthly materiality—is unlawfully appropriated and made to serve the etheric materials need of the nefarious Eighth Sphere.

The result is a planetary sphere made of mineralized, "densified" imaginations, a world of ghosts and specters lacking the subtlety of Old Moon. This means living thoughts and pure imaginations are weighted down with the infusion of mineral materiality, "a Moon-sphere filled with Earthly substantiality." It was as if the orderly progressive advancement from Old Moon to New Earth was interrupted—cosmically hijacked—by this "behind the scenes" machination of the Lucifer-Ahriman alliance. Now their Eighth Sphere is parasitically attached to Earth, but later, when it is sufficiently advanced, Lucifer and Ahriman will detach it, enabling it to "go its own way" in the cosmos. Their intention is that all of humanity and ultimately all seven spheres will disappear into this detached, free-ranging, black-hole vortex, the Eighth Sphere. So behind the scenes of ordinary perception, "while Lucifer sucks the juice out of the lemon, Ahriman presses it out, thereby hardening what remains."[22]

What remains could be the soul-less husk of a human being, Steiner warned. Lucifer and Ahriman strive collegially to drag human free will and all its issues, lawfully developed on Earth, into their illegitimate Eighth Sphere. When free will is transformed (or captured) into visionary clairvoyance, then it's already too late. Lucifer and Ahriman have sucked the individual as booty into their domain, where they conjure all sorts of things before him; so yet another Eighth Sphere specter is created. This translation is acutely active when the free will of "naive, credulous, superstitious people" is shackled into visionary clairvoyance; the "awful, terrible truth" is that while these individuals believe they've had an experience of immortality, "in their visions they see a part, or a product, of their souls being wrested away and prepared for the Eighth Sphere."[23]

This sweep of unaware human souls and their Earth-born spirituality into the illusory Eighth Sphere took place en masse during the nineteenth century's wave of Spiritualism, Steiner said. Even its underlying occult agenda and all the secret scheming of the brotherhoods were actually inspired by this Luciferic-Ahrimanic consortium. The occultists knew well that in the exchange between mediums and living humans, free will was being commandeered, unacknowledged, into the Eighth Sphere. The psychic contacts made by the mediums testified not to true links formed with the Eternal, but to what was continually disappearing from the Fourth Sphere. "Lucifer and Ahriman inspired the mediums, through whom they arranged the whole business, in order that people might be guided to the realm whence the dead were alleged to be speaking."

According to Steiner, Lucifer and Ahriman used the semblance of the dead as a psychic lure for the unwary. They seduced the mediums into cooperating in their cosmic hijack. It was as if they reasoned, "We shall capture men by alleging that the dead are in our domain." Then Lucifer and Ahriman could snatch away their souls into their burgeoning mists of illusion and egoity. Their choicest prize is the capture of a "whole soul" which is then lost from Earth evolution forever; their greatest victory would be the claim that "countless numbers of the dead had passed into their sphere."[24] Fully aware of this ever-present danger, Steiner cautioned his fellow Anthroposophists engaged in inner schooling to unfold clairvoyance to assiduously avoid being "duped" by anything connected with the Eighth Sphere.[25]

Again, the crux of the problem with the Eighth Sphere is the incompleted Old Moon astrality and its unlawful intermingling in human consciousness on Earth. During the Lemurian phase of human-cosmic unfoldment, when the present Moon was separating itself from Earth, Lucifer and Ahriman and their respective spirits intervened prematurely and unfavorably in human evolution. They drew humans down to the mineralized, tangible Earth too soon and unwisely enmeshed humanity's astral body and the lower elements of human nature in matter. The Luciferic hosts, whom Steiner called "retarded Old Moon-Beings," permeated the insufficiently prepared human astral body with their powers (which included the possibility of unfolding free activity in consciousness), thereby entangling the I, that precious gift of the Earth/Fourth Sphere, in this bewildering cloud of astral assaults and emotional desires. These Old Moon-Beings were "irregularly developed" and "backward beings" who rebelled during the ancient Moon evolution against the Old Sun spirits and became cosmic pariahs squatting subversively in an evolutionary backwater on the Old Moon. These regressive spirits naturally fell under the direct influence of Lucifer and Ahriman.

The Biblical myth of the temptation of Adam and Eve in the Garden of Eden by the wily serpent and his luscious golden apple of cosmic wisdom and awareness is an apt complementary image of this seduction by the spirits of the Eighth Sphere. The human astral body—the inexhaustible, mercurial body of desires, passions, and wishes—living on the material Earth was thereby subjected to the vertiginous gamut of influences and desires it should otherwise have worked out on the astral Old Moon. In other words, astral desires played out in an astral world represent a manageable proposition; but powerful urges of the astral body deployed in the mineralized "field of dreams," in which all self-initiated impulses and wishes could be made real and tangible, are too much for virginal, incarnating human souls. The terrible strain on the human soul was to have free will, self-awareness, individual materiality, and an inchoate, certainly untutored astral nature all at the same time. It guaranteed cognitive precocity.

The results of this impetuous, over-enthusiastic intervention were ambivalent at best, and possibly weighted towards the disastrous, said Steiner. "Because the Luciferic Spirits slipped into his astral body, man has come down into the world of sense, thereby falling prey to the evil but also acquiring the possibility of self-conscious freedom."[26] This essential dialectic of evil and freedom in the inner nature of humanity is the same ambivalent polarity of Spenista Mainyu and Angra Mainyu seen from a different perspective: the human soul is the target, the booty, the pivot, and the decisive factor in this cosmic struggle. As the Zoroastrian Gathas continually warned, and as Steiner's voluminous, meticulous descriptions inarguably show, this "superhuman warfare" is played out in human life and consciousness.

The fierce battle of Lucifer and Ahriman "moves through all the worlds and through every human life," said Steiner. Our physical organism doesn't belong to us, in fact; it is the battlefield for the "strongest attacks": the Luciferic powers converge on us from the left, the Ahrimanic forces assault us from the right. The fact that the Luciferic-Ahrimanic conflict is pitched within the heart of human consciousness, waged unilaterally in the core, pith, and periphery of each human, explains why the human is a double being, a cleaved Human. The human etheric body is a living, pictorial record of this polarization, said Steiner. The left side is "all shining and gleaming with radiant light, and the right half is wrapped in darkness and gloom."[27] Nor is the intensity of battle likely to ameliorate during the epoch of the consciousness soul; in fact, the further humanity evolves, the more precious the spoils of war become. In our time we must expect "the strongest possible forces of opposition" to be brought against us as we move forward on the intended path of evolution. We will be torn and tossed about in this complicated game, as Lucifer strives for universal freedom and Ahriman strains towards everlasting power and might. We are most vulnerable to Lucifer and Ahriman when for us a contradiction remains unnoticed, when some glaring inconsistency in feeling or thinking fails to arrest our attention— "when we have neither the strength nor the will to lay it bare."[28]

We need only consider the burgeoning pop field of virtual reality and Cyberia, which we briefly noted in Chapter 1, to see the negative (though alluring) side of this alliance. Here Ahrimanic technology, the product of high mechanistic intelligence, makes imaginal, virtual, experiential, and thus Luciferic worlds interactively available to individual journeyers. VR travelers manipulate imaginary, electronically-induced and computer-matrixed worlds in highly solipsistic pseudo-metaphysical encounters. From an anthroposophic view, virtual reality is nothing more than that: it is an insubstantial image, an electronic apparition, of an Imagination, but it is basically meretricious and will never lead one to an authentic one. The cognitive danger of course is that many people will settle for the *virtual* reality and never realize their immersion in this Cyberia showland effectively disqualifies them from apprehending the *real* reality. But then, from the point of view of this Ahrimanic-Luciferic alliance, that is precisely the intent.

Human cognitive vigilance is the only sure recourse against this cosmic struggle into which our consciousness and organic existence are interwoven. And as a powerful mentor to inspire this assiduous state of alertness, there stands Michael. The Luciferic element of free, self-aware, intelligent activity in consciousness was actually incorporated into humanity through the cooperation of Michael, as regent of cosmic intelligence. Michael undertook this incorporation as part of a long-range plan. Michael's constant activity on our behalf arms us against the infiltration of our evolving intelligence both by Luciferic influences, that aspire to inflate cognition, and by Ahrimanic influences, that seek to contract cognition.

The composite image of this relationship is the familiar tableau of Michael slaying the dragon. The dragon, Steiner said, represents all that enters our reason and intelligence of an Ahrimanic nature. The battle Michael wages against this symbolic dragon is in defense of cosmic intelligence, now earthed in humankind. Ahriman wants to make intelligence wholly of the Earth, a materialized, densified affair of the blood, reproduction, and genetic inheritance; Ahriman seeks to despiritualize it altogether. Lucifer strives to recelestialize intelligence, to estrange it from its rightful material context, the mineralized Fourth Sphere, Earth. Both endeavor to rip off human cognition and transplant it as building material in their nefarious Eighth Sphere. Michael resists all three tendencies on our behalf.

The Michael-deed, in cooperation with the voluntary self-illumination each human cultivates through one's reason, is to re-spiritualize cosmic intelligence in the context of materiality and earthly human life. Michael strives to birth pristine cosmic intelligence—divine, independent intellectuality—in living, organic, evolving human beings resident on Earth. Michael seeks to bring about the birth of cosmic intelligence in the Fourth Sphere, within the I-consciousness of incarnate human beings. Lucifer and Ahriman, in Steiner's view, both oppose Michael's work, in different but complementary ways. "Thus Michael stands in his activity between the Luciferic World-picture and the Ahrimanic World-intellect." Through the work of Michael, the Luciferic World-picture becomes a wisdom-rich World-revelation, and the Ahrimanic World-intellect becomes divine World-activity. "And in this World-activity lives the care of Christ for humanity"—the great Sun Spirit who mediates the balance between Lucifer and Ahriman in human life.[29]

Lucifer: The Inflation Out of Time

Lucifer's resumé is not as unilaterally pejorative as that of his Zo-roastrian lying colleague in human obstruction, Angra Mainyu, especially if we look past his post-Christ Event condemnation by the early Church Fathers like St. Jerome who equated the Light-Bearer with the Devil. The Hebrews equated Lucifer, whom they knew as *Helel ben Shahar* (Son of the Dawn), with the planet Venus, "the last proud star to defy sunrise," or Dawn (*Shahar*). As morning and evening star, Lucifer and Venus were considered the same—the Day Star; Lucifer/Venus was also known as Phos-phoros in recognition of the quality of his light. The Canaanites called Lucifer *Shahar* because he was the morning star god, the Light-Bringer who announced the daily birth of the Sun. His twin brother, *Shalem*, the evening star, announced the daily death of the Sun, speaking the Word of peace, *shalom*. Both Shahar and Shalem and their cycling relationship to the Sun were wor-shipped in Jerusalem, the House of Shalem.

Shahar and Shalem may have been symbolically equivalent to the Greek's Dioscuri or Heavenly Twins, Castor and Pollux, born of Leda's World Egg. "Both were born of the Great Mother Asherah in her world-womb aspect as Helel, 'the Pit.'"[30] This unusual interpretation of Pit and World Egg as somehow interchangeable evokes the neo-Zoroastrian view of Ahura Mazda and Angra Mainyu as emanations from Zurvan, the boundless circle of infinite Time. Lucifer's association with the Dawn is continued in the Greek mythic tradition, where he was known as *Phosphoros* ("Light-Bearer," from *phos*, "light" and *phoros*, "bringing") in complement to *Eosphoros* ("Dawn-Bearer"), both of which referred to the morning star, Venus. Eosphoros and consort Philonis conceived a daughter named *Stilbe* ("Flash"), whose name records the fact of the unusual brilliancy of the morning star. Eosphoros was conceived as the antecedent of both Sun and dawn, and was depicted as a youthful rider bearing a torch speeding forward on a white horse or chariot (reminiscent of another Greek solar hero, Phaethon, "the gleaming one"). Aphrodite eventually commandeered the radiant Eosphoros to serve as night-watcher in her temple.[31]

The pre-Christian image of Lucifer as Phosphoros, the Light-Bringer and day star, is crucial to our appreciation of this celestial being in his original, untainted form. Even the Bible, normally inflammatory with respect to Lucifer, contains corroborative allusions to him as the heavenly day star. "I am the root and the offspring of David, and the bright and morning star," declared Jesus (Revelation 22:16). "We have also a more sure word of prophecy; whereunto ye do well that ye take heed, as unto a light that shineth in a dark place, until the day dawn, and the day star arise in your hearts," announced Simon Peter, servant and apostle of Jesus Christ (2 Peter 1:19). The startling implication in both cases is that the Christ and Lucifer are closely linked in human evolution, and possibly, in some unsuspected way, are the same or mirror reflections of each other.

How is Lucifer, the fallen day star, pictured in anthroposophical thinking? Edouard Schuré (1841–1929), a close colleague of Steiner in the early days of Anthroposophy, presented a striking portrait of Lucifer in 1900 in his "antique drama" *Children of Lucifer*. A beautiful figure slowly appears above a chasm in the wild countryside. This is the Fallen Angel, seated on a planet "half riven and seamed with crevasses. One of his hands is chained to the globe by an iron ring riveted to the soil by a thunderbolt. In the other hand he proudly raises a torch in the darkness." Schuré graphically captures the tragic ambivalence of Lucifer as the imprisoned illuminator. As the drama unfolds, Schuré indicates that Lucifer's redemption will be achieved only through a human sacrificial act.[32] Steiner, too, vividly drew the countenance of Lucifer. He labored for seven years (1917–1924) on his massive sculptural imagination in wood, "Representative of Humanity," portraying Lucifer, Ahriman, and Christ in their respective relationships: Lucifer above, but plummeting; Ahriman below, groveling in a cave; and the Christ, standing upright, mediating the influences of both.

Lucifer's countenance is primarily a "mighty skull," a single form consisting of wings, ear, and larynx, emerging from reddish clouds. The whole person of Lucifer is concentrated into a face, a massive head whose features are as plastic and mobile as the fingers. Lucifer's face is elongated because he is all ear; even his brow-wings are part of "a long, drawn-out auricle." These sensitive birdlike wings, which emerge as wavy protuberances from the temples, feel about in the cosmic spaces, probing the universe for secrets and forces. Through the accentuated ears, Lucifer grasps what the wings have intuited, and through the larynx "this knowledge becomes the creative word that works and weaves in the forms of living beings," Steiner explained. He justified this strange intimacy between ear and larynx by the fact that on the Old Moon, ear and larynx were one organ; at that time, "Man was one great ear."[33] Through the composite form of larynx, ear, and wings, Lucifer lives in the harmony of the spheres. Lucifer's brow flows in a sweeping movement out towards the wings, which are broken, but his chin is underdeveloped and withdrawn because his true countenance emerges from his pulsating thorax. "Everything becomes cavernous ribbed wing, suffocating and drawn-in," after the once haughty celestial being has metamorphosed into "an expanding fluttering fall."[34]

The extant Hebrew and Greek legends preserved a mythic picture of Lucifer, and to this image Steiner added his sculptural imagination. We need now to penetrate the cultural facade erected before Lucifer and to understand the Light-Bringer's esoteric contribution to the evolution of humanity as Steiner conceived it. Principal among Lucifer's acts was that he made the human phantom visible as matter.

Old Saturn, Sun, and Moon had elaborated the human form, but prior to the appearance of Earth, the human still lacked physicality, and was an invisible phantom, a form in light. Then Lucifer poured forces and loaded substances into the network of the incorporeal human phantom "as one might load apples into a cart." The Human thereby became "opaque and tangible," said Steiner. As an apparently unavoidable corollary, this Luciferic penetration led to the disorganization and progressive destruction of the phantom of the physical body. The human physical body was prematurely hardened and the virginal human souls entered material forms that could not adequately counteract the destructive forces of organic life with their own "upbuilding" forces. Consequently, the physical body was never bestowed in its completeness. "The truth is that man in the course of the Earth-evolution lost the Form of the physical body, so that he no longer has what the Divine Beings had intended for him from the beginning of the Earth."[35] That primordial loss of the complete human Form in the translation into visible matter was exoterically recounted as the "Fall of Man."

The original intention was sound enough. Lucifer made the human form visible as matter so that physical humans could receive the gift of the individual *I*, of self-identity (or Ego), destined for the Earth phase of cosmic evolution. To be truly individuated, a human soul must be physically, individually embodied; to exercise *Freiheit*, the human soul must have a living, biological, visible context for the activity of free willing. Through descending deeply into matter, the human soul became freer and more independent than ever before. Paradoxically, only matter grants this freedom.

This kind of "segregated independence" is possible only in the visible domain of material Earth because even on the Old Moon, human souls were astrally intermingled and took individuality only through participation in the Group Soul. During the Lemurian epoch, the germinal seed of the human Ego was introduced under the aegis of Lucifer. With this the internal, perpetual war of virginal Ego and incompletely developed astral body began. The human Ego was set into a physical form whose astral nature, that is, the polymorphously passionate web of desires, now had the unique opportunity to apprehend—*and will to act on*—a visible, tangible, external sense world. It was a rich juxtaposition that produced confusion. "Yet it was necessary for man to come into this physical world of sense, for only there could he achieve his self-consciousness, his human egoity." [36]

This human egoity in a physically tangible base, however, would be the matrix for the free activity of intelligence, or *manas*, and therefore the prime justification for the Luciferic experiment in organic visibility. The gift of manas *was* the gift of corporeal self-identity, an equation that points to the core of Man as "the thinker," the user of intelligence.[37] Manas is central to our understanding of Lucifer's activity and Steiner's concept of the free activity of intelligence, so it's worthwhile to plumb the Indian philosophical texts for an elucidation.

Manas is the central organ of perception, both perceptive and active, that receives the separate sense impressions conveyed to it and stands ready to initiate willful action in response. Manas ascertains, discriminates, and doubts. It's often called the gatekeeper, or sense-controller, exemplifying attention; as such, this function means the "preventing of knowledge arising together." As the mind's gatekeeper, manas safeguards consciousness from being overwhelmed by a flood of sense data. Manas is the instrument of knowledge by which attention is focused on one thing at a time, translating sensations into percepts and percepts into concepts. But it's also an *upadhi*, a condition, imposition, or basis, that covers up, blinds, or limits the Atman, or pure Self, which is the knower.[38] Metaphorically speaking, the Self (*atman*) is the owner of a chariot which is the body; intuitive discernment and awareness (*buddhi*) is the charioteer, the bridle is the thinking faculty (*manas*), the horses are the sense-forces, and the ranging ground underneath the chariot are the objects of sense perception.[39]

The incessant dynamic activity of manas, this "ever-active mind organ" that reins in the galloping array of sensory information, actually underlies our self-conscious perception of external reality. Manas constructs external reality. Through the mental creations of manas, everything springs forth out of no-form into appearance as a "momentary imagination." Manas, state the Indian metaphysicians, is a hypothetical starting point, lacking actual reality, from which the manifold "dreams of appearance" that constitute our world emanate. The essence of manas is the activity, the momentum of world-building, and this is karma, the comparative deployment of action and reaction. "It is by the activity of manas that the subject-objectless pure consciousness assumes the form of a self-conscious ego. Manas thus consists of this constantly positing activity, the first moment of self-conscious activity leading in different directions." Through manas a self-conscious agent (the human) *posits* an external world. Manas *positions* the world. Manas is what makes it possible for the individually embodied human to conceive a world through the "positing" activities of perception. The world stands before us "due to the imagination of manas, like dreamland."[40]

Not only does manas position the world, but it also reflexively positions the Ego as intelligent world builder. The positing activity of manas, however dreamlike and imaginative, proceeds from a yet higher principle of "divine thought" called *Mahat*. Mahat, in the theosophical conception, is the "Lord in the Primary Creation" and "Supra-divine Intelligence"—in short, universal cognition. Mahat, as cosmic ideation, is transformed into manas, as human intellect; this transformation of Mahat to manas produces self-reflexivity in consciousness—in other words, self-awareness. This is the Second Creation, marking the birth of Egoism and I-consciousness. "When Mahat develops into the feeling of Self-consciousness-I then it assumes the name of Egoism." This means that manas, as the thinking faculty, is the basis for individuality in consciousness: *manas individualizes*. This "segregated independence" in cognition is the basis for the free activity of intelligence Lucifer had in mind for humans from the beginning. "Man" is manas individuated.

When the cosmic mind is focused in a principle (or limited by a basis, condition, or imposition, i.e., *upadhi*), the result is the consciousness of the individual Ego.[41] The limiting basis that transformed Mahat into manas was the human phantom made physically visible as individual human beings. The active agents in this process were Michael, regent of cosmic intelligence (Mahat), and Lucifer, regent of the free activity of human intelligence (manas). Potentially this cosmic translation of Mahat to manas would one day produce *Freiheit*, the freedom of spiritual activity.

But *Freiheit* would be a matter of careful, progressive elaboration through evolution. The Luciferic gift of manas—the world-positing, sense-organizing, mind-attentive doorkeeper of self-consciousness—was set into a materialized human form inflamed with an unresolved passionate astrality. This complicated level of human consciousness in which desire and mind are interwoven was called *Kama-Manas* in classical theosophy; the purified realm of the intellect, where the mind functions free from desire interwoven with materiality, was called Higher Manas. Manas intermingled with Old Moon astrality was the condition into which virginal humanity was inserted through the premature "visualization of Man" by Lucifer. "Whatever part of the astral body has been thus transformed by the 'I' is called Manas," said Steiner. "A man has just so much of Manas as he has created by his own efforts; part of his astral body is therefore always Manas." [42]

Manas, intended as the natural gift to incarnating humanity, thus had to be retrieved from the consequences of intermingling with an incompletely developed astral body. Lucifer, by his very nature, which is enthusiasm, exacerbated this situation by inflating the emotional soul life of the individual human. The Luciferic hosts penetrated the human astral body like "powerful rays," permeating it with passions, instincts, and desires, with the capacity for free, rapturous enthusiasm. Humans in material form came to crave the sense impressions of Earth. It's actually Lucifer's prescribed task to "tear" the soul life of humanity away from complete absorption in the physical-sensory world alone. Lucifer brings the light of the cosmos to materialized humanity as a celestial mnemonic. Lucifer's commission was to uplift, inspire, enthuse, and liberate the soul from the confines of materiality, to raise the soul's feeling life into artistic and philosophic imaginations. Through Lucifer's work, humankind was able to perceive the stars with an exalted warmth of consciousness; not only to heed the divinely inspired dictates of one's astral body, but to freely unfold impulses of one's own. "Lucifer is lord over everything of soul feeling in the physical sense world," said Steiner.

But Lucifer often overreaches his commission. In a surfeit of cosmic enthusiasm, Lucifer strives to detach this "feeling life of the soul" from the physical world, to spiritualize the imaginations "on a specially isolated island of spiritual existence composed of all the soul feeling he can seize"—the Eighth Sphere. Lucifer inspires a sensuous idealism, in which sensual instincts are sublimated into idealistic imaginations. This results in a will "pervaded by a sultry, voluptuous experience of the spiritual world." A good example of this is what Steiner called fevered, visionary mysticism, the heights of Midsummer madness, which is Lucifer's prime time in the yearly cycle. Lucifer acting in humanity is the tendency to become fantastic, to yield one-sidedly to fancy, to be seduced by the allure of beauty, to resort to "innermost inwardness," to indulge in excessive enthusiasm and emotional fanaticism.

Lucifer strains to transport our inner being out beyond the head into the vertiginously phosphoric cosmos. Lucifer yearns to envelop us through the suction of beauty in an exalted, sense-free, cosmic imagination. Lucifer is impatient with the limitations of Earth and time. The Light-Bearer wants to liberate the emotional soul life from its confining sensory base, to declare as independent the sensuous *I* enraptured with its manasic world-building potency. Once again, the trouble is timing. Permeated with unclarified selfhood, an unbridled astrality, and an incompletely individuated Ego, the human being is still, cosmically speaking, adolescent, and not quite ready for the Luciferic fantastic voyage.

Again, the condition of an unclarified astrally permeated egohood granted cognitive freedom but permitted intellectual error. When Lemurian humanity became individual, independent beings bearing a measure of inner freedom, they were no longer in such intimate resonance with the perfect guidance of the angelic realm. Through the gift of the individual Ego, the human soul walked in a new, ambiguous domain, semi-detached from the sureties of constant supersensible aegis. It was altogether necessary, if problematical, because by no other way than through cognitive free will could the newly incarnate humans come to inner freedom and true individuality.

Lucifer's intention was sound, but his timing was inappropriate, Steiner implied. The densification of the astral body was premature and precipitated an early process of deterioration. Illness, disease, decay, old age, and death came into the world as regents of organic limitation. Humanity should not lawfully have come into this measure of potential *Freiheit* until much later, in Atlantean times. In fact, humanity wasn't supposed to physically, visibly descend through incarnation into the sense world of Earth until the time period we now reckon as Atlantis. Through Lucifer's influence, humans became free beings, able to distinguish between good and evil (capable of what the Gnostics called "acquaintance"), able to exercise the "power of free decision," and capable of acting voluntarily out of one's inner impulses.[43] We were given a world to act upon as we willed but before we had gained the soul-spiritual maturity that would grant us the wisdom of the right use of will.

The possibility of free decision in undertaking actions originating from inner impulses inevitably introduced the possibility of error and thus evil. Error and evil resulted from actions inspired by unclarified manas. Manas, the rigorous, attentive gatekeeper of the sense doors on behalf of a young Ego struggling for balance and authority, was overwhelmed by the polymorphous opportunities for passionate fulfillment. Manasic world-building became individualized sensory gratification as Sun intelligence was misted over by Moon astrality. The possibility of free activity also meant the future was uncertain, indefinite. With the omniscient gods no longer supervising humanity, evolution was now ambiguously open-ended, a probable possibility, but no longer a guaranteed attainment. This troubling uncertainty was the price of cognitive freedom, but it birthed fear and self-doubt in the soul. Self-decision means self-responsibility, and this remains, even today, a freedom of frightening proportions. As we will, so shall it be, but when the will is asleep and self-reflexively unaware of itself, we may find ourselves running away in terror from what our wills have produced.

Lucifer's being, after all, is a cosmic ardency for freedom overplayed beyond its proper bounds. Lucifer's rightful domain lies beyond the Sun sphere, a trans-solar realm beyond the domain of the Christ who is our guide while we live as humans on Earth, said Steiner. But beyond Old Sun, Lucifer is our true mentor in the greater cosmos; there Lucifer is "still a brother of Christ" and in no way harmful to the human individuality. As we travel beyond the Sun in the life after death, "we need a new light-bearer who illumines our path into the universe." Lucifer is our uranian psychopomp, our instructor in the Mysteries beyond the Sun. The threshold of the Sun rearranges our perception of Lucifer and his relationship with the Christ. We sense Lucifer and Christ "side by side as equally justifiable powers, as brothers." This trans-solar Luciferic domain is completely unrelated to Earth, and there Lucifer is our illuminator, preparing us for our future incarnation, lighting our way through the spheres of Mars, Jupiter, and Saturn. In the transit from Sun to Mars, we discover that Lucifer is a legitimate power, an indispensable companion, and absolutely necessary because the individual human is not yet sufficiently mature to know where one's karma can best be worked out. Only the Mysteries beyond the Sun can reveal this.[44]

When we continue our cosmic after-death journey with Lucifer and Christ, we acquire "the right relationship to the progressive stream in evolution," explained Steiner. But the Luciferic enthusiasm of illumination cuts both ways. Lucifer, engaged in human egohood enmeshed in matter, is perpetually homesick for the rarefied celestial realm of unlimited imaginations, of boundless living thoughts, he left behind. He's always tugging and tearing at human materiality to recelestialize his originally sense-free intelligence, to reclaim that free-ranging manasic imagination with which he permeated humanity. But a certain "profound tragedy" aurically envelops Lucifer.

Lucifer is a spiritual intelligence whose true being is a remnant of the ancient past, whose soul life exists only in the earlier pre-earthly epochs, said Steiner. For these, Lucifer maintains a rivetingly sharp memory, a "wonderful cosmic nostalgia." He fights with the aid of his illustrious past to gain a foothold in the present and thereby to secure a future. Lucifer lives with a perpetual longing for his true home, the star Phosphoros (or Venus), which shines down on Earth as the cast-off "husk" of Lucifer.[45] Lucifer carries the memory of something humankind had before the descent into sensory life, of a pre-earthly Edenic state, but it's something that shouldn't have been preserved: "a longing for the passing moment and for all that has to do with time."[46] And because he misses it, Lucifer perpetually strives to reclaim it through human life. Lucifer strives to bring the eternal into the passing moment and thereby to capture Time.

Lucifer's "profound tragedy" is the agony of being caught in Time, of seeing cosmically unbounded Mahat working in an organic, manasic mortal body, of experiencing the constriction of cosmic intelligence by the pressure of materiality. Lucifer's cosmic enthusiasm for cognitive independence, for individualized intelligence, for world-building imaginations, cannot countenance the limitations of materialization that is the human experience of the Fourth Sphere called Earth. Why can't they be like me? Lucifer asks, swooping archangelically over the fields of human life like an exultant lark.

Lucifer wants to translate eternity into the temporal, inflating time, to carry what is proper to the realm of duration into the world of the transitory. Lucifer wants to dilate the passing moment, which is the inexorability of time (and the lawful regulator of biological Sun-dependent life) into eternity, into the boundless circle of infinite Time, the calm, undisturbed flow of uncreated Time. He wants to inject the atemporal spirituality of the supersensible worlds into the time-woven grid of Earth life. Time of the Long Dominion, the eternal human soul caught in Finite Time—this is Lucifer's true and everlasting foe.

Even so, individuality couldn't be accomplished in any way other than through the constrictive mortality of time-based material existence. It's as if, acting on humanity's behalf, Lucifer elects the exultation of cognitive individuality but rejects its concomitant price: time-bound mortality. He yearns to transfer the spiritual treasures of the supersensible world into the world of the senses as revelations. Luciferic spirituality *is* human intelligence, said Steiner, and through Lucifer humans acquired the faculty of using the organs of intellect, of speaking and thinking, of grasping a thought in solitude. But Lucifer is a being "forever striving to make the eternal, which otherwise is in constant movement and change, into the stable, temporal, and momentary, so that as something individual it can rejoice in its power to grow individually great."[47] According to Steiner, Lucifer had a chance 5,000 years ago to instill something of the eternal into nascent human intelligence. He did this through a unique human incarnation somewhere in Asia.

Steiner's assertion that Lucifer, one of the primordial spiritual beings of the universe, actually incarnated as a human being ("an earthly incarnation of Lucifer in a man of flesh and blood") is one of his odder conceptions, especially if taken literally. More likely, Steiner meant this in the same sense in which he described archangelic overlightings of the Hebrew prophets, and before them, the Indian and Atlantean sages. In those cases, the "incarnation" was the permeation of the etheric and astral bodies, and sometimes the Ego, of the patriarchs by the intelligent aegis of supersensible beings. The early third millennium B.C. marked the "incarnation of a supersensible Being," said Steiner, a remarkable event in Asia that "gave humanity something of immense brilliance."[48]

It was as if Lucifer, regent of human manas and hierophant of the Mysteries, momentarily took human biological form as a living fount of inspiration for the primeval, "pagan" wisdom culture. In that capacity he brought the ancient Rishis, the original teachers of a young humanity, the world of "intellectualistic thought," the domain of high reason and pictorial conceptions, and the ideal of a "cosmic and unconditioned activity of Intelligence and Will." Intellectually, Lucifer taught the Rishis how to fly. Lucifer, Steiner reminds us, is a proud spirit who prefers to "soar away" on the wings of free-ranging intelligence into the empyrean "where lofty visions open out." And he likes human company. Through the Luciferic influence, humans build imaginative pictures that surpass physical reality. Lucifer is the archangelic leaven that inspires "the airy viewpoint of a bird" in people, an updraft that lofts them high above actual life circumstances. The liability of this aerial ballet is "an excessive interest in our own concoctions," a conceptual self-absorption that regards with disinterest the affairs of our human fellows. In a deep sense, Lucifer cannot accept the consequences of what happened when humanity, through his efforts, was brought into physical substance.

This unconditioned activity of Luciferic intelligence strives to condense human sense impressions of the external world so they can "continuously shine as ideation" in consciousness. Lucifer wishes the physical world to revert to its ideational basis; he wants to extract the sense-free idea through the dissolution of its material expression. In a sense, Lucifer represents Goethean Idealist thinking taken to the extreme, to the abstract world where it is purely Idea without living substance or example. Lucifer desires a human world made of the *enthusiasm of ideas*—a picture world upheld by manas. But individuated manas is so potent that if it is fueled by unclarified fantasies that threaten to become realities, this could disorder the cosmos. "The constant tendency is to give a real substantial content to that which we form as an image in our spirit," commented Steiner.[49] That's the shortcoming today, but back then the Luciferic wisdom was of "the utmost benefit" to humanity, inspiring the impulse towards gnosis, or knowledge gained through direct "acquaintance" with reality.

At heart, the Luciferic tendency within material humanity is to reify ideations into a separate conceptual world, estranged from the organic earthly context. Lucifer prefers ideas in their purity, as if they never found expression, through densification, on Earth. Of course, this is the same manasic world-building principle at play in the living imaginations or thoughts of the gods, but somehow, when translated to Earth and practiced by humans, it becomes inappropriate to the intended goal of the elaboration of the human Ego in a psychophysical base. Lucifer clearly wants to pull humans away from the material Earth, Steiner observed. He wants to prevent humans from gaining a complete orientation in the physical plane, because, he feels, if they truly came to feel truly at home on Earth, they might altogether forget the supersensible pleasures of intelligence and sever their lifeline with the Light-Bearer.

Lucifer wants to pluck the human soul out of its confining corporeality, so that it is no more than "a vision of himself and is completely soul." This would free the human being to live in the cosmos as a "purely etheric being possessed of spirit and soul"— as if Earth never happened. Ideally, Lucifer prefers the human to be a "wholly moral being," an "etheric angel," an "automatically spiritual being"—individualized and thinking yet free of any physical nature, resident in an independent, vaporous Luciferic sheath (the Eighth Sphere) made of nonmaterial human imaginations. Lucifer wants to abandon the Earth to its material, mineralized fate, bereft of its spiritualized humans, who will have all relocated to his alluring sheath, concluded Steiner. But according to Valentin Tomberg, this Luciferic sheath is a false paradise made by Lucifer for his own grandeur from the "force of Imagination" he stole from Sophia, the Wisdom of God, at the Fall of Man.[50]

Between Sophia in the Pleroma and humanity on Earth stands Lucifer. Lucifer usurped and abused the "truth of the imaginative revelation of Sophia" for the purposes of creating a world, said Tomberg, who presents an impassioned indictment of Lucifer. Lucifer profoundly compromised Sophia's faculties of imagination, circumventing her revelatory function for human consciousness. Lucifer appropriated the imaginations of Sophia without cosmic sanction, then converted them into their opposite, a kind of obscuring wall of opacity. Sophia's "pictures of comprehensive truth" were transposed into a Luciferic sphere of lies—the false Paradise, "a false spiritual world" generating religious visions of "egoistic bliss." Cosmic falsehood is worse than wild fantasy, said Tomberg, because it's abused truth. This can be "tremendously corrupting" on faculties of knowledge not fully awakened by conscience. Abused truth in the context of unclarified manas spells cognitive disaster. Sophia's wisdom revelation shattered into pieces, then Lucifer reassembled the fragments in a different pattern—a Luciferic paisley, icons of a separate, meretricious world. "The shining wisdom of God was changed to the glittering garment of Lucifer," said Tomberg. Lucifer stole the imaginations of Sophia, which rendered the Mother of the World in her Wisdom aspect dumb, colorless, inactive and ineffective, the *mater dolorosa* of a sundered, fragmented wisdom.

Lucifer's "continual and terrible war" to tear humans away from their proper residence on Earth is played out unilaterally through every shell of human consciousness, into the deepest physical aspects of our being. Within the physical organism, Lucifer's sovereign domain is the head, the brain, and skull—the perfected, "noblest" organs of human thinking. In our time, the head is already in a retrogressive evolution and is in fact "dying." The human head actually developed long before the rest of the physical organism, Steiner said; what brought the human head out of its antecedent animal form into its present human shape was the Luciferic influence. The Luciferic spirits gained residency in the human head when Michael thrust them out of the supersensible world into the mineralized skull of the Human, and they've been there ever since.

But Lucifer is also with us in every breath we take. He enters the human physiology through the breathing, which is the doorway to the blood and circulatory system. The key to the breathing process is the etheric body. An etheric body that is over exuberant, too widely extended, too intensely inclined towards the starry world, produces "an excessively vigorous breathing process," and this provides the Luciferic forces their opportunity to enter the body. With every breath, Lucifer strives to "dissolve and evaporate" the materialized human, to lure it into the Luciferic "sea of colors and flowing light." Meanwhile, this airy etheric expansion and its corresponding soul feeling of "falsely mystical hopes," disorders the human blood and the "warmth process," the rightful carrier of the Ego. Anything that disorders the unfoldment of the human Ego de facto obstructs the Christ, whose sphere of influence is the Ego.

The Luciferic inflation, however, is only one half of the assault on the incarnate human, only one pole of that profound cosmic dialectic waged throughout every aspect of our life here in the Time of Long Dominion. Lucifer's manasic dilation out of matter is exquisitely counterpoised by Ahriman's intellectual compression into matter.

Ahriman: The Contraction into Time

Ever since the bifurcation of Boundless Time into the polarized beings of Lucifer and Ahriman, Lucifer has sought to fly free from the confines of finite time lived in matter with human intelligence secure in his talons. Meanwhile, Ahriman willingly dove headfirst into the weightiness, the gravity, of materiality, burying cosmic intellectuality deep in the Earth. Generally, Steiner's view of Ahriman is markedly less bleak than the Zoroastrian picture of Angra Mainyu as apocalyptic evil.

Ahriman, said Steiner, entered human evolution as a legitimate co-creator commissioned by the gods to be the rightful Lord of Death and the intellect. The gods appreciated Ahriman, if warily, as "a sage of death," a cosmic being necessary to the progressive unfoldment of human evolution. Ahriman's principal domain is the mineral kingdom, a world that is "utterly dead," but his sovereignty properly encompasses all of external nature. In the human sphere, Ahriman takes every opportunity to encourage humans in the exclusive, material use of their intellect.

Yet Ahriman's legitimate commission empowers him to deliver the passing moment and its valuable sensory contents back to eternity. In other words, Ahriman helps humans considerably in physical world activities; in this he is our "cherished companion," helping us gather the sense-world fruits that he wishes to return to the atemporal. Ahriman is an assiduous, compulsive saver: he preserves everything, gleaning all the "precious treasures" from each passing moment to lay upon the altar of eternity. Ahriman's great strongholds are libraries, filled with the "preserving jars of wisdom" in which knowledge has been separated, exteriorized from the human. Ahriman's obsession with preservation and avoiding change is so extreme, quipped Steiner, that he would stop the snake from shedding its skin.[51]

While Lucifer strives to capture Time by bringing the eternal into the passing moment, Ahriman in contrast struggles to capture Space from Time. Ahriman's basic problem is self-contraction; he suffers from a kind of ontological claustrophilia. From his own "self-love in acting," Ahriman's world has contracted into a frosty, darkened cavern of one being—his own; in this condition he affirms only himself and denies the rest of the world. For Ahriman, freedom means "the proud feeling of manifesting himself in the action," said Steiner, and that's why he needs more space: space for more matter, for more preservation, for more egoistical self-being. Ahriman needs space in which to materialize the spiritual world, to capture intelligence within materiality, and to hold humans spellbound and "fastened permanently" to the Earth.[52] That's the dangerous, "evil" side of an Ahriman working beyond his lawful domain in human life, an insidious influence that acutely overshadowed the materialistic nineteenth century beginning in the 1840s. So the *Druj* was alive and well in the century of materialism, said Steiner. Even in the supposedly psychic 1990s we cannot unequivocally declare ourselves exempt from the Ahrimanic deception. In fact, our time may present a perfect opportunity for Ahriman to work his craft at seducing human intellect away from Michaelic spirituality.

Ahriman appropriates the human intellect by encouraging us to form material, physical, sense-bound concepts to describe the supersensible world. Ahriman exerts a subtle corruption to the Luciferic pictorial, imaginative faculty; we start off building a concept of supersensible wisdom as being *like* a library, then without catching the exact moment, find we've slipped into a very concrete reification of librarians, desks, books, filing cabinets, due dates, and author indexes. We have unwittingly materialized—made it literal, turned it to stone—a supersensible reality. Ahriman tempts the intellect, struggling to form coherent concepts, to picture the subtle worlds according to physical laws and material activities. Through this conceptual gravity Ahriman anchors the human ever more deeply in the sensory world but in such a way that occults the presence of the spiritual. "In every illusion that matter is the sole reality, we must perceive the whispered promptings of Ahriman," Steiner warns us.

Ahriman is loathe for us to apprehend spiritually the supersensible world, to really approach it with subtle, pictorial, living imaginations, because these would free us from sense-bound gravity, which is his proper domain and base of action. The more we materialize our intellect and permeate our thinking only with the concerns of physical existence, the more remote become the supersensible worlds, and the more potently present looms Ahriman, who claims his sovereignty on Earth. Ahriman succeeds when humans gain acquaintance of the physical world in a non-spiritual way: that is, when humanity settles for a false gnosis, for acquaintance with the Lie, as the Zoroastrians would say.

Ahriman fosters the illusion that elemental matter is a reality in itself, that physical-sensory life is the consummation of existence. It's not hard to see how Ahriman's materialism effectively bars all outlook on the spiritual world for many people; an objective survey of the parameters of modern scientific theory and research demonstrates this readily. The arbiters of contemporary scientific and medical thinking almost unilaterally refuse to see through the material world to its true, spiritual foundations. Matter and the body have no causal relation to spirit and mind, they tell us endlessly. It's not just the external world that Ahriman materializes. He permeates human consciousness, too, with the conviction that the human is nothing more than a "completely developed animal," fighting for survival among the fittest, as Darwin, the nineteenth century's protégé of Ahrimanic thinking, so concretely expressed. That the human might be the living image of the Godhead is anathema to Ahriman and irritating to the physical scientists. Where Lucifer wants to pull the human soul out of the restrictive physical shell into the illusion of celestial freedom, Ahriman would discard the soul-spiritual core altogether, exalting instead the material sheath and everything that comes to expression through the body, like instincts and impulses, even the subhuman elements. By this, Ahriman aims to make human nature "more and more earthly."[53]

Ahriman's goal is to capture human intelligence within materiality and to subvert the innate world-imagining activity of manas. Ahriman wants to permeate manas with matter weighted down in time. He aspires to sever human thinking from its brain-bound foundation because he knows the brain moves already in a current of decay. Ahriman snatches human thinking out of this destructive current, making it on the one hand independent of the brain, yet strangely still operative within materialistic parameters established by the physical brain. As a result, Ahrimanic "shadows and phantoms" swarm through the physical world, disturbing the universal order.[54]

With a world populated with insubstantial shadows and phantoms of spirit-estranged human thinking, Ahriman actually seeks to destroy the human intellect. Of course, Ahriman doesn't see his actions as destructive; he just wants to exert his considerable influence, his being, on the way we use our cosmically bestowed intelligence. It is hard to argue with Ahriman: he is a brilliant sophist and will out-debate, out-maneuver, out-think us at every turn—as long as we let him choose the level of discourse. We must remember, too, that both Lucifer and Ahriman work to appropriate the cosmic intelligence from its regent, Michael, before it comes into full maturity in incarnate humanity, its recipient. Lucifer wants to inflate intellectuality beyond its sensory context, Ahriman seeks to contract intellectuality into a despiritualized material base. Through this titanic tug of war the lawful Michaelic functioning of the human intellect is imperiled.

From Ahriman intellectuality pours forth as "a cold and freezing, soulless cosmic impulse." The Ahrimanic style is a rigid logic unsoftened by compassion, unquickened by enthusiasm, unwarmed by a "heartfelt, inner relationship of soul between the human being and what he thinks and speaks and does."[55] Ahrimanic intellect is cool, calculating, mechanical, automatic, robotic, and

ruthlessly logical. Ahriman ossifies humans, hardens the inner being, calcifies their intellect; Ahriman instills the "superstition" of
materialism, sucking us dry, reducing our soul life to a brittle husk
of "prosaic philistinism."

Ahriman's "constant and fiercest" effort is to strangle individual intelligence, to carry if off for himself. Lucifer encourages
segregated independence, the rapture of a thought considered in
solitude, but Ahriman's pleasure is a soulless logical collectivity,
group thinking, group mind, the atavism of Group Souls. This is
Ahrimanized intellectuality in action. We find Ahriman's influence at play wherever the principle of differentiation is active.
Ahriman's speciality in human culture is to separate humans into
conflicting groups, tribes, genetic types, races, nationalities, denominations, sects—any specific, differentiated polity that de-
fines itself through taking patriotic, chauvinistic opposition to all
other polities. It is a kind of Balkanization of the soul, if you will.

Long ago this Ahrimanic energy of differentiation degraded
the primordial "one cosmic speech" into the multiplicity of different world languages. Ahriman was the architect of the legendary Tower of Babel that rendered human speech globally
cacophonous: after Babel, unilateral human understanding was
obstructed by walls of incomprehensible speech. Ahriman further differentiated humanity according to heredity, the blood,
and the nerve temperament. Ahriman's infiltration of the forces
of heredity particularly sowed confusion in the human soul life,
and it continues to distract allopathic medicine from discovering
the true spiritual foundations of catastrophic, degenerative dis-
eases, particularly those involving dysfunctional immune systems. Immunology is the table at which psychobiological identity
issues of self and not-self are negotiated—what's at stake is the
Ego. "The Ahrimanic powers succeed in ensuring that the Ego is
only very loosely connected with the human being," said Steiner.
This loose connection imparts ambiguity to the human I in regard to one's physical impulses, compromising the I's innate
healing response.[56]

Ahriman's opposition to individuality is an expression of his
"cold hatred" of everything that unfolds in freedom, which is
to say, everything Luciferic. In the politics of human spirituality, Lucifer is a radical, extolling liberation, while Ahriman is a

conservative, stomping out change and rationalizing bondage. Ahriman encourages us to fear the spiritual world in the "deepest foundations of our soul," and for good reason. Such a fear compels us to seek a haven in the material, the tangible, the sensory; the next step is the apotheosis of measure, number, and weight, the densification of the material world, in which everything subtle streaming in from universal space into the Earth is but more material for Ahriman's "cosmic machine."[57]

In a sense Ahriman commandeers human manas as mineralized intellectuality, the basic steel and concrete with which to build his cosmic machine. The slyness of the Ahrimanic deception is that we don't know we've been conscripted as unskilled laborers in Ahriman's factory. The Ahrimanic deception, as Steiner called it, works through the gamut of natural sciences, today's materialistic, mechanistic sciences, from astrophysics to microbiology. The Ahrimanic illusion is successful when scientists mistake a "ghostly" knowledge of nature, which is to say, a data base founded on concepts drawn exclusively from sense-bound information—"a superstitious empiricism"—for a "real knowledge" of nature, a Goethean approach which acknowledges its spiritual foundations, based on spiritual scientific investigation of the supersensible matrix underlying the physical world. "A right attitude in regard to the whole of modern science . . . will recognize that its knowledge is illusion," Steiner declared emphatically.[58]

Yet this right attitude can be easily overpowered by the dazzling face of Ahrimanic intelligence. "In Ahriman there stands before us a cosmic Being of the highest imaginable Intelligence, a cosmic Being who has already taken the Intelligence entirely into the individual, personal element," Steiner observed. Ahriman, like Lucifer, represents one face—albeit an unbalanced one—of a possible outcome of the disposition of the cosmic intelligence without the mediation of the Christ. Ahriman is the consummate debater, the master of conceptual manipulation and logical conclusiveness, an intellectual sophisticate with "a magnificent certainty of aim." Our unbriefed dialectical encounter with Ahriman alone quite likely would be shattering. In a sense we are fortunate we encounter Ahriman intermingled with Luciferic influences; Anthroposophy, with our welfare foremost in mind, would like us to encounter both through the Christ.

How would we respond to a brilliant philosopher who brands as stupid everything that doesn't exemplify intelligence in the context of "full personal individuality?" Those of us only moderately intelligent needn't worry. Ahriman, "a great and outstanding intelligence," seeks primarily the most gifted, the cleverest, the most advanced, the most acutely intelligent of humans for his administration. Quarry such as this—Nobel laureates in science and medicine, for example—are more worth his while. His intentions with respect to human evolution and the elaboration of cosmic intellectuality are thorough and overwhelming, Steiner said, and his means are versatile and devious. "For Ahriman by his brilliant gifts can find his way into everything—he can slip into the very style of a man."[59]

Ahriman slipped into one of the nineteenth century's most brilliant writers in his final period of decay, announced Steiner. Ahriman worked himself into "a man who had carried human faculties to the highest point of eminence"—Friedrich Nietzsche. The Ahrimanic presence was inarguably present in Nietzsche's last two books, *Ecce Homo* and *Anti-Christ*; this was a startling precedent because "for the first time Ahriman appeared as an author upon earth."[60] Nietzsche may have been one of Ahriman's most prominent corporate takeovers, but during Ahriman's ascendancy, underway since the fifteenth century, the craft of writing itself is in jeopardy. Ahriman struggles to keep thinking from flowing into the stream of death, which is to say, from permeation by the Mysteries of the supersensible. "Writing is the best means of keeping thoughts on the physical plane."[61]

We can expect a great deal more of Ahriman's materializing influence in the coming century as he moves into his flush of ascendancy in human culture on Earth. Before the end of the third millennium, or sometime between 2000–3000 A.D., Steiner predicted that the West will experience an "actual incarnation" of Ahriman "in the flesh." The implications of this are startling. The Ahrimanic influence intensifies continually in *preparation* for this unique incarnation. It's as if Ahriman, still working from the supersensible into the physical, sends phantoms, specters, and lies into the material world as an advance guard; these Ahrimanic emissaries work undercover, underground, to secure the necessary preparations for his apocalyptic negative epiphany. What will be of greatest possible advantage to Ahriman is an accentuation of our present state of "drowsy unawareness," our state of cognitive sleep in which we fail to apprehend symptoms of culture and irruptions in consciousness—"unspiritual currents"—as indications of Ahriman's approach. Most conspicuous among the preparatory Ahrimanic symptoms, said Steiner in 1919 (evidently scrying the California metaphysical boutique approach to spirituality prevalent at the end of the twentieth century), is a cultural attitude that fosters an easy, untrained, differentiated clairvoyance. In easy clairvoyance behold the signature of Ahriman.

Steiner envisioned Ahriman, much like Goethe's Mephistopheles, as deploying his "stupendous magical arts" to turn great numbers of men and women into seers. But Ahriman prefers a noncorroborable seership, a babble of competing psychics spouting sapphics to neophytes about nonconnected worlds. "Men would inevitably fall into strife on account of the sheer diversity of their visions." Ahriman will establish a great occult school, for the exultation of magical arts of "the greatest grandeur," through which what *must be* acquired through persistent, individual effort (according to legitimate human evolution in the time of the consciousness soul) will be lavished like honorary degrees upon the complacent, laid-back masses in a kind of Ahrimanic psychic Woodstock. In Ahriman's script, humans will live as spiritual materialists, free from any necessity for spiritual exertion, but laden down with psychic (though chimerical) treasures.[62]

We can already see aspects of this chaise-lounge approach to the spiritual in the Western floriation of California-style channelism. Brand-name psychics, with no evident pedigree of training or initiation, advertise the ease of "opening to channel," hailing it as "an accelerated spiritual growth path." There's no need, either, for any kind of serial training leading towards clairvoyance: "You do not need to develop your psychic abilities to become a good channel." Like solicitous nannies for adolescent debutantes, they urge us to "go out into the world as a channel" after a weekend seminar's intoxicating brush with the trance state somewhere in glamor-misted Marin or Orange County. Don't even think about allowing your "supersensible" blush to ripen into some form of wisdom, because "you often teach best what you have just learned." As one "supersensible" salesman pitched it, "This is it!

The time to Open to Channel is now. You've dreamed of it, read about it, thought about it, and now you will do it!"[63]

The trouble is when you "do it" you won't find DaBen, that being of "very radiant energy, loving and exacting, who has great caring," or Orin, that "very loving, wise, gentle being" ringing you in angelic halos. Instead, you'll confront the batlike cynical countenance of Ahriman overshadowing your every pronouncement; again, that's if you're lucky and can see what's before you. Most likely you will not, which is Ahriman's desire and Steiner's worry. Instead, you will behold something more pleasant, of your own making. Easy clairvoyance is Ahriman's speciality and chaiselounge psychics are his trademark. Steiner would invite every Monday-morning California channel to carefully ruminate upon his sculptural depiction of Ahriman.

Steiner's sculptural Ahriman is a forlorn figure, with a large human head, huge batlike wings flaring arthritically from a dragon's torso, crouching, writhing painfully in a dark cave. Ahriman's forehead is receding and undeveloped; the brow is made of shrunken bony forms, and his expression is "frivolously cynical." But his lower jaw, teeth, and chin are strikingly prominent as a gesture of masticatory power, the forces of the lower self, and his materialist attitude. This Ahrimanic chthonic worm is shackled by the gold of the Earth, fettered in chains of the planet's own paramount mineral. Metallity itself, Ahriman's dominion, ties him in bonds. Ahriman's limbs are crooked and ossified as though imprisoned in some "rigid language of form." His torso is entirely sclerotic, "engulfed in predominantly broken angular convex forms developing out of each other."[64] Even Ahriman's wings are spare and rigidified, beating out the quality of calcification and death. After all, his proper season is winter, in which all life is as if frozen in death. Ahriman writhes arthritically in this gesture of brittleness because he can't bear the compassion of the Christ above. He'll do anything to escape the radiant exudations of Christ's hands, which cause the "golden veins down in the rock depression to wind around Ahriman's body like strong cords and shackle him."[65]

Steiner's sculptural imagination of a chthonically potent Ahriman illustrates his way of working. Ahriman's influences in the physical world are characteristically subterranean and subversive, working through "inner fire forces of the earth." We find Ahriman's signature in such material upheavals as volcanoes, earthquakes, and other natural catastrophes, and to the degree that these cataclysms are obstructive, so much the better, for Ahriman is the prince of obstacles. Ahriman is also at home in the cold and watery, in the suction of gravity, in the planet's limestone. Ahriman works through the physical world to reduce life to a condition of "complete rigidification;" in the human organism, Ahriman acts through the digestive and metabolic systems, particularly the liver, to harden everything, producing sclerotic illnesses such as arthritis and arteriosclerosis. And through the materialization of manas, Ahriman dries up the human etheric body, so that it contracts and withers, incapable of living, world-building imaginations.

Ahriman is a subearthly, subconscious saboteur, a devious "morally lonely" agent who disdains to make his presence known. So he works below the threshold of ordinary human awareness, seething like lava, swelling like a volcanic force, building for a silent eruption into humanity's emotional soul life. He repudiates human morality, but affirms the transformation of each man and woman into "a sheer automaton of cleverness," an egoist embedded in the material world, as an exemplification of Ahrimanic morality. As we know now, Ahriman wants to sink manas into the four elements to forge his clever golden chains of materialized intellectuality.

Ahriman "prowls in the hidden parts of man's nature," down in the "deepest stratum of consciousness." In those cavernous extremities of consciousness the father of lies counsels us, whispering Mephistophelean suggestions from below the threshold of our awareness. Like an incubus, he permeates our dream life with great enticements to evil, coaching us from the shadows in the magical art of permeating our desire-nature and willing activity with the personal element. Then our action is motivated not by high ideals and divine inspirations, but by self-considerations and schemes for material aggrandizement. And because Ahriman prompts us hypnotically from within, those unfamiliar, unexplored outposts of our being in which we are normally asleep—our feelings, in which we dream, and our willing, in which we slumber—we are entirely vulnerable to his insinuations.

In this way, then, Ahriman claims human instinctuality as his dominion and the success of his imminent incarnation is assured.

The Human Equipoise between Lucifer and Ahriman

Zurvan's ambivalent progeny, as Steiner conceptualized Lucifer and Ahriman for us, however hateful, fearful, or generally inimical they might seem, nonetheless have a cosmically ordained role in human evolution. Their dynamic interplay is essential for the progressive unfoldment of human evolution and in the "deeper, spiritual ordering of the world," Steiner emphasized. Their dialectic is as inherent to creation as negative and positive polarities in electricity. "Evolution has need of hindrances in order that the right tempo can be maintained." The apparent opposition of Lucifer and Ahriman imparts weight to evolution, a thrustblock against which to push towards the Good. It was all part of the cosmic plan, anyway.

In the days before the Fall of the Human, the "Higher Powers of progressive evolution" made a contract with Lucifer and Ahriman, Steiner explained. Through a "deed of the Gods" humans were entangled in matter, which is to say, we began our cycle of materialized incarnations on Earth. We entered the world of matter, time, individuality, illness, and death. But this decision wasn't a human act; rather, it was a supersensible, divine decision laid upon a nascent humanity with the expectation that through this we would attain the powers of love and freedom. After the Fall of humanity, the primeval Old Moon teachers added another clause to the contract. Through this addendum they hoped to regulate the "extra-earthly" influences of Lucifer and Ahriman. Ahriman was permitted to exercise his maximum influence on human life *before* incarnation, employing the forces of heredity, but he could not interfere with humans after death, on their outward arc into the cosmos. Lucifer was allowed to wield his influence on humans *after* they had passed through the gates of death but not on the inward arc from the cosmos to Earth; Lucifer could employ the forces of climate, education, and modes of behavior as legitimate spheres of influence. These appointments defined their lawful jurisdiction.[66]

Today, a great many days and lives since the Fall, we might stand aghast before the tableau of Luciferic inflation and Ahrimanic contraction, were we able to see it in such a concentrated iconic form. We might fear Lucifer and hate Ahriman, but it's salutary to remember that within their "rightfully allotted place" in creation, Lucifer and Ahriman actually work beneficially on our behalf. In their own way, said Steiner, they both wish to "transform man into the spiritual," to spiritualize the Earth, and to imbue our world with "spiritual substance and with dense spiritual forces." Both Lucifer and Ahriman, as Zurvan's twin progeny and according to the measure of their being, negotiate the translation of cosmic intelligence, that world-creating activity of manas and the imaginative etheric thinking force of Sophia, into the context of a mineralized human individuality subject to time and mortality. In our human lives, then, we enact the ecstasy and the misery, the double valence of Zurvan's progeny caught in Time.

A proposition of this scale is inevitably ambivalent. Ahriman buries manas in matter, while Lucifer exalts manas in the ether. Ahriman permeates intellectuality with gravity, while Lucifer imbues imagination with levity. What transforms Lucifer and Ahriman from positive irritants to injurious opponents is when they operate outside their rightful domain. But who maintains the boundaries here? The Gods may have hammered out the original contract, and Lucifer and Ahriman may initiate action beyond their lawful spheres, but it's our *human* responsibility to bring their influences into the right relationship in consciousness, to establish equipoise between them.[67] And in this act of cosmic mediation between an inflationary Lucifer and a contracting Ahriman, Christ is our agent of equilibrium.

Human life is the scale beam in this equilibration, said Steiner. The fulcrum consists of Lucifer pulling upward, Ahriman pulling downward. Christ is the "exemplary" force that imparts balance, that brings the pendulum oscillations to rest in the warm center. "To keep the scales in perfect balance signifies the essential being of man, the state of equilibrium which represents the Christ Impulse."[68]

A realistic appraisal of the world requires us to acknowledge this triad of forces, Steiner emphasized. Our life in the world is an experience of hardening and dissolving, calcination and rejuvenation, in "perpetual alternation." But there is an "intervening space," even at the physical level of the human organism, a still haven from the perpetual oscillations of Lucifer and Ahriman. Jehovah, whom Steiner construed as a Moon-reflected aspect of the Christ, established this neutral ground at the original creation of humanity. This sanctuary sits in the form of a cube in the middle of the sternum, in the middle of the breathing process. "There it was that he so filled man with His own being, with His own magic breath, that the influence of this magic breath was able to extend into the regions in the rest of man that belong to Lucifer and Ahriman." In this unique cubic sanctum in the middle of the human, the breath of Christ (Jehovah) "enters directly into the spatial human being" and equipoise is attained.[69] Jehovah's cube in the human sternum assumes greater significance when we discuss World Pentecost in Section IV.

Steiner's *Representative of Humanity* sculpture reminds us that between the two opposing elements of Lucifer and Ahriman stands the Christ as the "impulse of equilibrium." Steiner likened the Christ equilibrium to a boat. Lucifer and Ahriman are the seething oceanic forces moving the world. To the degree a human (the sailor) is conscious of the Christ as a profound impulse working within him through the Ego, he steers his seacraft through the storms "in spite of everything because he sits in his Christ-boat."[70]

When we position ourselves in this Christ-boat, suffused with Christ-consciousness, the possibility opens up before us to establish a "spiritual bond of brotherhood" with our fellow boatmates despite the individuality of the Ego and the attendant impulses towards separation and selfishness. Lucifer gave humans freedom and independence; Ahriman introduced us to matter and material manipulation; then through the Mystery of Golgotha, Christ transmuted this freedom into love, and permeated this matter with spirit, transforming the influence of Lucifer and Ahriman into the Good.[71] But it's up to us individually to re-enact this transmutation of Lucifer and Ahriman into the Good. Christ set the example at Golgotha; now it's for us to recapitulate the Christ Event through the Imagination of Pentecost. This transmutation is really a catharsis, an initiation, a purgation of our Old Moon astrality, and superintending this profound life passage we find the double-faced Guardian of the Threshold.

CHAPTER 8

The Great Human Ideal on Earth

Encountering the Guardian of the Threshold

*T*HE GUARDIAN STANDS before the Threshold double-faced for our own protection. Do you truly wish to pass through? he asks, revealing to us a shocking picture. The supersensible worlds are perilous and fraught with danger for the unprepared, for those who stumble through unaware and untutored, without the authority of initiation. Steiner likened unauthorized entry into the spiritual worlds beyond the physical to putting your head into a swarming ant hill. With dismay you discover that immediately beyond the veil between the worlds is a "vortex of spiritual beings," most of them inimical to humankind. The beatific angels stand behind the inimical frontliners, awaiting our discernment. The possibilities for psychic disaster from this imprudent entry are considerable: misunderstanding, mistake, metaphysical error, severe psychic injury, self-projection, possession of self, and a lifelong habit of unhealthy, subjective mysticism. These are chief among the numerous dangers of an easy mediumship and an indolent clairvoyance that emerge without training and initiation.

Only through an initiatory clairvoyance can we safely, reliably *discriminate* between benevolent and malevolent spirits across the threshold. In Steiner's view, everything hinges on our faculty of supersensible discrimination—a skill that comes to us only through "arduous ordeals." Lucifer and Ahriman and their agents, we must remember, stand poised on the other side of the supersensible threshold, ready to bind our lotus flowers to our elemental backbone, to confound our percepts, distort our concepts, and generally scramble our experience. The moment we cross this spiritual threshold, we expose ourselves without mediation to the perennial cosmic dialectic of Lucifer and Ahriman. At that moment we are immediately and thoroughly irradiated with the full impact of the ambivalent consequences of their struggle in Time. Their irresolution is our confusion. Our muddle is their enhancement.

The supersensible worlds, both beyond and within the self, normally are sealed off from casual human access. Their spiritual contents are too potent, too potentially overwhelming and destructive, to be part of our ordinary mental continuum. Through ordinary sense-bound perception today most people are unable to see through the kaleidoscope of colors, sounds, scents, and shapes of the physical world into the subtle, formative world beyond, or to see through the pointillist night sky the majestic anatomies of celestial spiritual beings. Such a world is clearly implied, but most often Ariadne's thread that leads us out of the sensory labyrinth into true reality is difficult to find. The Guardian of the Threshold exists because most likely we would not psychologically survive the impact of the vision of the supersensible. Similarly, we suspect that our inner soul experiences conceal something deeper within, to which our access, too, is naturally blocked; we intuit that some other, more real, possibly autonomous, self lives autochthonously within our being.

What is blocked, then? "These are the two poles between which lie all vicissitudes of soul—fear of the void and the collapse into egotism," said Steiner.[1] Were we to penetrate directly beyond the external sense world into reality and the realm of the "upper gods," we would be confronted with the cosmic void, with the naked world of "mere idea," with the unfleshed cosmic imaginations and living thoughts of the universe. The experience could be devastating and annihilating. Conversely, were we to penetrate below the sealed membrane of our inner being and enter that chthonic realm of the "lower gods," we would be subjected to unbridled egotism, self-inflation, and the "blindly raging impulses of our own inner being." The key issue here is premature, unschooled entry. The supersensible world, both outer and inner, is a psychic Pandora's box of bewildering contents. Unauthorized entry is an especially problematic situation today as many people in the West blossom into a spontaneous psychism and nascent clairvoyance almost overnight, but almost always without training, preparation, or initiation. This trend is becoming more prevalent as the unfoldment of the consciousness soul nudges many women and men into an early blush with supersensible awareness. But without inner schooling, without mature, reliable mentors, if they fail to meet with the Guardians and slip past, how will they fare in the supersensible?

Esoteric tradition classically refers to these ontologically innate sealed doors in our being as the Guardians of the Threshold. Steiner construed the Guardian as twofold: the Lesser Guardian bars our entry within, the Greater Guardian blocks our access outward. We live, safely if numbly, in a hermetically sealed artificial box between two awesome expanses. In a strange paradox of relationship, our jailer is our benefactor. The twin-visaged Guardian is yet another mysterious, unsuspected cosmic being (like Michael, Sophia, Lucifer, and Ahriman) whose acquaintance we vitally need to make if we want to navigate the supersensible worlds with any degree of cognitive safety. The irony is that when we confront the Guardian in a "soul-shaking" initiation, we learn that this "other self within us" is our own Ego in disguise.

The Western occultist Dion Fortune illustrated the negative side of this principle vividly in her short story "The Scented Poppies." A man was using subtle techniques of black magic to commit serious occult offenses, including murder. When the case was brought to Doctor Taverner, Fortune's fictional white occultist, he decided to resolve the affair using occult means: he gave the probable offender clairvoyance, hoping this would smoke him out. "When a man gets the Sight, one of the first things he sees is his naked soul," explained Taverner, "and if that man was the one we think he is, it will probably be the last, for the soul that has perpetrated those cold-blooded murders will not bear looking at." Taverner was right; soon after, they heard a "blood-curdling yell," filled with terror and panic, as the culprit ran madly out of the building. "He has met the Guardian of the Threshold," said Taverner.[2]

So there on the threshold, as Doctor Taverner well knew, "we confront our own true ego." This "intensified self" disguises, or clothes, itself in our unique weaknesses, our failings—in short, in our unresolved Old Moon astrality. "Overcome with shame, we have to look at what we are, at what the Guardian has wrapped himself in."[3] The Guardian's raiment is made of the nightly dream contents of our unconsciousness, with the panoply of our inherited, unclarified emotional soul life of instincts, impulses, and passions, said Steiner. The Guardian is a terrifying, awesome imagination of our astral soul life in one composite image. In the vocabulary of Jungian depth analysis, the Guardian is the unintegrated Shadow looming on the threshold of the Self; as Jung said, individuation of the Self requires the incorporation of this ominous Shadow, cast by the rejected aspects of the personality, into the totality of one's psychological identity. The incorporation process itself has a transmutative effect on the Shadow, bringing it into the light of daytime consciousness and the Sun of the psyche, as Jung would say. In Greek mythology one image of the Guardian was the triple-headed hound, Cerberus, the noisome Spirit of the Pit, who guarded Hecate's underworld gates.

But whether it be spectral dog, the intimidating Shadow, or the Guardian of the Threshold, our legitimate, safe entry into the supersensible world depends entirely on our conscious, articulate exchange with this fundamentally *self-projected* mentor at the threshold. Standing before us we behold our Ego in the disguise of our unresolved karmic astrality, in the garment of lifetimes of neglect, suppression, and karmic liability.

The Guardian is also our initiator, because this riveting confrontation forces us to develop "truly genuine, unsparing self-knowledge" and the "faculty to differentiate truth from error" in the spiritual world. When we can discern the appearance of the Guardian as self-woven from our own unpurged astrality and emotional soul life, then we have made the foundational discrimination absolutely necessary for safe negotiation through the supersensible worlds. We can now distinguish what is subjectively self-projected from what is objectively cosmically existent. This is crucial in our cognitive activities across the threshold. We have to be able to recognize our own unfamiliar astral face in the Guardian's mirror before we can safely pass through and actually perceive something objective in the supersensible world. Then, with mature discrimination, we can behold first the impressions of, then indications of the activities of, then the actual "faces" of real, self-existent spiritual beings such as Michael and Sophia. It is a gradual, serial progression through imagination, intuition, and inspiration, as Steiner explained; this sequence is the lawful process of spiritual scientific initiation or what Steiner called inner schooling.

It is our responsibility to exercise clear judgment when confronted with unfamiliar spiritual beings. It is up to us to identify them correctly, and it is exceedingly easy to make errors in identification, even among the benevolent spiritual beings. But what if they are among the ranks of Luciferic or Ahrimanic beings, of ambivalent intent? What if we misidentify at this stage and with these risks? We need to query upon encountering spiritual beings: are they progressive or regressive spirits with respect to cosmic evolution? Are they aligned with Michael, Sophia, and the Christ? In the next chapter we'll examine the anthroposophical protocols for safe identification and negotiation. This chapter will focus on the disturbing consequences of failing to confront the Lesser and Greater Guardians of the Threshold as a result of easy mediumship and the circumvention of initiation.

Self Projection:
Failure to Meet the Lesser Guardian of the Threshold

One of the remarkable lessons we learn from the encounter with the Lesser Guardian of the Threshold is that prior to this meeting we had not seen our *true* being at all, said Steiner. Normally, and this is strange to consider, a person is aware of the contents of one's I, but is entirely unaware of the form or contents of the physical, etheric, and astral bodies.

In the early stages of an opening into clairvoyance, the threads that connect the activities of willing, feeling, and thinking in the astral and etheric bodies begin to loosen, and these functions, that had worked as a relatively single unit, now separate and act independently. The separation of the astral body from the unity of the human organism is a sudden potentization of the "sum-total of all the urges, desires, and passions accumulated in the course of successive lives on Earth." As we descend into the inner core of our being, the host of demonic forms that still lurk unresolved in the astral body suddenly loom up before us in a shocking confrontation. The Buddha's apocalyptic temptation by Mara under the Bodhi tree on the eve of his illumination was an example of this confrontation with one's own accumulated astrality.[4]

As shattering as this experience can be, it is inherently salutary, provided we work with it, because it establishes an irrefutable touchstone of what is one's own and what isn't. It may also counsel us in prudence, in taking little steps from this point onward as we approach the threshold. Without this chastening experience which is basically a self-confrontation, a person would be subject to endless supersensible deception because he would never be able to distinguish between "what he himself has carried over into that world and what in reality belongs to it." In terms of cognitive precision, this is crucial.[5] In the supersensible world everything is mobile and perpetually shape-shifting; cognitive mix-ups occur frequently and if our alertness falters, "one can mistake one's being for another."[6] It may sound flippant, but in the supersensible world, the spiritual beings, both friendly and inimical, do not wear identifying name badges; they assume that if we managed to get in, we know our way around, know the "personalities."

The encounter with the Lesser Guardian protects us from the glamors of *self*-ensnarement while evoking a sense of hidden self-shame. The important point here is that the Lesser Guardian shows us how much more we are than we thought ourselves to be, how much of us, mostly karmic inheritance, lives in the shadows of our awareness. The perception of one's own being in its true form uncovers this concealed shame because we realize, confronted by the frank evidence, how little progress we've made in clarifying our astrality and fulfilling our destiny. This is a quick way to deflate any undue sense of self-importance or psychic ability we may have developed; if we use it wisely, it is a seed that will generate prudence. The soul's imperfection (our personal karmic situation) when measured against the perfect structure of the physical sheaths (our phylogenetic inheritance) can exert an "overwhelmingly paralysing effect" upon one who sees this unprepared. The shame can consume one like fire.

This revelation of the incompletion, the imperfection, the fundamental immaturity of our inner being, the image of what we haven't yet done, can dissolve self-esteem, self-confidence, and self-consciousness, Steiner commented. We want to be chastened, even scourged, but not completely discouraged from taking any further action. The density of unfulfilled emotionality and unredeemed karma within the inner self can "seem horrifying," especially when its energies seem at every moment to be trying to entangle or capture us with tentacles. This is why Steiner called the Lesser Guardian our self-created supersensible Angel of Death, a spectral form made of "the hitherto invisible results" of our actions, feelings, and thoughts. Ordinarily, we don't encounter this Angel until after death. Normally, the "sentient body" interpolates as a veil between our waking consciousness and this inner astral image, and we are spared the shock every morning when we wake and reinsert ourselves into our physical and etheric bodies. But what we ordinarily do in the course of afterdeath activities, initiation compels us to perform while still incarnate, mainly because the results are more valuable if we are still alive.

But if we start "nibbling" at the supersensible as if it's a smorgasbord world of sweetmeats and "dainties," we're drawing the Lesser Guardian towards us, yet in such a way that we may entirely miss the *self* revelation of its presence. This indiscriminate nibbling fills our cognitive organs with "false illusory pictures," mirror images of the self, even hallucinations, all of which are "special booty" for Ahriman. Ahriman likes these "well-padded shadows and plump phantoms," and the more our supersensible images resemble scenarios of the physical world, the better. The result is that one mistakes one's inner projected world and astral body for the genuinely objective supersensible. This is a major, and common, error. The functions of thinking, feeling, and willing confront us as a "living trinity, experienced as three distinct entities;" in fact, when we encounter our astral self it, too, can appear in "multiple, spiritually objective copies." This *self* confrontation can plunge us without guidance into a vertiginous hall of mirrors.

This is the same tenor of experience that the Tibetan *Book of the Dead* describes as the *Bardo*, the in-between state, purgatory, that one encounters immediately after death; however, the Tibetan sages really intended the text to be a guide for the living as they negotiated the tortuous inner paths of initiation.[7] We are always facing ourselves. We are intimidated by our own independent thought-forms and misconstrue them as legitimate spiritual beings. The images may be fantastic and grotesque; we may be attacked by hideous animal forms or "dark demoniacal shadows," or assailed by creatures who are "distortions and caricatures" of sense-world beings. Beyond our ken, Lucifer creates separate shadowy beings, virtual images, animated pictures from aspects of our unresolved karma, then parades them, seductively or menacingly, before us, knowing we cannot tell the difference.[8]

The projected mirror images of our inner being seem to form a separate external world around us in astral space. It is a remarkably deceptive simulacrum, however, because the images are mirror-reversed. This means the moral weight of appearances is also reversed and we can be doubly fooled: a good quality appears as ugly, while vices are clothed in alluring beauty. Self-deception abounds because "the astral body is much cleverer than we are." Steiner called this seeming self-created astral world, *Kamaloca*.[9]

Normally after death, we are enclosed within Kamaloca for a period of review and clarification lasting the equivalent of about one third of our previous earthly life. In Kamaloca one resides purgatively "within the atmosphere of his own astral nature acquired on earth." Kamaloca is an environment made by the projection into external space of one's emotional subjectivity, a designer-theater of the soul. During initiation, supersensible nibbling, premature entry, or through unearned, easy clairvoyance, we enter Kamaloca while still physically embodied; in this context it's a far more treacherous, difficult region than in the after-death encounter because our cognition is so intimately tied to our sense-bound life. The less prepared we are, the more dangerous is Kamaloca; the less we appreciate how materialistic our supposedly spiritual views are, the more error we are prone to. We're imprisoned within ourselves in Kamaloca, enthralled by an "objective" world around us which is nothing more than the virtual projection of our wishes, desires, feelings, and moods—"this whole, damaging world of passion."

Kamaloca, then, is the problematical condition of being that confronts a person who slips unlawfully past the Lesser Guardian of the Threshold. In other words, if you slip past this Guardian and do not undergo the chastening, self-confronting experience it offers, then you wander through a cognitive minefield of your own projection, but without knowing it is yourself that comprises this astral environment. With the Lesser Guardian, you *know* you are being confronted with a tableau, certainly unfamiliar, of yourself. It is intimidating but safe. One who enters Kamaloca through by-passing the Guardian, while physically alive but without the "slow occult training of the soul"—that is, with no maps, inadequate preparation, little discriminative armament—walks blithely into an inchoate jungle, completely vulnerable to its amoral denizens. In occult training the individual is serially introduced to a personal, self-created Kamaloca and guided through the process of clarification and purging to a state of relatively objective cognition. Without this deliberate inner schooling, however, a person opening to psychism or easy mediumship is subject to a legion of deceptions. For example, the medium's own physiological processes are projected outwards as chromatic visions. This bizarre but common state Steiner called "abdomen clairvoyance," evoking the classical image of the "belly talkers" of Greece and Rome.

Abdomen clairvoyance generates visions—"the most sublime images, the most sublime radiating processes of color and form, the most beautiful clairvoyant images," even automatic previsions in time, said Steiner. But these are nothing more than subjectively spawned hallucinations originating in abnormalities of the physical organism. These multicolored tableaux can be "very seductive," producing "the most marvellous spiritual discoveries," but truthfully they are digestive fantasies, animated pictures of the metabolic, glandular, *physical* processes of the body. The medium's stunning vision is "perhaps only a passing indisposition of his liver or stomach after a more or less excellent midday meal," said Steiner.[10]

The etheric and astral forces at work in the formation, maintenance, and activity of the digestive organs reflect themselves in etheric pictures in what we could jokingly call an imagination of lunch. What this imagination projects before us are the spiritual aspects of the physical processes of digestion as a "revelation" of one's bodily life. Everything leading to mediumship, hallucinations or visions, said Steiner quite adamantly, proceed from "diseased" bodily organs which breathe their psycho-spiritual content into consciousness in a pathological way. These "psychopathic manifestations" actually submerge an individual's soul life more deeply into the physical body and act from a level *below* ordinary sense experience. Imaginative knowledge, gained through inner schooling in spiritual science, in contrast, works from a level that transcends sense perception.

Hallucinations of spiders or insects crawling over one's body, for example, actually derive from an agitated kidney system and not some infernal arachnoid infestation.[11] The visions of beautiful digestive color that belly clairvoyance creates actually make one *more* dependent on the sensory physical world and the biological forces of growth, digestion, and metabolism; they root one even deeper in the egoism of physical selfhood. Hallucinations, visionary experiences, telepathy, telekinesis, and teleplasty (the exudation of radiant etheric matter in human form), claimed Steiner, are all completely connected with the human's physical and etheric bodies; as such, they can "throw no light whatever upon the supersensible world." By contrast, the correct working of imagination, as a preliminary spiritual cognitive activity, makes us less dependent on organic, physical processes, and eventually liberates us from sensebound thinking altogether. Belly clairvoyance may be interesting, but, ontologically, it's an empty experience. "So the business may bring great successes but it still is not the right path, for it does not give us free mobility in the spiritual world."[12]

Mobility in Kamaloca can be like a wild ride on the "bumper" cars at an amusement park. We're very likely to careen into someone else's self-projected astral forms. Kamaloca is a multiplicity of externalized individualized worlds, all intermingling and cross-fertilizing—a vortex of projections. It is an uncorroborable terrain in which the possibility of scientific peer review and replication of experimental results is inconceivable. We may be thoroughly absorbed in our own astral extrapolations, yet our reveries may be literally punctuated by somebody else's astral detritus. As Steiner explained, in Kamaloca human souls experience, clarify, and transmute their astral bodies; it is like an alchemical laboratory. This activity produces psychic waste products that Steiner variously called astral remnants, astral corpses, or astral shells. These discarded remnants of astral alchemy are "constantly present" in our environment as anthropomorphic garbage. At the conclusion of the Kamaloca experience, the "untransformed portion" of the astral self is rejected as a hollow sheath. If it contains evil desires, inappropriate passions, or malevolent thought-forms, or if it originates from an individual who refused to cultivate any form of conscious spiritual cognition while alive, then this remnant can cause great damage in the world, becoming a "destructive center" that disrupts the air (or mental) element in human life. "The clairvoyant vision can observe in the atmospheric phenomena of the Earth for many years the noising of the astral bodies of the dead."[13]

This littering of the astral plane with cast-off human shells has important ramifications for contemporary channeling and mediumship. It helps us to clarify a widespread mistake in attribution. Mediums of the nineteenth century and trance channels of the late twentieth century claim they have contacted the authentic living spirits of the "dead." That may be their honest claim, but it's more likely a misinterpretation, said Steiner. What is far more likely is that they're contacting the loosened, distintegrating, anachronistic remnants of living, progressing souls, "thought-echoes" with a virtual, automatic sentience—cast-off remnants that are themselves, technically and really, dead.

This bewildering theater of misinterpretation also implicates the Akashic Records, our reading there, and subsequent claims we make about past lives. Again, we're dealing with the shadow play of dead phantoms. For example, the Akashic Records may preserve a *virtually* living image of Caesar true to his Roman life and appearance; yet the individuality of the Caesar soul may have already reincarnated many times since and even be present on the physical Earth at the time in which the medium "contacts" him. In modern language, we have encountered a virtual hologram of a departed living soul. What the medium contacts is the discarded astral shell of Caesar, but not the living soul. This kind of confusion commonly informed spiritualistic séances in Steiner's day. "The spiritualist imagines he is seeing a man who has died, when it is really only his Akasha picture." A medium might see the image of Goethe as he was in 1796; this image may well seem alive, may even answer questions with new information, with original answers that Goethe *might* have given, but it isn't

Goethe. Goethe is long gone; the psychic has been talking with a mirage.[14]

It's a startling fact that astral corpses can speak intelligently. Mediums readily misinterpret these voluble shells for the living spirits of deceased humans. The nineteenth-century spiritualist Langsdorf misinterpreted the astral husk of his metaphysical adversary, H. P. Blavatsky, for the real thing. Langsdorf was vehemently against all theories of reincarnation and always sought new grounds to refute anyone's claims, including Blavatsky's. When he encountered Blavatsky's astral remnant, "she" told him reincarnation was false and she wished she had never taught it. Steiner found this anecdote amusing and revealing. Blavatsky, when younger, had in fact opposed reincarnation. "She herself came to know better, but her error clung to her astral husk." And that husk of H.P.B. fooled Langsdorf, who conversed with a ghost of Blavatsky's former self; unfortunately, he passed his deception on to the world, where it continues to mislead people, added Steiner. [15]

Not only do mediums often channel the chimerical voices and vocalizing shells of the supersensible dead (in contrast to the supersensible living), but they often get things wrong when it comes to making past life determinations. Karmic and past life research is exceedingly deceptive. Accurate and genuine knowledge in this field is "extraordinarily difficult" to attain and among the most difficult of occult studies, said Steiner. "If you are satisfied with phantasy, then it is naturally easy, for you can make things fit in as you like." The rampant "foolishness" and "nonsense" in past life claims often grow out of the vanity and ambition of the mediums, of their attraction to glamor and the imprecision that comes with easy mediumship. "I can count as many as 25 or 26 Mary Magdalenes I have met in my lifetime!"[16] In a 1912 lecture cycle Steiner outlined an "absolutely good and sure" path for remembering one's own past lives "out of what actually exists" in the soul. "It is easier to imagine on all sorts of external grounds that one has been Marie Antoinette or Mary Magdalene, or somebody like that in a former incarnation."[17] No doubt Steiner would find that the Magdalene count is equally high today. But according to Steiner's criteria, we would have to conclude that people claiming Magdalene, and all the other celebrity reincarnations, as a past life have a mistaken conception. At least four major factors obstruct accuracy in past life research and most mediums and channels seem oblivious of them.

The first obstruction is a misreading of one's apparent identification and familiarity with the time period under investigation. The researcher seems to know all about the events and personalities of a time many centuries ago; this vignette of planetary time seems acutely familiar, notes the psychic. "Superficial students" conclude that this familiarity comes from an actual incarnation in that age, but most often this is incorrect; the connection is vicarious not participatory. The disarming sense of recognition, Steiner explained, comes from the life between death and rebirth in the Sun sphere, when students experience most vividly a connection with life on Earth, immersing themselves contemplatively like a supersensible scholar in the minutiae of that particular cultural epoch underway in physical life. "Earth life presented itself to you then as a 'beyond' very much as the supersensible life presents itself to you on Earth as a 'beyond.'"[18]

The second obstruction results from a basic inattention to self during a particular incarnation. We're more likely to recall incidents from a former life if during the actual moments of our experience, we possess a large measure of self-consciousness, with which we vividly imprint the incident in our karmic memory. We have to remember ourselves in a given moment of physical life to remember ourselves later in a subsequent incarnation; if not, we have nothing to remember, no hook with which to purchase a memory of a former time. Failing this, the lives and fortunes of prominent personalities around us get fixed in our etheric memory. An individual may recall a brilliant personality such as Queen Elizabeth I or Joan of Arc; the image may surface with vivid presence and undeniable verisimilitude. The mistake is to conclude that the current individual, on the strength of this memory, in fact *was* this former personality. All that is being recalled is the strong impression Queen Elizabeth made on such an individual with diminished self-awareness in that time period. So the real Queen Elizabeth, like Mary Magdalene, can observe a host of latter-day impersonators, none of them worthy of her imprimatur. Since this Elizabethan individuality failed to impress her own self-consciousness onto the etheric record at that time, her memory, active in a subsequent incarnation, regards her as a nonentity, remembering instead only what was most intensely noted, in this case, the Queen.

Third, the investigating medium must also factor in what Steiner called the principle of spiritual economy. This principle describes the preservation of valuable etheric, astral, and Ego bodies that are "transplanted in the spiritual soil of posterity," to act as impulses in later phases of world history. The etheric body, astral body, and Ego of an individual of high spiritual attainment will often be deployed in three different incarnational directions over time. "Disregarding this fact can easily lead to great misconceptions on the part of someone who investigates a human being's past with faulty clairvoyant methods." In this complex shuffling of being bodies, the individual bearing the etheric body of St. Francis, for example, could not accurately claim identity with the *I* of St. Francis, nor with his astral form. St. Francis' astral body was actually a copy of the astral body of Jesus, which itself had a complicated pedigree. The astral body of Nicholas of Cusa was transferred to Copernicus, although he didn't bear Cusa's Ego. The etheric body of Galileo was passed on to the Russian grammatist, Michail Lomonosov, but it would be completely wrong to say he was the reincarnation of Galileo.[19]

The fourth obstacle to accurate Akashic research is even more complex. The Mystery of Golgotha actually changed the karmic records of all individuals on Earth. You cannot find their "bad deeds" in the Akashic chronicle anymore, Steiner explained. Soul permeation by the Christ is the prerequisite for any kind of precision in Akashic Record investigation. Without this, the records won't tally. At the Mystery of Golgotha, Christ took upon himself the "objective debt" of everyone's guilty deeds (their "sins"), literally expunging them from the Akashic Records. This profound redemptive act did not absolve people from the inexorability of karmic justice; they still had to make amends and readjustments in subsequent lives, but their records were no longer a matter of public access.

Since the Christ bought up everyone's bad deeds, their Akashic Records were similarly purified. It makes research into lifetimes prior to Golgotha subject to continuous error because the records no longer show the bad deeds, although in post-Golgotha lifetimes people are still tacitly redeeming their karma. Entire karmic histories and planetary cultural chronicles prepared through occult research can be terribly inaccurate, Steiner commented. He indicated Theosophy's clairvoyant maven, Charles Leadbeater, as the most recent example. "I was not at all surprised that Leadbeater, who in reality knows nothing about Christ, should have made the most abstruse statements concerning the evolution of the Earth."[20]

Abstruse declarations about the supersensible world, especially if they are incorrect, is a form of occult malpractice that produces false, lingering, and dangerous results. Occult errors accumulate as thought-form pollution in the spiritual worlds. False results of spiritual inquiry by earlier "biased" occultists and "amateur mediums" actually reside in the supersensible as yet another epistemologically meretricious skin in the Kamalocan onion. There they confront us as living realities, living beings, and real powers when we make our own investigations—even though they are false.

It is not surprising, in light of this, that Steiner was exceedingly skeptical of most mediumistic claims about past life research, as we should be today. Simply consider the stakes: if the Brothers of the Left initially tried to prevent the dissemination of knowledge of reincarnation in the nineteenth-century Spiritualist phase, today, in the next episode, they can try to confuse, distort, obfuscate, and corrupt it, so that people form a mistaken idea of something that is true. A corrupted form does more epistemological damage than no form at all, or its suppression. Clairvoyants who speak "a great deal" about earlier incarnations "must be distrusted" and their reports considered fallacious, Steiner declared. He said that because mediums generally are not resistant to the powerful temptations of the astral world. They're easily deceived into misconstruing the Ahrimanically inspired ghosts and specters that take form from the rising mists of Kamaloca as authentic images of earlier incarnations; they don't see them as the Ahrimanic holograms they are. Unfortunately, this kind of occult malpractice piles "delusion after delusion" into the spiritual world.

This Kamalocan barque of occult garbage regularly unloads into the physical world. In the realm of the physically living, metaphysical mistakes stemming from faulty past life research

and the channeling of dead, astral remnants skews our understanding. Occult imprecision introduces entirely incorrect conceptions of the spiritual world. For example, in light of this, what
should we reasonably make of a trance channel such as Ellwood
Babbitt who claims to have manifested 300 different personalities
in direct voice channeling? Most channeling enthusiasts accept
this claim uncritically, genuinely believing that people like Edgar
Allan Poe and Will Rogers are just queuing up outside Babbitt's
awareness, dying for a chance at the microphone.

During the years 1967 to 1979, Babbitt claimed he channeled
Clarence Darrow, Sir Francis Bacon, Sigmund Freud, Socrates,
Abraham Lincoln, St. Luke, Pontius Pilate, Samuel Clemens, and
a great many more brand-name dead souls. And he did so in
good faith, even reverently, with no intention to misrepresent.
Even his colleague Charles Hapgood, an academic geographer
who tried to apply scientific precision to Babbitt's remarkable
claims, failed to acknowledge the deceptive activity of orating astral shells. Hapgood's clinical studies showed that during trance
channeling, Babbitt's brain waves and blood pressure were "radically different" for each manifested personality. For Hapgood,
this physically "proved" that other personalities were speaking
through Babbitt.[21] Like Babbitt, he misinterpreted discarded vocalizing astral corpses for the authentic spiritual presence of
former human beings; together, they disseminated this misattribution into the New Age channeling culture where it now inspires many others to the same error.

In America, this kind of misattribution can even get televised.
Shirley MacLaine's widely viewed *Out on a Limb* TV mini-series in
1987 featured "live" trance channeling by one of America's most
famous TV channels, Kevin Ryerson, guest of all the network talk
shows. Ryerson's astral celebrity show of spirit entities includes
John the Evangelist; Obadiah, a nineteenth century Haitian herbalist; Atun-Re, a Nubian from 1300 B.C.; Tom MacPherson, a sixteenth century Irish pickpocket; Japu, an Oriental storyteller,
circa 3000 B.C.; Little Elk, an Indian spirit; Ercon, denizen of the
UFO Arcumi; and "many other entities [who] have spontaneously
spoken through my trance state over the last fifteen years."

As far as Ryerson is concerned, these "spirit teachers" are supersensibly real as presented—and that's exactly how that nimble

Elizabethan thief MacPherson sees it, too. "I am not dead, I am very much alive. I consider myself as much a human being as you are, because I have personality, I have feelings, and I have ambitions." [22] Indeed he has, but it's the lower astral self of a simulacrum, a Kamalocan dummy animated by a living (although somnambulant) ventriloquist, Ryerson. It's a consummate act of impersonation that has fooled nearly everybody in Hollywood, set new standards for errors in spiritual investigation, and made Ryerson rich. It is those "noising" soul-corpses lingering in the astral atmosphere again, Steiner would say. Ryerson and his peers are channeling ghosts—ghosts with just enough residual spunk to say a few clever words to the television audience. "By far the greater majority of communications from the spirit world made by mediums stem from such souls and consist essentially of what they are striving to cast off." [23]

Perusing the mass of mediumistic reports available in his own day, Steiner noted that everything had a uniformly "strongly tendentious character;" he found this consistently propagandist tone suspicious. Further, most descriptions of the life after death were "entirely false," and this was especially so with material from mediums guided by the souls of *living* persons. We need to remember Steiner's revelations about the occult manipulations of the black lodges in nineteenth-century Spiritualism. Most mediums never contacted the legitimately dead at all, said Steiner; they were manifesting apparitions generated by the initiates of the lodges. If this is true, then what is the source of the voices of today's trance channels?

Technically, *medium*ship contact with the authentically dead is impossible. Transpirational contact through a *medium* is an existential oxymoron, Steiner said, and all claims of such contact are fallacious. It's impossible for a medium to actually enter the realm of the Dead, said Steiner, because "the very members of his being which belong to that realm have been made inoperative." Steiner was referring to the etheric, astral, and Ego bodies in a human's psychic constitution, members "which can be lifted out of the physical body." The mediums could never do this: they are but hollow instruments, empty reeds. Certifiable contact with the living dead requires the active, conscious removal of attention from the sense world and the officiating, awake presence of the I in the supersensible world. It is not something one can sleep through and competently perform. The nineteenth-century mediums couldn't do this, and most twentieth century channels similarly fall asleep on the job; some, like Ryerson, actually boast of their somnambulism. "I'm one of the very few people who literally gets paid for sleeping on the job," he said.

So the mediums never contacted the Dead; instead, they got the projected astral bodies of living people, projected by "initiates who had put themselves either in distant or close rapport with the mediums," Steiner explained. This led them astray into aberrations and false allegations and the promotion of a "great fallacy." Their cartographies of the life after death were woven not from objective truth, but from Luciferic teachings and Ahrimanic observations, all carefully manipulated by the unseen, unsuspected black lodges. Their "grotesque pronouncements" entered the world as major but unacknowledged sources of error.[24] The same metaphysical liability confronts us today at the close of the twentieth century. A great deal of the American channeling garden party may be skipping obliviously down the primrose path into a spiritual cul de sac. Our whole approach to cognitive expansion may similarly be at risk to Luciferic and Ahrimanic manipulation and distortion. In today's floriation of channeled guides sans credentials, many well-intentioned occult neophytes may find themselves routed unhappily into the developmental ditch from unreliable texts.

These false astral cartographies foster a legion of "materialist specter-seers," noted Steiner. Mediums of easy, unearned clairvoyance transfer their predominant attitude of love of the ease of thinking and feeling into their conduct in the spiritual worlds. These attitudes become cognitive habits that lead to the error of phenomenalism. Such people insist on seeing the supersensible world in the same terms as the physical world. This is evident in the spate of pseudo-occult movies since 1980 that have sought to domesticate the afterlife. Spiritual realities are couched in the same forms as physical sense-bound facts; metaphors and analogies are made literal, taken at face value. But when you domesticate the supersensible according to materialist tendencies, when you reconstruct the spiritual plane according to materialist principles, you do not perceive real spiritual beings at all. You get specters, ghosts, shells, and "condensed spirits." You get the literalization of metaphor, or in Alfred North Whitehead's famous expression, "misplaced concreteness."

This is "one dangerous extreme of error" that exists "in the widest circles," said Steiner. You're assured of slipping into unconsciousness in relation to the supersensible beings and processes if what you take into that world "is only an extract of sense reality." The specterseer finds only cast-off sheaths, useless withered remnants, the shells of dead shellfish—in short, "visible unreality." The profound spiritual error that arises here is to mistake what is dying and withering for what is fruitful and significant.[25] In other words, easy mediumship gives you only dead riches.

Specter-seers may be flourishing in America's affluent media capital, Hollywood. Hollywood is going to Heaven in the 1990s, declared *Time*. The hot new hero of the decade is the Dead, or nearly dead, or just back from the Dead. The decade of the Dead opened with *Ghost*, a semi-metaphysical blockbuster that combined transdimensional romance with a comic book dramatization of the astral plane. Clearly, robust spirits and friendly, intervening ghosts are *very* popular, and their shadowy forms are much in demand by cinematic moguls awakening to the capitalization of the Almighty. *Ghost* earned $500 million worldwide in its first year, which was sufficient to transform Demi Moore from *Ghost*'s skeptic (1990) to psychic in *The Butcher's Wife* (1991). Moore's conversion is impressive, and so is Hollywood's encore: a dozen more films about the "Great Beyond," moving out of the pipeline into theaters. Some of the heavenly renditions have "the depth of a shampoo commercial," quipped *Time*.[26] "Dying is depicted as a transitory state, at worst a move to a new neighborhood." In *Defending Your Life*, a spiritually unconscious ad executive after death reviews his bland life in Judgment City through televised excerpts mediated by a grouchy panel of judges. In *Bill & Ted's Bogus Journey* two suburban streetwise teenagers die, check out Hell, and return in a rock band.

The metaphysical message is gradually permeating materialist Hollywood, "a town devoted to the glorification of the earthly body and the display of riches"—in other words, the cultural synecdoche of the West. But the message comes through into mass culture cinematically skewed and materialized—Bill and Ted's journey *is* bogus. "Only so many times can you watch a dead person help a living person with a math test," quipped one actor. Or as an entertainment executive put it, "We all want to believe that death isn't so bad."[27]

Death, according to spiritual science, may not be so bad, but our beliefs may make a mess of the experience. The trouble is that what we believe may not correspond to what is. Long before Hollywood and its (financially lucrative) apotheosis of the intangible Beyond, Steiner rigorously drew the distinction between mediumistic tendencies and genuine spiritual knowledge. Mediums, Steiner noted ironically, are strongly averse to the discipline of spiritual science. The progressive cultivation of imaginative cognition is in fact counterproductive for the continuation of that void state of consciousness in which mediums ("instruments") operate. The anthroposophical habits of a person with an active, strongly conscious creative consciousness work "disturbingly" on the revelations of the psychic, Steiner commented in 1913. "A society composed of credulous followers," said Steiner, anticipating our time, "would be the very caricature of a society fit to cultivate spiritual knowledge."[28]

Possession of Self:
Failure to Meet the Greater Guardian of the Threshold

A society fit to cultivate spiritual knowledge is necessarily one comprised of individuals who have undergone the initiation with the double-faced Guardian of the Threshold. But a culture of easy clairvoyance discourages this kind of rigor and the precision of slow, serial training. Consequently, when we exempt ourselves from conscious cognition of the Lesser Guardian we get the illusions of self-projection. When we avoid the Greater Guardian we get the perfidy of self-possession. In either case the untrained soul gets dangerously entangled in the sticky webs of Kamaloca. If it's not self-inflation, it is possession of self by inimical elemental beings. With one's lotus flowers tied to the elemental backbone by Lucifer and Ahriman, and with one's astral eyes thereby impaired, the individual crosses the threshold naive and blind, his soul liable to error and exposed to every sort of inimical being around.

Quite likely a great many more supersensible explorers would actually elect the company of the Greater Guardian over the elemental beings if they could see them contiguously in a lineup. That is precisely the difficulty: we do not usually see them directly; more often, we experience their impact and effects on our cognition. The Greater Guardian is a "sublime luminous being" radiating an "indescribable splendor," said Steiner. "Union with him looms as a far distant ideal before the soul's vision." This higher light being seeks to use the individual's organs of thinking, feeling, and willing as instruments of soul power contributing to the "liberation" of humanity. [29] Our first contact with the Greater Guardian can be "absolutely astonishing," as Shirley MacLaine reported. "I saw the form of a very tall, overpoweringly confident, almost androgynous human being." This commanding figure was "extremely protective, full of patience, yet capable of great wrath, and seemed to 'know' all there was to know," commented MacLaine. "I am your higher unlimited self," the supersensible androgyne told her. "I am *never* away from you. I *am* you. I am your unlimited soul that guides and teaches you through each incarnation."[30]

MacLaine's description of her higher unlimited soul is a useful illustration of what Steiner had in mind when he spoke of the Greater Guardian. As MacLaine learned, her Guardian seemed to know a great deal; as Steiner would say, the Greater Guardian holds most of this knowledge in reserve until his protege is prepared. The Guardian holds this knowledge in reserve to protect us from devastation and loss of Ego by an unmediated experience of the cosmic void. On the other side of MacLaine's "supremely kind" Guardian looms the spiritual macrocosm. "When the Ego spreads over the Macrocosm," said Steiner, "it loses the faculty of self-awareness, rather as a drop loses its identity in a large vessel of water."[31] A premature surrender to the infinity of the spiritual macrocosm can result in the precipitous loss of I-consciousness. We have already seen how in the after-death experience in Kamaloca one's astrality is cinematically projected in a wraparound self-contained world. Similarly, in the life after death one's Ego dilates to fill the macrocosm in an apocalyptic cosmic homecoming; but that's to be expected because the human Ego, said Steiner, is a compression of all the constituents of the supersensible world.

The meeting with the Lesser Guardian initiates us into the time continuum of our being, while the Greater Guardian initiates us through a revelation of the "terrifying bewilderment" of unbounded space. Through the Lesser Guardian we get the time initiation, the encounter with the unresolved karmic accumulation of our being extended through time. Through the Greater Guardian we get the space initiation, the recognition of our Ego as a compression of the cosmos and the cosmos as an expansion of the I. It is imprudent to rush enthusiastically out into cosmic space, cautioned Steiner, because it's really "an empty and bottomless abyss." The phenomena of the spiritual macrocosm are "so mighty and awe-inspiring" that our sense-world concepts can not embrace them in any kind of rational model. The student stands before the cosmic void "with his ideas entirely dissipated into spiritual vapor," suffused with a "tremendous enhancement" of the fear of "losing oneself in cosmic distances."[32]

This is the compressed essence of the Greater Guardian's space initiation. However, for the purposes of integration and psychic stability, the cosmic revelation is gradual and serial. But if we circumvent this cosmically sanctioned initiation, we put ourselves at considerable risk to possession by inimical, clever elemental and cosmic beings who parasitically insinuate themselves into our soul to leech and pervert our powers of true spiritual cognition. At first exposure to this idea it is perhaps inevitable that a tone of paranoia is raised, but Steiner assures us this is a fact, and therefore a legitimate danger. Mediums and trance channels are among the most susceptible to this infiltration of self because they typically lack any training or occult preparation, and because they do not expect interference and perhaps are not aware of its possibility. The mechanics of mediumship itself set this up. The medium or channel often becomes an automaton, deserting the physical body and abandoning the conscious use of will, which is the proper activity of the human I. This is the trance of mediumship, the falling asleep of channeling. This is also the foundation for possession. We need only recall the unfortunate oxymoron expressed by Lasers/Jach Pursel, describing their working relationship as "objective full-trance channeling" to see the meretriciously benign face of possession.

The somnambulant trance channel surrenders conscious control over the physical and etheric bodies during the act of mediumship. They become "deserted territory," functioning like organic "automata," given up to the influence of the cosmos and its denizens, observed Steiner. If the energy of this cosmic influence is something histrionic like the "personalities" of Ramtha or Lazaris, the sleeping channel's body entertains viewers with dramatic gestures, voice changes, even warm hugs. At least possession by Ramtha, Lazaris, or Mafu is contractual and the human parties have some—albeit vague—idea of what they are surrendering to. The danger here is that it is only a partial idea; in a mediumship contract, one must take the other party's protestations of good will on faith. And while channelism's public relations experts tout this refurbished mediumship as the state-of-the-art, streamlined, even chic path to spiritual awakening, setting standards in effect for a whole range of other cognitive activities, with the disconnection of the medium's I-consciousness and will from the interdimensional communication, "such a man becomes a kind of automaton." The exchange becomes "simply a caricature of the workings of the spiritual upon man's bodily nature."[33] In other words, there is no spiritual scientific basis for channelism's exaltation of somnambulistic possession.

The trance channel is at high risk for soul infiltration by opportunistic elementals. Even "ordinary" people are not exempt from astral intruders as the recent movies *Aliens, Gremlins, Poltergeist,* and *Dracula* graphically remind us. Again, the products of Hollywood give us a fair indication of how these activities and phenomena are entering mass culture. "The instant the soul withdraws part of its activity from the body, injurious powers from the elemental kingdom may get hold of it," warns Steiner.[34] The medium's "undeveloped faculties of judgment" and inactive, unconscious will facilitate this invasion. "Pernicious forces" then insinuate themselves into one's being. The result is often a subversion of one's balanced moral nature, and a strange accentuation of defective qualities: untruthfulness, wrath, vindictiveness, heightened selfishness, and other "low" inclinations. Trance mediums may afterwards find themselves channeling through their behavior the desires, thoughts, and ambitions of really low-grade, unevolved spirits who anchor to equivalently undeveloped aspects of their Shadow.

Individuals who resist "really exact thinking," who will have nothing to do with the rigors of spiritual science, yet wish to experience the supersensible world, unknowingly enter into a de facto contractual alliance with "destructive beings" on the threshold of the "densely populated" spiritual worlds. It's only when one returns to his physical-etheric organism that one finds it inexplicably filled with "all sorts of ingredients," like a shaggy dog pimpled with burrs after a wild run. Even under ordinary, nonexploratory circumstances, the unattended being bodies of the typical human are transparent to a congeries of elemental squatters. The astral body, for example, hosts a throng of uninvited beings "embedded like the maggots in cheese."[35]

In fact, so rich is this supersensible commerce that throughout the whole of our life, "elemental beings stream in."[36] The physical circulation of lymph, for example, is not just a matter of fluids; "whole hosts" of elemental spirits move through the body through this circulation. When we eat food, it is not just carbohydrates and amino acids that enter our physical metabolism: we eat at the same time "definite spirits" that pass from the mouth to stomach then spread through the entire organism. Not even perfume is exempt from this insidious infiltration, said Steiner. "It is quite frightful to observe occultly what dissolute spirits insinuate themselves into the nose of persons out of their surroundings through many perfumes."[37]

If elemental infiltration of our human being bodies of this startling degree is the norm for ordinary, sense-world existence, its exponential heightening through mediumistic or channeling activities is staggering. The elementals' key is our "drowsy inattentiveness," the way we blithely park our unlocked physical, etheric, and astral bodies in the troublesome inner city of the supersensible worlds. Automatic writing, for example, potentially invites possession by elementary beings. The activity of writing in the context of a diminution of I-consciousness establishes the psychic habit of volitional surrender to controlling elementary beings. This is the first step towards making the soul an apartment complex for possessive spirits. "This type of human being can become possessed by elementary-spiritual beings."[38] A recent cartoon in a national literary magazine made this point graphically. A man stands at a podium under a spotlight clutching a large trophy, probably an Oscar. Half a dozen palm-sized elemental humans perch like newborn kittens on his body as he says, "And, of course, I want to thank all the little people!"[39]

After all, *who* is moving the hand across the page or flicking the fingers across the keyboard? Is it really the indefatigably literary soul of Honoré Balzac dying to write another installment in the human comedy? When are the credentials and resumé of our discarnate communicator ever presented? Do we have independent means of verifying these credentials? It is not farfetched to compare the dynamics of this situation with the nature of espionage. When read creatively, the literature and strategies of espionage are metaphysically instructive, especially the ideas of the mole (the unsuspected foreign agent highly placed in the opponent's camp) and disinformation (deliberate partial distortion of secret information to mislead the opponent). These are elements in a very clever sleight-of-hand, a strategy of deception and manipulation. If our reading of this activity is consistent with Steiner's indications about the mirror relationships of physical and supersensible worlds, then we must consider the possibilities that the contents of espionage reflect in our world strategies employed in the supersensible.

Readers of Whitley Strieber's harrowing UFO abduction narratives *Communion* and *Transformation*, however, may choose to withhold their testimonials for the friendly little people. Strieber called his frightening encounter with inimical elemental beings the "visitor experience." According to Strieber, a Stephen King-type novelist who favors the hyperbolic, "they" took him on "a fabulous and terrible journey" through his fears, intensifying his "worst imagining" a hundredfold as they dragged him through the "red terror of death," his "most suppressed dread," and just about everything emotional he had "buried" in himself. Four different anomalous beings "tormented" Strieber beginning in 1985. One was an enormous, extremely ugly robotic object, gray, scaly, with a network of wires at its extremities. The second type was short, stocky, with wide faces, glittering deep-set eyes, pug noses, broad human mouths; they were clothed in blue coveralls.

The third and most "provocative" of these quasi-human entities was five feet tall, slender, delicate, with a vestigial mouth and nose, and "extremely prominent and mesmerizing black slanted eyes." The fourth figure type was smaller, with the same head shape but "round black eyes like large buttons."[40]

Strieber's third class of elemental beings with black almond eyes and sharply ovoid face, has assumed the status of mass media icon for ambivalent, intriguing visitors from "elsewhere."[41] Strieber has a kind of bizarre conversion experience midway in his journey through unalleviated dread and physical rape by these visitors. "If I am right about them, [they] represent the most powerful of all forces acting in human culture." When these "fierce little figures" with black eyes like ovoid lakes stared into the "deepest core" of Strieber's being, he understood they sought the "very depth of the soul."

The visitors seek communion—whether we like it or not, as any attentive reader of Strieber's nasty account will add. The gray, scaly robotic visitors inserted a long, narrow triangular object into Strieber's rectum; then they performed another operation with needles and without consent on his head. "They have the ability to enter the mind and affect thought, and can accomplish amazing feats with this skill," comments a titillated Strieber. "They can affect the soul, even draw it out of the body, with technology that may possibly involve the use of high-intensity magnetic fields."[42] They even come redolent with the classic smell of fire and brimstone, said Strieber: "warm cheddar cheese with a hint of sulfur," sometimes the odor of smoldering cardboard or a potpourri of cheese and cinnamon.

Strieber writes a consummate thriller about these strange, communion-seeking visitors, whether it's an allegedly true narrative, as in *Communion* and *Transformation,* or a true-to-life fiction, like *Majestic.* But he is too uncritical to objectively see the *meaning* of this astral phenomenalism, which is involuntary possession of human souls by inimical Ahrimanic elemental beings masquerading, in our conceptualizations, as ETs. Strieber think's he's being assiduously critical and scientific by submitting himself to certifiable lie-detector tests, EEGs, MRI scans, psychological personality profiles, even psychiatric examinations—all in an effort to rule out subjective hallucinations as etiological factors in his "weird encounters," but surely he is up against intelligences whose manipulative devices can easily circumvent detection. Underlying the whole experience is "a very important, valuable, and genuine unknown," Strieber asserts. His hope is that "we will eventually face the fact that it is there, and begin a calm, objective, and intellectually sound effort to understand it."[43]

Anthroposophists disciplined in spiritual science should perk up with Strieber's call for an intellectually sound effort. The first objective observation this effort throws up is that Strieber misses a crucial point here. He continually diverts his own and the reader's attention to the epistemological problem of whether these events actually happened. The correct inquiry is rather, *where* did they happen? Either purposefully or through inadequate occult training, Strieber constantly portrays the abduction and communion events as material, physical occurrences, as interactions with extraordinary beings within our quotidian sensory reality. Quite likely this is an error in cognition and Strieber's encounters are unattended out-of-body astral encounters; or worse, they may be memory implants.[44]

Strieber's own materializing tendencies conspire with the Ahrimanic agenda of the entities to produce a physicalization of something inherently supersensible, if unsavory. And for what purpose? His narrative is electrified with negative adjectival sensationalism, his paragraphs are adrenalized catalogues of his fear, terror, dread, and torment. It's hardly the vocabulary of an edifying journey. Who needs this kind of experience, anyway? Strieber eventually exonerates the rapes, torture, and assaults of these fierce little marauders in an agapé of human egalitarianism, condoning their acts as if on behalf of our species. When we "achieve real relationship with the visitors," says Strieber, "there will be great wonder." The great wonder for any intelligent reader is why on Earth we would ever want to.

Strieber's errors in spiritual investigation provoke more than substantive literary criticism. His works are iconographically dangerous, the worst sort of cultural models of occult experience. His mass market exoneration of these inimical elemental abductors and their apotheosis through him (and others) into sublime extraterrestrial benefactors of high intelligence who, though misunderstood, are "the allies of our growth," is deleterious for the health of the consciousness soul. It is a cultural vaccination of a virulent strain of occult bacteria. Strieber, whose material formed the basis for a movie version of *Communion*, has unwittingly inserted a perniciously fraudulent icon into the cultural mainstream. The extraterrestrials duped Strieber; they're well on their way to duping millions of his readers. If this were the espionage business, we would call Strieber's work a disinformation plant.

The latest development in this disinformation campaign appeared in two "channeled" works *The Prism of Lyra* (1989) and *Visitors From Within* (1992). Here the almond-eyed ones, who claim they are residents of the constellation Lyra, credit themselves as the primordial Founders of the entire galactic family, the prismatic cosmogenitors of Sirius, the Pleiades, Orion, and Arcturus. "The Founders embodied the group consciousness of what eventually became humankind," the text informs us. "It is they who orchestrate humankind's evolution." We further learn that beings from Zeta Reticuli are the primary group behind the forcible abductions, which the authors whitewash as "temporary detainments."[45] More astonishingly, Royal and Priest challenge the readers "to use the abduction phenomenon as a tool for personal and planetary evolution."[46] With this kind of metaphysical misrepresentation, sanctioned by mass market and "New Age" authors, glorified by psychics, and avidly consumed by uncritical readers, the Ahrimanically inspired "Lyrans" have scored a prodigious occult coup.[47]

We find a revealing and alarming variation on this theme of elemental opportunism in the shamanistic-hallucinogenic odyssey of Terence McKenna as recounted in his recent *True Hallucinations*, an account of his formative experiments in the early 1970s in the Columbia Amazon with psilocybin, the psychoactive element in the *Stropharia cubensis* mushroom. McKenna is prominent and frequently quoted among those who argue for a resurgence of psychedelic experimentation in the 1990s. Through his "devotion" to psilocybin and the implications of his experiences under its influence, McKenna has emerged, as he puts it, as "a sort of mouthpiece for the incarnate Logos" and "turbo-charged" raver for psilocybin's "electrifying effect" and the "power and the promise of psychedelic dimensions." Basically, McKenna's "psilocybin-induced cognitive hallucination" convinced him that the transcendental awareness facilitated by this psychoactive mushroom enabled him and several colleagues to pass the Omega Point—an acme of human conscious evolution, as postulated by Teilhard de Chardin—and operate in the first few moments of the millennium in a world that had become "radically, fundamentally different."

Basically, the mushroom told McKenna that it is a "memory bank of galactic history" that, although alien, promises to open a potential for understanding that will obviate the petty concerns of Earth and history-bound humanity. During his moments of "tryptamine ecstasy," the "elves of hyperspace" whispered a "promise of special destiny" to McKenna. "For the loquacious mushrooms encountered there have spun a myth and issued a prophecy, in quite specific detail, of a planet-saving global shift of consciousness," he writes. In other words, anyone interested in *really* getting on with human conscious evolution ought to avail themselves of the galactic door-opening potential of psilocybin because it is the missing link in the development of human consciousness and language, says McKenna. Publishers, editors, agents, and marketing directors are assuring him that he is right, will be "big, have influence, and change the way people think." McKenna hopes they're right, regarding himself as "extremely fortunate" to have glimpsed, through psilocybin, a strange, beautiful new world and "to have made a marvellous pact with the alien gods who dwell there."[48]

What's wrong with McKenna's propositions? For one thing, a resurgence of psychoactive-induced hallucinogenic experiences in the 1990s is, in terms of human conscious evolution, anachronistic, regressive, and, as such, dangerous. The cultural impetus has come and gone, and our cognitive life has moved on since then. Western culture had its moment of startling if skewed lucidity in the 1960s; this mass initiation through psychedelic drugs served the purpose of momentarily affording many a glimpse of the supersensible worlds, although the glimpse generally came tremendously skewed and filtered by the unpurged astral body and the ambivalent nature of the astral plane itself. It was a vivid, arresting sampler, but you wouldn't want to drink the whole bottle. McKenna, a kind of hallucinogenic Pied Piper, has drunk it for two decades and is now successfully encouraging thousands of young Americans to take up psilocybin and crash the cognitive gates as metaphysically entitled neo-pagan, urban shamans. It's as if the lessons of the 1960s post-psychedelic experiment have all been forgotten. Those who survived the drug-experience psychologically intact, turned to meditation and Eastern spiritualities to consolidate and deepen their thirst for insight. Even Castaneda, in some respects the archetypal shamanic inductee, was taken off drugs by his teacher Don Juan Matus soon after they had served the purpose of forcefully shifting his habits of perception. Psilocybin-induced hallucinations were never meant to be a lifestyle, but this is what McKenna is apparently advocating with the glamor of higher-being endorsement from the mushroom itself. This is a path of considerable peril and probable folly.

We get a deeper perspective of Strieber's possession and McKenna's psilocybin exaltation by considering Steiner's analysis of the mechanics of possession in mediumship. The secret of mediumship, Steiner commented, is that it is an act of possession by Ahrimanic elemental beings concerned with humanity's future. These superintelligent beings actually pre-empt human conscious evolution and an open-ended future through their premature divulging of information that rightfully belongs to our future, and through their "extraordinary lucidity." These beings are "commissioned" from the supersensible world to keep an eye on human activities, said Steiner. Their rightful task is to preserve in escrow for the future what humans cannot transfer from one life to the next, such as technical achievements from earlier cultural epochs. "With the help of mediums they project into the present that which, in accordance with their mission, they ought to communicate to the future." Through the mediums, they "invade" the present, sacrificing their future mission in a zeal of revelation. The fact of mediumship itself implies that the future should perish for the "all important" present, said Steiner.[49]

The point of access for the elemental beings invading our present time from the future is the medium's physical brain, especially those parts which sustain Ego activity. This is the pineal gland at the base of the cerebellum, the source of the brow chakra and the seat of I-consciousness. When the medium or channel departs her physical and etheric bodies, and the Ego has vacated the brain, this "insulates" the pineal gland; it's also an open and "overwhelming" invitation for "certain entities" to slip in and establish residence in those parts of the medium's constitution that possess weight and gravity—the parts that are attracted to the Earth. As Steiner repeatedly cautioned his colleagues, "Mediums and those who experiment with mediums are unaware of the real processes involved."[50]

Once the brain and the precious pineal seat of the Ego are captured, the possessive elemental beings assault the nerve system, the seat of the will organization. The possessive spirits supplant the Ego in the medium as the director of the will. When elemental beings seize the medium's will activity, the normal faculties become lethargic, the body becomes "wholly passive," and dim, phantoms and shadows, normally permeated by the Ego, rise up autonomously, orchestrated by the elementals. As far as Steiner is concerned, this kind of total inertia ("a stupified, comatose condition") and the activation of atavistic phantoms are actually the prerequisites for mediumship and trance channeling. The medium slips unknowingly into a bizarre occult milieu in which elementary beings surround the brain like poisonous plants. We would be astonished, Steiner advised us, if we perceived the true activities of a spiritistic séance; we would find the entire circle of humans ringed by poisonous plants with demoniac beings emerging from the fruits and flowers. *Colchicum autumnale* and *Belladonna*, for example, are botanical mediums that permit noxious elemental beings from another world to enter ours as plant poisons. "For the most part [the medium] goes through a kind of cosmic thicket of poisonous plants that are activated from within and are part animal."[51]

What is paradoxical about this thicket of *Belladonna* is that these Ahrimanic beings possess a "vast, outstanding intelligence." Nor can we categorically deny that "authentic" information and spiritual revelations are actually transmitted by them through the mediums. But the transmission is possible only through an unlawful "trespass" of one relatively static world (supersensible) into another evolving world (ours). It is impossible for us to know objectively these trespassing elemental beings because our world is not their proper domain so they have no form appropriate for it; we cannot see them in terms that are cognitively meaningful to us. And since correct knowledge of them is not possible, this produces the "deceptive and highly hallucinative element" in everything connected with mediumship. This puts McKenna's marvellous pact in the "Devil's Paradise" in startling perspective and provides us reasonable grounds for rejecting this example as anything we should want to emulate as a means for gaining reliable cognition of the supersensible world. It may also be the occult reality behind walk-ins.

The phenomena of walk-ins was popularized by the internationally famous psychic Ruth Montgomery in a series of books, including *Strangers Among Us, Threshold to Tomorrow,* and *Aliens Among Us.* Her thesis is that more highly evolved extraterrestrials contractually inhabit the living bodies and complete the remaining lifespan of weary or dying human souls foundering at a crisis point. It may be an odd example of Steiner's principle of spiritual economy, in which physical bodies in motion shouldn't be wasted, or it may be another misunderstood form of elemental possession. In any case, it tends to de-emphasize the importance of being responsibly, humanly incarnate, setting up an alternative glamorous icon of higher pedigree possession. "Nowadays I seem to be stumbling into Walk-ins wherever I go," comments the genteel Montgomery. Her uncritical gentility, unfortunately, has helped create a glamorous New Age media image for this dubious category. Tens of thousands of these advanced space brothers are now squatting in midlife bodies, preparing for impressive Earth missions, her Guides told her. The pace of their easy incarnation has been accelerated at a rate not encountered since the closing days of Atlantis, Montgomery notes. The walk-ins are "striding forth" into contemporary culture "in great numbers to prepare earthlings for the coming shift," explained Montgomery's Guides. "They are more highly evolved, both spiritually and technologically, than earth people and have much to offer."[52] Doesn't this sound familiar?

So we have a contemporary scenario of progressive, technologically advanced walk-ins, powerful almond-eyed ETs, and thickets of spiritually superior beings all queuing up in the human being bodies and straining to pre-empt the rightful seat and activity of I-consciousness in men and women. We have a masterful disinformation campaign successfully exalting what is damaging, and condoning what is clearly forcible though devious possession. The consciousness soul is imperilled in every direction by this consummately orchestrated assault. The prudent thing to do is to meet the Guardians of the Threshold in the occultly prescribed manner and avoid the whole mess altogether—the illusions of self-projection and the ensnarements of self-possession.

Steiner warned us, after all, that in the imprudent moment in which we imprudently cross the threshold, without proper training, we are the prey of Lucifer and Ahriman. Their celestial size, their potency and agenda—the fundamental nature of their being—necessarily overwhelm us. Lucifer and Ahriman are too big a cosmic fact to handle on our own without considerable training. Time spent with the Guardians would have fortified us. Instead the profound existential issues posed by these complementary spiritual beings envelop us as a turbulent atmosphere. Their perpetual dialectic cleaves our spiritual being bodies in half and our cosmically immature Ego panics, scrambling for shelter like city dwellers in a wartime bombing raid.

When we fail to engage the Lesser Guardian in the time initiation, which is the revelation of the karmic self as an astral world, then Luciferic spirits capture time and enthrall us with a false, imaginary, self-projected world full of deceptive, unreal husks and shells. Luciferic spirits permeate the inner being, the unresolved, unrecognized karmic accretion of an individual's emotional life over time. Lucifer inflates this into an apparently external world. Lucifer strives to bring the eternal into the passing moment and thereby capture time. The Luciferic inflation is like a snake swallowing a rabbit. There's a monstrous bulge in a linear organic form. Lucifer wants dominion over time in human consciousness. Lucifer swallows the eternal moment on behalf of linear time by fooling us into misconstruing our subjective astrality (accumulations of self expressed in the passing moment) as an objective supersensible reality. The Luciferic inflation is thus the shadow side of the meeting with the Lesser Guardian.

When we refuse the encounter with the Greater Guardian in the space initiation, which is the revelation of the Ego as the substrate of the cosmos, then Ahrimanic spirits capture space and infiltrate our I-consciousness with intelligent but detrimental beings. Ahriman loads the physical organism with the immensity of space, giving what is insubstantial material weight. The Ahrimanic contraction is thus the shadow side of the meeting with the Greater

Guardian. Ahriman works perpetually to deliver temporality into eternity and thereby capture space from time. Ahriman wants dominion over space in human consciousness. He does this by infiltrating I-consciousness, the true seat of cosmic awareness, with spurious, parasitic supersensible denizens; their consciousness may be more expansive, but it's inappropriate, untimely, and injurious to humankind.

Lucifer and the Lesser Guardian, Ahriman and the Greater Guardian—these are complementary images of each other. When we approach the threshold as the result of spiritual scientific training, we encounter the Guardians who mediate our experience and usher us into a realm of cognitive certainty. When we refuse the discipline and prefer the sweet fruits of easy mediumship, we get Lucifer and Ahriman unmediated, a psychic shock sufficient to skew or paralyze I-based cognition. The Guardians are thus mediators between the microcosmic human and the macrocosmic Human, whose twin dialectical aspects are expressed as Lucifer caught in Time and Ahriman caught in Space. This implies that if Lucifer and Ahriman represent the complementary aspects of the cosmic Human on the other side of the threshold, then some other figure must subsume the complementarity of Lesser and Greater Guardians on this side. Steiner called this anthropomorphic composite the *Doppelgänger,* or Double, the image of a human's "new-born self."

"Man beholds his new-born self as another being standing before him, but he cannot perceive it completely," said Steiner. The Ego, expressed as the two Guardians, *must* be the first image confronting the human soul on the supersensible threshold. Initially, the Ego-Guardian image embodies all the emotional hindrances and karmic liabilities the individual will encounter in the unfoldment of the higher self. The Guardian assumes a largely individual shape for each man and woman. Through correct training, through the progressive elaboration of the lotus flowers of astral perception, "what he himself is appears to him as his first impression." Our first legitimately objective vision of the supersensible world is the unified image of our Double, the Ego.[53] But since the microcosmic human is the compression in time, space, and matter of the macrocosmic Human, this epiphany of the Ego at the threshold takes on cosmic significance. The composite Guardian becomes—in a sense is *transformed* into, through our initiation—the "Ideal of Man on Earth," said Steiner. "This guardian now transforms himself into the form of the Christ. The Christ shows Himself to the student as the 'great ideal of man on Earth.'"[54] When we successfully and conscientiously negotiate our passage across the threshold, the twofold guardian is transformed by our efforts into the great Human Ideal on Earth—the Christ.

Steiner said repeatedly that the Christ mediates the dialectic of Lucifer and Ahriman. He also explained that the Mystery of Golgotha was a great turning point in evolution. At that time comprehension of the Christ—"that is, of the original human Ego [*Ur-ich*]"—was withdrawn from clairvoyance and transferred to the Ego-soul of humanity. Through the self-generated forces of cognition and the elaboration of the consciousness soul, men and women of this fifth post-Atlantean cultural epoch can comprehend the Christ at Golgotha on their own. "Here, in the sight of all, stood One who represented what mankind had been before the coming of Lucifer and Ahriman." Christ as Son of Man represents the *Spirit of Humankind*, said Steiner. At Golgotha Christ stood garbed in the archetypal, ideal form originally intended for humans—"the true model of humanity before his fellow men." It is the kind of form "as I must make for myself through the most strenuous efforts of my soul," said Steiner, on behalf of the Christ.[55]

That Christ represents the ideal form of humanity before the influence of Lucifer and Ahriman implies that the form of Christ is a purified composite of both Lucifer and Ahriman, the bifurcated progeny of Zurvan, the calm flow of uncreated cosmic Time. The Christ in this capacity represents the ideal resolution and transcendence of the Lucifer/Ahriman polarity, or perhaps the dialectic resolved at a more evolved stage. It suggests that the transformation of the double-faced Guardian—first into the human higher self (*Doppelgänger*) and then into the great Human ideal on Earth (the Christ-permeated Ego)—into the numinous light form of the Christ is somehow a resolution to the trauma of the Holy Ghost caught in time and a redemption of what Steiner called the "human phantom," imperfect since the Fall.

What is the ideal for initiation at the threshold? The prepared human soul stands upon the supersensible threshold as the

Virgin Sophia—as the esoteric Christian tradition has always termed the cleansed, purified astral body, bearing within it the organs of perception of the spiritual world (the subject of the next chapter)—adorned like a bride for the celestial marriage with her intended consort, the Christ. Sophia is virginal because she—as an indwelling aspect of the human—has been purified and cleansed of sense-bound concepts through an inner alchemical process of training and development, as we'll see below. The indwelling Sophia is no longer liable to the Luciferic danger of self-inflation or the Ahrimanic peril of self-possession because the two Guardians of the Threshold have been met, treated with, and assimilated.

What comes next is almost too sublime to imagine; but *imagination*, as it turns out, is the key to both our comprehension and our preparation. Imagination will be the first act of the Virgin Sophia across the threshold. If the true form of the double-faced Guardian is actually the human Ego expressed in its ideal form as the Christ, then the true self of the candidate for admission into the supersensible worlds is the Virgin Sophia unfolded within us. In other words, through our inner soul activities we have unfolded the Virgin Sophia within, and "she" crosses the threshold on our behalf. The Virgin Sophia emerges in each of us through the development of what Steiner called imaginative cognition. This is spiritual scientific training in willed inner picture-making activity, image-consciousness, and etheric thinking. Through inner schooling, we restore imaginative force to Sophia, and with this restored picture-making force of imagination, we enter the spiritual worlds awake in our I-consciousness.

CHAPTER 9

The Virgin Sophia

The Restoration of Imaginative Force

through Inner Schooling

*W*E HAVE SEEN that the two Guardians of the Threshold mirror for us the necessary polarities of time and space, Lucifer and Ahriman, inherently active in our untransformed being. The Guardians thereby mirror the fundamental cleavage in the being of the Human, the cleavage of the Holy Ghost caught in time (Lucifer) and space (Ahriman) as it is played out microcosmically in every human. We have seen that when we fail to meet the Lesser Guardian (representing Lucifer), we are subject to self inflation, and when we fail to meet the Greater Guardian (representing Ahriman) we are vulnerable to self-possession. On the other hand, when we acknowledge each Guardian at the threshold, then we perceive the two Guardians as one composite Ego; then, through a transfiguration of the Guardian, we have before us the great Human ideal on Earth, the primordial Ego-Christ—before the bifurcation of Man (the Holy Ghost or Phantom) into Lucifer and Ahriman.[1] So the Christed form of the Human, the Christ Ego or I-consciousness, stands before us as the composite Guardian of the Threshold mirroring our potential, our destiny, and our necessity.

On the other side of the supersensible threshold—this side— stands what we bring to the encounter. What grants us safe and escorted passage through this interface between worlds is the Virgin Sophia, which we develop through our own inward process. The Virgin Sophia is an initiatory term from the Western Mystery tradition that refers to the deliberate, conscious clarification of

the astral body, or what the Gnostics called Lower Sophia (Achamod) living in humanity. According to Gnostic cosmology, the
passions of Lower Sophia outside the Pleroma were expressed as
the fourfold elemental, material world. Fire, air, earth, and water
are the elemental constituents in the cosmic emotions of Sophia
outside the Pleroma, which is the fullness of uncreated existence.
Our elemental affective life is the life of Lower Sophia in the material world.

Similarly, our psychophysical base is made of the fourfold passions of Sophia expressed through the elements. In fact, the elemental world of Lower Sophia comprises our extended being
bodies—physical, etheric, and astral. But we must remember this
is the Sophia clouded by her exile from the Pleroma, by the passions of a human individuality established in the material world.
We are dealing with the sublimity of Sophia predominantly uncul-
tivated within human intelligence. We particularly encounter the
ramifications of Lower Sophia's elemental passions in our astral
body as derived from the Old Moon phase of evolution. Into this
context we have co-mingled this fundamental elemental, passionate nature with our individual karmic exchange. Here we find the
cumulative results of what we've made of our passionate individuality in the material world over time; it is a composite of our interaction with Lower Sophia. Our Old Moon astrality represents the
permutations of manas, our thinking, world-making capacity of
mind, with Lower Sophia, the emotional implications of elemental
individuality—expressed over time in space. The alchemical transmutation of this births the Virgin Sophia within us, the clarified,
chastened, even scourged, and thereby *virginal* and untainted
Sophia principle. This does not happen of its own accord but must
be actively willed to happen. The only reliable way to do this is
through some form of systematic spiritual scientific training.

The activity of spiritual scientific training, then, is the progressive clarification of Lower Sophia in each human individuality.
"The refashioning of the astral body indirectly through Meditation and Concentration is called by the ancient name 'katharsis,'
or purification," said Steiner.[2] The result is a "cleansed, purified
astral body." Such a body is plastically reformed so that the higher
organs of perception, the chakras or lotus flowers, unfold into
cognitive activity. Through the clarified lotus flowers we begin

seeing with some objectivity in the astral world. "This cleansed, purified astral body, which bears within it at the moment of illumination none of the impure impressions of the physical world, but only the organs of perception of the spiritual world, is called in esoteric Christianity the 'pure, chaste, wise Virgin Sophia.'"[3]

The key here is the phrase "*impure* impressions of the physical world." This is Lower Sophia, her elemental affective life in the world as expressed through each of us. The impure impressions are clarified and rendered pure; the quality of this purity is called *virgin*, evocative of the pristine, primordial purity of cognition that was ours before humanity's phylogenetic incarnation. The passions of Lower Sophia expressed through human material individuality is another way of describing the Lucifer-Ahriman polarity constantly at play in human life. Lower Sophia, as it lives through us, is the theater for activities of Lucifer and Ahriman. Their activities produce the taints and *impure* impressions of the physical world that we seek to undo through inner schooling in spiritual science. Through the cultivation of the Virgin Sophia in us, we assiduously master this Lucifer-Ahriman dialectic implicit in the human individuality. Then we may pass beyond the double-faced Guardian at the threshold without hindrance, compromise, or deception.

The development of our higher organs of perception liberates manas, or cognitive force, in the astral body. This renders the individual capable of freely willed spiritual activity (*Freiheit*) on the basis of "pure impressions" of the spiritual worlds. As we know, Steiner equated unhindered supersensible perception with spiritual freedom. For perception to operate freely, manas must be unhindered. And when manas works as spiritual freedom, then the stage of imaginative cognition is possible and Sophia, as the Wisdom of God, can live within us. Using liberated manas we perform an initial act of spiritual freedom: the creation of an etheric imagination, or living picture.

All of this transpires at that profound mirroring interface, the two-way threshold of the supersensible and physical worlds. Essentially, we present the Virgin Sophia (the purified human astral body, capable of being permeated with wisdom) to the Christ Ego (the integral, ideal expression of the Human and the human I-consciousness and higher self, subsuming Lucifer and Ahriman) at the threshold. The threshold of course is the primordial boundary, with the pre-existent, nonbiological life on one side, and the Fall of the Human into biology, life, and time on the other. Some very important business is negotiated at this boundary between the worlds. Here Sophia, as the embodiment of cosmic intelligence, is permeated by the Christ, as the Logos and creative world-creating Word. Through this we become an individually true expression of Anthropos-Sophia. The Christ permeates Sophia with the impulse to speak as the Logos; this is the subject of a later chapter. How we unfold the Virgin Sophia is what spiritual scientific training, or inner cognitive schooling, is all about, and is the proper topic for the moment.

The path of inner schooling takes us in a regulated, orderly, reliable manner through the experience of crossing the threshold of the supersensible world. We make our passage without the pitfalls and dangers likely with an undisciplined, casual, mediumistic approach. The path of inner schooling, as outlined by Rudolf Steiner, is the antithesis of easy clairvoyance and channelism, as we have portrayed them. Spiritual scientific training insists on one golden rule: "For every one step that you take in the pursuit of higher knowledge, take three steps in the perfection of your own character."[4] The strict training of personal character is vital to successful occult preparation; in fact, it is the foundation for objective supersensible knowledge. The path of self-knowledge *is* the discipline of self-perfecting, explained Steiner. It's not something optional in the smorgasbord of spiritual development; it is unavoidable for a good reason. The issues presented by the Guardians must be dealt with. To be students we must constantly make an inner exertion to overcome egotism arising out of the whole psychophysical elemental nature of the human being. We students must very deliberately reshape our moral and intellectual character. That's because occult development presents us with a potential liability. As the Gnostics would say, we have to alchemically purify the world passions of Lower Sophia as they live in us; they are powerful and can batter us about severely. The process of inner schooling actually separates out the lower and higher natures of our human beingness. "One draws the lower nature out of the body like a sword from the scabbard, which then remains alone."[5] To chaperone this extracted passionate elementality, a concentrated extract of our own astral body, we desperately require precise training and preparation.

This lower nature, now isolated, can be quite intimidating. It's not something students of spiritual science would prudently wish to bring with them across the threshold. Thinking, feeling, and willing become three independent entities and if this trifurcation of the human being is not mastered, the schism can lead to all manner of excesses, to aberrant, atavistic, regressive, and negative behavior. Occult training (or spontaneous psychic opening) can make one, potentially, a very nasty fellow. The biographies of many mediums, trance channels, and psychics in the last hundred years reveal distressing examples of people who failed to master their inner psychic household and in whom the passionate selfhood ran amok. The gamut of evil, negative, and "gruesome" properties latent in the lower self suddenly erupt into full, irrefutable manifestation. The lower self tempts us from all directions because it is no longer restrained by the reasoned commingling with the higher self in the human individuality.

The inner balance of powers is terribly upset by our efforts at occult training. The path of occult development actually cleaves this *modus vivendi* and requires us to take our moral development firmly in hand. "In every aspect of life a demon lies in wait for him, ready to lead him astray."[6] Where does this self-created demon lead us astray to? Directly into the problematical hands of Ahriman and Lucifer across the threshold, into the fundamental ambivalence of humanity caught in time and space. That's the kind of issue we are up against across the threshold. That ambivalent warring destiny is ours if we make the boundary passage with an "immoral soul condition." This is a cognitive state Steiner described as stupefied and clouded, likely to produce nothing more than "fantastic imaginings."

But fantastic imaginings lead only to delusion and entanglement. All that our lotus flowers show us then are the tortuous involutions of Luciferic inflation and Ahrimanic contraction played out in the theater of our individuality. What we see is the profound *unresolved* ambivalence of humanity after the Fall; this of course is a transpersonal, phylogenetic liability affecting all of humanity. Spiritual scientific training is the systematic, progressive *resolution* of this macrocosmic bifurcation as expressed in the microcosmic human individuality. In other words, legitimate spiritual scientific training pits us against primordial issues to do with the descent of humankind from the celestial spheres at the beginning of time. Proper occult training has cosmic implications. It is crucial that we be able to find our bearings once we cross the threshold. "You are utterly alone with yourself, alone with your own inner world rising up within you."[7]

Our initial experience in the supersensible, then, is a self-woven imagination. We witness a great living picture "tableau which constitutes the etheric time-body of formative forces" of our psychophysical self as karmically elaborated over time and space. We really need to put the most uplifting, wholesome, and moral elements possible into this imagination. Morality, or ethical individualism, Steiner reminds us, is also a key factor in free spiritual perception and activity. It represents the will impulse liberated from unconscious karmic compulsions; the will becomes the ally of our etheric thinking, and together the liberated will and sense-free thinking grant us supersensible objectivity. Otherwise we're like somebody taking in the sensory world in a passive, drunken stupor, and all our statements about the supersensible world are in error.

Through a program of regular meditation and the cultivation of moral impulses, Steiner assured his students, they would find the proper orientation in the freshman foyers of the supersensible. Chief among the required moral impulses and preparatory experiences are a firmness in ethical judgment, certainty of character, keenness of conscience, courage, wakefulness, a resolute iron will, an indifference to pain developed through voluntary suffering, love, absolute calmness, and patience. Steiner laid particular emphasis on the necessity for an abiding patience. It's paramount to be capable of waiting to receive grace and inspiration, of enduring the time of inner ripening in a state of inner rest. As we are the mothers of our newborn clairvoyant cognition, inner ripening is spiritual gestation. Steiner advised students that it takes "often a very long time" before the lotus flowers are sufficiently developed to afford true clairvoyant cognition. Nor should we expect our moments of supersensible cognition to contain encyclopedic tomes of information or that we will have "immeasurable views" into the higher worlds every day. It isn't like that. We best prepare ourselves when we cultivate "a mood of expectation in restfulness of soul." And although it will irritate the psychic acquisitiveness rampant in Western and particularly American society, Steiner further admonished us to be content with even "the smallest fragment attained." We're not likely to come away from a single channeling experience with another 2,000 page *Urantia* text.

Through spiritual scientific training we incrementally refashion our astral body, purifying its manifold wayward, chaotic, passionately disorderly ways. Cultivating the habit of rhythm and repetition in our physical life is actually conducive to the regulation of the astral body. This might take the form of a meditation practice performed at the same time every day; or getting up in the morning at the same time, taking a walk, reading, writing, and other activities performed according to an unvarying time schedule. This rhythmicity is the principle behind monastic life, both Christian and Buddhist. The rhythm of the physical body—the most perfected part of the human being, permeated with Old Moon wisdom—works its way into our astral body and emotional nature. This physical rhythm implants itself there as an "example of spirituality." In practical terms, we impart rhythm to the astral body through daily meditative exercises practiced consistently at the same hour of the morning or evening.

One of the principal meditative practices Steiner recommended is objective self-observation and the control of the direction of thought. This is the student's "first obligation" in occult training. Here we become diligent, assiduous observers of what we experience within, in our thinking, feeling, and willing activities. We develop the strength of mental focus to hold our attention steady on one object; this is "thinking factually by means of inner force." Meticulous self-observation is crucial because it is only when we have self knowledge—know thoroughly and objectively that karmic panoply of passions, ideas, impulses, wishes, faults, and weaknesses that is our psychophysical self—that we can *distinguish* ourselves from all other spiritual beings across the threshold. It sounds strange but it is really a fact that we may encounter our self, or an expression of our astral body, across the threshold and have no idea that we are beholding ourselves. Cultivating the skill of self-distinction provides one with an identity tag for one's passionate individuality; thereafter we can recognize ourselves even when the self is mirrored before us as a great but unfamiliar cinematic image.

Inner schooling, then, trains us to be anthropologists of the lower self, scholars of the Lower Sophia resident in us. The rigorous insistence on inner truth is our standard in this fieldwork. We must develop a genuine knowledge and a mature estimate of our individual nature because, very soon, this individuality will confront us as a virtual image of the supersensible world. So it helps to know what you look like, especially when writ large in astral ink. The time of inner schooling is the best and really the only time to acquire this positive discipline of self-recognition and self-control, because at the supersensible threshold—experientially we might call it "through the looking-glass"—the "temptation to self-deception is immeasurably great," said Steiner.

Our susceptibility to self-deception at the threshold is further reduced through the development of additional moral-ethical qualities. We fortify our own soul forces through learning control of the will impulses; we develop equanimity and calmness in the face of joy and sorrow, maintain a positive, affirmative attitude towards the world, coupled with impartiality; we exhibit a style of active participation tempered by intelligent inner control. Authentic clairvoyance demands our *active* involvement in the objects of our perceptions. We need to participate in the "dynamic world of creative imagination" yet simultaneously exercise an "exceedingly strong" inner control. This means we can engage and disengage our attention, selectively, at will, in the supersensible tableau or the material reality around us. This is the gatekeeper function of manas, the "preventing of knowledge arising together" in an inchoate flood of spiritual impressions. Our inner life should be active, lively, and responsive, said Steiner, but tempered with prudence, common sense, and sober judgment; our cognitive forces should be at our will and disposal.

Our active, responsible participation in the dynamic world of creative imagination is the crux of the passage across the supersensible threshold. We do this successfully by developing imaginative cognition, the first stage of three in clairvoyance, and a foundation in anthroposophical schooling. Imaginative cognition is a form of willed lucid dreaming or vivid inner picture-making, willed creative visualizations. It elevates what otherwise dreams in our feelings into a matter of "complete, clear world cognition," into waking dreams permeated with a wisdom that indicates "another content" of reality. This other wisdom content is Sophia, the wisdom of God latent but unmanifest as Lower Sophia-Achamod in the fourfold elemental nature of humanity. Through imaginative cognition, we master fully conscious pictorial thinking; inherently this is an etheric reality.

Imaginative cognition gives us a picture-world, a complete survey of our etheric life and processes. Imaginative cognition is a pictorial revelation of our etheric body and through this the etheric cosmos into which our etheric individuality is woven. We confront our own etheric life, its memories, thoughts, forces, and life processes expressed over time, and understand how "the entire etheric cosmos lives in the individual human being." Within the human constitution, the etheric body, more rarified and finer than air, is in inner movement, when we are awake, in every area except the head, where it is at rest; at night, when we sleep, the etheric body begins to be in movement in the head as well. The etheric body is a time body, always in movement, containing "in one picture, our life in its movement and its actions," extending backward all the way to our birth.[8]

The life of the etheric cosmos within the human etheric individuality is one of constant motion and continuous transformation. The most keenly descriptive adjective for this etheric activity and one Steiner used all the time is *weaving.* The etheric cosmos weaves and pulses through our own etheric microcosm; what weave, of course, are cosmic thoughts, cosmic intelligence—"the World of Archetypal Images"—expressed as "mighty pictures." Imaginative cognition yields reflections of this unmediated cosmic intelligence. These come as colors, sounds, and smells, torn loose from their physical context; they appear before us as sense impressions "floating free in space." One no longer perceives colors or sounds as external activities; instead, the location of one's experience is *inside* the color picture, inside the sound. The incessant motion, the transformations, the etheric weavings and pulsings, the fullness of physically unmoored colors and sounds—these are pictures of the activities of spiritual beings. "In the imaginative world, everything speaks to man as if it were directly intelligent."[9]

Within the realm of our sensory experience, we look to the plant kingdom for elucidation of etheric imaginations. "In the plants we are seeing genuine Imaginations," said Steiner. Goethe's concept of the archetypal plant, the mobile essential form of the plant that metamorphoses prolifically as the entire plant kingdom, is an example of an etheric imagination. Goethe was repelled by the misconception implicit in the Linnaean system of botanical classification according to individual plant forms; for him Linnaeus' approach was suitable and accurate for classification of the mineral kingdom, but not the plant.

For this, a different kind of thought and observation was necessary, a more flexible, mobile concept capable of comprehending the plant kingdom as a unity. "Goethe, by means of mobile ideas, wanted to grasp the whole system of plant growth as a unity—so that he slipped out of one plant form, as it were, into another by metamorphosing the idea itself. This kind of observation with mobile ideas, was, in Goethe, doubtless the initial impulse toward an imaginative way of observing."[10] When we see a plant, what is visible is its higher, etheric nature, not its physical body; the plant's etheric form is filled out with physical matter, with mineral substance, with "little granules of physical matter." The physical form of the plant enables us to perceive its innate etheric form. That is why the etheric form of a plant is an example of an Imagination made visible through physical substance. All plants are Imaginations, said Steiner. "We have Imaginations all around us in the forms of the plant world."

Now, within the human, the etheric organization has a special relationship with the astral body. The lotus flowers, or chakras, in the astral body relay their spiritual impressions to our waking consciousness by way of imprinting pictures on the "soft wax" of the etheric body. This perceptual relay across the bodies is similar, at least metaphorically, to the way a closed-circuit video camera conveys information from the store to the back office. There is a lot of distortion and loss of image resolution, and it's usually in black and white, but the security officer gets the "picture." He gets the idea of what's happening out front in the store. The security guard may be only half-watching the television monitor, his mind roaming other "screens" at the same time. For our part, we need to maintain a heightened, unwavering vigilance, our eyes riveted to the etheric camera.

Through an "inner meditative exercising of the soul," we keep the "same clear presence of mind" in perceiving the etheric picture tableau as we present when understanding a concept elaborated from sense observations or scientific experimentation. We maintain that same "strictly critical" edge of aware intelligence. Imaginative cognition gives us picture-concepts, said Steiner. We best approach this "whole-idea complex" with the kind of resolute precision and impartiality we would bring to a mathematical problem. Mathematics contains nothing to which we can submit unconsciously, without the deliberate use of will. Thus "mathematizing" represents the activity of will as applied to imaginative cognition.

The key here is to radiate our will, with as much strength and intensity as we can muster, into the sphere of thinking. We infuse thinking with the force of will. Will is the spiritual fuel for imaginative cognition and thus the key to inner freedom. We must remember that generally we are awake in our thinking, we dream in our feelings, but we sleep in our willing. This is unfortunate because willing is the karmic foundation of our impulses and worldly actions; if we are asleep in our will, then we are compelled to act, but not free to act. When we actively marshal our will, rouse it from its habitual somnambulance and passivity, and kindle it into greater wakeful activity, then we can permeate our etheric thinking with its powerful volitional force. We make our will the ally of our thinking and etheric picture-making, or imaginative cognition. In imaginative cognition we purposefully "efface and exclude" thought contents from the sensory world and emotional configurations from the inner astral world. "Pure thinking may equally be called pure *will*," the key to inner freedom, outlined Steiner. Why does it give us inner freedom?

First, let's have a look at karma. Our karma is the cumulative momentum of our astral body and psychoemotional self over time and space. As such, it is a momentum we haven't recognized, because it "sleeps" unconsciously in the will. Normally this unrecognized karma impels us to actions through unconscious will impulses; we are moved to act, but we do not will ourselves to act. Before we know it, we have acted out of an uncognized karmic compulsion or necessity. This is hardly inner freedom. Second, let's examine our thinking. Our thinking, though relatively awake, which means possessing some degree of I-consciousness, or self-reflexive awareness, is articulate only within the world of elements and materiality. We think about sensory information; we think through sense-bound concepts derived from the mineral kingdom. We think in matter, in material terms, which is the densest, most contracted context for the activity of cosmic intelligence. At its worst, thinking materially is like shuffling around abstract ideas that are only empty shadows cast by inert substances. This degree of material slavishness is hardly inner freedom either.

So when we rouse the will, normally sleeping, into thinking, normally materialized, we revitalize these two fundamental aspects of human consciousness. Through this arousal we take a crucial step towards our conscious mastery of them. When our thinking is irradiated by will, it attains "such maturity" that it no longer draws in contents from the external material world, but works upon the picture revelations of the etheric body. "Its very life is of the nature of will."[11] Thinking becomes willful. Through the kindling of will we gain conscious mastery over manas, the innate world-making, gate-keeping activity of mind. Manas, as we learned above, represents the first moment of self-conscious activity, a self-positing activity leading in different directions. This is the basis for I-consciousness active in thinking. It gives the I a *position* in the world-making activity of manas. Willed thinking is a key to *Freiheit*, the freedom of spiritual activity; it's also a necessary precondition for imaginative picture consciousness.

The student's first and primary imagination is the externalization of oneself in a vista of "mighty" soul pictures in form, color, and tone. The first imagination is a vista of one's present earthly life and all the formative forces that produced it. This externalization of one's self as an imagination is inevitable and absolutely essential to the clear unfolding of clairvoyant cognition. Students who attempt to circumvent this occult necessity get their astrality served up as psychic visions of an apparently external spiritual world. Those who report Near-Death Experiences, in which their life passes dramatically in pictures before them, are experiencing this imaginative tableau of the etheric time body, encompassing the events of their life backwards to birth. "This is, to begin with, the first supersensible ability we can discover in ourselves."[12]

But those who bypass this stage get only an illusory self-projection that leads to no end of mistakes in perception. Through inner schooling we deliberately, knowingly project ourselves as objects of etheric imagination. This highlights another key point made by Steiner. In initiation knowledge, we ourselves are the object seeking a corresponding subject. We are properly concerned with how *we* are being thought by the cosmos. In other words, the standard object-subject relationship is reversed; our ability to undergo this fundamental reorientation or revisioning of our soul configuration is crucial. We behold ourselves in the mirror of an etheric imagination. This imagination becomes the object for contemplative reflection and through this the means for self-knowledge.

This preliminary imagination is actually a life tableau of all the organic elements and etheric formative forces that have built up our earthly life since birth. This tableau, in which we meticulously survey the whole of our inner life, is in reality "a structure of formative forces moving in the stream of time." Steiner also called it "the etheric time-body of formative forces." Through a kind of "morphological thinking" (thinking in forms), we behold an inwardly mobile thought-organism that lives and grows in time. This etheric life tableau is not spatial or linear; rather it is an organic structure constantly permutating through new forms, new pictures, unfolding as time-forms before us like a cinematic hologram. We regard this tableau as the objective form of the thought-forces of our individuality. The perception itself actually extricates our consciousness from the physical and etheric confines. Through imaginative consciousness, we become able to think independently of the physical body and to "live in free thoughts."[13] The etheric time-body, containing the retrospective of our live events, is a "colossus, this giant being in our soul." This "whole terrible specter" we behold, comprising the entirety of our life in the sense-bound world since birth, is like a gateway, that, finally, we must do away with, wipe from the slate of our awareness. "If we can get rid of it then something will appear for us that I would like to call a *more wakeful* consciousness."[14]

We are forewarned through the instructions of spiritual science not to mistake this grand reflected image woven of "the seductive artifices of [our] own soul imagery" for anything other than an astonishing self perception. A single viewing will not suffice. Not only does this imagination of oneself have a remarkably cinematic virtual reality, it comes with multiple, complementary views, like a Cubist painting in movie form. Up to twelve different dovetailing views of the Ego are possible in this imagination, like a miniature zodiac. In fact, the twelve views are possible because the same principle of relationship is at play here as between the twelve constellations of the zodiac and the Sun. After all, the zodiac represents twelve valid perceptions of the Sun, which is the Solar Logos. The human Ego is the Solar Logos expressed as I-consciousness. "So the human Ego is illumined from twelve different stations in the higher world."[15]

When we consider as a fact in itself the primary imagination of self as a projected world, this yields a valuable insight about the activities of the supersensible world. Imaginations represent the signs and thoughts of spiritual beings, said Steiner; they represent writings in an esoteric script in which our etheric and astral bodies are the paper. What we experience as mental thoughts are actually living beings active on the astral plane. Our thoughts are the shadowy mental images, the signs, of their activities, in the same way the abstract word "house" *signifies* the physical reality of a habitation. In the supersensible world spiritual beings express themselves as "teeming mental pictures and deeds;" these deeds cast their shadow-images into human awareness as thinking. In ancient times the human experience was to say, "I have the life of angels in my head," or "I have the life of the spirits of elemental beings in my head," but not, "I have a thought in my head." We did not think our own thoughts, but experienced the living thought processes of spiritual or elemental beings within our consciousness.

In images we find the origins of the world, after all. Images are the template of picture-concepts for the material world. The world first was an idea, an imagination, an etheric picture. The world is a cosmic thought, said Steiner. Our thinking, when it is etherically alive, really *is* the world in its antecedent conceptual state, a thought-picture of a material potentiality. When pure thought is gradually lit by this picture content, we think pictorially, "warmed through by glowing life." Images are behind everything around us, said Steiner. "It is into these images we enter when we immerse ourselves in the ocean of weaving thoughts."[16] This billowing, weaving world of thought-pictures is the echo of

Sophia's speech, the passionate, cosmically intelligent syllables of Sophia imagining a world of wisdom.

When we actively engage in imaginative cognition, we bring our awareness to the tip of the shadow-play activity of spiritual beings. Together, the etherically awake human and the astrally thoughtful spiritual beings jointly prepare an occult picture script. "You write down wholly in an inner soul process what is active through you."[17] The human supplies the content, the spiritual mentor supplies the grammar, and together they co-create a self-revealing tableau, an imagination. Like most first novels, our maiden voyage in imaginative consciousness is autobiographical and not particularly publishable; in other words, it has elucidative utility primarily for oneself. But it does teach us *how to write* using our immediate life biography—the contents of the etheric time-body—as the raw material. Later, when we master the art and mature through human experience, we can truly imagine new "fictional" worlds. It's as if the supersensible beings supervising our activity of imaginative cognition coach us in pictorial speech, in the craft of inner picture making. Until we consciously, willingly engage ourselves in this kind of remedial speech therapy, we are supersensibly mute, like Faulkner's madman full of the sound and fury of inarticulate Sophia bound in matter.

Yet even when we feel we're moving in the loquacious stream of pictorial imaginative speech, when we believe the gods are writing all over us and that we hold the keys for decipherment, prudence demands we should not relax our vigilance. We can not read passively. It's not like watching television; it must be interactive, participatory, wakeful. We can still be fooled. Imaginations must be tested for objective reality by a kind of deliberate banishment, a willed erasure of the entire picture content. If it comes back, it's probably real.

Steiner urged his anthroposophical colleagues undertaking inner schooling to challenge their imaginations. This means subjecting the picture tableau to the "active force of seeing." We actively extinguish (or banish) the image by a "resolutely active gaze," dissolving it into emptiness under the scrutiny of one's inner gaze. If the vision fails to reconstitute itself, then it was a self-projected phantom and objectively unreal; but if it returns, reassembling itself essentially as before, remaining stubbornly before us like a "solid fact," then it's a true picture and an objective fact. Then we know for certain we are engaged in a picture dialogue, in occult writing, in a genuine communication between our etheric cognition and authentic spiritual beings across the threshold. Researchers in the Akashic Records who do not regularly test their picture impressions through banishment, risk seeing the Akashic pictures "only as images of their own inner life."[18] It would be like superimposing your karmically variable face unknowingly over every image in a history text, so that it shows up everywhere, unaccountably, inaccurately, like Woody Allen's ubiquitous Zelig.

Why did Steiner insist so vigorously on the disciplines of spiritual scientific schooling? He understood that the preparation within each of us of the Virgin Sophia is actually the first stage in the recapitulation in reverse of the unfoldment of the world. As we noted before, spiritual science has cosmic ramifications; a great deal is at stake. Sophia left the Pleroma in search of a perception of the fullness of being; the passions of her exile precipitated and constituted the material world. Spiritual scientific training is like rolling up the long red carpet of organic life from the end, back towards the beginning again. Ultimately, we "roll" Sophia back into the Pleroma through our exertions. In this case, the carpet is human consciousness, while the rolling is the progressive, self-aware integration into the human individuality of ever more subtle forms of spiritual cognition. We roll ourselves up through the entire thought-woven universe of the celestial hierarchy—that is, cosmic intelligence, which is the thought-filled awareness of Sophia.

The first competent roll of the carpet, so to speak, is etheric imaginative cognition. Through our training, then, we progressively retrace our steps in the opposite direction by which we—and, phylogenetically, all of humanity—entered material manifestation. The equivalence of macrocosm and microcosm means we recapitulate in reverse the stages by which the elemental world unfolded into existence from the Pleroma, the calm, undisturbed flow of Cosmic Time. Our initiation retraces the stages by which the world came into being. The attainment of imaginative cognition is a cosmically important event with direct implications for the spiritual welfare of Lower Sophia.

The experiences of initiation and the course of clairvoyant unfoldment are individualized, yet there is a certain generic sequence of events. First, there is purification, in which the astral body is purged and cleansed of its moral defects and karmic accretions. Through this catharsis the lotus flowers unfold, astral perception becomes possible, and the Virgin Sophia emerges. Illumination is the second stage. Here the astral body imprints its visions and forms onto the mobile etheric body as living thoughts and imaginations which we interpret through the craft of occult reading. Third, we have the revelatory self-mirroring meeting with the Guardian of the Threshold. The fourth stage Steiner called Living in the Elements, in which we meet the sentient spirits behind the physical elements (e.g., earth element/gnomes; fire/salamanders; water/undines; air/sylphs). Finally, in the fifth stage, called Beholding the Sun at Midnight, we perceive, under conditions of material darkness, the presence of actual spiritual beings of the Sun. With this stage we become a human peer in the supersensible world.[19]

Just as a complete view of the Ego requires the integration of twelve potential views, so, too, does our understanding of the process of initiation benefit from different formulations. Steiner alternatively characterized this sequence of initiations that ushers us safely across the supersensible threshold as the Door of Death, the Door of the Elements, and the Door of the Sun. It's possible to legitimately enter the supersensible world through any of these three doors, Steiner granted, "but anyone wishing to follow the path to knowledge in its entirety will have to take the road to knowledge through all three doors."[20]

The first initiation, called the Portal of Death, is about divestment. Through this we drop all the ideas, concepts, and notions acquired through life in the physical world. The soul "dies away" from its attachment to intellectuality founded in the sensory world. It leaves behind all its material baggage, and enters the supersensible world shriven, bereft of ideation, empty of intellectual expectations. Ahriman, of course, encourages us to transport physical-world sensory concepts intact into the supersensible. Ahriman wants us to colonize the supersensible world with material concepts. But we must leave everything of our self and its threads of attachment to the physical world behind at the threshold; these threads are entirely ill suited to the supersensible realm, which is utterly different from the physical. The supersensible world is paradoxical, comprised of "independent individualities" that often work in apparent contradiction to one another. What is not surprising or paradoxical will probably strike us as grotesque instead. The only soul attainment we are permitted to carry across is our "powers of endurance." We emerge on the other side of this portal, our thinking activities scrubbed clean like a slate, and face "utter emptiness."

This nakedness is a conceptual death of the physical world as a factor in our awareness. We need plenty of courage to "allow our being to be built up anew." We enter a new cognitive domain free of conceptual anticipation, a realm in which our only guide will be "the thought that is beginning to assume life." This is another way of saying that our guide across the threshold is purified manas. Now our concepts of the supersensible emerge directly from our experience of this realm; they are fashioned directly out of the living etheric reality cognized through thinking. They are no longer concepts made of projections from the sense-bound world. Manas posits a new etheric world before us, showing us where to position I-consciousness. Through a rigorous meditative focussing on certain preselected thoughts, by making them the "absolute center" of our conscious mind and identifying with them completely, we actually create a new autonomous being. "The thought assumes the form of a winged human head that continues into indefiniteness." And with this winged head as a "new spiritual eye," we fly unencumbered into the direct experience of spontaneous cosmic thinking.[21] Of course, we still have to look out for the lion.

Through the second major initiation, the Door of the Elements, we encounter the lion. The lion is an old mystical symbol for the fearsome power of the human will operating out of control in the supersensible world. For the Gnostics, the upstart Demiurge named Ariel-Ialdabaoth had a lion's face. The raging lion is a symbolic mirroring of our own unchecked will activity freed from material life. The lion represents the unbridled force of egotism that threatens to devour us, the terrific force of willing for *me*. Lucifer wants us to pass through the Portal of the Elements without seeing the lion; this would accentuate our innate selfishness such that we'd try to rule the world through heightened will impelled by personal egotism. As the Tarot counsels, we must attain the strength of the lion, holding its mouth open with our bare hands. The lion must be controlled so that "our will is alive within the whole of thought life." Yet this same potency of will in living union with the thought world can generate a feeling of "abject terror." And if the lion doesn't unsettle us, most likely the dragon will.

In the third initiation, the Portal of the Sun, we encounter the dragon. In this legitimately scheduled meeting, both Lucifer and Ahriman conspire to make the dragon invisible to us. Our subconscious collaborates with Lucifer and Ahriman because this dragon is an ugly creation, readily inspiring aversion. It's the instinctual rage of the four elements operating as human selfhood. This wild dragon paramountly has to do with ourselves, with the sun forces of digestion and other organic processes, with our lowest, elemental nature. It is the "tissue of instincts and feelings, all of our idiocies, all our vanities, our pride and self-seeking and also our basest instincts." As we approach the mirror of the Portal of the Sun without prevarication, and without being distracted by Lucifer and Ahriman, we acknowledge ourselves as a raging dragon.[22] The acknowledgment itself is a kind of dragon-slaying, a mastery through recognition.

Our forthright encounters with the dragon and lion and our divestment of sensory thoughts at the Portal of Death are each important alchemical stages in the purification of the astral body. Out of the carcasses of the lion and dragon emerges the wise Virgin Sophia. The bottleneck in unfolding unencumbered cognition is always the human astral body, selfhood permeated with Lower Sophia's passionate elemental nature. This is another way of saying the main obstacle to unfolding clear supersensible cognition is the tendency of Lucifer and Ahriman to tie our chakras in knots. They are the twin embodiments of unresolved passionate selfhood, of I-consciousness entangled in the perplexities of tangible individuality lived out in time and space.

It's truly an old story, this astral body entanglement. It encompasses what exoteric tradition mournfully calls the Fall of humanity. According to Steiner, the astral body entanglement and the Fall of humanity both implicate an unresolved aspect of Old

Moon history. To clarify this history, we must delve into a very old period of evolution. The astral body, created during Old Moon, is consequently the carrier of Old Moon picture-consciousness, which is like today's dream-filled sleep. These Old Moon pictures were not precise likenesses of objects, but volatile, floating, and symbolic images. The human being was still a completely etheric being, lacking any mineral substance, which would not be incorporated into the organism until the next phase of evolution, called Earth. "His soul became active in a way that was definitely dreamlike, consisting of dream images." Humans lived under the constant tutelage of superior spiritual beings and powers that flowed and floated into them during Old Moon.[23] As such, humans were not capable of independent thinking or self-willed moral impulses. During the Old Moon phase, the Spirits of Personality "inoculated the astral body with selfhood." This was a problematical infusion that encouraged the development of the passionate instinctual nature.

The trouble was that the inoculation occurred just *below* the threshold of awareness. Humans didn't see the Spirits of Personality (whom Steiner also called Sons of Life) nor did they hear them directly either. Even so, these Spirits provoked images in human consciousness that were not so much copies of the outer world as powerful upwelling dream symbols. There was no inner freedom in this. "Conduct based on perception admits of freedom of choice, while action under the influence of the pictures indicated is impelled by a dull urge." Of course, cognitive freedom was not possible a priori during Old Moon evolution; this would require the inclusion of mineral substance into the human organization during Earth evolution. The Spirits of Personality worked up these dull urges through what today we might call subliminal persuasion. Their dream pictures were "genuine formative forces" sufficient to set the whole inner being of a human into activity. These formative forces woven of upwelling symbolic pictures actually shaped the human being accordingly. "He became, as it were, a copy of his processes of consciousness." Again, there was no freedom of spiritual activity in this kind of morphogenetic elaboration.[24]

Eventually, the Old Moon humans gained an imaginative perception of the Sons of Life as "etheric soul forms." These were images still unconnected with anything materialized. The sentient and intellectual souls, and later the sense organs, of Old Moon humans were not autonomous or self-expressive at that stage. The Sons of Life used them to achieve their own human stage; this, incidentally, perfected for them these organs of consciousness. In Steiner's cosmogony, the spiritual evolution of the cosmos, hierarchy, and humanity are interdependent but staggered events. In other words, the members of the three hierarchies evolve serially ahead of physicalized humanity through a sequence of forms. Through this perfecting through the Sons of Life, the undeveloped human souls entered into a reciprocal relationship with the Sons of Life such that Old Moon humans felt overshadowed by their tutelary Son of Life. Of the Old Moon human it could easily be said: "He experiences himself as the instrument of this higher being." It is interesting that one of the most commonly heard words to describe the role of the medium in contemporary trance channeling is that one is an "instrument" of a more developed spiritual being.

This unequal relationship may still exist today atavistically in mediums and trance channels who are always calling themselves "instruments" of some more exalted spiritual entity. But instruments are passive and inert; they can't use themselves; they can only be used by skilled (more advanced) practitioners. Why should anyone aspire to be an instrument rather than a free agent? An instrument is not an active participant in the Michaelic unfoldment of I-consciousness and *Freiheit*. Human consciousness regarded as an instrument of the gods is what Steiner always called atavistic elementary clairvoyance, a condition anachronistically unsuitable for our epoch. In light of this, we could reasonably construe much of contemporary channeling as a regressive, atavistic continuation of the Old Moon "instrumental" relationship of the Sons of Life with humans who haven't developed their sentient and intellectual souls sufficiently for independent self-expression. A relationship that the contemporary medium defers to with respectful humility may from another angle be seen as regrettable, unacceptable regression. What is most upsetting here is that this whole inverted scenario enters mass culture as a glamorous example of standard procedure, as an indication of the way things are supposed to be.

With this perspective in mind, it's instructive to consider what kind of inner schooling many of today's brand-name channels have undergone. Or have they? In Steiner's view, there simply is no way around deliberate inner soul-development as a preparation for the encounter with the supersensible worlds. The casual, no-effort, chaise-lounge approach will never do. Steiner outlined this necessity in strong, straightforward expressions. Students need "inwardly disciplined, systematic meditation," a "strictly disciplined mode of perception," and "absolutely scrupulous and exact methods." These qualities of exactitude are best developed in a regular, systematic occult practice. Steiner also emphasized that higher knowledge grows out of fully developed, *whole* soul-spiritual human being who unfolds all her forces "harmoniously and intensively."

One isn't psychic on demand, then haphazardly materialistic the rest of the time. One is cognitively dilated as a new condition of being; it is a full time change of soul configuration. Students penetrate the spiritual worlds through an "intensification of the cognitive forces" already at play in ordinary life. Through exercises of the will, students transform their passionate nature, emancipating desires from the human emotional organization. Then, through concentrated meditations, they experience free thinking from the physical body, first strengthening it so that it can live within its own content, then permeating it with active will. With this self-transformation as the foundation, occult students then approach the supersensible threshold with an attitude that is conscientious and critical; fortified with this they have some assurance of cognizing reality.

The range of intellectual background and occult training among well-known contemporary trance channels is considerable. Yet we find that rarely does it satisfy any of these criteria. Most channels have a blasé, Cinderella attitude of sudden riches, like a financial windfall from a forgotten dowager. Judging by their own accounts, it seems almost nobody completes any kind of systematic training. The way people become trance channels is like the plot of the 1950s TV show, *The Millionaire*. An anonymous benefactor hands you a check for one million dollars, and suddenly you are blushingly rich. We see far more often that mediumship in our time arises spontaneously, as an act of psychic serendipity, or perhaps as a karmic gift. It's hardly ever accompanied by any deliberate training, verification, or self-purification; it is accepted, and marketed, at face value. Channelism has generated a plethora of pop metaphysicians, a *commedia dell 'arte* troupe of freelance ontologists. As Elizabeth Fuller, a psychic publicist for the Edgar Cayce "sleeping prophet" approach to spiritual cognition, puts it, "Everyone is psychic."

One of America's most "celebrated" trance channels and probably among its wealthiest is Jach Pursel, spokesman for Lazaris. On the eve of Lazaris' debut in 1972, Pursel was a "mid-management" regional insurance supervisor in Florida. For him, "meditation was a euphemism for napping." But one evening during a slightly more active meditation Pursel started to spontaneously visualize. "I saw things! I saw things *spontaneously*! This was a first! The rapid-fire images culminated as I experienced this wonderful man standing in front of me." Pursel's fondness for napping returned when this wonderful man calling himself Lazaris began speaking through him, answering the questions of Pursel's wife. "The questions were great. The answers were boring. Maybe that's why I fell asleep."[25] Pursel's compatriot in somnambulance, and equally affluent for her efforts, is Ramtha's J. Z. Knight. She was a housewife and a former cable television executive when the Lemurian guru strode translucently into her kitchen one day while she was whimsically balancing a crystal pyramid on her head.

When the multiple fragment entity called Michael presented itself through the planchette of her Ouija board in 1970, Jessica Lansing was 32, a well-educated professional publicist with an interest in parapsychology. Lansing, who apparently regarded the Ouija board as something akin to a party game, was "somewhat upset and probably rather frightened" when Michael suddenly irrupted into her life. "It was alarming, sitting there with this board and planchette, getting words that made sense that I didn't have any control over." She felt it shouldn't be happening and wondered why she had been selected. "I mean, look at me. I'm a sensible married woman. I'm not exactly the sort of woman usually exploring the occult."[26] Nor was Jeanette Kandl, voice for King David of the Israelites, any better prepared for her initiation into trance channeling. She attended a meditation meeting put on by one of Edgar Cayce's A.R.E. groups. She was "completely unfamiliar with either metaphysics or meditation," felt she didn't "meditate very well," and was "quite unnerved by the experience at first." It didn't help when a trance medium conveyed the incontrovertible directive from a spirit: "You are going to be a deep-trance medium."[27]

That's how Mentor wrote his way into the life of Meredith Lady Young. Back in 1981, Young was 37, married, and a mother of two children, enjoying "all the embellishments of a successful suburban life in Connecticut." When the automatic writing began spontaneously, she saw herself as "a complete amateur," untutored in making sense of human consciousness or tackling major issues of spirituality. "I *felt* words—real words—crowding into my mind. My hand moved in response, writing what was being mentally transmitted in this mysterious manner." Although Young felt she participated in the transmission, she remained "partially anesthetized" as the first 47 pages of automatic words "grew from within me."[28]

The supersensible world didn't take Kevin Ryerson as much by surprise as it did his colleagues Pursel, Knight, Lansing, and Young, although it did put him to sleep. Ryerson studied the works and meditation techniques of Edgar Cayce and "consciously developed" his ESP abilities through psychometry, divining, and inspired writing. By 1969, when he graduated high school, Ryerson felt he had the equivalent of "a self-taught bachelor's degree in parapsychology." His first trance was spontaneous although "by no means against my will." Ryerson had intended to emulate Cayce's access to "superconscious mind resources" but got discarnate entities instead. He rounded off his occult training by completing a two-year theological program at the University of Life in Arizona from which he emerged credentialed as "a teacher of metaphysics and a trance channel."[29]

Robert Monroe, a former broadcasting executive, created his own occult credentials through his unique "frequent flyer" program of astral journeys. After a spontaneous introduction to the supersensible world in 1958, Monroe developed a reliable electronic means, called Hemi-Sync, of inducing out-of-the-body astral experiences (OBEs). Monroe correlated specific sound wave frequencies with different effects in consciousness. Hemi-Sync, or hemispheric synchronization, uses electronic sound patterns to entrain both brain hemispheres (physical seats of the so-called rational and intuitive aspects of mind). Hemi-Sync, as Monroe sees it, is the sound frequency petard that launches one out of the body, while staying awake. His books are a fairly wild experiential cartography of the astral "rings." The popular Gateway Program is all about experimenting with the calibrations of astral launch— "self-exploration and discovery," Monroe calls it—set in a supervised, electronically enhanced environment. "Participants learn to move into what is called Focus 12," explains Monroe, "where all physical-data input is shut off and the consciousness can reach out and begin to perceive in ways other than through the five senses."[30]

Elizabeth Fitzhugh, channel for Orion, initially studied the channeled texts of Jane Roberts, took "ESP Awareness" classes, then enrolled in the Gateway Program at the Monroe Institute of Applied Sciences in Virginia. After an initial telepathic encounter with a discarnate boy, and promptings from "the inner voice of guidance," Fitzhugh decided to take on the mantle of channeling, with one provision. Acknowledging her "responsibility of cognizance," she insisted that as a voice channel she would work *with* the energies transmitted, be actively engaged while relatively awake with the spiritual being named Orion. Cognizance for Fitzhugh means awareness at a distance, like hearing the echoes of words. "The final choice of entering into this work," Orion assured her, "would always come through [her] conscious agreement and interaction."[31]

One of the most popular channels of the 1990s is Barbara Marciniak who claims to have transmitted information from "the Pleiadians" since May 1988 when they spontaneously irrupted in her awareness while traveling with a metaphysical group through Greece. "Something impulsed me with the notion to begin to channel," she recounts in *Bringers of the Dawn,* her collation of 400 hours of trance-channeled Pleiadian transmissions. This "urge" expressed itself in a whispered voice dissimilar to her own and eventually described itself laconically as "the Pleiadians." The contact was a blissful union, soothing, full of wisdom and peace, filling her with "a deep sense of wonder," Marciniak notes. She agreed to cooperate with them, "conditionally" offering them the use of her body as a speaking medium. Then she makes two alarming statements.

First, Marciniak says that now (1992, four years after the contact) she lives in "fine accord" with the Pleiadians and feels truly "more ET than human...and my life has become a Pleiadian mystery play." This is problematic because through it she tacitly demeans her humanness in favor of an undocumented alien presence; further, she posits them as outside, separate, and better than her human being, which is not only an irresponsible example to set for a gullible public, but, metaphysically speaking, insofar as the cosmos (which includes the Pleiades) is the Supersensible Human on the macrocosmic scale, incorrect. Second, she relinquishes her critical skepticism and declines to investigate "the Pleiadians" to substantiate their intentions. "Never having been a great investor in worry, it became quite easy for me to move into the Pleiadian moment of letting go, as they created a life of their own through me.... My job was to manage and be a physical steward for their energies." Here Marciniak equates cognitive discrimination—which is the Michaelic requirement of the consciousness soul—with "worry" and slips into that Pollyannish New Age passivity that seems to equate sharp thinking with an embarrassing neurosis. She takes the "easy" route of compliance and divestment, gladly surrendering her own cognitive life and independent I-consciousness for a subservient stewardship of alien energy. Is this an example one would wish to emulate? Whoever said "the Pleiadians" were the good guys in the cosmic struggle for the soul of humanity?[32]

Mary-Margaret Moore's entry into the work of channeling, Bartholomew, also required her conscious agreement. But it was framed against a background unconventional for psychics. Moore's friends often queried her, "How could an educated and reasonably intelligent woman like you deal with being a psychic?" Her background was "strongly Zen," a rigorous form of Buddhism that officially excoriates any psychic or occult phenomena, especially contact with discarnate entities. Zen Masters aren't likely to admit even Elder Brothers like Bartholomew as epistemologically valid. But Moore, a de facto Zen apostate, was impressed with the "usefulness" of Bartholomew's energy and its "vaster point of view," though she was wary of precipitating a "karmic mess" through her involvement. She resolved to bring to the exchange as much consciousness as possible. "First and foremost, I decided to stand responsible for the validity of all the information that was being given."[33]

Ken Carey took the matter of conscious responsibility one step further. He resolved always to test the validity of his transmissions from the angels against his own "better judgment." His first "blending with the angel" nonplussed him. "The thoughts, the ideas, the scope of the images—I was not used to thinking in such terms." He felt unprepared for the encounter, was often mentally incapable of following the material, and at first "balked in outright disbelief." Yet he had prepared himself during the 1970s through a rural, agrarian life-style in Missouri, de-emphasizing "outer media" while tuning into "inner media." He regarded himself as a biological radio. Carey's process of accessing supersensible information is not channeling, he insists. He doesn't go into trance, doesn't lose consciousness, doesn't change his voice or accent. "*I* am fully present throughout the experience," says Carey, who sees this contact with "higher-frequency awareness" as an organic process innate in every child.[34]

That higher-frequency awareness is innate in young children is a statement with which Steiner would concur. But it's unlikely he would condone channelism's style, especially as demonstrated by the examples presented at the beginning of this brief survey. The anthroposophical attitude cannot support the general absence of any willed, conscious, systematic occult training that is de rigeur today among contemporary men and women "opening to channel." This is the wrong kind of divestment, the wrong way to pass through the Portal of Death. As potential consumers of channeled material alleging to speak truthfully of the supersensible worlds, we must be assiduously critical of its contents and origins.

Much of today's popularly available channeled and occult material results from a remarkable passivity, an indifferent somnambulance, an involuntary engagement, an ahistorical metaphysical posture. It is not the result of spiritual science. Spirit entities erupt without notice into the lives of unprepared men and women and their pronouncements are accorded truth and respect. This is an epistemologically suspect, even dangerous, trend. As we gather from the examples cited above, the participation of

I-consciousness in the encounter is considered optional. Self-purification, inner ripening, spiritual scientific protocols, exercises in will and sense-free thinking, meditative concentration, meeting the Guardians of the Threshold, recognizing Lucifer and Ahriman looming over the chakras—these are hardly ever mentioned.

Instead, the dubious values of easy mediumship, meditative napping, and psychism-as-spirituality are promoted by well-compensated channels and their *controls*, as spirit entities were once accurately called. After all, instruments are controlled by their users; that is the purpose and destiny of an instrument. Spiritual attainment following strenuous personal effort is tacitly seen as an aberration. Why struggle? Shirley MacLaine danced in the light with her higher self on the ballroom floor of glamorous Atlantean incarnations when a therapist inserted an acupuncture needle in her brow chakra. It wasn't any different from watching a movie at home, and it took no more effort. Why bother to develop etheric imaginations when you can so easily insert an astral entertainment video in your head, as if it were a VCR? Hemi-Sync brain wave entrainment will send you out on exciting OBEs, or you can meet your beatific spirit guide through past life regression and hypnosis. The "New Age" concept of channeling is so skewed that one medium actually wrote: "I also heard that unless the channeler was unconscious, the material coming through was not totally pure."[35]

The correlation of consciousness with purity is apt though inverted. Unless the channeler brings the force of I-consciousness into the encounter at the supersensible threshold, the likelihood that transmissions received have any purity, accuracy, or validity, is minimal at best. As far as field data goes, such transmissions are even less consequential than hearsay and vague anecdotes. Spiritual scientists as scholars of the supersensible would never accept them. Take the case of Swedish visionary Emmanuel Swedenborg (1688–1772).

Swedenborg at mid-life ascended to seership on a foundation of "an eminently serious and conscientious scientific approach," said Steiner. Swedenborg's scientific achievements and competence were formidable, and should have well prepared him for unsullied entrance into the supersensible worlds. But Swedenborg was still subject to "all kinds of illusions" in spite of his

rigorous scientific preparation. Where did he go wrong? Swedenborg brought his physical plane habits of perception into the spiritual worlds; he insisted on observing spiritual beings as objects of
his perception, just as he beheld trees and humans in the material world. The result was that he perceived real spiritual beings in
a false guise, in a form he imposed on them. He clothed his seemingly objective perceptions with "emotion-filled thinking [full] of
subjective content." He never divested his pure thinking, or cognition, of the emotional motives normal to his personal, subjective mind. Swedenborg wasn't able to conceive of a world of pure
thoughts or pure concepts. But it's only when "thinking itself that
is doing the thinking" becomes the touchstone of our supersensible experience, when thinking contains only pure thoughts, that
"divine content, the content that comes from above, can flow in."
Otherwise, we are subject to "perversions of mystical thinking"
and "mystical monkey business," chides Steiner. Most of the available visionary literature of his time, added Steiner, was rife with
"illusions of this sort."[36]

If Swedenborg's supersensible cognition was this subjectively biased, how are we to regard the descriptions of the spiritual worlds
from today's channels, mediums, and savants, who almost universally lack any kind of scientific preparation or rigorous meditative
training? The implications are unsettling. We must reasonably in-
quire if such a channel's cognition hasn't instead been appropriated by Lucifer and Ahriman or infiltrated by intelligent but
maligned elementary beings as a cosmic reward for their psychic
nonchalance and occult disregard for the Guardians. There are
deeper, more troubling questions. Is the unstudied, untutored,
lackadaisical approach to the supersensible encounter predominant in contemporary channelism setting a culturally damaging
standard? Is the California sleeping millionaire trance prophet today's state-of-the-art for channelism? And does this Ahrimanic
easy mediumship further or hinder the incarnation of Sophia
within humanity in the epoch of the consciousness soul? These
are important questions that must be raised.

A response formulated according to a spiritual scientific attitude would have to conclude that channelism's standards are
radically damaging, that trance channels are not in any way exemplary of correct occult practices, and that none of this serves the

restoration of imaginative force to Sophia. If anything, it further alienates Sophia within matter through the Ahrimanizing of spirituality and cognition. Valentin Tomberg stated Sophia's case very strongly: "The tragic path of the Sophia has its counterpart in the human soul in that the human soul also has been deprived of the power of forming truth: the power of Imagination has become subjective fantasy with an inward leaning to the fantastic." The soul's capacity to create its own imaginations has lost its force and truth-value, said Tomberg. Like Sophia, the human soul, swathed in egotism, has grown dumb. All it sees are subjective fantasies which it mistakes for cosmic imaginations. Tomberg reminds us that the destinies of the "true soul-being" of humanity on Earth and Sophia in the spiritual world are similar, if not equivalent.[37] If humanity succumbs to the Ahrimanization of cosmic intelligence, so does Sophia as its bearer.

In earlier times, people remembered that Sophia represented the archetype of the human soul. This means that when an individual purified the astral body of its disturbing sheath of egotistic desires, so that the true, inner soul-being could emerge as the microcosmic Virgin Sophia, this act of catharsis was also a cosmically redemptive act for the macrocosmic Sophia in the spiritual world. Holographically speaking, there is only one Sophia distributed fractally throughout the created world. Sophia is an activity, a process of consciousness manifest at different levels and scales of being. The redemption of Sophia in human consciousness is, holographically, the redemption of Sophia as the 30th Aion outside the Pleroma. We must remember the basic equations: humanity equals the microcosmic Human; the macrocosmic Human equals the cosmos. And Sophia is a fundamental activity in consciousness implicit in the cosmos at either level of expression, either cosmic Human or human. When Sophia is redeemed in individual humans, then Sophia is redeemed in the collectivity of the cosmic Human. When the Virgin Sophia is born in the human consciousness soul, then the living force of imaginative cognition arises again as the life force of her being. The individual beholds mighty pictures and spiritual symbols, signs of authentic activities, indications of the weaving of cosmic intelligence, of the living thoughts of manifold spiritual beings across the threshold. Then Sophia truly comes into her own through the cognition of humanity. This gives us an idea of the negative consequences presented by channelism without occult standards.

With the Virgin Sophia we have the first indication of cosmic intelligence arising purely, founded in the I-conscious, awake human individuality. Imagination *is* Sophia's cognition; the mighty supersensible cosmic picture tableau *is* Sophia's intelligence. Sophia's great tableau of the "etheric time-body of formative forces" is the cosmos itself, the thoughts of the hierarchies arising in activity, the etheric, dynamic thought-life of the world itself. Sophia beholds this. It is her self-knowledge. It's just a question of scale, whether we refer to the macrocosmic or microcosmic Sophia. The imagination of Sophia unfolds as a majestic tableau of cosmic intelligence, as the fullness of cosmic intellectuality, activity, and presence—the Wisdom of God. Sophia bears the cosmic intelligence promised to humanity; more precisely, Sophia *is* this cosmic intelligence; it is her cognitive life. Sophia's imagination is the vision of her pictorial, morphological thinking, arrayed in scintillating form as the cosmos itself. It's the perpetually mutable, constantly growing, dynamically weaving thought-organism. It is cosmic intelligence as the "structure of formative forces moving in the stream of time." It is potentially ours, too, when we achieve the Virgin Sophia as a foundation.

Sophia's imagination is the projected body of her self-knowledge—cosmic intelligence itself. This is the joy of Michael's desiring, that Sophia should behold the cosmic intelligence as a living imagination in the context of individual I-consciousness. When Sophia comes to know herself through this cosmic imaginative tableau, this living thought projection of her "true soul-being," then the stage is set for the redemption of the Human.

The secret here is that humans individually redeem the cosmic Human through birthing the Virgin Sophia. That is why channelism and its products are such a dangerous, counterproductive digression; yet the *fact* of its existence is, paradoxically, a positive, salutary indication of something more exalted working its way into human spiritual evolution. It is the preparation, the early symptoms of ripeness, for the initiation called the Imagination of Pentecost, the subject of the remainder of the book. The Virgin Sophia in exoteric terms is the Madonna, the mother who births the Christ. Esoterically, Sophia is the consort of the Christ, and their union is the Gnostic syzygy (or pairing up) of Intelligence and Logos, concept and percept, manas and mahat. Their syzygy generates speech, Logos-permeated, world-creating speech in the act of Pentecost—the subject of our final chapters.

For now, let us bear in mind that the incarnation of Sophia within the human individuality means men and women become individual points of anthropomorphized Sophia—*anthroposophists*, positioned for syzygy with the Christ, the great Human Ideal on Earth. This syzygy of Sophia and Christ heals the primordial cleavage in humanity; it reunifies Lucifer and Ahriman into the single being Lucifer always was. Goethe was right: there is only an ambivalent Mephistopheles. The incarnation of Sophia through an anthroposophically positioned humanity necessarily leads to the resurrection of the Holy Ghost caught and bifurcated in Time.

The Resurrection of the Holy Ghost

Christ in Relation to the Cleaved Lucifer

*I*NCREASINGLY throughout the remaining days of the twentieth century, Steiner said in 1920, the inner schism and "most significant disharmony" in humans will rise up into consciousness, demanding a resolution. Men and women will feel acutely torn between their sense of "dwarf-like" material existence as hermits of the Earth and their upwelling intuition that each man and woman is in fact a cosmic being of unlimited scope. This will become the most urgent of all questions, how to reconcile our apparently limited physical individuality with a deep intuition that we are in truth cosmic beings. What is lacking is proof, grounds for certainty, some way of integrating the twin aspects of the human riddle, grounds for trusting the equation, continually put forward by Steiner, that microcosm equals macrocosm.

Out of "grey spiritual depths" the Christ will reveal himself to us as that living proof, addressing us spiritually, within etheric cognition. The Christ's presence *is* the solution; the Logos is the connection, the point of coherence. This will be the new experience of the Christ, said Steiner; it will be a revelation of cosmic identity arising out of the attunement and need of human souls. The Christ reveals the human as a picture of the living spirit, as a cosmic thought, showing us incontrovertibly that human organology is a mirror of the cosmos. What Steiner means here is that in the life processes of our body's organs—heart, lung, liver, kidneys, spleen—we behold the microcosmic expression of the life of the planets and stars. This is why Steiner always emphasized that self-knowledge is knowledge of the world; our human organs were formed out of cosmic processes and activities.[1]

To appreciate how the epiphanous presence of the Christ is the solution to this primordial riddle, we need to understand how big the body of Christ is. The form of the physical human, explained Steiner, is a living picture of the cooperative activities of all the supersensible hierarchies. The human form is an apparency, a virtual image, of our true being in the supersensible world, a real being that is as large as the cosmos. For example, the activity of angels lives in our thinking; in our human speech we find the Archangels; and we find the Archai working through all our will-imbued actions. In the pulsating forces of the blood, home of the human Ego, live the Third Hierarchy (Angels, Archangels, Archai); the Second Hierarchy (Exusiai, Dynamis, and Kyriotetes) occupy our internal organs; and the beings of the First Hierarchy (Seraphim, Cherubim, Thrones) indwell the etheric body. The outer human form is a picture of the working together, the cosmic activity and processes, of all the supersensible hierarchical beings. Humans live on Earth among "the revelations of the individual spirits"; our entire life is a dramatic struggle within the Being and outer garment of the Divine.[2]

Whose *idea* was all this? The human is actually a cosmic thought, one of the "links in the thought-logic of the cosmos," said Steiner. Our whole world-system is the "consolidated clairvoyance" of the hierarchies. When these cosmic beings think, they think humans. As humans, we belong with our entire being to the regency of cosmic thought. We live embedded within the mighty thoughts of the three hierarchies; it is not inexact to say we are the living, mineralized imagination of the hierarchies. To these cosmically thinking beings, individual humans are like single letters in a book, which their logic function organizes into sentences and paragraphs of meaning. We are "consumed as spiritual food and serve as nourishment" for these cosmic creator-thinkers. As humans, we enter material incarnation with a "grand, mighty content," the handiwork of countless spiritual beings creating through thought the "most wondrous structure" of our physical organism. We need only remember the Gnostic account of the creation of Adam, the "natural body" of the immortal First Human—Anthropos—through the contribution of 365 angels. As the Nag Hammadi documents tell us, "They all worked on it until, limb for limb, the natural and the material body was completed by them.... And all the angels and demons worked until they had constructed the natural body."[3] The physical, etheric, and astral sheaths of the human constitution are entire worlds for the activities and processes of spiritual beings. When we move, speak, feel, think, or will, all these human activities are really the supersensible life processes of individual Spirits expressed in matter. The human rightly feels "intergrown with the entire cosmic structure" despite the fact that one feels completely independent, the possessor of the uniquely human I-consciousness. "Man is so complex because he is truly a mirror-image of the spiritual world."[4]

The physical human is the macrocosmic Human turned inside out. All that is outside as the cosmos and which we experience as our extended spiritual being bodies in the life after death and preceding birth, contracts and turns inside out, becoming the interior of the physical human on Earth. All the forces and agencies in the cosmos cooperate to generate the physical human. "The cosmic germ of man's physical body is experienced in his pre-earthly existence as a cosmos."[5] This "majestic universe" contracts and shrinks together to form the spiritual then etheric then physical body of humankind. This cosmic germ is immense, the human's future physical body expanded to be a universe. Human organology is the contracted expression of cosmology; in the life of the heart, liver, and kidneys, we experience the supersensible activities of the stars and planets. Every organ is in effect the terrestrial counterpart of a divine-spiritual Being, said Steiner, who added, "Behold Cosmic Man through human organology."[6]

In the Old Saturn phase of cosmic unfoldment, the entire cosmos appeared as a gigantic cosmic being, as a Cosmic Human. This Cosmic Human was the sum-total of "the inner-organic, cooperative activity of generations of Gods." Other wisdom traditions, such as Qabala, call this Cosmic Human the Adam Kadmon, explaining how its body occupied the whole of the *Otz Chaim*, the Tree of Life. The body of the terrestrial human was assembled through the principal contributions of the spiritual beings of the zodiac, the twelve faces of the human individuality. Through the contributions of the *Tierkreis*, the "animal circle" of

the zodiac, the hierarchies assembled the inner organs of the
Cosmic Human from the animal group souls of the zodiac.[7] Taurus, the animal group soul of the bull, created the human neck;
Pisces, the animal group soul for fish, made the feet. Exoteric astrology acknowledges this co-creative participation in its standard
attributions, such as Taurus rules the neck, Pisces rules the feet.
When we say the zodiac builds the human organs from the supersensible animal consciousness, it's simply another vocabulary for
the Gnostic statement that the passions of Sophia outside the
Pleroma precipitated the four elements of matter and thus the
material world. The animal group souls of the animal circle, or
zodiac, are the twelvefold elaboration in the context of material
selfhood of these four elemental passions of Sophia. Both systems
are ways of indicating the lower, instinctual, biological, animal nature of the human individuality. They also highlight the evolutionary relationship of humanity with the animal kingdom.

Reversing orthodox thinking, or what he suggested was its mis-
perception, Steiner put forward the idea that the animal forms
represent the cast-off, prematurely congealed forms of the human in the process of evolving its form. Thus the animal kingdom is innately part of the human totality, forming the basis,
through its group soul qualities, of its astrality, or emotional, passionate nature. Animal forms are the "hardened physiognomical
expressions of human passions." In the very early days of Lemuria, the human form was mobile and pliant, so plastic, in fact,
that through the force of emotions in the astral body, these passions made metamorphozing imprints in the physiognomy of the
human. The various passions and thoughts assumed temporary
form through the mobile plasticity of the human form. "A large
proportion of our present higher animals are nothing other than
human beings who were so entangled in their passions that they
became hardened and ceased to evolve further." In other words,
we may see our evolutionary past in the animal forms; we may see
in the animals our "degenerated descendants." We must be careful to appreciate Steiner's subtlety here. He does not argue that
humans evolved out of, or from, the animal kingdom, as did Darwin and the materialist evolutionists; rather he argues that the animal forms are biologically hardened human emotional states
extrapolated out during an early phase of evolution (specifically,

before the Sun separated from the Earth). In the animal kingdom we see a "great tapestry" made from the hardened expressions of "every conceivable characteristic and thought" of human
emotion.[8]

Incarnating humans, in assembling their form from the constituents of the cosmos, from the animal group souls of the zodiac, surround this twelvefold inner, elemental nature with a
sheath woven out of thought. This is the thought-full etheric
body which bears the imprint of the "cosmic archetypal picture,"
the entire thought-weaving activity of the creative hierarchies.
Ordinarily after death, humans see objectively what this form really is, what their true self looks like: the radiant, shining body of
the supersensible Human. "This cosmic picture of man shines
spiritually [as] the luminous picture of his own form."[9] Here, an-
chored in the human etheric body with its "grand, mighty content," is the "cosmic archetypal picture" of the spiritual Human.
As Steiner often declared: "O Man, thou art the condensed image of the world! O World, thou art the being of Man poured
out into infinite space!" With this, we have arrived at a crucial
point.[10] This impression of the supersensible Human is the
phantom, the primordial form in radiant light of the Cosmic
Human from which every human physical individuality is cop-
ied. This Cosmic Human is the same Adam Kadmon, described
by Qabala, and Phanes, the egg-born Ur-human of light, described by the Orphic Mysteries. We may take the words phantom, ghost, Supersensible Human, and cosmic form as
interchangeable evocations of the bringing forth in light of the
image of Cosmic Human, the Anthropos. The human phantom,
the thought-full etheric body with its might cosmic content, is
the anthropomorphic expression of the Cosmic Human. There
is a new link to add to this sequence, a correlation implied but
not stated outright by Steiner. The Holy Ghost takes form as Cosmic Human, as the human phantom. Cosmic Human bears the
form in light of the Holy Ghost (or phantom). Cosmic Human
is, literally, the Light-Bringer, in which the light (*phos*) is brought
forth (*phoros*) as an image.[11]

This human phantom is the composite form of divine spirituality, the morphological totality of the thought-weavings and spiritual activities of all the hierarchies of the cosmos expressed as a

single radiant, anthropomorphosed body of light. Esoteric Christianity calls this emanation of divine spirituality the Logos or Word. The human form is "the vesture of the Logos," said Steiner. "Everything is an incarnation of the Logos," all things in the world—mineral, plant, animal kingdoms, the stars and planets, and human intelligence that encompasses the world—"first come forth into existence from the Logos." The Logos is the point of coherence, of cosmos-organizing self-aware intelligence, the primordial I-consciousness inhabiting the being bodies of the Cosmic Human who is woven of the complete activities of all the spiritual hierarchies. The Christ is the I-consciousness that makes the Cosmic Human, who comprises the activities and processes of all the supersensible constituents, coherent. Esoteric astrology tells us the Logos is the coherence of the stars (from *aster*, meaning "stars": aster-logos); Anthroposophy tells us that Man and its microcosmic expression as human beings, is the vesture of the Logos, the manifest body of the Word. Here we are dealing with what Georg Kühlewind calls the Logos-structure of the world. Our world is not made of things but words structured by the Logos as a text that may be read by us, as beings with I-consciousness. "Only an I-being has a 'world.' And I-beings have a world only because the world has the nature and structure of the word, the Logos, which in turn is accessible only to I-beings."[12]

The Logos calls forth the world. The world, the universe, is the spoken Word of the Logos. The cosmos is a "universal resounding," a starry euphony of everything that is spoken by the celestial beings in continuous acts of self-revelation, a universe revealing itself through morphogenetic syllables—all this is the Logos. The one word that summarizes, encapsulates, epitomizes, and *is* the cosmos: this is the Logos. The cosmos is the vesture, the garment of the Logos. This cosmic body or vesture of the Logos Word is the human phantom, which is Supersensible Human as the cosmic form in light. Its miniaturized, condensed, contracted expression is the human, biological, tangible individuality, each and every woman and man. Macrocosmic Human is the microcosmic human: the phantom in light, the phantom in matter. The human being is the Logos made flesh, the Word incarnate. A revelation looms implicit in this syllogism. Before the Mystery of Golgotha, the Logos was only an appearance. With the physical incarnation of the Christ on Earth and the completion of the Mystery of Golgotha, Christ united with this cosmic appearance and made it tangible through his own being. Through Golgotha, "the apparent Logos [was] born upon Earth as real Logos."[13] Before we can understand this equation, we need to insert another supersensible being in between the Logos and human fleshly individuality. This is Phosphoros, the Light-Bringer who bears the form (the phantom, ghost, or vesture) of the cosmos as the Human; the Light-Bringer is known in Western esotericism as Lucifer.[14] Again, this is not stated as such by Steiner, but in my estimation it is implicit and perhaps intended in the body of his work. As the phantom of the Cosmic Human is none other than the Holy Ghost, and as Phosphoros-Lucifer is the Light-Bringer, bearing the form of the Cosmic Human in light, we are led inescapably to the conclusion that *Lucifer is the Holy Ghost*, the bearer of the phantom, or ghost, of the Supersensible Human. This remarkable discovery further implies that *Lucifer and Ahriman are in truth one being, the Light-Bearer*. Lucifer is the single progeny of Zurvan; as such, Lucifer is only relatively, apparently, cleaved into the warring halves of Lucifer and Ahriman. Lucifer is the singular Holy Ghost as Cosmic Human caught in Time and Space, and thus rendered ambivalent as Lucifer/Ahriman, through the biological individuality of humanity.

Lucifer brings the light forward into visibility as form. Form inherently individualizes. Form means two; form *is* two, object and ground, manifestation and context. In this we find the origin of all the difficulty with selfhood and the spirit of independence which is Lucifer. Lucifer, in Western thinking, was the ultimate scapegoat for the scission of unity from the beginning of human incarnation. *Lucifer is the Fall*; the entire life story of Lucifer, his deeds and aspirations, is the Fall of humanity itself. That is because Lucifer bears (or expresses through his manifestation, his showing forth) the form that individualizes light. Human individuality is the microcosm of Lucifer's macrocosmic individuality. The individualization of light as form is the Fall, the primordial scission, the awful cleavage in the Holy Ghost. Humanity *is* the Fall; microcosmic human individuality is the Fall redivivus. The individualization of Human as a cosmos of light itself is the Fall. The polarized drama played out in human biology is merely an intensification of this archetypal dialectic. Individuality in biological form is only twice as problematical as individuality in cosmic form.

Lucifer's expansive being was constricted into a biological time organism—*bio-Logos*, the Logos operating within material, organic, evolving life. This event precipitated a cleavage or polarity in the singularity of the Holy Ghost, the image of the Supersensible Human. Time, biology, matter, evolution, individual form—these are all inherently dualistic conditions, growth striving against inertia, stasis conflicting with change. Lucifer's being, caught in the matrix of biological time, was cleaved, producing Lucifer and Ahriman. It was the incarnation into human individual visibility, into time-dependent matter, that created all the problems. Visibility polarizes. The movement from celestial transparency to terrestrial opacity, from the phantom of Man to the tangibility of human—this precipitated the ambivalence we have experienced in the Holy Ghost ever since. But it also made possible the eventual development of spiritual freedom and cognitive autonomy—*Freiheit*—within humanity. It is what will make the Michaelic respiritualization of cosmic intelligence possible through humanity. The scission of Lucifer was teleologically redemptive and ontologically necessary.

One day, when Lucifer is redeemed and his singularity re-established, then long-range purpose of this intention, its sacrificial gesture on behalf of a nascent humanity, will be acknowledged and made fruitful. Steiner's characterizations of the Lucifer-Ahriman cosmic polarity are apt: Lucifer, the expansive, celestial Human, striving to regain existence in uncreated cosmic Time with the Unbegotten Father, Zurvan; Ahriman, the contracting, terrestrial Human striving towards deeper penetration into time and matter. The titanic struggles within the cleaved being of Lucifer generate the multiplicity of fetters to independent cognition in the context of time, biology, matter, and individuality—our felt lives. This profound existential turmoil is inexorably played out in the being bodies of all humans over time. The *angst* of the Holy Ghost caught in time and space is a prime feature of our daily awareness.

The identity of Lucifer with Ahriman and Lucifer with the Holy Ghost is more than an intellectual syllogism. Not only does independent clairvoyant perception confirm this equation, but Steiner's own declarations in his apocalyptic lecture *The Deed of Christ* and in his provocative lecture cycle *The East in the Light of the West* (both in 1909) actually establish the spiritual scientific foundations for a reformulation of this basic dialectic within the Living being of Anthroposophia. In our time, the living Being Anthroposophia desperately requires the fruits of a fresh appraisal of Lucifer and Ahriman. The cosmic cleavage in humanity continues to tear terrestrial humans apart. The Fall of humanity must be redeemed in our own conceptual life, within the process of cognition, even within Anthroposophy—no, *especially* within Anthroposophy.

Steiner himself evidenced a puzzling ambivalence or inconsistency in his formulations of the Lucifer-Ahriman dialectic during the 25 years of his public ministry. First he took one position, then he took another. It was evidently not possible in the first two decades of the twentieth century for Steiner to bring forth the full teachings about Lucifer. To construe the redeemed Lucifer as the Holy Ghost is for Western culture a radical proposition; similarly, to comprehend Lucifer and Ahriman as a single spiritual being is for the mainstream Anthroposophical Movement an equally unsettling contention. We have heresy on our hands, in either case; yet we may also have an iconoclasm of double potency. Steiner actually established all the preliminaries for this conclusion. In fact, we note with surprise that Steiner's view of Lucifer, as he expressed it up until approximately 1909, was radically different from the bleak Zoroastrian dialectical formulations that he articulated in all the years that followed, until his death in 1925. His pre-1910 statements are much more in accord with the deeper truth of a singular Lucifer as the Holy Ghost that needs to be brought forward at the end of the twentieth century as a redemptive impulse.

"Lucifer is the *bearer* of the Light—Christ *is* the Light!" Steiner announced in 1909. Another name for the Light-Bearer who brings forth the Light which is the Christ is *Christophor*, the Christ-Bringer. Another phrase from early Christianity to express this relationship was *Christus verus Luciferus*, meaning, "Christ is the *true* (*verus*) Light-Bearer." In a remarkably straightforward equation, this says Christ *is* Lucifer, not Christ *contra* Lucifer, which was the

Zoroastrian dialectic Steiner later forwarded. Thus, to call Lucifer *Christophor* means the vesture of the Logos is Lucifer. Lucifer bears the body which is the light of the Christ. The cosmic form of humanity individualized as Lucifer is the light of Christ: Lucifer is the Christophoric Human. Lucifer incarnates the Holy Ghost. "This 'Holy Spirit' is none other than the Lucifer-Spirit resurrected now in higher, purer glory—the Spirit of independent understanding, wisdom-woven."[15] Steiner cites a prophecy made by the Christ when on Earth: "Ye shall be illumined by the new Spirit, by the Holy Spirit!"

Lucifer wished to give humanity the Ego-impulse of independent individuality and individualized cosmic intelligence. As Kühlewind teaches us, only I-beings can have and know the world. Lucifer anticipated the potential *Freiheit* of humanity; his mission in effect was to make it happen. Lucifer understood the full implications of a biological humanity, of his self-aware individuality expressed materially through billions of individualized men and women. But the Luciferic gift of the Ego occurred at a time when men and women were not sufficiently mature to handle independence in the context of tangible, biological individuality, explains Steiner. That is, humans were given cognitive individuality in the context of the Lower Sophia, the unpurged passionate astrality of Old Moon. The Ego-impulse, the carte blanche of selfhood, tore humans "asunder." They were unable to freely develop love for one another in the context of free selfhood. Spiritual beings must love; only humans can choose to. The idea was that humans, given individual visible, mineralized form, given the Ego which made I-consciousness and cognitive autonomy possible, would then freely develop moral impulses, inspired by the Christ, and leading to fellowship and community as the fruits of fraternal love.

This implicates the purpose of the planet itself; just as Old Moon is called the Planet of Wisdom, in which wisdom permeated all things as their root substance, so the Earth is destined to be the Planet of Love. Over time, the love principle is to be spiritualized on Earth so that, as our gift to the next phase of evolution, the Jupiter stage, all earthly beings will be filled with love. To achieve this exalted goal, humanity must wean itself from its group soul identity, from bonds forged on the basis of blood relationships and ethnic consanguinity. Instead there must be independent egos in direct relationship; "only thus could true love develop," says Steiner. It was—and remains—a bold plan.

At Golgotha, the Christ appeared as the "real Logos" in human individuality on Earth, making possible what through Lucifer had been potential and appearance. This was "the great love-principle of Christ which brings the egos together, which makes communities of individuals."[16] Christ brought the impulse of the Sun's inner spiritual radiation to complement the physical sunlight already manifest on Earth. Through this gift of a "spirit seed" for humanity's future, the Christ Sun would irradiate humans from within their being.[17] Christ exemplified the spirit of freedom couched in a human individuality. Christ represents the perfection of I-consciousness within the embodied individuality of Lucifer. Christ is the resolution of the agonizing duality of tangible individuality versus cosmic unity, selfhood versus God—the basic cleavage in humanity. Since Golgotha, "the torch of the resurrected Lucifer, of the Lucifer transformed into the good, blazons the way for Christ."[18] Lucifer, resurrected into a new form, can now unite with the Christ as the "good Spirit."

We are dealing with some very large concepts here—the singularity of Lucifer and Ahriman, Lucifer as the Holy Ghost or phantom of the Cosmic Human, the *resurrection* of Lucifer as the good Spirit, Lucifer as Christophor, Lucifer's *union* with Christ, the Logos becoming real and tangible on Earth. These all require fuller explication. We will spend the remainder of this chapter fulfilling that necessity because this new understanding of the relationship of Lucifer and Christ within the being of humanity is crucial to our preparations for the Imagination of Pentecost.

Let's start with the first big idea, that of the singularity of Lucifer and Ahriman. Steiner implied this through but not after 1909 in his Christophor concept, but after that year he recanted, and thereafter presented instead the unrelievedly darker, Zoroastrian dualism of Lucifer and Ahriman. It's hard to understand precisely why Steiner changed his position. It is likely that, for the purposes of vivid description, he created this dialectic as a literary or metaphysical device. The climate of Steiner's times and the negative aspect of the Germanic temperament probably precluded any bolder formulation. At the level of inner truth

Lucifer and Ahriman are one being, but at a dualistic or polarity-based level of experience, Lucifer and Ahriman could be seen conceptually as separate. This cognitive duality itself is the cleavage of the Holy Ghost, the primordial bifurcation in the being bodies of the Cosmic Human, perpetuated in anthroposophical conceptions.

We find support for the singularity of Lucifer in the original teachings of Theosophy. H. P. Blavatsky may have neglected the Christ, as Steiner rightly criticized her, but her statements about Lucifer in *The Secret Doctrine* are predominantly in alignment with the view of a singular Lucifer put forward here.

According to Blavatsky, the Western esoteric tradition knew Lucifer under different names: the Astral Light, the Sidereal Virgin, the *Mysterium Magnum*, and the Aether (as a reflection of Akasha). It was the Latin scholastics who transformed the "universal soul and Pleroma, the *vehicle of Light* and the receptacle of all the forms, a force spread throughout the whole universe," into Satan, or the negative Lucifer as humanity's foe. The Astral Light was the cause of existence, said Blavatsky; it fills the infinity of space; it is Space itself, the matrix of the universe "from which all that exists is born by separation or *differentiation*." In antiquity and in truth, Blavatsky asserted, Lucifer was the name of that spiritual being who presided over the light of truth. When we say "truth," this brings Sophia into the equation as the true revelation of the totality of cosmic intelligence. In fact, Blavatsky further correlates Sophia and Lucifer by citing a Gnostic source that said Sophia resides in the planet Venus or Lucifer; presumably, this statement is to be understood symbolically and not literally. To the profane, the Astral Light may be God and Devil at once. According to this view, Lucifer is divine and terrestrial light, the Holy Ghost, and Satan, if we like. And the Luciferic Astral Light, "the manifested effects of the two who are one, guided and attracted by ourselves, is the Karma of humanity."[19]

With Blavatsky's formulations we have intimations of a close correlation of Lucifer with Sophia, the Light-Bringer as differentiated Astral Light presiding over the totality of cosmic intelligence. Blavatsky doesn't hesitate to state that the dialectic of Lucifer and Satan (substitute: Ahriman) is apparent but not real, that it is a polarity articulated through human karma (substitute:

conceptual habit). The Fall was the result of enhanced human cognition, true knowledge, acquaintance, and wisdom, provided by "our intelligent liberator and Saviour from pure animalism"— Lucifer, who in cognitive life represents the quickening spirit of Manas, the independent human mind. Lucifer, claimed Blavatsky, was the "first Archangel who sprang from the depths of Chaos: *Lux*, Luminous Son of the Morning, the individualization of Space-filled intelligence." Lucifer is the "incorporeal man who contains in himself the divine Idea."

As attractive as this arcane exoneration of Lucifer as the unblemished Son of the Morning might be, we have to be careful with Blavatsky. She ignores the Christ. She mistakenly equates Lucifer with the Logos as the intelligence of the Astral Light, rather than beings its form-bearer. Lucifer was the "Blazing Dragon of Wisdom," Blavatsky declared, reminding us that the dragon was an ancient glyph for the Astral Light, the primordial principle which meant the "wisdom of chaos." That's why she concluded Lucifer is the Logos in his highest aspect, and the Adversary in his lowest aspect, both of which are reflected in the human Ego.[20]

This is elegant but only half-true. Here we come up against the ontological limitations of Theosophy, whose roots were fundamentally pre-Golgotha, if not anti-Golgotha. Blavatsky was correct in stating that the ambivalent dialectic within Lucifer (as Lucifer/Satan, Lucifer/Ahriman) is played out in the human individuality through karma. But she blurred the subtle distinction between light and its form-bearer. Blavatsky understood the struggles of Lucifer and Ahriman as polarities within a single being, but she incorrectly called this being the Logos. Yet, when she used the phrase "Blazing Dragon of Wisdom," she implied that Lucifer, as the dragon of light, embodied the wisdom of Sophia, whose soul life is the continuing revelation of cosmic intelligence. Steiner appreciated the distinction between Logos and Lucifer, but insisted on a trinity of Lucifer against Ahriman, mediated by the Christ. With Blavatsky in mind, we observe that the relationship of Christ and Lucifer is symbiotic but not isomorphic.

Following the Gnostics, we could say that Lucifer is the Human, Christ is "Son of Man" (the Human). Lucifer is the Logos individualized. Lucifer is the Astral Light expressed as cosmic selfhood. Lucifer is cosmic intelligence (Sophia) in independent form. Through Lucifer, Space, which is the domain of the Logos, assumed form, assumed an appearance in light. As Steiner succinctly said, Lucifer bears the Light, Christ is the Light; thus Lucifer is the Christophor, the Christ-Bringer. This is inconsistent with saying that the Christ mediates the dialectic between Lucifer and Ahriman, which was Steiner's later position. In his pre-1909 formulations, Steiner posited a much more intimate, interdependent relationship between Lucifer and Christ. Another way of saying this is Christ is the I-consciousness of Lucifer's individuality, the Logos that coheres the cosmic form Lucifer wears as individualized Sophianic body. Steiner described the relationship in yet another way when he spoke of the Children of Lucifer and the Brothers of Christ.

In the course of world cultural evolution towards an apprehension of Christ and Lucifer, two fundamental spiritual streams emerged. In what Steiner designated the northern evolutionary stream, spiritual vision created the outer, objective, cosmic aspect of the image of divinity, while the southern stream presented the "invisible soul-image of the godhead in the inner life," the earthly image of divinity. The outer aspect was called Apollo, while the inner picture was called Dionysos. Apollo, said Steiner, was an "intimation" of the Christ but not the Christ itself; but for the Greeks Dionysos was the actual garment of the inner Lucifer, "illumined in the inner being of man by a light invisible to outward sight, and which has to be acquired by the process of individual perfecting."[21]

In ancient times, both Christ as the upper cosmic god and Lucifer as the nether god within the human soul dwelt contiguously in human consciousness. Initiates beheld Lucifer through the veil of the inner soul world, and beheld Christ through the veil of the external sense world. Looking below, they found Dionysos; penetrating upwards, they beheld Apollo. In fact, in the first post-Atlantean cultural epoch of India, the rishis taught the unity of spiritual life, stressing the equivalence of approaching the supersensible either externally or internally. Later in the Western Mysteries, the human initiate descended into the soul depths of the lower gods and encountered Dionysos.

Over time the Luciferic-Dionysiac inner reality "sank into darkness" and was harder to reach, more fraught with problems. Candidates for initiation were told that "if they descended while yet unpurified and immature, these Luciferic beings would only appear in distorted images, as wild demons who would tempt them to all sorts of evil."[22] This is the origin of the fear of the name of Lucifer, contends Steiner, and the basis for all subsequent terrible descriptions of the nether world. At the time of Golgotha, Lucifer became invisible to human cognition when his path cut across the incoming Christ. Humans could no longer perceive Lucifer through the veil of their inner soul-life, because the Luciferic impulse, which had impregnated the human etheric body, became exhausted, Steiner explains. When the etheric body was only loosely connected with the physical and was still outside it, Luciferic spiritual currents were "perpetually pouring" into it. This was the primordial light out of which the etheric body sprang forth, "the light from the realm of Lucifer." In those early days, a human experienced these currents as "the most inward element of his being" and as a powerful inheritance from pre-Atlantean evolution.

The Mystery of Golgotha marked a "complete reversal" of the human relationship to Christ and Lucifer. "Man's vision will become reversed," Steiner foretold. Christ, penetrating the Earth, became an inner spiritual reality, while Lucifer, ascending, shone forth as an outer cosmic god. Lucifer will appear in "ever greater radiance in the outer world," while the Christ will be apprehended within human soul life as an indwelling reality. In the future, "the Christ will to an ever greater degree be realized by inner spiritual meditation and Lucifer will be found when the gaze is directed outwards into cosmic regions."

In this reversed condition, candidates for initiation must allow themselves to be borne outwards to the light by the Light-Bringer, Lucifer himself. Steiner foresaw a "new influx of the Luciferic principle." Through this ascension, Lucifer will "intensify our understanding and comprehension" of the world, while the Christ will "strengthen us perpetually within." Luciferic forces will stream into the etheric body from outside, while the Christ will dwell within us as our true I-consciousness. Lucifer, by permeating our etheric thinking body with cosmic vitality, the spirit of independent intellectuality, and cognitive freedom, will give us the "faculty for describing and understanding the Christ." Again, as Steiner outlined it in 1909 in *The East in the Light of the West*, the working relationship of Lucifer and the Christ is close and collegial, not adversarial.

This remarkable revivification of the relationship of the Light and the Light-Bearer, of Logos and Lucifer, is the reintegration of the two diverse evolutionary streams—the outer path to Apollo-Christ, and the inner penetration to Dionysos-Lucifer. The Christ provides the substance while Lucifer gives the form. Together, their union generates vital new impulses for human spiritual evolution. Their union heralds "the inner and essential kernel of the spiritual stream which must flow through the Western channel." We will gaze upwards to Phosphoros the Light-Bearer, said Steiner and "revere" him as the spiritual being through which we alone "learn to understand the whole of the deep, inner meaning of the Christ." Lucifer becomes our psychopomp in our inner world journey to the Christ within. Lucifer will guide us to the "safety of a luminous spiritual life," while the Christ leads us to "inner warmth of the soul." Anthroposophy's mission, as Steiner conceived it at that time, was to encourage the symbols of these two worlds to "unite themselves in love."[23] This can only be interpreted as an agapé of Logos and Lucifer.

As an integrated symbol of this new union in love of Lucifer and Christ, in 1909 Steiner presented the Cross of the Christ in the Star of Lucifer.[24] Steiner's older colleague, Edouard Schuré (1841–1929) put forward the same image nine years earlier in his antique drama *Children of Lucifer*. This is the post-Golgotha formulation of their symbiotic relationship as Schuré understood it. Let us tease out what is implied in this image. Previous to Golgotha it was different. Let's take the whole of human time before Golgotha as comprising the residual momentum of Creation. At creation Lucifer appeared in light bearing the form of the Human. The symbol for this epiphany was the Star of Christ on the Cross of Lucifer. Lucifer's Cross is the anthropomorphic light body of the Human extended in the four directions of time and space. The Cross is the individualization of light into form, here presented as a condensed, abstract image of the human. The Star of Christ is the primordial point of light, the Logos, the fundamental I-consciousness shining within the individualized body of Lucifer. The Logos shone as a brilliant point of self-awareness within the manifested form of the Holy Ghost.

This symbol was turned inside out at Golgotha, because at Golgotha the Christ and Lucifer reversed their positions with respect to human cognition and evolution. Golgotha marks the turning around in human planetary evolution at the deepest seat of consciousness. Golgotha commenced the redemption implied by Lucifer's primordial teleological sacrifice of his wholeness. This second, reversed symbol (the Cross of the Christ in the Star of Lucifer) is actually an image of the redemption of Lucifer accomplished through the Mystery of Golgotha. "The Spirit who has brought man freedom will appear again in a new form: *Luciferus*, the sovereign Bearer of Light, will be redeemed."[25] The Christ entered material human incarnation upon the Cross of the four elements in time and space. The Christ incarnated into the elemental world of Lower Sophia. Lucifer ascended into the cosmos, towards the Pleroma and the Aionic world of Sophia.

Let's examine these reversible symbols once more. The symbol for creation is the Star of Christ within the Cross of Lucifer. The body of the cosmos appears, comprised of the totality of the thoughts, deeds, formative forces, and presences of all the supersensible hierarchies; this is Sophia's body of manas revelations, as Tomberg pointed out earlier. This cosmic body is the Human, the perfect holy image of existence, the Holy Ghost (form-phantom). The body of the Human is the totality of cosmic intelligence, which is the imagination of Sophia. The imagination of Sophia (that is, the living, weaving, dynamic thought-picture that is Sophia's cognition) is constituted by the Christ, embodied as Human, and brought forward into visibility by Lucifer as the Light-Bearer. The intended transmission of this cosmic intelligence to incarnate humanity is safeguarded over time by Michael. A picture—an Imagination, if you will—begins to emerge of the interdependent relationship of Sophia, Lucifer, Christ, and Michael in the life of humanity and with respect to the disposition of cosmic intelligence.

As the form-bearer of cosmic intelligence, as Sophia's representative, Lucifer has Manas, the fundamental capacity of mind that posits individuality through the act of perception and conception, which is to say, cognition. The (Hu)Man is Manas embodied; the Human is the one who thinks, the one who participates in the cosmic wisdom imagination of Sophia. The Human—and its microcosmic expression as humanity—is the one who rightfully claims the imagination of Sophia. Lucifer as Human embodies individualized Manas because Manas posits individuality; manas makes differentiated worlds out of the unity of Mahat. Through its gatekeeper function, Manas prevents the simultaneous arising together of sense impressions which, at this level, is the staggering totality of cosmic intelligence. Manas differentiates this overwhelming totality into a time sequence, into an imaginative tableau, an etheric time-body of formative forces, an unfolding, transfiguring thought-organism of perpetual revelation. This makes serialized, individualized perception of Sophia's conceptions possible. The imagination of Sophia, glimpsed through etheric cognition, is the cosmic totality of the thoughts of the gods, the "web of soul-light wisdom" from which the universe sprang, in which "everything was written in living prototype."

Basically, everything has to slow down a little and get compartmentalized, otherwise individual cognition is impossible. There would be only the totality but no knower. Lucifer may possess Manas, which makes serialized perception possible, but it is the Logos that wields the tool. It's the Logos who is present as I-consciousness, as self-aware Manas in the act of positing a differentiated world from the cosmic totality. Christ is the I-consciousness wielding the manas deeds of differentiation. Christ is the I-consciousness present that bridges the gulf between Lucifer and Sophia, percept and concept, between individuality and totality. Lucifer *is* the individuality, but the Christ is the one who reflexively *knows* this. With Lucifer there is perception; with Sophia, conception; but with Christ the percepts of Lucifer and the concepts of Sophia become the knowledge of cognition. The Logos is the integral simultaneity of being individualized and infinite, of Human and Unbegotten Father. Christ says *I AM!* and closes the gap between the eternal *AM* and the individualized *I*. This is the Star of Christ in the Cross of Lucifer.

The reversal of this image through Golgotha to the Cross of Christ in the Star of Lucifer marks the redemptive permeation of humanity by the Christ, the Son of Man (which is to say, the Cosmic Human or Anthropos). The macrocosmic form of the Human and the microcosmic body of humanity, symbolized by the cross, are so thoroughly permeated by the Christ that what was initially a single point of Logos awareness bursts into a supernova, an enveloping sphere. The Christ Ego, or I-consciousness, completely irradiates the form of the Human, both the Luciferic prototype, and its biological copies, as man and woman. Before one would say, Not I but the Christ in me; now it becomes, Not in me, but I in the Christ.

The Luciferic manasic individuality is subsumed by the Logos. Sophia's cosmic intelligence is made coherent by the Logos. The Luciferic individuality (the Cross) completes its incarnation as biologically individuated humanity, as selfhood in flesh. Now the human I-consciousness dilates to fill all of space, which is the domain of the Logos (the Star). This symbol represents the respiritualization of cosmic cognition after its Fall into material incarnation, biological individuality, and astral selfhood. It marks the maturity of individualized, independent manas and its successful elevation into cognitive peership in the supersensible worlds. The first symbol (the Star of Christ on the Cross of Lucifer) indicates the emergence of cosmic intelligence out of the Pleroma into the context of a manasic individuality. The second symbol (the Cross of the Christ in the Star of Lucifer) marks the raising of this spiritualized, Logos-permeated individuality into cosmic, spiritual cognition at the threshold of the Pleroma, or the Unbegotten Father. As the Christ said, I am the way back to the Father.

The Mystery of Golgotha was the first step on the return to the Unbegotten Father. Golgotha initiated a profound movement in planetary and human spiritual evolution. The Christ Event turned creation inside out, making redemption imminent. The Christ Event reversed the Fall, making it an Ascent. Through Golgotha, said Steiner, the Christ redeemed the human Ego and phantom by restoring two missing parts to the human etheric body. By implication, the Christ redeemed Zurvan's progeny, Lucifer, the Holy Ghost caught in Time, through the Mystery of Golgotha. Again, with this point, I extend indications by Steiner to their self-evident conclusion. To understand the dynamics of this redemption through Golgotha, we must review Steiner's information about Lemurian humanity.

During the epoch of ancient Lemuria, human biological individuality was elaborated on Earth. Luciferic forces had already insinuated themselves into the human astral body and were about to impregnate the etheric life body as well. This potentiality was unacceptable to the "cosmic Powers" in charge and they removed two aspects of the human ether body, preserving them in supersensible safety for a later time. Unfortunately, this preservation also hobbled the integrity of the etheric body, making it impossible for incarnating humans to deploy the full range of etheric activities. The etheric body has four parts, explains Steiner: warmth-ether, light-ether, tone-ether, and life-ether. The etheric was born during Sun evolution through the work of the Kyriotetes, the Spirits of Wisdom, who gave light of their own being to form the fourfold ether.

The Kyriotetes' etheric light was given to serve the states of matter through its elemental states. First there was the etheric light that is close to warmth, or warmth-ether, then light-ether, which was formative for air, tone-ether came next for liquid, then life-ether to form the solid, or earth element. "The ether evolves through the soul spiritual activity of the hierarchies."[26] Warmth-ether, expressed in human will and the Ego, and light-ether, expressed in human feeling and the astral body, were retained by Lemurian humanity. But tone or sound-ether, pertaining to thinking, and life-ether, pertaining to sense and meaning, were kept out of human reach. By this retention of the two ethers, the "power freely and arbitrarily to penetrate" the thought-ether and sense-ether was withdrawn from men and women and preserved in the world of the Gods.[27]

Steiner's description of the tone-ether and life-ether aspects of the human etheric body are difficult to understand but very important to our understanding of the accomplishment of Golgotha. Essentially, the tone-ether (the etheric substrate for the element of water, or liquid) pertains to the transition from cosmic tone to thoughts and words. The finer etheric element of sound permeates light. Steiner gave the term tone or sound ether to "what works within substances as an organizing principle," causing chemical combinations and chemical analyses, and governing the chemical affinities of matter, in whose context the ringing or tones organize matter, or the chemical basis of life, the way tones organize powder on the Chladni glass plates, as demonstrated in the science of cymatics. A still higher etheric mode than sound, the Word-cosmic speech—"thrills through space and pours itself out into the sound-ether."[28]

The tone which lives in the air is an etheric reality; the tone-ether pervades the air and works through the human fluid organism. In the human constitution, our etheric body lives through the water component of the physical body. The tones derive from the supersensible region of the Music of the Spheres, that tone-rich domain of "universal resounding," of manifold cosmic words, the multiplicity of words spoken forth from the one Heavenly Word, the Logos. "What is Christ in His true form? *The Divine Creative Word!*" The tone-ether works through the fluid organism of the human, generating thoughts and the pictorial, conceptual, thinking process of the etheric body. The transition from the ethers to the physical organization, across the dimensions, is profound. "All this goes down into the air organism as a source of *light*, into the fluid organism as a source of *tone*, into the solid organism as a source of *life*."[29]

The trouble is, before Golgotha these universal thoughts were not our own and were not subject to our will activity. For each man and woman the life of feeling (light ether) and will (warmth-ether) were personal, but no individual was able to form thoughts alone, unassisted by supersensible agencies. Steiner expressed the rationale behind this decision in this way: "If thoughts were as individual as feelings, we should never understand one another." Thus thought and meaning were withheld from the power of arbitrary human will and preserved for a later time when humanity might have achieved the requisite maturity to accommodate these two ethers. This is another way of saying that prior to Golgotha, Sophia, as the power of conceptualization and the imagination of cosmic intelligence, was unable to incarnate in microcosmic humanity. Anthroposophy was not possible before Golgotha. Further, the physical body tended to intrude on the etheric thought-body, contracting their dynamic weaving life and pictorial-conceptual process into abstract, mental concepts. This densification of thoughts had ramifications throughout the etheric body. "Theoretical thoughts *cool down* the warmth organism, *paralyze* the sources of Light, *deaden* the sources of Tone, *extinguish* Life."[30]

The tone-ether and the Sophia revelation of cosmic intelligence both imply the Logos, which is the heart of the life-ether (or meaning-ether). The Logos coheres the sequence of light, tone, thought, and life; the Logos gives the sequence meaning. In fact, in this fourfold human etheric body we can see the dynamic interplay of four mighty celestial beings, negotiating the transfer of cosmic intelligence to human biological individuality. It's really a four-way drama of the Sun, which births the etheric body. In the light-ether (air element/feeling), we find Lucifer, permeating the human with selfhood. In the warmth-ether (fire element/willing), we find Michael, regent of cosmic intelligence, infusing will. In the tone-ether (water element/thinking), resides Sophia, the revelation of the totality of cosmic intelligence. In the life-ether (earth element/meaning), we find the Christ, the Logos that imparts meaning to the threefold activity of cosmic intelligence in the Human, expressed through Lucifer, Michael, and Sophia.

When the tone-ether and life-ether were withdrawn from human use, "the power freely and arbitrarily to penetrate the thought-ether and the sense-ether (meaning-ether) was withdrawn" from humanity. As Steiner explained it, words, which express our thoughts, originate in the tone-ether. These expressive forms send vibrations through etheric space or the tone-ether because "tone or sound is only the shadow of the actual thought-vibrations." The inner essence of our thoughts, the quality that imparts meaning to them, belongs to the life-ether.[31] Not to have access to tone-ether and life-ether clearly impedes our cognitive freedom.

The Fall of the Human, through the creation of humanity in biology during Lemuria, sundered the fourfold integrity of the etheric activity of cosmic intelligence. The redemption of the Human at Golgotha through the incarnation of the Christ within the Cross of Lucifer restored it. With Golgotha, the etheric body became whole again as the two withheld parts, the tone-ether (thoughts) and life-ether (meaning), were restored. With this restitution, humanity gained full independent access to the revelations of cosmic intelligence. With Golgotha, Sophia could incarnate in humanity and men and women could become anthroposophists., Sophia-bearers. Golgotha repatriated the exiled human soul with its country of origin. "With his soul he really belongs to the region of the Music of the Spheres and to the region of the Word, of the living Cosmic Ether."

Humanity's original endowment of a fourfold etheric constitution was restored through Christ. "The soul becomes whole again for the first time by taking the Christ into itself." The experience is a "wonderful feeling" of returning to that "primal cosmic home of the soul of man [from] which Christ descended."[32] The rekindling of tone in our etheric fluid organism, since Golgotha, resounds in the cosmos as part of the Music of the Spheres. "Moral ideals stimulate the warmth organism, producing in the air organism—sources of *Light*; producing in the fluid organism—sources of *Tone*; producing in the solid organism—seeds of *Life*."[33] With this primordial return, no longer were thought and meaning withheld from the "power of arbitrary human will." At Golgotha, the divine-spiritual Word became flesh and the apparent Logos became the real Logos. Ever since, humanity has had the potentiality of tone-ether, or thought, and life-ether, or meaning, at its discretion. Christ in his true form is the Divine Creative Word as preserved since the Lemurian epoch, said Steiner. For the first time in Earth history, this Divine Spiritual Word descended into an individual human etheric body, entering Jesus during the Baptism by John. The Word became flesh. With Golgotha and the restoration of the two missing parts of the etheric, the human phantom, or light-form prototype of the physical body, was redeemed. What rose out of the grave was the Risen Body of Christ, the pure perfect phantom, "the spiritual cell, the body which overcame death, the body of Christ Jesus." The Resurrection literally signified the rescue of the human Ego, said Steiner. In an entirely unprecedented planetary event, Christ gave humanity his immortal body of light. "His Resurrection is the coming to birth of a new member of human nature—an incorruptible body."[34]

When we declare, as Steiner did, that at Golgotha Christ redeemed the human phantom, that Christ rescued the human Ego, and that Christ presented to humanity a risen body of light, we are incontrovertibly saying this: through this act, Christ thereby redeemed the Light-Bearer, Lucifer. Lucifer was redeemed at Golgotha. The resurrected body of the human phantom was Lucifer's. The majestic ascension of Christ was a tableau of the risen form of Lucifer, the form-bearer of Man. Golgotha was the redemptive turning point in Lucifer's primordial teleology. "But I shall rise again out of my darkness, I shall break my chains asunder," declares Lucifer in Schure's *Children of Lucifer*. "A day will come when we shall reign together upon Earth, He the Messiah, come down from Heaven, and I the Archangel risen again from the Abyss."[35] That day began at Golgotha when through the Christ Event the Holy Ghost, the body of the Human called Lucifer, was resurrected. As such, this planetary event is still in progress at the close of the twentieth century; in fact, it is not yet clearly recognized for what it was.

Lucifer ascending is the vindication of his cosmic egoity, the justification for what his critics have always called Lucifer's pride and blasphemy. Lucifer's unabashed egoism is justified, said Steiner, because the Human is the cosmos and the cosmos is the Human and both are the perfect image of God. Lucifer was only stating a big fact. Lucifer understood that self-knowledge opens one up to the essential being of the world, so that one knows unarguably that both *I am* and *I am the world* are equally true statements. It doesn't matter if you're macrocosmic Man or microcosmic human—the ubiquity of the Holy Ghost as the vehicle for the I-consciousness of the world is the same.

In a radically provocative essay called *Individualism in Philosophy* (1899), Steiner argued that the human soul is the actual location of everything attributed to God. The self-aware human I-consciousness can engage fully in the fundamental being of everything in creation, and the Ego does not need to postulate or invent any divinity foreign to itself. That is a bold pronouncement, and of course that's not the story of Western philosophy or religious thinking. Granting carte blanche for what seems like total cosmic solipsism was too intimidating for the Church fathers or the patriarchs of philosophy. Humans have cleverly projected this positively unsettling truth of human cosmic identity outwards as sin and blasphemy. Steiner brilliantly traces the ontological history of this human evasion of self-responsibility to accept the human I as the creative source of the world from Thales,

Parmenides, and Plato, through Kant, Spinoza, Hegel, and Nietzsche. The aim of this continuing Western discussion within the being of Philo-Sophia, said Steiner, has been to discover the basis for true individualism or egoity, the place of the individual I within humanity and the cosmos, not as an inner or outer projection but as an essential, cognizable being.

Western philosophy and the way men and women have lived their inner soul life for millennia have been a tragicomedy of "this great human self-deception." Nobody ever seems to get it, or else, getting it, they run instantly away in existential fright. Nobody catches manas in action as it posits individualities, worlds, and hierarchies. Everyone is always retreating from the outrageous proposition Lucifer put before humanity. It's an ironic chronicle of deliberate "human self-estrangement," this human propensity to establish one's *I* as an outside, external being or differentiated hierarchy. We regard our inner being as something outer. We establish a world order, with rulers, lawgivers, and gods. We project outside us a whole creation to which we then humbly subordinate ourselves. But we forget or refuse to acknowledge that the contents of this world have sprung from the human spirit, from our own I-consciousness. Since humans don't dare to pronounce themselves "the pinnacle of creation," they invent gods in their own image and let the world be ruled by them. Humans always shrink back from the recognition that what they have as an external creation is actually self-created. People forget what the gift of Manas implies about the substantiality and origin of the apparent world. Manas posits worlds; Manas gives worlds a position. "He feels himself too weak to carry the world. Therefore he saddles someone else with this burden. Man glorifies his child but without wanting to acknowledge his own fatherhood."[36]

Steiner's essay unrelentingly traces this evasive dialectic in human consciousness up through the latest nineteenth-century formulations of Schopenhauer, Stirner, and Nietzsche. Without exception, and with increasing subtlety, all the major Western thinkers slipped away from the uncomfortable recognition of the world-creating primacy of the human Ego. This is just another way of rejecting Lucifer. When we repudiate our manasic world-positing activity and with it our responsibility as world-fathers, the next step is to project the blame for the imposition onto Lucifer, our benefactor. Since we cannot claim our rightful authorship, we excoriate our writing teacher, our literary mentor. We truly blaspheme Lucifer when we designate his unabashed egoity as sinful. *The Philosophy of Spiritual Activity* (1894) wasn't an apologia for the denigrated Lucifer, but with this watershed anthroposophical text, Steiner tried to resolve the Western collective failure in responsibility with a taut precision. He would not let a single philosopher squeeze sophistically out of his exacting analysis. Steiner contended that his formulations on *Freiheit* finally achieved the view towards which the evolution of Western philosophy had been striving since Greece.

We can observe the I in its cognitive activity and we can thereby comprehend the I in the act of thinking, Steiner declared. In the cognitive process, we receive the essential being of things from within ourselves. Each of us can defensibly state, "I therefore have the essential being of the world within myself." But if we posit the world-being as foreign and separate from ourselves, which is essentially the history of Western philosophy, there is no possibility for freely willed action. To construe the lawfulness of the world as existing outside the actor is "inner unfreedom," Steiner said. On the other hand, when this lawfulness is posited out of the doer himself, this is an act of inner freedom. This is ethical individualism, or morality, arising out of free cognition, or *Freiheit*.

"To give oneself the laws of one's actions out of oneself means to act as a free individual," explained Steiner. "The consideration of the cognitive process shows the human being that he can find the laws of his action only within himself." Isn't this what Lucifer's egoity is all about? Isn't the singular Lucifer really our mentor? When the I is comprehended in the act of thinking, it understands it is neither dependent on nor answerable to anything other than itself. The I knows that it is located within the lawfulness of everything because it is its source.[37] The Mystery of Golgotha brought the Christ into manic world-positing; it permeated Luciferic individuality with the Logos, thereby perfecting the I.

Golgotha restored the singularity of Lucifer by healing the primordial rift in the being of the Holy Ghost between a dilating Lucifer and a contracting Ahriman. The ambivalence of the double-faced Guardians at the supersensible threshold was resolved. Humankind beheld the great Human ideal on Earth as Lucifer ascending, in the risen cosmic body of the Human. With the restoration of the singular Lucifer through Golgotha, the *triune* being of the Holy Ghost could now be revealed. The triune Holy Ghost is Lucifer, Sophia, and Michael, a celestial constellation around the Sun of cosmic intelligence. The Holy Ghost is really triune Manas, the three aspects of Man, the one who thinks. The triune Manas, the Holy Ghost, Cosmic Man—all are about *Wisdom In the Human.*

In this simple phrase we find Sophia (*Wisdom*), Michael, (*In*), and Lucifer (*Human*). The Holy Ghost is Wisdom in the Human. Wisdom in the Human is Anthroposophy: the living being Anthropos-Sophia. This has been the sequence of the book as well: Michael's Dawn, Sophia's Wisdom, and now Lucifer's Human. The mission of anthroposophy ever since the Fall of the Human has been to achieve the incarnation of the Holy Ghost in matter, as Wisdom in the Human living in human cognitive individuality. It is a threefold activity: Michael facilitates the implantation of Wisdom (Sophia) in Man (Lucifer). That is why I designate Michael's role with the word "in." Michael puts the intelligence *in* (to) the Human and humanity.

Let's review the matter of Wisdom in the Human. The wisdom of the Human is Sophia, the imaginative cognition of cosmic intelligence, the dynamic picture of the cosmic totality of the thoughts, deeds, and activities of all created worlds and beings. Sophia imparts to the Human and thereby, humanity, the "prevenient Manas-revelation, the knowledge of that which gives meaning to all separate cognitions," as Tomberg eloquently put it.

Michael is the one who is like unto God. Michael embodies the original intention of intelligence, the purity of cosmic intelligence in its *preindividuated* state. Michael is the active regent, the guardian of Sophia's virgin Manas-revelation, who transfers Sophia, as the revelation of cosmic intelligence, into a context of individualized, independent, human cognition, which is Lucifer. Michael puts Sophia *in* Lucifer. Michael is the verb in the transfer of cosmic intelligence from a nonindividuated into an individualized context. As Tomberg said, Michael "guides the whole revelation of the Sophia so that it may be absorbed by the best forces of Man's consciousness-soul." Michael is the "fiery Prince of Thought in the universe," as Steiner said.

345

Lucifer is the absorber, the anthropomorphic form-bearer, the bearer of individuated intelligence who brings the cosmic light into separate, independent, freely acting form. Lucifer is the individuated free Sophia, the inverse of Michael who is the preindividuated unfree Sophia. This is acutely paradoxical, but we must remember freedom is only possible in matter through human material individuality. When Lucifer individualized himself in matter, Sophia fell into freedom. Michael, as Lucifer's mirror-image and Sophia's champion, guides the cosmically excruciating process.

What's the point of the whole experiment? The point is to bring the Son of Man into matter. To make the Word flesh. To incarnate the Logos. The Holy Ghost, now appreciated as the triune Michael, Sophia, Lucifer, is the home of the Christ who is the Logos and Son of Man. Michael is Christ's standard-bearer, maintaining humanity's original relation with divine spirituality and the Logos. Lucifer is the *Christophor*, the Christ-bringer. Sophia is the Christ's divine consort, his syzygy among the Aions of the Pleroma. Through Sophia, the triune Holy Ghost, as the Human achieves syzygy with Christ, as Son of Man. The Christ as Logos, the Light of the Human, is the cognizing, self-reflexively aware consciousness that *knows*, that *is* the Cosmic Intelligence in its act of knowing. Christ is the I-consciousness at the heart of intelligence. Through the Christ-Logos, the Human knows itself. Through the Christ-Logos, the Holy Ghost, as the trinity of Michael, Sophia, and Lucifer, has *acquaintance* (gnosis) of the unbegotten Father, Zurvan of uncreated endless Time, through his emanations, Mind and Truth. The Human becomes aware of itself knowing. The Human cognizes itself *as* knowing. The Human knows this knowing as the cosmos itself, the concentrated expression of Cosmic Intelligence.

This is cognitive freedom, *Freiheit*. Humanity knows this knowing is his own being. This is the human experience of Mind and Truth, the fruit of Anthroposophy. It's the raison d'etre of physical incarnation and the "fall" of Sophia towards her divine syzygy with the Son of Man. This act of phylogenetic cognition completes the Creation, as Kühlewind explains. When we learn how to read the Logos script of the world as a written text, instead of seeing only things, this will lead us to complete our true reality.

"The meaning of creation—the hidden part of the cosmic creative word—was to help humanity reach this point of understanding. The *new meaning*, the new reality, arises through our own continuing of creation."[38]

And where is the whole experiment headed? What is the destiny of the triune Holy Ghost of the Human resurrected and ascending after Golgotha? It is going to the Star of Christ, the Star of Lucifer, what Steiner enigmatically called "the good auric Star" of the Human. The triune Holy Ghost of Michael, Sophia, and Lucifer is itself one aspect of the sublime trinity described as Father, Son of Man, and Holy Ghost (or Father, Logos, and Man; or matter, light, and energy). As we will hear in the final section—Speaking—this fundamental trinity itself is part of the good auric Star and through this Star, Wisdom in the Human wishes to Speak.

PART IV

"SPEAKING"

THE GOOD AURIC STAR
OF THE HUMAN

CHAPTER 11

Sophia's Syzygy

The Trinity of Michael, Sophia, and Lucifer

*W*ITH THE DAWN, Lucifer, magnificent and crowned, comes with angels to his supersensible emerald situated at the El Tule tree here outside Oaxaca in southern Mexico. This is an epiphany of stunning importance: the resurrected Lucifer, whole again, radiant with light, the phosphoric image of the Human, returning to his place of original terrestrial contact with humanity. Lucifer returns to El Tule because that's where he established his emerald heart on Earth at the beginning of time. El Tule and the Oaxaca environs have been Lucifer's esoteric Mystery center ever since. The venerable cedar before us with its circlet of meditators at this high point in the event popularly called Harmonic Convergence in mid-August 1987—a unique moment of synchronous reverence—forms the link between the physical, etheric, and astral planes. Of course to ordinary perception there is simply an old, fat cedar tree in a rural Mexican churchyard; but to clairvoyant perception there is a supersensible geometrical form of massive proportions (the emerald) occupying this particular node in the planet's etheric geography. The tree marks the spot that is a supersensible conduit that will carry Lucifer's initiatory impulse this morning to the emerald hearts of millions of women and men similarly meditatively poised around the planet, and to Gaia, the I-consciousness of the planet Herself.

Lucifer, the Shining one, the Dawn-Bringer, the Light-Bearer, absolutely dwarfs the El Tule tree, which is venerable in its own right, being an estimated 2,000 years old and massive in girth.

Lucifer's emerald heart alone fills my field of inner vision. It is gigantic, sheer-sided, like a double-terminated quartz crystal enlarged ten-thousandfold, as if seen through a green filter. The paradox is that this same phosphoric emerald that I am beholding through El Tule is inside each of us, in miniature. Here, in both locations, planetary and human anatomical, Lucifer established his presence long ago for human consciousness as the individuality of humanity. The gift of the emerald so long ago from Lucifer as a self-sacrifice on behalf of humanity is what made the human Ego and its cognitive autonomy a possibility. It gives us access to Sophia's revelations of cosmic intelligence. Through this planetary event peaking this morning, Lucifer illumines the astral sphere around the Earth, feeding illumination of a specific and individualized type into those who have any degree of receptivity at an astral or higher mental level. It's an epochal day in which many will cross the supersensible threshold, not assailed by an inimicable Lucifer but escorted by an exulting mentor. As such, it is a moment of grace. The sheer potency of Lucifer's unsullied presence shifts our attention to inside the emerald.

It is very different on the inside of the emerald. My impression is of an immense hexagonal cathedral filled with many thousands of people, masses of angels, and scores of members of the White Brotherhood (the human ascended hierarchy). The attention of this supersensible conclave is drawn toward the domed ceiling of the cathedral where, set like a jewel in the center of the domed canopy above us, is an object that appears as a brilliant multifaceted crystal, adamant with intensity—a single star shining so hard it forms geometric surfaces, like a diamond. The impulse arises in me to travel to the seed center of this star crystal. The first vista is an open twilight space among the billions of galactic stars. I have the vivid impression of floating blissfully in an angelic body of light; still, this is not the seed center. Then it's as if the same adamantine, infinitely faceted diamond appears again at a yet more subtle level of perception, but it is situated in no recognizable framework of space or time. All my bodies drop away: human, supersensible, angelic. I am here, formless, aware, within this primordial star, in an imagination of the Star Absolute.

The event popularly known as the Harmonic Convergence, which occurred principally between August 16 and 18, 1987, was observed by millions of participants and ridiculed by the world media. Owing to the cynicism of the mainstream media and a certain inflationary tendency among new age supporters of the event, many equated the event with either an expected mass landing of benign UFOs or the expectation of flocks of pentecostal convergers descending beatifically from mountain tops speaking in tongues. Neither happened, which is why for the most part people wrote the event off as inconsequential, a kind of neo-Woodstock recidivistic whimsy. It wasn't.

The impetus behind the world event was the interpretation of ancient Mayan calendrical predictions by scholar-mystic Jose Argüelles that this particular period of time in August would represent a crucial pivot in time requiring the earnest focus in consciousness of thousands of men and women stationed at "sacred sites" around the globe. The event was publicized and previewed for a year in advance. The truth and significance of this globally observed event has been largely overlooked and unarticulated, lost in a fog of wisecracks or indifference. This is so because basically it was an interior, interdimensional event, staged with reference to the planet's etheric geography or web of geopoints popularly called sacred sites; the event's full impact will be (and is already) felt continuously and increasingly over the next several decades. Something happened of paramount importance with respect both to our entire post-Atlantean epoch of human evolution and the future of the Christ Impulse on Earth. As Steiner said so often, important, pivotal events in human and planetary history often pass us by for the most part unmarked or misunderstood.

My inner impressions of this event, reported above (and at the beginning of Chapter 1), represent a perspective that I contend is consistent with the heart of Anthroposophy and Steiner's indications. Certainly, one perspective does not encompass the totality of a planetary event such as this and we must remember that Steiner always insisted we must weave together at least twelve contiguous impressions (a full zodiacal circuit) to get a reasonably objective conception of the substance of an event. Similarly, there are key items in Steiner's teachings—the auric Star, the dodecahedral Stone of Love, the Grail, etheric geography of the Mystery centers, the Arthur stream, World Pentecost—that, at least in terms of his material available in English, he never adequately explained or worked through to their final implications.

So we have the foundation in Steiner's published works for these subjects, but not the discussion of their extrapolations and ramifications for Anthroposophy. In the last two chapters, on the basis of my inner work with Steiner's material, I propose to make these extrapolations and explore their ramifications for an evolving Anthroposophy on the edge of the twenty-first century. It is my impression that, nearly seventy years after Steiner's death, the times have ripened, the unfolding of the consciousness soul has moved forward a notch, and certain of his preliminary indications may now perhaps be taken a little further than was publicly possible by 1925.

One of the most enigmatic of Steiner's legacies to us two generations after his work at Dornach is his occasional references to the "auric Star." During the momentous days of the Christmas Meeting in 1923 at Dornach, Steiner invoked this star during his ritual of laying the Foundation Stone for the new Goetheanum. "And if we prove worthy of this aim, we shall see that a good star will hold sway over what is willed from here. Follow this good star, my dear friends! We shall see whither the Gods will lead us by the light of this star."[1] Steiner fluctuated in his attributions to this guiding Star. In 1904 he said the Christ soul shines as an auric radiant Star. The Star that accompanies the evolution of humankind and that shone before the Magi approaching Bethlehem was, according to Steiner, the "soul of Christ himself," which was "aglow with Buddhi, in very truth a star." In the body of Jesus shines the Christ Star, the soul of Christ in the cave of the body, declared Steiner. This shining is a reality in the astral world, he insisted, and an enactment of the Lesser Mysteries. When we are led by a Star, this means nothing else than seeing the soul itself as a Star.[2] Then in 1909, when he was working publicly with Edouard Schuré, Steiner attributed this star to Lucifer. Lucifer's Star, if we surrender to it, can enlighten us "every moment as to the rightness and indubitableness of the spiritual ideas within us. The Star of Lucifer, which comes to us when clairvoyant investigation speaks, throws its light on what only seems to be night and changes it into day."[3] Around this time, Steiner also attributed this Star to Zoroaster, whose name means "Golden Star." Zoroaster was the "Star of Humanity," the "Star of Splendor" whose presence heralded the great Sun Being, Christ.[4] Gnomic references to the Star as something radiantly present within human individuals later appeared in two of Steiner's mystery dramas, *Portal of Initiation* (1910) and *The Soul's Probation* (1911).[5] Like the Magi of the East, we must "find the Star through the power of that which is true Spiritual Science," Steiner encouraged anthroposophists in 1920.[6]

Steiner left many intriguing clues about the nature, location, and purpose of this Star. It is the auric soul of Christ, the golden essence of the Sun-being Zoroaster, the phosphoric brow of Lucifer, the powerful guiding light within women and men, and somehow the fruit of anthroposophical effort. Traditionally, the Star's appearance is commemorated on January 6, at the Festival of the Three Kings, or Epiphany, the original date for Christmas. Epiphany marks the "appearing forth" of the light. On that pivotal day in human and planetary history, the Star of Bethlehem guided the three Magi, Caspar, Melchior, and Balthazar, to the newborn Jesus child, whom they beheld with adoration. According to Steiner's lifelong disciple Walter Johannes Stein (1891–1957), the Star of Bethlehem and its relation to the Mystery of the Christ incarnation has a microcosmic, individualized meaning as well. Stein writes: "Whenever and wherever on the earth a child is born, the star of the higher self comes to rest over the tabernacle of the body."[7] The Epiphany also marked an esoteric event. On that day, after Jesus was baptized in the River Jordan, the Christ-Being entered his human sheaths, "whereby new and quickening forces poured into earthly existence," said Steiner. Thus the Christ was born on Earth through Master Jesus, and the Star epiphanically heralded this incarnation. But if the Star announced the birth of the Christ on Earth, is it, as Steiner suggested, actually the *same* as the Christ?

My own inner work in recent years suggests that the Star is in fact an additional constituent of the supersensible hierarchy. If we conceive of the Three Hierarchies as a triangle of nine angelic families, then the Star represents the tenth, at the heart of it all. Or maybe it should be the eleventh, as Steiner clearly reserved the tenth hierarchical position for Humanity as the Hierarchy of Love and Freedom. As such, it is difficult to incorporate the Star into Steiner's model of three hierarchies because he never mentioned it in this context. Inversely, the triangulation of the Three Hierarchies represent an aspect of the Star. If we understand the Three Hierarchies to represent the totality of formative forces and spiritual intelligences active in the cosmos, then we must appreciate the Star as the first point, the summation, the alpha and omega of the cosmic extrapolation, and, despite the paradox, as the point before it all unfolded, too.

In this chapter I intend to expand on Steiner's sketchy indications about the Star so that their full impact may be registered in our time. Technically, the Star precedes even the Saturn phase of cosmic evolution. Similarly, the trinity of Michael, Lucifer, and Sophia, as the threefold supersensible face of the Human, whose body is the hierarchically woven cosmos, also represents an aspect of the Star. Outside of Anthroposophy, this Star has been known by many names, although always in a somewhat veiled or oblique sense. In the Hebrew angelologies, it is *Ophanim* ("Wheels"), an exalted angelic family whose work encompasses cosmic multiples of zodiacs. In Sanskrit, the Star is *Nimitta*; in Tibetan, *Rigpa*; in Qabala, *Ain Soph*. Schuré was right when he attributed speech to the radiant golden-cored Star that appeared above the chasm of Lucifer. When the Star shifts dimensions from primordial point of absolute light (*Nimitta*) to manifest angelic family (*Ophanim*), it is as vocal and communicative as any other intelligence in the supersensible world. Steiner never revealed the inner workings of his occult meditations and explorations, but it's quite likely he had cognitive contact with the Star (as the Ophanim), but attributed its identity to the soul of Christ.

That's not entirely inaccurate because the Star conducts souls *to* the Christ as a kind of celestial psychopomp. The activity of the Star of Bethlehem, showing the Magi the way to the Christ, is archetypally true: the Star always points the way to the Christ revelation. The Star is the epiphany of the Christ. That Steiner often mistook the Star for the Christ doesn't particularly affect the truthfulness of his disclosures. During our time, the Christ must be brought forward within the personal sphere of men and women as a direct experience. Steiner clearly acknowledged this as the quintessential spiritual event for the epoch of the consciousness soul; beginning with the mid-twentieth century, this would become increasingly a common experience. The Christ-Principle, he said, is a "wonderful seed for all future time," capable of delivering to us "apocalyptic wisdom, the new and true knowledge of the spirit."[8]

The Star is part of the experience of the Christ-Principle, the beginning of what might be called the realization of the Christ within the Buddha Body. The contents of this new formulation will be presented below. The Star is the potential for the Christ in each human to awaken in the Buddha Body (or Philosopher's Stone), which is another name for the light body of the awakened one. The Star is the means by which Steiner's prophecy—that Pauline Christianity will unite with Buddhism as the Christ leads human souls into the Land of Light called Shambhala—will be fulfilled. The epiphany of the Star is also the starting point for the experience of the Imagination of Pentecost as the fulfillment of the next phase of Anthroposophy.

The epiphanous appearance of the Star before the Magi on their way to Bethlehem was a special event, a rare manifestation in outer visibility of this inner essential point of light. Where is the Star normally? The Star is the finest, tiniest, brightest point of light within Devachan, the world of Light—yet it is accessed in the context of the human body. Steiner acknowledged the bodily location of the Star. The human body is a cave, a grotto, a hollow, in which the soul dwells, said Steiner. "In the body of Jesus shines the Christ Star, the soul of Christ." In Steiner's *Portal of Initiation*, the initiate Benedictus says to Johannes, the spiritual student, "I see your Star in its full radiance." So may each of us legitimately say today: "I see the Star blazing as a brilliant pinprick of light at the center of your being." Specifically, the Star is found two finger widths above the belly button and the same distance inside. To be precise, this is not to say the Star is anatomically embedded in the flesh of this bodily region; rather, this point is roughly the midpoint of the body and provides a stable, balanced point of reference, within our physical constitution for a reality that is at the center of our spiritual body.

The Star shines at the center of our ninefold constitution, as a tiny blazing point of light, as the first Star, as a scintillating pinprick at the heart of the Spirit-Man, Life-Spirit, Spirit-Self, the threefold Ego, the astral, etheric, and physical bodies—yet beyond them all. The Star responds remarkably to a warmth of regard, to the presence of an inner smile, to our breathing consciously with an attitude of unconditional love. This is a specific preliminary meditative practice that may be practiced at any time by anybody to arrive at the same results, as described below. The Star responds positively to this fullness of human attention focused on the wave of the breath. After a period of concentration, we find the Star flashes "supernova" and turns us inside out as its light extends to the outermost limits of the personal sphere, into the Buddha Body (the Buddhic shell, the Body of Light), or what Steiner called Spirit-Man. This happens when the Star becomes concentrated within itself, so it is on the outside of us rather than on the inside. When the Star is nova, we are inside it; well might Steiner say that now supersensible eyes behold us objectively as an epiphany on Earth.

The Star is truly at the center of the drama, whether it's played out in the terrestrial or cosmic theater. In the Tree of Life, the Star is the point of light above the crown; in the galaxy, the Star is represented by Polaris; in the human organism, the star is the first, monadic point preceding all differentiation. It is the Star of the drama of life. In the drama of the Trinity, the Father, Son, and Holy Ghost (or light, energy, and matter), the Star is at the heart of it all. Lucifer's mission is to expiate his Star. Michael's mission is to facilitate the Star. Sophia's mission is to follow the Star back to the Father. The Christ's mission is to awaken to the Star, while bringing the Father to Earth. The Star's destiny is to return to the Sun Absolute. Humanity's mission is to awaken to the Star within matter as the doorway to the Christ experience. That's where Lucifer's emerald comes in. Even though it is correct to say that the Star blazes at the center of our being, it is equally true to declare: the Star beckons to us from inside the emerald. As we will suggest below, the emerald of Lucifer is the Foundation Stone of Anthroposophy.

Steiner laid the Foundation Stone for the Goetheanum twice, first in 1913, then again in 1923. On the evening of September 20, 1913, in the midst of a torrential rain storm and accompanied by about forty stalwart Anthroposophists, Steiner placed the Foundation Stone (a double pentagonal dodecahedron, made of copper) into the hill at Dornach. Steiner invoked the hierarchies to favorably oversee his group's intentions with the new Goetheanum and to ward away from the aspiring human souls the "darkness of chaos" and the "dark Ahriman clouding vision." The "doubly twelve-membered form" of the Foundation Stone (meaning, two twelve-faceted forms), Steiner said, represents "the striving human soul immersed as microcosm in the macrocosm." The stone is "an emblem of the human soul." The dodecahedral emblem was formed according to "the cosmic images of the human soul" and as the cornerstone of the human "who desires to seek for himself in the spirit, to feel himself in the world's soul, to divine himself in the world's Ego."[9] The stone symbolized knowledge, love, and strong courage, and would be a stumbling block for Anthroposophy's enemies. The act of laying the stone was an integral aspect of the mission of the Earth itself, Steiner told his colleagues. Because this act was so significant, it would have a high price. "We are only at the beginning of our difficulties, but let us go forward with a firm confidence in the ultimate victory of the spirit."[10]

The difficulties Steiner foresaw were exceedingly painful as nine years later the Goetheanum burned to the ground on New Year's Eve, 1922, presumably set off by arsonists belonging to occult groups opposed to Steiner's work.[11] One year later at the famous 1923 Christmas Meeting in Dornach, Steiner rededicated himself, the Anthroposophical Society, and the eventually reborn Goetheanum, in a second Foundation Stone ritual. The original copper double-dodecahedral stone, buried in Dornach Hill in 1913, miraculously survived the destruction of the Goetheanum. This time on Christmas Day, 1923, Steiner "laid" a meditative Foundation Stone in the hearts of the 800 members present in the Schreinerei—and in the hearts of all the future members, too—by reading an initiation poem he had written for the occasion. Steiner called this spiritual invocation "the dodecahedral imaginative Form of Love" and the "dodecahedral Stone of Love." On this subtler oracular, word-stone, which Steiner invoked through meditative prayer and verse, "we will erect the building of which the stones will be the individual work done by us severally, in all our groups, as we go out into the wide world."[12]Anthroposophists ever since have described this Christmas Meeting in rapt, even mystical terms. For Friedrich Hiebel, who was one of the 800 present, "The consecrated hour of the Laying of the Foundation Stone immersed us in a miracle of a new baptismal process that in its changing nature defies any subsequent description."[13] For Rudolf Grosse, the conference was a supersensible event, a Mystery consecration and an act of spiritual creation coordinated by Steiner the master builder; it marked the beginning of a "Cosmic Turning Point of Time" and a new cosmic age.[14] The Christmas Meeting Foundation Stone experience was an almost public Mystery deed, "whose deep significance will only reveal itself to mankind as time goes on," commented F. W. Zeylmans Van Emmichoven. The whole of Anthroposophy was reborn in the Foundation Stone meditation; through this great Mystery event a seed was sown making it possible for the entire world to become a temple, "wherever human souls live and work out of the Foundation Stone's power."[15] In the estimation of Bernard Lievegoed, the Christmas event was "the great cultic deed" whereby Steiner laid the Foundation Stone of the "new Mysteries" as a culmination of all the antecedent Mystery streams of Europe.[16]

In a similar vein, the Christmas Meeting was for Sergei Prokofieff in its full spiritual experience and "unshakable reality" the "true Whitsun for Anthroposophists." It was a profound revelation that awaited ripening and comprehension by Anthroposophists throughout time. The Christmas Meeting was the beginning of the fulfillment of the grand promise of the Michaelic fifteenth-century supersensible Mystery school, an essential act in the group karma of Anthroposophists over time. "For Whitsun [Pentecost] is the festival of the spiritual knowledge of what once occurred *as fact* on the physical plane but which, at that time, could not yet be comprehended in the depths of its hidden essence." Prokofieff offered another insight which is an important clue. In its "most hidden essence," the Foundation Stone is "the true expression of the esoteric being of the Grail." The Christmas Meeting, Prokofieff added, was a living expression of "these new Michael Mysteries (which) are, in their deepest esoteric essence, none other than the Grail Mysteries renewed by the Time-Spirit."[17]

The correlation of Steiner's dodecahedral Foundation Stone with the Holy Grail brings us to a remarkable insight about Lucifer.

The Grail is Lucifer's dodecahedral heart. We have to fill in a few steps in the spiritual syllogism before the necessity of this conclusion becomes apparent. Steiner provides the key bridging link. In his lectures that accompanied the presentation of Schuré's *Children of Lucifer* Steiner noted that according to a "wonderfully beautiful legend," when Lucifer fell from Heaven to Earth a precious stone fell out of his crown. "Out of the stone which fell from Lucifer's crown was made the Holy Grail." Steiner is accurately reporting information preserved in the thirteenth century Grail initiation text called *Parzival* by Wolfram von Eschenbach. This is what the old hermit at Fontane la Salvaesche told Parzival: "When Lucifer and the Trinity began to war with each other, those who did not take sides, worthy, noble angels, had to descend to earth to that Stone which is forever incorruptible.... This Stone is also called 'The Gral.'"[18]

We might conceive of Lucifer's crown as a corona of accompanying angels and spiritual beings; the stone that would become the Grail and thereby prepare the way for the Logos, "shone like a wondrous jewel." Then the Archangel Michael struck the "stone of light" from Lucifer's crown, "and he then descended to live amongst men, forming himself into a vessel to receive the blood of Christ. The vessel became known as the sacred chalice which held within it the sun host," or the spiritual intelligences of the inner Sun. As such, the Grail story is about the history of wisdom (knowledge as reflected light) descending to Earth from above— "wisdom which resolves itself into love."[19]

Lucifer's stone afterwards was first used at the Last Supper as a serving vessel and then later at Golgotha to collect the blood of Christ Jesus at the crucifixion. Angels (and/or Joseph of Arimathea and his colleagues) then brought the sanctified chalice to the West, to facilitate among Westerners a true understanding of the Christ principle. The Christ principle pertains in essence to the incarnation of the human Ego, the Word made flesh. "This precious stone is in a certain respect nothing else ... than the full power of the Ego," said Steiner, which had to be prepared for "a new and more intelligent beholding of the radiance of Lucifer's Star."[20] All of this is mythological parlance for Steiner's notable metaphysical declaration, quoted earlier, that Lucifer *bears* the light but Christ *is* the light. Out of his own substance (the stone in his crown) Lucifer prepares the Grail which contains the light of Christ (the Logos and the Sun intelligences), which, in physical terms, is the holy blood, the Grail for the I-consciousness.

Every human may become the Christ-I, which exists as an immortal ideal, yet, paradoxically, elements of the Christ consciousness are born in history by specific individuals to serve the purposes of planetary and human evolution. According to the principle of spiritual economy, multiple copies of the Christ-Ego exist. Apparently with the sixteenth century, copies of the Christ-Ego began to "weave" themselves into the human egos of a few individualities, including Christian Rosenkreutz, the founder of the Rosicrucian school. Actually "countless" copies of Christ's Ego were preserved for posterity, said Steiner. After the Mystery of Golgotha, the Christ Ego was "multiplied into an infinite number of copies," a plethora still present today in the supersensible world for humans who have made themselves "mature enough to find it."[21] The process of finding copies of the Christ Ego—which is really just another way of saying the etheric perception of the Christ—is the achievement of the Holy Grail. The new bearers of the Christ Ego, for whom the statement "Not I, but the Christ in me" is correct, become the "true *Christophori,*" the authentic Christ-bringers.

Let's review the sequence so far. Lucifer's stone is transformed into the Holy Grail, which bears the Christ blood to the West. By Christ blood, we mean the full potency of the Ego, or the incarnatory force of I-consciousness, as exemplified by Christ. Then, a cabal of initiates called the Brotherhood of the Holy Grail, Steiner informs us, collected the blood of Christ, which was "the expression and copy of His ego," which itself was "the eternal ego into which any human ego can be transformed." The Mystery of the higher Ego was preserved in the Grail, and in the Grail lives the I-consciousness, "united with the eternal and immortal," with the Mystery of the Christ-I.

This Brotherhood recognized the need to preserve the Christ Force and Christ-Impulse, represented by the Ego dissolved in the blood, in "a silent, deep Mystery" outside of culture and knowledge until "a suitable moment" arrived for its revelation. It was not so much the case that this Brotherhood literally preserved the physical blood; what they maintained in prudent secrecy until the ripe moment of cultural evolution was the means by which the human Ego could be permeated by the eternal Christ I consciousness, now incorporated with the substance of Earth, and carried in the flesh through the blood, which is the organ for the Ego in the physical body. In other words, in the Mystery of the Grail we find the secret of the Word made flesh, the I-consciousness incarnate, capable of receiving the cosmic imaginations of Sophia. The Mystery of the Grail, said Steiner, is the same as the Mystery of the Blood—and that is the Mystery of Golgotha, the Christ Event.

The "concealed knowledge" of the Grail started to reverse itself and become revealed knowledge at the 1923 Christmas Meeting at Dornach. The inner force of the Christ Ego and its "all encompassing 'archetype of love,'" preserved in multiple copies in the Holy Grail, began to permeate Anthroposophists from that moment forward. That is why Steiner declared: "We see that the highest imaginable ideal of human evolution results from the 'knowledge of the Grail': the spiritualization that man acquires through his own efforts."[22] In a sense, the 800 anthroposophists assembled in the Schreinerei that Christmas week underwent a Mystery initiation, facilitated by Steiner, as modern-day Knights of the Holy Grail. It is not whimsical to evoke this category from Western Celtic mythology, for it actually represents something profound, and, from the vantage point of initiation into the esoteric Christian stream, it is an impulse that is still relevant. As Walter Johannes Stein notes in reference to the theme of King Arthur: "To take up in earnest the suggestions of Rudolf Steiner would be to carry the Arthurian tradition livingly into the future."[23] Through their own efforts and insights as "Grail Knights," the Schreinerei anthroposophists would attain a "copy" of the Christ Ego—a permeation of their individualized I-consciousness (the I AM) with the Christ Logos (the eternal, cosmic I AM).

These connections made, we are still left with two links in our full appreciation of the Christmas Meeting unestablished. Why did Steiner specifically use a dodecahedron (a twelve-sided regular geometric solid, one of only five existing in nature) as the Foundation Stone? Why did he inaugurate this cycle of the new Mysteries specifically at Dornach Hill?

Let us consider the matter of the Foundation Stone first. In my evocation of supersensible events of the Harmonic Convergence of 1987 and of earlier, pre-Lemurian formative days of the Earth, mention was made of the heart of Lucifer as a green emerald. I mentioned that it is present on a planetary level, within the nexus of etheric geography, and within the subtle anatomy of individual humans. The individualized emeralds are all holographic replicas of the original, single emerald, which is an expression of the heart of Lucifer, the form-bearer of the Human as we outlined in the previous chapter. The emerald is present on at least three levels: as Lucifer's cosmic heart; as a geomantic node in the planet; as a subtle node in the human organization. As above, so below, and in the middle, too. For supersensible perception, the emerald within the human stands two inches high, top to bottom, like a double-terminated crystal, beginning at the third rib down on the right side of the sternum.

Technically, the emerald corresponds to what Hindu Tantric iconography describes as the *Ananda-kanda*, the inner, esoteric heart chakra. In this standard Eastern model, the lotus flowers of the heart are twofold: there is an outer, twelve-petalled heart chakra called *Anahata*, and an inner, eight-petalled heart chakra called *Ananda-kanda*. When I make mention of a green emerald a few inches long, I am using a physical image to evoke a supersensible reality; it is somewhat accurate to describe the emerald within the human constitution as an electromagnetic doorway within the subtle body, approximately at the interface between etheric and astral bodies. It is green because that is the color, or radiation, most consistently reported by clairvoyants as occupying that region of the human aura. As the heart chakra is midway in the sevenfold sequence of lotus wheels, so is the color green at the midpoint in the color spectrum. My contention here is that this green emerald inner heart chakra, present in every incarnate human, is the same green stone fallen from the crown of Lucifer, as described by Eschenbach and Steiner—that it is the Grail, or the source of the Grail.[24]

Now, what is the purpose of the emerald within the human constitution? In terms of yogic analysis, the ananda-kanda lotus center is the ether or spiritual heart, in which one meditates upon the Godhead and requests enlightenment. Traditionally, this center is depicted as having a jewelled altar and a special wish-fulfilling tree. This *Kalpataru*, or celestial wishing-tree, grants all that one asks, and leads to spiritual awakening. The emerald was implanted in the human biophysical organism as a gift from Lucifer and the Exousiai (Elohim, or Spirits of Form) at the point in the Lemurian epoch when the human form was brought into matter, into its final stage of mineralization on Earth. Lucifer implanted the emerald within every incarnating human beginning with the introduction of individuality and visibility in the early Lemurian epoch. To facilitate the realization of human individuality within matter and the incarnation of cosmic intelligence within individualized human beings, Lucifer petitioned the hierarchies that a means might be provided to insure the realization of this possibility.

It was of course inherently paradoxical, because the means had to be fluid enough to allow for free will and voluntary choice. Nobody *had* to use this means; it was voluntary and optional. The means was a little six-sided doorway in the electromagnetic field of the heart chakra in the shape of an emerald. Lucifer was willing to give of his own spiritual substance to a nascent humanity; as such, Lucifer became creatively entangled—or karmically invested—over time in the incarnational history of humanity on Earth. It could not be any other way because each of us bears Lucifer's heart as our own inner, etheric, or spiritual, heart center—the heart within the heart. Additionally, because the Earth was designed to be a planetary expression of the macrocosmic Human, truly a designer planet based on the archetypal, ideal form of the Human—a concept within the province of etheric geography, or geomancy, which I will discuss below—Lucifer implanted a copy of his emerald at a specific etheric location on the planet: the environs of El Tule, outside Oaxaca, in southern Mexico. On the planetary level, the emerald at El Tule has an inner heart chakra function within the spiritual beingness of the Earth equivalent to that the emerald has within the human constitution. At both levels, human and planetary, we have a holographic virtual image of the heart or stone of Lucifer.

Lucifer's emerald, or stone, is the means through which cosmic intelligence is individualized in humanity. Through the Grail, it provides a receptacle or chalice for the Logos; with the Logos awakened in us (the Christ blood in the Grail), the revelations of Sophianic cosmic intelligence are open to our cognition. The emerald is the foundation stone within individualized humanity for love and cosmic intelligence. The emerald is an access point for Love from Above—celestial, angelic, hierarchical unconditional love—in the heart within the heart because *inside* the emerald is the Holy Grail. The emerald stone is like a carapace enclosing the Holy Grail. The confirmation of this architecture is the fruit of a meditative experience, which I will describe below.

One feature of the Harmonic Convergence was to bring thousands of women and men inside the emerald, within viewing distance of the Grail. This event of 1987 involved the mass convergence of human souls within the emerald heart of Lucifer, the foundation stone for the awakening of cosmic intelligence on Earth. It presented the unprecedented opportunity for a mass initiation of individuals within the Christ Mystery of I-consciousness, which is the Grail experience. Since the emerald is the foundation for the individualization of cosmic intelligence, this necessarily guarantees the presence of the trinity of the Holy Ghost—Michael, Sophia, and Lucifer—as equally active agents in the Christed initiation within the emerald. If we are looking for Michael, Sophia, or Lucifer, we are certain to find them within the emerald. And the best way to look for them inside the emerald is with the Star.

The good auric Star frequently mentioned by Steiner guides us to the emerald, just as the Star of Bethlehem guided the Magi. When the Star goes supernova, through the warmth of our concentration, it brings us to the threshold of the emerald, as if to a doorway. In this case, the emerald has six doorways (six facets), any of which will grant us entry. Each of the six sides of the emerald is an aspect of the truth of oneself: understanding, knowledge, compassion, intuition, peace, and bliss. Each of these sides has to be balanced within the individual. Each individual may approach the emerald from different sides dependent upon one's differing characteristics. When any side of the green emerald's outer layer is penetrated, it reveals the light within—the *source* of the light whose illumination invokes an experience beyond the normal framework of time-space continuity and one's sense of the "experiencer." The light it contains is beyond any description. Therefore, we progress gently towards something which is not dependent upon the ordinary sense of "going towards"; that is probably why many interpret the word Grail as meaning *grada-lis*, "gradually, step by step, attained by degrees."

The experience I am describing here is of course a supersensible one, requiring precise, wakeful steps in developing an etheric imagination. Entry requires concentration, focus, image-building, inward wakefulness, and the warmth of Love which animates the imagination of the emerald. When human beings begin to awaken the Luciferian aspects of themselves, the emerald glows within. It is a positive aspect of the Lord of Light (Lucifer) awakening in the One. It's a crucial, foundational step in Lucifer's long return to the Unbegotten Father after a prolonged sojourn in matter.

When a human begins to awaken spiritually to other men or women, when the Love in one individual meets the same Love in another, then the emerald awakens. Christ is present within the emerald, within the "innermost core of human nature," said Steiner, as the seed of love in the eternal Ego, the primordial I-consciousness. Or, as we indicated above, the Logos is the light inside the Grail made of Lucifer's substance. Wisdom is the precondition of love, Steiner emphasized, and love is the result of wisdom reborn in the Ego. "In earth humanity this power of love must take its beginning, and the 'cosmos of wisdom' unfolds itself into a '*cosmos of love.*'"[25] Another name for this prototypal Love is the Christ Ego. There is intensively only one emerald. The five billion humans now occupying the planet in the 1990s all bear individual copies of the one emerald of Lucifer. When all those who concentrate their attention on their emeralds awaken spontaneously at the same moment in time and space, then Lucifer will unite again with the Father.

Now we must introduce a geometrical aspect to complete the link between the emerald stone of Lucifer and Steiner's dodecahedral Stone of Love. The "double-terminated" emerald has six equal facets yet when seen from a slightly different angle it is actually a cube, which is also six-sided. The perception of the emerald as cube is central to our understanding. In the Western alchemical vocabulary, the five elements (earth, fire, air, water, and ether) are each represented by a regular polyhedron. These geometrical forms are known as Platonic Solids, mainly because it was Plato, describing a cosmology based on geometric symbolism in the *Timaeus*, who most conspicuously among the ancients whose texts are still extant discussed this fact. As we know, for Plato, true reality consisted of archetypal ideas which cast pale, transitory reflections as phenomena of the physical world; these primordial ideas cannot be perceived by the senses, but only through pure reason, or what Steiner would call imaginative cognition. "Geometry was the language recommended by Plato as the clearest model by which to describe this metaphysical realm."[26] At the same time, "In Plato's system, geometrical symbolism was held to account for all known states of matter."[27]

Geometry teaches us that there are only five volumes (regular polyhedra) in which all the edges and interior angles are equal; only five geometrical forms satisfy these conditions. These are the cube (6 sides or "hedra," faces) tetrahedron (4), octahedron (8), icosahedron (20), and dodecahedron (12). Each of these is correlated with an element, or, according to occult perception, embodies the physical element at an ideal, prematerial level, respectively: earth, fire, air, water, ether. These essential forms "have in themselves, and through their analogues with the elements, the power to shape the material world."[28] In this sequence of five essential geometric volumes we have evidence of "the mathematics of the cosmic mind." Precise geometrical equations and mathematical laws describe the relationships among these five, and the lawful progression of their generation, one to the next, to form a nest (or maze) of polyhedra, which is the underlying geometric matrix of the physical world.

The six-sided cube is the Platonic Solid (the ideal, prematerial, geometrical form of an element) for the substance earth. The element earth (not the planet Earth) is the epitome of matter as the densification of spirit. The cube, structurally, represents stability, solidity, and immovability; as such, it is an apt metaphor for the element earth and for matter itself. The cube represents "fully embodied, fully manifested Man within the Solar System," explains Theosophical geometrician L. Gordon Plummer.[29]

It might be useful here to remember Lower Sophia's five passions outside the Pleroma that precipitated the material world. Insofar as Sophia's passions generated the world of the five elements, we are justified in suggesting that each of these fundamental passions (as the Gnostic texts tell us: grief, fear, bewilderment, ignorance, and conversion) was expressed first as a Platonic Solid, then materially, as an element of matter. The Gnostic cosmology is characteristically bleak in its attributions of Lower Sophia's passions, but according to this model we can propose a sequence of Platonic Solids as they precede the physical world. Ignorance is the six-sided cube, the regular solid for earth; fear is the four-sided tetrahedron, fire; bewilderment is the eight-sided Solid for air; grief is the twenty-faceted icosahedron, water; and the dodecahedron, the twelve-sided Platonic Solid for ether, represents conversion, the turning point—and the way out of the nested maze of polyhedra. In other words, I am suggesting we consider Sophia's fivefold elemental passions to be represented by the sequence of generation and nesting among the five Platonic Solids.

In this cycling through Sophia's passions and the polygonal building blocks of matter, we move from the *ignorance* of the cube (earth) to the *conversion* through the dodecahedron (ether). We may now correlate the six-sided cube (earth element) with the twelve-sided dodecahedron (ether), thereby revealing an important link in the syllogism. It is geometrically demonstrable that the cube is the dodecahedron when it is ratcheted or spun five times, that is, when you can see the five turns (or perspectives) as if frozen in space; or, put differently, five cubes make the dodecahedron.[30] This is another way of saying that the cube of earth (the stable density of matter) is converted by turning into the dodecahedron of ether (the most innately spiritualized of the elements). Like the oroboros, the end is in the beginning, the etheric dodecahedron is in the material cube.

The implications of this geometric fact are rich. Lucifer implanted the possibility of conversion (to dodecahedron-ether) within the densest base of material ignorance (from cube-earth). The conversion to spirit is implicit in matter; or we might say, matter is prespiritualized, awaiting our conversion to complete its awakening. All it takes to convert the cube of matter to the dodecahedron of ether is a fivefold ratcheting. To speak of the cube spinning is the same as to describe the four dimensional time-body of the Platonic Solids in geometrical transformation from cube to dodecahedron. Another expression for this five-fold ratcheting is the pentagram, the five-sided figure traditionally associated with Christ; functionally, the pentagram is the bridge that links the cube with the dodecahedron. The pentagram is the fivefold ratcheting of the cube, frozen in space for our perception, as it forms the dodecahedron. "Some Christian mystics associate the pentagram with Christ as both God and man. It is the Logos aspect of reason and word." The five wounds of Jesus at the crucifixion, according to this insight, might also be associated with the five senses that register the material world.[31] According to this geometrical symbolism, the pentagram of Christ accomplishes the conversion of the material cube to the spiritualized dodecahedron. This observation helps us appreciate that through his "precious stone" Lucifer implanted the greatest possibility of freedom—the possibility of freely willed conversion, a re-*turning* to the supersensible light of the Unbegotten Father—within the most intractable expression of matter, the cube of earth. And Lucifer counted on the Christ to facilitate the conversion.

This last observation enables us to make the final link in this series of connections. Steiner's dodecahedral Foundation Stone is essentially equivalent to the six-sided emerald stone of Lucifer. Therefore, the dodecahedron (stone) *is* the emerald heart (stone and Grail) of Lucifer. The dodecahedral Stone of Love and the emerald are fundamentally identical and differ only according to perspective. This introduces yet another aspect behind Steiner's very precise choice of the dodecahedral form for his Foundation Stone. It has to do with the Akashic Records.

The emerald dodecahedral Foundation Stone is integral to the translation of cosmic intelligence into individualized form for an important reason. That reason is the Akashic Records. Akasha means ether, which exists at different levels. We know that the etheric body is the human time "library" of all life events and thinking, and the dodecahedron is the Platonic Solid for the element of ether. This Akashic feature exists at the soul level, surrounded by (or constituted of) the ether element in the shape of a dodecahedron (the twelve-sided polyhedron, each face of which is a pentagon). The element ether is the time-body, the repository of records of events, the origin of formative forces, and the carrier of the thought-weavings of the cosmos. In the human organism, the etheric body contains historical, biographical records of the life of that individuality as lived in time. On the planetary and extraplanetary level, the Akashic Records fulfill the same function, containing records of planetary, solar, galactic, and cosmic time events. It is really a matter of scale because the Akashic Records function holographically and hierarchically; the Records exist at many different levels of complexity and time reference, from the individual human to the cosmic. At any level, it is like a library, a great time-body memory bank.

So, in choosing the dodecahedron as his Foundation Stone, Steiner implicitly identified this regular polyhedron's esoteric function as the template or access point for the Akashic Records and thereby indicated that this fact was of paramount importance for future anthroposophical events at the Goetheanum. The selection of the dodecahedron, whether coincidental or deliberate, is crucial to Steiner's intention. Access to the great time library of the Akashic Records enables an individual to check the relative accuracy of an occult statement made by somebody else; it is a means for peer review of spiritual scientific research. It is the means for knowing directly and independently; as such, it is crucial to the achievement of the consciousness soul and the Michaelic respiritualization of cosmic intelligence. The dodecahedral Foundation Stone as Akashic Records is the promise of the Michaelic consciousness-soul epoch: individually independent cognition that is corroborable by others. We appreciate in Steiner's astute selection of the dodecahedron as the Foundation Stone a rich hierarchy of symbolism and esoteric truth. Steiner's prodigious efforts to develop the protocols and guidelines for a spiritual scientific methodology were intended to make this access to the Akashic Records unilaterally possible to every aspiring individual.

The dodecahedron (or emerald) is thus the access point for the Akashic Records. We know already that the dodecahedron and cube are essentially identical, only differing by perspective. This means the Akashic Records has something to do with the heart of Lucifer, which is the six-sided emerald/cube. On the basis of this we can state: the Akashic Record *is* Lucifer's heart and thus the dodecahedral foundation stone; as such, it is the vehicle for Sophia's tableau of cosmic memory and intelligence—Sophia's "prevenient Manas-revelation," as Tomberg put it, or Sophia's imagination, as we noted earlier. This means that when we access the precious stone of Lucifer, the dodecahedral imaginative Form of Love of Steiner, the cube, the emerald, the source of the Grail, the etheric time-body of weaving thoughts, the Akashic Records—it is all the same place. It is all a revelation of cosmic intelligence appropriate to the scale or level of access. All of this went into the ground at Dornach Hill in 1913 and into the hearts of the Schreinerei participants in 1923 as part of Steiner's Foundation Stone ceremony. The emerald is the Schreinerei within the human organization, the theater for the cosmic drama of intelligence. Lucifer provides the means, Michael facilitates it, Sophia is the revelation, and as we will see below, Christ is the *speaking forth* from this matrix.

The totality of the enactment is the awakened, oracular intelligence of the Holy Ghost: the human *speaking*. Since every human has the emerald, every individual has the possibility of unimpeded access, or independent conscious cognition, and the means to speak from this context, to *speak as the Logos*. In other words, the emerald facilitates the individualization of spiritualized cosmic intelligence and its living expression as the spoken word. Ultimately, the Grail is a speech Mystery, the Word made oracular.

We undertake all of this on Lucifer's behalf. After all, Lucifer undertook a great deal on our behalf a long time ago. So our efforts today are reciprocally necessary and urgent. When Lucifer unites with the Unbegotten Father, then Lucifer on his own level experiences the apocalyptic conversion from the ignorance of matter to the revelation of unity. Then is the phantom of the Human truly redeemed.

Let's review our picture to date. The Holy Grail is the transformation of Lucifer's precious stone. Lucifer's emerald is actually the esoteric housing of the Holy Grail, located within the inner heart chakra. The Grail contains countless copies of the Christ Ego, which means the potential for every human individual to undergo the Christed initiation. This stone is the emerald heart of Lucifer, expressed equivalently as a cube, for matter, or dodecahedron, for etheric conversion. The emerald is also an equivalent expression for the Akashic Records. The purpose of the emerald is to translate cosmic intelligence, through the Trinity of the Holy Ghost of Michael, Sophia, and Lucifer, into individualized, biologically tangible humans. The direct revelation of cosmic intelligence through the Christed initiation within the emerald transforms wisdom into love. Finally, Steiner used Lucifer's emerald twice as the prototype for his dodecahedral Foundation Stone ritual at Dornach in 1913 and 1923.

We need to add another crucial element to our consideration. This new factor will help us answer the second question of why Steiner located his twice-built Goetheanum at Dornach Hill. To answer this, we need to acknowledge the occult fact that the planet has an etheric body just as the human does and with an equivalently complex anatomy and physiology. Steiner never quite explicitly described the planet web or Earth's energy-consciousness matrix in these terms. He made oblique references to the energy dynamics at various Mystery centers, but he did not publicly outline his views on a subject Anthroposophists call etheric geography. Yet the existence of this subtle formative field around the planet is clearly implied in all he said and it is crucial to the conclusions I have in mind. Again, it is a matter of extending his indications on the basis of contemporary thought and inner research to develop a fuller picture.

Steiner discussed the palpable etheric aura of the ancient Mystery centers such as Ephesus and Tintagel. In his profound lectures on the *Gospel of St. John*, Steiner explained how the Earth is embedded in overlapping etheric and astral auric bodies. He said a clairvoyant observing the planet from afar and over time would have noted that with the Mystery of Golgotha the color of the planetary aura changed. It changed at the precise moment when the blood of the crucified Christ permeated the physical soil of Earth. This was a unique moment when all spiritual-earthly relationships reconfigured. This transformation registered in the planetary aura. "Because the Logos began to unite with the Earth, the Earth's aura became changed." From that point forward, it became absolutely correct to regard the entire planet as the body of Christ. The Logos united with the "psychospiritual being" of the Earth. Christ points to the ground and proclaims: "This is My Body!" With Golgotha, Christ permeated the material planet with the fecund, cosmic forces of the Logos. Through this act, the Christ created a "new light center," which is for all time "interwoven with the Earth's aura."[32]

The Logos force initially was an astral light, but over the course of human evolution, it will become an etheric light and finally a physical light as our material planet gradually transforms into a sun. The Christ force created a "sphere" or "spiritual ring" of Christ light around the planet which, through the sustained pressure of spiritual momentum, will convert the elemental Earth into a blazing Star. After Golgotha, the Earth began to shine with a new radiance; eventually, it will become a "luminous body, a sun body," as men and women take up the "radiant force" that Christ imparted to the Earth through Golgotha. We see on the planetary level the same potential conversion of cube-earth to dodecahedron-ether (or Sun, because the Sun is the source of the etheric), that we examined in the personal human sphere. Once again, Christ is the transformative energy. "While we behold the dying Christ, we stand in the presence of the genesis of a new sun," said Steiner, "for death becomes the seed of a new sun in the universe."[33]

The destiny of Earth is to return to the Sun. A long time ago in cosmic history, Old Sun (and later, Old Moon) separated from Earth. With this separation, not only did the physical sunlight depart the Earth, but the intelligence of the Sun left, too. "The spiritual and soul beings at whose head stood the Elohim, the real Spirits of Light, the denizens of the Sun"—these Sun-beings departed with Old Sun. But when the evolving Earth once again unites with the Sun and becomes a Star in the cosmos, humans together with the Elohim, "will then occupy the same field of action." Golgotha was the foundational event in this path of cosmic return. "For through the Event of Golgotha, which bound the force of the Elohim in the sun to the earth—in other words the force of the Logos—the impulse was given which will again eventually impel one Logos-force toward the other."[34]

It is the Logos-force acting within individual humans that will facilitate the transformation of Earth to Sun. As each individual woman and man willingly takes up the Christ energy within through an etheric perception, an etheric imagination, then the Earth grows progressively brighter. The means through which we take up the Christ-force is the emerald; the means by which the Earth is transformed into a Star is the planetary web, its etheric geography. And the place where the two movements come together is the emerald present in multiple holographic copies throughout the etheric geography of the planet.

Now we can consider Dornach in a broader context. For what *supersensible* reason did Steiner enact both dodecahedral foundations at Dornach Hill? We must look beyond the obvious reasons, such as the fact that Dornach Hill was the Anthroposophical Society's property and therefore the only and logical place for a dedication. There is the incidental, historical fact that the nearby village of Arlesheim, at the base of Dornach Hill, was once prominent in the European Grail Mysteries as a hermitage under the tutelage of St. Odille, the seventh-century patron saint of Grail Knights, and later, in the ninth century, Hugo of Tours, the leader of that century's Grail impulse. There is reason to believe that in the thirteenth-century Wolfram von Eschenbach based his figure of Treverizent, the Grail custodian, on Hugo.[35]

So there was an established lineage for Dornach as a Mystery center within the Grail stream. But we need to penetrate deeper to the underlying fundamental appropriateness within the evolutionary scheme of Earth and humanity for the Foundation Stone enactment at Dornach. On the surface of events, around September 1912, an enthusiastic member of the German Section of the Theosophical Society named Dr. Grossheintz invited Rudolf Steiner and Marie von Sivers to visit their newly acquired hilltop property near Basel, Switzerland. Grossheintz' invitation was propitiously timed. Steiner was having difficulties in obtaining permission from municipal authorities in Munich for his con-construction plans for what he was then calling the *Johannes-Bau* (St. John's Building), which would be the central headquarters for the anthroposophical movement in Europe.

Steiner walked the hill, examined the landscape around Dornach, even looked into the subterranean grottos in Arlesheim at the base of Dornach Hill. During his walk, Steiner contemplated the "peculiar spiritual cloudlike formation which we may designate as the etheric aura" at Dornach. He knew that "a kind of etheric aura towers up" over every topographical area on the planet.[36] Later he spoke of "the special etheric sheath which had surrounded the ancient true Mystery Centers" and that was present at Dornach from its beginning. Dornach Hill had "Mystery secrets" which Steiner planned to articulate through the Goetheanum as a living building dedicated to speech.[37] Steiner's first visit to Dornach Hill left him inexplicably gloomy; afterwards, Marie von Sivers speculated that Steiner very likely had foreseen the eventual destruction of the first Goetheanum by fire. After the Munich authorities refused him permission to build, Steiner returned to Dornach in May 1913 and accepted Dr. Grossheintz' gift of Dornach Hill. Four months later at the autumnal equinox, Steiner laid the first Foundation Stone for the Goetheanum on the site, certain that in Dornach "a central point for spiritual knowledge will be created."

Present at Dornach Hill, even today, is a subtle feature that makes it entirely possible to make the site a central point for spiritual knowledge. Sitting supersensibly at Dornach Hill like a lustrous jewel in its setting is an emerald in a landscape zodiac. This is a geomantic expression of the positioning of the emerald within the human organization. We know from life science disciplines like anatomy, Chinese acupuncture, and Tantric yoga that the human body, both materially and energetically, is stunningly complex. The same is true for the planet when we consider its subtle consciousness-energy matrix, or etheric geography. One feature that facilitates higher consciousness functions in humanity through the planetary web is called a landscape zodiac. This is a large supersensible star imprint, an etheric template of the constellations of the zodiac existing as a living formative force overlighting a variable portion of the landscape. Each landscape zodiac is an initiatory supersensible temple with an energy anatomy equivalent to the human chakras. There are about 500 landscape zodiacs around the world varying in size from less than a mile to over one hundred miles in diameter.

One of the best known of such geomantic features is located at Glastonbury, in Somerset, England. Known generally as the Glastonbury (or Avalon) Temple of the Stars, this geomantic feature, which is about twenty miles in diameter, is exoterically described as a recapitulation in landscape topography of the standard morphological features of the signs of the zodiac. Those who have written about this mythologically based landscape zodiac suggest its origin might date back to the Chaldean epoch, some five thousand years ago at least; others argue for an Atlantean origin. The suggestion is also made that King Arthur's Knights of the Holy

Grail used the etheric zodiacal temple as a basis for their inner questing, as the Round Table. "The Round Table, laid out in the form of a zodiac over the country around the [Glastonbury] Tor, was the conceptual creation of a civilization which appears to have risen some 4,000 years ago, at the beginning of the age of Aries," remarks noted geomantic scholar John Michell. "Its religion was based on a solar myth within the twelve-part framework of the zodiac, and the leader of its twelve ruling gods was a British version of Apollo, namely Arthur."[38]

The landscape zodiac is all about myths in the landscape, or what one commentator calls geomythics. "Imaginative Symbolism was physically writ large across the geomantic terrain of Avalon's Holy Ground. Everything is really symbolically physical and physically symbolic. It is also an excellent description of the Glastonbury Zodiac; those vast nature/star effigies that dreamingly spin on the Round Table of earth, the rich, seminal emanations of the Living Thoughts of God."[39] For another Glastonbury exegist, the Somerset star temple is "Merlin's Atlantean Temple of Initiation, a Great Synchronicity Machine." The zodiac is "a Grand Ideal latent in the Somerset landscape," keyed to the spiritual-magical unfoldment of human consciousness and based on the Qabala. "Each star temple within the Somerset zodiac represents a progressive stage of initiation," such that formerly men and women purposefully transited the starry landscape as part of a cycle of initiations. [40]

In other words, the landscape zodiac represents a large etheric Mystery center coordinated with the spiritual intelligences of the cosmos. From my own investigations, I can report the impression that the landscape zodiac represents an interactive, experiential, miniaturized virtual image of the principal stars and constellations of the galaxy; underlying this image is the form and consciousness of the Human, the Holy Ghost. The zodiac exists to provide the revelation of this face of the Human as a direct inner initiatory experience. We might reinvoke the Gnostic example of Sophia casting the image of the "immortal man of light" or "Adam of Light" on the waters (the etheric element) for the humbling of the arrogant Ialdabaoth. This Sophianic image is the composite face of the zodiac as templated on the landscape through its etheric body.[41]

We gain a deeper sense of the experience of such an etheric temple by considering the way Steiner described the quality of the ancient Indian etheric clairvoyance. At that time, the initiate rose out of his physical body into his etheric body, and from there "he looked all around him at the cosmic totality of the thought of the gods, whence the world sprang forth." The initiate wove around himself an etheric, cosmic net out of the thoughts of the gods; to him, this world-web of thought was like a "soul-light" pervading the world. The initiate perceived "soul-light pervaded by spiritual wisdom" in which everything was written in living prototype, "entirely woven of and irradiated by the soul of the light, truth and knowledge poured."[42]

With this preliminary sense of the complexity of etheric geography, we discover that Dornach Hill and environs sit at the center of a landscape zodiac about 14 miles wide. This zodiac has a planetary context which we can suggest by referring again to the twelve-sided dodecahedron. Plato left a hint for us in his *Timaeus* when he described the Earth, when seen "from above," as being like a leather ball sewn in twelve equal sections: in other words, a dodecahedron. It is a geometric fact that each face of a dodecahedron is a pentagon, which is a five-sided figure. If we visualize a twelve-sided dodecahedron as a form made of light superimposed over the physical Earth, then the planet's surface is divided into twelve domains, each of which is contained by a pentagon. As such, we might term each topographical pentagon a pentagonal face. Each pentagonal face is subject to a specific astrological influence; just as with the twelve principal signs in the traditional zodiac, one sign influences each pentagonal face for a long period of time.

The Dornach zodiac, or star template, resides within one aspect of the dodecahedral planet web, one pentagonal face, over which the living etheric energy of Aquarius is active. Aquarius, astrologically, is the "quality of time" of the coming era, literally the New Age about which so much has been said.[43] At the center of the Dornach zodiac temple, and occupying the energetic position of the heart within the heart chakra of its energy configuration, sits the supersensible emerald. Aquarian energy is also entirely in accord with the requirements of the elaboration of the consciousness soul. Aquarius encourages the development of strongly individuated, spiritually independent men and women capable of working collegially in a common spiritual project. Aquarian energy is decidedly Michaelic. The multinational consortium of builders who cooperated in the wartime construction of the Goetheanum is an excellent example.

To speak esoterically for a moment, the Christmas Meeting of 1923 actually took place, supersensibly, under an Aquarian aegis and within the emerald at Dornach in the heart of its landscape zodiac. Through the spiritual potency of his Foundation Stone meditative prayer and the force of his own spiritual presence, coupled with significant hierarchical spiritual presence, Steiner facilitated the initiation *in the emerald* of the 800 Anthroposophists present in the Schreinerei. Steiner inducted his fellow Anthroposophists into the emerald heart of Lucifer. Both the Schreinerei meeting in Dornach of 1923 and the Harmonic Convergence through El Tule in 1987 took place inside the emerald, the Foundation Stone for cosmic intelligence within the Human. This means the Christmas Meeting in fact took place within the heart or "precious stone" of Lucifer. In light of this, the Harmonic Convergence was a continuation, on a much larger scale, of the same spiritual ceremony performed at the Shreinerei; even though it did not have strictly anthroposophical contents, the location and function and spiritual impact of this convergence within the emerald were legitimately part of this same continuum involving the redemption of the Holy Ghost. In 1923, Steiner essentially "brought" his colleagues into the emerald wherein they had the opportunity to supersensibly behold the Holy Grail and to experience the permeation of their individual Ego with the Christ-I. In 1987, Lucifer essentially met his human colleagues inside the emerald where they had a brush by the Holy Ghost.

Steiner's Aquarian emerald initiation was momentous for world history as well, imparting an invaluable spiritual impulse to a tumultuous century in which the destiny of the Slavic peoples would play a paramount role, first under Communism, then under relative autonomy. All of Slavic central and eastern Europe and the western half of Russia are situated within this same Aquarian pentagonal face of the planet web. The Aquarian impulse is currently influencing this entire region, throughout this century. Steiner's Christmas Meeting within the emerald was truly a key supersensible foundation stone for the liberation and future ascendancy of the Slavic countries. It was a significant gesture on behalf of the coming Jupiter phase of evolution and its spiritual requirements. Steiner had prophesied that the Slavs would carry the spiritual impulse for the next cultural epoch. In the early days of the twentieth century, "dreams of Pan-Slavism" were thoroughly discussed by the secret brotherhoods of Europe, who envisaged them as a dominant folk element of the future. "For in the folk spirit of all that is gathered together as the Slav peoples, there lives what, one day in the future, will furnish the material for the spiritual stream of the sixth post-Atlantean epoch."[44] This is the future of course, and if current events in the Balkans are indicative, it is probably the distant future as the process of divesting personal and cultural identity from various ancient group souls, tribal allegiances, and archangelic folk souls is clearly a painful, torturous, if not apocalyptic experience.

Steiner's act of spiritual mentorship illumined the landscape zodiac with the new Aquarian energy of our day. In his Foundation Stone Meditation, delivered on December 25, 1923, Steiner exhorted his fellow Anthroposophists to "truly *live*" in "the All-World-Being of Man." The spiritual force of his Meditation was itself a sufficient inducement for many to supersensibly engage another part of their awareness in the "All-World-Being of Man." The fact that they were situated at the heart center of a holographic representation of this "All-World-Being of Man" made their spiritual efforts that week that much more significant. As we appreciate that the Christmas Meeting virtually took place within the emerald heart of Lucifer, the Light-Bearer of humanity, situated at Dornach within a complex supersensible etheric geography, we can see that through his invocations Steiner ushered many across the threshold into the presence of the Grail.

We can take inspiration from Sergei Prokofieff's forceful insight into the supersensible reality of the Christmas Meeting which, he said, marked the descent of the Michaelic Grail into the hearts and souls of human beings. Both for that unique fortnight at Dornach and forward into the twentieth and twenty-first centuries, Prokofieff envisioned "the circle of Michaelic Grail Knights, the community of the new guardians of the Holy Chalice, the Holy

Stone." The "renewed image" of the Grail must arise from "the depths of the new revelation of Anthropos-Sophia—the Wisdom of the Holy Spirit concerning man."[45] The Christmas Meeting was a seed laid in the soul of humankind that must bear fruit at the end of the twentieth century as the culmination of anthroposophical development and as the "completion of the New Mysteries," said Prokofieff.[46]

Prokofieff's observations gain more significance when we consider an additional factor in this model of etheric geography. With apologies for the mounting complexity of this subject, I must point out that the entire spiritual form of the planet, the etheric anatomy of the Earth, is situated within Lucifer's emerald. The planet Earth is contained within the dodecahedral Foundation Stone of Lucifer. It is useful to visualize our blue-white globular planet as enveloped in a delicate living web of light, a consciousness-energy matrix with a definite geometrical form. At one level of perception, the form of the planet web is the dodecahedron for ether (technically, it is a composite of the dodecahedron and the icosahedron for water, with either 120 faces or 12 faces, depending on your perspective). As we learned from our consideration of how the six-sided cube-emerald ratchets five times to form the twelve-faceted dodecahedron, the planetary dodecahedron is equivalent to the cube-emerald. Thus the etheric form of the Earth is a cube, emerald, dodecahedron, again, varying only by perspective.

This means the planet exists within the emerald heart of Lucifer *and* the holographically miniaturized emerald within each individual human. Each of us holds the Earth within the inner heart chakra, the emerald inside the human. The Earth is doubly held in this emerald regard: through the macrocosmic emerald in Lucifer's heart, and through the microcosmic emerald in each human's heart chakra. The ramifications of this fact are startling. The redemption of the cleaved Lucifer *is* the redemption of the environmentally-ravaged Earth; they are in no way separate or even sequential. In this redemptive act humans are the crucial factor.

In our own time at the close of the twentieth century, we can imaginatively penetrate to that same supersensible experience Steiner facilitated in his anthroposophical colleagues in the

Schreinerei. The Christed initiation in the emerald (Foundation Stone) is inherently atemporal. This means in a real sense the Christmas Meeting within the emerald is still in progress; in a timeless sense, we can join those souls from 1923 in the Shreinerei through the emerald. What, really, is the Christmas Meeting that so profoundly set the course of the Anthroposophical Society from that point forward? It is the living work of Anthroposophy within the dodecahedral imaginative Form of Love which is Lucifer's heart. It is the vessel for the cosmic imaginations of Sophia, Her Manas-revelations of cosmic intelligence. The way into the emerald always starts with the Star. In the next few paragraphs I relate the actual steps in the formation of an imagination that will position us in virtually the same supersensible space inside the emerald as at the 1923 Schreinerei convocation.[46]

In the first stage, through the warmth of our concentration, the Star at the midpoint of our being goes supernova. We identify the Star as a tiny pinprick of blazing light at the center of our being. When we breathe as Love from Above to the Star—patiently, without struggle—it grows larger and larger. Eventually, it becomes bigger than us, envelops us in a flash, then disappears. When that happens, we say the Star has gone supernova. Before, the Star was inside us; now, we are inside the Star. It has turned inside out as the result of our concentration. We, as a point of consciousness, are the Star. All around us we perceive a pale blue empty sphere of unlimited dimension and no content. Our awareness extends throughout this sphere; our awareness is this pale blue sphere. It's as if we are free-falling without a body in an infinite blue emptiness. Everywhere we look, it is pale blue spaciousness.[47]

In the second stage, we enter the emerald. We project our inner six-sided green emerald outwards as a large visualization before us. We build the living thought-picture of a six-sided, translucent, green emerald looming before us as massive as a Gothic cathedral. Everything turns inside out when we enter the emerald by "walking" through one of its six permeable facets. In any case, ether is the medium for records-keeping. From the outside, the emerald has the appearance of the Emerald Tablets of Hermes Trismegistus. On the inside of the emerald, the green tablets are like windows; as such, they have information for the creation of worlds and human life.

A great deal awaits our discovery inside the emerald, but in this exercise we need to be selective. We find before us a majestic, glistening round table as if carved from the purest marble. The Round Table here is an imagination of the composite of the twelve signs of the zodiac, the twelve archetypal spiritual beings who comprise the zodiac. We draw up one of the many dozens of available seats around this table and sit down. We may notice others seated around the table, possibly some of the Michaelic Grail Knights Prokofieff extolled. With this observation, we may appreciate the confluence of the Grail Stream and the Arthur Stream within the emerald heart of Lucifer. The Round Table is a legendary image from the Arthur mythic cycle. The Grail is the consummate symbol of esoteric Christianity, later appended to the pre-Christian Arthur cycle, according to Church and Celtic scholars. The Akashic Records reveal a common origin for the Arthur and Grail revelations as components of a primordial, integral Mystery tradition.

In the third stage, once inside the emerald and seated at the table, we encounter the Holy Grail. However, we do not behold the golden chalice as an object separate or outside of ourselves. Surprisingly, in this third stage we *become* the Golden Grail. From the center of the table a brilliant point of golden light appears. It swells into a magnificent golden Sun. This is what Steiner called *das Sonnenhafte* ("Sun-quality"), the inner true spiritual Sun shining in our innermost recess.[48] As if we are speeding towards this inner Sun, it fills our field of vision (or sense of spatial identity) until it envelops us completely. Our sense of physical, spatial, bodily definition dissolves. Instead, we are golden everywhere, just as earlier we were uniformly pale blue. The golden light congeals, or is sculpted, into a shape: the Grail chalice with two handles. Where once was our physical body in terms of our perception, now there is the hollow interior of the chalice. Our sense of the volume occupied by our physical body disappears; in this hollow space is now the hollow inside of the Grail. In the space immediately around, within the confines of our aura, is the inside of the Grail bowl. It is paradoxical to say, but it is our experience now that where our body isn't, now there are the curving inner sides of the Grail. Our point of spatial identity is the entire Grail chalice, which is to say, we are omnipresent as the Grail. We have entered the Sun-body, the expression of individuation and the vessel for I-consciousness known as the Grail. The Golden Grail is the expression of Self individuation, of all the aspects of our astral, emotional, zodiacal self welded together into one integral receptive whole.

In the fourth stage, we are permeated by the Christ. The Grail chalice, which is now our supersensible body of manifestation, is the context for the Christed initiation. We reside within the paradox of the emptiness of the hollow center of the Grail and the definite encompassing form of the Golden Grail around us. We observe we are a single point of consciousness, an awareness that posits I AM! This subtle point of I-consciousness is located at the center of our head, at the bottom of the brain, essentially in between the pineal and pituitary gland. We become aware of an enveloping scarlet sphere, a scarlet globe of a soft, unfathomably warm, loving, almost ineffable presence. We let go while remaining vigilantly aware of the proceedings. It is a wakeful crucifixion.

It is as if our I AM! is stained with a drop of spiritual blood, a droplet of scarlet cosmic potency. This scarlet "blood" slowly permeates our I-consciousness, that individualized self-aware consciousness that continually posits *I AM!* The scarlet permeation is complete when it dissolves our personal, individualized voice of *I AM!* which in a very subtle substitution becomes, *Not I, but the Christ in me.* The Christ is the one saying *I AM!* within consciousness. The Christ permeates the blood circulating throughout the body; the Christ is awake in all the cells, organs, bones, and processes of the body, as the Awakener living in the material substance of the body.[49]

This brings us to the fifth stage in this imagination inside the emerald. When the Logos permeates our individual I AM! our consciousness expands to fill, potentially, all of space. In a sense, the Logos is the connective space between everything. Our spatial parameters become infinitely flexible depending on the "muscular" range of our cognition. Thus, in the fifth stage we enter the "Buddha Body."

This is a term from Buddhist traditions, most notably the Tibetan, to describe a category of manifestation that is not the physical human body but an aspect of the awakened Buddha appearing before occult perception. The term Buddha Body is

not meant to indicate the specific body of a unique spiritual being called Buddha; rather it indicates, as does the Grail, a generic
form, a stage of initiation or awareness, available to any human
being. In Buddhist language, the Buddha, who represents the
awakened one, can occupy three levels of manifestation, three in-
terpenetrating spheres (called *trikaya*, "three bodies"), just like
ice, water, and steam. Similarly, the Buddha has three attributes:
speech, mind, and body. It is a personification of a principle of
pure wisdom.[50] The Buddha Body is the *Sambhogakaya*, the Body
(*kaya*) of Wealth, or Visionary being; it represents a stage in the
manifestation of consciousness. "The Mystery of the Body is here
not that of materiality, of physical embodiment, but the mystery
of boundlessness, the all-embracing wholeness, of the 'universal
body.'"[51]

Perhaps the closest equivalent image we have in the Western
Mystery tradition is the Philosopher's Stone. Granted, this is an
arcane term that has been variously interpreted; Steiner, for example, described it publicly as carbon, implying its potential alchemical transmutation into diamond. One interpretation useful
here is suggested by Walter Johannes Stein who likens the Philosopher's Stone to the totality of the being bodies (or sheaths:
etheric, astral, and beyond) of the human. Following early indications by the medieval alchemist Basilius Valentinus, Stein suggests
that "the whole creation of the stone was the creation of the human being." Building the Stone (or discovering it) is the inner alchemical process of purifying the innate carbon of the human
into the spiritual diamond. The secret of the Philosopher's Stone
is about the "constitution of the healthy body, the faithful soul,
and the victorious spirit. For those are the substances which constitute the Philosopher's Stone ... [which] is the human being."[52]

Were we to see this Philosopher's Stone or Buddha Body from
the outside (which is possible because this particular auric shell
exists on many levels of scale, like an onion), we would see it as
an eight-sided polygon called an octahedron. This is the Platonic
Solid for the air element, which is the vessel for Mind. This octahedron is variously called the Buddha Body, the Miracle or Diamond Body, and the Light Body. It is the empty form of the
Awakened One, extensible throughout all space. Why do we call
the octahedron *Buddha Body*? It represents the sphere of *budh*,

which means "awakening." *Budh* means to wake, to rise from sleep, to come to one's senses, to regain consciousness, to recognize, to mark, to recover from a swoon, to gain presence of mind, to return to consciousness. *Budh* is the intuitive intelligence, the *Buddhi* or Life-Spirit, the spiritual product of the purification and transmutation of the etheric Sun-body, as Steiner described it. *Budh* is the enlightenment body of the awakened Christ, the manifestation form of the Logos at that level of expression. Through this initiation, the Christ Logos awakens in the individual man or woman within the octahedral body of light. The Christ-permeated I awakens in the wisdom, light body.

As with our experience in stage three, when we experienced ourself as the Grail, the Buddha Body (or Philosopher's Stone) is the fullness of form that the emptiness of the Logos takes. The Christed I-consciousness resides within the extensible body of Light. The Buddha Body is inherently paradoxical from a material frame of reference. As the Buddhist teachings remind us, form equals emptiness; emptiness equals form. Out of emptiness, form is generated. Form generates emptiness. The form of the Buddha Body is an expression of emptiness. When emptiness is made manifest, it manifests as the Buddha Body. The content of the Grail is emptiness. The Living Water flowing through the Grail indicates the Grail's emptiness. The Living Water is the truth of consciousness being approached within emptiness. The emptiness is expressed as the Buddha Body through the truth of the Living Water. The Buddha Body is the body of Light. It is the octahedron made manifest. It is the complete octave, a complete spectrum. It is known also as the Rainbow Body or Light Abode of Bliss.

With our imagination of the Buddha Body, we complete the supersensible scaffolding implicit in the Christed Initiation in the Buddha Body. It is possible, on the basis of this imagination, to go further, into the domain of the ascended human hierarchy and the starfields of the Great Bear and then into the realm of the Cosmic Logos and certain aspects of Sirius. But what we have presented will suffice for now. We have induced ourselves into that same supersensible region in which the true Christmas Meeting transpired. This initiation explicitly integrates Buddhist and Christian terms and images, but this synergy shouldn't surprise

Anthroposophists. Steiner forthrightly declared that the Christ would lead contemporary men and women into the land of light, the Buddhist Shambhala; he further stated that with the twentieth century we would begin the momentous synthesis of Pauline Christianity and Eastern Buddhism. Evidently, seeds of this fusion were present in the 1923 Christmas Meeting Foundation Stone meditation. We can add to these indications Steiner's observation that the Buddha's *Sambhogakaya* formed the astral sheath of the "Nathan Jesus" and was therefore a constituent of the complex manifestation form of the Christ.[53] This further amplifies the nature of the linkage of the Christ and Buddha streams and their differing vocabularies.

With this explication of the imagination in the emerald, we gain an important insight into the Sun Mystery. As Steiner said, the spiritual nature of the Sun was always the basis of the ancient Mystery tradition, long before the physical incarnation of the Logos through Master Jesus in historical time; and it will continue to be the basis far into the future. What changes in the course of human evolution is our proximity to the Sun in the experience of the Mystery initiation. As we mature into the requisites of the epoch of the consciousness soul, we draw much closer, intimately so if we choose, to the source of the Sun Mysteries within the human spiritual organization itself. The Sun Mystery initiation takes place within the emerald which is the etheric Sun-body in the human spiritual organization. In a sense, the emerald is the Sun Mystery center within the human being. This becomes clear when we trace our course *into* material incarnation from the Sun; this is the same as reversing the order of the stages in the Christed initiation in the Buddha Body as we explained them above. Incoming, we start with the Buddha Body or Philosopher's Stone.

The Christ is the Logos conscious as I AM! within the body of the awakened one, the Buddha. The Logos operates at different levels, including the cosmic and solar; as the Cosmic Logos, it works through Sirius, the brightest star in the galaxy; as the Solar Logos, it works through the Sun of our solar system. From the viewpoint of life on Earth in this solar system, the Sun is the point of Logos that imparts coherence to the cosmic pith of stars: the Sun is the *astro-logos*; astrology is the science of this coherence.

The Sun does this most conspicuously through the twelve constellations, or Houses of the Zodiac, arranged along the ecliptic of the galaxy, the apparent path of the Sun. If we understand the Sun to represent the totality of the Self, then the zodiacal circuit represents its differentiation into twelve complementary images. In traditional Western iconography, there are two representations for this: one is the Round Table, a personification of the ecliptic; the other is a chalice of gold—the Holy Grail—with the inscriptions of the twelve zodiacal signs around the outer rim. The Logos differentiates itself through the twelvefold individuality of the Sun, through the unified field of Sun-beings whose body is the golden Grail.

The Grail as such is an imagination of the twelvefold life of the Sun, whose body is the cosmos. It is the zodiacal chalice, twelve images fused into one through the golden alchemy of the Sun, for I-consciousness. The inscriptions on the perimeter of the Grail signify the twelvefold spiritual formative forces that create the cosmos as an individuality unified (made coherent) through the Sun. The Grail represents the individuated state of the human being, the twelve aspects of the Self integrated, balanced, and unified. The effulgence of the Grail is the life of the golden Sun, the outer spiritual radiance of this cosmic individuality. In the sequence of our emerald imagination above, first the golden Sun then the Grail appeared at the center of the Round Table. The Round Table is actually the mirror reflection of the Grail. Here the cosmic totality, the unified body of the Sun-beings, has further differentiated into the twelve astrological-astronomical positions of the cosmos, or the twelvefold zodiacal structure of human consciousness.

The Grail, the golden Sun effulgence, and the Round Table, the personified ecliptic, are also situated within the emerald. The emerald is the Sun Mystery center—the Grail Castle in a sense—in whose interior stands the Holy Grail. The emerald is the etheric manifestation body of the Sun, the Logos expressed as Life: this means ether and time. The emerald is like a swinging door, opening into time or nontime, depending on which way we are transiting. Within the emerald is the undisturbed flow of cosmic Time, the Zoroastrian Zurvan, the Gnostic Pleroma, or the mythic Saturn-Kronos before he was bound in the Pit. The Pentecostal illumination by the Holy Spirit and the Sophianic revelation of cosmic intelligence transpire inside the emerald. Outside the emerald, there is the manifest, material world of biology, the Logos in life. The Akashic time chronicles, spanning cosmic, planetary, and individual time (the Zoroastrian Finite Time, or the Gnostic Lower Sophia) are accessed on the outer surface of the emerald (after one has completed the first two stages in the imagination of the emerald). The swinging door, then, is the surface or membrane of the emerald itself. Inside we find the integral spiritual life of the Sun; outside we find the material biological life enlivened by the Sun.

One of the insights of the Sun Mystery is the understanding that this teeming inner spiritual life of the Sun is holographically, microcosmically present within the human organization. We bear the Sun Mystery within our human organization, in the emerald. Through the emerald we have access to the Akashic Records and to the human ascended hierarchy, what is usually called the White Brotherhood. We find the point of access to this within the individualized emerald present in the etheric body of each man and woman. In fact, the epicenter or heart of the human etheric body is the emerald. We know that during the Old Sun phase of cosmic evolution the Elohim helped to create the human etheric body. They translated the living Logos into Life. This precipitated the etheric Sun-life body made of the weaving, living thoughts, cosmic pictures, and tones (mantric "words") of the Gods. The Sun-body is the matrix in which individualized human intelligence is made possible.

During the planetary epoch of Lemuria, this Sun-body was transferred into human biological individuality when the emerald, representing the condensed, miniaturized Sun-body, was implanted in every incarnating woman and man. This was tantamount to implanting the entire Sun Mystery into the human organization in concentrated (but not abridged) form through the emerald, or inner heart chakra. This implantation called for a turning inside-out of the Sun. From the solar viewpoint, the six-sided emerald, or cube, is the furthermost manifestation body of the Sun, in terms of its proximity to incarnate humanity. From the terrestrial viewpoint, the twelve-sided dodecahedron is the subtlest spiritual body, the closest to the Sun. In essence, at this delicate boundary, the dodecahedron turns inside out to become the cube-emerald. The geometrical relationship between emerald-cube and dodecahedron demonstrably supports this statement which is used here more for its metaphorical suggestiveness.

The emerald was implanted within Lemurian humanity as it underwent the transition to physical tangibility and psychic individuality for the first time in human phylogenetic history. Humanity gained biological selfhood. The emerald was a reminder of the Sun Mystery within the emotional body, the Old Moon astral forces, or the elemental world of Lower Sophia. Another name in the Western tradition for this complex is the Pit. The Pit, among other things, indicates the first three chakras—*Muladhara* (base), *Svadisthana* (sacral), *Manipura* (solar plexus)—pertaining to physical survival, procreation, and selfhood in the context of biological individuality. The Pit is a perhaps severe but accurate expression of the difficulties of matter—the red maw of unilluminated selfhood—the elemental emotionality of individuality, the unrefined passions of Lower Sophia.[54]

When the Sun turned inside out and was miniaturized within humanity as the emerald, this was the moment in which the Holy Ghost was caught in Time. The Cosmic Human fell into the earthly Pit. Cosmic individuality got snared in biological selfhood. All metaphors of the Fall lead back to the Sun. From Lucifer's heliocentric point of view, the movement of energy into matter, or the Sun into biological individuality, was a problematic undertaking. When the Sun turned inside out and took up holographic residence within the human as the emerald, Time began. This was the moment of the withdrawal of Old Sun from the Earth. The Sun, now outside Earth, became the regulator of time; the Sun in fact became Time itself in this new relationship. Within each human individuality, the Sun was bound as the emerald in the Pit of biological selfhood, like the Buddhist jewel in the mud-grown lotus. The emerald as the Sun within the biological human is the energetic heart of the etheric time, life, and thinking Sun-body.

As we noted earlier, the Earth itself, when comprehended in its spiritual, anatomical form, is situated within this same emerald-dodecahedral Sun-body. More precisely, the physical, elemental Earth emanated forth *from* this spiritual anatomy in the same way that human individuality became physically tangible. In either case, the emerald Sun-body is the key to the translation, in either direction: inbound, towards manifestation, or outbound, towards resurrection. The way we make the Earth a Christed Star is the same way we redeem the Holy Ghost caught in Time—through the Sun Mystery within the emerald. The means in this two-way event have to do with Pentecost, the descent of the Holy Spirit upon the crowns of the apostles of Christ.

This is properly the subject of the final chapter but for our purposes here it must be noted that the experience of Pentecost happens *inside* the emerald. When Steiner foresees a future in which World Pentecost is the norm, there is no place this can happen but inside the emerald—*inside* the Foundation Stone. The twelve Apostles of Christ or the twelve Knights of the Round Table—either way, their location is about the Round Table inside the emerald or Sun-body. Technically, in terms of the imagination presented above, the Apostles or Grail Knights at the moment of Pentecost are situated within the Buddha Body. The contact of the Holy Spirit with their crown chakras initiates inspired speech; they are moved to *speak as the Logos.*

Let's consider the Shreinerei meeting once again as synecdochal for the future World Pentecost. There stood Steiner and his 800 fellow anthroposophists, inside the supersensible emerald at Dornach Hill, inside the Foundation Stone itself, inside the inner heart chakra of an etheric zodiacal imagination of the Cosmic Human overlaid on the physical landscape under the influence of Aquarius, and inside a physical building, the Goetheanum, whose esoteric dedication was as *the House of Speech.* What finer place than this to launch an impulse for World Pentecost, for inspired Logos-speaking, than inside the House of Speech. The experience of Pentecost, entered into in the context of our material individuality but, in terms of the placement of consciousness, within the emerald, is the way we knit both sides of the Sun together, the six-sided emerald inside and the twelve-sided dodecahedron outside. The new *imagination* of Pentecost as a Sophianic speaking forth as the Logos, creating worlds of meaning and manifestation, is the fruit of this synthesis.

The emerald truly is the House of Speech. In that apocalyptic moment of Pentecostal illumination, the walls of the emerald resound with the mantric speech of the Solar Logos, the Logos working through the Sun: *Ar-thur! Ar-thur!* It may surprise many that the mantric key to the Arthurian Mystery is contained in the name itself of its predominant figure: Arthur. *Ar-thur!* is the activating sound of the Solar Logos working through the Sun inside the emerald. The first syllable *Ar* is the Sun aspect; the second syllable *Thur!* is the Word aspect or Logos, meaning growth and change. A third syllable, *hum!* is appended to ground the energy. The mantra *Ar-thur-hum!* is spoken out loud by living men and women with their consciousness present within the emerald.

As the sound of the Solar Logos, *Ar-thur!* means the Word made flesh. The spiritual force behind the *Ar-thur!* sound, the angelic intelligence that utters the *six* syllables—intoning each letter of *Ar-thur!*—of the Word, is the Elohim, the formative spiritual beings of the Sun. In his commentary on the Gospel of St. John, Steiner said that the Sun, which is the symbol for the Logos, is the expression of six Elohim. The historical appearance of Christ Jesus means that the "forces of the six Elohim, or of the Logos, were incarnated in Jesus of Nazareth . . . (as) the inner force of the sun, the force of the Logos-Love, assumed a physical human form. . . . He Who was there in the visible world is an actual incarnation of the six sun Elohim, of the Logos!"[55] These six Sun Elohim are that same Gnostic solar lion and Demiurge, Ialdabaoth.[56]

Thus when six Elohim are focused within one consciousness, the Christ becomes manifest as the Logos. The sound of the Logos working through the Sun is the six Elohimic letters of *Arthur!* When the Christ became manifest as flesh, the Logos had completed its involutionary arc from Logos (Saturn) to Life (Sun) to Light (Moon) to Flesh (Earth). Previous to the Mystery of Golgotha Arthur as Solar Logos had represented the Logos in its closest proximity to humanity living on the Earth. Arthur stands between Adam (Lemurian humanity) and the Christed Human (the threefold Holy Ghost of Michael, Sophia, and Lucifer permeated by the Logos). Before the Mystery of Golgotha, said Steiner, "the Knights of King Arthur received into themselves the Sun-Spirit, that is to say, the Christ as He was in pre-Christian times."[57] After Golgotha—the unique incarnation of the Logos in the flesh of a human in which the Logos was born on Earth without mediation—Arthur, as Solar Logos, as the Elohimic *Ar-thur!*, remains as the spiritual mid-way station between humanity and the Logos in the Christed initiation within the emerald.

Just as Steiner emphasized repeatedly that one of Anthroposophy's missions was to bring the public's attention to the insufficiently recognized planetary significance of the Mystery of Golgotha, so, too, in our own day is it incumbent on us not to overlook the critical supersensible events that are shaping our present and forming our future evolution. One such epochal event was the Harmonic Convergence of August 16–18, 1987, in which Lucifer came with the dawn. Hardly anyone saw him because they were looking for something outside, while he came to people from within. Lucifer converged upon humanity within the Foundation Stone, Steiner's dodecahedral imaginative Form of Love. The Harmonic Convergence was a planetary conclave and Sun initiation within the emerald, the supersensible overture to a profound renewal of the destiny of the Logos expressed as Life and Logos in the Flesh—the macrocosmic Human as held enthralled in the Pit by microcosmic humanity.

In effect, the Convergence was the next turn in Steiner's 1923 Christmas Meeting and Cosmic Turning Point of Time. At the Schreinerei in 1923, 800 men and women supersensibly took the initiation within the emerald; sixty-four years later, several million underwent the new Mystery of the Sun initiation within the emerald, underwent the preliminaries for *the Christed initiation in the Buddha Body.* Both events—not to overlook the numerous micro-events that have occurred since as repercussions of the spiritual force set in motion by the Christmas Meeting and the Harmonic Convergence—are overtures to a planetary epiphany Steiner envisioned called World Pentecost.

For many who meditated vigilant in consciousness during the days of the Convergence, Lucifer precipitated an awakening in etheric vision. This planetary event validated individual visionary experience as a way of developing personal trust in the potential veracity of inner guidance unmediated by external spiritual authorities. In this sense, it was the quintessential overture to the requisites of Aquarian spirituality. The validation of individual spiritual perception laid the foundation for the blossoming of independent cognition, provided the unavoidable purificatory stage of the Virgin Sophia is completed by each individual. The initiation in the emerald in essence *is* the exercise of independent cognition. It moves towards the fulfillment of Lucifer's mission, which is to shift human consciousness from where it is to the Christed Initiation in the Buddha Body. It's about bringing the energy aspect of matter into consciousness. Through this initiation, Lucifer and Sophia are reconciled, Sophia regains her cosmic imaginations, and is fructified by the Logos in the moment of her long-awaited syzygy with Her consort, the Christ. For the Imagination of Pentecost, the trinity of the Human, as Michael, Sophia, and Lucifer, must be restored to wholeness. The Holy Ghost must be resurrected from the Pit of Time. Sophia must regain her syzygy with the Christ.

Through this cosmic event, Sophia is restored to syzygy with the Christ-Logos but in the historical context of the emanated Earth. In other words, Sophia's restitution takes place in historical (planetary) time, in the context of the elemental world She created in her wanderings outside the Pleroma. It would be of no cosmic benefit for Sophia as Divine Wisdom to re-attain her syzygy within the Pleroma, because then the emanation and evolution of the cosmos through Saturn, Sun, Moon, and Earth phases would have been in vain. Instead, the plan—the necessity—was to restore Sophia's syzygy through the mineralized Earth and its incarnate humanity. When Sophia is reconciled with Lucifer, which means, when the Trinity of the Holy Ghost (the Human, Anthropos) is healed through our cognitive work, and when the Christ permeates the Human with the force of the Logos, then the *Paraclete*, the divine Comforter, is born in our lives.[58]

St. John used the word *Paraclete* five times in his Gospel to suggest the presence of the Holy Spirit as comforter, advocate, consoler, helper, teacher, intercessor. The ascended Christ indicated he would send the Paraclete to the Apostles from the Father to be the eternal, abiding presence among them. The Paraclete, as the Holy Spirit, would be the Witness of the Truth of the Christ's mission through Jesus. The Paraclete would descend unseen, unacknowledged, during Pentecost, and thereafter abide with the Apostles as an indwelling, spiritually comforting presence in their hearts. Whether the Paraclete is the ascended Christ returned or whether Christ sent "another Paraclete" to abide with the Apostles is immaterial. It is basically a way of stating that the Christ would forevermore abide in the heart of the Human—the trinity of Michael, Sophia, and Lucifer, as the Holy Ghost—expressed through the microcosmic human, individual men and women.

Valentin Tomberg gives the Paraclete a slight shift in nuance when he identifies it as the unified Lucifer and Sophia receiving the Christ. At the moment of Pentecost, Lucifer surrendered himself to Sophia, and became one with the Sophia-impulse, says Tomberg. When the influence of Lucifer merged with Sophia's, the Paraclete was manifested. "And Lucifer's attitude of service towards the impulse of Sophia resulted not only in Sophianic revelation reaching the souls of men in undisturbed form, but also in the fact that Lucifer radiated from *himself* the inspiring flame of its enthusiasm and joy." Because the same spirit who had brought about the isolation of souls was now bringing forth the unifying fires of enthusiasm for the reunion of souls, the birth, or appearance, of the Paraclete was made possible, Tomberg argues. The birth of the Paraclete filled the Apostles with "new wine" which was "the Spirit of the Pentecostal revelation, the Paraclete."[59]

When the trinity of the Holy Ghost as the Human was restored with the reconciliation of Lucifer, Sophia, and Michael, then the Logos could be revealed to the Apostles directly through "undisturbed" cosmic imaginations. What was experienced two thousand years ago during Pentecost by the twelve Apostles is now, in our epoch of the consciousness soul, available unilaterally to all men and women. First there was the Christ, then the twelve Apostles, then thousands of women and men, as part of the unfolding of World Pentecost. What was Pentecost at the time of the Christ becomes World Pentecost in our day, filled with undisturbed cosmic imaginations—the Imaginations of Pentecost.

The revelation of the undisturbed cosmic imaginations of Sophia as the imagination of Pentecost, moves humans to speak *as* the Logos, to sound forth Logos-inspired syllables, words, and sentences in one's native language. The Imagination of Pentecost is Wisdom in the Human *Speaking* the fulfillment of Anthroposophy. The Imagination of Pentecost gives speech to Sophia, elicits creative speaking that sounds forth from within the emerald within every woman and man. It sounds forth from within humanity, within the planet, within the heart of the Human, within Lucifer's emerald—as Logos-inspired speech.

This is the matter for our final chapter, but let us remember in closing here that it all comes back to the Star, the good auric Star of the Human, as Steiner called it. The Sun Mystery of the emerald dissolves into the profounder Mystery of the Star. Each individual must understand that tiny point of light called the Star, which is Sophia anthropomorphized. It's important that we understand the nature of Anthroposophy, that Sophia is anthropomorphized, brought into human life, through each individual. Steiner was an exemplary point of anthropomorphic Sophia; Steiner was the human embodiment of the living being Anthropos-Sophia, and, as such, he is an emulable ideal. The philosophical aspect was generated in him, as it can be in all of us, through his understanding of this process by which Sophia enters livingly into Human and human.

Giving Speech to Sophia

The Imagination of Pentecost

in the House of Speech

S INCE THE MYSTERY OF GOLGOTHA, the experience of Pentecost has been a perennially available event, as if at our fingertips. There was first the apostolic Pentecost; later, there was Steiner's Christmas Meeting; more recently, there has been the Harmonic Convergence. Always, it is a progressive movement towards *World* Pentecost; always, it is an induction facilitated by the Holy Spirit to bring us within the Foundation Stone, inside the emerald, into the etheric body of the Sun.[1]Pentecost is the Mystery of the Foundation Stone that inspires us to speak as the Logos. In the original Pentecost, as recorded in the Gospels, the twelve Apostles were "all with one accord in one place." This means they were seated collegially, expectantly, at the Round Table within the Sun-body of the emerald. First there was a "rushing mighty wind," then "cloven tongues of fire" sat on their crown chakras; as they were filled with the Holy Spirit, they were inspired to "speak in foreign tongues" so that every man and woman heard them speak "in his own language."[2] Each Apostle was moved to speak individually as lucidly, as warmly, as appropriately—*as* the Logos. Through Pentecost, the Logos gained twelve more lucid, mellifluous tongues; through World Pentecost, potentially every human voice is the expressive means for the Logos. Through Pentecost, the Logos spoke twelvefold, but through World Pentecost, the Logos speaks a millionfold.

The apostolic Pentecost is the archetype of World Pentecost, an indication of what we may expect during our own Pentecostal initiation within the Foundation Stone. Let us take a moment to consider how Steiner interpreted the experience at Pentecost. For the Apostles the moment of Pentecost was like being awakened from a dream by the descent from the cosmos of "the Substance of all-prevailing Love" (or the Spirit of Cosmic Love, or the primal force of Love). The twelve who had constellated around the Christ felt "quickened" from on high, "wakened to life by the primal force of Love," as if transformed, their souls made anew. The transpersonal Love dormant within each inner heart emerald spontaneously awoke and moved each to impassioned speech, to a stunning, lucid mellifluosity, with unlimited cognitive range and expressive potency. It was as if they could say *anything* and say it perfectly well.

It was as if life lived through them as speaking while the world witnessed a new, diffusive epiphany of the Logos speaking in the flesh. Instantly they were able to express themselves in speech in such a way that everyone, at whatever station of spiritual or intellectual development, could understand them and from this warm, lucid speaking, take consolation and sustenance. They could "read the deepest, innermost secrets of the soul"; they felt within themselves a new understanding of things that before they could not grasp. At last they understood the Mystery of Golgotha and could communicate this insight in such a way that could quicken the spirituality of their listeners. They were spiritual mellifluosity incarnate; the full range of speaking lived in them as unobstructed potentiality. They felt themselves capable of bringing consolation to every different individual through their enwarming speech. They felt capable of relating "new things and again things ever new." In fact, so strong was the force of the Logos that Apostles felt called, "through the power of the Christ Impulse working within them, to let speak the fiery tongues, the individualized Holy Spirit within them." Each felt the Holy Spirit speaking out of his own inner being; each felt he heard the Word continually sounding through all the ages. It was inspired speech, so much so that the transcripts of their insights, the Gospels, "speak with the tongues of Angels and not with the tongues of men." [3]

Each Apostle, inspired by "the Spirit of Cosmic Love," was able to say precisely what was needed, to proclaim spontaneously and meaningfully life-bestowing "Christ words" as if he were individu-ally permeated with the deepest wisdom of the Logos, the fullest understanding of life, possessed of all the imaginations of Sophia. With the Christ Impulse living in them, moving them to speech, individualizing itself through their own I-consciousness, "it was poured forth so that for ever the Gospel of Christ may relate new things and again things ever new." Each new speaking brought forward a newness, a revelation from the storehouse of the cosmic imaginations of Sophia. It was the "individualized soul-worlds of the Holy Spirit, the fiery tongues, the individualized spirit awak-ening in our souls," said Steiner.

The secret of Pentecost, or Whitsun as it was later called, is that the single man or woman individually receives the Holy Spirit, through which the Christ Impulse becomes individualized in each. The message of Ascension, which precedes Whitsun by ten days, is that the Christ Impulse came to pass for humankind on Earth; the challenge of Pentecost is to make the revelation of the Logos indi-vidual, for each of us to birth the Holy Spirit within. Easter gives us the power to develop these experiences, but Pentecost is the "fruit of this power's unfolding." With Pentecost, "the power of the Christ in you has become a power of your own souls." Looking ahead to the future, Steiner said Pentecost would be the festival of "united soul-endeavor" for the harmony of feeling necessary for the "incarnation of a common spirit." Pentecost represents the "immortality of the I," and the I represents "our continual resur-rection in the spirit, our renewed life in the spiritual world."[4]

Steiner further relates that the Apostles had a vision of the fu-ture of Christianity, in which they felt themselves as though sur-rounded by thousands of future disciples of Christ, drawn from all the peoples of Earth, and felt that all of them would one day have the power "to proclaim the Gospel in words that will be un-derstandable."[5] This is an imaginative tableau portraying the fu-ture Christ-inspired event Steiner called World Pentecost. In a 1923 lecture Steiner indicated that World Pentecost was the mes-sage of Anthroposophy. Anthroposophy's mission was to bring to humankind a "perpetual Whitsun Mystery," which, he argued, humanity "sorely needs" for its redemption and salvation. "Then the healing Spirit will speak to a new faculty of understanding in men—the Spirit by whom the sickness of human souls is healed, the Spirit sent by Christ. And then will come that which is a need of all mankind: WORLD-PENTECOST!" [6]

The key point about Pentecost is that it marks the individualization of the Christ impulse. Each Apostle, each true Anthroposophist, each Harmonic Converger, each woman or man who at any time undertakes the initiation within the emerald, is quickened potentially to speak as the Logos. Here we must note a curious reversal, too. It is entirely true, existentially speaking, that it is *Not I but the Christ in me*, however, it is equally true that *the face of the Christ is your own*. The Logos has no face until each of us presents it in the world, when we speak as the Logos. Master Jesus is not what the Logos looks like; the face of Jesus is Jesus' face. Yet, paradoxically, the Christ so permeated Master Jesus that Jesus' face was the face of the Logos, individualized. This is the key to the paradox. Each human face, as a result of Christ permeation, is the legitimate face of the Logos, following the example set by Jesus.

The Logos gained a human face when Master Jesus provided the incarnational sheaths. The Logos gains many faces when we each allow the Christ to incarnate through our speaking. Then the face of the Logos is our own individual countenance, speaking as the Logos. This is the individualization of the Logos in the flesh in the massive epiphany Steiner called World Pentecost. The Word is made multiply manifest in the flesh. When we speak as the Logos, when the Christ Impulse lives individually within us, we are fulfilling the Michaelic requisites of the consciousness soul. We have secured the transferral of the impulse of the Mystery of Golgotha through two thousand years of time into our own lives at the close of the twentieth century and at the threshold of the third millennium. The Logos is born a thousandfold, then a millionfold, on Earth as we give speech to Sophia in ceaseless loquacity. The Earth is the place for speech, for I-speaking. As Steiner said, Pentecost is a festival of the future in which men and women stand filled with the "expectancy" of receiving the Holy Spirit. "And the power of the Christ in you has become a power of your own souls," explained Steiner, and you can feel that "the Holy Spirit speaks out of [your] own inner being." [7]

What precisely is it that is speaking? It's the Logos, the primordial, eternal Word, says Steiner, the "eternal, creating wisdom." What sounds forth from the Pentecostal inspiration within the

Foundation Stone is Wisdom In the Human Speaking. This is living *Anthroposophy*. Clearly this is a word expressive of cosmic imagination and perfectly suited to its task. It is Sophia speaking forth Her cosmic imaginations out of the incendiary enthusiasm of Pentecost. It is the Sophia in the Human, in humans, speaking. A tremendous cosmic event occurred at Pentecost, said Valentin Tomberg: "The dumbness of the Sophia-being ceased, and she was again able to reveal herself by speech." From that moment on, Sophia could pour her influence into the waking day-consciousness of humanity on Earth. No longer was she obstructed by Lucifer's barrier of falsehood. Now Lucifer "conducted the revelations of the Sophia undistorted through his sphere of falsehood by means of the dedication of his whole being." [8] We might reformulate Tomberg's essentially accurate but bleakly nuanced views by saying that with the resurrection of the cleaved Lucifer as the Human through the Mystery of Golgotha, and with the restoration of the primordial trinity of the Holy Ghost, of Lucifer, Sophia, and Michael as the Human, the cognition, embodiment, and expression of cosmic intelligence could proceed without distortions or obstructions, and be established in the flesh of Earth. On this basis may we give speech to Sophia.

Another name for this restored cosmic trinity of the Human is the Virgin Sophia. That's because Sophia's purificatory catharsis takes place within the individual consciousness of each human as a result of the cleansing of the Old Moon astral body. When the human astral body no longer contains impure impressions of the physical world but has spiritual organs awake and competent for supersensible perception, then "the pure, chaste, wise Virgin Sophia" within the individual man or woman encounters the Cosmic Ego, the I-consciousness of the Christ Logos. When the Virgin Sophia within us is permeated by the I-consciousness of the Christ, we become the "instrument" for the spiritual Being of the Sun. "His personal ego has been eclipsed, which means that at such moments it has become impersonal and it is the Cosmic Universal Ego that is using his ego as its instrument through which to speak." [9] If we must use the word "instrument," then it should be in Steiner's sense of a wakeful, impersonal eclipse.

This permeation by the Holy Spirit inciting us to inspired speech full of the force of the Logos is possible only in the context of an astral body which resembles the Virgin Sophia. Then, through permeation by this "living element," we bring forth "ideas that are inwardly alive" which we express with "all our soul warmth and all our soul light." It is as if the Christ teaches us *how* to speak, as if through the Christ we speak for the *first* time. If this is true, then clearly we have terribly undervalued the potency of speech. We cannot reach this primacy of speaking without first cultivating the Virgin Sophia, making ourselves virginal and inwardly prepared for speaking. Then we create the world anew through speaking out of the living imaginations of Sophia. "Clairvoyance in true spirituality can bring both soul warmth and soul light into intellectuality," said Steiner.[10] The world may then see what anthroposophists "have to say *out of* themselves." The human being lights up as the "star of humanity," as the good auric Star of the Human speaking through the Sun. As this speaking Star, speaking through the etheric Sun-body of the emerald, our speech becomes the expression of a new "spiritual humanism" that teaches us to consider "what is revealed in us as Sophia, namely anthroposophia."[11] In other words, through Pentecost we become a revelation in speaking—a revelation even to ourselves. A large measure of the expectancy of Pentecost is to expect to be profoundly surprised by our own speech, to hear our own voice carrying the timbre of the Logos.

One reasonably inquires next: In what way is channeling not anthroposophical speaking? Steiner says that in Pentecostal speech we are instruments for the Logos; similarly, the trance channels claim they are instruments for higher spiritual beings. Is there any difference between these two instrumentalities? The trance communications of contemporary channels and mediums is arguably *not* true anthroposophical speech, yet the *fact* of channeling is itself an important symptom of the imminence of World Pentecost. It's a sign of the coming of true speech. After all, in one of his most impassioned commentaries on the Mystery of Christ, Steiner referred to the Virgin Sophia moved to speech by the Cosmic Ego as an instrument. The intelligences behind most channels today similarly refer to their sleeping prophets as instruments. The crucial difference is that Anthroposophy insists that the instrument be active—actively present, actively awake, actively cognizant, actively permeated, actively speaking. In channeling, by contrast, it is perfectly de rigeur to sleep through the entire event and read the transcripts like the morning paper at breakfast. We are confronted with the danger today of mistaking channeling, which is a symptom of World Pentecost, for speaking as the Logos, which is its fruit.

The fact that late twentieth-century channeling distinguishes itself principally through the vehicle of speech from nineteenth-century mediumship and its materialized astral phenomena, closet apparitions, and automatic writing, is indicative of the coming of age of World Pentecost. If the speech component of channeling were not so prominent, we would have reasonable grounds to regard the whole event as recidivistic nineteenth-century mediumship, as the atavistic resurfacing of earlier oracular traditions of belly-talking. Even so, channeling almost unilaterally is not anthroposophic speaking for two reasons.

First, the majority of practitioners have not undergone the required stage of preparing the Virgin Sophia. As a result, whatever degree of inspiration they might receive from the Holy Spirit is woefully entangled with the unresolved Old Moon astrality of their own biological selfhood. Their pronouncements are epistemologically suspect. In effect, they are channeling unexpiated aspects of their Old Moon self. Second, the majority of channelers speak while in trance, which means they are not awake in their communications, they are not present in their I-consciousness in the act of speaking. Their messages from beyond are thus ontologically suspect. There is no guarantee that the *who* of the speaking is inspired by the force of the Logos and that the *what* of the speaking has any supersensible accuracy. Trance channeling is really a profound disservice to the Logos and to human evolution. It also represents a potential detour from the lawful unfolding of the consciousness soul, if it is taken to be the state-of-the-art for inspired speaking. The contention of this book is that it must not be. The Logos is not represented in trance channeling nor are the requisites of the consciousness soul honored. Trance channeling establishes a very misleading cultural impression of what the state-of-the-art for spiritual speaking might be. Despite these limitations, what is particularly important in our epoch of the consciousness soul heading towards World Pentecost is not the contents, which we should prudently disregard for the most part, but the *fact* of oracular trance, mediumistic, or channeling activity. The fact that this jejune speaking is happening is itself an important symptom. It is a legitimate sign of the unfolding of the Michaelic consciousness soul. But we must assiduously guard against accepting the phenomenon of trance channeling as an end in itself, which is what the dark brotherhoods would prefer; it is only a symptom of a possibility struggling to emerge.

Channeling is a *stutter* in the Logos, a *stammer* in the speech of the Holy Spirit. The words of channeling are massively filtered through the Old Moon astrality of biological selfhood. The original impulse *may* be authentic (but not always, depending on deliberate supersensible obstruction and the strategies of the Brothers of the Left), but the communications are suspect. Channeling is the unintelligible glossalalic voice of the Logos radically distorted by Achamod, the unresolved passions of Lower Sophia living within each human individuality. It is a movement from the supersensible attempting to break into speech, but getting inextricably enmeshed and disfigured at the threshold between worlds. The Guardian of the Threshold has not been empowered to translate the Logos into living intelligent words because we have not prepared the Virgin Sophia in ourselves. So the communications get enmeshed in that primordial cleavage in the being of Lucifer at the threshold, because we haven't assumed the responsibility to prepare ourselves.

The result is not the voice of the independent individual human Ego, and it certainly isn't "poetically constructed speech," as Steiner said of Logos-speech. Yet perhaps if only a homeopathic essence of the Logos comes through, even this minutest aspect of the force of the Logos will not be without value. "One needed only to speak in halting words to become a witness of God," said Steiner. "Even in the simplest, stammering words it was possible to become a witness of the Divine; it need be only single words without meter." A man or woman who finds God in the I AM! bears witness of Divine Speech or "God's language," said Steiner, "even in his stammering words—and he finds the way to God."[12]

The fact of oracular channeling—not its dubious contents or glamorous attributions, but the *fact* that it is happening around us—could widen the materialistic Western cultural aperture to embrace the supersensible world as a possible fact of reality. The sheer momentum of this supersensible impulse to speech through human "instruments" could be culturally transformative; meanwhile, we can prudently discount most of the contents or at least subject them to reasonable peer review and scrutiny. We really must: our metaphysical future depends on the discriminations we make at this time. We could take this grassroots blossoming of channeling, this arising of oracular speech from out of the democratic polity, as the stammered, stuttered, inarticulate syllables of a bound and gagged Holy Ghost struggling to speak freely again after so many millennia of silence. This is a perilous moment in the young life of the consciousness soul. Our keenest discrimination is required. We could follow the fragmented voices back to the Logos, or we could mistake an atrocious translation for the original words of the poet and take the garbled message at face value.

We must also appreciate the obfuscating strategies of the Brothers of the Left. It plays wonderfully into their hands when we mistake channeling for speaking as the Logos. It supports their plans perfectly when we mistake a *symptom* of the imminence of World Pentecost for its arrival and accomplishment. Why has the spiritual world initiated yet another "centennial effort" in this last quarter of the twentieth century, as evidenced by the wealth of signs of expanding cognition? So that we might have the experience of the Christed initiation in the Buddha Body, the perpetual Christmas Meeting and Whitsun inside the Schreinerei of the Foundation Stone, and from this, give speech to Sophia by speaking as the Logos. How can this lawful goal by thwarted? By convincing us that we may bypass the stage of preparing the Virgin Sophia, which is to say, dispense with the requisite of rigorous inner training in spiritual science.

One can easily see ways in which the much-touted "New Age" has been co-opted, subtly corrupted, by the machinations of the Brothers of the Left. Consider its strongly unscientific and anti-scientific attitude, its laissez-faire lack of peer review standards, its imprimatur of passivity and noneffort, its grandiosity, and all of it filtered through an Eastern Hindu-Buddhist bias. To a large extent the precocious, self-advertising Western new age is largely the progeny of that occult deal H. P. Blavatsky was forced to cut with the American and Indian lodges to get out of her occult imprisonment. As we noted earlier, she was forced to strongly emphasize Eastern spirituality and metaphysics in her emerging Theosophy as a condition of release. As such, those invidious lodges commandeered the late twentieth century new age with their own ancient, and, according to Rudolf Steiner, largely spiritually anachronistic thought forms.

Today, as the 1990s mature, we see increasingly the degeneration of this Eastern metaphysical content into new age bromides and trivialities in the service of personal comfort and modest self-improvement. These qualities—passivity, antiscience, grandiosity, Eastern biases—can be inimical to the interests and development of anthroposophical spiritual science which emphasizes active inner activity; mathematical, scientific epistemological rigor; sober, daytime conscious concept-building; and an appreciation of the Christ Event. When we study the phenomena of the new age critically, especially in accordance with Steiner's polarity of Luciferic inflation and Ahrimanic contraction, we see, on the one hand, Ahrimanic spiritual materialism, a grievous densification of spiritual conceptions into mundane, physical terms; on the other, we see a Luciferic grandiosity of unqualified, unchallenged subjectivity. In short: the worst of both tendencies.

The sullied Sophia, the wandering whore, Sophia Prunikos, can never wed the Christ and receive her deserved syzygy with the divine consort. Only the Virgin Sophia may, and this depends entirely on us and the efforts we choose to make on her behalf. The Brothers of the Left would strongly prefer that we give our true oracular potency away in false attributions to vague, uncredentialed spiritual presences just across the threshold. They would have us miss the Christ within us by misattributing the voice of the Logos to other spiritual beings, and not to ourselves. Equally effective would be a state of self-inflation so bilious as to identify literally with the resurrected Christ and to believe one is the Christ's sole representative. They would have us fail in the transition from Theo-Sophia to Anthropos-Sophia, and to keep giving entranced voice to disembodied intelligences of ambivalent intent. What we must do, if we are to pass through this crucial test in the life of the consciousness soul, is to individualize the Christ Impulse, to make it a living soul power within us, the very life of the larynx.

Women and men are spontaneously speaking forth words of the Spirit. The trouble is, the "eternal, creating wisdom" of the Logos is almost completely lost within the unclarified, passionate body of Lower Sophia. Borrowing the Gnostic imagery, we might say that contemporary channelers speak like the Gnostic Demiurge Ialdabaoth, "impious in his arrogance," unaware of the existence of yet two higher, far more exalted beings, "Man" (the Cosmic Human or Anthropos) and Son of Man, the Christ. In this sense, the phenomena of oracular channeling recreates the negative aspects of Ialdabaoth, remythologizing the Gnostic usurper as a new cultural icon. Like the Ialdabaoth of Gnostic myth, the contemporary channeler reveling at the psychic garden party is bound for a radical sobering.

After all, the impious Demiurge was crushed and humbled when his mother, Divine Sophia, cast the reflection of Anthropos on the waters and put Ialdabaoth in his proper place. Similarly, the living example of a woman or man who truly speaks as the Logos, who speaks awake, warmly, lucidly, from within the presence of the Christ, from the Sun-body as the Star of humanity, from within the Pentecostal emerald, in full command of the Akashic time chronicles, from out of a Christed larynx—such an example will have the same chastening effect on this meretricious cultural icon as it had on Ialdabaoth waking up to the diviner realities beyond his ken. In our own authentic moment of the Virgin Sophia speaking as the Logos, we apprehend the sleeping trance prophet as nothing more than an epistemological imposter. The long-awaited emergence of a new state-of-the-art always refigures the entire field.

In our moment of authentic Spirit-permeated speaking, of speaking as the Logos, what speech is it? What is the language we speak? According to Valentin Tomberg, that speech is the Pentecostal speaking of the "risen soul." It is the voice of the ascended Christ, speaking a "language which was a kind of resurrection of the original human speech...not of the divided nations, but of the human soul."[13] Steiner took this perception a step further. The Christ spoke the speech of the Elohim, the six Sun-spirits of Form whose combined focus made the Logos manifest as the Christ in flesh. The Christ "taught as the Exousiai teach," proclaimed the original text of the Gospel of St. Mark, which means

Christ Jesus spoke with the power of the Elohim. "It was their forces in the body of Christ which enabled Him to teach 'with authority.'"[14]

The speech of the Elohim is Sun-speech. Their etheric syllables are broadcast by the dodecahedral imaginative Form of Love, the emerald Foundation Stone. Earlier I said that at dawn on Harmonic Convergence morning, Lucifer returned to Earth plumed with the Elohim. Another way of presenting this same supersensible reality is to say that the Elohim accompanying Lucifer represented the sixfold Sun-heart of Lucifer, the six facets on the emerald. The creative force of the Elohim expresses itself through Lucifer in the sixfold facets of the emerald. It is as if each Elohim speaks through one facet of the six-sided cube-emerald. The emerald is thus the Elohim's *Sun-larynx*. The Sun speaks through this emerald Foundation Stone, and by speaks, I mean creates. The emerald is the larynx of the Sun-Body of the Elohim. It is how they speak worlds and humans into creation: speech creates, the Word is made flesh and matter.

The speech of the Elohim is literally Pentecostal speech, the overfull momentum of the *fiftieth* moving inexorably into speaking. The word Pentecost literally means "the fiftieth." Why is Pentecost the fiftieth? It is not the fiftieth solely because it is observed fifty calendar days after Easter. It is the fiftieth for a geometric reason. The sum of the facets of the five Platonic Solids (the archetypal polygonal forms of the elemental passions of Lower Sophia from which the material world was precipitated) is fifty. Here is the arithmetic of the faces of matter: tetrahedron/fire, 4; cube/earth, 6; octahedron/air, 8; dodecahedron/ether, 12; icosahedron/water, 20. The Pentecostal summation is 50. The five states of matter have fifty faces; when the fiftieth is achieved, Pentecost is possible. It is as if the fivefold passionate nature of Lower Sophia, the *fiftieth* of Sophia, is then seized by the Logos to become the mouthpiece for the Elohim in a cosmic paroxysm of Sun-speaking resounding through the green speech-broadcasting "walls" of the emerald.[15]

Insofar as the configuration of the Earth's etheric anatomy is an emerald cube/dodecahedron, this is the House of Speech for the Elohim and the Mystery center for World Pentecost. Through the planetary emerald, not just the Upper Room, but the entire Earth is the location for World Pentecost. Let me suggest an image here. Imagine yourself to be the Earth itself, the blue-white planetary globe. You perceive that your body is situated within a geometric structure, a six-sided double-terminated green crystal or an emerald cube, depending on your perspective. Each of the six facets is like a translucent window; in each window is an Elohim, a vast spiritual being in the form of an angel who is speaking. Their speech is what creates the geometric shape of the green hexagon in the first place. Their speech is the emerald cube surrounding you, which is to say, your etheric dimension, your Sun-body which transmits formative forces to your physical planetary body and its biospheric life. As a planetary being, you live within a House of Speech spoken by the Elohim Sun-spirits. As such, you live within a cosmic larynx. This Sun-larynx is the source of your life. It is the Foundation Stone of your life. When you raise your perceptions to this etheric imagination, you bring yourself to the verge of the fiftieth, to the point of Pentecostal cognition from the etheric dodecahedron. Inspired by the Elohim, words form on the tip of your tongue. You are poised to speak on behalf of the five states of matter. With enough practice and guidance, you can do what the Elohim do. That's the secret of the larynx, of the fiftieth of Pentecost.

The Pentecostal fiftieth is the full oracular force of the purified Achamod, the wise, chaste, pure Virgin Sophia moved to speech. At Pentecost, the Logos permeates the fiftieth of Sophia and she regains her divine syzygy through Elohimic speech. The fiftieth of Sophia, expressed geometrically, is the dodecahedral Foundation Stone, the emerald Heart of Lucifer, in which the other four Platonic Solids are polygonally implicit. The fiftieth is the completion of the nest of polyhedra, or the full, sequential generation of the five states of matter. The emerald is the Sun larynx of the Elohim. It's the means by which they create entire worlds, through which they translate the Word as Life into the Word as Flesh.

Through speaking, the Elohim shift the Logos as etheric Life within the emerald into the Logos as biological Life in the flesh. The Elohim turn the emerald inside out; they implant the body of the Sun in the body of flesh. Through this Elohimic translation, we move from life within the emerald Sun to life under the dodecahderal Sun. We shift from living inside the Sun to the Sun living inside us. The emerald is the swinging door between inner and outer Sun. The emerald door swings open in response to Logos-speaking: the Elohim speak it open as the Logos within the Sun; we speak it open as the Sun-Logos within humanity. Thus the Solar Logos is the Word made manifest, the energy of the Sun expressed through communication.

Christ spoke the speech of the Elohim with authority. We, too, can speak with Logos authority following our Pentecostal inspiration. We, too, can speak the living speech of the Elohim. This is what the consciousness soul, the etheric perception of the Christ, the Michaelic dawn, Aquarian spirituality, and Anthroposophy itself are all about: speaking individually with true authority. When we speak with authority, we speak as *authors*—creators, originators, writing worlds into being through living speech. Christ-inspired speech is truly world-creative, just as St. John declared: In the Beginning was the Word. The six Sun Elohim, focused as one, manifested the Logos in flesh. The Word was made flesh through Elohim speech. The Elohim spoke authoritatively and the Christ became flesh. Similarly, our Christ-inspired human speech is authorial. Our speech is eurythmic, with a beautiful, harmonious rhythm. Eurythmy, Steiner's art of the larynx, is central to our speaking the imagination of Pentecost.

Our speaking recreates the etheric human being as a "very complicated air-form," said Steiner. In his lectures on eurythmy as visible speech in 1924, he indicated that as we speak the alphabet out loud from *a* to *z*, this intonation creates a very complicated air-form made of letters, a complex word. This word form is the human etheric body itself; the etheric body is woven of spoken letters, the origins of the eurythmy gestures. My body in effect is made of the alphabet. When the etheric body speaks, it doesn't use the tongue but the limbs; when the larynx makes words, the etheric body dances them. "This etheric man is the Word which contains within it the entire alphabet, born from out of the creative human larynx. So if we were to go through the whole alphabet, we should in the consecutive sounds, unfold the mystery of man. In speech the human being himself is fashioned." The etheric body represents the birth of an air-form through the creative larynx, "a birth of the whole etheric man when the alphabet is spoken aloud," said Steiner.[16] After all, *In the beginning was the Word,* our Western traditions continually remind us, just as the Eastern spiritualities emphasize the creative force of mantras. But with Steiner's astounding observation, this near platitude suddenly springs into meaning. "God eurythmetizes, and as the result of His eurythmy there arises the form of man."[17]

The etheric human being is a revelation of the spoken Word comprising the entire alphabet. The etheric body is a complex sentence made of the letters of the alphabet. The etheric body is authored through the Sun-speech of the Elohim as a body made of words. The etheric human, then, is the word made of the complete spoken alphabet. The Human is spoken forth, not written; the creative language is oral, the meaning is tonal. Speech is implicit in the origin of the human being. Steiner prophesied that one day the human larynx would replace the genitals as the reproductive organ for generating new human life. He talked about the "womb of the Word," and how through the creative larynx a birth continuously takes place in the process of speech. "Speech is always the bringing to birth of parts of the etheric man. The etheric larynx and its sheath, the physical larynx, are a metamorphosis of the uterus."[18]

This primogenitive speaking is eternally present in the human etheric body as the formative intelligence of the Sun. Living speech recreates the etheric, thoughtful, thinking human. This means that speaking, arising out of the undistorted imaginations of Sophia, redeems, resurrects, and recreates the etheric Sun-body of the human. We resurrect our thoughts through living speech and launch ourselves back to the Sun through a kind of verbal petard. This is the fruit of Anthroposophy: *Wisdom In the Human Speaking the redeemed Human out of the larynx womb of the Word.* This is the Imagination of Pentecost, a speaking forth of world-creating living pictures carried on the Logos-force of human words.

The dodecahedral larynx filled with the intelligence of the Akashic time chronicles and the cosmic imaginations of Sophia, the Sun as cosmic Elohimic larynx, the emerald Foundation Stone as the vocal cords of the Sun—in these images we find the key to the redemption of living etheric thinking for that life of the constantly weaving, always new, always newly revealing, cosmic imagination of Sophia quickened by the Logos into spontaneous creative speaking. Through this we perform true acts of manas, of world-positing, recreating the world and the Human as new intelligent air-forms. The Gnostics might say this marks the recovery of the First Anthropos, the "Begetter, Self-Perfected Mind," the one who thinks, and through thinking, creates, manasically positing the world, sending forth the new creation as "the barque of air." Or, as the contemporary Hungarian anthroposophist Georg Kühlewind eloquently puts it, "The world consists entirely of words, of communicability. The world is a transparent, *speaking* world."[19]

Since the alphabet is an expression of the Mystery of the Human, we need to appreciate its cosmic grammar of vowels and consonants. Grammar, we understand, is profoundly generative. The Mystery of the Human as alphabet implicates the cosmos. "All the single letters of the alphabet are actually formed as images of what lives in the cosmos," said Steiner. The totality of the spoken alphabet is the "original primal sentence," the "lost archetypal word" through which the divine revealed itself to humanity and for which the esoteric community has constantly sought. The cosmos reveals itself through the spoken word. Stars scintillate meaningfully within each letter of the cosmic script. Even today in our intensely materialistic milieu of language in service of commerce, the alphabet can be revelatory. It is all a question of how we speak, of what moves in us as we speak and from us out into the world. The stars of the cosmos speak through us; our words are made of their spiritual substance; we birth the constellations and planets on Earth when we speak as the Logos. This means we can retrace our steps back "to times when cosmic being still revealed itself in the inner organism of speech."[20]

Clairaudient perception of the human etheric and physical body, said Steiner, uncovers the tones of the cosmos, also called the Music of the Spheres, sounding in two-part harmony. Clairaudiently, in our etheric Sun-body and physical Saturn-body, we hear the Music of the Spheres speaking in tones. The vowels represent the movements of the planets sounding in the etheric body, while the consonants represent the fixed stars of the zodiac echoing in the physical body. In vowels, we have the planets;

in consonants, the stars. The zodiacal consonants echo in the physical body, while the planetary movements sing vowels in the etheric; the astral body records the experiences of the planets in motion, and the Ego "is the perception of the echo of the Zodiac," said Steiner. Tones or occult music embody us, at these four levels of our being.

With this understanding of the orchestration of the human musical bodies, we pass the threshold into what Steiner called "concrete cosmic speech." The human is a cosmic musical instrument. The Ego represents the compression into a single point of consciousness of everything that fills out the whole of measureless cosmic space. "We think we have an individual human being in front of us, but this individual is a picture, on a certain spot, of the whole world." The Human, Steiner said, "is an actual pictured microcosm of the reality of the macrocosm."[21] The alphabet, at least long ago in the time of the "original, instinctive human wisdom," was a revelation of astronomy; through contemplation of individual letters, humans gained acquaintance with the spiritual essence of individual stars as these stars lived in them. The Music of the Spheres was a wonderful heuristic cosmic instrument, "and behind it are the gods of the planets who play upon this instrument of the zodiac."[22] Each planet causes a constellation to resound differently, said Steiner.[23] The human organism, sculpturally appreciated, is also a musical instrument, made of the twelve primeval consonants shaped sculpturally according to earth conditions. But these earthly consonants perpetually long for the "soulful" vowels alive in the imaginative realm—"a tonal world colored in a variety of ways in vowels...a singing world of vowels."[24] This singing world of soulful vowels has another nuance. Just as each letter of the alphabet is a revelation of the life of an individual star, so, too, an individual human's form represents the toning of a spiritual "word." Each instrument, though generically identical (from the Human template), is yet individually unique (as karmic humans). The soul signature of each human is an "infinitely expressive word, a warmth filled creative word." Each soul word is a revelation to the cosmos of what that individual human uniquely is, a revelation of precisely the way that I AM! is in that soul individuality. Each soul word is the Logos individualized as each human speaks forth his or her own being, said

Steiner. The Human is the symphony of the creative Word and the perpetual revelation of the Logos. "The human souls are themselves words; their symphony is the symphony of the spoken Cosmic Word in its very being."[25]

This soul word is an expression of the individualized Logos, the fruit of individually experienced Pentecost; but the collectivity of the individual soul words, the symphony of the creative Word, represents the act of World Pentecost. It represents the new, perpetual Christmas Meeting within the Foundation Stone. Pentecostal speech—lucid, articulate, transmissive—is symphonic. The Foundation Stone is the House of symphonic speech. Emeralds reverberate across the human landscape. That is why Steiner established the physical Goetheanum upon the dodecahedral stone at Dornach Hill. The Goetheanum would be synecdochal as the House of Speech (*Haus der Sprache*, Steiner called it) for the remainder of the epoch of the consciousness soul. The Goetheanum, as the seed Steiner planted within the Aquarian emerald of Dornach Hill, will itself seed the planet in the coming time with the living impulse of *anthroposophical speaking*.

It all turns on our speaking. The universe gives us the Logos. The Earth endows us with speech. The Christ restores to us the living source of speech. Pentecost inspires us to speak syllables of the Sun through the physical larynx. Then we speak, spontaneously, manasically, awake in our I-consciousness, awakened to our I-consciousness through this speaking as the Logos. We awaken through speaking. The voice rouses us from slumber into apocalyptic clairvoyance. Our Logos-speech restores the "lost unison between thinking and speaking," a fusion originally intended for humanity by the Elohim at the beginning of time and human phylogenetic incarnation.

The Fall of the Human sundered thinking from speaking and the world has been cognitively cleaved ever since. Through the primordial cleavage of Lucifer in the descent of humankind into visibility, the *concept* was unreeved from the *sounds* of language; the sound-tones no longer carried the pictorial meaning. Words lost their life, intelligence degenerated into intellectuality, what was vivid became abstract. Speaking lost its *generative* potency and the Sun-speaking Elohim were exiled from the Earth. The word-sword of the Logos was broken. Eschenbach's *Parzival* describes a sword broken into pieces that must be welded together again by the Grail Knight. The word-sword, the power of the spoken voice, personified as an etheric sword, has atrophied, lost its powers and keen edge, shattered. The Knight must take the sword back to the Well of Kunneware, the source of a magic spring where the sword "will become whole again from the flow of water." The living (etheric) waters of the Logos heal the broken word-sword. The pieces of the sword must be refitted precisely, to reconstitute the signs of the zodiac, originally inscribed on the blade. Further, the Knight must perform the task beneath the rock and before daylight, which is to say, with supersensible cognition not based on sensory-world thinking. Then there is the matter of the magic spell, without which the proceedings will be fruitless. "For the magic spell which welds together the shattered word-sword is LOVE, the Love of Christ, the word made flesh."[26]

Why must the word-sword be restored? The answer to this basic question highlights the central purpose of the Grail Quest and Arthurian mythos. The sword must be reforged to heal Anfortas, the wounded Fisher King, who once misused the sword and grievously wounded himself in the groin. Anfortas' misuse of the divine sword was called the Dolorous Stroke. As such, he lost his generative powers, turned his kingdom into the Wasteland, and languished for years in the Grail Castle. The vital link between his root chakra (source of the creative) and his brow and crown chakras (source of divine insight) is impaired. As a result of this wound he cannot remember his divine origin; his memory function, based in his etheric body, is not functioning. He lives in the presence of the Grail (in a body with the emerald Foundation Stone), but lacks the power (the generative force of the Logos) to use the Grail to heal himself. Once the sword was a single blade, once speaking and thinking were one generative force, once humankind had the Logos—potency of the gods—but the King (nascent I-consciousness) misused it, and now it is a broken sword. Only the Christed Grail Knight, Parzival—the evolved human, the Mystery initiate, in whom "Not I, but the Christ in me," is the functional truth—has the consummate spiritual skill to wield the word-sword in a healing way. Through Parzival, the *Maimed* Fisher King becomes, once again, the *Rich* Fisher King.

Whose sword was this originally? It was the Elohim's, humanity's prime-parents, as the Gnostic myths tell us: lion-faced Ialdabaoth, the Demiurge. After all, their world-creating powers (word-sword or the Sun-larynx of the emerald) were awesome, as the Gnostic texts tell us. "Now the prime parent Ialdabaoth, since he possessed great authorities, created heavens for each of his offspring through verbal expression—created them beautiful, as dwelling places—and in each heaven he created great glories, seven times excellent."[27] But the Elohim's great verbal authority would be surpassed one day by that of Adam, immortal Human of light, the one to come who would be "mightier" than they. As the Gnostics recount it, Ialdabaoth was terribly upset with this prospect and considerably "jealous." In particular, Ialdabaoth disliked Adam because he was luminous with the Epinoia (Sophia's awakening light), "he could think better than they," and he would not, like them, be ignorant of "whence he had come into being." Adam's thinking "was superior to all those who had made him."[28]

It is always daunting for us humans to remember that in many respects humanity is the unalloyed envy of the creator gods, especially the Elohim, our "prime parents"—who have lived so closely with us over the eons since our phylogenetic incarnation. The Elohim may have divine awareness, but they lack self-awareness, which is a form of independence, and, because of this, the option of freely willed spiritual activity. They *must* act in accord with the Good, unlike humans who may choose to, or not. The Elohim may be close to God, but as humans we may become one with Divinity while in physical base; this the Elohim cannot do. Nor can they lawfully enter into human form and enjoy that superiority in thinking, except, perhaps, on special commission, and only for limited periods, as in the world epoch of the Giants. And, most galling for Ialdabaoth, humans potentially can "think better" which means, wield the word-sword with greater skill, authority, and freely given Love than their prime parents.

The Biblical image of the human David besting the giant Goliath (the Philistine) and *taking his sword* perfectly illustrates this relationship. "Then David ran and stood over the Philistine, and took his sword and drew it out of its sheath, and killed him, and cut off his head with it." (1 Samuel 17: 50) The tableau is repeated later in the Grail tradition when King Arthur outfights "the fiercest giant" at St. Michael's Mount in Cornwall. Defeating the giant, Arthur "cuts off his genitors," then orders Sir Kay "to smite off the giant's head and to set it upon a truncheon of a spear, and bear it to Sir Howell, and tell him that his enemy was slain."[29] In either case, we see dramatized the reluctant transmission of the lawful right to use the word-sword from Elohim to initiate human.

Perhaps the Gnostic texts, the Biblical account, and the Grail accounts cast the Elohim unfairly in a truculent, adversarial relationship to the true disposition of cosmic intelligence, as represented by the word-sword. After all, they comprise the corona on the emerald crown of Lucifer and, as such, they are committed to the successful translation of the force of the Logos in speech from the supersensible Human to the earthly human. So, the rediscovery of the Foundation Stone in the epoch of the Michaelic consciousness soul reverses their exile from human consciousness. The Mystery of Golgotha gave the Earth and humanity the evolutionary momentum of the Logos. The Apostolic Pentecost exemplified the way to reeve speaking with thinking, but the coming World Pentecost will be its planetary fulfillment. Through the recovery of living speech, once again men and women will speak words "permeated with their innermost feelings," experiencing the mental image within the sound. That's because the meaning and tone ethers were restored to humanity with the resurrection of the Holy Ghost at Golgotha, and they are now at our service. With the restoration of the meaning and tone ethers, speaking is reunited with thinking; the word-sword is reforged and the human larynx becomes primogenitive, capable of generating etheric forms, of healing the human phantom.

With the healing of the primordial cleavage of Lucifer, what had been his apparent appropriation of the imaginations of Sophia was now transmuted into a *transmission* of the Manas revelations of Sophia. Lucifer transmits the imaginations of Sophia permeated with the force of the Logos—and we, individual human beings, speak them, weaving a new dynamic imagination. From the moment of Golgotha onward, the Sophia imagination permeated the Logos sound, and cosmic intelligence was reborn as human speaking. The Imagination of Pentecost is truly a speaking, an anthroposophical speaking: Sophia in the Human speaking humanly. The mental image, the concept, the imagination, is "carried on the wings of the word," as the cleft between speaking and forming mental images is sealed.[30] The restoration of thinking and speaking through the Imagination of Pentecost is Anthroposophy renewed and fulfilled as Wisdom In the Human Speaking. The imagination is the living, creative unison of thinking and speaking, inspired in the moment of Pentecost within the Sun-Mystery temple of the emerald, in its full generative, world-creating potency. Through Pentecost, Sophia regains her syzygy with Christ Jesus; through the Imagination of Pentecost, we give speech to Sophia who speaks the Human and the World anew into being.

A living speaking is speech in which the conceptual is one with the sounds, in which human words impart this twofold reality, weaving living imaginations in the cognition of listeners. The etheric is born in Earth, as a life medium. Ideally, any human language can carry the force of the Logos through living imaginations, which is why the Biblical description of Pentecost said that the multitude was confounded "because that every man heard them speak in his own language." (Acts 2:8) As Georg Kühlewind says, when we become aware of the Logos, we discover that all words lead back to the Logos. The Logos sounds within each word, each sentence, as a tonal barque of air set forth by the Christ-inspired speaker. The Word rings true in each word as the Logos individualizes through spoken language. We gain "a living experience of what resides in a sound of speech." Pentecost is "a resounding word-filled event. The Spirit is all word, not sight."[31]

The revelation awaiting us is actually within the humanly incarnate context as we illumine the Human—speak the Human forth—through our living speaking. The supersensibly ineffable reveals itself in speaking, through our verbal acts. The Unbegotten Father surprises us by his presence within matter. The Logos seizes the larynx and we give speech that testifies to the Christ's presence in our human beingness. Speech is testimonial to the Father's presence in matter. Speech is healing, restitutive. The Star conducts us to the Christ within the emerald, and the Christ takes us back to the Father, the Star Absolute. We understand the radical insight moving in Steiner when he wrote *Individualism in Philosophy*. At this dilation of consciousness, we must take complete responsibility for our manasic potency as world-creators.

Any of us may say: When I speak as the Logos, I am the authority of last resort. Through the purity of the Logos we exhibit neither the self-inflation of Lucifer nor the materialist contraction of Ahriman. In this way we talk our way out of the tight corner of matter, out of Sophia's polygonal nest of the elements, out to the place of the *fiftieth*, where suddenly we are turned—converted—to speech.

The world unconditionally requires this of us. At this stage in human evolution, as we mature into the consciousness soul, and at this stage in our planetary evolution, as Gaia matures towards her Jupiter phase as a Christed star, the process requires more than ever that we speak creatively as the Logos. It insists that we speak from what Steiner called "the living Christ-Impulse, the speech-forming power," and, through this Logos force, that we *re-speak the world*. From out of the emerald larynx, the dodecahedral imaginative Form of Love, we declare the Foundation Stone for a new world, a new humanity. We reunite the Earth with the Sun through our living speech. At the beginning of Time, the Sun was turned inside out revealing the Earth. This time we turn the Earth inside out to uncover the Sun. As always, the emerald is the means, the interface between dimensional expressions of the same reality. It is crucial that we reveal the Sun within Earth, within the human, through speaking, here at the close of the twentieth century and the second post-Golgotha millennium.

In large measure, this is why we are here on Earth in the first place. It's our phylogenetic raison d'etre. Humankind has a spiritual task to discharge on Earth. As we know, the human being is the life of the entire cosmos; the zodiacal consonants, the planetary vowels, the musical tones of the supersensible hierachical spheres—all these live in us. The Earth needs to speak to the cosmos. The Earth in its etheric anatomy lives within the emerald Foundation Stone; this means the Earth is a planetary larynx. When the Logos moves us to speak, we speak on behalf of the Earth. More precisely, we speak as the Elohim through the Earth as planetary larynx. Our Logos—inspired speaking *is* the planet speaking to the cosmos. The dodecahedral imaginative Form of Love expressed as planet Earth is our authorial voice speaking in the cosmos.

This isn't human largesse or self-aggrandizement on a monstrous scale by any means. Our authorial role was mandated by Lucifer and the Elohim at the phylogenetic beginning of Time when they implanted the emerald within each human individuality. Our task as humankind living on Earth is to mature into accepting the responsibility of the Elohim to recreate our host planet through manasic speech, to give speech to Sophia through her reflection, Gaia. The intelligence of the Earth star is the Human itself, declared Steiner. The Human is Lord of the Earth because the Earth is made in the Human's likeness. As we noted in an earlier chapter, the design principle of the etheric geography of Earth is astro-Sophia, the wisdom of Sophia expressed in stars. When we clairvoyantly penetrate the etheric anatomy of Earth, we find the galaxy; and when we intuit the essential morphology of the galaxy living on Earth, we behold the divine image of the Human cast upon the waters. And when we speak as the Logos from a prepared geomantic context such as Dornach—or any of the hundreds of zodiacal geopoints around the planet—we speak on behalf of the Cosmic Human and its planetary imprint. "The all-essential causes of what happens on the earth do not lie outside man; they lie within mankind. The truth is that the responsibility for the course of earth existence through ages of cosmic time, lies with humanity."[32]

Our task as the resident spiritual intelligence of the planet is to make the Earth the planet of Love, said Steiner. Love is the fruit of the Christed initiation within the emerald. It is the Logos force that connects everything in the interdependent web of being—human, planetary, cosmic, universal. When we bring this same energy of universal connection into our speaking, we permeate the world with Love. This task must be fulfilled yet we must willingly, freely, voluntarily comply. We are compelled to act freely. The hierarchies expect us to nourish the cosmos as our part in the process of reciprocal maintenance. The mission of the Earth, Steiner explained, is to achieve the perfect equilibrium among three antecedent elements in cosmic evolution. These are the Saturn mission, which is the imprinting of will; the Sun-mission, which is the imprinting of thought; and the Moon-mission, the imprinting of feeling. These three antecedent cosmic missions of willing, thinking, and feeling are made coherent through I-consciousness, the unique endowment for Earth. All things return to the Logos. Love is the new fourth element that connects willing, thinking, and feeling. "Love can only develop in a world when an absolute equilibrium comes about between the three forces." And Love can be expressed only in the context of an awakened I-consciousness.[33]

Our task, then, is to move in freedom towards Love. Our eventual success in this divinely ordained assignment establishes humanity as the tenth hierarchy, as the Spirit of Freedom and Love. What makes Love possible? That each human be in possession of I-consciousness, that each be cognitively independent, capable of *Freiheit*. "The bearer of love can only be the independent ego which develops by degrees in the course of evolution of the Earth," said Steiner.

This has perennially been the Michaelic goal since the phylogenetic descent of the Human into Lemurian materiality.[34] Michael awaits this complete incarnation of unrestricted, undistorted cosmic intelligence into the I-consciousness of men and women biologically individualized, living on Earth. Michael, the psychopomp of the Logos, puts the Logos *in* the intelligence. The Christ warms and spiritualizes the intelligence with the Love of the Unbegotten Father. The Logos creates loving bonds among individual humans, connecting them emerald to emerald. The Christ is the historical "living Force," always present, who exemplifies freedom of the heart and freely willed fraternity. The Christ knits men and women fraternally through their participation in the emerald Foundation Stone, the threshold of the Imagination of Pentecost. "And men will learn to understand this bond of brother-love as perfected spiritualized Christianity."[35]

This is the Logos collegiality of the Foundation Stone and the aspiration of Anthroposophy. This fraternity from emerald to emerald will feed not only the Earth but the cosmos, that "gigantic organism which needs nourishment." The cosmos needs new incentives for the movement of its stars, Steiner said, and this nourishment has to come from our illumined, independent human experiences. Our spiritual exaltation is food for the angels. Cosmos becomes the Human and the Human becomes cosmos in a perpetual recycling.

The cosmos, after all, is essentially the body of the Holy Ghost extrapolated across measureless space. Just as all words lead back to the Logos, so all emeralds return to the one emerald, to the Heart of the Human. The original Foundation Stone is the heart of the Holy Ghost, the triune cosmic being of the Human, the *One Who Thinks*, as mediated through Michael, Sophia, and Lucifer. Anthroposophy, as Steiner said, is a cosmic event. The Imagination of Pentecost is the planetary fulfillment of the cosmic aspiration of Anthroposophy to manifest *Wisdom In the Human Speaking* on Earth.

NOTES

CHAPTER 1

1. Stahl, "Channel Hopping," *Playboy,* December 1987, 131.
2. Vaz, *Spirit in the Land: Beyond Time and Space with America's Channelers,* 13.
3. Sullivan, "New Age to Dawn in August, Seers Say, and Malibu is Ready," *Wall Street Journal,* June 23, 1987.
4. Simmons, *The Emerging New Age.*
5. Ostling, "The Church Search," *Time,* April 5, 1993.
6. Steinfels, "Conversations: Charting the Currents of Belief for the Generation that Rebelled," *The New York Times,* May 30, 1993. See also: Wade Clark Roof, *A Generation of Seekers: The Spiritual Journeys of the Baby Boom Generation,* Harper-San Francisco, 1993.
7. Kosmin, Barry A., and Lachman, Seymour P. *One Nation Under God: Religion in Contemporary American Society.* Harmony Books, New York, 1993.
8. Webb, "The Occult Establishment," in *Not Necessarily the New Age* ed. Robert Basil, 54–83.
9. Donner, *Being-in-Dreaming: An Initiation into the Sorcerer's World;* and Abelar, *The Sorcerer's Crossing: A Woman's Journey;* Valencia and Kent, *Queen of Dreams: The Story of a Yaqui Dreaming Woman.*
10. Johnston, David. "Spiritual Seekers Borrow Indian Ways," *The New York Times,* December 27, 1993.
11. McKenna, *True Hallucinations;* and *The Archaic Revival.* See also: "Tripping but Not Falling," Trip Gabriel, *The New York Times,* May 2, 1993, which calls McKenna "the Timothy Leary (and much more) of the discreetly psychedelic 90s" and "an aging Deadhead with some tightly reasoned, seemingly preposterous notions" which he frequently presents to audiences of equal mixture of "psychonauts, cyberpunks, and slightly befuddled mycologists."
12. Goswami, *The Self-Aware Universe—How Consciousness Creates the Material World.*
13. Zajonc, *Catching the Light: The Entwined History of Light and Mind.*
14. Leviton, Richard. "God Incarnate," *Yoga Journal,* January/February 1994.
15. Markides, *The Magus of Strovolos: The Extraordinary World of a Spiritual Healer; Homage to the Sun: The Wisdom of the Magus of Strovolos; Fire in the Heart: Healers, Sages and Mystics.* See also Richard Leviton, "Journey to the Magi: An Interview with Kyriacos Markides."
16. Specifically, Sophy Burnham's *A Book of Angels* (566,000 copies sold) and *Angel Letters* (200,000 copies); *Ask Your Angels* (270,000 copies) by Timothy Wyllie, Alma Daniel, Andrew Ramer; Malcolm Godwin's *Angels, An Endangered Species;* Joan Webster Anderson's *Where Angels Walk: True Stories of Heavenly Visitors* (published 1992; 400,000 copies sold by the end of 1993); a quartet of angel studies by Terry Lynn Taylor including *Messengers of LIght, Guardians of Hope, Answers from the Angels* (total sales: 320,000 copies); *Touched by Angels* (65,000 copies) by Eileen Elias Freeman; *Angels and Aliens,* by Keith Thompson (1991). Since it was first published in 1975, Billy Graham's *Angels: God's Secret Agents* has sold 2.6 million copies. Angels gained prominent, even iconic,

expression on Broadway in 1993. Tony Kushner won the 1993 Pulitzer Prize (and 9 Tony awards) for his Broadway play *Angels in America: Millennium Approaches*, which was about homosexuals, AIDS, and the nation's spiritual hypocrisy, and in which an angel appears on stage at the end of the play's first part... crashing through a bedroom ceiling where a young man lies dying of AIDS. With an impassive expression, the angel declares: "Greetings, prophet; the great work begins: the messenger has arrived." (See David Richards, "An Epic All Right, But It's the Details and Future that Counts," *The New York Times*, May 16, 1993.) Concurrently on Broadway, in another play called *Morisol* by José Rivera, a guardian angel deserts her human charge to help a rebellion in heaven against an old, dying God. For more on dolphin channeling, see Richard Leviton, "Listening to Kajuba: Communications with the Dolphins."

17. Gibbs, Nancy. "Angels Among Us," *Time*, December 27, 1993.

18. Woodward, Kenneth L. "Angels," *Newsweek*, December 27, 1993.

19. Prager, Emily. "The Dressing Room—New Year's, Angels, and Me," *The New York Times*, December 26, 1993.

20. Hutchison, *Megabrain: New Tools and Techniques for Brain Growth and Mind Expansion*; see also Leviton, "Would the Buddha Use a Mind Machine?"

21. R. U. Sirius, "Editorial," *Mondo 2000*, No. 2, 1990, 9.

22. Elmer-Dewitt, "Cyberpunk!" *Time*, February 8, 1993.

23. Rheingold, *Virtual Reality.*

24. Barlow, "Being in Nothingness," *Mondo 2000*, No 2, 1990, 34–43.

25. Jaron Lanier, in "Jaron Lanier is Virtually Sure," *The New Yorker*, December 27, 1993.

26. Crevier, *AI, The Tumultuous History of the Search for Artificial Intelligence.*

27. For example: *Ghost Story* (1981), *Poltergeist* (1982, with two sequels), *Gremlins* (1984), *Ghostbusters* (1984; and sequel,1989), and *Aliens* (1986; and sequel, 1992), *Beetle Juice* (1988), *Communion* (1989), *Fire in the Sky* (1993).

28. Specifically: *Heaven Can Wait* (1978), *Resurrection* (1980), *Bliss* (1985), *Made in Heaven* (1987), *Heaven* (1987), *Ghost of a Chance* (1987), *Wings of Desire* (1988), *Field of Dreams* (1989), *Always* (1989), *Ghost* (1990), *Jacob's Ladder* (1990), *Flatliners* (1990), *Ghost Dad* (1990), and *Defending Your Life* (1991), *Heart and Souls* (1993), *Faraway, So Close* (1993). There were notable earlier pioneering features about angels: *Gabriel Over the White House* (1933), *Topper* (1937), *It's a Wonderful Life* (1940), *The Bishop's Wife* (1947).

29. Basil, "'A Vast Spiritual Kindergarten:' Talking With Brad Steiger," in *Not Necessarily the New Age*, 226–249.

30. Carman, "One Flew Over the Cuckoo Limb," *San Francisco Chronicle*, October 17, 1986.

31. Gardner, "Isness Is Her Business," *New York Review of Books*, April 19, 1987, 16–19.

32. Ibid.

33. Specifically: Bell Bell, a giggling six-year-old Atlantean; Barking Tree, a deceased Hopi Indian; Matea, a 35,000-year-old black female spice trader; Merlin, the fabled magus of King Arthur's Camelot; and Kajuba, the alleged group-soul of a dolphin pod. From Kathleen Hughes, "For Personal Insights, Try Some Channels Out of this World," *Wall Street Journal*, April 1, 1987.

34. Levine, *U. S. News & World Report*, February 9, 1987; Smith, *Los Angeles Times*, December 5, 1986; Stahl, *Playboy*, December 1987; George Hackett, with Pamela Abramson, "Ramtha: A Voice from Beyond," *Newsweek*,15 December 1986; "She's Having the Time of her Lives," *People Weekly*, January 1987; "Voices from Beyond: The Chanellers," *People Weekly*, January 1987; Otto Friedric, "New Age Harmonies," *Time*, December 7, 1987; Deborah Sontag, "Reverence and Rigidity in the New Age," *The New York Times*, October 5, 1992.

35. Cornell, "Idea of Hell Loses its Wallop," *San Francisco Chronicle*, 28 May 1986, cited in Klimo, *Channeling: Investigations on Receiving Information from Paranormal Sources*, 3.

36. *USA Weekend*, January 9–11, 1987.

37. Greeley, "Mysticism Goes Mainstream," *American Health*, January–February 1987, 47–49, quoted in Basil, *Not Necessarily the New Age*, 10. Also Philip E. Ross, "Science? Nyet" *Scientific American*, June 1991, 17, 20.

38. George Gallup Jr., "The Twilight Zone," excerpted in *Life Times*, No. 5,1988.

39. Melton, "An Interpretive View of the Development of American Religions," in *The Encyclopedia of American Religions*, xix, xlvii.

40. Also: Hilarion, formerly one of Theosophy's revered living Mahatmas (1977); Pretty Flower, a Zulie Indian woman from ancient Arizona, now living in spirit form "to uplift the vibration of the planet toward the light of the universe" (1985); Mafu, a first century Pompeian leper "illumined master, guru and deity unto myself" (1986).

41 . Others include: Jason, a soul unit composed of twelve parts, including the channel as twelfth (1981); the Eternals, "the Holy Spirit, the power of God, Elohim, Yahweh, Krishna, Christ, the total consciousness, the supermind of the All Powerful" (1983); Mentor, "multidimensional beings from another more spiritually evolved plane" (1984); Silver Ray, "from the Supreme Council of Creation in the Omniverse, the creator of your planet and your individual soul" (1985); Telstar, five "interdimensional, intergalactic beings named Adam, John, Miribi, Mikail, and Isadora" (1986).

42. Van Tassel, quoted by Klimo, *Channeling*, 54.

43. Silarra and Savizar are ET walk-ins newly arrived in Sedona, Arizona who began publicizing their cosmic grandeur in New Age media beginning in 1988 as if they were the hottest new starlets in Hollywood. "We are the third team of ET walk-ins who have inhabited these bodies. We are ET masters. We have come here to co-create Heaven on Earth with other masters.... There are millions of us here...in service to Earth's awakening." Their mission began on July 14, 1988 with the "descension of a new spirit for Extraterrestrial Earth Mission.... Soon, Planet Earth will become a Star and all beings that live here will be in Light bodies." Source: Extraterrestrial Earth Mission flyer, P.O. Box 2846, Sedona, AZ 86336, circa 1989.

44. Panshin, *The World Beyond the Hill: Science Fiction and the Quest for Transcendence.*

45. Carey, *The Starseed Transmissions: An Extraterrestrial Report*, 2–4. Also Gitta Mallasz, a Hungarian graphic artist, published a remarkable account of "angel dialogues" received during 1943 in a Nazi concentration camp (*Talking With Angels*, 1979). Julie Redstone, a Ph.D. psychologist and psychic counselor, offered the guidance of the Archangel Michael in *Teaching the Heart to Sing* (1989).

46. "We are dedicated to the full activation of the Angelic Presence upon planet Earth. Our purpose is to serve as facilitators to bring our vast, starry Angelic family together. We shall fly as one sacred white Dove whose combined essence transcends our individual selves as we return home to the Star that we are." From: Solara Antara Amaa-Ra, *The Starry Messenger.*

47. Klimo, *Channeling,* 66.

48. In late 1992 J. Z. Knight was the subject of a lawsuit filed by her fifth husband, who claimed that Ramtha had bullied him into accepting a meager divorce settlement and had dissuaded him from seeking medical attention for AIDS. Allegedly during their business partnership they had grossed up to $4 million a year on Ramtha industries and products. The problematic question for the judge was whether to allow the celebrity spirit Ramtha to testify in the case. "I trusted him implicitly," reflected the former husband of Ramtha. "He was all-knowing and omnipresent." After the court case, he changed his view considerably, contending that Ramtha's attraction was based on "mind control techniques." From Egan, "Worldly and the Spiritual Clash in New Age Divorce," *The New York Times,* September 25, 1992.

49. Spangler, *Channeling in the New Age,* 40.

50. Sanaya Roman, a former California marketing consultant channeling Orin (since 1977), and Duane Packer, a former geophysicist and the mouthpiece for DaBen (since 1982), teamed up to encourage people in "opening to channel." They equated psychic contact with "a high level guide" with "accelerated" spiritual growth, psychic calisthenics with spiritual practice, such that channeling was virtually tantamount to identification with "your Higher Self." For Roman and Packer, channeling was the chic, affordable do-it-yourself guru kit as if they sat poised on the threshold of a channeling franchise. Channeling is egalitarian, said the authors, the essence of a democratic society, and readers were encouraged to open their own mystical boutiques. Strenuous effort was discouraged. "Give yourself permission to have valuable and worthwhile things, such as your spiritual growth, come easily. It takes far less time and energy to grow through joy than to grow through struggle....Spiritual growth does not have to be a step-by-step process; it can be instantaneous.... Spiritual growth is not something you work hard for. How much more fun it would be to trade stories about how easily things came!" From Sanaya Roman, *Spiritual Growth: Being Your Higher Self,* 110,112.

51. Klimo, *Channeling,* 27.

52. Steiner, *From Symptom to Reality in Modern History,* 35,158,159, 187, 188.

53. For a precis of the broad strokes of this argument see Leviton, "The Imagination of Pentecost: Rudolf Steiner & Contemporary Spirituality," *The Quest,* Fall 1993, Vol. 6, No. 3; Leviton, "Die Wahre Basis der Seherschaft," *Esotera,* February 1993; for the full version of the opening anecdote from El Tule, see Leviton, "The Lord of the Tree Returns: A Perspective on the Harmonic Convergence," *Life Times,* No. 5, 1988.

54. These experiences are recounted in my *Joseph's Seed,* Nimitta Press (1994).

55. Steiner, *The Mission of the Archangel Michael.*

56. Stein, *The Ninth Century and the Holy Grail,* xiii.

CHAPTER 2

1. The difference between cognition and perception is important and is at the core of Steiner's epistemology, particularly in his foundational text *The Philosophy of Spiritual Activity.* This is a difficult text, requiring long, careful consideration. For the present let us say perception is the awareness of objects, activities, presences, contents in the world; cognition is the act of knowing, comprehending them, conceptually understanding what they are.

2. Steiner, *The Reappearance of Christ in the Etheric,* 40.

3. The Akashic Records is a term from the occult vocabulary that refers to a meticulous permanent imprint of human physical events upon the *akasha,* or etheric substance of the world. To call this etheric imprint a library is in part metaphorical, but it has a functional reality. Clairvoyants, including Steiner, are able to selectively cognize the records in the Akasha of particular human events at earlier times in history. In a general sense, the etheric records are perceived as something like video tableaux, with greater or lesser detail available, depending on one's interest and ability. The Akashic Records are a planetary version of the memory records in the individual human etheric body which become instantly available to men and women at the point of death, or apparent death (and formerly, through initiation experiences) as in Near-Death Experiences; here an individual is presented with a time picture of one's entire life. The recording medium, again, is the human etheric body. The concept will make more sense both later in this chapter and much later in the book.

4. Steiner, *Karmic Relationships: Esoteric Studies,* Vol. 4, 46.

5. Steiner, *Reappearance,* 7.

6. Steiner, *The Gospel of St. Matthew,* 181, 182, 190.

7. There is some indication of change in this situation. *ReVision* (Spring 1991, Vol. 13, No. 1/Summer 1991, Vol. 14, No. 1) devoted an entire issue to "Rudolf Steiner and American Thought."

8. Steiner, *Planetary Spheres and Their Influence on Man's Life on Earth and in Spiritual Worlds,* 26.

9. Steiner, *The True Nature of the Second Coming,* 35–38.

10. Rudolf Steiner, *The Gospel of St. John and Its Relation to the Other Gospels,* Anthroposophic Press, Spring Valley, NY, 1948, pp. 55–56.

11. Like cognition, the term Logos is also complex, requiring long reflection. Considerably helpful in this work are the insights of Georg Kühlewind in *Becoming Aware of the Logos,* 16, 19, 20, 25, 27: "Logos is not word, law, sense, reason, measure, etc. It is everything that makes these possible: a *common relationship to the world,* a common world. It is the connecting element....*This* world exists *for* and *through* the speaker, through the Logos....The world consists entirely of words, of communicability....The world is a *transparent,* speaking world....The first, primal beginning was the Logos becoming aware of itself.... It is the Logos itself, indeed, that makes possible this sight that penetrates back to the primal beginning....The primal beginning *is* the Logos....-The Creator...in pointing with the word, he shows himself, and is revealed. This is the primal revelation, creation itself." See also Georg Kühlewind's *The Logos Structure of the World: Language as Model of Reality.* Also illuminating is the anthroposophical art of eurythmy in which the word-composition of the human etheric body is revealed through dancelike movements.

12. Steiner, "The Cosmic Word and Individual Man," 1–14.

13. Ibid. 1–14.

14. Steiner, *Eurythmy as Visible Speech*, 26, 27, 29, 36. See Leviton, "The ABCs of Movement."

15. Steiner, *Cosmosophy*, Volume 1, 39–42, 58-61, 125–126.

16. Steiner, *The Principle of Spiritual Economy*, 58.

17. Steiner, "Easter: The Mystery of the Future," in *The Festivals and Their Meaning*, 209.

18. Steiner, *The Occult Movement in the Nineteenth Century*, 109.

19. Steiner, *Toward Imagination: Culture and the Individual*, 36.

20. The temptation to expect and describe the Second coming as imminent physical fact is exceedingly hard to resist at the end of the twentieth century. In January 1993, for example, the devoted followers of Grand Rebbe Menachem Mendel Schneerson, world leader of the Lubavitcher Hasidim, based in Crown Heights, New York, agonized whether their ninety-year-old leader had proclaimed himself the King Messiah. Eventually Schneerson, incapacitated from a stroke, declined the mantle. See Ari L. Goldman, "Debate of Messianic Proportions," *The New York Times*, January 29, 1993.

21. Steiner, *The Destinies of Individuals and of Nations*, 97, 146, 164. Also "The Etheric Body as a Reflection of the Universe," 324.

22. Steiner, *The Presence of the Dead on the Spiritual Path*, 39–41.

23. This is demonstrated in the activities of various Steiner-inspired social initiatives, most notably, in the U.S., by the Fellowship Community of Spring Valley, New York, under the mentorship of Paul Scharff, M.D., and Ann Scharff. Here we see how the social process of community life can support the development of etheric cognition. "We work with the Dead for the sake of their lives. We work with Christ in the ether so we do not kill one another to have etheric forces needed for the new Mysteries," says Paul Scharff. "Social unfolding requires ether forces. The old way, through the slaughter of the innocents, is old-fashioned; the new way is through forgiveness on the way to the Christ." See Richard Leviton, "The Fellowship Community," and Leviton, "Awakening to Community: Fellowship Community's Living Alternative."

24. Steiner, *Presence*, 39.

CHAPTER 3

1. Steiner, *Karmic Relationships: Esoteric Studies*, Vol. 3, 167–169.

2. Steiner, *Anthroposophical Leading Thoughts*, 98–99.

3. Ibid. 54, 76–78, 98–99, 111.

4. Ibid. 84.

5. Ibid. 58.

6. Steiner, *Karmic Relationships: Esoteric Studies*, Vol. 3, 58.

7. Ibid. 6–170.

8. Steiner, *Christianity as Mystical Fact*,

9. Steiner, *Karmic Relationships: Esoteric Studies*, Volume 8, 80–83.

10. Steiner, *How Can Mankind Find the Christ Again?*, 92–95. Steiner, *The Driving Force of Spiritual Powers in World History*, 31–33, 41, 54–57.

11. Steiner, *Karmic Relationships: Esoteric Studies*, Volume 3, 93.

12. Steiner, *Anthroposophical Leading Thoughts*, 122–124.
13. Steiner, *Karmic Relationships: Esoteric Studies*, Volume 4, 89–90, 126 128
14. Steiner, *The Cosmic New Year*, 80–82, 88, 163.
15. Steiner, *Materialism and the Task of Anthroposophy*, 261–62.
16. Steiner, *The Wrong and Right Use of Esoteric Knowledge*, 41.
17. Steiner, *The True Nature of the Second Coming*, 22–23, 29–30, 62.
18. Steiner, *From Jesus to Christ*, 171.
19. Steiner, *Anthroposophical Leading Thoughts*, 138.
20. Throughout this book I will use the term "imagination," which is a key word in anthroposophy. For Steiner this word had a special meaning. It does not mean a fanciful, contrived, conjuration of the mind, an imagining, which has little correspondence to manifest reality. It does mean, or seek to evoke, a living pictorial tableau, a dynamic thought picture generated from the mind or intellectuality of the "gods" as evidence of their cosmic thinking. By definition such an imagination finds its context in the etheric body, through the Sun forces of the Exousiai. An imagination is the thought matrix, the living picture, from which physical reality manifests. Later in the book I will examine the structure and attainment of imaginations in the anthroposophical training.
21. Steiner, *Earthly Knowledge and Heavenly Wisdom*; Steiner, *The Driving Force of Spiritual Powers in World History*, 90–92
22. I am indebted to Paul Scharff, M.D., for this elucidation of the functions of thinking, feeling, and willing, from a March 2, 1993, private correspondence.
23. Steiner, *Materialism and the Task of Anthroposophy*, 178–182, 260. Steiner, *The Driving Force of Spiritual Powers in World History*, 66, 71, 90–92.
24. Steiner, *Anthroposophical Leading Thoughts*, 53–54.
25. Evidence of this struggle to prepare the conditions for the Jupiter phase have already been lucidly summarized, in different terminology, by Benjamin R. Barber, in "Jihad Vs. McWorld," *The Atlantic Monthly*, March 1992. "The two axial principles of our age—tribalism and globalism—clash at every point," Barber writes, as "the planet is falling precipitantly apart *and* coming reluctantly together at the very same moment."
26. Steiner, *The Gospel of St. John*, 115.
27. Steiner, *The Gospel of St. Luke*, 93, 100.
28. Steiner, *Background to the Gospel of St. Mark*, 153–155, 162.
29. Steiner, *The Reappearance of Christ in the Etheric*, 87–88. Steiner, *The True Nature of the Second Coming*, 78–81.
30. Steiner, *Karmic Relationships: Esoteric Studies*, Volume 4, 11–13, 78. Volume 7, 137.

CHAPTER 4

1 Hardinge, *Modern American Spiritualism.*, 29.
2. Ibid. 39.
3. Klimo, *Channeling*, 98.
4. Ibid. 55.
5. Steiner, *Materialism and the Task of Anthroposophy*, 163.
6. Steiner, *The Course of My Life*, 251–252. Also, Steiner, *Materialism and the Task of Anthroposophy*, 163.

7. Steiner, *Friedrich Nietzsche, Fighter for Freedom*, 39, 117, 153, 201.

8. Steiner, *Goethean Science*, 182.

9. Steiner, *Goethe's World View*, 33, 93.

10. Steiner, *The Course of My Life*, 193–198.

11. Steiner, *The Riddle of Man*, 40, 42, 45.

12. Steiner, *Individualism in Philosophy*, 51–52.

13. Steiner, *The Course of My Life*, 278–279.

14. Wilson, *The Occult: A History*, 284.

15. Melton, *The Encyclopedia of American Religions*, 118.

16. Podmore, *Modern Spiritualism: A History and a Criticism*, Volume 1, xii, xiv, 3.

17. Smith, *The Journal of Joseph: The Personal History of a Modern Prophet*, 5.

18. Hardinge, *Modern American Spiritualism*, 27–28.

19. Podmore, *Modern Spiritualism*, Vol. 1, 303, 547.

20. Hardinge, *Modern American Spiritualism*, 273.

21. Fields, *How the Swans Came to the Lake: A Narrative History of Buddhism in America*, 83–84.

22. Podmore, *Modern Spiritualism*, Vol. 1, 194.

23. Wilson, *Poltergeist, A Study in Destructive Haunting*, 137–140.

24. *Podmore, Modern Spiritualism*, Vol. 1, 269, 272, 276.

25. Ibid. 237. Not all spirit writing during the Spiritualist heyday was this involuntary. Andrew Jackson Davis (1826–1910), the "Poughkeepsie seer," medical clairvoyant, and spiritual healer, compiled his reports about a spirit country he called "Summerland." Davis wrote some major texts in this field, such as *The Principles of Nature* (1847) and a five volume treatise, *The Great Harmonia* (1850). In both Davis combined a Swedenborgian cosmology with Charles Fourier socialism. Robert Dale Owen (1801–1877) was a utopian-socialist, journalist, and, formerly, a famous agnostic, who, after a Spiritualist conversion experience, summarized spirit activities in his popular *Footfalls on the Boundary of Another World* (1860).

26. Supernormal or psychic photography in America began on October 5, 1861, in a Boston, Massachusetts, studio when a ghostly figure inexplicably appeared in the self-portraits of amateur photographer William H. Mumler, who identified the apparition as his deceased cousin. Mumler's print attracted great interest among Spiritualists, especially when he affirmed: "This photograph was taken by myself of myself and there was not a living soul in the room beside myself." Mumler described himself as "a medium for taking spirit photographs," and reported a trembling, enervating sensation in his arm during the original photo session indicating, he presumed, a spirit presence. Sets of Mumler's psychic photographs were sold all over the U.S. and Europe and he became the center of considerable controversy. See: Cyril Permutt, *Photographing the Spirit World: Images from Beyond the Spectrum*.

27. Doyle, *The History of Spiritualism*, Volume II, 123–124, 145–146.

28. Podmore, *Modern Spiritualism*, Vol. 1, 246–247.

29. There had been the famous Seeress of Prevorst, Frau Frederic Hauffe. In the 1820s, this German "magnetic somnambule" slipped into prolonged trances in which she demonstrated prophetic clairvoyance, communications with "phantasmal figures" and ghosts of the deceased, movements, noises, disturbances of physical objects, and "extraordinary revelations on things spiritual."

The intermixture of Hauffe's physical phenomena with her revelations, in complement to those from other early nineteenth-century German "magnetists," were foundation stones for European Spiritualism. Ibid. 99–109.

30. Kardec, *Experimental Spiritism—Book on Mediums; or, Guide for Mediums and Invocators*, 420, 33.

31. Klimo, *Channeling*, 101.

32. Kardec, *Experimental Spiritism—Book on Mediums; or, Guide for Mediums and Invocators*, 201.

33. Berger, *The Encyclopedia of Parapsychology and Psychical Research*, 275. Also, Westen, *Channelers: A New Age Directory*, 48.

34. Murphet, *Yankee Beacon of Buddhist Light*, 25.

35. Henry S. Olcott, quoted in Gomes, *The Dawning of the Theosophical Movement*, 32.

36. Doyle, *History of Spiritualism*, Vol. 1, 263.

37. Blavatsky, in Gomes, *Dawning*, 28–31.

38. Ibid. 38.

39. Murphet, *Yankee Beacon of Buddhist Light*, 24.

40. Gomes, *Dawning*, 62.

41. Blavatsky, *Isis Unveiled*, Volume II, 587.

42. Blavatsky, *Collected Writings*, Volume II, 108–110. Also, Ryan, *H.P. Blavatsky and the Theosophical Movement*, 47.

43. Blavatsky, *Collected Writings*, Volume I, 192.

44. Ibid. 53, 73.

45. Henry S. Olcott, quoted in Gomes, *Dawning*, 80.

46. Howell, *The Astral Body and Other Astral Phenomena*, 192–201. Howell further notes that it was common for "quite ordinary people" on the astral plane. "burning with the desire to pose as great world-teachers," to pose as "self-appointed preceptors," imitating the appearance of great adepts, masters, even archangels. At the same time, these mediocre astral spirits would flatter the medium "into believing that he or she is the sole channel for some exclusive and transcendent teaching." In light of this simulacrum, Howell urged his readers to attach no more importance to the communications of such astral poseurs than one does to advice given in the physical world; to subject it, in other words, to the careful examination of conscience and intellect. "A man is no more infallible because he happens to be dead than when he was physically alive."

47. Blavatsky, in Gomes, *Dawning*, 38, 62, 80, 180. A.E. Powell, a Theosophist writing in 1925, (*The Etheric Double*, 88–90) summarized the views of Blavatsky, Leadbeater, Besant, and others, on the matter of mediumship and etheric materializations. The medium is "an abnormally organized person," subject to "nervous strain and disturbance" on account of the ease with which the etheric body separates itself from the physical body. "The Etheric Double, when extruded, largely supplies the physical basis for 'materializations,'" usually observed, clairvoyantly, "oozing" out of the left side of the medium. This extrusion exacts a "terrible drain on the vitality" of the medium, leaving members of a seance afterward in a state of collapse; in many instances, enervated mediums become "drunkards" taking stimulants to restore their vitality loss. Etheric extrusions can happen only in "conditions of perfect passivity" in the medium; further, "any attempt to assert the individuality or to think connectedly, immediately weakens the materialized form, or brings it back into the 'cabinet.'"

48. Blavatsky, *Collected Writings*, Vol. I, 73.

49. Blavatsky, *Collected Writings*, Vol. II, 87–106.

50. Ibid. 500–507.

51. Ibid. 105.

52. Knoche, "Foreword," in Blavatsky, *H.P. Blavatsky to the American Conventions*, ix.

53. H.P. Blavatsky, *Collected Writings*, Vol. II, 6.

54. Wachmeister, *Reminiscences of H.P. Blavatsky and The Secret Doctrine*, 38.

55. Blavatsky, *Collected Writings*, Vol. II, 5–8,18, 26, 29.

56. Manas will concern us in greater detail later in the book. For the present, we may take manas to mean the capacity of thought, all mental faculties and activities, the intellectual, rational function of consciousness, through which we receive impressions of the world, thereby enabling us to doubt, make decisions, and translate will into action.

57. H.P. Blavatsky, *Collected Writings*, Vol. II, 38.

58. Ryan, *H. P. Blavatsky*, 19,110.

59. Blavatsky, quoted in Geoffrey A. Barborka, *H.P. Blavatsky, Tibet and Tulku*, 121.

60. Leadbeater, *The Masters and the Path*, 213.

61. Ibid.186.

62. Mills, *100 Years of Theosophy: A History of the Theosophical Society in America*, 31, 39, 60–62, 70, 100, 99.

63. Jayakar, *Krishnamurti*, 22.

64. Besant, *An Autobiography*, 300.

65. Ibid. 308, 314.

66. Nethercot, *The First Five Lives of Annie Besant*, 304–306.

67. Ibid. 304–306.

68. Ibid. 23, 24, 30, 31, 64.

69. Ibid. 65.

70. Ibid. 65, 73, 75.

71. Steiner, *Awakening to Community*, 47; Steiner, *The Occult Movement in the Nineteenth Century and Its Relation to Modern Culture*, 28.

72. Steiner, *Psychoanalysis & Spiritual Psychology*, 91.

CHAPTER 5

1. Steiner, *Inner Impulses of Evolution*, 73–75.

2. Christopher Bamford, Introduction, in Harrison, *The Transcendental Universe*, 56.

3. There is evidence suggesting the principle lodge behind the eruption of Spiritualism and the opposition to Theosophy and Blavatsky was a group called the Hermetic Brotherhood of Luxor, with roots traceable back to the 1780s in Vienna. The H.B. of L. evidenced a "veiled but continual opposition to the Theosophical Society," writes Christopher Bamford, and "a deep hostility toward the evolutionary spiritual and global perspective Theosophy has come to stand for." Ibid. 37, 52.

4. Harrison, *The Transcendental Universe*, 86.

5. Steiner, *The Karma of Untruthfulness*, Volume I, 226–228. Also, Steiner, *The Occult Movement in the Nineteenth Century*, 15–20.

6 . Harrison, *The Transcendental Universe*, 85.

7. Ibid. 69–70.

8. Steiner, *The Karma of Untruthfulness*, 228–232. Steiner, *The Occult Movement in the Nineteenth Century*, 34–36.

9. Harrison, *The Transcendental Universe*, 87.

10. Steiner, *The Occult Movement*, 106.

11. Steiner, quoted in Christopher Bamford, "Introduction," to Harrison, *The Transcendental Universe*, 17.

12. Steiner, *The Reappearance of Christ in the Etheric*, 147,148, 155, 156.

13. Steiner, *The True Nature of the Second Coming*, 41, 75.

14. Steiner, *The Occult Movement* 31–33.

15. Steiner, *The Course of My Life*, 301.

16. Steiner, *The Philosophy of Spiritual Activity*, 3, 10, 262.

17. Steiner *The Course of My Life*, 250, 251.

18. Steiner, *Earthly Knowledge and Heavenly Wisdom*, 3, 8, 9, 11.

19. Ibid. 3,8,9. Also, *The Driving Force*, 52–55, 58–59, 77–78. Also, *The Course of My Life*, 250–251.

20. Steiner, *Cosmosophy*, Vol. 1, 173–175.

21. Ibid. 106, 121.

22. The term "Human" is used throughout this book in a nongender specific way. Technically, in esoteric terms, the term "Man" is also nongender specific, in acknowledgment of its ancient occult signification to mean the human being (as a male/female composite) as the "one who thinks," from the Sanskrit, Manas. Man is the incarnation of Manas. However, to avoid any misunderstanding or supposition of gender bias, the term "Human" is used instead of "Man." The subject is treated in considerable detail in Section III, "The Holy Ghost Caught in Time."

23. Steiner, *The Course of My Life*, 239–2 41.

24. Steiner, *The Occult Movement*, 26, 114.

25. Prokofieff, *Rudolf Steiner and the Founding of the New Mysteries*, 4.

26. In the view of C. G. Harrison, Blavatsky's *The Secret Doctrine* had many shortcomings. It was "exceedingly faulty, both in regard to its cosmogenesis and its anthropogenesis," it was "tinctured and pervaded" by her personality, while her "passionate invective," "sectarian animus" in favor of all non-Christian systems, and her "perversion" of inconvenient facts, seriously impairs its value as a scientific work, also that "all combine to render her a most unsafe guide to the Higher Wisdom." See: Harrison, *The Transcendental Universe*, 70.

27. Steiner, *The Occult Movement*, 47.

28. Steiner, *Goethe's World View*, 99.

29. Ibid. 155–156, 20–21.

30. Steiner, *Karmic Relationships: Esoteric Studies*, Vol. 4, 95.

31. According to the *Oxford English Dictionary*, the term also appeared in a work by Bailey in 1742 who described anthroposophy as "the knowledge of the nature of man;" then in 1841 a work by T. Hook quipped "our boasted professor of anthroposophy."

32. The linguistic progression of the root *Soph* reveals a metaphysical lesson about the decline of wisdom as a direct revelation. *Soph* (or *Sof, Suf, Suhf*) is

Qabalistic-Hebrew for boundless Time, infinite, unmanifest being. *Sophia* is the feminine expression of divine wisdom but in a fallen state, outside of Soph. *Sophos* is the wise, skilled one, *sopher*, the scribe, bookman of wisdom—teaching, communicating aspects of the fallen wisdom; *sophic*, is wisdom gained through a secret process; *sophiology*, the eternal and created Sophia, or wisdom. *Sophist* embodies seeming wisdom, mental cleverness, fallacious reasoner, conceptual adulteration, which degenerates further, as *sophisticate*, to empty knowledge, *sophomore*, and *sopor*, lethargic sleep.

33. Jonas, *The Gnostic Religion: The Message of the Alien God and the Beginnings of Christianity*, 179–181.

34. "The Apocryphon of John," in Robinson, *The Nag Hammadi Library in English*, 111. Also, "On The Origin of the World," 175.

35. Pagels, *The Gnostic Gospels*, 53–54.

36. Again, as with the term *Man*, the term *Adam* is used here as a fundamental non-genderized term. Adam is the composite name for the primal Human as manifested in matter, encompassing male and female aspects of biological humanity. Here I follow the indications of Qabalist Carlo Suares (*The Cipher of Genesis*, 1970) who decodes Adam as "the *aleph* (A) in the blood (DAM)," meaning the spiritual principle incarnate in a blood-based being. Use of the pronoun "he" in this context is purely for simplicity of reference, to avoid awkward though politically correct constructions such as "s/he," or "he or she," etc.

37. Blavatsky, *The Secret Doctrine*, Vol. II, 42–45, 242–247, 72–73, 196–197, 352–355, 434–435.

38. E.F. Scott, "Gnosticism," in *Encyclopedia of Religion and Ethics*, Vol. VI, ed. James Hastings, 236.

39. Hans Jonas, "Gnosticism," in *The Encyclopedia of Philosophy*, Vol. 3, ed. Paul Edwards, 340.

40. Steiner, *The Search for the New Isis, Divine Sophia*, 17–25, 38.

41. Steiner, *Christ and the Spiritual World*, 22–28.

42. Steiner, *The Gospel of St. John*, 46–47.

43. Tomberg, *Anthroposophical Studies of the Old Testament*, 174–176, 183–184.

44. Howell, *The Web in the Sea*, 113.

45. Tomberg, *Anthroposophical Studies of the New Testament*, 185.

46. Steiner, *Karmic Relationships: Esoteric Studies*, Vol. 7, 15–16.

47. Steiner, *The Change in the Path to Supersensible Knowledge*, 11–12.

48. Steiner, *The Fifth Gospel*, 9.

49. Steiner, *The Spiritual Guidance of Man*, 25, 28, 30, 32, 39, 45, 54–55, 75.

50. Ibid. 37.

51. Steiner, *The Mystery of the Trinity and The Mission of the Spirit*, 144–145.

CHAPTER 6

1. The increasing use of creative visualizations in psychotherapy and holistic, empirical medicine since the 1970s qualifies as another prominent sign of cognitive expansion in the Michaelic age. O. Carl Simonton pioneered the medical use of creative mental imagery as a therapy against cancer (*Getting*

Well Again, 1978); Shakti Gawain (*Creative Visualization*, 1979) and Jeanne Achterberg (*Imagery in Healing*, 1985) extended the field with more popular and clinical work. The concept is taking hold among the scientists, too, as evidenced by the innovative work of Francisco Varela relating immunology and cognitive models (*The Embodied Mind: Cognitive Science and Human Experience*, 1992). In these examples, the emphasis is to create a mental image whose contents are related to physical organs or processes, either in their dysfunctional or ideal state; then to energetically apply the image to the physical organs as they are situated within the body. In the case of certain forms of Tibetan Buddhism now popular in America, the mental images have no direct relation to the sense world and, typically, consist of complex mandalas and portrayals of deities. In either case, the Western mind is gradually exercising itself in willfully building and maintaining mental images, thereby preparing itself for the kind of sense-free etheric thinking and picture-making Steiner had in mind.

2. Steiner, *An Outline of Occult Science*, 279–285, 293–294.

3. Steiner, *Knowledge of the Higher Worlds and Its Attainment*, 62, 144, 167, 184.

4. Steiner, *Inner Impulses of Evolution*, 76.

5. Steiner, *How Can Mankind Find the Christ Again?* 167–169.

6. Steiner, *Theosophy*, 154–157, 168.

7. Steiner, *The Presence of the Dead on the Spiritual Path*, 6–8, 17.

8. Steiner, *The Stages of Higher Knowledge*, xii, xiv, 19, 72.

9. Steiner, *Macrocosm and Microcosm*, 148.

10. Steiner, *Three Lectures on the Mystery Dramas*, 14, 39.

11. The Sabian cycle of symbols, one for each of the 360 degrees, was formulated by Marc Edmund Jones, among others, and reported by Dane Rudhyar in *The Astrology of Personality*, Scrvire/Wassenaar, Netherlands, 1963 (p. 334): "What is seen in the Degree is the archetypal 'quality' of whatever occurs within its boundaries; the potential selfhood of any life manifestation focused therein. The zodiac, considered as a complete cyclic series of Degrees, becomes much more than a representation of collective energies. It becomes the universal womb of significances. It becomes Time in its highest sense: A cyclic series of creative moments which are 'wombs of souls,' each of which releases a 'quality' that becomes the 'monad' of every entity reaching independent existence within that moment.... That there are 360 of such Degrees means that there are, *from a planetary viewpoint*, as many basic types or modalities of individual selfhood on Earth; as many 'meanings' incarnate as 'groups of human beings.'" In Rudhyar's estimation, the development of the Sabian Symbols represents "a momentous astrological revelation, the significance and import of which may loom larger and larger as the years pass." (p. 336)

12. Steiner, *True and False Paths in Spiritual Investigation*, 194–197, 218.

13. Steiner, *The Presence of the Dead on the Spiritual Path*, 14–15, 50.

14. Steiner, *Materialism and the Task of Anthroposophy*, 5–6, 162–163.

15. Steiner, *Knowledge of the Higher Worlds and Its Attainment*, 78–79.

16. See Richard Leviton, Review of "A Rosicrucian Notebook," *The Quest*, Summer 1993, 84, 86.

17. Steiner, "Meditation and Concentration," 7–10. Also, "Brain Thinking as Spiritual Activity," 22–24.

18. Steiner, *The Course of My Life*, 174–175, 181, 237–239.

19. Rittelmeyer, *Rudolf Steiner Enters My Life*, 56–57, 123.

20. Bro, *Edgar Cayce on Religion and Psychic Experience*, 19–23.

21. Rota, *Welcome Home: A Time for Uniting*, 6–7.

22. Elkins, Rueckert, McCarty, *The Ra Material*, 51.

23. Kandl, *In the Beginning: Conversations with David*, Vol. 1, x, 5.

24. Hapgood, *Talks With Christ and His Teachers Through the Psychic Gift of Elwood Babbitt*, xviii, xx, xxi.

25. Cooke, *The New Mediumship*, 52.

26. Ryerson and Harolde, *Spirit Communication: The Soul's Path*, 5–8.

27. Knight, *A State of Mind: My Story*, 11, 369–373.

28. Montgomery, with Garland, *Ruth Montgomery: Herald of the New Age*, vii.

29. Hatford, *Letters from Janice*, ix.

30. Bailey, *The Unfinished Autobiography*, 164.

31. Skutch, *Journey Without Distance: The Story Behind A Course in Miracles*, 56.

32. Bernard, *Why You Are Who You Are: A Psychic Conversation with Richard*, 12–13.

33. White and Swainson, *Gildas Communicates: The Story and the Scripts*, 20, 27.

34. Roberts, *The Coming of Seth*, 23–24, 29.

35. Roberts, *The Seth Material*, 2–3.

36. Ibid. 6–7.

37. Goettsche and Fogg, *Down to Earth: The Jason Journal*, 11–13.

38. Fitzhugh, *The Orion Material: Perspectives of Awareness*, 204–205, 210–211.

39. Moore, *"I Come as a Brother"—A Remembrance of Illusions*, i–iii.

40. Spangler, *Channeling in the New Age*, 1.

41. Carey, *Vision*, xvi; *The Starseed Transmissions: An Extraterrestrial Report*, 1–2; Carey, *Return of the Bird Tribes*, xxii, xvii.

42. Wetzl, trans. *The Bridge Over the River*, vi, vii.

43. Ibid. 88.

44. Steiner, *Awakening to Community*, 155–159.

45. Steiner, *The Significance of Spiritual Research for Moral Action*, 7.

46. Steiner, *The Spiritual Hierarchies and Their Reflection in the Physical World*, 28.

47. Steiner, *The Stages of Higher Knowledge*, 37.

48. Steiner, *Background to the Gospel of St. Mark*, 25.

49. Ibid. 15–16, 23–24, 165.

50. Steiner, *An Outline of Occult Science*, xii, xiii, 18–19, 107, 294.

51. Steiner, in *The Living Being "Anthroposophia,"* by Rudolf Grosse, 1–3.

52. Steiner, *Karmic Relationships: Esoteric Studies*, Vol. 7, 47.

53. Steiner, *Karmic Relationships: Esoteric Studies*, Vol. 6, 84, 121–122. Also, Steiner, in *The Christmas Foundation: Beginning of a New Cosmic Age*, by Rudolf Grosse, 9, 10, 75, 93. Also Steiner, *Festivals*, 275.

54. Steiner, *World History in the Light of Anthroposophy*, 137, 142, 146–149. Also, Steiner in Grosse, *The Christmas Foundation*, 89.

55. Steiner, *The Fifth Gospel*, 40–41.

CHAPTER 7

1. Graves and Patai, *The Hebrew Myths: The Book of Genesis*, 57.

2. Technically, Zurvan is generally regarded as a post-Zarathustran heresy that nonetheless resolved certain key problems in his original conceptions. Variations in the English spelling include Steiner's translated usage of *Zeruane Akarene*; H. P. Blavatsky's *Zeruana Akerne*, *Zervan* and *Zrvan*. The Zoroastrian scholar R. C. Zaehner apparently standardized the spelling as *Zurvan*.

3. Steiner, *The Gospel of St. Matthew*, 38.

4. Blavatsky, *The Secret Doctrine*, I, 113–114; II, 233, 488.

5. Boyce, *Zoroastrians, Their Religious Beliefs and Practices*, 25–26.

6. Zaehner, *The Teachings of the Magi*, 31–33, 37.

7. Ahura Mazda is often called *Ormazd* but this is an adulteration of the Pahlavi *Auharmazd*, which derived from the Avestan Persian *Auramazda*, or Ahura-Mazda. Mazdah is the Iranian form for the Sanskrit *medhas*, which means "science." Ahura comes from the Sanskrit *asura*, the name for gods, deities, and spirits of power, such as the Indian Varuna, sometimes called "the wise Asura." (James Hastings, "Ormazd," in *Encyclopedia of Religion and Ethics*, Vol. 9, 566–570.)

8. These are variants on the name now written as Ahriman. In Gathic Avestan, the being's name was *Angra Mainyu*; in Younger Avesta, it was *Anra Mainyu*; in Pahlavi, *Ahraman*, which the Greeks translated as *Areimanios*; in modern Persian, *Ahriman*. The original meaning was "enemy spirit, spiritual foe," from *anra* (inimical) and *mainyu* (spirit). (Hastings, "Ahriman," *Encyclopedia of Religion* I, 267.)

9. *Asha* is the Persian form of the Indian word *arta*, meaning justice, truth, the law of men, gods, and the universe. It derives from the Vedic *rta*, for which Varuna was India's ancient god-protector. The implication is that Ahura-Mazda was the Persian successor to Varuna as Lord of the *asha/arta*. The *Amesha Spenta* were "typically Iranian transformations of the earlier Indo-Iranian gods (Adityas). Ahura Mazda, the supreme God, has taken the place of Varuna," wrote J. P. de Menasce, in "Ancient Persian Religion," in *New Catholic Encyclopedia*, XIV, 162–166.

10. Again, the antecedent Indian connection is suggested with the name *Druj*, which may have been a cultural translation of a minor demon mentioned in the *Rig Veda* as *Druh*, who represented malice and hatred. (Dhalla, *History of Zoroastrianism*, 91–94, 265, 259, 391–386).

11. Ibid.

12. Hastings, *Encyclopedia of Religion*, I, 267; IX, 566–567.

13. Ibid.

14. The name itself preserves the arch-demon qualities of Zoroaster's Angra Mainyu. Mephistopheles is a compound of the Hebrew *mephitz*, "destroyer," and *tophel*, "liar," which itself is short for *tophel sheqer*, "falsehood plasterer." A related word, *mephitic*, means poisonous, pestilential, noxious vaporous exhalation of the Earth.

15. Kaufmann, "Introduction," *Goethe's Faust*, trans. by Walter Kaufmann, 22–23.

16. Steiner, *The Mission of the Archangel Michael*, 10, 17–18.

17. Ibid. 10.

18. Steiner, *Goethe's Standard of the Soul*, 44–46.
19. Steiner, *Secrets of the Threshold*, 29, 52–54, 127.
20. Ibid. 52–54, 136, 176.
21. Steiner, *The Occult Movement in the Nineteenth Century*, 78, 80, 82–83, 85.
22. Steiner, *Inner Impulses of Evolution*, 24.
23. Steiner, *The Occult Movement in the Nineteenth Century*, 91.
24. Ibid. 91–92.
25. The Eighth Sphere is a vexingly obscure matter in Steiner's writing, and an issue that taxed a number of occultists, including A.P. Sinnett in *Esoteric Buddhism*, and C. G. Harrison in *The Transcendental Universe*. According to Harrison, writing in 1893, Sinnett's account (1884), locating the Eighth Sphere with the Moon, was "utterly misleading," and a profanation of the mysteries about which he was patently "ignorant." The Mystery of the Eighth Sphere, claimed Harrison, "is a key to the problem of evil in the Universe," involving knowledge "pertaining to some of the very highest mysteries." According to Valentin Tomberg (*Anthroposophical Studies of the Old Testament*, 21–24), the Eighth Sphere is an unnatural or unlawful sphere, or phase of existence, outside the lawful sevenfold stream of cosmic evolution, created by the three Hierarchies of Evil. It is situated between the Earth and the Moon, and partakes of elements of the Moon and the Earth's interior. Regarding its substance nature, it is primarily absorptive and suctional, made of an electromagnetic specter substance neither alive nor dead; as such, it is Ahriman's citadel in the cosmos. "For Ahriman is that being in the Cosmos who is striving to absorb all that exists into himself."
26. Steiner, *The Deed of Christ*, 17.
27. Steiner, *The Balance in the World and Man, Lucifer and Ahriman*, 22–24.
28. Steiner, *The Occult Movement in the Nineteenth Century*, 116.
29. Steiner, *Anthroposophical Leading Thoughts*, 111.
30. Walker, *The Woman's Encyclopedia of Myths and Secrets*, 551–553.
31. Fox, "Greek and Roman," *The Mythology of All Races*, Vol. 1, 247.
32. Schuré, *Children of Lucifer—An Antique Drama in Five Acts*, 278.
33. Steiner, *The Four Seasons and the Archangels*, 53. *The Destinies of Individuals and of Nations*, 199–200. "The Etheric Body as a Reflection of the Universe," 325.
34. Fant, Klingborg, Wilkes, *Rudolf Steiner's Sculpture in Dornach*, p.60.
35. Steiner, *From Jesus to Christ*, 114–116, 125–127. Also, *The Gospel of St. John and Its Relation to the Other Gospels*, 88–89.
36. Steiner, *The Gospel of St. John and Its Relation to the Other Gospels*, 83.
37. The English word Man derives from the Sanskrit root "man," which comes from the Sanskrit verb "to think." Man means "thinker;" the human is thereby named by his/her most characteristic attribute: intelligence. In Indian mythology, *Manu* was the first-born human; in Indian theosophy, the mental plane of intellect working free from the flesh is called *manasic*.
38. Muller, *The Six Systems of Indian Philosophy*, 213, 330, 502–503, 546–548.
39. Zimmer, *Philosophies of India*, Ed. Joseph Campbell, 228, 321,363–364.
40. Dasgupta, *A History of Indian Philosophy*, Vol. II, 232–238, 366.
41. Blavatsky, *The Secret Doctrine*, I, 13, 75, 329, 454.
42. Steiner, *At the Gates of Spiritual Science*, 15.

43. Steiner, *The Christ Impulse and the Development of Ego Consciousness*, 52–54.
44. Steiner, *Life Between Death and Rebirth*, 19–20, 140, 292–296.
45. Steiner, *Wonders of the World*, 77.
46. Steiner, *Initiation, Eternity, and the Passing Moment*, 112.
47. Ibid. 103–104, 120.
48. Steiner, *The Ahrimanic Deception*, 3–5. Also, *The Influences of Lucifer and Ahriman*, 10, 53–55.
49. Steiner, *Anthroposophical Leading Thoughts*, 108,146, 182. Also, *The Mission of the Archangel Michael*, 40.
50. Tomberg, *Anthroposophical Studies of the New Testament*, 184–185.
51. Steiner, *Initiation, Eternity, and the Passing Moment*, 124–128.
52. Steiner, *Anthroposophical Leading Thoughts*, 99.
53. Steiner, *Mystery Knowledge & Mystery Centres*, 26–27.
54. Steiner, *Secrets of the Threshold*, 21–22.
55. Steiner, *Anthroposophical Leading Thoughts*, 97–98.
56. Steiner, *Mystery Knowledge & Mystery Centres*, 28–30. Also, *The Ahrimanic Deception*, 14. *The Influences of Lucifer and Ahriman*, 13–14, 42–45, 55–56.
57. Steiner, *Occult Science and Occult Development*, 6.
58. Steiner, *The Ahrimanic Deception*, 10–12, 19.
59. Steiner, *Karmic Relationships*, Vol. 3, 126, 158–160.
60. Ibid. 175.
61. Steiner, *Secrets of the Threshold*, 86.
62. Steiner, *The Influences of Lucifer and Ahriman*, 58–59.
63. Roman and Packer, *Opening to Channel*, 79, 97,191.
64. Fant, et al., *Rudolf Steiner's Sculpture in Dornach*, 18.
65. Steiner, *Christ in Relation to Lucifer and Ahriman*, 3.
66. Steiner, *Mystery Knowledge & Mystery Centres*, 31–32. *From Jesus to Christ*, 57.
67. Steiner, *Secrets of the Threshold*, 19, 81, 85, 95. *Karmic Relationships*, Vol. 2, 242. *The Balance in the World and Man*, 15, 32. *Wonders of the World*, 67. *Mystery Knowledge & Mystery Centres*, 26–27.
68. Steiner, *The Mission of the Archangel Michael*, 9–10, 14.
69. Steiner, *The Balance in the World and Man*, 30–31.
70. Steiner, *The Etheric Body as a Reflection of the Universe*, 327.
71. Steiner, *The Gospel of St. John and Its Relation to the Other Gospels*, 93–94.

CHAPTER 8

1. Steiner, *Wonders of the World*, 178.
2. Fortune, *The Secrets of Doctor Taverner*, 89–90.
3. Steiner, *Secrets of the Threshold*, 130–132.
4. Steiner, *Background to the Gospel of St. Mark*, 82–83.
5. Steiner, *An Outline of Occult Science*, 332.
6. Steiner, *Secrets of the Threshold*, 118.
7. When the soul wakes up in the after-death state and understands he has died,

a subjective panorama is set out before him. "On his awakening in the Second *Bardo,* there dawn upon him symbolic visions, one by one, the hallucinations created by the *karmic* reflexes of actions done by him in the earth-plane body. What he has thought and what he has done become objective: thought-forms, having been consciously visualized and allowed to take root and grow and blossom and produce, now pass in a solemn and mighty panorama, as the consciousness-content of his personality." From the Introduction, W.Y. Evans-Wentz, *The Tibetan Book of the Dead,* 29.

8. Steiner, *Secrets of the Threshold,* 116–118.

9. *Kamaloca* is a Sanskrit term Steiner appropriated from Theosophical descriptions of the supersensible world. Kamaloca is the place (*loca*) of desires and pleasures (*Kama*), a region of burning desire and cleansing fire similar to the Western conception of purgatory. Kamaloca is an intermediate condition of being in which the manifold desires, passions, impulses of the astral body, that is to say, the emotional soul life of the human, are manifested, clarified and purged. Kamaloca is accessed normally in the after-death experience, after the etheric body has been shed; here one reviews the uncognized contents of one's nighttime consciousness and the full panoply of worldly karmic effects resulting from action inspired by the astral, emotional nature. Kamaloca can also be accessed consciously during the physical lifetime through an initiatory process or "accidentally" through unschooled psychism.

10. Steiner, "Meditation and Concentration: Three Kinds of Clairvoyance," 7–8, 13–14, 22–24. Also, "Manifestations of the Unconscious: Dreams, Hallucinations, Visions, Somnambulism, Mediumship," 24–26, 34. *Philosophy, Cosmology and Religion,* 125.

11. Steiner, *Psychoanalysis and Spiritual Psychology,* 124, 132.

12. Steiner, *The Destinies of Individuals and of Nations,* 139.

13. Steiner, *The Wrong and Right Use of Esoteric Knowledge,* 15.

14. Steiner, *At the Gates of Spiritual Science,* 25–26.

15. Ibid. 34–35.

16. Steiner, *Karmic Relationships,* Vol. 4, 25.

17. Steiner, *Reincarnation and Karma: Two Fundamental Truths of Human Existence* 37.

18. Steiner, *Supersensible Man,* 58.

19. Steiner, *The Principle of Spiritual Economy,* 7, 10–11.

20. Steiner, *Christ and the Human Soul,* 49–51.

21. Hapgood, *Talks With Christ and His Teachers,* xviii–xx.

22. Ryerson and Harolde, *Spirit Communication: The Soul's Path,* 14–17.

23. Steiner, *Life Between Death and Rebirth,* 242.

24. Steiner, *The Occult Movement in the Nineteenth Century,* 21, 27, 29, 58, 61.

25. Steiner, *Errors in Spiritual Investigation,* 12–14.

26. Smilgis, "Hollywood Goes to Heaven," *Time,* June 3, 1991, 70–71.

27. Ibid.

28. Steiner, "Manifestations of the Unconscious," 6.

29. Steiner, *Knowledge of the Higher Worlds and Its Attainment,* 254–257.

30. MacLaine, *Dancing in the Light,* 334–335.

31. Steiner, *Macrocosm and Microcosm,* 21.

32. Steiner, *Wonders of the World,* 183.

33. Steiner, "Manifestations of the Unconscious," 27–29.

34. Steiner, *The Stages of Higher Knowledge,* 14.

35. Steiner, *The Influence of Spiritual Beings Upon Man,* 2, 5, 9, 14.

36. Steiner, *The Spiritual Hierarchies and Their Reflection in the Physical World,* 21–22.

37. Steiner, *The Influence of Spiritual Beings Upon Man,* 12–15.

38. Steiner, *True and False Paths in Spiritual Investigation,* 147.

39. Wilson, *The New Yorker,* April 2, 1990, 34.

40. Strieber, *Communion: A True Story,* 20, 161, 253, 301.

41 This visual icon appears on the mass market covers of Strieber's *Communion* (1987), *Transformation* (1988), *Majestic* (1989), and the promotional material for the movie version of *Communion* (1989). It also appears on the paperback covers of Budd Hopkin's *Missing Time* (1981), *Intruders* (1987); and a channeled work *The Prism of Lyra* (1989), by Lyssa Royal and Keith Priest.

42. Strieber, *Transformation: The Breakthrough,* 236, 240–241.

43. Ibid. 248.

44. This is an intensely vexatious subject. The reference to memory plants derives from Philip Dick's science fiction work, *We Can Remember for You Wholesale,* which was produced cinematically as *Total Recall* (1990). Here, a man has the memories of a wonderful vacation electronically imprinted in his mind by a computer; he is relieved of the physical necessity of actually taking the vacation. Through a memory implant, he has the virtual experience of a vacation.

45. Royal, Priest, *The Prism of Lyra: An Exploration of Human Galactic Heritage,* 11–15.

46. Royal Priest Research 1993 Catalog, Scottsdale, 1993, 5.

47. There is another dimension to this which is more upsetting in its implications. In 1993 a major Hollywood film was released called *Fire in the Sky,* which chronicled allegedly true events from the late 1970s in which an Arizona logger was abducted by alien ETs, ruthlessly experimented upon—from his point of view, physically tortured—and released. This movie was one of the few ET movies that have come out in the last 8 years since the mid-1980s heyday. But in the gap between *ET* (1983) and *Fire in the Sky* (1993) something profound has shifted. While *ET* was the epiphany of the alien visitor, *Fire in the Sky* was its negative, shadow, nightmare side, the apocalypse of alien as torturer. But why this fall from grace in a decade? Why this shift from grace to fear? It is instructive to consider in what ways this kind of mass culture iconographic shift serves the interests of the Brothers of the Left. Obviously, if encounters across the threshold are stamped with fear, people become reluctant to make any forays; this retreat also fosters a regressive materialism, a return to the familiar ontological comforts of home in the physical world. In *Fire in the Sky* it was the logger's curiosity that literally brought him into the abductive environment; had he been incurious or simply frightened, like his companions, he would not have been picked up and psychically damaged. As things turned out, there was no positive, transformative benefit to him from this brutal experience; he survived it, then sought to forget it. The abduction phenomenon is growing in prevalence and in recent years, since the books by Strieber and Hopkins, has had a negative, fearful, brutish atmosphere. Prudence counsels that we must not take these experiences, as reported, at face

value, as being literally accurate as presented. There is a significant possibility that some of them, to a degree, are false memory transplants, engineered by the Brothers of the Left, to foster a general ambiance of fear, distrust, and paralysis sufficient to keep us away from the threshold with false ideas about the world beyond. The same dynamics are appearing in the phenomenon called "satanic ritual abuse" and "recovered memory." It is at least a working hypothesis, backed by some clinical work, that false memories of abuse may be implanted   through hypnotic suggestion and "believed with assuredness as one believes real memories." See Lawrence Wright, "Remembering Satan, Part II," *The New Yorker,* May 24, 1993, 69.

48. McKenna, *True Hallucinations,* xi, xii, 111, 157, 160, 226.

49. Steiner, *True and False Paths in Spiritual Investigation,* 156–157, 162.

50. Ibid. 157, 164–165, 167.

51. Ibid. 162.

52. Montgomery, *Threshold to Tomorrow,* 1, 9. Also, *Aliens Among Us,* 143.

53. Steiner, *An Outline of Occult Science,* 328, 340–341, 345.

54. Ibid. 345

55. Steiner, *The Gospel of St. Mark,* 239–240.

CHAPTER 9

1. In making the connection between Human and Holy Ghost, or Phantom, I am unavoidably jumping ahead to a conception I will introduce later in the book, namely, that the Human, or the Holy Ghost/Phantom is a trinity comprised of Michael, Lucifer/Ahriman, and Sophia, redeemed by the Christ at Golgotha.

2. Steiner, *The Gospel of St. John,* 169, 174, 179.

3. Ibid. 179.

4. Steiner, *Knowledge of the Higher Worlds and Its Attainment,* 69.

5. Steiner, *Esoteric Development,* 8–9.

6. Ibid. 9.

7. Steiner, *Initiation, Eternity, and the Passing Moment,* 86.

8. Steiner, *The Mystery of the Trinity and The Mission of the Spirit,* 79–80.

9. Steiner, *The Stages of Higher Knowledge,* 26–27.

10. Steiner, *The Mystery of the Trinity and The Mission of the Spirit,* 30–31.

11. Steiner, *The Bridge Between Universal Spirituality and the Physical Constitution of Man,* 50–52.

12. Steiner, *The Mystery of the Trinity and The Mission of the Spirit,* 80.

13. Steiner, *Self-Consciousness, The Spiritual Human Being,* 13, 44, 48–49, 57, 65, 88.

14. Steiner, *The Mystery of the Trinity and The Mission of the Spirit,* 85.

15. Steiner, *Macrocosm and Microcosm,* 159.

16. Steiner, *The Destinies of Individuals and of Nations,* 237.

17. Steiner, "Learning to Understand the Spiritual World," 10–11; Also, *Occult Reading and Occult Hearing,* 27, 47.

18. Steiner, *Psychoanalysis and Spiritual Psychology,* 90, 112.

19. Steiner, *The East in the Light of the West,* 24–39.

20. Steiner, *The Destinies of Individuals and of Nations*, 129.
21. Ibid. 130–134. Also, *Esoteric Development*, 167–168.
22. Steiner, *The Destinies of Individuals and of Nations*, 140–141. Also, *Esoteric Development*, 175–176.
23. Steiner, *Polarities in the Evolution of Mankind*, 5.
24. Steiner, *An Outline of Occult Science*, 159–160. Also, *Cosmic Memory*, 197–199, 208.
25. Pursel, *Lazaris, The Sacred Journey: You and Your Higher Self*, ii, iii.
26. Yarbro, *Messages From Michael*, 17, 21, 23.
27. Kandl, *In The Beginning*, ix.
28. Young, *Agartha, A Journey to the Stars*, 30, 31, 36.
29. Ryerson and Harolde, *Spirit Communications*, 12–13.
30. Monroe, *Far Journeys*, 29.
31. Fitzhugh, *The Orion Material*, 204, 205, 210, 211.
32. Marciniak, *Bringers of the Dawn*, xxiv–xxvii.
33. Moore, *From the Heart of a Gentle Brother*, i, ii.
34. Carey, *Return of the Bird Tribes*, xvi, xvii. Also, *Starseed: The Third Millennium*, xii.
35. Rota, *Welcome Home*, 3.
36. Steiner, *Community Life, Inner Development, Sexuality, and the Spiritual Teacher*, 40,45,47,52,75, 76.
37. Tomberg, *Anthroposophic Studies of the New Testament*, 185.

CHAPTER 10

1. Steiner, *The New Spirituality and the Christ Experience of the Twentieth Century*, 117–118.
2. Steiner, "The Cosmic Word and Individual Man," 12–14.
3. "The Apocryphon of John," in Robinson, *The Nag Hammadi Library*, 115.
4. Steiner, *The Reappearance of Christ in the Etheric*, 136.
5. Steiner, *Philosophy, Cosmology, and Religion*, 87.
6. Steiner, *True and False Paths in Spiritual Investigation*, 202, 217.
7. Steiner, *Cosmosophy*, Vol. 1, 99, 101–102,114–116.
8. Steiner, *Universe, Earth and Man*, 93–95.
9. Steiner, *Supersensible Man*, 26–27.
10. Steiner, *Cosmosophy*, Vol. 1, 120–121.
11. The word "phantom" comes from the Greek *phantein*, meaning *eidolon*, or image. The confusing English term *ghost* is equivalent to phantom and *phantein*, meaning the form or image of the human in light. Other Greek roots explicate phantasm from *phantasma*, *phantazo*, meaning "to make visible," *phaino*, "to show," *phantazein*, "to bring before the mind," *phanero*, meaning "visible, manifest." The basic root appears to be *phan*, "to shine, appear." The meaning of the root *phan* is closely related to *phos*, "light," as in *Phosphoros*, the Light-Bringer. Again, the sense is the form made visible as light, or the light bearing visible, radiant form, the form bringing light into a visible image.
12. Kühlewind, *The Logos-Structure of the World*, 13, 17.

13. Steiner, "The Cosmic Word and Individual Man," 10–11.

14. The truth of Lucifer is an open secret. Lucifer derives from the Latin *lux*, meaning "light" (also *lucis*) and *ferre*, "to bring." Lucifer in Latin means exactly the same as Phosphoros in Greek: "light bringer."

15. Steiner, *The Deed of Christ*, 18.

16. Steiner, *The Apocalypse of St. John*, 130–131.

17. Steiner, *Universe, Earth and Man*, 105–106.

18. Steiner, *The Deed of Christ*, 18.

19. Blavatsky, *The Secret Doctrine*, Vol. 2, 511–513.

20. Ibid. Vol. 1,70–73; Vol. 2, 162, 513.

21. Steiner, *The East in the Light of the West*, 88, 94–95.

22. Ibid. 113–118.

23. Ibid. 6–7, 97–99, 118–125, 130–132, 136–137.

24. Ibid. 5.

25. Steiner, *The Deed of Christ*, 23.

26. Scharff, *Holy Nights—Contemplations on the Christmas Foundation Meeting of 1923*, 67.

27. Steiner, *The Gospel of St. Luke*, 140–142.

28. Steiner, *Genesis: Secrets of the Bible Story of Creation*, 28, 49–52, 69.

29. Steiner, *The Bridge Between Universal Spirituality and the Physical Constitution of Man*, 14–17, 33–38.

30. Ibid. 38.

31. Steiner, *The Gospel of St. Luke*, 141–142.

32. Steiner, *Christ and the Human Soul*, 63–64, 68.

33. Steiner, *The Bridge Between Universal Spirituality and the Physical Constitution of Man*, 14–17, 33–38.

34. Steiner, *From Jesus to Christ*, 113–114, 128–132.

35. Schuré, *The Children of Lucifer*, 347.

36. Steiner, *Individualism in Philosophy*, i, ii, 23–28, 33, 34, 38.

37. Ibid.60, 74.

38. Kühlewind, *The Logos-Structure of the World*, 18.

CHAPTER 11

1. Steiner, *The Foundation Stone*, 57.

2. Steiner, *The Festivals and Their Meaning*, 92–93.

3. Steiner, *The East in the Light of the West*, 3–5.

4. Steiner, *The Gospel of St. Luke*, 100.

5. *The Portal of Initiation* (in *Four Mystery Dramas*) has three references to the Star. "You must live through each terror/to which illusion can give birth/before the truth reveals itself to you:/thus speaks your star." (63). "My son, you have stood firm so far;/you will progress still further/I see your star in its full radiance." (74) "I could behold your star/it shines in its full power." (140). *The Soul's Probation* (in *Four Mystery Dramas*) has one reference." With forces won like this, my soul/beholds Johannes' star with certainty...." (127). In Edouard Schuré's *Children of Lucifer* (published in 1900) the Star

gets prominent play. The Star gleams on Lucifer's forehead; he describes himself as "I the Star of the Archangels." When he fell, the Star on his brow faded. (279). Later in the Sanctuary of the Unknown God, a Star appears above the chasm, vivid white surrounding a golden core, glittering like a sun as a voice spoke out of it. "Light! I hear my living Star! . . . By their sacrifice, Heroic Love has regained divine Wisdom; the Rebel Angel has found again his lost Star." (360).

6. Steiner, *The Search for the New Isis, Divine Sophia*, 13.

7. Stein quotes Plutarch who noted that in addition to the soul submerged in the earthly body, "the human being has another and purer part, hovering outside him like a star above his head." This is the Daimon or Genius that guides one throughout life, added Plutarch. "This star that illumines our path is ever carried and protected by the Angel-being who guards us throughout life," wrote Stein. He notes that Zoroaster's name means "living and radiant star." Zoroaster was so called because "the star which is there in every human being was present in his case in a unique and high degree." The star is the power of the soul itself, body-free, present at the birth of every human being, said Stein. "In the Jesus child, of course, the star was visible in a unique radiance." From Stein, *The Death of Merlin: Arthurian Myth and Alchemy*, 22–23.

8. Steiner, *Universe, Earth and Man*, 36.

9. Van Emmichoven, *The Foundation Stone*, 19.

10. Easton, *Rudolf Steiner: Herald of a New Epoch*, 195–197.

11. Steiner was considered the Nazi's foremost occult enemy in their formative work up until his death in 1925. According to Trevor Ravenscroft (*The Spear of Destiny*, 262–263, 289), a cabal of black magicians and Western occultists, including the Thule Gesellschaft, surrounded and abetted Adolf Hitler in his rise to power in Germany. They considered Rudolf Steiner, whom they saw as the leading figure of an extensive circle of Grail Initiates, to be their archenemy. Plans made to assassinate Steiner at a Munich railway station in 1922 were only barely thwarted. "The prime reason for burning down the Goetheanum was to destroy a huge woodcarving of the Trinity of Evil," Steiner's Representative of Man, which apparently infuriated Hitler. Hitler also blamed Steiner as a war criminal responsible for Germany's failure to win World War I through undue influence in 1914 with General Helmuth von Moltke. The Nazis also opposed Steiner because through his clairvoyance he was aware of their occult machinations and sought to make public their secret, invidious projects.

12. Easton, *Rudolf Steiner: Herald of a New Epoch*, 329.

13. Hiebel, *Time of Decision with Rudolf Steiner*, 212.

14. Grosse, *The Christmas Foundation: Beginning of a New Cosmic Age*, 12, 73, 75, 76, 129.

15. Van Emmichoven, *The Foundation Stone*, 19, 36, 50.

16. Lievegoed, *Mystery Streams in Europe and the New Mysteries*, 81.

17. Prokofieff, *Rudolf Steiner and the Founding of the New Mysteries*, 286, 287, 298, 303.

18. Eschenbach, *Parzival*, 239–240.

19. Ravenscroft, *The Cup of Destiny: The Quest for the Grail*, 35–36.

20. Steiner, *The East in the Light of the West*, 4.

21. Steiner, *The Principle of Spiritual Economy*, 113, 114, 155, 156.

22. Steiner, *An Outline of Occult Science*, 357, 356, 362.

23. Stein, *The Death of Merlin: Arthurian Myth and Alchemy*, 130.

24. For an experiential introduction to the emerald and meditative exercises working with this supersensible reality, consult: Richard Leviton, *Lovely Lucifer: A Workbook in the Christed Initiation in the Buddha Body.*

25. Stein, *The Death of Merlin: Arthurian Myth and Alchemy*, 364–365.

26. Lawlor, *Sacred Geometry: Philosophy and Practice*, 9.

27. Pennick, *Sacred Geometry: Symbolism and Purpose in Religious Structures*, 24.

28. Lawlor, *Sacred Geometry: Philosophy and Practice*, 96.

29. Plummer, *The Mathematics of the Cosmic Mind: A Study in Mathematical Symbolism*, 25–26.

30. L. Gordon Plummer helps us with this correlation with the following remark (p. 26): "The Cube with its 12 edges fits perfectly within the Dodecahedron with its 12 faces.... We see that each face of the Dodecahedron is crossed by a line; and upon closer observation, it will be seen that these lines form the Cube."

31. Howell, *The Web in the Sea: Jung, Sophia, and the Geometry of the Soul*, 219.

32. Steiner, *The Gospel of St. John in Relation to the Other Gospels*, 270–271. Also, *The Gospel of St. John*, 111.

33. Steiner, *The Gospel of St. John in Relation to the Other Gospels*, 253.

34. Steiner, *The Gospel of St. John*, 112–113.

35. Ravenscroft, *The Cup of Destiny: The Quest for the Grail*, 49, 53–55.

36. Steiner, *The Mission of Folk Souls*, 16.

37. Grosse, *The Christmas Foundation*, 66.

38. Michell, *New Light on the Ancient Mystery of Glastonbury*, 62–63.

39. Roberts, *Geomancy—A Synthonal Re-appraisal*; and Anthony Roberts, editor, *Glastonbury—Ancient Avalon.*

40. Coon, *Elliptical Navigations Through the Multitudinous Aethyrs of Avalon.*

41. Leviton, "Zodiacal Circles of Light: Landscape Zodiac Temples of Britain;" "Ley Lines & The Meaning of Adam."

42. Steiner, *The East in the Light of the West*, 167–168.

43. Platt, *The Qualities of Time, Volume I: Contributions Towards a Modern Understanding of How the Cosmos Works in Man.*

44. Steiner, *The Karma of Untruthfulness*, Vol.I, 7, 34.

45. Prokofieff, *Rudolf Steiner and the Founding of the New Mysteries*, 300–303.

46. For a complete description of this imagination and information about zodiacs as the Image of the Human, see: Richard Leviton, "A Primer on Landscape Zodiacs and the Discipline of Spiritual Geomancy."

47. The blue sphere was known to Steiner, according to Stewart Easton: "But Steiner states that within the astral body as seen by the clairvoyant there is an 'emptiness' that may in a sense be compared with the blue sky....So the 'empty space' in the astral body in which the 'I' incarnates likewise appears blue to the clairvoyant, but there is not even a suspicion of 'cloudiness' in this blue to indicate the presence of such an 'entity' as the 'I'...." (Easton, *Man and World in the Light of Anthroposophy*, 146.)

48. Sergei Prokofieff elucidates the concept of the inner Sun-quality. "This must become the fundamental experience of the new Michael-epoch: 'The Sun-quality (*das Sonnenhafte*), which through many long ages the human being has received only from the Cosmos, will begin to shine in the innermost recesses of the soul. Man will learn to speak of an 'inner Sun'... will see his own being which walks on the Earth guided by the Sun, as Sun-guided (*sonnengefuhrt*)." (Sergei Prokofieff, *Rudolf Steiner and the Founding of the New Mysteries*, 301–302.

49. Alice Howell puts this eloquently: "Perhaps the vessel Aquarius carries is none other than Sophia's cup, the treasured mystical Grail that held the wine of Christ-consciousness, the pure spirit of love, shed for us all, whoever we are, so long as we are humble and ecumenical enough to receive it in the spirit it was given, to circulate it as mystical blood, and share it with joy and gratitude." (Howell, *The Dove in the Stone: Finding the Sacred in the Commonplace*, 105.)

50. "The Sambhogakaya, or 'Body of Wealth,' is the dimension of the essence of the elements that make up the gross material world, a subtle dimension of light appearing in a wealth of forms which can only be perceived through the development of visionary capacity and mental clarity." (Namkhai Norbu, *The Crystal and the Way of Light: Sutra, Tantra and Dzogchen*, edited by John Shane, 130.) The Sambhogakaya is the "Body of Delight, the body of Buddhas who in a 'Buddha-paradise' enjoy the truth that they embody.... [It is] the experience of the ecstasy of enlightenment, of the dharma-mind of the Buddha and the patriarchs, and of the spiritual practices transmitted by them." As a form body for the Buddha, it is a means "for conveying the experience of the absolute.... The *Sambhogakaya* represents the qualities of the Dharmakaya [unified cosmic consciousness, the body of Truth] and is considered to arise directly out of it. Its forms are expressed in iconography as... visualized deities [which] become a means of communication with the highest reality." (From: Ingrid Fischer-Schreiber, Franz-Karl Ehrhard, Michael S. Diener, *The Shambhala Dictionary of Buddhism and Zen*, trans. by Michael H. Kohn, 229–230.) The Sambhogakaya is "the jewel of the inspirational 'Body of Bliss,' in which the Enlightened Ones appear before the inner eye in the splendor of their virtues and accomplishments. From this wondrous vision flows the inspiration of all immortal art, highest wisdom, and profound truth, expressed in mantric speech and poetry." (Lama Anagarika Govinda, *Creative Meditation and Multidimensional Consciousness*, 92.) Govinda also notes (in *Foundations of Tibetan Mysticism*, 148) that within the Buddhist model of the five sheaths of human consciousness, the Buddha Body (Body of Inspiration, Body of Bliss, or *Sambhogakaya*) corresponds to the fifth sheaf, *ananda-maya-kosa*, "the body of the highest, universal consciousness, nourished and sustained by exalted joy... only experienced in a state of enlightenment, or in the highest state of meditation (*dhyana*)."

51. Govinda, *Foundations of Tibetan Mysticism*, 225.

52. Stein, *The Death of Merlin: Arthurian Myth and Alchemy*, 120, 136.

53. Steiner described this aspect of the Buddha as *Nirmanakaya*, but this is technically inaccurate. As discussed above, Buddhism describes three bodies of the Buddha in its doctrine of Trikaya: *Nirmanakaya*, the physical appearance body (kaya) or body of transformation; *Sambhogakaya*, the light or astral body, the heavenly body of bliss; and *Dharmakaya*, the truth body, which is virtually

unmanifest and formless, the body of ineffable foundational reality. Insofar as the Buddha's *kaya* informed the astral body of the Nathan Jesus, this would have to be the *Sambhogakaya*.

54. The justification for this interpretation of the PIT may be found in the Qabala. Qabalistically, PIT means Peh (mouth) plus Yod (Hand) plus Tau (chalice). Peh is associated in Tarot symbology with Mars, the color red. Tau is associated with the color black, with Saturn, and indicates a cross or crucifix of the 4 elements, incarnation, the chalice, the limitations and restrictions of matter and time. Yod is the Hand, the Hermit, associated with grey, Virgo, and is the dispenser of light. The symbolism of the PIT is straightforward: the gaping redblack maw of matter, under the influence of Saturn and Mars, with only the beneficent hand of Virgo as a potential key of redemption. The PIT is human biological incarnation with selfhood limited to the parameters of the unevolved first 3 chakras: survival, procreation, aggressive me-ness. For the celestially paranoid, those who view incarnation with reservation, as Steiner once said of his anthroposophical contemporaries, the PIT is the bloody black grin of the Devil. In Qabalistic psychology, the PIT also refers to the *Nephesch*, the unredeemed Virgin animal soul of man, associated with the base of the Tree of Life. The PIT equals *Nephesch*, the unredeemed dragon of materiality, the unconscious animal soul. Thus the lower three chakras comprise the PIT, the site of seduction, where Lucifer was seduced and became the Holy Ghost caught in Time.

55. Steiner, *The Gospel of St. John*, 54–55.

56. The Sun Elohim, like the Gnostic Ialdabaoth, are the progeny of Sophia and the "prime parent" of the cosmos ("the ruler out of the waters, having great authority within him and ignorant of whence he had come into being") who create the seven archons of the planets. Ialdabaoth and the 365 angels co-create Adam as microcosmic Man. The number 365 is the solar time index, the individual cosmic letters of Man, which means humankind was expelled from the timeless into the time-dominated, from Sun-life to Earth-life, or biology.

57. Steiner, *Karmic Relationships*, Vol. 8, 77.

58. *Paraclete* comes from the Greek *parakletos*, which means comforter, advocate, and consoler, and *paraklein*, which means to summon to one's aid as an adviser, called in, summoned to help.

59. Tomberg, *Anthroposophical Studies of the New Testament*, 188, 193.

CHAPTER 12

1. *Pentecost*, from *Pente Kostus*, meaning "fiftieth," is the Greek translation of the older Hebrew word *Shavuot* (or *Shabuot*), literally meaning "weeks," and later meaning the "festival of Weeks." Shavuot was celebrated 50 days after the offering of the barley sheaf made in the Temple of Jerusalem on the second day of Passover; in other words, 7 weeks and one day afterwards. The Hebrews commemorated this fiftieth day as marking the consecration of their ancestors by God as a "holy people" on Mount Sinai when Moses received the covenant of the Torah; for this reason the day is also called *Zeman Matan Toratenu*, "the Season of the giving [to us] of [our] Torah." In the Christian faith, Pentecost, often called Whitsun, or Whit Sunday, is observed 50 days after Easter.

2. The Greek phrase is *lalein eterais glossais*, "to speak in foreign tongues," which we now translate as glossalalia. As glossalalia or Pentecostal speech has evolved, typically it is in code as initially unintelligible, "foreign" speech. The classic Biblical description of Pentecost is in 2 Acts 1–41.

3. Steiner, *Building Stones for an Understanding of the Mystery of Golgotha*, 104.

4. Steiner, *The Fifth Gospel*, 26–27. Also, *The Festivals and Their Meaning*, 255, 259, 264, 269, 275, 268, 305. Also, *Toward Imagination: Culture and the Individual*, 5–6.

5. Steiner, *The Festivals and Their Meaning*, 259.

6. Ibid. 288–289.

7. Ibid. 264.

8. Tomberg, *Anthroposophical Studies of the New Testament*, 186.

9. Steiner, *The Gospel of St. John*, 179.

10. According to Friedrich Rittelmeyer, who scrutinized Steiner relentlessly for spiritual flaws before accepting him as his mentor, Steiner exemplified this principle in his deportment while lecturing. "I realized then how a man in the very Presence of Christ speaks of Christ. There was something more than devotional reverence in the words. In freedom and reverence a man was looking up to Christ Whose Presence was quite near....Anyone who witnessed this could doubt no longer but that a fully authorized servant of Christ was standing before him." (*Rudolf Steiner Enters My Life*, 91.)

11. Steiner, *Earthly Knowledge and Heavenly Wisdom*, 65–68, 124, 130–131.

12. Steiner, *The Gospel of St. John*, 93–94.

13. Tomberg, *Anthroposophical Studies of the New Testament*, 189–190.

14. Steiner, *Background to the Gospel of St. Mark*, 219–220.

15. Pentecostal speech represents the 50 faces of the five Platonic Solids in unified speech. Thus the number for Sun Speech is 50, Pentecost. In Qabala, there is mention of the 50 Gates of Binah. In the Tree of Life, Binah is the sphere of the Cosmic Mother, the matrix of the five phases of matter. In the chakra system of Tantric yoga, the summation of the petals of the six chakras (root to brow) and the formative syllables, expressed in Sanskrit, that activate them, total 50—which is the number of letters in the Sanskrit alphabet. As the chakras represent the formative etheric forces of the five elements as they organize physical matter, we find a further elucidation of Steiner's prescient remark that the complete alphabet (Sanskrit with 50 letter/sounds) is the complete person (formative forces of the chakras).

16. Steiner, *Eurythmy as Visible Speech*, 23–34.

17. Ibid. 36.

18. Ibid. 30.

19. Kühlewind, *Becoming Aware of the Logos*, 16.

20. Steiner, *The Alphabet*, 1–4.

21. Ibid. 5–16.

22. Steiner in Easton, *Man and World in Light of Anthroposophy*, 240.

23. Steiner's concept of the gods playing the zodiacal musical instrument by sounding different planets is a restatement of the Gnostic idea of *Heimarmene*. For the Gnostics this was inexorable fate, cosmic necessity as decreed by the seven Archons, the planetary rulers created by Ialdabaoth.

24. Steiner, *The Inner Nature of Music and the Experience of Tone*, 33–34, 38–40, 42–44.

25. Steiner, *Supersensible Man*, 39–41.

26. Ravenscroft, *The Spear of Destiny*, 181–182.

27. "On the Origin of the World," in Robinson, ed., *The Nag Hammadi Library in English*, 174.

28. "The Apocryphon of John," in Robinson, ed., *The Nag Hammadi Library in English*, 116.

29. Malory, *Le Morte d'Arthur*, Vol. 1, 176.

30. Steiner, *The Lost Unison Between Speaking and Thinking*, 25–27, 37.

31. Kühlewind, *Becoming Aware of the Logos*, 38.

32. Steiner, *Rosicrucianism and Modern Initiation*, 56, 60. Also, *Lucifer and Ahriman*, 76.

33. Steiner, *The Mission of the Folk Souls*, 65–66.

34. Steiner, *The Gospel of St. John*, 47–49.

35. Steiner, *The Apocalypse of St. John*, 24.

BIBLIOGRAPHY

Abelar, Taisha. *The Sorcerer's Crossing: A Woman's Journey.* Viking Arkana, New York, 1992.

Ahern, Geoffrey. *Sun at Midnight: The Rudolf Steiner Movement and the Western Esoteric Tradition.* The Aquarian Press, Wellingborough, U.K.,1984.

Amaa-Ra, Solara Antara. *The Starry Messenger.* Star-Borne Unlimited, Portal, AZ, Vol. 1, No. 1, 1990.

Bailey, Alice A. *The Unfinished Autobiography.* Lucis Publishing Company, New York, 1951.

Barber, Benjamin R. "Jihad Vs. McWorld." *The Atlantic Monthly*, March 1992.

Barborka, Geoffrey A. *H.P. Blavatsky, Tibet and Tulku.* The Theosophical Publishing House, Adyar/Madras, 1966.

Barlow, John Perry. "Being in Nothingness." *Mondo 2000*, No. 2, 1990.

Basil, Robert, ed., *Not Necessarily the New Age.* Prometheus Books, Buffalo, NY,1988.

Belyi, Andrei; Turgenieff, Aasya; and Voloschin, Margarita. *Reminiscences of Rudolf Steiner.* Adonis Press, Ghent, NY,1987.

Berger, Arthur S., and Berger, Joyce. *The Encyclopedia of Parapsychology and Psychical Research.* Paragon House, New York, 1991.

Bernard, Graham. *Why You Are Who You Are: A Psychic Conversation with Richard.* Destiny Books, Rochester, 1985.

Besant, Annie. *An Autobiography.* Theosophical Publishing House, Adyar/Madras, 1893.

—— and Leadbeater, C.W. *Talks on the Path of Occultism, Vol 1: At the Feet of the Master.* Theosophical Publishing House, Adyar, 1926.

Blavatsky, H. P. *Collected Writings,* Vol. 1, 1874–1878. Theosophical Publishing House, Wheaton, IL, 1966.

—— *Collected Writings,* Volume II, 1879–1880. The Theosophical Publishing House, Wheaton, IL, 1966.

—— *H. P. Blavatsky to the American Conventions.* Theosophical University Press, Pasadena, CA,1979.

—— *Isis Unveiled.* Theosophical University Press, Pasadena, CA, 1977.

—— *The Secret Doctrine.* Theosophical University Press, Pasadena, CA, 1977.

—— *Studies in Occultism.* Theosophical University Press, Pasadena, CA, 1987.

—— *Transactions of the Blavatsky Lodge.* Theosophical University Press, Pasadena, CA, 1946.

Bohm, Werner. *Chakras-Roots of Power.* Samuel Weiser, York Beach, ME,1991.

Boyce, Mary. *Zoroastrians, Their Religious Beliefs and Practices.* Routledge & Kegan Paul, London, 1979.

Boyle, Nicholas. *Goethe: The Poet and the Age,* Vol. I, *The Poetry of Desire.* Oxford University Press, New York, 1992.

Bro, Harmon H. *Edgar Cayce on Religion and Psychic Experience.* Warner Books, New York, 1970; reissued 1988.

Carey, Ken. *Return of the Bird Tribes.* Uni-Sun, Kansas City, 1988.

—— *Starseed: The Third Millennium.* HarperSan Francisco, CA,1991.

—— *The Starseed Transmissions: An Extraterrestrial Report.* Uni-Sun, Kansas City, 1982.

—— *Vision.* Uni-Sun, Kansas City, 1985.

Carman, John. "One Flew Over the Cuckoo Limb." *San Francisco Chronicle,* October 17, 1986.

Cooke, Grace. *The New Mediumship.* White Eagle Publishing Trust, Liss, U.K., 1965.

Coon, Robert. *Elliptical Navigations Through the Multitudinous Aethyrs of Avalon.* Excalibur Press, Street, U.K., 1984.

Cranston, Sylvia. *H.P.B—The Extraordinary Life & Influence of Helena Blavatsky.* Jeremy P. Tarcher/G.P. Putnam's Sons, New York, 1993.

Crevier, Daniel. *AI, The Tumultuous History of the Search for Artificial Intelligence.* Basic Books, New York, 1993.

Dasgupta, Surendranath. *A History of Indian Philosophy.* Cambridge University Press, Cambridge, 1968.

de Menasce, J. P. in "Ancient Persian Religion," in *New Catholic Encyclopedia.* McGraw Hill Book Company, New York, 1967.

Dhalla, Maneckji Nusservanji. *History of Zoroastrianism.* Oxford University Press, New York, 1938.

Donner, Florinda. *Being-in-Dreaming: An Initiation into the Sorcerer's World.* HarperSanFrancisco, CA, 1991.

Doresse, Jean. *The Secret Books of the Egyptian Gnostics.* Inner Traditions International, Rochester, VT, 1986.

Doyle, Arthur Conan. *The History of Spiritualism.* Cassell and Company, London, 1926.

Easton, Stewart C. *Man and World in the Light of Anthroposophy.* Anthroposophic Press, Hudson, NY, 1989.

—— *Rudolf Steiner: Herald of a New Epoch.* Anthroposophic Press, Spring Valley, NY, 1980.

Edmunds, Francis. *From Thinking to Living: The Work of Rudolf Steiner.* Element Books, Shaftesbury, U.K., 1990.

Egan, Timothy. "Worldly and the Spiritual Clash in New Age Divorce." *The New York Times,* September 25, 1992.

Elkins, Don; Rueckert, Carla; and McCarty, James Allen. *The Ra Material: An Ancient Astronaut Speaks.* The Donning Company, Norfolk, 1984.

Elmer-Dewitt, Philip. "Cyberpunk!" *Time,* February 8, 1993.

Eschenbach, Wolfram von. *Parzival.* Translated by A. T. Hatto, Penguin Books, New York, 1980.

Evans-Wentz, W. Y. *The Tibetan Book of the Dead.* Oxford University Press, New York, 1960.

Fant, Ake; Klingborg, Arne A.; and Wilkes, John. *Rudolf Steiner's Sculpture in Dornach.* Rudolf Steiner Press, London, 1975.

Fields, Rick. *How the Swans Came to the Lake: A Narrative History of Buddhism in America,.* Shambhala, Boulder, CO, 1981.

Fischer-Schreiber, Ingrid; Ehrhard, Franz-Karl; and Diener, Michael S. *The Shambhala Dictionary of Buddhism and Zen.* Translated by Michael H. Kohn, Shambhala, Boston, 1991.

Fitzhugh, Elisabeth. *The Orion Material: Perspectives of Awareness.* Synchronicity Press, Takoma Park, MD., 1987.

Fortune, Dion. *The Secrets of Doctor Taverner.* The Aquarian Press, Wellingborough, U.K., 1989.

Fox, William Sherwood. "Greek and Roman," *The Mythology of All Races.* Cooper Square Publishers, New York, 1964.

Friedric, Otto, "New Age Harmonies." *Time,* December 7, 1987.

Gabriel, Trip. "Tripping but Not Falling." *The New York Times,* May 2, 1993.

Gardner, Martin. "Isness Is Her Business." *New York Review of Books,* April 19, 1987.

Goettsche, Ron; and Fogg, Bob. *Down to Earth: The Jason Journal.* Synergy Publishers, Denver, 1984.

Goldman, Ari L. "Debate of Messianic Proportions." *The New York Times,* January 29, 1993.

Gomes, Michael. *The Dawning of the Theosophical Movement.* Quest/Theosophical Publishing House, Wheaton, IL, 1987.

Goswami, Amit. *The Self-Aware Universe—How Consciousness Creates the Material World.* Jeremy P. Tarcher/G.P. Putnam's & Sons, New York, 1993.

Govinda, Lama Anagarika. *Creative Meditation and Multidimensional Consciousness.* Unwin Paperbacks, London, 1977.

―― *Foundations of Tibetan Mysticism.* Samuel Weiser, York Beach, ME,1969.

Graves, Robert; and Patai, Raphael. *The Hebrew Myths: The Book of Genesis.* Doubleday & Company, New York, 1964.

Greeley, Andrew. "Mysticism Goes Mainstream." *American Health,* January-February 1987.

Grosse, Rudolf. *The Christmas Foundation: Beginning of a New Cosmic Age.* Steiner Book Centre, North Vancouver, Canada, 1984.

―― *The Living Being "Anthroposophia."* Steiner Book Centre, North Vancouver, 1986.

Hackett, George with Abramson, Pamela. "Ramtha: A Voice from Beyond." *Newsweek,* December 15, 1986.

Hapgood, Charles H. *Talks With Christ and His Teachers Through the Psychic Gift of Elwood Babbitt.* Fine Line Books, Turners Falls, MA, 1981.

Hardinge, Emma. *Modern American Spiritualism: A Twenty Year's Record of the Communion Between Earth and the World of Spirits.* University Books, New Hyde Park, NY, 1970 (reprint of 1870 edition).

Harrison, C. G. *The Transcendental Universe.* Lindisfarne Press, Hudson, NY, 1993.

Hastings, James. "Ormazd," in *Encyclopedia of Religion and Ethics.* Charles Scribner's Sons, New York, 1914.

Hatford, Wayne. *Letters from Janice.* Uni-Sun Books, Kansas City, 1987. Hiebel, Friedrich. *Time of Decision with Rudolf Steiner.* Anthroposophic Press, Hudson, 1989.

Howell, Alice O. *The Dove in the Stone: Finding the Sacred in the Commonplace.* Quest Books, Wheaton, IL, 1988.

―― *The Web in the Sea: Jung, Sophia, and the Geometry of the Soul.* QuestBooks, Wheaton, IL, 1993.

Hughes, Kathleen. "For Personal Insights, Try Some Channels Out of this World." *Wall Street Journal,* April 1, 1987.

Hutchison, Michael. *Megabrain: New Tools and Techniques for Brain Growth and Mind Expansion.* Ballantine Books, New York, 1986.

Jayakar, Pupal. *Krishnamurti.* Harper & Row, New York, 1986.

Jonas, Hans. "Gnosticism," in *The Encyclopedia of Philosophy,* Vol. 3. Paul Edwards, Editor-in-Chief. The Macmillan Company & The Free Press, New York, 1967.

—— *The Gnostic Religion: The Message of the Alien God and the Beginnings of Christianity.* 2nd ed. Beacon Press, Boston, 1963.

Kandl, Jeanette. *In the Beginning: Conversations with David.* Vol. 1, Harbinger House, Tucson, AZ, 1988.

Kardec, Allan. *Experimental Spiritism—Book on Mediums; or, Guide for Mediums and Invocators.* Samuel Weiser, York Beach, ME, 1970.

Kaufmann, Walter. "Introduction," *Goethe's Faust.* Translated by Walter Kaufmann, Anchor Books/Doubleday, Garden City, NY, 1961.

Klimo, Jon. *Channeling: Investigations on Receiving Information from Paranormal Sources.* Jeremy P. Tarcher, Los Angeles, 1987.

Knight, J. Z. *A State of Mind: My Story.* Warner Books, New York, 1987.

Kühlewind, Georg. *Becoming Aware of the Logos.* Lindisfarne Press, West Stockbridge, MA, 1985.

—— *The Logos-Structure of the World: Language as Model of Reality.* Lindisfarne Press, Hudson, NY, 1993.

Lawlor, Robert. *Sacred Geometry: Philosophy and Practice.* Thames and Hudson, London, 1982.

Leadbeater, Charles W. *The Masters and the Path.* Theosophical Publishing House, Adyar, India, 1925.

Leviton, Richard. "A Primer on Landscape Zodiacs and the Discipline of Spiritual Geomancy." Nimitta Press, Goshen, MA, 1991.

—— "Awakening to Community: Fellowship Community's Living Alternative." Mercury Press, Spring Valley, NY, 1992.

—— "Die Wahre Basis der Seherschaft." *Esotera,* February 1993.

—— "Journey to the Magi: An Interview with Kyriacos Markides." *Yoga Journal,* September/October 1990.

—— "Ley Lines & The Meaning of Adam." in *Anti-Gravity and the World Grid,* ed. by David Hatcher Childress. Adventures Unlimited Press, Stelle, IL, 1987.

—— "Listening to Kajuba: Communications with the Dolphins." *Magical Blend,* January 1989.

—— "From the Cradle to the Grave." *Yoga Journal,* July/August 1993.

—— "The Imagination of Pentecost: Rudolf Steiner & Contemporary Spirituality." *The Quest,* Fall 1993, Vol. 6, No. 3.

—— "The Lord of the Tree Returns: A Perspective on the Harmonic Convergence." *Life Times,* No. 5, 1988.

—— "Would the Buddha Use a Mind Machine?" *Yoga Journal,* November/December 1992.

—— "Zodiacal Circles of Light: Landscape Zodiac Temples of Britain." Nimitta Press, Goshen, MA, 1992.

—— *Lovely Lucifer: A Workbook in the Christed Initiation in the Buddha Body.* Nimitta Press, Goshen, MA, 1993.

—— "The ABCs of Movement." *Yoga Journal*, July/August 1993.

—— Review of "A Rosicrucian Notebook." *The Quest*, Summer 1993.

Lievegoed, B.C.J. *Mystery Streams in Europe and the New Mysteries.* Anthroposophic Press, Spring Valley, NY,1982.

Lissau Rudi. *Rudolf Steiner: Life, Work, Inner Path and Social Initiatives.* Hawthorn Press, Stroud, U.K., 1987.

MacLaine, Shirley. *Dancing in the Light.* Bantam Books, New York, 1985.

Malory, Sir Thomas. *Le Morte d'Arthur.* Penguin Books, New York, 1969.

Marciniak, Barbara. *Bringers of the Dawn: Teachings from the Pleiadians.* Bear & Company, Santa Fe, 1992.

Markides, Kyriacos C. *Fire in the Heart: Healers, Sages and Mystics.* Paragon House, New York, 1990.

—— *Homage to the Sun: The Wisdom of the Magus of Strovolos.* Arkana/Routledge & Kegan Paul/Methuen, New York, 1987.

—— *The Magus of Strovolos: The Extraordinary World of a Spiritual Healer.* Arkana/Routledge & Kegan Paul, London, 1985.

Martin, Stoddard. *Orthodox Heresy: The Rise of "Magic" as Religion and its Relation to Literature.* St. Martin's Press, New York, 1989.

Matthews, Caitlin. *Sophia-Goddess of Wisdom, The Divine Feminine from Black Goddess to World Soul.* Mandala/Grafton/Harper Collins, London, 1991.

McKenna, Terence. *The Archaic Revival.* HarperSanFrancisco, CA, 1992.

—— *True Hallucinations.* HarperSanFrancisco, CA, 1993.

Mead, G. R. S. *Pistis Sophia: A Gnostic Gospel.* Spiritual Science Library, Blauvelt, NY, 1984.

Melton, J. Gordon. "An Interpretive View of the Development of American Religions," in *The Encyclopedia of American Religions*, 3rd Edition. Gale Research, Detroit, MI, 1989.

Michell, John. *New Light on the Ancient Mystery of Glastonbury.* Gothic Image Publications, Glastonbury, U.K., 1990.

Mills, Joy. *100 Years of Theosophy: A History of the Theosophical Society in America.* Theosophical Publishing House, Wheaton, IL, 1987.

Monroe, Robert. *Far Journeys.* Doubleday & Company, Garden City, New York, 1985.

Montgomery, Ruth. *Threshold to Tomorrow.* Fawcett Crest, New York, 1982.

—— *Aliens Among Us.* Fawcett Crest, New York, 1985.

—— with Garland, Joanne. *Ruth Montgomery: Herald of the New Age.* Fawcett Crest, New York, 1986.

Moore, Mary-Margaret. *From the Heart of a Gentle Brother.* High Mesa Press, Taos, 1987.

—— *"I Come as a Brother"—A Remembrance of Illusions.* High Mesa Press, Taos, 1986.

Muller, F. Max. *The Six Systems of Indian Philosophy.* Longmans, Green, & Co., London, 1899.

Murphet, Howard. *When Daylight Comes: Biography of Helena Petrovna Blavatsky.* Quest Books, Wheaton, IL, 1975.

—— *Yankee Beacon of Buddhist Light: Life of Col. Henry S. Olcott.* Theosophical Publishing House, Wheaton, IL, 1988.

Nesfield-Cookson, Bernard. *Rudolf Steiner's Vision of Love: Spiritual Science and the Logic of the Heart.* Crucible, Aquarian Press, Wellingborough, U.K., 1989.

Nethercot, Arthur H. *The First Five Lives of Annie Besant.* University of Chicago Press, Chicago, 1960.

Norbu, Namkhai. *The Crystal and the Way of Light: Sutra, Tantra and Dzogchen.* ed. by John Shane. Routledge & Kegan Paul, New York, 1986.

Ostling, Richard N. "The Church Search." *Time,* April 5, 1993.

Pagels, Elaine. *The Gnostic Gospels.* Random House, New York, 1979.

Panshin, Alexei and Panshin, Cory. *The World Beyond the Hill: Science Fiction and the Quest for Transcendence.* Jeremy P. Tarcher, Inc., Los Angeles, 1989.

Pennick, Nigel. *Sacred Geometry: Symbolism and Purpose in Religious Structures.* Turnstone Press, Wellingborough, U.K., 1980.

Permutt, Cyril. *Photographing the Spirit World: Images from Beyond the Spectrum.* The Aquarian Press, Wellingborough, U.K., 1988.

Pfeiffer, E.E. *The Task of the Archangel Michael.* Mercury Press, Spring Valley, NY, 1985.

Platt, Paul. *The Qualities of Time,* Vol. 1. *Contributions Towards a Modern Understanding of How the Cosmos Works in Man,* Star Cross Press, Sheffield, MA, 1986.

Plummer, L. Gordon. *The Mathematics of the Cosmic Mind: A Study in Mathematical Symbolism.* The Theosophical Publishing House, Wheaton, IL, 1982.

Podmore, Frank. *Modern Spiritualism: A History and a Criticism.* Methuen & Company, London, 1902.

Powell, A.E. *The Etheric Double: The Health Aura of Man.* Quest Books, Wheaton, IL, 1969.

—— *The Astral Body and Other Astral Phenomena.* Quest Books (5th edition), Wheaton, IL, 1992.

Prokofieff, Sergei. *Rudolf Steiner and the Founding of the New Mysteries.* Rudolf Steiner Press, London, 1986.

Pursel, Jach. *Lazaris, The Sacred Journey: You and Your Higher Self.* Concept: Synergy Publishing, Beverly Hills, CA, 1987.

Ravenscroft, Trevor. *The Spear of Destiny.* Samuel Weiser, York Beach, ME, 1982.

—— *The Cup of Destiny: The Quest for the Grail.* Samuel Weiser, York Beach, ME, 1988.

Rheingold, Howard. *Virtual Reality.* Summit Books, Simon & Schuster, New York, 1991.

Rittelmeyer, Friedrich. *Rudolf Steiner Enters My Life.* Floris Books, Edinburgh, U.K., 1982.

Roberts, Anthony. *Geomancy—A Synthonal Re-appraisal.* Zodiac House, Westhay, U.K., 1981.

—— editor, *Glastonbury—Ancient Avalon.* New Jerusalem, Rider, London, 1978.

Roberts, Jane. *The Coming of Seth.* Pocket Books, New York, 1966.

—— *The Seth Material.* Prentice-Hall, New York, 1970.

Robinson, James A. General Editor. *The Nag Hammadi Library in English,* Revised Ed., Harper & Row, San Francisco, 1988.

Roman, Sanaya. *Spiritual Growth: Being Your Higher Self.* H.J. Kramer, Tiburon, 1989.

—— and Packer, Duane. *Opening to Channel.* H.J. Kramer, Tiburon, 1987.

Roof, Wade Clark. *A Generation of Seekers: The Spiritual Journeys of the Baby Boom Generation.* HarperSanFrancisco, CA, 1993.

Ross, Philip E. "Science? *Nyet*" *Scientific American,* June 1991.

Rota, Eileen. *Welcome Home: A Time for Uniting.* Sand Castle Publishing, Virginia Beach, VA, 1988.

Royal, Lyssa and Priest, Keith. *The Prism of Lyra: An Exploration of Human Galactic Heritage.* Royal Priest Research, Sedona, AZ, 1990.

Rudhyar, Dane. *The Astrology of Personality.* Servire/Wassenaar, Netherlands, 1963.

Rushkoff, Douglas. *Siberia: Life in the Trenches of Hyperspace.* HarperSan Francisco, 1994.

Ryan, Charles J. *H.P. Blavatsky and the Theosophical Movement.* Theosophical University Press, Pasadena, CA, 1937.

Ryerson, Kevin, and Harolde, Stephanie. *Spirit Communication: The Soul's Path.* Bantam Books, New York, 1989.

Savitch, Marie. *Marie Steiner-von Sivers: Fellow Worker with Rudolf Steiner.* Rudolf Steiner Press, London, 1967.

Scharff, Paul. *Holy Nights—Contemplations on the Christmas Foundation Meeting of 1923.* Mercury Press, Spring Valley, NY, 1991.

Schiller, Paul Eugen. *Rudolf Steiner and Initiation.* Anthroposophic Press, Spring Valley, NY, 1981.

Schuré, Edouard. *Children of Lucifer—An Antique Drama in Five Acts.* Spiritual Science Library, Blauvelt, NY, 1986.

Scott, E.F. "Gnosticism," in *Encyclopedia of Religion and Ethics,* Vol. 6. Edited by James Hastings. Charles Scribner's Sons, New York, 1914.

Shepherd, A. P. *Scientist of the Invisible: Rudolf Steiner, A Biography.* Inner Traditions International, Rochester, VT, 1983.

Simmons, J.L. *The Emerging New Age.* Bear & Company, Santa Fe, NM, 1990.

Sinnett, A.P. *The Mahatma Letters.* Transcribed by A. Trevor Barker. Theosophical University Press, Pasadena, CA, 1975.

Sirius, R.U. "Editorial." *Mondo 2000*, No. 2, 1990.

Skutch, Robert. *Journey Without Distance: The Story Behind A Course in Miracles.* Celestial Arts, Berkeley, CA, 1984.

Smilgis, Martha. "Hollywood Goes to Heaven." *Time,* June 3, 1991.

Smith, Joseph. *The Journal of Joseph: The Personal History of a Modern Prophet.* Compiled by Leland R. Nelson, Council Press, Mapleton, UT, 1979.

Sontag, Deborah. "Reverence and Rigidity in the New Age." *The New York Times,* October 5, 1992.

Spangler, David. *Channeling in the New Age.* Morningtown Press, Issaquah, 1988.

Stahl, Jerry. "Channel Hopping." *Playboy,* December 1987.

Stein, Walter Johannes. *The Death of Merlin: Arthurian Myth and Alchemy.* Floris Books, Edinburgh, U.K., 1989.

—— *The Ninth Century and the Holy Grail.* Temple Lodge Press, London, 1988.

Steiner, Rudolf. *Ancient European Clairvoyance.* Rudolf Steiner Nachlassverwaltung, Dornach, May 1, 1909.

—— *Ancient Myths and the New Isis Mystery.* Anthroposophic Press, Hudson, NY, 1994.

—— *An Outline of Occult Science.* Anthroposophic Press, Spring Valley, NY, 1972.

—— *Anthroposophical Leading Thoughts.* Rudolf Steiner Press, London, 1985.

—— *Anthroposophy, An Introduction.* Rudolf Steiner Press, London, 1983.

—— *Anthroposophy and Christianity.* Anthroposophic Press, Spring Valley, NY, 1985.

—— *Aspects of Human Evolution.* Anthroposophic Press, Hudson, NY, 1987.

—— *At the Gates of Spiritual Science.* Rudolf Steiner Press, London, 1986.

—— *Awakening to Community.* Anthroposophic Press, Spring Valley, NY, 1974.

—— *Background to the Gospel of St. Mark.* Rudolf Steiner Press, London, 1968.

—— "Brain Thinking as Spiritual Activity." Unpublished lecture, Dornach, Switzerland, 1 May 1915.

—— *Building Stones for an Understanding of the Mystery of Golgotha.* Rudolf Steiner Press, London, 1985.

—— *Christ and the Human Soul.* Rudolf Steiner Press, London,1972.

—— *Christ and the Spiritual World.* Rudolf Steiner Press, London, 1963.

—— *Christ in Relation to Lucifer and Ahriman.* Anthroposophic Press, Spring Valley, NY, 1978.

—— *Christianity as Mystical Fact.* Anthroposophic Press, Hudson, NY, 1986.

—— *Christianity in Human Evolution.* Anthroposophic Press, Spring Valley, NY, 1979.

—— *Community Life, Inner Development, Sexuality, and the Spiritual Teacher.* Anthroposophic Press, Hudson, NY, 1991.

—— *Cosmic Memory: Prehistory of Earth and Man.* Harper & Row, New York, 1981.

—— *Cosmosophy,* Vol. 1. Anthroposophic Press, Spring Valley, NY, 1985.

—— *Creative Speech: The Nature of Speech Formation.* Rudolf Steiner Press, London, 1978.

—— *Deeper Secrets of Human History in the Light of the Gospel of St. Matthew.* Rudolf Steiner Press, London, 1987.

—— *Earthly Knowledge and Heavenly Wisdom.* Anthroposophic Press, Hudson, NY, 1991.

—— *Errors in Spiritual Investigation.* Mercury Press, Spring Valley, NY, 1983.

—— *Errors in Spiritual Research Meeting the Guardian of the Threshold.* Mercury Press, Spring Valley, NY, 1983.

—— *Esoteric Christianity and the Mission of Christian Rosenkreutz.* Rudolf Steiner Press, London, 1984.

—— *Esoteric Development.* Anthroposophic Press, Spring Valley, NY, 1982.

—— *Eurythmy as Visible Speech.* Rudolf Steiner Press, London, 1984.

—— *Exoteric and Esoteric Christianity.* Steiner Book Centre, North Vancouver, n.d.

—— *Facing Karma.* Anthroposophic Press, Spring Valley, NY, 1979.

—— *Four Mystery Dramas.* Steiner Book Centre, North Vancouver, 1973.

—— *Friedrich Nietzsche, Fighter for Freedom.* Spiritual Science Library, Blauvelt, NY, 1985.

—— *From Buddha to Christ.* Anthroposophic Press, Hudson, NY, 1978.

—— *From Jesus to Christ.* Rudolf Steiner Press, London, 1973.

—— *From Symptom to Reality in Modern History.* Rudolf Steiner Press, London, 1976.

—— *Genesis: Secrets of the Bible Story of Creation.* Rudolf Steiner Press, London, 1982.

—— *Goethe's Standard of the Soul.* Anthroposophical Publishing Company, London, 1925.

—— *Goethe's World View.* Mercury Press, Spring Valley, NY, 1985.

—— *Goethean Science.* Mercury Press, Spring Valley, NY, 1988.

—— *How Can Mankind Find the Christ Again?* Anthroposophic Press, Hudson, NY, 1984.

—— *Individualism in Philosophy.* Mercury Press, Spring Valley, NY, 1989.

—— *Initiation, Eternity, and the Passing Moment.* Anthroposophic Press, Spring Valley, NY, 1980.

—— *Inner Impulses of Evolution.* Anthroposophic Press, Spring Valley, NY, 1984.

—— *Isis and Madonna.* Mercury Press, Spring Valley, NY, 1987.

—— *Jesus and Christ.* Anthroposophic Press, Spring Valley, NY, 1976.

—— *Karmic Relationships: Esoteric Studies.* 8 volumes. Rudolf Steiner Press, London, 1975.

—— *Knowledge and Initiation.* Steiner Book Centre, North Vancouver, n.d

—— *Knowledge of the Higher Worlds and Its Attainment.* Anthroposophic Press, Hudson, NY, 1947.

—— *Learning to See into the Spiritual World.* Anthroposophic Press, Hudson, NY, 1990.

—— "Learning to Understand the Spiritual World." Unpublished lecture, April 18, 1914.

—— *Life Between Death and Rebirth.* Anthroposophic Press, New York, 1968.

—— *Links Between the Living and the Dead.* Anthroposophical Publishing Company, London 1960.

—— *Macrocosm and Microcosm.* Rudolf Steiner Press, London, 1968.

—— *Man as a Picture of the Living Spirit.* Rudolf Steiner Press, London, 1972.

—— *Man as Symphony of the Creative Word.* Rudolf Steiner Press, London, 1970.

—— *Man in the Past, the Present, and the Future.* Rudolf Steiner Press, London, 1966.

—— *Man's Being, His Destiny, and World Evolution.* Anthroposophic Press, Spring Valley, NY, 1984.

—— *Man's Life on Earth and in the Spiritual Worlds.* Anthroposophical Society, London, 1922.

—— "Manifestations of the Unconscious: Dreams, Hallucinations, Visions, Somnambulism, Mediumship." Unpublished lecture, 1918.

—— *Materialism and the Task of Anthroposophy.* Anthroposophic Press, Hudson, NY, 1987.

—— "Meditation and Concentration: Three Kinds of Clairvoyance." Unpublished lecture, Dornach, Switzerland, March 27, 1915.

—— *Michaelmas and the Soul Forces of Man.* Anthroposophic Press, Spring Valley, NY, 1982.

—— *Mystery Knowledge & Mystery Centres.* Rudolf Steiner Press, London, 1973.

—— *Occult Reading and Occult Hearing.* Rudolf Steiner Press, London, 1975.

—— *Occult Science and Occult Development.* Rudolf Steiner Press, London, 1983.

—— *Occult Signs and Symbols.* Anthroposophic Press, Hudson, NY, 1972.

—— *Paths to Knowledge of Higher Worlds.* Steiner Book Centre, North Vancouver, 1980.

—— "On the Connection of the Living and the Dead." Anthroposophical Movement, London, Vol. V., No. 45, November 4, 1928.

—— *On the Life of the Soul.* Anthroposophic Press, Spring Valley, NY, 1985.

—— "On the Relationship with the Dead." *Goetheanum News*, Dornach, 39th volume, No. 2/3, March/April, 1971.

—— *Philosophy, Cosmology and Religion*. Anthroposophic Press, Spring Valley, NY, 1984.

—— *Planetary Spheres and Their Influence on Man's Life on Earth and in Spiritual Worlds*. Rudolf Steiner Press, London, 1982.

—— "Pneumatosophy: Finding and Formulating the Cosmic Word in In-Breathing and Out-Breathing," Anthroposophical Press, New York, lecture from April 1, 1922.

—— *Polarities in the Evolution of Mankind*. Rudolf Steiner Press, London, 1987.

—— *Practical Training in Thought*. Anthroposophic Press, Spring Valley, NY, 1985.

—— *Pre-Earthly Deeds of Christ*. Steiner Book Centre, North Vancouver, 1976.

—— *Preparing for the Sixth Epoch*. Anthroposophic Press, Spring Valley, NY, 1979.

—— *Psychoanalysis & Spiritual Psychology*. Anthroposophic Press, Hudson, NY, 1990.

—— *Reincarnation and Karma: Two Fundamental Truths of Human Existence*. Anthroposophic Press, Hudson, NY, 1992.

—— *Rosicrucian Esotericism*. Anthroposophic Press, Spring Valley, NY, 1978.

—— *Rosicrucianism and Modern Initiation*. Rudolf Steiner Press, London, 1982.

—— *Secrets of the Threshold*. Anthroposophic Press, Hudson, NY, 1987.

—— *Self-Consciousness, The Spiritual Human Being*. Spiritual Science Library, Blauvelt, NY, 1986.

—— *Self-Education: Autobiographical Reflections, 1861-1893*. Mercury Press, Spring Valley, NY, 1985.

—— *Spiritual Beings in the Heavenly Bodies & in the Kingdoms of Nature*. Anthroposophic Press, Hudson, NY, 1992.

—— *Spiritual Research: Methods and Results*. Steinerbooks, Blauvelt, NY, 1981.

—— *St. John's Tide*. Mercury Press, Spring Valley, NY, 1984.

—— *Supersensible Man*. Anthroposophical Publishing Company, London, 1961.

—— *The Ahrimanic Deception*. Anthroposophic Press, Spring Valley, NY, 1985.

—— *The Alphabet*. Mercury Press, Spring Valley, NY, 1982.

—— *The Apocalypse of St. John*. Rudolf Steiner Press, London, 1977.

—— *The Balance in the World and Man, Lucifer and Ahriman*. Steiner Book Centre, North Vancouver, 1977.

—— *The Being of Man and His Future Evolution*. Rudolf Steiner Press, London, 1981.

—— *The Bridge Between Universal Spirituality and the Physical Constitution of Man*. Anthroposophic Press, Spring Valley, NY, 1958.

—— *The Challenge of the Times*. Anthroposophic Press, Spring Valley, NY, 1941.

—— *The Change in the Path to Supersensible Knowledge*. Steiner Book Centre, North Vancouver, 1982.

—— *The Christ Impulse and the Development of Ego Consciousness*. Anthroposophic Press, Spring Valley, NY, 1976.

—— *The Concepts of Original Sin and Grace*. Rudolf Steiner Press, London, 1973.

—— *The Cosmic New Year*. Rudolf Steiner Publishing Company, London, 1938.

—— "The Cosmic Word and Individual Man." Single lecture, Rudolf Steiner Nachlassverwaltung, Dornach, Switzerland, May 2, 1923.

—— *The Course of My Life* (2nd edition). Anthroposophic Press, Hudson, NY, 1986.

—— *The Cycle of the Year as Breathing Process of the Earth.* Anthroposophic Press, Hudson, NY, 1988.

——*The Dead Are with Us.* Rudolf Steiner Press, London, 1985.

—— *The Deed of Christ.* Steiner Book Centre, North Vancouver, 1976.

—— *The Destinies of Individuals and of Nations.* Rudolf Steiner Press, London, 1986.

—— *The Driving Force of Spiritual Powers in World History.* Steiner Book Centre, North Vancouver, 1972.

—— *The East in the Light of the West.* Spiritual Science Library, Blauvelt, NY, 1986.

—— "The Errors of Spiritual Investigation." Unpublished lecture, November 27, 1912.

—— *The Easter Festival in the Evolution of the Mysteries.* Anthroposophic Press, Hudson, NY, 1987.

—— "The Etheric Body as a Reflection of the Universe." *Anthroposophic News Sheet.* Dornach, Switzerland, September 29, 1940.

—— *The Etherisation of the Blood.* Rudolf Steiner Press, London,1985.

—— *The Festivals and Their Meaning.* Rudolf Steiner Press, London, 1981.

—— *The Fifth Gospel.* Rudolf Steiner Press, London, 1968.

—— *The Foundation Stone.* Rudolf Steiner Press, London, 1979.

—— *The Four Sacrifices of Christ.* Anthroposophic Press, Spring Valley, NY, 1981.

—— *The Four Seasons and the Archangels.* Rudolf Steiner Press, London, 1984.

—— "The Future Jupiter and Its Beings." Unpublished lecture, January 3, 1915.

—— *The Gospel of St. John.* Anthroposophic Press, Hudson, NY, 1962.

—— *The Gospel of St. John and Its Relation to the Other Gospels.* Anthroposophic Press, Spring Valley, NY, 1982.

—— *The Gospel of St. Luke.* Rudolf Steiner Press, London, 1964.

—— *The Gospel of St. Mark.* Rudolf Steiner Publishing Co., London, 1938.

—— *The Gospel of St. Matthew.* Rudolf Steiner Press, London, 1965.

—— *The History of Spiritism and The History of Hypnotism and Somnambulism.* Anthroposophic Press, New York, 1943.

—— *The Holy Grail.* Compiled by Steven Roboz. Steiner Book Centre, North Vancouver, 1984.

—— *The Human Soul in Relation to World Evolution.* Anthroposophic Press, Spring Valley, NY, 1984.

—— *The Influence of Spiritual Beings Upon Man.* Anthroposophic Press, Spring Valley, NY, 1961.

—— *The Influences of Lucifer and Ahriman.* Steiner Book Centre, North Vancouver, 1984.

—— *The Inner Development of Man.* Anthroposophic Press, Spring Valley, NY, 1985.

—— *The Inner Nature of Music and the Experience of Tone.* Anthroposophic Press, Hudson, NY, 1983.

—— *The Karma of Untruthfulness.* Vol. 1, Rudolf Steiner Press, London, 1988.

—— *The Lost Unison Between Speaking and Thinking.* Mercury Press, Spring Valley, NY, 1984.

Bibliography

—— *The Michael Mystery.* St. George Publications, Spring Valley, NY, 1984.

—— *The Mission of the Archangel Michael* (2nd edition), Anthroposophic Press, Spring Valley, NY, 1961.

—— *The Mission of Folk Souls.* Anthroposophical Publishing Company, London, 1929.

—— *The Mystery of the Trinity and The Mission of the Spirit.* Anthroposophic Press, Hudson, NY, 1991.

—— *The New Spirituality and the Christ Experience of the Twentieth Century.* Rudolf Steiner Press, London, 1988.

—— *The Occult Movement in the Nineteenth Century.* Rudolf Steiner Press, London, 1973.

—— *The Origin of Suffering, The Origin of Evil, Illness, and Death.* Steiner Book Centre, North Vancouver, 1980.

—— *The Philosophy of Spiritual Activity.* Anthroposophic Press, Hudson, NY, 1986.

—— *The Presence of the Dead on the Spiritual Path.* Anthroposophic Press, Hudson, NY, 1990.

—— *The Principle of Spiritual Economy.* Anthroposophic Press, Hudson, NY, 1986.

—— *The Realm of Language.* Mercury Press, Spring Valley, NY, 1984.

—— *The Reappearance of the Christ in the Etheric.* Anthroposophic Press, Spring Valley, NY, 1983.

—— "The Recovery of the Living Source of Speech." Anthroposophical Society in America, New York, single lecture, April 13, 1923.

—— *The Riddle of Man.* Mercury Press, Spring Valley, NY, 1990.

—— *The Search for the New Isis, Divine Sophia.* Mercury Press, Spring Valley, NY, 1983.

—— *The Significance of Spiritual Research for Moral Action.* Anthroposophic Press, Spring Valley, NY, 1981.

—— *The Spiritual Guidance of Man.* Anthroposophic Press, Spring Valley, NY, 1950.

—— *The Spiritual Hierarchies and Their Reflection in the Physical World.* Anthroposophic Press, Spring Valley, NY, 1970.

—— *The Stages of Higher Knowledge.* Anthroposophic Press, Spring Valley, NY, 1967.

—— *The Sun Initiation of the Druid Priest and His Moon-Science.* Rudolf Steiner Press, London, 1966.

—— *The Ten Commandments and the Sermon on the Mount.* Anthroposophic Press, Spring Valley, NY, 1978.

—— *The True Nature of the Second Coming.* Rudolf Steiner Press, London, 1971.

—— *The Universal Human: The Evolution of Individuality.* Anthroposophic Press, Hudson, NY, 1990.

—— *The Waking of the Human Soul and the Forming of Destiny.* Steiner Book Centre, North Vancouver, 1983.

—— *The Work of the Angels in Man's Astral Body.* Rudolf Steiner Press, London, 1988.

—— *The Wrong and Right Use of Esoteric Knowledge.* Rudolf Steiner Press, London, 1966.

—— *Theosophy.* Anthroposophic Press, Hudson, NY, 1971.

—— *Theosophy of the Rosicrucian.* Rudolf Steiner Press, London, 1981.

—— *Three Lectures on the Mystery Dramas.* Anthroposophic Press, Spring Valley, NY, 1983.

—— *Toward Imagination: Culture and the Individual.* Anthroposophic Press, Hudson, NY, 1990.

—— *True and False Paths in Spiritual Investigation.* Rudolf Steiner Press, London, 1985.

—— *Turning Points in Spiritual History.* Spiritual Science Library, Blauvelt, NY, 1987.

—— *Universe, Earth and Man.* Rudolf Steiner Press, London, 1987.

—— *Wonders of the World, Ordeals of the Soul, Revelations of the Spirit.* Rudolf Steiner Press, London, 1983.

—— *World History in the Light of Anthroposophy.* Rudolf Steiner Press, London, 1977.

Steinfels, Peter. "Conversations: Charting the Currents of Belief for the Generation that Rebelled." *The New York Times,* May 30, 1993.

Strieber, Whitley. *Transformation: The Breakthrough.* Beech Tree Books, New York, 1988.

—— *Communion: A True Story.* Avon Books, New York, 1987.

Suares, Carlo. *The Qabala Trilogy.* Shambhala, Boston, 1985.

Sullivan, Meg. "New Age to Dawn in August, Seers Say, and Malibu is Ready." *Wall Street Journal,* June 23, 1987.

Tomberg, Valentin. *Anthroposophical Studies of the Old Testament.* Candeur Manuscripts, Spring Valley, NY, 1985.

—— *Anthroposophical Studies of the New Testament.* Candeur Manuscripts, Spring Valley, NY, 1985.

—— *Inner Development.* Candeur Manuscripts, Spring Valley, NY, 1983.

Valencia, Heather, and Kent, Rolly. *Queen of Dreams; The Story of a Yaqui Dreaming Woman.* Simon & Schuster, New York, 1991

Van Emmichoven, F.W. Zeylmans. *The Foundation Stone.* Rudolf Steiner Press, London, 1963.

Vaz, Mark Cotta. *Spirit in the Land: Beyond Time and Space with America's Channelers.* Signet/New American Library, New York, 1988.

Wachmeister, Countess Constance. *Reminiscences of H.P. Blavatsky and The Secret Doctrine.* Theosophical Publishing House, Wheaton, IL, 1976.

Walker, Barbara G. *The Woman's Encyclopedia of Myths and Secrets.* Harper & Row, San Francisco, 1983.

Webb, James. "The Occult Establishment." in *Not Necessarily the New Age* Ed. by Robert Basil. Prometheus Books, Buffalo, NY, 1988.

Westen, Robin. *Channelers: A New Age Directory.* Perigee/Putnam Publishing, New York, 1988.

Wetzl, Joseph, translator. *The Bridge Over the River.* Anthroposophic Press, Spring Valley, NY, 1974.

White, Ruth, and Swainson, Mary. *Gildas Communicates: The Story and the Scripts.* Neville Spearman, Sudbury, U.K., 1971.

Wilson, Colin. *Poltergeist, A Study in Destructive Haunting.* Llewellyn Publications, St. Paul, MN, 1993.

—— *The Occult: A History.* Vintage Books, New York, 1973.

Wilson, Gahan. *The New Yorker.* April 2, 1990.

Wright, Lawrence. "Remembering Satan, Part II." *The New Yorker,* May 24, 1993.

Yarbro, Chelsea Quinn. *Messages From Michael.* Berkley Books, New York, 1979.

Young, Meredith Lady. *Agartha, A Journey to the Stars.* Stillpoint Publishing, Walpole, NH, 1984.

Zaehner, R.C. *The Teachings of the Magi.* George Allen & Unwin, London, 1956.

Zajonc, Arthur. *Catching the Light: The Entwined History of Light and Mind.* Bantam Books, New York, 1993.

Zimmer, Heinrich. *Philosophies of India.* Edited by Joseph Campbell. Bollingen Series XXVI, Pantheon Books, New York, 1951.